TRILATERAL PERSPECTIVES ON INTERNATIONAL LEGAL ISSUES:

RELEVANCE OF DOMESTIC LAW AND POLICY

Michael K. Young
Yuji Iwasawa
Editors

Transnational Publishers, Inc.
Irvington, NY 10533

Library of Congress Cataloging-in-Publication Data

Trilateral perspectives on international legal issues : relevance of
domestic law and policy / edited by Michael K. Young & Yuji Iwasawa
    p. cm.
  Includes bibliographical references and index.
  ISBN 1-57105-003-5
  1. International law. I. Young, Michael K. II. Iwasawa, Yugi,
1954-
JX3091.T75 1995
341—dc20   95-1376
                                                 CIP

CONTENTS

PART II

**EXTRATERRITORIAL APPLICATION OF DOMESTIC LAW IN THE FIELD OF TRADE
AND ECONOMIC REGULATION AND THE EFFECT OF RESPONSES BY THE
INTERNATIONAL LEGAL COMMUNITY**

Contents

PART III
INTERNATIONAL LEGAL PERSPECTIVES ON JAPAN—NORTH AMERICAN (U.S./CANADA) ECONOMIC FRICTIONS

PART IV
ADJUSTMENT AND DEVELOPMENT OF PROCEDURES FOR THE SETTLEMENT OF INTERNATIONAL DISPUTES

PART V
INTERNATIONAL PEACEMAKING AND PEACEKEEPING ACTIVITIES IN THE POST-COLD WAR WORLD AND ITS RELATIONSHIP TO DOMESTIC IMPLEMENTATION OF INTERNATIONAL OBLIGATIONS

Contents

| PREFACE

Shigeru Kozai

The idea of the Trilateral Project originated two years ago, when Professor Louis Henkin, the former President of the American Society of International Law, proposed in a letter to me collaborative programs among ASIL, CCIL, and JAIL. His letter expressed "a particular need to become more familiar with the research and thinking of our Japanese colleagues. Because of language and distance, we have regrettably not had a great deal of exposure to your leading scholars and practitioners in the field of international law."

I was rather surprised by this observation and immediately decided to respond positively to his kind proposal. Such an international symposium seemed the appropriate first-step toward correcting whatever "isolation" Japanese international law scholars may be experiencing and to promoting trilateral communication and dialogue.

A brief survey of Japan's encounters with and experiences in international law might illuminate the discussions which follow in this volume. In the early seventeenth century, after nearly a century of friendly relations with several European States, Japan reacted to fear of possible political domination by the Roman Catholic Church by adopting a policy of national isolation (*sakoku*). The doors to all foreign intercourse were closed, except for a strictly regulated Dutch and Chinese trade at Nagasaki. For the next two centuries, during which modern international law emerged and developed in Europe, Tokugawa Japan had no knowledge or access to Western legal systems, with books on such subjects considered contraband.

Japan first became acquainted with international law in the mid-nineteenth century, when forced to open her doors to the outside world and to conclude a series of treaties with the Western powers. After futile attempts by various maritime powers, the United States finally succeeded in opening Japan to world trade and concluding a bilateral treaty. Commodore Matthew Perry arrived in 1853, bearing a letter from President Fillmore for the Japanese Emperor.

Records indicate that Perry invoked neither the "law of nations" nor "international law" but resorted to threats of force and war.[1] On one occasion the Governor of Uraga asked Perry not to carry out a survey of the harbor and bay because it was against Japanese law. Perry replied that "though the Japanese laws forbade such surveys the American laws commanded them, and that he was as much bound to obey the American as [the Governor] was the Japanese laws."[2] Here we see an early example of the "extraterritorial application of domestic law" by the United States.

During the negotiation of the Treaty of Amity the following year, Perry's coercive attitude was resisted by the Japanese Commissioner who used *burakashi* tactics, a colloquial expression at that time meaning "protraction or evasion." A similar pattern is observed even today in U.S.-Japanese trade negotiations.

Unlike Perry, Townsend Harris, the first American Consul-General to conclude a treaty of commerce with Japan, used a more persuasive method. He frequently referred to the "law of nations" to support his positions. His approach necessitated that Bakufu officials acquire a fragmentary knowledge of international law.

In late 1864, the American missionary William Martin completed a Chinese translation of Henry Wheaton's *Elements of International Law* and published it in Beijing under the title *Wan Kuo Kung Fa.*[3] Though Martin's work was not considered a translation but a paraphrased interpretation of Wheaton, it was favorably received by Japanese intellectuals and politicians in the closing days of the Tokugawa regime. The fact that most Japanese first learned about the Western law of nations through Martin's Chinese version strengthened the tendency of the Japanese, without any knowledge of Western legal systems, to view international law not so much a system of positive laws, but rather as a set of principles of justice commonly applied to international relations.

The real creative work in this field was done by Shusuke Nishi (later Amane Nishi), the first Japanese student to receive a Western legal education at Leiden, the Netherlands, where he studied under Professor Simon Vissering. In 1868, he published a Japanese translation of Vissering's lectures on the law of nations under the title Vissering's Public Law of All Nations [*Vissering-shi, Bankoku kōhō*]. It was Nishi who clearly grasped the positivist concept of the law of nations. In contrast to Martin's free translation, Nishi's textbook was written in a strictly legalistic manner, using accurate terms to faithfully represent the positive Western

---

1.   When asked by Bakufu officials to go to Nagasaki to deliver the President's letter, "since under Japanese law business relating to foreign countries cannot be transacted here in Uraga, but at Nagasaki," Perry replied that he would never consent to such an arrangement, "and he would go ashore with a sufficient force and deliver [it], whatever the consequences might be." The frightened official reluctantly received the letter "in opposition to   Japanese law." CORRESPONDENCE RELATIVE TO THE NAVAL EXPEDITION TO JAPAN, Senate Doc. No. 34, 33d Cong., 2d Sess. 45 (1854).

2.   CORRESPONDENCE RELATIVE TO THE NAVAL EXPEDITION TO JAPAN, Senate Doc. No. 34, 33d Cong., 2d Sess. 45 (1854).

3.   Literally, "the public law of all nations."

law of nations based on treaties and customs of the modern nations of Europe.

In 1868, shortly after the Tokugawa Shogun returned political power to the Emperor in Kyoto, the newly established government issued various proclamations and decrees in which we find the law of nations frequently invoked. The new Meiji government thus expressed its will to observe strictly the international agreements concluded by its predecessor with the Western powers.

However, the new Japanese regime soon began to realize the "unequal" character of treaty provisions such as extraterritoriality and the unilateral nature of conventional tariffs and of the most-favored-nation clause. For example, Nishi's textbook clearly stated the discrepancy between the European practice of subjecting foreigners to the territorial jurisdiction of the state and the Asian system of consular jurisdiction. Consequently, in June 1871, the Japanese Minister of Foreign Affairs notified treaty powers' representatives of Japan's intention to demand a revision of the treaties.

But the Meiji leaders soon realized that the road was by no means an easy one, and that in order to obtain her objective, Japan would first have to reform her juridical system and adopt the laws of Western states. As a result of strenuous efforts to adopt a Western legal system for two decades, a constitution and criminal, civil and other codes were promulgated in Japan. The police and the judicial system were drastically reformed based on Western models.

In 1893, at the Hamburg Conference of the International Law Association (ILA), Japan succeeded in obtaining a resolution favoring abolition of the consular jurisdiction system for Japan. Finally, in July 1894, the first new treaty of commerce based on equality was concluded between the British Empire and Japan. Other nations soon followed suit. Four decades after her initial encounter with international law, Japan had obtained full membership in the family of nations.

Both in the Sino-Japanese War (1894-5) and the Russo-Japanese War (1904-5), Japan carefully adhered to the international rules of war. Legal advisers accompanied her armed forces and fleet, in order to give advice about the conduct of warfare. It was mainly to research the law of belligerency that our Japanese Association of International Law was founded in 1897.

Unfortunately, after Japan's victory over Russia, her attitude toward foreign relations began to change. Having developed into an imperialistic power herself, she tended to rely more on force than law. During the dark age of militarism from 1931 to 1945, Japan often disregarded international rules, and, after withdrawing from the League of Nations, Japan became isolated again from the international community.

Following the end of World War II, Japan made a fresh start in her international life. Her new constitution, which repudiated militaristic policies of the past and devoted Japan to pacifism, renounced war and abolished armaments. Later, however, this pacifism encountered a real test when Japan became a member of the United Nations and her government proclaimed "U.N.-centered diplomacy" as its fundamental policy of close cooperation with U.N. activities. Since then, the crucial issue for the Japanese has been how to reconcile these opposing positions.

In the wake of the Gulf War, the Japanese Diet, after long and heated debates, adopted the Law Concerning Cooperation in UN Peace-Keeping Operations. The law was a product of compromise. Because of constitutional constraints, the Japanese contribution was strictly limited to the traditional "consent-type" U.N. peacekeeping operations. In the field of traditional peacekeeping, Canada is regarded as a leading peacekeeper with a long record of positive contributions. Japan has much to learn from Canada's many experiences.

In both international security and foreign trade, the United States, Canada, and Japan share common interests for a stable international legal order. As we approach the next century, our three nations will need to foster much closer ties. Toward that end, I sincerely hope that this symposium will provide a forum for heartfelt discussions on issues of common interest. Ours is admittedly a small step towards a hopefully giant start.

Shigeru Kozai
Immediate Past-President
Japanese Association of International Law

December 1995

| PREFACE

Edith Brown Weiss
H. Scott Fairley

In July 1994, the Japanese Association of International Law, the American Society of International Law, and the Canadian Council on International Law held the first trilateral program on international law in Tokyo, Japan. Participants explored different perspectives on important international legal issues of concern to the three countries.

Some of the collaborative ties which contributed to the trilateral symposium began in conjunction with a previous Annual Meeting of the Canadian Council, in association with the Japanese Association of International Law, held at Ottawa in 1990. This meeting focused on international law themes of mutual interest, and the presidents Professor Armand de Mestral and Professor Soji Yamamoto, assisted by many others, established an ongoing relationship between the two organizations which former American Society President Peter Trooboff carried forward in aid of the 1994 event.

In 1900 the U.S. Supreme Court in the famous case of *The Paquete Habana*, referred to a Japanese source, *Takahashi's International Law*, to help determine relevant international legal rules. Today more than ever, scholars, jurists, practicing lawyers and others need to be informed about and to understand international legal scholarship written from various cultural perspectives.

The trilateral symposium was a remarkable event in advancing understanding of different perspectives on international legal issues. Thirty scholars (fifteen from Japan, ten from the United States, and five from Canada) presented papers on five topics of special interest to the three countries: the development of international law, with special attention to environment and ocean issues; extraterritorial application of national laws; economic frictions between Japan and North America; settlement of international disputes; and international peacekeeping/peacemaking and domestic implementation.

It is hard to capture the intellectual excitement which permeated this symposium. Participants shared knowledge, forthrightly analyzed legal problems, examined different perspectives and advanced their mutual understanding of complex issues.

This volume presents the written results of the 1994 symposium. In particular, we are delighted to make available the important theoretical and practical scholarship of Japanese legal scholars to a non-Japanese audience. We hope that in reading this book, readers will more fully appreciate the breadth and the quality of scholarship in Japan. Much of Japanese scholarship on international law has not been accessible in the West, because of language barriers, but it should be. All of us have much to learn from each other.

We hope that this symposium will inaugurate a sustained program of cooperation and scholarly exchange among the three organizations of international law. In March 1996, in Atlanta and in Washington, D.C., scholars from the three organizations will again meet to explore new topics and to continue a dialogue and exchange of perspectives.

There are many people who have made this publication possible. Foremost, we are especially grateful to our Japanese hosts for organizing the symposium and for their very generous and impeccable hospitality. All the participants carry cherished memories of the Tokyo symposium and the subsequent fora in Kyoto and Hiroshima.

The editors of this volume Professors Michael Young and Yuji Iwasawa and their assistants, in particular, Batia Zareh, deserve special thanks for their great dedication and outstanding work in bringing the papers to publication. They have acted with exceptional insight, skill, efficiency, and grace.

It has been a particular pleasure to work with the President of the Japanese Association of International Law at that time, Professor Shigeru Kozai. We are especially grateful to Professor Kozai for this crucial leadership in shepherding this event to conclusion and for his arrangement of the Kyoto symposium. Special thanks also go to Professor Shinya Murase, for his superb assistance in planning for the event.

Edith Brown Weiss
President
American Society of International Law

H. Scott Fairley
Immediate Past-President
Canadian Council on International Law

January 1996

| INTRODUCTION

This should be a time of celebration for international lawyers. At long last, the polarization between East and West that supposedly paralyzed the international community has disappeared. Concerted action on myriad international problems, long overdue, should finally be possible.

The need for such action, moreover, has never been greater. The potentially far-reaching impact of each country's actions on the global commons, indeed, on the environmental well-being of every other country, has become increasingly apparent, as has the urgency of the need to address collectively these problems. The need to extend a multilateral discipline to trade in all sorts of goods, as well as services and investment, likewise has never been greater or more immediate. Interaction between states as well as between states and the citizens of different states is also at an all-time high.

Nevertheless, pessimism, not optimism, is generally the order of the day. While environmental concerns are undoubtedly important, the developmental needs of the South remain substantial and the South urgently insists that these needs be addressed first. Although all agree in principle that trade should be freeer, protectionist pressures—sometimes for developmental, but often for even less grandiose reasons—are as great as any time since the end of World War II. Even in the face of vastly increasing interaction between states and supposedly greatly strengthened multilateral institutions, unilateral action is rampant. Low intensity conflicts both within and between states also have increased markedly with the demise of the draconian discipline of the Cold War.

Even the most basic conceptual building block of modern international law—the nation-state—has come under attack. From above, the concept is called into question by the formation of an increasing number of supra-national entities to address collectively a growing range of problems whose solutions were previously the exclusive province of national governments. From below, the concept is challenged by numerous internal conflicts· that undermine the territorial, governmental and political integrity of many countries, most visibly perhaps in countries that comprised the former Soviet bloc.

At the very time the need for concerted international action is at its greatest and the prospects for successful results should be at their brightest, developments around the globe have shaken confidence in the ability of traditional international rules, institutions and processes to solve these pressing problems. When solutions to these international problems are successfully devised, moreover, it is clear that the nature of the institutions, rule-formation processes and dispute resolution mechanisms often bear only passing resemblance to their Cold War forebearers and even less to their pre-war counterparts. In short, it is clear that the form and function of international law is changing dramatically.

The pace and direction of that change is often unclear, however, and, from the perspective of international lawyers, invariably deeply underconceptualized. Answers to the most fundamental questions are still lacking. What will the new international order look like? What will be its basic building blocks? What form will the new institutions and resultant rules take and how will they function? Who will participate in rule formation and dispute resolution? In what ways can countries legitimately encourage participation in rule making and subsequent adherence to the resulting rules? What effect will these new rules and institutions have on pressing global problems that demand attention?

It was to address some of these issues that this project was conceived and undertaken. Under the auspices of the American Society of International Law (ASIL), the Japanese Association of International Law (JAIL), and the Canadian Council on International Law (CCIL), panels of prominent international law scholars, practitioners and diplomats from the United States, Japan and Canada were asked to analyze critical areas of international law, as well as to highlight important developments and predict future directions that the law might take.

The result of that request is this volume. These papers were first circulated in advance of a conference held in Tokyo in the summer of 1994. Participants were asked to read the papers and come to Japan prepared to comment on the larger themes that emerged from these papers. The bulk of the two-day conference was then spent discussing the papers and the over-arching themes in detail. Papers were revised substantially in light of these comments and this volume was produced. Each chapter of this volume begins with a brief summary of the conference discussion of the papers contained in that chapter.

In part by design and in part by fortunate coincidence, virtually all the papers address two major themes of international law, namely, law-making and law enforcement. The first two Parts deal principally with the first issue, rule formation in the international arena. Part One discusses this issue directly, focussing not only on the creation of conventional binding norms and rules, but also on the development of new forms of international law, called by one author "soft law," which guide and shape the behavior of nations. Both the norm formation process and the effect on the behavior of states are different than more conventional international rules; nevertheless, the content of the rules is often quite specific and the pressure to comply great. An increase in international "law" of this type may well be one of the more important and interesting byproducts of the decline in East-West polarization.

The second Part examines the ways in which countries attempt, sometimes successfully but almost invariably acrimoniously, to impose domestically developed norms on other countries. Interestingly, while all the authors see the predictable difficulties of such extraterritorial application, a few also discuss important benefits that accrue to the international order when a country challenges its counterparts to live up to higher standards of behavior in areas in which delay in the rule formation process is problematic or other factors impede the development of necessary norms and rules. Especially engaging are the authors' discussions of the ways in which domestic rules increasingly shape and influence the development of international norms. This ability to give vent to domestically developed standards in international settings is arguably one of the more prominent, and certainly one of the more provocative results of the demise of the Cold War.

The next two Parts focus principally on dispute resolution, exploring both norm creation and norm enforcement. Part Three examines these issues through the prism of bilateral trade and economic disputes. The chapters focus on dispute resolution as a mechanism with two fundamental purposes: first, to clarify the international standards with which the countries must comply; and, second, to encourage compliance with the agreed-upon norms.

It is important to point out that dispute resolution in these cases has this dual function, especially the norm clarification function, at least in part because the subject matter under consideration is economic. Certainty and predictability are highly prized attributes of legal rules in the economic arena. An entrepreneur's success or failure is determined in no small measure by his or her ability to make accurate predictive calculations. Negotiated rules can provide some degree of much needed specificity, but large areas of uncertainty invariably remain and dispute resolution can often play a highly useful, if not decisive role in reducing that uncertainty. In all events, all the authors described an enhanced need for efficient and effective dispute resolution in this area and some are even brave enough to predict some degree of satisfaction of that need.

Part Four focuses on dispute resolution in general, examining more broadly its role as a device to insure compliance with agreed-upon international norms and standards. The authors examine a broad array of mechanisms, ranging from very informal conciliation procedures and good offices to the highly structured and formal International Court of Justice. Interestingly, the reader of these papers might be left with the impression that the demise of the Cold War may precipitate a decided shift towards the more informal processes and away from the highly structured, more formal mechanisms. This is not a result one would necessarily have predicted, or, it is important to stress, one with which all the authors of these papers would agree. Still, in light of the tone and logic of these papers, it is interesting to speculate whether the decrease in East-West tension will actually encourage more informal cooperation and dispute resolution and even less large-scale, formal institution building.

Chapter Five turns to enforcement, pure and simple, examining the increase in opportunities for international peacekeeping and peacemaking activities. Naturally, the role of the United Nations comes in for particularly close scrutiny. At the same time, the experiences of individual countries are also examined in great detail. Perhaps the most compelling aspect of this part is the careful examination of the interplay between the requirements of domestic politics and the needs and interests of the international community. Conflict between international needs and domestic requirements is frequent, and, in the absence of extraordinary political leadership, the latter, just as frequently, prevails over the former. While these conclusions are not likely to startle the reader, what is striking is the degree to which these obvious insights are ignored at the international level, with international leaders and organizations getting far ahead of anything the domestic traffic will bear. The need to structure an international order that is adequately attentive to domestic political constraints is clear and imperative, while, as the authors well note, only rarely, if ever, satisfied.

Of course no introduction can do justice to the richness and complexities of the chapters contained in this volume. At the same time, I hope that even these few words will whet the readers' appetites for a more careful examination of this book. I am confident they will not be disappointed.

In conclusion it is vital that I express gratitude to the many people and institutions whose contributions made this complex undertaking possible. First, sincere appreciation is due to the three International Law Societies, their leaders, their members and their employees. The presidents of all three societies, Edith Brown Weiss of the ASIL, Shigeru Kozai of the JAIL, and Scott Fairley of the CCIL, attended this conference and lent invaluable support every step of the way. Their members were equally unstinting with their time and energy, including the JAIL Organizing Committee, chaired by Professor Shigeru Kozai and directed by Professor Shinya Murase, whose efforts on behalf of this project were truly extraordinary. The remainder of the committee was comprised of Mr. Tetsuo Ito and Professors Yoshiro Matsui, Naoya Okuwaki, Masato Dogauchi, Akira Kotera, Atsuko Kanehara, and Miyako Tatematsu, all of whom also deserve high priase. Thanks also must go in equal measure to the liaisons for the CCIL, Professor Armand de Mestral and Mr. Maurice Copithorne, and the ASIL Organizing Committee, including Professor Louis Henkin, also former president of the ASIL, Professor Anne-Marie Burley, and Mr. Peter D. Trooboff, who deserves special mention for his unstinting support and generous expenditure of time at every juncture and without whose guidance and assistance this project simply would not have been possible.

Equally important, each society lent its staff, without whose logistical support the conference and this subsequent volume would not have been realized. While it is always difficult to single out any individual for fear of neglecting others who are equally deserving, Dr. Charlotte Ku, Executive Director of the American Society of International Law, merits special mention. Her contributions for the past two years have gone well above and beyond the call of duty and this enterprise is, in many important respects, her's. The staff of Sophia University's School of Law Graduate Programs was also extraordinarily helpful in making all the necessary arrangements in Japan. They include Mr. Masato Nakamura, Ms. Keiko Ko, Ms. Hisako Kanda, and Ms. Megumi Abe.

Certain organizations also provided important logistical and financial support, without which we would not have been able to function. The International House of Japan and its incomparable staff, under the most able leadership of Mr. Mikio Kato, provided excellent facilities and accommodations for the conference in Tokyo. The following corporations and organizations provided essential financial support: the Japan Foundation Center for Global Partnership, the Tokyo Club, Mitsubishi Bank, Meiji Life Insurance, Mitsubishi Heavy Industries, Ltd., Mitsubishi Motors Corporation, Mitsubishi Corporation, Mitsubishi Electric

Corporation, Mitsubishi Trust and Banking Corporation, the Tokio Marine and Fire Insurance Co., Ltd., Sumitomo Chemical Industries, Ltd., Daiichi Kangyo Bank, Sanwa Bank, and Nomura Foundation for Social Science. The Pacific 2000 Fund of the Department of Foreign Affairs and International Trade of the Governement of Canada has also contributed to the successful completion of this project.

The Japanese Ministry of Foreign Affairs graciously sponsored a reception for the participants in Tokyo, while the Canadian Embassy in Japan hosted a luncheon and the U.S. Embassy, under the guidance of Ambassador Walter Mondale, arranged for dinner at the home of the Deputy Chief of Mission, Mr. Rust Demming. These events allowed the participants to continue their consideration of these important issues in extraordinarily congenial surroundings, while providing an opportunity to interact with a variety of diplomats, who, after all, are often the formulators and the executors of the international rules about which we debated. Each occasion was not only most enjoyable, but highly productive and we are grateful for the generosity and consideration of the respective foreign ministries.

Transnational Publishers, and the various editors assigned to this project, have also been a pleasure to work with. In particular, Ms. Heike Fenton and Ms. Esther Gueft have worked tirelessly to produce a volume worthy of their fine press.

We also received considerable logistical support from the School of Law of Columbia University and thanks are owed to Dean Lance Liebman for allowing this use of the school's resources. Special thanks must also go to the Columbia students, along with a former Columbia student and a lawyer, who we only half-jokingly nominated as an honorary former Columbia student, who performed yeoman's service as reporters for the various conference sessions. Their excellent reports, along with appropriate acknowledgements, are contained throughout this volume.

Most important, I must thank Ms. Batia Zareh, just graduated from Columbia Law School, who spent most of the past two years shepherding this project and this book from conception to completion. As every author in this volume well knows, Batia was the first and last editor of every piece. She spent countless hours examining each chapter for logical consistency, grammatical fluidity and citational accuracy. For months on end Batia was in the office before me and left well after me. She spent so many weekends on the project that nasty looks and occasional snide comments from her many too-frequently ignored friends became a daily part of my routine. Words cannot do justice to her efforts. Her service in the cause was simply extraordinary. Batia, thank you!

Thanks are also due, of course, to my fine co-editor, who truly made this a transnational project. Professor Yuji Iwasawa performed exceptionally able service on both sides of the Pacific and, as our co-editorship indicates, this volume is as much his as anyone else's.

One word about form: though some of our Japanese contributors would have preferred otherwise, we made an editorial decision to put all Japanese names in this book in Western style, given name first and surname last.

Finally, I would like to thank all of the authors for their impressive contributions. Each produced a noteworthy work at the outset and then strove assiduously to improve it between the time of the conference and publication. From the very beginning this has been a collaborative effort in its truest sense. To have had the opportunity of working with such fine scholars has been a pleasure and a privilege. For the efforts and patience of each of the authors, I am most grateful.

Michael K. Young
Fuyo Professor Japanese Law
Director, Center for Japanese Legal Studies
Columbia University

December 27, 1995
New York, New York

SOME RECENT DEVELOPMENTS IN U.N. PEACEKEEPING AND THEIR IMPLICATIONS FOR ITS FUTURE

Hisashi Owada
Permanent Representative of Japan to the United Nations

I deem it a privilege to have this opportunity to share with you my own thoughts on some aspects of the new developments that have been taking place in the field of peacekeeping activities of the United Nations in recent years and to consider their legal and political implications.

I. NEW TRENDS IN U.N. PEACEKEEPING

U.N. peacekeeping operations have a long history, but in recent years they have undergone drastic modifications to cope with the diverse international and regional conflicts that have erupted since the end of the Cold War. I wish to begin by commenting on several major changes that have come about in the practice of recent U.N. peacekeeping activities.

First of all, their mandates have become much more complex and comprehensive. An operation is no longer expected simply to maintain a cease-fire, as has been the case with peacekeeping operations of the traditional type. Its mandate may now include a broad range of activities such as election monitoring, de-mining, refugee repatriation, troop demobilization, monitoring human rights, and support for national reconstruction. In other words, U.N. peacekeeping operations are increasingly expected to assist in nation building, expanding beyond their classical paramilitary roles along the ceasefire line into the realm of control over the civilian administration. The U.N. effort in Cambodia was a prime example of this new type of peacekeeping operation.

Second, as peacekeeping operations are expanding in scope, and especially as they are growing in importance in the field of humanitarian assistance activities, in particular within countries where there is civil war and where the central authority has collapsed, a novel approach to make this operation effective through some enforcement action, if necessary, has emerged. Thus, the concept of peace enforcement, as proposed by the Secretary-General in his "Agenda for Peace" of

April 1992, was put to its practical test for the first time in UNOSOM II in Somalia for this and other wider purposes as a new feature of U.N. peacekeeping operations. Discussions continue as to the feasibility of peace enforcement measures and the necessary conditions for their inclusion in future peacekeeping operations.

The third development which merits our attention is that of preventive deployment. This new peacekeeping mechanism has already been put into practice in the former Yugoslav Republic of Macedonia, and a General Assembly resolution has affirmed its validity. A keen interest is emerging to explore the applicability of preventive deployment in situations of potential conflict and to consider how it might be further developed and made readily available as a preemptive measure wherever there is a potential conflict.

The fourth development I wish to note is the growing weight of the civilian component in peacekeeping operations. As U.N. peacekeeping operations have become more comprehensive, the role of civilian personnel—particularly in the fields of election monitoring, security, administration, and humanitarian assistance—has grown more important. The mobilization and training of such personnel and their deployment in the field in an integrated manner has come to demand a careful study. And with this development, guaranteeing their safety has become an important issue.

Finally, as a result of all these new developments, peacekeeping operations have become larger and more costly. UNTAC in Cambodia and UNOSOM II in Somalia each deployed more than 20,000 personnel, and UNPROFOR in Yugoslavia more than 30,000. The cost of each of these operations came to over U.S. $1 billion. As might be expected, these large-scale operations have placed a tremendous financial burden on the United Nations. But they have also raised the question as to whether the United Nations is in fact capable—in terms of expertise, equipment, and general preparedness—of meeting the demands that are being made of it. Thus, the two most urgent issues facing member states of the United Nations today are financing and organizational reform.

II. MEASURES SUGGESTED TO IMPROVE PERFORMANCE

In the light of this changing vista of U.N. peacekeeping operations, many discussions have been held both within and outside the United Nations on how to improve their effectiveness and efficiency as well as on how to promote the cooperation of the member states in such operations. It would be useful at this juncture to take stock of a number of significant points that have emerged in the course of these discussions:

1) In planning and preparing a peacekeeping operation, it is imperative to bear in mind that every international conflict is unique, shaped by historical, ethnic, and social experiences of the disputing parties, and that peacekeeping requirements are different for each conflict. Thus, when the

Security Council decides to launch a peacekeeping operation, its decision is to be based upon as thorough and precise information on the nature and prognosis of the conflict as possible. The dispatch of a U.N. factfinding mission to the site of a conflict at an early stage has proved to be productive in this regard.

2) A peacekeeping operation should have an achievable objective, and its mandate and duration should be clearly and precisely defined. It must be conducted as effectively as possible, with the limited financial and human resources that are available and within a reasonable period of time. It might be useful to introduce a sunset clause to avoid the undue prolongation of deployment.

3) The command and control structure of the United Nations should be consolidated in the field and at headquarters, so as to better integrate troops. This aspect of the problem has been gaining particular importance as the whole scope of the U.N. peacekeeping operations has been expanding to comprise not only military elements but also humanitarian and other civilian elements working in the same field, though conceivably for different purposes. Attempts to improve coordination between the military and humanitarian and other civilian aspects of peacekeeping operations are underway, especially in view of the increasingly greater role played by the civilian component.

4) Without the understanding and support of the people in the host country, a peacekeeping operation cannot achieve its objectives. Those who have dedicated themselves to restoring peace and stability in a nation have sometimes been misunderstood and even rejected by the very people they were trying to help. The success of public information strategy through radio pursued in Cambodia suggests that a more proactive approach to gain public understanding on peacekeeping operations by the local population can be effective, if staffed with competent personnel who are in close contact with the population they are meant to reach.

5) It is noteworthy that the arrangement is now in place whereby some 70,000 personnel from approximately thirty countries are available for peacekeeping operations on a standby basis. In view of the growing importance of civilians in peacekeeping activities, it would be useful to establish a standby force of civilian personnel as well, which member states could provide upon the urgent request of the United Nations.

6) It is important to enhance the positive support and cooperation of Member states in relation to the Council's decisionmaking process. Toward this end, informal and frequent consultations among the

Secretariat, troop-contributing countries, major financial donors, and Security Council members should be held on a regular basis. Indeed, unless such efforts are made, the Council will not enjoy the full and necessary support of contributing countries in launching a new peacekeeping operation.

7)   The training of peacekeepers is also of great importance. The troops that participate in U.N. peacekeeping operations come from many different countries with different cultural backgrounds, and thus reflect a range of attitudes and experiences. Although it might not be possible to unite these different troops under a common ideological banner, it would nevertheless be necessary that they recognize minimal common rules of peacekeeping activities. The establishment of peacekeeping training centers or the reinforcement of existing training courses for cadres of troops could enhance the U.N. command and control function in the field and foster a "U.N. culture" among the troops of the various member states.

8)   The safety of personnel engaged in peacekeeping is a serious issue, and one that could affect the future of U.N. peacekeeping operations. In light of the discussions held in the Security Council and the General Assembly, as well as the report issued by the Secretary-General in August 1993 on this subject, efforts in the following two directions will probably be urgently needed. First, renewed efforts are needed to achieve a degree of integration and accountability among various bodies to ensure the security of U.N. personnel. Toward this end, the activities of the U.N. Headquarters (Office of the Security Coordinator) should be strengthened with expert staff to assist the Security Coordinator. Second, whenever the Security Council contemplates launching a peacekeeping operation, it should weigh in its consideration of the matter the security aspect of the personnel involved. The Secretariat, for its part, has the responsibility to inform the Council as to whether the Secretary-General has been given sufficient means and resources to protect the lives of those who are engaged in the peacekeeping operation in question.

III. MAJOR PROBLEMS OF LAW AND POLICY TO BE EXAMINED

While keeping in mind these points that have emerged out of the discussions on the present state of U.N. peacekeeping activities, I wish to focus my deliberation today on four issues, all of which raise important and interesting points of law and policy on peacekeeping and which warrant our careful scrutiny as we consider the future of U.N. peacekeeping operations.

a.   Impact of Peace-Enforcement upon Humanitarian Assistance

First of all, let me touch upon the relevance of the "peace-enforcement" dimension to be operated under Chapter VII of the Charter to the U.N. peacekeeping operation, with particular reference to its impact upon humanitarian assistance.

As the Secretary-General pointed out in his "Agenda for Peace," ceasefires have often been agreed to but not complied with, and the United Nations has sometimes been called upon to send forces to restore and maintain the ceasefire. This task can on occasion exceed the mission of peacekeeping forces and the expectations of peacekeeping force contributors. Under such circumstances, the Secretary-General has recommended that the Security Council consider the utilization of peace-enforcement units in clearly defined circumstances and with their terms of reference specified in advance. In the view of the Secretary-General's recommendation, such peace-enforcement units are warranted as a provisional measure under Article 40 of the Charter; they should be distinguished from the forces under Article 43 in that the mission of forces under Article 43 would be to respond to outright aggression, imminent or actual, although in both cases the measures to be taken will presumably be "enforcement measures" taken to maintain or restore international peace and security in the face of a "threat to the peace, breach of the peace or act of aggression."

Very often, when the authority of a central government has completely collapsed and competing factions within the country are engaged in acts of violence, a peacekeeping force may be required to ensure that humanitarian assistance be delivered to those for whom it is destined. Under such special circumstances the concept of peace enforcement as proposed by the Secretary-General would seem to have certain validity.

Thus, in the case of Somalia, a typical example, what started as a traditional peacekeeping operation established by Security Council Resolution 751 (1992)[1] was later transformed into a modified UNOSOM (UNOSOM II) by Security Council Resolution 814 (1993), with an expanded mandate to cover what can only be regarded as an enforcement action under Chapter VII of the Charter.[2]

---

1.   In Security Council Resolution 751 (1992), a United Nations Operation in Somalia (UNOSOM) was entrusted with the task, *inter alia*, of monitoring the ceasefire in Mogadishu (para. 3) and of facilitating an immediate and effective cessation of hostilities and the maintenance of a ceasefire throughout the country in order to promote the process of reconciliation and political settlement in Somalia and of providing urgent humanitarian assistance (para. 7).

2.   The Security Council, declaring that it was acting under Chapter VII, decided to expand the mandate to include the following military tasks:

(b)   To prevent any resumption of violence and if necessary, take

In the case of the former Yugoslavia, a United Nations Protection Force (UNPROFOR) was established by Security Council Resolution 743 (1992) as a peacekeeping operation of the traditional type, with the mandate to consolidate the ceasefire and thus to facilitate the negotiation of an overall political settlement. By a series of subsequent Security Council resolutions, and in particular by Security Council Resolution 836 (1993), new functions were added to the original mandate of UNPROFOR in such a way that the Security Council, acting under Chapter VII of the Charter, decided to extend the mandate of UNPROFOR, to the end of ensuring full respect for the safe areas free from armed attacks and from any other hostile act.[3]

These new developments in the practice of U.N. peacekeeping are totally novel and designed to cope with the new situation in which the U.N. peacekeeping activities are increasingly facing the task of restoring order and bringing about

---

appropriate action against any faction that violates or threatens to violate the cessation of hostilities;

(f) To protect, as required, the personnel, installations and equipments of the United Nations and its agencies, ICRC as well as NOGs and to take such forceful action as may be required to neutralize armed elements that attack, or threaten to attack, such facilities and personnel . . . .

3.   The relevant part of Resolution 836 (1993) reads as follows:

[The Security Council]

. . . .

5.   *Decides* to extend the mandate of UNPROFOR in order to enable it to deter attacks against the safe areas, to monitor the ceasefire, to promote the withdrawal of military or paramilitary units other than those of the Government of the Republic of Bosnia and Herzegovina and to occupy some key points on the ground, in addition to participating in the delivery of humanitarian relief to the population;

. . . .

9.   *Authorizes* UNPROFOR, in carrying out these new mandates, acting in self-defense, to take the necessary measures, including the use of force, in reply to bombardments against the safe areas by any of the parties or to armed incursions into them or in the event of any deliberate obstruction in or around those areas to the freedom of movement by UNPROFOR or of protected humanitarian convoys;

10. *Decides* that member states, acting nationally and through regional organizations or arrangements, may take all necessary measures, through the use of air power, in and around the safe areas, to support UNPROFOR in the performance of its mandate set out above. (Emphasis original.)

favorable conditions for ensuring emergency humanitarian assistance to the local population and displaced persons in distress. To that extent, the rationale behind such an innovation is understandable.

It should be noted, however, that the essential nature of the operation changes once the borderline between the peacekeeping operation under Chapter VI crosses into the territory of action under Chapter VII. Whereas the basic characteristic of a traditional peacekeeping operation is to remain within the realm of Chapter VI and therefore to remain neutral to the respective positions of the parties to the conflict, an enforcement action under Chapter VII by its nature is an action to enforce certain rules against one of the parties or both. Admittedly, the rules in question to be enforced may be norms of humanitarian law and prescriptions based on humanitarian consideration, having nothing to do with the merits of the dispute or the basis of the conflict.   Nevertheless, the very fact of resorting to an enforcement action against one of the parties could transform the position of the United Nations from that of an impartial nonparty intervening solely to keep peace into that of an actor intervening in the conflict itself.

The dilemma that this situation could pose to the peacekeepers of the United Nations and its affiliated agencies engaged in humanitarian assistance in the conflict is obvious. The moment the United Nations itself becomes a party to the conflict as an agent for law enforcement, it can no longer be expected to effectively carry out its functions for offering humanitarian assistance to the victims of the conflict, standing aloof and neutral to the conflict itself.

This dichotomy demonstrates the delicate point involved in crossing the border between peacekeeping and peace-enforcement, however closely interlinked the two may be with each other in terms of achieving the goal of restoring peace in a situation of conflict. The ill-fated precedent in the case of UNOSOM II in Somalia should serve as a caution against the tendency of combining the two into one operation.   A failure to distinguish clearly between impartial and essentially consent-oriented activities, which is the essence of peacekeeping, on the one hand, and a coercive approach designed to impose a desired outcome, which is the essence of peace-enforcement, on the other, could bring about a grave security risk to the deployed peacekeepers. The experience in Somalia has taught us to be cautious in invoking the provisions of Chapter VII of the Charter for launching what is essentially a peacekeeping operation.   Although UNOSOM II was presented as a new category of operation sanctioned under Chapter VII, its success ultimately depended on obtaining maximum local support and preserving the image of the United Nations as a disinterested and impartial actor engaged in political and social reconstruction.

At a minimum, any enforcement action must be carefully planned and the time-tested principle of impartiality carefully weighed against the need for taking any action containing an element of enforcement, so that the peacekeepers themselves do not become victim to the conflict. It would seem useful in this connection to engage in a comprehensive *post-mortem* exercise on the operation in Somalia in order to ascertain whether the outcome would have been different if the operation had been conducted in a more cautious and less peremptory manner to avoid the risk of antagonizing the local population.[4]

b.   Importance of Peace Process as Framework for Peacekeeping

Second, it seems of critical importance to the success of a peacekeeping operation that it is prepared and implemented as an integral part of a well designed, comprehensive plan to achieve the objective of a political settlement. The traditional peacekeeping operation, deployed to prevent the recurrence or escalation of a conflict by intervening between the disputing parties, has a better chance of bringing about a durable peace if it is conducted as part of a broader political effort for the restoration of peace and national reconciliation. The Cambodian operation is a case in point; it is believed that the secret of its success lay in its comprehensive and multifaceted approach. Because the situation in Cambodia was extremely complex, it would have been futile simply to deploy a traditional peacekeeping force there. Intense diplomatic efforts were first necessary to bring about a degree of national reconciliation, which was consolidated through the Paris Agreement. Japan, together with other like-minded countries, played a decisive role in those efforts which were pursued in close coordination with the permanent members of the Security Council. Under the Paris Agreement, a framework was established for efforts to restore peace in Cambodia. UNTAC was then launched with a mandate that included a wide range of tasks, from the organization and conduct of elections to civil administration. Involving some 22,000 personnel, it was the costliest operation ever launched by the United Nations. But equally important were the parallel and concerted diplomatic efforts to create a political environment that would be conducive to durable peace, as well as the provision of economic assistance for the rehabilitation and reconstruction of the war-torn nation, which laid the groundwork for an economic recovery plan to be implemented once the elections were held. It is believed that this well-planned operation could serve as a model for future United Nations efforts.

---

4.   In fact a Commission of Inquiry was set up to investigate the armed attack on UNOSOM II. The report, published in June 1994, concludes on the issue of enforcement as follows:

> The United Nations should refrain from undertaking further peace enforcement actions within the internal conflicts of states. If the United Nations decides nevertheless to undertake enforcement operation, the mandate should be limited to specific objectives and the use of force would be applied as the ultimate means after all peaceful remedies have been exhausted.

c.   Preventive Deployment as Part of Peacekeeping

If the purpose of U.N. peacekeeping consists in maintaining and consolidating a precarious peace, which in many cases comes about in the form of the establishment of a ceasefire, there is no reason why we should wait until after the conflict has erupted in order to achieve the same purpose.

In conditions of a crisis within a country, preventive deployment of U.N. peacekeeping units could serve to maintain calm and peace by offering an impartial deterrence to the crisis, provided that all the parties involved in the crisis give their consent for such deployment. Here, however, the question arises as to whether all the preconditions for the establishment of a traditional peacekeeping operation in an international conflict, including the principle of consent of the parties, will have to be met before such deployment.

From a doctrinal point of view, one could argue that such a deployment of forces might legitimately take place when the Government of the territory makes a formal request for the deployment, on the analogy of the doctrine of "intervention by invitation," since no other sovereign State is involved in the conflictual situation.[5]

One wonders, however, whether here also the basic philosophy of peacekeeping which gives priority to the maintenance of peace on the basis of principles of impartiality and consent, would not counsel us caution in our approach to this new, potentially fertile area for U.N. peacekeeping. This will particularly be the case if preventive deployment is envisaged for the purpose of safeguarding humanitarian interests of a local population whose welfare could be jeopardized by the eruption of a major internal disorder or crises.[6]

Be that as it may, we can cite as a successful case of this preventive deployment the example of U.N. troop deployment in Macedonia, which has succeeded in preventing the conflict in the former Yugoslavia from spilling across the border and in enhancing Macedonia's sense of security. On the strength of this successful precedent, we can probably say with a degree of confidence that the potential of preventive deployment should be more fully explored in relation to situations that are likely to threaten international peace and security. By the same token, sending U.N. investigation missions to areas where there is the danger of a

---

5.   General Assembly Resolution 47/120 of October 8, 1993, reaffirms that "a United Nations preventive deployment . . . should be undertaken *with the consent of and, in principle, on the basis of a request by the Member State* or Member states involved, having taken into account the positions of other States concerned *and all other relevant factors.*" (Emphasis added.)

6.   It is relevant to recall in this context the guiding principles annexed to General Assembly Resolution 46/182 of Dec. 19, 1991, which stresses, *inter alia*, that "humanitarian assistance must be provided in accordance with the principles of humanity, *neutrality* and *impartiality.*" (Emphasis added.)

conflict erupting, under the same conditions that are valid for preventive deployment, could be extremely useful in the context of preventive diplomacy.

In a similar vein, we could also explore the utility of economic and humanitarian assistance in defusing situations that could lead to conflict. It would be helpful if the United Nations closely monitored even subtle changes in politically volatile regions and if neighboring countries were requested to provide up-to-date information on these regions.

d.   Problem of Selectivity in Peacekeeping

Finally, what is probably the most critical issue for U.N. peacekeeping efforts for the future is that of securing cooperation of Member states in contributing human and financial resources to make the peacekeeping activities of the United Nations a success. The success or the failure of the United Nations in the field of peacekeeping depends primarily on the political will of the Member states to cooperate in contributing necessary resources.

Naturally, we must continue to encourage the Secretariat to improve its administrative and budgetary management of the operations, as well as to strengthen the system of audit and inspection in order to ensure accountability and enhance the mechanism of financial control. Member states should thoroughly scrutinize the present system of planning, budgeting and managing administration to consider ways of streamlining it.

Again, it is all too clear that the present piecemeal approach of budgeting for only a few months at a time and of considering the financing of each operation separately is partly responsible for operations that are inadequately planned and poorly administered.

Nonetheless, we must accept the stark reality of the post-Cold War world that hostilities on a regional level, based on ethnic, tribal, religious and other differences as well as internal conflicts stemming from the collapse of a government within a country, are rampant, and that the demand upon the United Nations for its peacekeeping mission will far outweigh the supply.

Already, the financial burden of the existing U.N. peacekeeping operations risks depleting the financial resources of the United Nations, even threatening to shake the very foundation of this organization if the present tendency of peacekeeping operations continues to expand in an unbridled manner. But the problem is not limited to the danger of depletion in financial resources. The availability of human resources for effective peacekeeping in all of the conflictual and troubled spots of the world is increasingly a grave problem for the United Nations, to the extent that peacekeeping operations of the United Nations are basically dependent on the voluntary cooperation of its Member states.

Under such circumstances, we inevitably must think about the application of some principle of selectivity in responding to the need for U.N. peacekeeping operations, however desirable it might be for the United Nations to be able to respond to all the crises in the world. We may perhaps have to reconcile ourselves to the reality that the capacity of the United Nations is not unlimited.

The real question will probably not be whether the principle of selectivity is desirable so much as what kind of criteria for selectivity will have to be applied in introducing this principle into this field.

With this in mind, the Clinton Administration of the United States recently announced its "Policy on Reforming Multilateral Peace Operations" in the form of a "Presidential Decision Directive" (PDD). The directive recognizes that "territorial disputes, armed ethnic conflicts, civil wars (many of which could spill across international borders) and the collapse of governmental authority in some States are among the current threats to peace." While many of these conflicts may not directly threaten American interests, their cumulative effect is significant. On the basis of this recognition, the directive tries to define the role of U.N. and other "multilateral peace operations" in U.S. foreign policy as being "part of National Security Strategy and National Military Strategy of the United States." On this premise, the directive aims to ensure that "our use of peacekeeping is *selective* and *more effective*." (Emphasis added.) The PDD sets out to list eight elements, as "the factors the Administration will consider when deciding whether to support a new U.N. peace operation."[7]

This is clearly not the place to pass a definitive judgment on the validity of each of these factors as elements for selectivity. However, it is noteworthy that the top priority factor to be considered is that "U.N. involvement advances U.S. interests," as well as an international community of interest. As a policy directive of a U.S. administration, sensitive to the reaction of the public involved, this may be understandable. Nevertheless, it would seem to me that here lies a crucial point

---

7.   The PDD 25 in question states as follows:

The Administration will consider the factors below when deciding whether to vote for a proposed new U.N. peace operation (Chapter VI or Chapter VII) or to support a regionally-sponsored peace operation:

(a)   U.N. involvement advances U.S. interests, and there is an international community of interest.
(b)   There is a threat to or breach of international peace and security.
(c)   There are clear objectives.
(d)   For traditional peacekeeping operations, a cease-fire should be in place and the consent of the parties obtained.
(e)   For peace-enforcement operations, the threat to international peace and security is considered significant.
(f)   The means to accomplish the mission are available.
(g)   The political, economic and humanitarian consequences of inaction by the international community are considered unacceptable.
(h)   The operation's anticipated duration is tied to clear objectives and realistic criteria for ending the operation.

that any government of the Member states of the United Nations will have to ponder upon in all seriousness, if the effectiveness of U.N. peacekeeping operation is to be enhanced over the long term. It is that such criteria for selectivity will have to be brought in as a common yardstick for action by the Membership of the United Nations as a whole, based on the consideration of how best we can promote the public policy of the international community that the United Nations represents, rather than from the viewpoint of whether the operation will serve the purpose of promoting a narrowly defined national interest of a Member state or a group of Member states.

At this time, when U.N. peacekeeping operations play an ever greater role in the maintenance of public order in the confused world of the post-Cold War era, it is absolutely essential that the organization, in its strategy, planning and budgetary and logistic management in peacekeeping, be guided by this consideration of public policy of the international community, with a view to safeguarding and promoting certain essential community values. For this purpose, it is important to develop and consolidate a system that will enable us to effect overall control over U.N. peacekeeping from such a perspective and to ensure that the operation be effectively and efficiently performed.

PART I
INTERNATIONAL LAWMAKING IN THE CONTEMPORARY WORLD WITH EMPHASIS ON THE LAW OF THE SEA AND ENVIRONMENTAL LAW

| SUMMARY

Alex V. Chachkes

Custom and treaty have normally been adequate to address the challenges of international lawmaking. But the products of custom and treaty and the time required for their production make it unlikely that these traditional instruments, at least in their current form, provide adequate solutions to many contemporary international legal problems. The laws of the sea and environment are paradigmatic of the problems facing international lawmakers. Foremost, all states utilize and exploit the global environment and the world's seas. Events such as the nuclear accident at Chernobyl and long-range threats, such as global warming, all provide acute reminders of our environmental interdependency. Worldwide interest in using global resources, such as the sea for mineral or navigational purposes, highlights the pressing need for higher levels of international cooperation than in the past. We have also come to understand better the irreversibility of the environmental impact of many of the actions we take. The difficulty of reaching agreement internationally on these issues is exacerbated by the complexity of accounting for the positions of states of varying geographic size, political might, level of development, and financial resources. The domestic effects of tighter international environmental standards might slightly alter the lifestyle of the citizens of one state, but they might devastate the economy of another. Regulation of fishing on the high seas might slightly raise prices in certain countries, but may totally eliminate major industries in another. Further, the process of international lawmaking has become increasingly complex as the interests and influence of non-state actors in the process has grown.

Surveying the various mechanisms of international lawmaking, it is impossible to point to a single lawmaking mechanism most suited to address the needs of the contemporary world. The sources of international law and the processes by which it is made are as different as the disputes between states, and the environmental problems that cause them.

The most straightforward form of international lawmaking has always been the treaty. The treaty, though, is not proving to be a particularly good instrument for solving contemporary environmental and law of the sea disputes. The complexity of these problems requires that rules be codified into precise, comprehensive

3

regulations, complete with enforcement and dispute resolution procedures. But this takes time, time we may not always have. The tension between preservation of the global environment and states' claims on what they believe is their fair share of the Earth's resources makes resolution of these problems through comprehensive treaties even more problematic. Indeed, not a single law of the sea or environmental treaty commands universal, much less comprehensive, membership.

Developing states also sense a significant disparity between their power and that of the rich industrial North in the traditional treatymaking process. Developing states always have an equal stake in the global environment, but often have the most to lose from the imposition of environmental constraints. Further, as Professor Jonathan I. Charney commented, treaties often leave the hardest questions for later solution. Finally, "treaty congestion" may result from the over 900 international legal instruments dealing with the environment. Overwhelming numbers of separate secretariats, monitoring systems, participant meetings and funding, Professor Edith Brown Weiss pointed out, raise concerns of comprehension, consistency, and manageability.

Other traditional sources of international law may also be inadequate to the task. As Professor Ryuichi Ida stressed, the customary norm formation process is largely a product of bilateral relations between a relatively small number of states, mainly in Europe. The scope of international problems has widened to include those states formerly excluded from the formation process. These new voices must be heard. The character of these new participants, however, may considerably increase the difficulty of formulating customary norms. These new states include both developing countries, which lack the bargaining power that comes with economic strength, as well as the former communist nations, which challenge the validity and applicability of norms formulated without their consent. The participation of nations whose primary concerns are feeding and clothing their citizens also challenges the traditional normative assumptions, creating the need for more situationally normative legal instruments. Finally, in light of the immediacy of many environmental problems, the customary international norm formation process is at once too lengthy, often requiring decades before a norm is adequately established, and much too general in the resultant norms.

From what source, if not treaty or the norms of the North, will new laws come? Some authors point to the traditional approach of customary international law: state practice and *opinio juris*. Others have suggested "soft law" as a source for international law. "Soft law," a concept that has gained currency in the past fifteen years, is the process whereby states reach agreement on international action that is limited in its substantive legal content. "Soft law" is the legal precedent and norms that are derived from the residue of weak treaty provisions and legal instruments that are themselves incapable of constituting legal norms. Examples include codes of conduct, intergovernmental conference declarations, U.N. General Assembly resolutions, and memoranda of understanding. "Soft law" serves two functions: (1) as a template for negotiation of treaties; and (2) as evidence of the development of state practice and *opinio juris*, catalyzing the development of customary international law. "Soft law" is pre-customary norm, but, nonetheless, may be respected by a "well developed state," according to Professor Linda C. Reif. Professor Ida remarked that, while not binding, "soft law" legitimatizes state conduct. Thus, "soft law" codifies a state's commitment, giving its action something greater than mere moral obligation.

All commentators agreed, though, that "soft law" is fraught with problems. According to Professor Ida, the very idea of "soft law" is defined by its lack of commitment. "A charming name," but what do we mean by labeling a norm as "soft," Professor Ida queried. When states speak of legal rights and duties, they inevitably rely on "hard law" to justify the imposition of sanctions on violators. Further, as expressed by Professor Shinya Murase, the strengthening of "soft law" has the tendency to undermine "hard law," as states, aware that a weak commitment in writing could provide evidence to support a "soft law" claim, qualify even their weak commitments. Professor Charney reiterated, "soft law" acts only as a guide, reflecting no concrete state commitment, at least no commitment that might be enforced by an offended state.

Professor Mamoru Koga expressed concern that "soft law" might diminish the voices of the minority, as most international bodies contributing to the sum of decisions that determine "soft law" express a perspective predicated on Northern values. Professor Jackson expressed concern that "soft law" has been used in the past to evade the domestic lawmaking process required to pass "hard law," i.e., the treaty ratification process. Professor Charney answered that as an alternative to the opaque traditional treatymaking process, this drawback might just be acceptable.

Professor Charney also outlined another alternative to customary law: "general international law." Similar conceptually to customary law, "general international law," he argued, is a product of international community norm consensus formed around the discrete decisions of the international community. A product of organizations such as the U.N. General Assembly and diplomatic conferences, it differs from customary law in that it creates law, even where no custom has been present. This gives "general international law" an immediacy that may allow it to address many international environmental problems in a more timely fashion than customary international law. "General international law" is also generally the product of fora that are universal, transparent and consensual. Thus, the creation of this type of law differs from customary law, being derived from express acceptance. An example of general international law is the ban on mineral development in Antarctica that developed out of the Madrid protocol; although this was a product of the Antarctic treaty process, it is rapidly moving toward universal acceptance.

Professor Ida raised four concerns about the concept of "general international law." First, it is not necessarily the product of fora open to all states. Second, much like customary law, the rules for identification of the law's precise norms and standards are vague. Third, state obligation is difficult to identify. Finally, there are no standards for enforcement of what are only arguably very unclear violations of admittedly unclear standards.

One conference participant questioned these very categories of law formation, suggesting instead that any categorical approach to understanding law should turn upon the strength of that legal form to encourage states toward compliance with an agreed-upon goal; concepts of "soft" versus "hard" should be replaced with "binding" versus "nonbinding." The panelists, though, were reluctant to discard the labels "hard" and "soft" as practical categories in the context of law formation.

Particularly, panelists rejoined that the "hard" and "soft" labels are connotations different in kind: the appellations "hard" and "soft" refer to the form and quality of a legal source. As Professor Ida pointed out, "soft" forms of law demarcate tendencies toward norm-creation, but are not a recognized form of law. The form of a legal source, its hardness or softness, also reflects the degree of commitment and ability of that law to bind, a distinction particularly relevant when considering procedures for dealing with violations.

The panelists also discussed the idea of the consensual action of states binding one another versus consensual action imposing single state, unilateral sanctions as a framework for the understanding of international law. True, the common conception of an environmental or law of the sea conflict is that arising from multi-state action, e.g., deep sea mining, chlorofluorocarbon use, or auto emission. But not uncommon are situations where unilateral imposition might be necessary to preserve the global environment.

Professor Franck identified another form of international lawmaking—the creation of what he labelled "super hard law"—necessitated by the need for definitive, unilateral, and speedy action to address a concrete problem of global dimension. A good example of the creation of this type of lawmaking mechanism is the recent action of the United Nations Security Council (UNSC) in creating a Yugoslav War Crimes Tribunal, complete with a legal charter, powers of judging, securing evidence and imposing law on offenders (sentencing). This, and other cases (Kuwait/Iraq border hostility, *Lockerbie* extradition rulings), create rulings that bind every state without treaty. Professor Franck queried whether it might not be possible to use similar "legislation" to address environmental acts that threaten environmental peace and security.

Many were skeptical as to the validity or even applicability of "super-hard law" to environmental transgressions. Would the expansion of UNSC rulings to address nonaggressive acts undermine the legitimacy of the international security system by reducing state support for such UNSC declarations in cases of true military aggression? Is "super-hard law" even within the competence of the UNSC or U.N. Charter? Could "super-hard law" be appropriately directed against multilateral actions? What would restrain the UNSC from imposing the will of the majority (e.g., members of the Security Council; the North) on the minority (e.g., nonmembers; the South)?

Professor Michael Young questioned whether the inadequacy of current international lawmaking mechanisms might not encourage states to take unilateral steps to protect the environment. Professor Charney seemed to agree, noting that under traditional international law transgressions in these areas are often dealt with *ex post facto* for lack of concrete rules. Earlier recognition of internationally binding rules, whether from "soft law" or "general international law," might discourage unilateral action. Professor Reif expressed similar concerns over the lack of existing legal rules pertaining to the environment. She noted a clear, more definitive articulation of a "human right:" the right to a "healthy or safe environment" would discourage states from unilaterally causing irreparable environmental damage.

The panelists next examined another relatively recent international law development: the framework mechanisms for open, multiparty consensual creation of concrete commitments. This approach has been employed in the laws of the environment and the sea, either through standing institutions, like the U.N. Security Council, or *ad hoc* ones, such as the three United Nations Conferences on the Law of the Sea (UNCLOS I to III), the United Nations Conference on Environment and Development (UNCED) and the General Agreement on Tariffs and Trade (GATT).

The goal of framework conventions is to combine normative universalism with universal participation, flexible obligations, and continuous modification of standards and targets in light of scientific uncertainty. In a framework convention, voices of less developed states are often accommodated. As Prof. Reif pointed out, the inclusion of developmental interests in UNCED, as its very name indicates, symbolizes the intent to enfranchise the representatives of traditionally ignored countries. For countries more concerned with clothing and feeding their citizens than protecting the whales, conferences like the Rio Conference have provided useful fora for debates about balancing and coordinating economic and environmental concerns, rather than merely enhancing environmental restrictions. Professor Koga remarked that the UNCLOS III was a "great laboratory workshop on international law" in this respect. UNCED also capitalized upon the experience of UNCLOS II by using a preparatory phrase to limit lengthy negotiations at the conference itself.

The latter half of the panel discussion focused upon the role of the public in the international law of the sea and environment. What is the role of the public? Has a norm emerged for public access to information and public participation in the decisionmaking process? Is there an emerging international procedural right to effective public access to domestic judicial administrative process? Is the very idea of a "public right" contingent upon biased conceptions of autonomy inherent in Western universalism or is this an idea that can and should be generalized to all civilized countries?

The nongovernmental organization (NGO) has been the main conduit for effective expression of public opinion outside of state representation. Professor Reif saw the public, particularly through the NGO, as pushing the lawmaking process from a closed and state-driven process to an open and private-entity driven process. On the "macro" level, increased public participation though NGOs has directly facilitated the creation of "soft law" (e.g., standards, codes, etc., issued by such bodies as the International Chamber of Commerce and the International Standards Organization). Public entities, being "closer to the ground" than the states, can also effectively monitor environmental well being, supplementing the efforts of the state. NGOs also provide valuable perspective and suggestions regarding appropriate areas for regulation. Since the public often has different priorities than the state, wider public participation necessarily expands the scope of the discussion.

On a local, or "micro" level, examination of the relationship between a state and its citizens reveals that greater public participation facilitates the expression of the public desire for a healthy and safe environment. The public is, of course, the first harmed by any environmental degradation. The fluid interaction between a state and its citizens encourages the flow of information, grassroots level monitoring and continuous researching and updating of scientific knowledge.

Indeed, NGOs might serve to fill a possible "gap" between the delegates to international organizations and the people they represent. Professor Jackson wondered whether delegates from countries with limited financial resources might receive inadequate or insufficient instruction and information from their governments and whether NGOs might help fill that informational gap. Professor Charney opined that NGOs might be particularly influential in some of the newer lawmaking forums, such as "general international law."

It was generally agreed that effective procedural devices for the public to interact with lawmakers and lawmaking groups encourages effective creation and implementation of environmental goals. The panelists queried, however, whether these procedural rights have been recognized by the international community. Professor Reif saw no customary procedural right, only rights expressed by treaties. Some thought, however, that "soft law" developments, at the very least, indicated a developing consensus in certain geographic regions regarding these procedural rights. This is especially true in regions with well developed interest groups.

NGO participation is unquestionably of increasing importance. Professor Weiss cited examples of extensive NGO participation in the rule-making fora of the Convention on International Trade in Endangered Species (CITIES). There, the role of the NGO has always been important, but recently NGOs have outnumbered governments on the floor. NGOs have also become much more sophisticated in their lobbying efforts, focussing not only on their own government, but also on the governments of other countries. Governments may also even find extra-legal use for their NGOs, encouraging them to lobby other governments or even other branches within the same government.

Professor Iwamura pointed out that even when NGOs are excluded by the lawmaking forum, they still may play a key role, exerting considerable influence behind-the-scenes. Professor Weiss agreed, citing the First International Tropical Timber Agreement. NGO pressure influenced the adoption of provisions that were not on the agenda of participating governments.

The most direct participation in the international environmental lawmaking process of NGOs to date has been in the framework conventions. When participation is direct, the framework may get all the ensuing benefits attached to listening to a nonstate interest. This may be problematic, though, as the lesser developed countries might reasonably express some doubt as to whether larger, usually Western NGOs, represent truly international environmental interests. Voices from these countries have questioned whether these NGOs are strongly slanted toward the interests of the developed world. Professor Atsuko Kanehara questioned whether NGOs' participation in the lawmaking process should properly be the subject of regulation under international law. NGO participation does facilitate increased transparency of the international lawmaking process, though at the same time it may further weaken the voice of the already under-represented states and interests.

Professor Kanehara reiterated that NGOs are indispensable in helping governing bodies gather and disseminate information as well as deal with scientific uncertainty. Since the public is significantly affected by international environmental rules (e.g., the phasing out of CFCs), the public ought to have a say in the lawmaking process. Yet Professor Kanehara saw the state of the law regarding NGO participation in international lawmaking uncertain at best. NGOs have been formally granted procedural rights (e.g., NGOs were given formal legal status in the World Heritage Convention as official observers), but most international framework agreements leave the matter to the states. Little was made, moreover, of the possibility that decisionmaking within the NGOs might be undemocratic in nature. Further, NGOs may be completely unrepresentative in nature, which may result in a less representative international process if NGOs are given a substantial voice in the international lawmaking process. These and other problems also need much more careful examination before NGOs are given even greater rights in the international arena.

Finally, the limits of NGO participation should also not be ignored. NGOs may be susceptible, as Professor Charney pointed out, to "populist and chauvinistic" impulses. As an example, he cited the parochial NGO approaches regarding the 200 mile economic zone and the disruption that occasioned on species-wide monitoring and management. Professor Koga expressed concern that non-American NGOs tend to be less developed, and thus less effective and prone to influence by American NGOs. This problem, along with many others, must be considered if NGOs are to be made an institutional part of the international lawmaking process.

The panel then turned to the relationship between the nature of an agreement's dispute resolution mechanisms and the process of implementation and compliance. It would seem, ostensibly, that compulsory dispute resolution mechanisms would have the greatest influence on implementation and compliance. Professor Kanehara argued that agreements with binding force and dispute resolution procedures strongly encourage compliance. Professor Ida reiterated that parties enter agreements only reluctantly and thus rules that can be invoked before a court, thereby insuring compliance, are necessary. Professor Detlev Vagts added that states must know the content of the rules that will be applied before they are willing to submit to third-party resolution.

Professor Charney suggested that compulsory dispute settlement under UNCLOS serves two purposes. First, it resolves concrete disputes between the parties. Second, the threat of compulsory settlement encourages compliance. The UNCLOS settlement process did have a shortcoming in this respect: the parties to the UNCLOS dispute resolution procedures convention represent only a narrow sector of the international community. Thus, universal application of UNCLOS provisions will be weakened if participation in the dispute resolution mechanism is not broadened.

The central difficulty in the creation of a universally binding dispute resolution process is the inability of states parties to reach agreement on a single mechanism. This difficulty was apparent in recent framework conventions, such as the Vienna Convention and the Convention on Climate Change. Both the right to a certain level of environmental protection and an obligation to provide such protection were recognized, but these rights were qualified by the various positions of the individual states. Given that some states may be willing, but unable to contribute adequately to the protection of the global environment, treaty regimes may also need to contain inducements to encourage compliance, as well as penalties for noncompliance.

Whether because of limits on infrastructure, experience in environmental protection or state of industrial development, not all states can make equal contributions. Individual capacities must be taken into account. Thus, framework agreements often take a dual approach, including incentives for compliance and penalties for noncompliance. This approach was exemplified in the preparatory work for UNCED. Working Group 3, concerned with compliance, outlined procedures to bring noncompliance to the attention of all state parties; to invoke measures if reports are not properly filed; and to offer technical and financial incentives to complying states. Thus, rather than sanctions alone, compliance was to be encouraged by incentives and noncompliance discouraged by the threat of adverse publicity.

Requiring states to publicize their strategies for compliance, so that instances of possible noncompliance can be identified and rectified early, may also be a useful technique to encourage uniform treaty interpretation, as well as compliance. At a minimum, this will discourage unilateral interpretations of treaty obligation.

Compliance might also be influenced by the extent to which the parties attempt to accommodate diverse needs and interests in the treaties themselves. Professor Maureen Irish, using the environmental side agreements of North American Free Trade Agreement (NAFTA) as an example, questioned whether treaties should obligate the parties to enforce domestic legal standards. Professor Reif agreed that the NAFTA side agreements are a departure from past practice. These agreements clearly call for increased public participation, due process, and domestic judicial procedures. Yet, Professor Reif remarked that these agreements have only nonbinding dispute resolution techniques, and thus avoid imposing any country's standards on the others. Specifically, the NAFTA side agreements call for conciliation, non binding third-party recommendations, and discretionary treatment of complaints by the newly established Commission.

Several conference participants argued that the emphasis on dispute resolution mechanisms was misleading. The reasons for compliance or noncompliance are much broader than the mere availability of dispute resolution mechanisms. Mr. Keith Highet suggested that dispute resolution is not necessarily about one party's "winning" a dispute in court, since states generally have little idea in advance of the position they will take in future disputes. This is evidenced in compromissory clauses: general agreements that any question or subject raised by another party to the treaty concerning the treaty subject matter will go to court. Rather, to some extent, dispute resolution should be viewed as just that, a way to resolve disagreements over the proper interpretation of a treaty or a point of international law, not only as an incentive to comply with treaty provisions.

Professor Weiss reiterated that it is not essential to rely primarily on the formal process of dispute resolution, particularly in the international law of the environment. Various mechanisms have reduced dramatically the need for confrontation. Such mechanisms include meetings of parties, subcommittees and working groups, draft reports and assistance to states to develop the local capacity to monitor reports (as offered in the Implementation Committee of the Montreal Protocol). Professor Charney added that compulsory dispute settlement is part of the political process, not contrary to it.

CONCLUSION

The challenges of international lawmaking have increased with various global developments. Professor Weiss highlighted just a few, including "the linkage of environmental protection with economic development and competitiveness, the blurring of the clear distinctions between international and national or local occurrences, the rise of nonstate actors, both corporate and environmental, and the increasingly rapid rate of change in many aspects of society, including our scientific understanding of problems." Traditional international sources of law have proved inadequate to address these challenges; change is needed. The increasing capacity of humankind to alter the environment on an increasingly greater scale has made this an issue of the utmost urgency. International recognition of the gravity of these concerns has resulted in some successes, such as the Vienna Convention. At the same time, many contentious issues remain unresolved and others arise. The international legal community must continue its quest to find suitable and effective international legal processes and instruments to deal with these issues.

INTERNATIONAL LAWMAKING IN THE CONTEXT OF THE LAW OF THE SEA AND THE GLOBAL ENVIRONMENT

Jonathan I. Charney

I. INTRODUCTION

In 1992, the United Nations Conference on Environment and Development commemorated the twentieth anniversary of the 1972 Stockholm Conference on the Human Environment. Stockholm marked the beginning of intense international concentration on global environmental concerns. The year 1972 also marked the commencement of the negotiations of the Third United Nations Conference on the Law of the Sea. The resultant 1982 Convention on the Law of the Sea entered into force in the fall of 1994.[1] The international community responded to these

---

1. United Nations Convention on the Law of the Sea [hereinafter *LOS Convention*], *opened for signature* December 10, 1982, Preamble, U.N. Doc. A/CONF.62/122 (1982), *reprinted in* UNITED NATIONS, OFFICIAL TEXT OF THE UNITED NATIONS CONVENTION ON THE LAW OF THE SEA WITH ANNEXES AND INDEX, U.N. Sales No. E.83.V.5 1983. For the status of the signatories and parties, see *Status of the United Nations Convention on the Law of the Sea*, 25 LAW OF THE SEA BULLETIN, June 1994, at 1. The number of ratifications has increased since that publication. The United States voted in favor of the 1994 UNGA resolution endorsing the entry into force of the Convention and the 1994 Agreement resolving the disputes over the deep sea-bed regime. G.A. Res. 48/263 (1994), *reprinted at* 33 I.L.M. 1309 (1994). The executive branch of the United States submitted the LOS Convention to the U.S. Senate on October 7, 1994, for its advice and consent to United States ratification. UNITED NATIONS CONVENTION ON THE LAW OF THE SEA, WITH ANNEXES, AND THE AGREEMENT RELATING TO THE IMPLEMENTATION OF PART XI OF THE UNITED NATIONS CONVENTION ON THE LAW OF THE SEA, WITH ANNEX, MESSAGE FROM THE PRESIDENT OF THE UNITED STATES, S. Doc. No. 103–39, 103d Cong., 2d Sess. (1994).

conferences by producing substantial new international law for the environment and for the seas. Interestingly, these efforts also contributed to the evolution of the lawmaking process. This chapter explores the evolution of the lawmaking process in response to the demand for new international law in these areas. I examine first the role of treaty-based international law. Next, I critique the role of customary international law in the development of contemporary international law of the environment and of the sea. Finally, I explore the value of general international law in these areas. All of these subjects are vital to contemporary international law. While the contribution of customary international law may have peaked, treaty-based law will play an increasingly significant role. The full importance of general international law, however, may not yet be appreciated.

II. TREATIES

Treaties are important sources of rights and obligations in international environmental law[2] and the law of the sea.[3] They often comprise text that details the rights and obligations of state parties, providing easily accessible statements of black letter law to guide government decisionmakers and bureaucrats. States commit themselves to abide by the treaty-based rules when they become parties; thus, questions concerning the binding force of the rules set out in treaties are not likely to arise. As written documents, treaties may not only establish general rights and obligations, but may also create detailed and specific rules that can be fixed at the time of the treaty negotiation.

In addition, institutions or other procedures may be created to revise those rules or develop new rules after the treaty enters into force. International

---

2.   For collections of major environment treaties *see* INTERNATIONAL PROTECTION OF THE ENVIRONMENT: TREATIES AND RELATED DOCUMENTS (Bernd Rüster & Bruno Simma eds., 1975–1992 & Supps.); and WORLD TREATIES FOR THE PROTECTION OF THE ENVIRONMENT (Tullio Scovazzi & Tullio Treves eds., 1992 & 1992 Supp.).

3.   Many international agreements pertain to the law of the sea. In addition to the 1982 LOS Convention, *supra* note 1, a key role was played by the four 1958 Geneva Conventions on the Law of the Sea: Convention on the Territorial Sea and the Contiguous Zone, 29 Apr. 1958, 15 U.S.T. 1606, T.I.A.S. No. 5639, 516 U.N.T.S. 205; Convention on the Continental Shelf, Apr. 29, 1958, 15 U.S.T. 471, T.I.A.S. 5578, 499 U.N.T.S. 311; Convention on the High Seas, Apr. 29, 1958, 13 U.S.T. 2313, T.I.A.S. No. 5200, 450 U.N.T.S. 82; Convention on Fishing and Conservation of the Living Resources of the High Seas, the Living Resources of the Seas, Apr. 29, 1958, 17 U.S.T. 138, T.I.A.S. No. 5969, 559 U.N.T.S. 285. These and other international agreements are collected in: NATIONAL LEGISLATION AND TREATIES RELATED TO THE TERRITORIAL SEA, THE CONTIGUOUS ZONE, THE CONTINENTAL SHELF, THE HIGH SEAS AND TO FISHING AND CONSERVATION OF THE LIVING RESOURCES OF THE SEA (United Nations Legislative Series); NEW DIRECTIONS IN THE LAW OF THE SEA (Houston S. Lay, Robin Churchill, Myron Nordquist comp. & eds., 1973–1981); and NEW DIRECTIONS IN THE LAW OF THE SEA (Kenneth R. Simmonds comp. & ed., 1983).

environmental treaties therefore often have annexes and protocols that set out the detailed obligations of the parties.[4] Specific fora are created or authorized to revise these obligations as developments require.[5] Additional obligations may be made binding on the parties based on consent to the original treaty or a special procedure created to secure the necessary future commitments.[6] Finally, treaties may establish mechanisms to monitor compliance,[7] settle disputes,[8] and enforce obligations.[9] Similar mechanisms are integral to the 1982 Convention on the Law of the Sea and other oceans agreements.[10] Treaties, therefore, are valuable in establishing international legal regimes in the best tradition of positive law.

On the other hand, treaty-based solutions to international law issues are inherently limited. While treaties may be rapidly negotiated and entered into force, the negotiation of important, complex treaties often takes years, especially if many states participate in the negotiations. After years of preparatory work, the substantive law of the sea negotiations took over ten years to conclude the text finally adopted in 1982. Even twelve years after that adoption, further substantive consultations were required to resolve differences that presented obstacles to widespread acceptance of the LOS Convention.[11] Once a treaty is adopted, another

---

4.   *E.g.*, Convention on the Control of Transboundary Movements of Hazardous Wastes and their Disposal, done Basel, March 22, 1989, Annexes I–III, 28 I.L.M. 657 (1989).

5.   *E.g., id.* art. 18.

6.   *E.g., id.* arts. 17 and 18.

7.   *E.g., id.* arts. 6, 10, 13, 15.5, 16.

8.   *E.g., id.* art. 20 and Annex VI.

9.   *E.g., id.* arts. 12, 15.2, 15.5(c).

10.   The details are found in the LOS Convention itself, as well as its nine Annexes, *supra* note 1.   Amendment procedures are provided in LOS Convention, arts. 312–314; compliance and enforcement is addressed in the deep sea-bed regime through the Assembly, Council, Secretariat, and the Legal and Technical Commission, arts. 160, 162, 165, 166–169, 175 (audit of the Authority), 184–185 (suspension); further details are provided in Annex III, *Basic Conditions of Prospecting, Exploration and Exploitation*; compliance with spatial limits to jurisdiction is supported by the obligation to publish these limits on navigational charts, LOS Convention, art. 17; certain coastal state enforcement authority is granted in cases of violations of the rights of innocent passage, transit passage, and archipelagic passage, arts. 21, 25, 26, 42, 43, 54; rights of the coastal state in the Exclusive Economic Zone (EEZ) and continental shelf are specified, arts. 56, 77; environmental enforcement provisions are granted for flag states, coastal states and port states, arts. 213–222; state responsibility is recognized for environmental damage, art. 235; notification and cooperation with the coastal state regarding marine scientific research in the EEZ is required, arts. 245–253; and important compulsory dispute settlement systems are established, arts. 279–299.

11.   *See* Statement by Ambassador Madeleine K. Albright, United States Permanent Representative to the United Nations, (Apr. 27, 1993), U.S.U.N. Press Release 55-(93) (Apr. 27, 1993), *reprinted in* U.S. Enters Sea-bed Negotiations, OCEANS POL'Y NEWS, Apr. 1993, at 2; Jonathan I. Charney, *The United States and the Revision of the 1982 Convention on the*

long period of time may pass before states commit themselves to the treaty by signature and ratification or accession and the necessary number of such commitments is accumulated to bring the agreement into force. While the Law of the Sea Convention was concluded in 1982, twelve years passed before it entered into force.[12] On the other hand, sometimes multilateral treaties enter into force relatively quickly, especially those that focus on general obligations and contain few details or require relatively few state parties to bring them into force.[13]

Finally, treaties may directly bind state parties only; nonparty states may only be directly bound with their consent.[14] Widespread adherence to treaties is unlikely, and universal or even nearly universal participation is almost impossible. Treaty-based obligations may thus bind only sectors of the international community, which may prove inadequate if the solution to a problem requires broader participation. This inadequacy is particularly acute as regards the law of the sea, since the deep sea-bed regime presented an obstacle to widespread participation,[15] but navigational, environmental, and resource issues also required global participation in order to be optimally effective. Nearly universal, if not universal, commitment is necessary for successful resolution of major environmental problems of global concern, e.g., climate change and ozone depletion.

Law of the Sea, 23 OCEAN DEV. & INT'L L. 279 (1992); David E. Pitt, *U.S. Seeks to 'Fix' Mining Provisions of Sea Treaty*, N.Y. TIMES, Aug. 28, 1993, at A3. *See also* Steven Greenhouse, *U.S., After Negotiating Changes, Is Set to Sign Pact on Sea Mining*, N.Y. TIMES, Mar. 10, 1994, at A14, cols. 1– 4.

12. *See supra* note 1.

13. After signature at the 1992 United Nations Conference on Environment and Development (UNCED), the Convention on Biological Diversity (done at Rio de Janeiro, June 5, 1992), 31 I.L.M. 818 (1992) obtained the thirty necessary ratifications to enter into force on Dec. 29, 1993. *United Nations Biodiversity Treaty to Take Effect December 29; UNEP Executive Director Says*, BNA INT'L ENV'T DAILY, Oct. 5, 1993. The Framework Convention on Climate Change was signed just prior to UNCED (done at New York, May 9, 1992, 31 I.L.M. 849 (1992)). It entered into force with the necessary fifty ratifications on Mar. 21, 1994. *United Nations Climate Change Convention to Enter into force March 21, 1994*, BNA INT'L ENV'T DAILY, Jan. 10, 1993.

14. Vienna Convention on the Law of Treaties, May 23, 1969, Preamble, arts. 34–38, 1155 U.N.T.S. 331, *reprinted in* 8 INT. LEG. MAT. 679 (1969); *See* Jonathan I. Charney, *The Antarctic System and Customary International Law, in* INTERNATIONAL LAW FOR ANTARCTICA 55, 63–68 (Francesco Francioni & Tullio Scovazzi eds., 1987).

15. The deep sea-bed regime is set out in Part XI of the LOS Convention, arts. 133–191 and Annexes III and IV, *supra* note 1. Aspects of this regime were essentially superseded by the 1994 Agreement on the deep sea-bed regime, *supra* note 1. For a discussion of the problems with the deep sea-bed regime of the 1982 LOS Convention text *see* Jonathan I. Charney, *The United States and the Revision of the Convention on the Law of the Sea*, 23 OCEAN DEV. & INT'L L. 279 (1992). For a discussion of the 1994 Agreement *see* Jonathan I. Charney, *U.S. Provisional Application of the 1994 Deep Sea-bed Agreement*, 88 AM. JOUR. INT'L L. 705 (1994).

III. GENERAL INTERNATIONAL LAW

a. Traditional Approaches

The traditional alternative (or complement) to a treaty-based solution is customary international law. Customary international law is the product of state practice and *opinio juris* that produces norms of international law. Although international organizations may not be established by custom, customary international law is capable of sustaining most rights or obligations that might also be established by treaty. State practice and *opinio juris* could support a general norm or a specific and detailed rule of behavior. No specific act of consent is required by any state; rather, acceptance by the international community supported by other states' acquiescence is sufficient to confirm a rule of customary international law.[16] Thus, as compared to treaties, universal or nearly universal law may be attainable through customary international law. It is therefore not surprising that customary international law is the foundation for modern international law of the sea and the environment. This is evident in general environmental obligations founded upon traditional tort-based state responsibility rules and the freedoms of the seas.[17]

While in theory customary international law may be equal to or superior to treaty-based law, in reality it is severely limited. Traditional customary international law emanating from state practice and *opinio juris* may take a considerable amount of time to mature. State practice and *opinio juris* may establish general norms, but are less likely to yield detailed and finely tuned legal rules—the sort of rules that are increasingly required to provide solutions to contemporary international problems. Furthermore, unlike the traditional subjects of international law (war, treaties, diplomatic relations, navigation in the sea), state practice in international relations necessary to support a nascent rule of customary international environmental law is not easily developed. The practices, if any, in this field are likely to be domestic and diverse. Even if a practice exists, it is unlikely that sufficient evidence of it will come to the attention of the international community and give rise to an *opinio juris*. Considerable time and attention is required to develop the necessary consensus of state practice to sustain traditional customary international law for any but the most general rules relating to the environment.

---

16.   *See* Jonathan I. Charney, *Universal International Law*, 87 AM. JOUR. INT'L L. 529, 536–42 (1993).

17.   The traditionally cited Trail Smelter (Trail Smelter Arbitral Tribunal, Decision of Apr. 16, 1938 (U.S. v. Can.), 33 AM. JOUR. INT'L L. 182 (1939); Trail Smelter Arbitral Tribunal, Decision of Mar. 11, 1941 (U.S. v. Can.), 35 AM. JOUR. INT'L L. 712 (1941)), Corfu Channel (Corfu Channel Case (Alb./U.K.), 1949 ICJ REP. 4 (Apr. 19)), and Lake Lanoux (Lake Lanoux Arbitration (Fr. v. Sp.), 24 INT'L L. REP. 101 (1957) (Nov. 16)) cases certainly loom large in this field.

Finally, it is difficult to marshal direct evidence of state practice. Even if such practice is known, it is often so laden with the peculiarities of the circumstances that it is almost impossible to draw general conclusions. For example, the recently concluded study of international maritime boundary practice directed by this author did gather considerable evidence of state practices but, despite a common framework and physical commonalities, political, economic, geographic, and historical differences provided reasons to consider each solution unique.[18] Although international maritime boundaries may be unusual, individual circumstances often distinguish state practice, regardless of the subject. This renders conclusions on the uniformity of state practice the product of subjective rather than objective analyses. Traditional customary international law is, therefore, unlikely to serve as a primary vehicle for any but the most general kind of new international environmental law. In the law of the sea, new uses and activities provide little time for state practice and *opinio juris* to develop sufficiently to fix norms for new and potentially damaging activities, e.g., long-line pelagic driftnet fishing.

b. Contemporary Developments—General International Law

Much of contemporary international law of the environment and of the sea is based upon *general* international law. It is not treaty-based law, since states are not required to be parties to treaties establishing or codifying rights or obligations. Nor is this really customary-based law, since no custom (that is, uniform state practice over time) may exist (although it is often classified as a form of customary law). This general international law is rather the product of an international community consensus formed around the normative status of discrete decisions at international fora. These decisions have increasingly been accepted as legislative in character, and often are considered sufficient to give rise to new law. This international lawmaking process is particularly salient in the two areas that are the focus of this paper: the law of the sea and law of the environment.[19]

Traditional accounts describe customary international lawmaking as an amorphous process in which a pattern of behavior by states acting in their own interest over a long period of time (state practice) is coupled with the conclusion that such practice reflects a legal obligation (*opinio juris*). Treaties may codify the practice in normative terms and writers may characterize these developments as general obligations. It eventually becomes well established that new international

---

18.   Jonathan I. Charney, *Introduction, in* INTERNATIONAL MARITIME BOUNDARIES xxiii, xlii (Jonathan I. Charney & Lewis M. Alexander, eds., 1992).

19. *See generally* Charney, *supra* note 15;   Pierre-Marie Dupuy, *Soft Law and International Law of the Environment,* 12 MICH. JOUR. INT'L L. 420 (1991); and Geoffrey Palmer, *New Ways to Make International Environmental Law,* 86 AM. JOUR. INT'L L. 259 (1992).

law on the subject has emerged.[20] The judgments in the *Paquete Habana*,[21] *Lotus*,[22] and *North Sea*[23] cases epitomize this process. Traditional customary law formation may have sufficed when both the scope of international law and the number of states were limited. Today, however, the subject matter of international law has expanded to encompass areas that were traditionally the preserve of states' domestic jurisdiction. States have dramatically increased in number and diversity, making access to and analysis of state practice almost impossible. This is the case even though new technologies provide access to a large quantity of information. Effective use of that information for proof of state practice and *opinio juris* is virtually impossible. At the same time, much pertinent information remains hidden. Although customary law still may be created in the traditional manner, that process has increasingly given way in recent years to a more structured method, especially in the instant areas.

Rather than state practice and *opinio juris,* multilateral fora often play a central role in creating and shaping contemporary international law. These fora include the United Nations General Assembly, regional organizations, and standing and *ad hoc* multilateral diplomatic conferences, as well as international organizations devoted to specialized subjects. Today, major developments in international law are often begun or supported by proposals, reports, resolutions, draft treaties or protocols debated in such fora. There, representatives of states and other interested nongovernmental groups assemble to address international problems of mutual concern and sometimes reach a consensus that is expressed in normative terms capable of general application. At other times, the potential new law evolves through the medium of international relations or the practices of specialized international institutions. Then, at later stages, they are addressed at the appropriate international fora. The debate and decisions reached at those fora draw attention to the rules under consideration and help to shape and crystallize them.

The authoritative status of the debates at these multilateral fora depends on many factors. Central to the issue is the clarity with which the fact that the rule under consideration reflects a refinement, codification, crystallization, or progressive development of international law is communicated to the participating states. Of crucial importance also is the degree of support given to the rule under consideration. Adoption of the rule by the forum in accordance with its procedures for decisionmaking may be neither necessary nor sufficient. On the other hand, unanimous support is not required. Consensus, defined as the lack of expressed objection to the rule by any participant, may often suffice. Participants who do not express a position on the rule are, of course, considered to have tacitly consented.

---

20. *E.g.,* RESTATEMENT (THIRD) OF THE FOREIGN RELATIONS LAW OF THE UNITED STATES §§ 102, 103 at 24–35 (1987) [hereinafter RESTATEMENT].

21. The Paquete Habana, 175 U.S. 677 (1900).

22. The S.S. "Lotus" (Fr. v. Turk.), 1927 P.C.I.J. (ser. A) No. 10 (Sept. 7).

23. North Sea Continental Shelf (FRG/Den.; FRG/Neth.), 1969 I.C.J. REP. 3 (Feb. 20).

Even opposition by a small number of participating states may not stop the movement of the proposed rule into law. But support for the rule must be widespread and encompass all interest groups. It therefore is significant whether the objections, if any, demonstrate that an important group of states is opposed—thus precluding the widespread support of the international community—or whether only minor and relatively isolated states are in opposition. The effect of the dissent depends upon the number of objecting states, the nature of their objections, the importance of the interests the objecting states seek to protect, and their geopolitical standing relative to the states that support the proposed rule. Moreover, objections may go to the heart of the rule under consideration or to merely subsidiary issues.

The discussions at such fora are necessarily communicated to all states and other interested parties. According to some customary law analysts, the work and the products of those fora may be characterized as state practice and/or *opinio juris*.[24] Certainly, the fora may substantially move the solutions toward acquiring the status of international law. Those solutions that are also positively received by the international community through indications of support, such as state practice, will rapidly be absorbed into international law, notwithstanding the technical legal status of the form in which they emerged from the multilateral forum.

How much, if any, evidence of state practice and/or *opinio juris* is required from events outside of the forum considering the rule depends upon the facts of each case. To be sure, proof of *opinio juris* and state practice has never been objectively evident; it must depend on subjective interpretations of the facts and motivations of state officials.[25] Furthermore, considerable flexibility exists regarding, for example, what constitutes practice, the required period of time and its continuity, and the required generality of state participation.[26] This flexibility—indeed, some might say uncertainty—is all the more apparent today with the dramatic increase in the number of states and in the data that might be utilized.[27] These increasing difficulties have made the relatively objective and transparent

---

24. Gennady M. Danilenko, *The Theory of International Customary Law*, 31 GER. Y.B. INT'L L. 9, 37, 38 (1988); Rosalyn Higgins, *The Role of Resolutions of International Organizations in the Process of Creating Norms in the International System, in* INTERNATIONAL LAW AND THE INTERNATIONAL SYSTEM 21 (W. E. Butler ed., 1987); G. I. Tunkin, *The Role of Resolutions of International Organizations in Creating Norms of International Law, in id.* at 5, 12, 14, 17; ANTHONY A. D'AMATO, THE CONCEPT OF CUSTOM IN INTERNATIONAL LAW 104, 162, 165, 271 (1972).

25. *See* Peter Haggenmacher, *La Doctrine des deux éléments du droit coutumier dans la pratique de la Cour internationale,* 90 REVUE GÉNÉRALE DE DROIT INTERNATIONAL PUBLIQUE 5 (1986).

26. *See* Hiram E. Chodosh, *Neither Treaty Nor Custom: The Emergence of Declarative International Law,* 26 TEX. INT'L L. J. 87, 100–5 (1991), and references therein.

27. *See* Louis B. Sohn, *"Generally Accepted" International Rules*, 61 WASH. L. REV. 1073 (1986).

activities of international institutions in this regard more salient. The clearer the rule debated, the clearer the intention to promote a rule of generally applicable international law and the stronger the consensus in favor of the rule the less need there is for evidence from outside the forum.[28] Similar attention paid by the same or other fora may further strengthen the case for the rule. When these signals are weak, confirmation of the normative status of the rule may be sought in declarations by states outside the forum and in other evidence of *opinio juris* and/or state practice before or after the meeting of the forum.[29] In theory, however, a single clearly phrased and strongly endorsed declaration at a nearly universal diplomatic forum could be sufficient to establish new international law.[30]

The process outlined above differs significantly from the traditional understanding of the customary lawmaking process, which requires general practice over time joined with an *opinio juris*. It is more accurate to denominate this law *general international law*, as the International Court has done on numerous occasions.[31]

---

28. *See generally* Frederic L. Kirgis, Jr., *Custom on a Sliding Scale*, 81 AM. JOUR. INT'L L. 146 (1987).

29. *See* Sohn, *supra* note 27; Luigi Condorelli, *Custom, in* INTERNATIONAL LAW: ACHIEVEMENTS AND PROSPECTS 205 (Mohammed Bedjaoui ed., 1991); Antonio Cassese, *The Geneva Protocols of 1977 on the Humanitarian Law of Armed Conflict and Customary International Law*, 3 UCLA PACIFIC BASIN L.J. 55 (1984). The latter two authors do not appear to be willing to dispense with proof of state practice in any case. Sohn appears willing to do so.

30. Of course, reality may never be that unambiguous. Furthermore, any norm that attracts such definite and widespread support would necessarily be echoed in pronouncements and/or actions extrinsic to the forum. When that happens, precious little, if any, such evidence should be needed.

31. *E.g.*, Elettronica Sicula S.p.A. (ELSI) (U.S. v. It.), 1989 I.C.J. REP. 15, 66, para. 111 (July 20); Border and Transborder Armed Actions (Nicar. v. Hond.), Jurisdiction and Admissibility, 1988 I.C.J. REP. 69, 85, para. 35 (Dec. 20); Continental Shelf (Libyan Arab Jamahiriya/Malta), 1985 I.C.J. REP. 13, 39, 55, paras. 46, 76 (June 3); Military and Paramilitary Activities in and against Nicaragua (Nicar. v. U.S.), Jurisdiction and Admissibility, 1984 I.C.J. REP. 392, 422–24, paras. 69, 71, 73 (Nov. 26); Delimitation of the Maritime Boundary in the Gulf of Maine Area (Can./U.S.), 1984 I.C.J. REP. 246, 293, 294, 297, 299, 302, 303, 339, paras. 91, 94, 106, 107, 111, 112, 122, 123, 230 (Oct. 12); Continental Shelf (Tunis./Libyan Arab Jamahiriya), 1982 I.C.J. REP. 18, 38, 47, 74, paras. 24, 46, 100 (Feb. 24); Interpretation of the Agreement of Mar. 25, 1951 between the WHO and Egypt, 1980 I.C.J. REP. 73, 90, 92, 95, paras. 37, 41, 48 (Advisory Opinion of Dec. 20); United States Diplomatic and Consular Staff in Tehran (U.S. v. Iran), 1980 I.C.J. REP. 3, 31, 33, 41, 43, 44, paras. 62, 69, 90, 94, 95 (May 24); Aegean Sea Continental Shelf (Greece v. Turk.), 1978 I.C.J. REP. 3, 32, paras. 76, 77 (Dec. 19); Legal Consequences for States of the Continued Presence of South Africa in Namibia (South West Africa) notwithstanding S.C.R. 276 (1970), 1971 I.C.J. REP. 16, 47, 55, paras. 96, 121 (Advisory Opinion of June 21); Barcelona Traction, Light and Power Co., Ltd. (New Application: 1962) (Belg. v. Spain), 1970 I.C.J. REP. 3, 32, 38, 46, paras. 34, 54, 87, 88 (Feb. 5); North Sea Continental Shelf (F.R.G./Den.; F.R.G./Neth.), 1969 I.C.J. REP. 3, 28, 38, 42, paras. 37, 63, 73 (Feb.

Whatever its proper appellation, the lawmaking process is substantially advanced by the activities of these multilateral fora. In addition, this is a deliberative process that often approximates the legislative process found in the more centralized legal systems of nation states.

I do not intend to suggest, however, that multilateral fora have independent legislative authority. They do not, although some argue that the United Nations General Assembly exercises legislative authority when it adopts and terms resolutions as declarations of international law.[32] Nor do I intend to suggest that upon adoption or entry into force, all generally applicable treaty texts become *ipso facto* and *ab initio* international law.[33] Rather, the products of multilateral fora substantially advance and formalize the international lawmaking process,[34] making possible the rapid entry into force of new international law. Decisions made at such fora, support for the generally applicable rule, and written publication of the proposed rule giving full notice to the international legal community call for an early response. If the response is affirmative (even if tacit), the rule may enter into law, thereby avoiding some of the mysteries of customary lawmaking. This process also permits broader and more effective participation by all states and other

---

20). *See also* Georges Abi-Saab, *Discussion, in* CHANGE AND STABILITY IN INTERNATIONAL LAW-MAKING 10 (Antonio Cassese & Joseph H. H. Weiler eds., 1988).

The use of this label appears to be consistent with art. 38 of the Court's Statute since "international custom" is only "*evidence* of a *general* practice *accepted* as law." INTERNATIONAL COURT OF JUSTICE, STATUTE, art. 38 (emphasis added).

32. *See generally* Military and Paramilitary Activities in and against Nicaragua (Nicar. v. U.S.), Merits, 1986 I.C.J. REP. 14 (June 27); Western Sahara, 1975 I.C.J. REP. 12 (Advisory Opinion of Oct. 16); Texaco Overseas Petroleum Co. & California Asiatic Oil Co. v. Libyan Arab Republic (Jan. 19, 1977), 17 I.L.M. 1 (1978); THEODOR MERON, HUMAN RIGHTS AND HUMANITARIAN NORMS AS CUSTOMARY LAW 86 (1989); Higgins, *supra* note 24, at 21, 21–26; ANTONIO CASSESE, INTERNATIONAL LAW IN A DIVIDED WORLD 193–94 (1986); Oscar Schachter, *International Law in Theory and Practice*, 178 RECUEIL DES COURS 9, 110–32 (1982 V); Christopher C. Joyner, *U.N. General Assembly Resolutions and International Law: Rethinking the Contemporary Dynamics of Norm-Creation*, 11 CAL. W. INT'L L. J. 445 (1981).

33. D'Amato maintains that they do automatically establish customary law. Anthony D'Amato, *The Concept of Human Rights in International Law*, 82 COLUM. L. REV. 1110 (1982); D'AMATO, *supra* note 24, at 104, 110, 164.

34. Various writers have made similar, though not as broad, suggestions. *E.g.*, MERON, *supra* note 32, at 86, 93, 113; Schachter, *supra* note 32, at 127–30, 133; Oscar Schachter, *Entangled Treaty and Custom, in* INTERNATIONAL LAW AT A TIME OF PERPLEXITY 717, 722, 732, 734 (Yoram Dinstein ed., 1988); Eduardo Jiménez de Aréchaga, *Intervention, in* CHANGE AND STABILITY IN INTERNATIONAL LAW-MAKING, *supra* note 31, at 27, 29–30; Higgins, *supra* note 24; Louis B. Sohn, *The Law of the Sea: Customary International Law Developments*, 34 Am. U.L. REV. 271 (1985).

interested groups and allows for the legitimate operation of tacit consent.[35] Detailed rules may be established through this process. While the process may be abused, it is less open to abuse and miscommunication than classical customary lawmaking. States are increasingly aware that the work of multilateral fora contributes to the development of general international law and, therefore, they take discussions at those fora seriously. If the process is as transparent as it appears, the interests and wills of states are now better served than before.

There are many examples of this process in action. Two prominent developments in the law of the sea occurred shortly after consensus was reached at the Third United Nations Conference on the Law of the Sea, with the rapid acceptance of both the 200-nautical-mile exclusive economic zone and the 12-nautical-mile territorial sea.[36] Early in the subsequent period, principles adopted by the Stockholm Conference on the Human Environment in 1972, especially Principle 21, emerged as established international law.[37] Those conferences communicated

---

35. For support of the view that the facilitation of communication and exchange of views on potential international law norms accelerates the international lawmaking process, *see* South West Africa (Eth. v. S. Afr.; Liber. v. S. Afr.), Second Phase, 1966 I.C.J. REP. 6, 291 (July 18) (Tanaka, J., diss. op.); Condorelli, *supra* note 29, at 190, 201.

36. *See* Continental Shelf (Libyan Arab Jamahiriya/Malta), 1985 I.C.J. Rep. 13, 29–30, 32–34, paras. 26–28, 31–34 (June 3); Delimitation of the Maritime Boundary in the Gulf of Maine Area (Can./U.S.), 1984 I.C.J. Rep. 246, 294-95, paras. 94–96 (Oct. 12); Restatement, *supra* note 19, at 5; Jonathan I. Charney, *The United States and the Law of the Sea after UNCLOS III—The Impact of General International Law*, 46 LAW & CONTEMP. PROBS. 38, 44–48 (1983). *See also* Philip Allott, *Mare Nostrum: A New International Law of the Sea*, 86 AM. JOUR. INT'L L. 764 (1992). In contrast, no progress was made on fixing the maximum breadth of the territorial sea during and after the U.N. Conference on the Law of the Sea of 1958 and the Second United Nations Conference on the Law of the Sea of 1960, since no consensus was reached by the participating states. *See* ANN L. HOLLICK, U.S. FOREIGN POLICY AND THE LAW OF THE SEA 135–59 (1981).

37. Principle 21 states: "States have, in accordance with the Charter of the United Nations and the principle of international law, the sovereign right to exploit their own resources pursuant to their own environmental policies, and the responsibility to ensure that activities within their jurisdiction or control do not cause damage to the environment of other states or of areas beyond the limits of national jurisdiction." *Report of the United Nations Conference on the Human Environment*, adopted June 16, 1972, Stockholm, U.N. Doc. A/Conf.48/14 & Corr. 1, 11 I.L.M. 1416, 1420 (1972).

Laura Pineschi, *The Antarctic Treaty System and General Rules of International Environmental Law, in* INTERNATIONAL LAW FOR ANTARCTICA, 187 (Francesco Francioni & Tullio Scovazzi eds., 1987); RESTATEMENT, *supra* note 20, § 601 reporters' note 1, § 602 reporters' note 1; Boleslaw Adam Boczek, *The Protection of the Antarctic Ecosystem: A Study in International Environmental Law*, 13 OCEAN DEV. & INT'L L. 347, 389 (1983); Richard B. Bilder, *The Present Legal and Political Situation in Antarctica, in* THE NEW NATIONALISM AND THE USE OF COMMON SPACES: ISSUES IN MARINE POLLUTION AND THE EXPLOITATION OF ANTARCTICA 167, 193–94 (Jonathan I. Charney ed., 1982); Günther Handl, *Territorial Sovereignty and the Problem of Transnational Pollution*, 69 AM. JOUR.

to all states that new rules of international law were under consideration. With the positive responses, the new rules came into law—even though the decisions and discussions in question had not traditionally been considered legally authoritative for general international law.[38] Owing to the pervasiveness of multilateral fora in international environmental law and the law of the sea, solutions to issues with pronounced lawmaking potential are likely to pass through one or more such fora toward becoming international law. For them, this process replaces the traditional customary lawmaking process.

We can today witness the continuing development of international law of the sea and of the environment through the general international lawmaking process. The United Nations is currently focusing on improving the management of high seas fish stocks beyond coastal state resource zones. Recently, United Nations resolutions declared extremely long pelagic high seas driftnet fishing illegal.[39] This resolution is reported to have "eradicated" that practice.[40] Also evolving is a mandatory system for managing high seas fisheries through greater cooperation and coordination of states active in the fishery in question.[41] Parties to the Antarctic

---

INT'L L. 50, 67 (1975); Cooperation in the Field of Economics, of Science and Technology and of the Environment, pt. 5, Environment, Conference on Security and Cooperation in Europe [CSCE], Final Act, August 1, 1975, secs. 1(a)(1), 1(a)(10), 73 DEP'T ST. BULL. 323 (1975), *reprinted in* 14 I.L.M. 1292, 1307 (1975).

38. These norms have been found in nonbinding resolutions of standing and *ad hoc* intergovernmental forums, and in draft treaties that have not entered into force. The Vienna Convention on the Law of Treaties, the 1982 Convention on the Law of the Sea, the Human Rights Covenants, and the Geneva Protocols all gave rise to general international law prior to their entry into force.

39. *Large-Scale Pelagic Drift-Net Fishing and Its Impact on the Living Marine Resources of the World's Oceans and Seas,* G.A. Res. 44/225, Dec. 22, 1989, U.N. Doc. A/RES/44/225, Mar. 15, 1990, 29 I.L.M. 555 (1990); and *Large Scale Pelagic Drift-Net Fishing and Its Impact on the Living Marine Resources of the World's Oceans and Seas,* G.A. Res 46/215 (Dec. 20, 1991), U.N. Doc. A/Res. 46/215 (Feb. 10, 1992), 31 I.L.M. 241 (1992). *See* William T. Burke, Mark Freeberg and Edward L. Miles, *The United Nations Resolutions on Driftnet Fishing: An Unsustainable Precedent for High Seas and Coastal Fisheries,* 25 OCEAN DEV. & INT'L L. 127, 128 (1994); Barbara Kwiatkowska, *The High Seas Fisheries Regime: At a Point of No Return?* 8 INT'L JOUR. MAR. & COASTAL L. 327, 329 (1993).

40. Burke, Freeberg, and Miles, *supra* note 39, at 178. *See also* Convention for the Prohibition of Fishing with Long Driftnets in the South Pacific, done November 24, 1989, Wellington, 29 I.L.M. 1454 (1990).

41. *See Implementation of the Decisions and Recommendations of the United Nations Conference on Environment and Development; Sustainable Use and Conservation of the Marine Living Resources of the High Seas,* United Nations Conference on Straddling Fish Stocks and Highly Migratory Fish Stocks, Report of the Secretary-General, U.N. Doc. A/48/479 (Oct. 7, 1994) p. 14; Kwiatkowska, *supra* note 39. Thus, in 1994 agreement was reached among the states active in the Bering Sea fisheries to ban fishing in the high seas

Treaty recently produced a new Protocol banning for an indefinite period mineral resource development of Antarctica.[42] This ban will effectively bind all states as general international law, even though most are not parties to the Antarctic Treaty or the Protocol. In 1993 the adverse reaction of the international community to the dumping at sea of low-level nuclear waste by Russia yielded an amendment to the London Dumping Convention that totally banned such dumping.[43] The ban will likely become normative for all states.

It is true that for many years the 1982 Convention on the Law of the Sea was not in force. The debates, communications, and consensus at the negotiations and the adoption of the text, however, radically changed much of the general international law of the sea.[44] The many products of the United Nations Conference on Environment and Development (UNCED) will produce significant new general international law beyond treaty obligations.[45] UNCED has certainly, for example, enhanced the rights of states from whose territories unique biological resources are taken for commercial development,[46] strengthened the precautionary principle as a rule of international law,[47] and reinforced the requirement that

---

areas beyond 200-nautical-miles from the coastlines of the surrounding states (the "donut hole"). *U.S. and Russia Agree on Bering Sea Fishing*, N.Y. TIMES, Jan. 13, 1994, at A10, cols. 4–5.

42. Protocol on Environmental Protection to the Antarctic Treaty, *done* Madrid Oct. 4, 1991, 30 I.L.M. 1461 (1991).

43. The decision was taken on November 12, 1993, to enter into force one hundred days later. David E. Pitt, *Russia Is Pressed on Nuclear Waste Dumping*, N.Y. TIMES, Dec. 5, 1993, 4B, col. 1; *Ban Is Now in Force on Nuclear Dumping*, N.Y. TIMES, Feb. 22, 1994, at A4, col. 1. *All Signatories to the London Convention Except Russia Accept Total Ban on Dumping*, INT'L ENVIR. RPTR., Feb. 23, 1994, at 156.

44. *See* Charney, *supra* note 36. See papers prepared by the Panel on the Law of Ocean Uses: *United States Interests in the Law of the Sea Convention*, 88 AM. JOUR. INT'L L 167 (1994); *U.S. Interests and the United Nations Convention on the Law of the Sea*, 21 OCEAN DEV. & INT'L L 373 (1990); *Statement by Expert Panel: Deep Sea-bed Mining and the 1982 Convention on the Law of the Sea*, 82 AM. JOUR. INT'L L. 363 (1988); *Exchange Between Expert Panel and Reagan Administration Officials on Non-Seabed-Mining Provisions of LOS Treaty*, 79 AM. JOUR. INT'L L. 151 (1985). *See also* Allott, *supra* note 36.

45. *See generally* United Nations Conference on Environment and Development, 31 I.L.M. 814 (1992), and documents reprinted therein; James Brooke, *The Earth Summit: Four of the Varied Faces in the Global Crowd at the Rio Gathering*, N.Y. TIMES, June 11, 1992, at A12; William K. Stevens, *Earth Summit Finds the Years of Optimism Are Fading Memory*, N.Y. TIMES, June 9, 1992, at C4.

46. Convention on Biological Diversity, *supra* note 13.

47. Rio Declaration on Environment and Development, Principle 15, U.N. Doc. A/Conf.151/5/Rev. 1 (June 13, 1992, 31 I.L.M. 874 (1992); Framework Convention on Climate Change, *supra* note 13, art. 3.3; Convention on Biological Diversity, *supra* note 13, art. 8.

environmental impact assessments be conducted when activities that pose substantial risks to the environment are planned.[48]

IV. CONCLUSION

Much international environmental law of the sea and of the environment requires the detail, precision, and institutions that may best be provided by treaty-based regimes. Treaties are a popular and critical vehicle for solving international environmental and oceans issues. Treaties are inadequate, however, when law is needed to bind most, if not all, states or to rapidly establish new and exacting norms. The traditional customary lawmaking process is equally unsuitable. This need is satisfied, however, by general international law.

General international law is central to the evolution of international law of the future. It permits the international community to establish new international law relatively rapidly, it may generate detailed rules of law, and it may create law that is binding on virtually all, if not all, states.[49] General international law may be the preferred source in developing widely applicable, new international laws of the sea and of the environment, in particular. Certainly, the availability of *ad hoc* diplomatic conferences, as well as standing fora to debate, publicize, and endorse treaty and nontreaty texts provides a formidable tool for diplomats seeking to promote new international law.

---

48. Rio Declaration, *supra* note 47, Principle 17; Convention on Biological Diversity, *supra* note 13, art. 7; Framework Convention on Climate Change, *supra* note 13, arts. 4(e) and (f); Nonlegally binding authoritative statement of principles for a global consensus on the management, conservation, and sustainable development of all types of forests, para 8(h), U.N. Doc. A/CONF. 151/6/Rev.1 (June 13, 1992), 31 I.L.M. 315 (1994).

49. The general international lawmaking process may create international law that is binding on all states. Even if a few states object, they may be bound by a determination of a strong consensus of the international community. Under a community based system of law, the community may establish rules binding on all its members, so long as support is widespread and strong and notwithstanding the objections of a few, isolated states. No constitutional foundation of the international legal system forbids this and contemporary developments confirm this conclusion. For my analysis of this issue see, Charney, *supra* note 16.

INTERNATIONAL LAWMAKING PROCESS IN TRANSITION? A COMPARATIVE AND CRITICAL ANALYSIS OF RECENT INTERNATIONAL NORM-MAKING PROCESS

Ryuichi Ida

I. INTRODUCTION—THE CONTEMPORARY PHENOMENON OF MULTILATERALISM IN THE FORMATION OF INTERNATIONAL LAW

International lawmaking is, in a sense, a function of a given international community. The era in which customary rules or customary norm formation processes were in their glory mainly consisted of bilateral relations among a relatively small number of states centered in Europe. Since then, the number of states has multiplied, international relations have developed considerably in volume and in quality, and some important heterogeneity has been introduced through the appearance of socialist countries and of newly independent states. In these circumstances, the flourishing of international organizations and the increased importance of multilateral intercourse, as well as the increase of bilateral relations, have a manifestly great impact on various branches of contemporary international law.[1]

A problematique of traditional international law is that the newcomers to the international community, such as socialist states and developing countries, did not take part in the formation process of existing rules. Socialist states denied the validity of "capitalist" international law, while developing nations exposed their

---

1. Multilateralism, first in politics and then in law, had made an appearance only after 1815. The Congress of Vienna was the beginning of the era of "common interest," though not yet "community interest." This notion was the basis of development of multilateralism. For concise and accurate analysis of the evolution, *see*, PAUL REUTER, INTRODUCTION AU DROIT DES TRAITES 14–22 (1985).

"contestation"[2] to the automatic applicability of existing norms formulated without their consent. Such a phenomenon may be characterized as legal voluntarism.

On the other hand, new frontiers in international affairs have arisen, such as development, outer space, and environment; there have been only few existing rules applicable to these fields. Here also, opposition is apparent, as between developing countries and developed countries, or as between states capable of space activities and those technologically yet incompetent.

In such circumstances, especially of the postwar world, the international community has groped for some new norm-setting process, such as codification through multilateral treaties or international quasi-legislation through resolutions of international organization.

The following is a discussion of significant change in the international norm-making process in the framework of the above-mentioned situation.

II. THE TRADITIONAL LAWMAKING METHOD AND ITS INADAPTABILITY TO THE CONTEMPORARY MULTILATERALISM OF RELATIONS

Traditional ways of making international rules consist of two modalities: customary norm and treaty. The shortcomings of each of the processes relative to the urgent need of new rules will be examined.

a. Customary Rules

(1) Theoretical Concept of Customary Rulemaking

It is generally admitted that, in order to establish customary rules, two elements are required: state practice and *opinio juris*. A doctrinal controversy exists in this regard, however.[3] Some maintain that, as *opinio juris* should be recognized only through the state practice, the latter is the true and only factor of formation of customary rules.[4] Others assert that state practice is taken into consideration only

---

2.   MOHAMED BEDJAOUI, POUR UN NOUVEL ORDRE ECONOMIQUE INTERNATIONAL 59–60 (1979); *See*, R. P. Anand, *Attitude of the Asian-African States toward Certain Problems of International Law*, 15 INT'L & COMP. L.Q. 55 (1965); *See generally* THIRD WORLD ATTITUDES TOWARD INTERNATIONAL LAW (F.E. Snyder & Surakiart Sathiratai, eds.) at 851 (1965).

3.   Prof. D'Amato's point on Prof. Gény's doctrine is instructive. ANTHONY D'AMATO, THE CONCEPT OF CUSTOM IN INTERNATIONAL LAW 48–49 (1971). The International Court of Justice expressed the traditional view on the matter in North Sea Continental Shelf, 1969 I.C.J. 3, 44.

4.   *See, e.g.*, HANS KELSEN, Théorie du droit international coutumier, 1 REVUE INTERNAT-IONALE DE LA THEORIE DU DROIT (Nouvelle série) 253, 264–266 (1939);   PAUL GUGGENHEIM, TRAITE DE DROIT INTERNATIONAL PUBLIC 47–48 (1953).

for the purpose of finding the *opinio juris*.[5] Although such a controversy has long existed and has been of importance regarding a theory on sources of international law, a contemporary understanding of the debate is centered on how each doctrine explains that a new rule would be recognized if created in the framework of customary norm-making process in a situation in which state practice is not general (e.g., space law in 1950s and 1960s), or where the international community urgently needs some new rules.

(2) Inefficiency of This Modality to Meet the Urgent Need

A customary norm requires in general a considerable length of time to be established. The International Court of Justice (ICJ) accorded some ten years for a customary rule to be established in its judgment on the *North Sea Continental Shelf* case. A period of ten years, however, is too long to wait. In ten years the situation could change and the created custom could be outmoded. How can we shorten the time factor? How can customary law make up the time?

Professor Bin Cheng's doctrine of "instant" customary law[6] is an attempt to answer these questions. He tried to take resolutions of the General Assembly of the United Nations as representative of *opinio juris*, though actual state practice relating to space activities was quite limited (only the United States and the USSR could realize a conquest of outer space). He saw in a resolution of the United Nations General Assembly (UNGA) and the declaration of two super states a firm creation of a customary international rule; thus, time could be accelerated in his doctrine.

His theory contains some weak points. Affirmative votes cannot be considered as the will of states to be bound by resolution since UNGA resolutions have only value as recommendations, not of binding force. It is difficult to recognize the general character of a rule so created when only two states, the United States and the USSR, possessed the capability for space activities. Treaties must be distinguished from binding resolutions, since the latter does not require any formal procedure other than voting. These issues do not have sufficient and reasonable answers.

Any other doctrine based on the theory of customary sources is equally unconvincing. In fact, the theory of custom has been developed in situations in

---

5. *See, e.g.*, Bin Cheng, *United Nations Resolutions on Outer Space: "Instant" International Customary Law?* 5 IND. J. INT'L L. 23, 36 (1965); DIONISIO ANZILOTTI, 1 COURS DE DROIT INTERNATIONAL 73–79 (1929) (French Translation of CORSO DI DIRITTO INTERNAZIONALE (3rd. ed. 1928)); Gregory Tunkin, *Remarks on the Juridical Nature of Customary Norms of International Law*, 40 CAL. L. REV. 419, 423 (1961); GENNADY M. DANILENKO, *The Theory of International Customary Law* GER.Y.B. INT'L L. 9, 11–14 (1988) (asserting a customary rule is tacit agreement).

6. Bin Cheng, *United Nations Resolutions on Outer Space: "Instant" International Customary Law?*, 5 IND. J. INT'L L. , 23 (1965).

which international relations were individualist,[7] and therefore mainly on a bilateral basis. The will (*opinio*) of each state was expressed individually[8] through state conduct in each situation in which a state was required to act in one way or in another. A collective mode of expression of will was not generally known or used.

International circumstances have changed, especially as a result of the phenomenon of the international organization.[9] The multilateralization of relations is a characteristic of our time. The theory of custom could hardly survive in its original form; some other theory of sources must emerge so that the role of international organization or, at least, of multilateral fora can be clearly evaluated.

b. Treaties

Proliferation of multilateral treaties is a contemporary tendency of international lawmaking.[10] It has some advantages and disadvantages. As indicated above, newcomers to the international community, especially newly independent states, have been claiming an active participation to the formation of international law. In this respect, treaty-making through multilateral fora offers a good opportunity. These developing countries are not only assured to participate in the norm-setting process, but are also enabled to make their demands reflected in the text through an automatic majority in almost all the international conferences or institutions. Moreover, states need not wait as many years to set up rules as for custom, and a rule so established is generally free of ambiguity in its content.

On the other hand, a treaty requires ratification for entry into force. This ratification stage is a notorious disadvantage of conventional norm creation. Multilateral treaties, even if the contracting states reach agreement on drafting, take years, and sometimes more than ten years pass before entry into force.[11] Further,

---

7.   Charles De Visscher, *Coutume et Traité en Droit International Public*, R.G.D.I.P. 353, 354 (1955). He clearly points out that the impact of the intensity and complexity of international relations on international law sources is crucial.

8.   B. Cheng, *Custom: The Future of General State Practice in a Divided World, in* THE STRUCTURE AND PROCESS OF INTERNATIONAL LAW 531–532 (R. St. J. MacDonald and D.M. Johnson, eds., 1986).

9.   Michel Virally shows us the meaning and impact of the phenomenon of the international organization on international relations and law, and the use of the multilateral diplomacy, in his lecture at The Hague. Michel Virally, *Panorama de Droit International Public: Cours Général de Droit International Public*, 183 R.C.A.D.I. 9, 251 (1983).

10.   Reuter, *supra* note 1, at 13; Michel Virally, *The Sources of International Law*, MANUAL OF PUBLIC INTERNATIONAL LAW 128 (Max Sørensen ed., 1968).

11.   Notoriously, the two International Covenants on Human Rights took ten years to take effect, the Vienna Convention on the Law of Treaties eleven years, and the United Nations Convention on Law of the Sea twelve years. A recent and outstanding example is the 1982 UNCLOS, which was adopted in 1982 and entered into force on November 16, 1994.

the legal clarity of words and phrases is not always ensured as a result of various conflicts and compromises of interests in the negotiation process.[12]

Thus, norm-making by way of treaty has the two faces of Janus. To take a form of treaty or not, that is the question for states when speedy creation of new rules or prompt reform of the existing norms is necessary.

c. Codification Through the International Law Commission

(1) Basic Characteristics of Lawmaking Through the ILC

Attempts at progressive development of international law and its codification are not new. International efforts in this regard go back to the Congress of Vienna in the nineteenth century, which culminated in The Hague Conferences in 1899 and in 1907. The League of Nations also trusted this task to the Committee of Experts, which prepared a list of subjects ripe for codification, as well as "bases of discussion." It also convened The Hague Codification Conference in 1930, the result of which was rather disappointing since the rules on territorial water and on responsibility were left disagreed upon.[13]

The idea of progressive codification was renewed by nations through creation of the International Law Commission of the United Nations (ILC). Although the Commission was at the outset given two different tasks—progressive development and codification—the distinction between the two was later amalgamated.

The Commission was expected to combine "the requirements of sound learning with the realities of political life."[14] The Commission was first composed of fifteen members of recognized competence in international law and in their personal capacity. The respect for such personal status should be based on professionalism that is independent from individual national interests. Theoretical perfection in the elaboration and drafting of the whole set of rules to be codified should be envisaged and expected.

Such professionalism seems, however, to have been hindered by political considerations.[15] Geographical distribution of seats, work on a part-time basis, and an increase in number of members are factors that politicize elections. Consider-

---

12. A famous example is UNCLOS, arts. 74, 83 (concerning the delimitation of the EEZ and the continental shelf between adjacent states).

13. *See* R.P. DHOKALIA, THE CODIFICATION OF PUBLIC INTERNATIONAL LAW 76–143 (1970).

14. Shabtai Rosenne, *The International Law Commission 1949–1959*, 36 BRIT. Y.B. INT'L. L. 107, 120 (1960).

15. B. Graefrath, *The International Law Commission Tomorrow: Improving Its Organization and Methods of Work*, 85 AM. J. INT'L L. 595, 600 (1991); IAN M. SINCLAIR, THE INTERNATIONAL LAW COMMISSION 14 (1987).

ations of a political nature[16] are certainly not to be neglected, so that governments will later accept the draft articles elaborated in the Commission. On this point, the Sixth Committee of the General Assembly, however, tends to reject a draft that is politically unacceptable rather than to revise or amend phrases or principles.[17]

(2) Outcomes of the Works of the Commission

The Commission first selected fourteen topics, nine of which resulted in final drafts or model rules; all others, save one (state responsibility), are not currently topics for consideration. Some sixteen subjects were added as the Commission's work progressed and as international relations evolved. The result of its work so far might be said to be fruitful and productive.

The above-mentioned aspects of professionalism, however, offset the Commission's conduct of work.[18] The Commission works rigidly, is careful in its research of the practices, doctrines and opinions of governments, and always seeks consensus among its members.[19] The process of work on one topic or on another is very time-consuming, while the term for work in a year is only twelve weeks, with not more than ten meetings a week. The delay of work has therefore often been a main subject of criticism.[20] This might cause distrust of the Commission's capability to accomplish the task in time. For example, two of four topics discussed by the Commission in its forty-fifth session (1993) have been considered from the very beginning of its existence (state responsibility and Draft Code of Offenses against Peace and Security of Mankind), and one of the remaining two for more than ten years (international liability). None of these three topics has yet finished its first reading of the entire draft articles phase.

In addition to these shortcomings, the Commission and the Sixth Committee are said to be rather passive regarding the aspect of progressive development over that of codification.[21] Thus some important topics that might have normally been treated by the Commission have been taken by other organs (e.g., the Committee on the Peaceful Uses of the Sea-bed and Ocean Floor; the Committee on the Peaceful Uses of Outer Space; the Committee on the Definition of Aggression), or by creating another organ of codification, which is the United Nations Commission of International Trade Law (UNCITRAL).

---

16. Sinclair, however, in describing the politicization of election admits some advantages to the mixture of academic lawyers, practitioners and diplomats in its composition. Sinclair, *supra* note 15, at 16–17.

17. HERBERT BRIGGS, THE INTERNATIONAL LAW COMMISSION 360 (1965).

18. *See generally* Sinclair, *supra* note 15, at 32–44, on the work methods of this commission.

19. Briggs, *supra* note 17, at 239.

20. B.G. RAMCHARAN, THE INTERNATIONAL LAW COMMISSION 38–56 (1977) briefly shows some principal defects of the working methods and suggests possible improvements.

21. Sinclair, *supra* note 15, at 28–29.

The General Assembly, very much aware of this unfavorable situation, asked the Commission to speed up its task; the Commission itself is also making efforts to improve the efficiency of its method. The Commission thus, on the one hand, constituted a working group to prepare a draft articles,[22] while the task of preparation and preliminary drafting had been so far entrusted to the Special Rapporteur; on the other hand, it accorded to the Drafting Committee the ability to possibly redraft the draft articles proposed by the Special Rapporteur, such redrafting having been entrusted to the Special Rapporteur himself.

While we may expect in the near future some significant improvements in its working method and its efficiency, at least three important fields, to be considered in the next section, have been treated outside the International Law Commission. All three belong not to codification but to progressive development.

III. NEW SYSTEM OF LAWMAKING PROCESS?

Recent developments and changes in international lawmaking are quite significant in three aspects: the instrument itself, the process of treaty conclusion, and the types of provisions and obligations introduced. A treatment of these aspects in three areas with particular relevance to new lawmaking processes follows.

a. The International Law of Development

Newly independent states and their relations with developed countries create a new strata in international law. Developing countries wish to catch up with developed countries—a challenge that international law had never been confronted with, nor been ready to deal with effectively. These historical and structural patterns, coupled with an impatience on the part of developing countries, created an urgency for new rules.[23]

---

22. Such a working method was very useful for the drafting of the statute of an International Criminal Court; substantial drafting of the whole statute was accomplished in only two sessions of the Commission. This speedy work seems principally due to an appropriate sizing of the working group (nineteen members, and open to all others, but usually only ten to fifteen were present in the discussion).

23. The international law of development has been developed by French scholars, of which the guiding article is Michel Virally, *Vers un Droit International du Développement,* XI A.F.D.I. 3 (1965). For this analysis we turn to Oscar Schachter, *The Evolving International Law of Development,* 15 COLUM. J. TRANSN'L L. 1 (1976). An interesting discussion on the making of this law was done in a colloquium in 1982 in Aix-en-Provence: C.R.E.S.M., LA FORMATION DES NORMES EN DROIT INTERNATIONAL DU DEVELOPPEMENT (1984).

(1) The Norm-Creating Role of General Assembly Resolutions

In the field of international law of development, the resolutions of international organizations, in particular those of General Assembly of the United Nations,[24] are assigned to play a central role of normativity. Contrary to the heavy process of customary rules and of multilateral treaty-making, resolutions are more easily adopted and less rigidly invoked than conventional instruments, and are less time-consuming than custom. It is on this point that developing countries have relied in order to express their claims to developed countries for the aid for development.

The concept of international law of development is based on the ideology of social justice and solidarity in the international community. Developing countries, for whom developing by themselves once they achieve independence is almost impossible, claim "real equality"[25] of international relations. They therefore firmly wish to be treated in a preferential manner in all spheres of relations so as to recover the difference in degree of development. They also challenge the applicability of existing international legal norms established before they gained independence, especially in international economic law, which is, in their view, law created among the rich. The international law of development is thus a law of protest. The law is given a new function, which is to change the structure of international relations.

This branch of law deviates greatly from its positivist conception; the law here is rather an instrument of protest and reform. The fundamental function of law is no longer only to settle disputes but also to set up the objectives and guiding principles to realize true equality in the international community. Such claims were represented by the concept of the "New International Economic Order" during the 1970s. These norms are not greatly edified in the form of customary law because it would take too much time. Nor are treaty rules apt to meet the problem, as the treaty-making process from negotiation to entry into force is too long for matters of North-South opposition, there is an uncertainty of entry into force, and the negotiations would inevitably reflect real bargaining power or would fail.

Developing countries chose to utilize the General Assembly of the United Nations and other organs as norm-setting institutions. The claims of developing countries were legitimate but were not in conformity with existing rules, rendering legality and legitimacy in conflict. The *lex lata* should be replaced or supplemented by the *lex ferenda* in the framework of North-South relations and as urgently as

---

24. A thorough study on the normative relations of U.N.G.A. resolutions with customary international law and treaties is given in Krzysztof Skubiszewski, *Institut de Droit International, Resolutions of the General Assembly of the United Nations—Provisional Report*, 61-I ANNUAIRE DE L'INSTITUT DE DROIT INTERNATIONAL, 110–125, 144–149 (1985); *id.*, Michel Virally, 298, 299–300. *See also*, OSCAR SCHACHTER, INTERNATIONAL LAW IN THEORY AND PRACTICE, 84–105 (1991).

25. On the concept of "real equality," *see* Ryuichi Ida, *La structure juridique de la Charte des droits et devoirs économiques des Etats*, in NEW DIRECTIONS IN INTERNATIONAL LAW—FESTSCHRIFT W. ABENDROTH, 118, 127–132 (R.G. Girardot et al. eds., 1982).

possible. International organizations, the General Assembly of the United Nations among others, are the most suitable fora for such normative diplomacy.

(2) Relative Normativity?[26]

A resolution of an international organization is characterized by its facility of formation and adoption as well as by its practical flexibility of use, which is exactly the reason that developing countries chose the resolution as an instrument of normative strategy.

The question arises as to how states become legally bound by the acts of international organizations. Apart from decisions of the Security Council, the resolutions of the General Assembly and of almost all other institutions are only recommendations and not more. Can nonbinding text be transformed into a legally binding instrument?[27]

The first element of an answer can be found in the function of *opinio juris* for the consolidation of legality of custom. Bin Cheng's "instant custom" doctrine can aid in recognizing some legal binding force to a resolution. This *opinio* may be reinforced through repeated adoption of resolutions containing the same principles or objectives. The repetition and cross reference of the same principles in many different resolutions may have more weight than simple facts. A similar concept is often applied when accumulation of bilateral and multilateral conventions is considered to have a norm-generating effect.

The form of the text is also significant. A form of pseudo-treaty, such as the Charter of Economic Rights and Duties of States or Council on Security and Cooperation in Europe (CSCE) Helsinki Final Act, imports some legal value to the text, although the former example is a recommendation[28] and the latter clearly stipulated as nonlegally binding in nature.[29] Some other factors, such as circumstances of adoption, results of voting (unanimity, consensus, or majority), explanations of votes, reservations to the resolution, etc., should be taken into account.

---

26. Prosper Weil, *Vers Une normativité relative en droit international?* 78 R.G.D.I.P. 6 (1982); *see also* Richard Baxter, *International Law in "Her Infinite Variety,"* 29 INT'L & COMP. L.Q. 549 (1980).

27. Many important writings are devoted to this problem of normativity. *See* a leading conception of R.J.Dupuy, *Droit déclaratoire et droit programmatoire: de la coutume sauvage à la soft law, in* S.F.D.I., L'ELABORATION DU DROIT INTERNATIONAL PUBLIC 132 (1976); *see also* Michel Virally, *Textes internationaux ayant une portée juridique dans les relations mutuelles entre leurs auteurs et textes qui en sont dépourvus—Rapport provisoire, in* 60-I ANNUAIRE DE L'INSTITUT DE DROIT INTERNATIONAL 166–374 (1985).

28. Subrata Roy Chowdhury, *Legal Status of the Charter of Economic Rights and Duties of States, in* LEGAL ASPECTS OF A NEW INTERNATIONAL ECONOMIC ORDER 82 (Kamal Hossain ed. 1980).

29. Michel Virally, *Sur la notion d'accord,* FESTSCHRIFT BINDSCHEDLER 159, 166–172 (1980).

Left to be determined is the exact meaning of binding force for these resolutions and other similar instruments, which is discussed below.

b. The 1982 United Nations Convention on the Law of the Sea (UNCLOS)

The law of the sea is not a new branch, but the rapid progress of science and technology has urged the international community to reform the existing rules. This necessity, along with increasing concern of developing states over the resources of the sea and the seabed, introduced some particularities into the lawmaking process.

(1) Evolution of the Law of the Sea in the Context of UNCLOS III

Four Geneva Conventions on the law of the sea were based on the work of the ILC. In 1949 the ILC, employing a Special Rapporteur, Prof. Jean-Pierre-Adrien François, undertook the task of codifying the law of the sea. The diplomatic conference was convened in 1958 and 1960 for the adoption of a law of the sea convention on the basis of the ILC final draft of some seventy-three articles. In fact, four conventions and one protocol on the settlement of disputes were adopted, leaving the question of the width of the territorial sea open. In this lawmaking process, the ILC played the central role; these conventions can be considered codification in its proper sense.

Since 1960, however, newly independent states, which could scarcely have participated in drafting the provisions of Geneva Conventions, argued for a reconsideration of the law of the sea, as they felt unable to gain sufficient benefits from the ocean resources under the existing conventions. The new starting point for the reform was a proposal presented by Maltese Ambassador Arvid Pardo in 1967, which launched a long process of negotiation for the reform of the law of the sea in its entirety.[30]

While the main opposition remained, consisting of commercial and strategic interests before 1958 conventions, the technological development and the appearance on the international scene of developing countries considerably changed the basic structure of the law of the sea. Particular attention should have been paid to the developing countries' legitimate preoccupation with a probable division of the deep seabed and ocean floor by developed countries possessing high technology. In fact, the core conception of the law of the sea to be newly restructured was

---

30.   In 1967, at the First Committee of the General Assembly, Ambassador Pardo declared that the seabed and the ocean floor beyond the limits of national jurisdiction were a Common Heritage of Mankind and should be used for peaceful purposes, and that the needs of the developing countries should be taken into consideration in a preferential manner. His initial statement, proposing to elaborate an international regime and rules concerning only the seabed and the ocean floor through the aforementioned new conception, triggered vigorous challenges by the developing countries to the overall existing law of the sea.

appropriation of the sea by coastal states. As the negotiation was premised upon this conception, structural change can be understood on four levels:[31]

1) The law of the sea is no longer only rules concerning water, but should be treated in a multidimensional function;
2) The sea is the object of appropriation (territorialization) in addition to the place of communication;
3) The law of freedom from sovereignty is transformed into the law of control by sovereignty;
4) The law considerably lost its impersonal and universal character, but consists of different rules each applicable to each situation, which is situational law.

Such structural change is reflected in the long process of negotiation.

(2) Characteristics of the Lawmaking Process in the UNCLOS

Some basic characteristics of this process can be pointed out as follows:

(a) Politicization of the Process

The preparation of this process was done by a political body,[32] the Sea-Bed Committee, and not by the ILC; this indicates the outstanding political character of the whole process.[33] Political consideration overrode legal perfectionism, the latter having been assured by the ILC's work. Unfortunately, and apart from the Declaration of Principles, the Sea-Bed Committee did not present any draft, leaving the first task for the UNCLOS to draw up draft articles. The ILC counted only twenty-five members to accomplish the task of drafting, while the Sea-Bed Committee numbered first, forty-two members, and later, eighty-six, and the UNCLOS had 165 states and some other entities (the number of participating states to the two previous conferences was eighty-six and eighty-eight).

What is significant is that the first session of the UNCLOS III was devoted to the question of organization and procedure, the outcome of which was the adoption of consensus as a formal procedure and negotiation by "package deal." Such a procedure gave a justified pretext for compromise of interests; this is also of very political nature.

---

31. R.J. DUPUY, L'OCEAN PARTAGE 15–38 (1979).

32. A. DE MARFFY, A HANDBOOK ON THE NEW LAW OF THE SEA 162 (R.J. Dupuy and D. Vignes eds., 1991).

33. Guy De Lacharrière, *La réforme de droit de la mer et le rôle de la Conférence des Nations Unies, in* LE NOUVEAU DROIT INTERNATIONAL DE LA MER 1, 5 (Daniel Bardonnet & Michel Virally eds., 1983); JEAN PIERRE LEVY, LA CONFERENCE DES NATIONS UNIES SUR LE DROIT DE LA MER 39 (1983) (pointing out that the first decision of procedure, i.e., creation of a Special Committee, determined a political character of the question).

(b) Multidimension of Conflicts and Compromises of Interests

Strategic and political interests prevailed over commercial ones. The sea is at the same time a place of military operation and a space of defense of sovereignty. Many topics were discussed from this viewpoint, like the outer limits of the territorial sea, innocent passage, international straits, archipelagic waters, and so on.

The natural resources element was also decisive, and encompassed not only halieutic resources, which had been traditionally and continued to be a main object of utilization, but also mineral resources in the seabed and ocean floor, which offer enormous economic expectations. The economic dimension of this negotiation should therefore have never been neglected at all. The notion of a common heritage of mankind being accepted, the problem was, and remains partly even now, how and by whom the mineral resources in the deep seabed can be exploited.

Environmental considerations became a sensitive issue at negotiation. Numerous incidents of petrol pollution and increasing amounts of harmful wastes inabsorbable by the sea forced the states to consider this problem. The concern of coastal states in particular was so considerable that UNCLOS III deemed pollution to be an impediment to free passage.

(c) Special Negotiating Methods: Consensus and Package Deal

To make necessary demands and concessions based upon a balance of different interests, the Conference took up two important procedural arrangements: consensus and package deal.[34] The question of procedure was a particularly difficult one in the first phase of the UNCLOS III process, for it would reflect political considerations on what and how negotiating states would make concessions without suffering a unilateral bad bargain. Adoption of texts by voting was rarely made, and consensus was the major and formal method of decisionmaking as stated above. According to this method, voting would not be envisaged on a substantial question as long as a possibility of consensus subsists. This principle was first adopted by a "gentlemen's agreement" in 1973, and later annexed to the Rules of Procedure[35] of the Conference. Such a procedural technique, while taking considerable time to generate an agreement, assured that, once adopted, the text would meet no opposition.

The second unique method of negotiation was that of "package deal." As the interests confronted were quite varied for each of the participating countries, each issue could not be separately discussed. The classic method of diplomatic

---

34. *See generally* G. Plant, *The Third United Nations Conference on the Law of the Sea and Preparatory Commission: Models for United Nations Law-Making*, 36 INT'L & COMP. L.Q. 525 (1989); for consensus in the UNCLOS III, *see* Barry Buzan, *Negotiating by Consensus*, 75 AM. J. INT'L L. 325 (1981); for package deal, *see* H. Caminos & M.R. Molitor, *Progressive Development and Package Deal*, 79 AM. J. INT'L L. 871 (1985).

35. Rules 37 and 19 explicitly provide this procedure.

negotiation was insufficient and inapplicable, with none of the issues independent from the others. Accordingly, all the issues, either interdependent of or irrelevant to the others, were discussed together in the whole context of the law of the sea. The product is in the form of a single but detailed convention of 320 articles, together with nine annexes and four resolutions.

However, such multibarter dealings in the UNCLOS, based on the combination of consensus and package deal, had undesirable repercussions.[36] First, the result could be obtained only after all the discussion would have been completed. This is one reason for the marathon negotiation of UNCLOS III. Second, the true and precise meaning of each provision is not clear in itself, since the package-deal approach conceals the context in which the words and phrases of the text were drafted. One eminent example is the U.S.–Soviet joint proposal on transit passage of international straits. This historic proposal was paired with their acceptance of a twelve-mile territorial sea.

(d) Burgeoning Informalism

Related to the above-mentioned particularities of negotiation, the process was highlighted by its general utilization of informalism. States exchanged their contentions with each other without formal draft articles until the tenth session (resumed). Formal meetings at every level were exceptional. Many informal bodies were established: working groups, negotiation groups, the working group of twenty-one, coordinators group, and others.[37] Formal bodies also met frequently on an informal basis.

Moreover, informal documents played a crucial role in determining the text of articles; a series of negotiating texts[38] were used throughout the Conference as real drafts of convention, and it is only at the tenth session (resumed) that first *formal* draft convention[39] was presented. Only such informalism could lead the negotiation to the conclusion of a convention composed of an amalgam of package deals. Along this line, presidents and personalities of different bodies and of various levels played a critical role in each part of the negotiation.[40]

---

36. Robert Jennings, *Law-making and Package Deal*, *in* MELANGES OFFERTS A PAUL REUTER—LE DROIT INTERNATIONAL: UNITÉ ET DIVERSITÉ 347, 353 (1981).

37. *See* LEVY, *supra* note 33, at 78–79 (list of groups).

38. Informal Single Negotiating Text (ISNT), Revised Single Negotiating Text (RSNT), Informal Composite Negotiating Text (ICNT), ICNT Rev.1, ICNT Rev.2, and Draft Convention—Informal Text.

39. U.N. Doc. A/CONF.62/L.78 (1981).

40. Levy, *supra* note 33, at 68. *The Final Act of the Conference*, reproduced in 21 I.L.M. 1245–53 (1982) (apparently shows the importance of groups and personalities in the conduct of negotiation process).

(3) Preparatory Process for Effective Implementation Before the Entry Into Force

A treaty itself is not the general final objective. Without effective application, the rules stipulated in the treaty lose their reason for existence. The follow-up system of the UNCLOS thus merits consideration. We must recognize the importance of follow-up mechanisms even in a non legally-binding instrument like the CSCE Helsinki Final Act.

Resolution I of the Conference decided to establish the Preparatory Committee (PrepCom) for the International Sea-bed Authority and International Tribunal of the Law of the Sea. The PrepCom's function is twofold: procedural and substantial.

The procedural task is to present draft rules of procedures of the authority, while the substantive mandate of PrepCom, which is set by Resolutions I and II, is to exercise the powers and functions of the authority assigned by Resolution II concerning pioneer activities. The real purpose of PrepCom is to assure pioneer activities of some highly developed countries in line with the provisions of the Convention; in that sense, PrepCom plays the role of supervisor of signatory states before entry into force of the Convention.

The Vienna Convention on the Law of Treaties provides an obligation not to prevent the object and purpose of the treaty before its entry into force. This obligation, based on good faith, does not necessarily urge the states to make an institutionalized system, nor does it require omission of an obstacle or a disturbing act. The PrepCom system provides positive measures to prepare the prompt and effective functioning immediately after the entry into force of the UNCLOS.

PrepCom was expected to establish a seabed exploitation mechanism, which the Convention itself could not provide in detail. This mechanism should have taken into account the preoccupation of developing countries and the technological and economic developments. The Convention is rigid by nature because of its legality, but it is certain to make an indispensable adjustment for the evolution from signature to entry into force. The PrepCom system is charged to fill such a gap and provide a channel to begin functioning. The result is that the agreement on the implementation of Part XI was adopted by the UN General Assembly on July 28, 1994, just before the entry into force of the UNCLOS itself; it provides some changes to the original system without taking the formal convention procedure of revision. The difficulties of implementation of the original provisions of the UNCLOS having been already indicated from the beginning and the surrounding technological, scientific, economic, or political conditions having evolved during these some ten years, it results that a part of the original text may become no more applicable even before the entry into force.

c. UNCED and International Environmental Conventions

Much will be discussed on the content of the international environmental law by other panelists. Here we are trying to point out some peculiar lawmaking techniques taken in the United Nations Conference on Environment and Development (UNCED).[41]

(1) Several Negotiation Fora in Parallel

UNCED itself was not a conference intended to make law. UNCED adopted three instruments, namely, Agenda 21, the Rio Declaration and the Forest Statement, all of which are non legally-binding in character. Parallel to these instruments, two conventions, the Climate Change Convention and the Bio-Diversity Convention, were opened for signature by the participating states of the Conference. Each of these conventions was prepared in a framework other than UNCED. Three aforementioned texts adopted in UNCED had been prepared by the Preparatory Committee for UNCED, the Climate Change Convention was adopted by the Intergovernmental Negotiating Committee (INC) on Climate Change established by the UNGA, and the Bio-Diversity Convention was prepared by INC on Bio-Diversity and adopted by the Conference for Adoption.

This parallel negotiation was not planned[42] from the beginning, but the importance of UNCED presented a good chance to promote and develop international environmental cooperation with binding instruments. UNCED was enhanced by making available for signing at the Conference two binding legal documents. At UNCED itself, only nonbinding instruments were negotiated and signed, producing results which many considered insufficient. Such parallelism of different fora and their coordination made the UNCED framework fruitful.

The difference from the UNCLOS III framework derives from the very nature of the subject with which each conference dealt. The sea is one and integrated; only the means and types of utilization differ from each other. The environment, on the contrary, though interrelated, does not have an integrated physical feature. Such a parallel and separate system of normmaking process might be more suitable.

---

41. An appropriate presentation of lawmaking process in the UNCED is given by Akiho Shibata, *International Law-Making Process in the United Nations: Comparative Analysis of UNCED and UNCLOS III*, 24 CAL. W. INT'L L.J. 17, 17–53 (1993).

42. The whole negotiation concerning the environment and the development up to the UNCED seems, however, to form a real "system" of negotiations. *See* Pamela Chasek, *The Negotiating System of Environment and Development*, *in* NEGOTIATING INTERNATIONAL REGIMES, 20, 23–24 (Bertram I. Spector et al. eds., 1994).

(2) Continuing Norm-Setting Processes—A "Never Ending Story"

International environmental law is a daily evolving field. Technological development, changes in economic situation, sophistication of lifestyle, and modernization of developing countries are factors that determine the evolution of the human environment. Legal norms must follow, or even precede, this evolution.[43] Norm-creating techniques must therefore be innovated.

The framework convention is part of this flow. The Climate Change Convention and the Ozone Layer Convention are of such specificity; each presents a field for future development and precision.

There are, in fact, three types of "framework" treaties: (1) one determines standards and goals itself, while concrete measures of achieving these standards and goals are left to the discretion of each state party (e.g., the Climate Change Convention of 1992); (2) another sets up only institutions and organs; precise rules are provided by following agreements or protocols of implementation (e.g., the Vienna Convention of Ozone Layer Protection and the Montreal Protocol); (3) the last establishes a set of general and global standards and principles; states make bilateral or small-sized agreements in each relevant circumstance (e.g., the proposed scheme by the ILC in the Draft Articles on the Non-Navigational Use of International Watercourses adopted on first reading).[44]

Because technological knowledge often must "catch up" with environmental phenomena, legal norms should be established as a basic framework while avoiding too much rigidity in each provision. This process means, however, that norm-setting in international environmental law will never be finished:[45] herein lies the question of legal stability and the difficulty of determination of specific rights and duties at a given moment in a given relation.

---

43. Pierre-Marie Dupuy, *Soft Law and the International Law of the Environment*, 12 MICH. J. INT'L L. 420, 421 (1991).

44. Art. 3, para. 1: "Watercourse State may enter into one or more agreements,...which apply and adjust the provisions of the present articles to the characteristics and uses of a particular internation watercourse or part thereof." The commentary to this article indicates that this formula of a "framework agreement" provides a promising solution to the problem of the diversity of international watercouses and the needs of general principles and rules. DRAFT ARTICLES ON THE LAW OF THE NON-NAVIGATIONAL USES OF INTERNATIONAL WATERCOURSES AND COMMENTARIES THERETO, PROVISIONALLY ADOPTED ON FIRST READING BY THE INTERNATIONAL LAW COMMISSION AT ITS FORTY-THIRD SESSION (mimeo.), 13–14 (Sept. 1991).

45. *Id.* at 421.

(3) A New Actor in the Lawmaking Process: Nongovernmental Organizations

Many nongovernmental organizations (NGOs) participated directly or indirectly in the UNCED negotiation.[46] The role of the NGO in international environmental protection is highly appreciated and the quality of its work is often high. There are numerous NGOs on a transnational or a domestic scale. The status of NGOs as observers in interstate fora does not mean much in itself, but the effectiveness and the efficiency of the information offered by NGOs and of their supervision is to be noted.

The influence of NGOs over domestic and foreign policy is so great in almost all democratic countries that governments cannot thoroughly ignore what the NGOs propose, even though the final political decision is made by the government. There are some national delegations in which members of NGOs take part in international conferences, and sometimes governments make use of NGOs to either reinforce or justify their decisions. There also cases in which a government may feel harassed by an NGO; regardless of the sentiment, however, the government should take into consideration that there is an opposing position.

A NGO is composed of motivated persons, each taking part in the movement volitionally. Individuals have access to the norm-creating process through NGOs and thus democratize the process and the rules.

IV. CONCLUSION—A DIALECTIC OF LEGALISM AND POLITICISM

The contemporary phenomena of multilateralism in the international lawmaking firmly stands on a dialectic of the legal and the political.[47] Policy-oriented lawmaking, relative normativity and soft law, and democratization on an interstate and on a transnational level all emerge prominently from this examination.

---

46. About 1500 NGOs are said to have participated in the UNCED. STANLEY P. JOHNSON, THE EARTH SUMMIT 4 (1993). For interesting remarks on the efficiency and the frustration in their participation, *see* Ann Doherty, *The Role of Nongovernmental Organizations in UNCED, in* NEGOTIATING INTERNATIONAL REGIMES, *supra* note 40, at 199–218. For the significance of the participation of NGOs in the international scene and its impact on international law, *see generally* MARIO BETTATI & P.M. DUPUY, LES ONG ET LE DROIT INTERNATIONAL (1986). The part played by the transnational corporations in some fields of international law is already familiar to us; *see* Jonathan I. Charney, *Transnational Corporations and Developing Public International Law*, DUKE L. J. 748 (1983).

47. An excellent analysis of the interrelationship between policy and law in the process of lawmaking, especially in the UNCLOS negotiation, is suggested by GUY LADREIT DE LACHARRIERE, LA POLITIQUE JURIDIQUE EXTERIEURE (1983). The author was the head of legal department of the French Ministry of foreign affairs in the UNCLOS negotiating process.

a. Policy-Oriented Lawmaking

Although the eminent role of the ILC in lawmaking remains, the requirements and expectations of governments vary. Prior to the 1970s, the world legal community had been of essentially European origin. Similar if not identical legal thinking and reasoning was an assurance in the establishment of a common legal order. Legality was of primary value. With the increased participation in the lawmaking process of formerly excluded nations, however, it became much more difficult to agree upon rules and to create a mutually acceptable legal regime. Established rules are often rejected by newly independent states.

Today the law is predominately an instrument for the realization of national interests and policy. International law, as a tool of foreign policy or as an obstacle to it, has served either to limit or to justify the acts of states, mainly by settling disputes. The law today, especially in the three fields mentioned above, establishes the objectives, the direction, and the framework of state conduct toward the realization of various interests. The interests of each state as well as the community interest should be assured as widely as possible; no individual interest can be neglected without compensation. Consensus procedure and package-deal negotiation are two main tools of this comprehensive approach. The product of such an approach, i.e., international law, necessarily reflects this policy-oriented process through different new conceptions: programatory law, framework conventions, follow-up procedures, and so forth.

The law, however, requires objectivity. A rule that reflects a concrete interest of one state or of another should not be in itself a legal rule. To objectify complicated political products, some technics, such as adoption by consensus, informal negotiation, or a comprehensive approach, are used. The law thus embodies a complex of community interests and national or group interests. A lawmaking forum creates legal norms with plenty of political overtones.

b. Relative Normativity—"Soft Law Phenomena"

Priority so given to the politicism over legalism leads us to a risk of relative normativity. Politicization of law is not surprising, for the law has been and is always one of the most effective instruments for stability in a given society. However, politicism as described previously means that states feel less confined in the sphere of law, have more discretion in their conduct, and remain peacefully in a somewhat ambiguous legal situation.

Another face of contemporary multilateralism, which may be called "legalization of political instrument," is also present. States make use of resolutions of the General Assembly or of texts of a conference to extract legal constraints, which, by the nature of such texts, are normally not specified. This emerges in response to the inadaptability of traditional processes of formation of norms to the evolution of international society, as well as to the revolutionary character of norms required. Thus, to assign a legal nature to a nonlegal text or to reduce a substantial legal value from a formally legal text means to tentatively depart from the traditional closed circle of formation of norms in order to reform the process. The notion of "soft law"[48] is a representative one. This notion indicates a contemporary international situation in which the legality and the legitimacy of states' conduct does not always coincide. Confrontations thus arise between the freedom of conduct of states based on existing international law, on the one hand, and the public interests and the global welfare derived from the conception of an "International Community," on the other.

"Soft law" or similar expressions, however, do not necessarily assure the precise scope and meaning of rights and obligations involved. We do recognize a phenomenon named "soft law," but it is nothing more, nothing less than its name suggests. To classify a rule in the category of soft law does not enable us to clearly know what degree of normativity we are dealing with, whether and when a rule before us is to be hard law, and what will be the responsibility of a soft illegal act. Soft law is an excellent qualification of a social phenomenon, but it lacks strictness as an analytical tool.

c. Democratization on an Interstate Level and Transnational Level

The democratization of the norm formation process appears on two levels. One is naturally the interstate level, on which newcomers to the traditional legal community, i.e., socialist states and developing countries, especially the latter, claimed permission to and now do participate in every lawmaking forum, and even often play an active role in the reform or creation of norms.

Democratization on a transnational level is also of note. An outstanding role played by various NGOs in the formation, observance, and application of international law of the environment demands recognition that sovereign states—the traditional monopolizers of norm creation—yield to nonstate entities in this area on a substantial, not formal, level. Such appearance by NGOs reveals, as Prof. Georges Scelle taught about seventy years ago, that the final addressee of international law is the individual.

---

48. On this notion and a criticism thereof, see Ryuichi Ida, *La formation des normes internationales dans un monde en mutation—Critique de la notion de soft law, in* LE DROIT INTERNATIONAL AU SERVICE DE LA PAIX, DE LA JUSTICE ET DU DEVELOPPE-MENT—MELANGES MICHEL VIRALLY 333–340 (1991).

METHODS OF INTERNATIONAL REGULATION FOR GLOBAL ENVIRONMENTAL PROTECTION: A REAPPRAISAL OF INTERNATIONAL LAWMAKING

Atsuko Kanehara

I. INTRODUCTION

In the field of international environmental protection, international law has devised various lawmaking methods in order to cope effectively with environmental problems which have remarkable characteristics.[1] The focus of this chapter is on the framework convention, which is the notable and characteristic method of international lawmaking in the domain of global environmental protection, in particular to the protection of the ozone layer and stabilization of global climate change. As for the former, the 1985 Vienna Convention for the Protection of Ozone Layer[2] and the 1987 Montreal Protocol on Substances that Deplete the Ozone Layer,[3] and as to the latter, the 1992 U.N. Framework Convention on Climate

---

1. Edith Brown Weiss, *International Environmental Law: Contemporary Issues and the Emergence of a New World Order*, 81 GEO. L.J., 675, 675–94 (1993); Günter Handl, *Environmental Security and Global Change: The Challenge to International Law, in* ENVIRONMENTAL PROTECTION AND INTERNATIONAL LAW 59, 61–71 (W. Lang, *et al.* eds., 1991); Geoffrey Palmer, *New Way to Make International Environmental Law*, 86 AM. J. INT'L L. 259, 259–83 (1992); Shinya Murase, *Chikyū Kankyō Hogo ni Kansuru Kokusai Rippō Katei no Shomondai* [*Problems of International Lawmaking on Global Environmental Protection*], *in* CHIYKU KANKYO TO SEIJI [GLOBAL ENVIRONMENT AND POLITICS] 217, 218–22 (Okita *et al.* eds. 1990).
2. The Vienna Convention for the Protection of Ozone Layer, Mar. 22, 1985, 26 I.L.M. 1516 (1987) [hereinafter *1985 Vienna Convention*].
3. The Montreal Protocol on Substances that Deplete the Ozone Layer, Sept. 16, 1987, 26 I.L.M. 1541 (1987) [hereinafter 1987 Montreal Protocol].

Change[4] are now in force.

This chapter will examine framework conventions and, in particular, methods to regulate the behavior of states, namely, how to restrict the freedom of states and how to induce or lead them to do what is legally required. The scope herein therefore will not be confined to considering the framework conventions as the most effective international lawmaking method to enhance global environmental protection; rather, the focus will be placed upon the meaning and the function of "framework" formulated in those conventions.

Framework conventions regularly set forth general principles of global environmental protection, and contain legal, moral and political commitments of states toward environmental protection. They are regularly supplemented by protocols which stipulate detailed and specific obligations and are also supposed to undergo a periodic review in accordance with the progress of the pertinent scientific or technological knowledge.

This combination of a framework convention with a protocol is, in fact, an attempt to off-set the scientific uncertainty with which global environmental problems are inevitably confronted.[5] Apart from the meaning of the term "framework" as generally recognized, this chapter expands the definition to the linkage of all functions fulfilled by various kinds of provisions within the framework conventions, namely, the provisions of either substantial or procedural legal obligations and legal procedures. By this linkage of functions, it is proposed that the framework conventions can establish a unique mechanism for the regulation of the behavior of states for global environmental protection.

Section II provides a brief survey of the normative state of affairs which existed before the adoption of framework conventions. Such a survey is essential in order to understand fully what the requirements are for framework conventions. Sections III–V then examine three major points of framework conventions in order to consider how framework conventions satisfy these requirements by unique methods for the regulation of states' behavior: (1) the content and nature of the legal interest provided for by the framework conventions, which form the basic structure of the "framework;" (2) the manner in which obligations are expressed by the framework conventions; and (3) the way in which a unique mechanism for implementation may work within the framework conventions.

II. THE NORMATIVE STATE OF AFFAIRS PRECEDING THE ADOPTION OF FRAMEWORK CONVENTIONS FOR GLOBAL ENVIRONMENTAL PROTECTION

The most salient features of the normative state of affairs preceding adoption of the framework conventions for global environmental protection are the important

---

4.   The United Nations Framework Convention on Climate Change, May 9, 1992, 31 I.L.M. 849 (1992) [hereinafter 1992 Framework Convention].

5.   Weiss, *supra* note 1, at 687–88.

activities of international organizations and the proliferation of "soft laws."[6]

International organizations such as the United Nations and the United Nations Enivronment Programme (UNEP) play essential roles for international environmental protection. In addition, the important function of regional organizations, for example, in enacting general principles or setting eco-standards in the form of European Community directives or OECD recommendations cannot be overemphasized. These organizations offer states an opportunity for continuous and structural cooperation on environmental protection. In these organizations, states engage in ongoing negotiations about environmental problems, which may result in a common normative consciousness among states. Such a common normative consciousness often crystallizes into resolutions and declarations adopted by those international institutions or by international conferences. This may explain why such a large number of soft laws has proliferated on the subject of environmental protection.

In terms of international lawmaking on global environmental protection, the contributions of the activities of international organizations and of soft laws can be summarized in the following two points. First, soft laws formulate the goals which are frequently expressed in a series of political statements or values. Even if they are drafted in general or indefinite terms, for example, to protect the ozone layer or to stabilize climate change, the extensive use of soft laws in which general goals are set may bring about a common and strong understanding for all states that they should cooperate and act in concert on a global basis to protect the environment.

There does remain one fundamental and difficult task for the framework conventions, namely, to formulate enforceable legal principles and legal procedures so as to achieve the goals already recognized by states. Although most soft laws formulate goals, they stop short of formulating concrete or enforceable legal

---

6.   As for "soft laws," there have been a number of definitions suggested. Here, however, I follow the general consensus on the definition of "soft laws" as instruments in non-legal form, for example, resolutions of international organizations, declarations adopted at international conferences, codes of conduct and so on. The United Nations Environment Programme took the initiative toward the 1985 Vienna Convention. Among soft laws relating to ozone layer protection, for example, there is the United Nations Environment Program: Nairobi Declaration on the State of Worldwide Environment, para. 2, U.N. Doc. UNEP/Gc/ INF.5 (1982).

More soft laws can be found regarding the stabilization of climate change than ozone layer protection. Examples include: as United Nations General Assembly resolutions, the Protection of Global Climate for Present and Future Generations of Mankind, G.A. Res. 43/53, U.N. GAOR, 43rd sess., Supp. No. 49, at 133, U.N. Doc. A/43/49 (1988); as declaration of an international conference, the Declaration of The Hague on the Atmosphere of Mar. 11, 1989, 28 I.L.M. 1308 (1989); and as activities of the European Community, the European Communities Council Resolution of June 21, 1989, on the Greenhouse Effect and the Community, Official Journal of the European Communities, 1989, C183/4 etc. *See also* Pierre-Marie Dupuy, *Soft Law and the International Law of the Environment*, 12 MICH. J. INT'L L. 420, 420–35 (1991).

obligations. The framework conventions, therefore, should be enforceable legal instruments for achieving the goal of the protection of the global environment.

As for the second contribution of the activities of international organizations and soft laws, it must be recognized that the framework conventions on the global environment are themselves the product of the work of these institutions and organizations. Examples include the 1992 Framework Convention and the 1992 Convention on the Biological Diversity which were drafted through international organizational work and adopted during the 1992 United Nations Conference on the Environment and the Development (UNCED) with states participating from all over the world. What is most important is that throughout the entire stage of negotiating, drafting and adopting these framework conventions, there has undoubtedly been a strong desire to create universal international law for global environmental protection. Framework conventions on the global environment are expected, above all, to formulate legal principles and procedures which are able to be accepted by as many states as possible.

To that end, universal conventions are more in demand now than ever before. There has been no opportunity to make other types of conventions with a limited number of parties and which could be used as a legal method for coping with global environmental problems.

Another point regarding the normative state of affairs preceding adoption of the framework conventions is related to the hybrid composition of modern international society. Because the number of independent states has drastically increased following the Second World War, it is very difficult for international law to develop and make effective international law rules. This is because the effectiveness of many rules greatly depends on the extent to which the individual situations of states are considered in a flexible manner.

To protect the global environment, for instance, the regulation of chlorofluorocarbons (CFCs) that deplete the ozone layer and the reduction of greenhouse gases are necessary. To achieve this goal, it may be necessary to change, for example, the established lifestyle of individuals in each country. This means that global environmental law should extend its regulations to economic, social, cultural, and other areas which have so far been within the domestic jurisdiction of each sovereign state and upon which international law has not touched. These factors naturally vary from state to state, making obvious the necessity to consider each state's specific circumstances as much as possible. Such an approach is indispensable to making the relevant obligations truly effective.

This requirement for individual state consideration is closely related to the universalism at which the conventions on the global environmental protection aim. The conventions need to provide for flexible obligations when considering the different and variable situations of individual states to ensure their universal acceptance.[7] As previously seen, framework conventions on the global environment

---

7.   Incentives have been offered to developing countries especially in recent environmental agreements. The incentives, such as technical assistance and technological transfer, are also

should be legal instruments in order to achieve the actual goals which have been recognized already by states in their extensive use of soft laws. Framework conventions also should satisfy fully the two related and, in some cases, contradictory requirements of universal participation in the conventions at a global level and individual consideration of the abilities and situations of each state.

For this purpose, the framework conventions develop newiy devised methods for regulating states' behavior. The next section will examine these methods in the "framework," and begin with the problems of the legal interest stipulated by the framework conventions, the content and nature of which form the basic structure of the "framework."

III. THE CONTENT AND NATURE OF THE LEGAL INTEREST OF PROTECTING THE GLOBAL ENVIRONMENT

The protection of the ozone layer and the stabilization of a global climate are defined as a legal interest in framework conventions. By so doing, the framework conventions regard the ozone layer and global climate as "a unitary whole" of the global environment and not as an environment divisible among the states or regions.

This recognition is also clearly included in the concept of the "common concern of mankind' in the 1992 Framework Convention.[8] The 1992 Convention on the Biological Diversity is based on the same basic concept or principle.[9] The nature of the legal interest so prescribed by the framework conventions determines the legal relations among states in the context of global environmental protection. They may be determined by reference to "who may enjoy the legal interest" and "to whom States are supposed to owe their obligations."

The stipulation of obligations to protect the global environment as a unitary whole ideally means that every state has the right to the global environment as a unitary whole while at the same time sharing the obligation to protect the global environment as a member of the international community. The legal interest of protecting the global environment therefore belongs to the international community as a whole or to all the states of the world, and, states must protect the global environment for the international community as a whole or for all states, since it is

---

devices to make those agreements universally acceptable.

8.   Preamble. Alan E. Boyle, *International Law and the Protection of Global Atmosphere: Concepts, Categories and Principles, in* INTERNATIONAL LAW AND GLOBAL CLIMATE CHANGE 7–13 (Robin Churchill and David Freestone eds., 1991); W. Riphagen, *The International Concern for the Environment as Expressed in the Concepts of the "Common Heritage of Mankind" and of "Shared Natural Resources," in* TRENDS IN ENVIRONMENTAL POLLUTION AND LAW 343, 343–62 (Michael Bothe ed., 1980).

9.   The Convention on Biological Diversity, May 22, 1992, preamble, 31 I.L.M. 818 (1992).

an obligation *erga omnes*.[10]

This conception of an obligation *erga omnes* cannot work properly without appropriate institutional and procedural support. This bolstering could be found, for example, in the evolution of an international judicial procedure which would include a sort of *actio popularis*, or, in the establishment of a global institution which could enact global environmental policy on behalf of the international community.

At this stage of development of an international society, there are treaty regimes[11] which provide an alternative butressing function. The framework conventions may be interpreted as such, since they prescribe the legal interest for the protection of the global environment, which belongs to the treaty regime as a whole. States party therefore owe the obligation to protect the global environment to the treaty regime itself.

According to this basic stance of the framework conventions, within the treaty regime reciprocal consideration or barter of interests among a limited number of states is not allowed. To do so would permit the states in question to derogate from the concerted action needed to achieve the common objective of the treaty regime. Framework conventions thus transcend the principle of reciprocity and preclude the balancing of interests among a limited number of sstates. In this sense, the legal relations of states within the treaty regime are not reciprocal, and states, in principle, individually share the obligation to protect the global environment.[12]

The legal relations among states party is closely related to the problem of what the framework conventions require of them, how they contribute to the concerted actions required by the conventions, and also, the problem of dispute settlement or noncompliance, which will be discussed below.

IV. THE MANNER IN WHICH OBLIGATIONS ARE EXPRESSED BY THE FRAMEWORK CONVENTIONS ON THE GLOBAL ENVIRONMENT

The framework conventions provide for general and procedural obligations. However, they stop short of formulating more concrete and enforceable obligations. This is partly because protocols are expected to provide for concrete obligations or standards. The 1987 Montreal Protocol stipulates numerical standards to

---

10.   Frederic L. Kirgis, Jr., *Standing to Challenge Human Endeavors That Could Change the Climate*, 84 AM. J. INT'L L., 525, 528–29 (1990).

11.   Environmental agreements frequently go beyond a mere statement of principles, rights, and duties. In order to achieve the goal of the protection of the environment, they also establish a "treaty regime"—a nexus of continuing relationships for cooperation by the states party specialized groups, international institutions and so on. Oscar Schachter, *The Greening of International Law, in* HUMANITÉ ET DROIT INTERNATIONAL 271, 275–76 (Melanges René-Jean Dupuy, 1991) and INTERNATIONAL LAW IN THEORY AND PRACTICE 80–81 (1991).

12.   Boyle, *supra* note 8, at 8.

implement the 1985 Vienna Convention. As to the 1992 Framework Convention, a protocol for its implementation is planned. More important, however, the particular expression of obligations in the framework conventions was intentionally used to promote the realization of universal acceptance. The indefinite and abstract way of expressing these general obligations in the framework conventions can be considered a "safe guard" for states, allowing for a flexible interpretation of the obligations to implement them according to the ability and specific situation of each state.

In other words, these framework conventions clearly deny the necessity of an international unification of obligations. They stipulate "qualified obligations" and allow for the "differentiation of obligations." The framework conventions provide for such obligations by including a flexible approach through the use of clauses such as "to take appropriate measures" and "to take measures commensurate with each state's ability." These are the "qualified obligations." In some cases the framework conventions expressly admit preferential treatment of developing countries, as seen in the "differentiation of obligations." Both are undoubtedly the methods by which each state's individual circumstances may be considered in as flexible a manner as possible.[13]

The framework conventions stand in contrast to the other international environmental agreements in their method of providing for the obligations. In international law, generally, states can be regulated most effectively under legal instruments which stipulate obligations in as concrete and specific a manner as possible. This holds true for international environmental law and, generally, international environmental agreements impose not only a general or abstract obligation to protect the environment but also an obligation to observe concrete eco-standards derived therefrom, and to take specific domestic regulatory measures.[14]

The method of regulating the behavior of states in the framework conventions is different from that of international agreements in other fields of international environmental protection where the obligations of states are clear and concrete in terms of eco-standards and where the implementation of internationally "unified" eco-standards is essential.

By contrast, the framework conventions first provide for the general goal and general obligation to take cooperative and concerted action. The most important

---

13. *See, e.g.*, art. 2 of the 1985 Vienna Convention, art. 5 of the 1987 Montreal Protocol, and arts. 3 & 4 of the 1992 Framework Convention. SCHACHTER, INTERNATIONAL LAW IN THEORY AND PRACTICE, *supra* note 11, at 368–372 (1991); Peter H. Sand, *International Cooperation: The Environmental Experience, in* PRESERVING THE GLOBAL ENVIRONMENT 236, 240–56 (Jessica T. Mathews ed., 1991).

14. As a typical example, art. 4 of the 1973 International Convention for the Prevention of Pollution from Ships requires states party to take particular legislative measures. International Convention for the Prevention of Pollution from Ships, Nov. 2, 1973, 12 I.L.M. 1319 (1983). Paolo Contini & Peter H. Sand, *Method to Expedite Environment Protection: International Ecostandards*, 66 AM. J. INT'L L. 37, 39–47 (1972).

object of framework conventions is imposing the obligation on as many states as possible to take concerted action. Obligations in concrete and definite terms are not included in framework conventions. Thus, the most important feature of the framework conventions is that as many states as possible are required to perform "certain" obligations with a view to contributing to "internationally concerted action"; it is not the determination or unification of the "extent of the concrete contribution."

The framework conventions on global environmental protection require states party to make "appropriate" contributions which are shared in good faith, taking into consideration their individual circumstances. They must make the "appropriate" contributions to realize the legal interest of protecting the global environment, which all of them enjoy as members of the treaty regime. The importance, again, is that for the achievement of the goal of global environmental protection, "concerted action" should be taken under the framework conventions concerned in a continuous and steady manner in order to further the improvement of the global environment.

Under the treaty regime on ozone layer protection, the 1987 Montreal Protocol supplementing the 1985 Vienna Convention provided for concrete standards to reduce emissions of ozone depleting substances. The treaty regime on ozone layer protection is not, however, a legal instrument that mainly aims at imposing clear and concrete obligations for regulating the behavior of states.

First, the treaty regime for ozone layer protection grants the states party great discretion in choosing domestic regulatory measures to implement the numerical standards set out therein. The treaty regime does not stipulate clear and concrete obligations "in a definite manner." Second, but more important, the treaty regime provides for "qualified obligations" and allows for "the differentiation of obligations" which, as mentioned before, are the notable characteristics commonly realized in the treaty regimes on global environmental protection.[15] These characteristics of the treaty regime are, accordingly, of greater signifigance than the setting of numerical standards in the 1987 Montreal Protocol.

As observed above, the normative state of affairs preceding the framework conventions raised expectations that they formulate enforceable legal principles and legal procedures so as to realize the goal of protecting the global environment in

---

15. Furthermore, regarding the problems of environmental protection on the global level, similar supplementary protocols are being planned. It should be noted, however, that in the ozone layer protection regime, it was possible to provide for the relevant eco-standards only because of the particular feature of that problem: the ozone depleting substances such as the CFCs are now specified with a high degree of scientific certainty, and also the production sources of CFCs can readily be identified. This is not the case with the other global environmental problems. The relevant factors vary according to specific problems of the global environment. We cannot expect that a certain eco-standard and certain control measures can always be applicable as effective means for enhancing global environmental protection. It should be noted, therefore, that effective regulating methods contained in the framework conventions are essential.

fact. The framework conventions unfortunately do not appear to successfully complete the tasks required because of a lack of clarity and concreteness of the obligations to be undertaken by states party.

Instead, the framework conventions have an implementation mechanism which is also characteristic. How this particular implementation mechanism can induce states to contribute to an internationally concerted action by restricting the freedom of states is examined below.

V. THE IMPLEMENTATION OF INTERNATIONALLY CONCERTED ACTIONS

While states party are required to contribute to a "concerted action" for the common purpose of global environmental protection, the contents of the "concerted action" and the concrete obligations arising therefrom are left to the discretion of each state, though within a designated limit. There must be a certain procedure to impose restrictions on or to regulate the unilateral application or interpretation of those flexible obligations, otherwise, the normativity to be realized through the conventions would be seriously encroached upon by the unilateral interpretation of each state. It follows that for effective implementation, in the first place, a procedure is required to restrain the discretion of states in their determination of "what the concerted action should be" and "to what extent each state should make contributions in the concerted action." Second, a procedure to rectify or, if necessary, eliminate state behavior that deviates from or impedes the "concerted action" which needs to be implemented continuously and steadily is also needed. It is not important to entail international responsibility of or impose sanctions upon those states which deviate from or impede the "concerted action;" what matters here is to make states contribute in a continuous and steady manner in order to secure the "concerted action." Thus, what is needed is another procedure to verify and ensure the performance of obligations by states.[16]

Regarding the first procedure above, the state practice of international cooperation has ripened into a customary obligation regarding the protection of the environment, other than the global environment, in the form of international cooperation for environmental assessment and procedures such as prior notification and prior consultation.[17] These procedures can restrict the unilateral actions by

---

16. Alan E. Boyle, *State Responsibility for Breach of Obligations to Protect the Global Environment, in* CONTROL OVER COMPLIANCE WITH INTERNATIONAL LAW 69, 69–82 (William E. Butler ed., 1990).

17. *Survey of State Practice Relevant to International Liability for Injurious Consequences Arising Out of Acts Not Prohibited by International Law,* U.N. Doc. A/CN 4–384 (1984); Günter Handl, *The Principle of "Equitable Use" as Applied to Internationally Shared Resources: Its Role in Resolving Potential International Disputes over Transfrontier Pollution,* 14 REVUE BELGIQUE DU DROIT INTERNATIONAL 41, 55–63 (1978–79); Soji Yamamoto, *Kokusai Hunsō ni Okeru Kyōgi Seido no Hensitu* [*Change in Nature of Consultation for International Dispute Settlement*], *in* KOKUSAI HUNSŌ NO HEIWATEKI

states when there are no clear obligations imposed thereon or when there are only those obligations which are general and abstract enough to permit, to a considerable extent, each State's discretion of unilateral interpretation.[18]

The framework conventions also provide for environmental assessment and procedures which assume functions similar to those of prior notification or prior consultation procedures. These are exercised through certain international bodies under the relevant treaty regime. The legal concept of "common concern" for the global environment as a unitary whole can work properly under such institutional mechanisms, where appropriate.[19]

The framework conventions contain abundant provisions on international cooperation in legal, scientific and technical fields and in the exercise of research and systematic assessment.[20] The Conference of the Contracting Parties is required to keep under continuous review the implementation of the convention by examining the most recent information collected through international cooperative measures.[21] Thus, the Conference of the Parties, backed by the international cooperation of states, institutionally fulfills the function of collective implementation, which is normally beyond the ability of an individual state.

The framework conventions impose on states an obligation to transmit information on the policies and measures that they have adopted in their implementation of the convention.[22] The Conference of the Parties should be entitled to review the measures and policies adopted by a state in advance of enforcement and to make necessary recommendations. The scope of a unilateral decision permitted to each state on what and how it should contribute to the concerted action under the treaty regime could be adequately confined in a more effective way if the Conference of the Contracting Parties or some implementing body could duly review the appropriateness of the measures and policies adopted by each state regarding the required concerted action. In such a case, the Conference could fulfill the function of an "institutionalized prior consultation" corresponding to the prior consultation normally practiced between two states on a bilateral basis.

KAIKETSU TO KOKUSAIHŌ [PEACEFUL SETTLEMENT OF INTERNATIONAL DISPUTES AND INTERNATIONAL LAW]: ESSAYS IN CELEBRATION OF THE 60TH ANNIVERSARY OF TAKESHI MINAGAWA 215, 231–243 (1981). Atsuko Kanehara, *The Significance of the Japanese Proposal of "Pledge and Review" Process in Growing International Environmental Law*, 35 JAPAN ANN. INT'L L. 1, 4–12 (1992).

18. Kanehara, *id.* at 10–11.

19. PATRICIA W. BIRNIE & ALAN E. BOYLE, INTERNATIONAL LAW AND THE ENVIRONMENT 160–79 (1990).

20. Arts. 3 and 4 of the 1985 Vienna Convention and arts. 3 and 4 of the 1992 Framework Convention.

21. Art. 6 of the 1985 Vienna Convention and art. 7 of the 1992 Framework Convention.

22. Art. 5 of the 1985 Vienna Convention and art. 12 of the 1992 Framework Convention.

As to the second point above, dispute settlement clauses are usually contained in the framework conventions on global environmental protection.[23] These dispute settlement provisions may not work as expected, however, because the dispute concerning a state party's noncompliance with the treaty regime is different from a confrontational type of dispute between rival states as is presupposed by traditional dispute settlement clauses.[24]

As previously noted, the legal interest of protecting the global environment duly belongs to the treaty regime as a whole. Deviation from or impediment to concerted action by an individual state under the treaty regime is therefore regarded as an infringement on the common interest of all the states party. A dispute concerning the alleged noncompliance of an individual state could also have a confrontational aspect between that noncomplying state party and the other states party. In order to effectuate the common interest by continuing and maintaining the concerted action under the treaty regime, it is more important to make the alleged noncomplying state implement fully the prescribed obligation than to define its international responsibility for the alleged breach or to impose sanctions against that state.

To this end, the "Non-Compliance Procedure" adopted in 1992 by the Conference of the Parties to the Montreal Protocol on the protection of the ozone layer deserves attention.[25] Under the "Non-Compliance Procedure," any state party is entitled to address its reservation regarding another state party's implementation of its obligation under the Protocol. Thereafter, the Implementation Committee is required to decide upon and to call for steps to bring about full compliance with the Protocol by taking appropriate measures including issuing cautions, suspending the operation of a treaty, suspending the specific rights and privileges under the Protocol or, most important, giving appropriate assistance.

The advantages of the "Non-Compliance Procedure" appear to be two fold. First, it duly allows for a form of standing for "any state party" to address its reservation regarding another state party's implementation of its obligation. Any state party can have such standing so as to ensure due performance of the Protocol on behalf of the treaty regime. This must result from the notion that the legal interest for protecting the ozone layer belongs to the treaty regime. Second, the inclusion of the principle of supporting the measures to be taken by the non-complying state party reflects the importance attached by the treaty regime to making the state party contribute in a continuous and steady manner in order to further the concerted action.

---

23 . Art. 11 of the 1985 Vienna Convention and art. 14 of the 1992 Framework Convention.

24. Thomas Gehring, *International Environmental Regimes: Dynamic Sectoral Legal System*, 1 Y.B. INT'L ENVTL. L. 35, 50–54 (1990).

25. Art. 8, U.N. Doc. UNEP/Ozl.Pro.4/15. Martti Koskenniemi, *Breach of Treaty or Non-Compliance? Reflections on the Enforcement of the Montreal Protocol*, 3 Y.B. INT'L ENVTL. L. 123, 123–162 (1992).

The "Noncompliance Procedure" established under the Montreal Protocol is aimed at attaining compliance with the concrete standards for the reduction of emissions of ozone depleting substances. In cases where no concrete eco-standards are set, it is desirable that a framework convention on global environmental protection should contain an implementation mechanism in the form of a "Report and Review" system, which may be similar to the supervisory procedures established in the field of human rights.[26]

In relation to both the first and second points above, the implementation mechanism for the stabilization of a global climate called "Pledge and Review," which Japan proposed in the 1992 UNCED is a useful and a practical technique.[27] According to this proposal, each state commits itself to setting the standards to be observed. Such a voluntary pledge is combined with an institutional review by a competent international body. The "Pledge and Review" procedure requires, in principle, that each state individually pledge target reduction in greenhouse gas emissions as a unilateral interpretation of the general obligation to stabilize the global climate under the framework convention. The "Pledge and Review" procedure also requires that an implementating institution review "internationally" the strategies adopted by that state before and after its performance. Here, the reflection of the legal concept of "common concern of mankind" and the idea that the legal interest of stabilizing the global climate belongs to the treaty regime as a whole are clearly demonstrated.

The Japanese proposal, unfortunately, was not adopted and, in practice, the 1992 Framework Convention merely imposes on states an obligation to communicate information on the relevant policies and measures adopted by them. If the "Pledge and Review" procedure had been included in the 1992 Framework Convention, it could have resulted in a unique procedure which strikes a desirable balance between conflicting considerations: the unilateralism of pledges by individual states on the one hand and the universalism of review realized through competent international institutions on the other.[28]

VI. CONCLUDING REMARKS

The "framework" of the framework conventions on global environmental protection has herein been examined mainly by focusing on the methods included for the regulation of state behavior. The framework conventions stipulate the legal interest of protecting the global environment as a unitary whole. This has been recognized recently by states in their extensive use of soft laws in the resolution of the problem. The legal interest belongs to the treaty regime as a whole. As a result, each state party should share the obligation of protecting the global environment.

---

26. Handl, *supra* note 1, at 71–72.

27. Kanehara, *supra* note 17, at 20–21.

28. *Id.* at 20–32.

Above all, the framework conventions require that as many states as possible take part in an internationally concerted action. Each state party, therefore, should make an "appropriate" contribution to the action according to its individual ability and situation.

Additionally, the framework conventions create particular mechanisms to implement the action in a steady and secure manner, although they do not yet seem to be sufficiently effective. Examples of such mechanisms are the procedures which restrict the unilateral interpretation by states of their obligations and which ensure their implementation of the obligations. The entire method included in the framework conventions for regulating states thus can be realized through the "framework," which links the whole of the functions by various provisions in the treaty regime.

The method of regulating the behavior of states in the framework conventions is markedly different from that of most international law rules. International law, generally, has tried to impose on states obligations in as concrete and specific a manner as possible, and to regulate effectively their behavior. International law often stipulates judicial arbitration as a final procedure for dispute settlement. It has been suggested that the most effective means for exercising and protecting legal rights is the provision of enforceable rights and obligations in concrete terms so that courts can apply and interpret those rules easily.

In comparison with these traditional and ordinary means for regulating the behavior of states, the mushrooming of so many instruments with universal application may have a paradoxical impact on the normativity of international law in general, since their prescribed obligations lack clarity and have only mild implementation mechanisms. Nevertheless, the particular method used in the framework conventions is the most original and novel device that international law has developed when faced with global problems such as the protection of the environment.

These global problems, which include human rights, development, world trade and environment, have steadily grown. An application of general and universal international law is seen as a strong solution. However, the formulation of a universal international law may face certain difficulties. Firstly, new problems very often require a change in the fundamental structure and principles of international law. Second, individual situations and relevant factors vary from state to state. It is accordingly difficult to make conventions that prescribe detailed and specific obligations which are enforceable for each problem, and which are universally acceptable.

One result from this normative state of affairs is a proliferation of soft laws to regulate these problems. International scholars have already considered the possibility of a new formal source of international law different from the traditional ones of custom and treaty.[29] Furthermore, some scholars regard soft laws as

---

29. There is a vast body of literature concerning this problem. *See especially*, C.M. Chinkin, *The Challenge of Soft Law: Development and Change in International Law*, 38

significant new sources of general and universal international law.

While the doctrinal development of international legal sources deserves an in-depth examination, if soft laws were recognized as new sources of international law so as to acquire legally binding force, they would not always impact global problems in a practical and effective manner. Most soft laws governing the protection of a global environment formulate only general goals or general principles and stop short of formulating principles and obligations which are truly enforceable. Even in cases where soft laws set forth detailed and specific obligations or have a legally binding force, their universal effectiveness would depend on whether states can accept and observe their obligations. It is doubtful that most states are ready to accept detailed and specific obligations on problems such as global environmental protection where necessary changes must be drastic and socially widespread, for instance, in the cases of the reduction of ozone-layer-depleting CFCs and the reduction of greenhouse gases, and where feasibility depends heavily on the specific circumstances of each state concerned.

What is required, therefore, in international law is not only the development of new sources of law which have binding force or new legislative procedures within some institutional and organizational work, but newly devised methods to regulate states universally in as practical and effective a manner as possible. The new and unique method realized within the framework conventions on global environmental protection is a valuable tool for developing a universally acceptable rule of international law. For this reason, the unique legal characteristics of the method herein described should be regarded as a product of the physiology rather than of the pathology of law.

INT'L & COMP. L.Q. 850, 850–866 (1989); Ignaz Seidel-Hohenveldern, *International Economic Soft Law*, 163 RECUEIL DES COURS 164, 164–246 (1980); Joseph Gold, *Strengthening the Soft International Law of Exchange Arrangements*, 77 AM. J. INT'L L. 443, 443–489 (1983); Prosper Weil, *Towards Relative Normativity in International Law?*, 77 AM. J. INT'L L. 413, 413–442 (1983). Naoya Okuwaki, *Kokurenhō Taikei ni Okeru Kokusairippō no Sonritukiban - Rekishiteki Haikei to Mondai no Shozai* [*Theoretical Basis of International Legislation in the System of the United Nations Law—Reflection on Historical Background*], in KOKUSAIHŌ, KOKUSAI RENGŌ TO NIHON [INTERNATIONAL LAW, THE UNITED NATIONS AND JAPAN]: ESSAYS IN CELEBRATION OF THE 60TH ANNIVERSARY OF YUICHI TAKANO 77, 91–120 (Yasuaki Onuma ed. 1987), and *Kokuren Shisutemu to Kokusaihō* [*The United Nations Law System and International Law*], in SHAKAIHENDŌ NO NAKANO HO [LAW IN SOCIAL CHANGE] 49, 62–79; Shinya Murase, *Gendai Kokusaiho ni Okeru Hōgenron no Dōyō—Kokusai Rippōron no Zenteiteki Kosatsu toshite* [*The Changing Views on the Sources of International Laws*] 25 RIKKYO HŌGAKU 81, 96–109.

REVIEW OF TREATY NEGOTIATING PROCEDURES FOR INTERNATIONAL LAWMAKING: LESSONS FROM UNCLOS III

Mamoru Koga

I. INTRODUCTION

The number of resolutions adopted by international organizations is increasing year by year. Some of these resolutions function as lawmaking. Among them, the resolutions of the United Nations General Assembly express the intention of states on legal issues or *opinio juris* regarding customary norms.[1] A resolution of an international organization is adaptable to changing circumstances so that it can effectively respond to new problems. Prompt measures taken by resolution are especially necessary in new fields, such as in environmental law. Since the membership of the United Nations includes almost all countries of the world, resolutions of its General Assembly play an important role in the development of law in new fields. So-called "soft-law," a norm on the way to formation through such resolutions, is flexible enough to bring about a new regime.

However, the resolutions of the U.N. General Assembly made by majority vote only function as recommendations; they do not bind U.N. members legally. Had resolutions passed by majority vote been binding, states might have refused to join the United Nations for fear of being bound by resolutions against which they voted. The resolutions of international organizations therefore do not create definite rights and obligations of states.

---

1. McWhinney emphasizes the lawmaking role of the U.N. Genereal Assembly and notes that, ". . . the General Assembly resolution has become the prime instrument for the remaking of the old international law in the image of the new Third World majority." E. McWHINNY, UNITED NATIONS LAW MAKING 57 (1984).

It is more efficient to deal with issues requiring lawmaking measures in a clearly binding treaty rather than through resolutions. In major areas of international law, the resolutions of the U.N. General Assembly have been supplemented by definite multilateral treaties.[2]

While resolutions can be flexible responses to new situations and doubtless have played an important role in the development of law, the establishment of new regimes by treaty is more desirable for legal certainty. A universally approved multilateral treaty creates law in a new field; many multilateral treaties have been concluded which make new regimes in controversial areas of international law. Many treaties are comprehensive, packaging together basic principles, concrete rights, and obligations of member countries, an organizational structure for managing the regime, and procedure for conflict resolution.[3]

In order to respond to new situations, the fixed text of a treaty may be inadequate and some supplementary resolutions under the treaty may be necessary. For such subsequent resolutions to be sound, a treaty acceptable to many countries is pursued. Thus, treatymaking skills that can increase the degree of state compliance are of great importance.[4] "Negotiation skills" play an important role. In this regard, reviewing the procedure used in the Law of the Sea Conference may be a useful starting point.

a. Review of Procedures in the Law of the Sea Conference

The law of the sea provides useful materials for studying the development of the lawmaking process. The first norms of international law emerged in this field and the first attempt to codify international law was made in this area. Codification in the form of a general treaty was tried at the 1930 Hague Conference. At that time, only the regime of the high seas and the territorial sea was known.

Both the First United Nations Conference on the Law of Sea (UNCLOS I) in

---

2. McWhinney points out that the "soft law" of the General Assembly resolution often ends up as "hard law." *Id.* at 79. After discussing the supplemental role of soft law to the traditional sources (treaties and customary law), Van Hoof states that ". . . international legal doctrine, while recognizing the existence to the so-called 'soft-law' and acknowledging the importance of exploring the 'gray area,' should make every effort to 'narrow down the gray area.'" G. J. H. VAN HOOF, RETHINKING THE SOURCE OF INTERNATIONAL LAW 191 (1983).

3. The Charter of the United Nations and other treaties establishing major international organizations are typical examples of this type, however, the more systematic example may be the U.N. Convention of the Law of the Sea.

4. Even after the Law of the Sea Conference, there are fit examples for the relationship between the negotiation skill and its lawmaking role, such as the ozone layer treaties. This chapter, however, is intended to contribute to the volume by introducing the earlier lessons. For the negotiation on the London Revision 1990 to the 1987 Montreal Protocol on Substances That Deplete the Ozone Layer, *see* R. E. BENEDICK, OZONE DIPLOMACY —NEW DIRECTIONS IN SAFEGUARDING THE PLANET 163–98 (1991).

1958 and the Second Conference (UNCLOS II) in 1960 followed a typical process of codification. The United Nations International Law Commission (ILC) prepared the four draft treaties for the diplomatic meeting. UNCLOS I adopted them with a few amendments. However, UNCLOS II failed to agree on the width of the territorial sea. The Convention of the Territorial Sea came into effect without this key provision. While UNCLOS I was essentially a legal process, UNCLOS II was entirely political. This difference was a future source of confusion. Although an important part of the codification of customary law is the legal process, the political process is indispensible to resolving a politically controversial issue such as the width of the territorial sea. This suggests that treaty negotiations by diplomats will be more important in new law fields.[5]

Negotiation at the Third United Nations Conference on the Law of the Sea (UNCLOS III, 1973–1982) was political from its outset. To prepare a draft treaty, the Sea-bed Committee in 1968 set up two sub-committees for special study, law and technology. Most of the committee members were diplomats serving as specialists, making this membership fundamentally different from that of the ILC.

Negotiation of the deep seabed regime became more complicated, since the exploitation of seabed resources was an undeveloped industry and major interests were involved. The special and problematic features of deep seabed resources (manganese nodules) are that: (1) land-based resources equivalent to manganese nodules are monopolized by a few countries, mainly developing countries; (2) the land-based resources will be depleted in the twenty-first century; (3) the metals contained in the resources are essential for new technologies such as space rockets and jet planes; and (4) the technology for exploitation of seabed resources, though not yet fully developed, is said to be owned by a few developed countries.[6]

Preparatory work by the ILC was not appropriate in the new order of the seabed; drafting on the basis of precedent is not possible in a new field such as this. The international conference system was instead considered appropriate since it would lead to political decisionmaking through negotiation.

While UNCLOS III had a draft prepared by the Sea-bed Committee,[7] it was too simple to use as the basis of negotiation. The Sea-bed Committee was expected to prepare a draft corresponding to an ILC draft, but could not because of the lack of agreement among members. UNCLOS III therefore had to begin diplomatic negotiations without a single reference text. Instead the Conference itself undertook the task of preparatory work.

Commenting on the unique UNCLOS III process, Judge Oda said in his

---

5.   In the case of codification of customary law, the political authority of the U.N. General Assembly stems from the number of Member states and adoption by a large majority. M. E. VILLIGER, CUSTOMARY INTERNATIONAL LAW AND TREATIES 144 (1985).

6.   A. M. POST, DEEPSEA MINING AND THE LAW OF THE SEA 19–30 (1983).

7.   U.N. Doc. A/9021. For the works of the Sea-bed Committee see S. ODA, THE LAW OF THE SEA IN OUR TIME —II, THE UNITED NATIONS SEABED COMMITTEE 1968–1973 (1977).

dissenting opinion in the *Continental Shelf* case that "[s]uch procedure and method is an experiment without precedent in the history of international law, and thus UNCLOS III can be described as a great laboratory workshop of international law."[8] He referred to the "package deal" and the consensus method in connection with the legal status of articles on the continental shelf in the Draft Convention. There were many novel procedures in the negotiation of UNCLOS III, but all were adopted for a single purpose: the widest possible acceptance of the final Convention.

In 1974 the second session of UNCLOS III adopted a gentlemen's agreement stating that, "[t]he Conference should make every effort to reach agreement by way of consensus and there should be no voting until all efforts at consensus have been exhausted."[9] Because of this agreement, UNCLOS III labored for ten years in pursuit of a compromise that would secure the widest possible acceptance. Had the Conference given up the consensus approach and proceeded by voting, it would most likely have ended around 1978. The result of the Conference was eventually adopted by a vote and then refused by many developed countries. Nevertheless, the effort should be appreciated as a strenuous and sustained attempt to make a general treaty that would be accepted and complied with universally. As such, it has enormous value as a lesson for future lawmaking procedure.

(1) Consensus Rule

UNCLOS III did not proceed to voting until the adoption of the Draft Convention in 1982. There were many decisions made before then, which were adopted by consensus. Making a decision by majority vote is an easy way to reach a result, but it fixes the conflict of opinions. Even though a majority wins in the voting, this does not mean that the consequence will be fruitful. A decision without the support of broad substantive agreement is inefficient. For this reason, the consensus rule was introduced.

The consensus rule was often used even before UNCLOS III, mainly by the U.N. General Assembly in the 1960s. The distinctive feature of the procedure as used by UNCLOS III was the concerted effort to reach general agreement and avoid voting. The President of the Conference and Chairmen of the Committees held many consultations between conflicting parties, suspending the meeting whenever any clear conflict was apparent. Such consultations were held before the Committee meeting under the parties' sponsorship. After reaching a basic agreement among the parties, the meeting was resumed, and the chairman called

---

8.   Case Concerning the Continental Shelf (Tunsia/Libyan Arab Jamahiriya), 1982 I.C.J. 17(Feb.24) at 171.

9.   UNCLOS III, Rules of Procedure, Annex, U.N. Doc. A/Conf.62/30 Rev. 3 (1981). *See also* United Nations, Third United Conference on the Law of the Sea, Official Records, Vol.1, 41–53 (1975).

for a statement of each party for their clarification and satisfaction, reconfirming that there was no objection.

In this process, the consultation stage is the most important. Many incidents may have led to a breakup of the Conference, which were successfully navigated by the efforts of the Chairman. A typical example of this procedure was seen in the 11th Session just before voting for the Draft Convention. The President declared that formal amendments should be submitted between April 8 and 13. Upon this invitation, thirty-one amendments were submitted to the Secretariat and voting on the amendments was deferred under Rule 33. The President of the Conference withdrew from the Plenary Meeting to concentrate on consultations with the sponsoring countries to persuade them not to press for a vote on their amendment proposals. As a result, twenty-nine amendments were withdrawn, with some conditions or clarifications. Two amendments, made by Spain and Turkey, were put to a vote and rejected.[10] After this decision, the Draft Convention became the only formal text of the Law of the Sea Convention.

Committee II also adopted the "rule of silence," which regards a basic proposal without any express objection as generally supported. This enabled the consideration of the text to proceed efficiently, although it did stimulate many objections by some participants. These objections were eventually withdrawn or simply ignored because other major participants that did not express any objection were regarded as supporting the original text. The objectors were given the right only to have their statement written in the official records, which they expected to have some legal implications. The legal status of the record is still not clear, however.

The rule of silence was useful in masking minor dissatisfactions and preventing the appearance of sharp conflicts. Despite these merits, the procedure only postponed clear settlement, as many countries continued dissatisfied until the final stage, as shown by the many formal amendments submitted in the 11th Session, as mentioned above. Some of them had been negotiated in the early stages of the Conference and had been deemed to have been settled by compromise.[11]

Consensus procedure is apparently difficult to apply to controversial issues in which major interests are involved. For such issues, however, majority voting is even more inappropriate because it solidifies the conflicts of opinion. Consensus procedure is therefore effective for issues where the conflict is minor; for highly controversial issues, consensus must be supplemented by other procedures.

---

10. *Id.* at 87–155 (1984).

11. In referring to the procedure used at this Conference, Simma states, "[a]s is often the case, this method is chosen precisely in order to compel basic agreement which is in reality lacking. Failure is thus built into the treaty." B. Simma, *Consent: Strains in the Treaty System, in* THE STRUCTURE AND PROCESS OF INTERNATIONAL LAW: ESSAYS IN LEGAL PHILOSOPHY DOCTRINE AND THEORY 488 (R. St.J. Macdonald & D. M. Johnston eds., 1983).

(2) Package Deal

The "package deal" is a negotiating technique that links issues and promotes a compromise by combining unfavorable articles with favorable ones. There were many kinds of packages in UNCLOS III. The issues surrounding the traditional law of the sea made one package. Strait passage and economic zones were dealt with as a separate package in the Second Committee.

As the articles on the deep seabed regime became increasingly unfavorable to developed countries, a general package was devised to promote a compromise. First, the deep seabed items were combined with articles on navigation. Some countries expected that the United States would sign the Convention in order to assure favorable transit passage in spite of the seabed articles.

When that failed, the second package combined the reserved area (parallel system) with production limitation (production policy). Former U.S. Secretary of State Henry Kissinger proposed this package. This instead led to protracted negotiations and the United States rejection of the Convention. The third package was the linkage of the articles on the obligation of operators with the review clause. This package was called the "mini-package." It may, however, be better to see this package as a variety of deals. The last five years of the Conference were spent in this negotiation.[12] These articles are filled with many "safeguards" or limiting clauses, which are traces of compromise balancing among the conflicted participants.

The purpose of a package deal is to promote a compromise on controversial issues. It supplements the consensus procedure in this way. Sometimes, it is more effective in important issues. However, some difficulties appeared in the package deals of UNCLOS III. First, the package approach cannot be effective when each member persists in its particular interests. Compromise dealing is possible only if all members evaluate their interests *comparatively*. Second, a package deal becomes impossible if many packages are so intricately linked that negotiators cannot identify whether their interests are involved. In such cases, negotiations generally focus only on the articles which are unfavorable to them. Third, if a negotiating party can get one element of the package easily by another method, the dealing will be meaningless. An example of this was seen in 1983, when President Ronald Reagan proclaimed the establishment of the economic zone. Developing countries blamed the United States for preempting the UNCLOS III package,[13] to which the United States replied that the economic zone was recognized as a rule of customary law. Rules of customary law should therefore not be invoked in treaty negotiations.

---

12. For the informal negotiation during this period mainly regarding financial arrangements, *see* J. K. SEBENIUS, NEGOTIATING THE LAW OF THE SEA 13–48 (1984).

13. Statement by the Chairman of the Group of 77, delivered on Aug. 13, 1984, U.N. Doc. LOS/PCN/48.

(3) Group Negotiation

UNCLOS III dealt with many issues which were very different in nature. Thus, it tried a variety of negotiation groupings during its ten years. Informal meetings and group negotiations had been used also in other conferences. However, the number and variety of fora in UNCLOS III may be considered as one of its distinctive features.

The fora can be classified into two types. One is a variation on the idea of a sub-committee, examples of which are the "negotiating group" and "working group." Seven negotiating groups were established in 1978 to concentrate on seven core issues. Each group had a coordinator as the chairman and an assisting team composed of diplomats from several countries. Any representative was allowed to attend and speak. These meetings were "informal," meaning that there were to be no published records, although most countries had their staffs record the meetings.

The "Working Group 21," (WG-21) established in the First Committee of the following year was a more efficient forum. Only twenty-one members selected from each group were allowed to speak, although other countries' diplomats were permitted to observe the discussions. In WG-21 meetings representatives were identified by their own names, not by that of their country.

The second type of forum is a consultative body sponsored by the Conference President or a Committee Chairman. Each group entrusted with a particular issue was led by an influential person designated from among the representatives. Prominent examples of this type of body were the Evensen Group and the Nandan Group, named after their chairmen, each of whom brought into full play his abilities to develop a compromise text on a particular issue.[14]

Besides these fora, various groups were established to promote negotiation. Regional groups and interest groups served to simplify the interrelationship among participants. These are common in any conference dealing with a multilateral treaty. Additionally, the President created some private bodies, such as "friends" and "collegium," which consisted of the Chairman of each Committee, a representative of the U.N. Secretary-General, leading participants, and others. These functioned as a kind of task force to manage and coordinate the Conference.

To the casual observer, it may have seemed that the President was looking for the best method by trial and error. However, UNCLOS III was really a laboratory for experiments in negotiating procedure. By dividing the negotiating forum into several smaller groups, the Conference became more complicated, especially in the

---

14. Although the President of the Conference summed up the groups as a feature of this Conference, there is no reference in his article, and no official document records the activities of these informal meetings. T. T. B. Koh, *Negotiating a New World Order for the Sea,* 24 VA. J. INT'L L. 78–2 (1984). Some semi-formal groups were introduced in the Final Act of the Conference. U.N. Doc., The Law of the Sea, 1649 U.N. Sales No. E. 83 V. 5 (1983).

First Committee.   Similar issues were discussed in different groups with overlapping concerns. Although group negotiation was designed for efficiency, it resulted in making this Conference even more political and controversial.

b. Possible New Negotiating Procedures— A Suggestion

The aim of UNCLOS III was to create a concrete regime in the framework of treaty law. It was necessary to make a stable regime by written agreement in order to secure a comprehensive compromise in the conflict between developed and developing countries, and between coastal and shipping countries.

The law of the sea, a traditional area of international law, has, by dint of its long history, a solid base of rules established by customary norm. There is also a complicated network of domestic law and international law applicable to maritime affairs. A global order and regional or local orders form a systematized body of law. Moreover, the demand of tests for judgment in dispute settlement is higher in maritime issues, owing to many conflicts among national interests.

There are differences between the law of the sea and environmental law. The law of global warming and the ozone layer offers the following examples:

1)   the history of environmental law is rather short and national practices supporting the law are few, requiring creation of a completely new set of laws;

2)   it is more important to establish guidelines for countries to coordinate their activities to achieve a goal (e.g., the ratio of reduction of emission) than to set up a mechanism for dispute settlement. If some countries fail to reach the goal, neither international dispute settlement nor sanctions are immediately necessary;

3)   the implementation of environmental law mostly depends on the domestic law and policy of each country. For example, the emission of carbon dioxide gas has a connection with the life style and culture of people and the legal situation of that country's society.

On the other hand, the law of the sea has given rise to problems between countries in the international sphere. Accordingly, it tends to involve more political conflicts.

The UNCLOS III was expected, as a forum, to realize the concept of a New International Economic Order in the serious confrontation between "North" and "South" in the 1970s. It was the first full-scale international conference for "collective bargaining," in which almost all developing countries united and endeavored to solve the North-South problem. The meetings of the conference therefore were preceded by political bargaining, in which scientific knowledge was referred to only where it had political benefit. As a result, the seabed regime has become a very artificial regime despite the nature of the subject and the market principle.

This artificiality resulted because the legal regime was negotiated before any concrete business or scientific data on the seabed were gathered. For a legal regime involving natural science, it is necessary to prepare a draft which takes account of scientific data.

UNCED made good use of the lesson of UNCLOS III. First, the drafting was preceded by office work before the diplomatic conference in order to avoid a long negotiation period. Second, it did not stipulate detailed provisions, but was limited to agreement on basic principles and guidelines. Consequently, the substance of environmental law depends on further implementation in conjunction with domestic legislation and the adoption of bilateral treaties.

Today, as global problems increase, the demand on treatymaking by diplomatic conference is greater. As stated previously, the codification work done by the ILC is adequate in an area where there are many customary norms, but is not appropriate where political negotiations are connected with national interests.

The UNCLOS III, where the drafting work and political decisionmaking processes were combined, took a long period of time and many drafts before it was successfully concluded. The expense of regularly sending a mission to UNCLOS III was a heavy burden for small developing countries, particulary those with a GNP per capita of less than U.S. $1,000 dollars. The conference continued for ten years and did not yield a benefit commensurate with its costs, a lesson which the leaders of UNCED took into consideration. Accordingly, improvements in the negotiation procedure still exist.

(1) Extension of Participants —Drafting Work by Experts

In a new field of law, the ILC seems not to function well. For codification treaties, the ILC researches many previous cases and collates the existing laws for a diplomatic conference. While diplomatic negotiations are still held in these new fields, there may be a stage where the substance of a treaty is examined from scientific, economic, and sociological perspectives in order to insure the objectivity of a treaty.

In this respect, some nonstate actors, such as scientists and experts from international organizations, may contribute to the work. Even in current conferences, scientists, and economists are consulted. However, usually there is no forum in which such experts discuss a specialized draft.

In UNCLOS III, many scientists and economists from developed countries played an active role in the negotiation of some provisions (e.g., the definition of the continental shelf or the financial arrangements of seabed exploitation), but they, too, were affected by the policy of their countries. Although sub-committees were established for the consideration of scientific data, they became fora for political bargaining. The desirability of a draft by neutral scientists and economists in the preparatory stages is therefore evident.

(2) Strengthening International Organizations

The role of international organizations is important in providing neutral experts to the conference. Neutrality is a virtue of international organizations, although their organs are small in comparison with the governmental organizations of each nation. International organizations, such as the United Nations, have organs in the Secretariat with a research function and mandate to submit information to the General Assembly and the Security Council. The research ability of the organs is much smaller than that of the governmental institutions of member countries.

In Japan, the Ministry of International Trade and Industries (MITI) directs a variety of institutes, each with many scientists and well-equipped laboratories. These groups carry out many joint programs with company experts. Their opinions are taken into consideration before any industrial laws are drafted by the appropriate officials. Such an objective process should also be introduced to the international lawmaking regimes.

(3) Promoting the NGOs of Developing Countries

Nongovernmental Organizations (NGOs) have recently gained influence in the review of implementation of treaties and drafting of laws in Western countries. The general public is also playing an increased role in monitoring the implementation of the treaties and laws concerning environmental issues. Many global issues are related to the public life and the cooperation of the public is useful and necessary. Accordingly, a promising international regime in this area would be one that has cooperative relations with NGOs.

As prerequisite, however, significant problems of NGOs must be solved. Currently, NGOs exist and are active only in some Western developed countries. Although NGOs exist in some developing countries, they are branches of or modeled on NGOs of developed nations and rarely came into being fueled by domestic motives. The activities of NGOs are influenced by the cultural values of their members. Granting a major role to NGOs might result in the introduction of the values of only Western people to the global regime. The freedom of participation by NGOs does not always guarantee the equality of peoples.

The growth of the NGO in developing countries is essential to the giving of an important role to NGOs in securing equality. For that purpose, the supply of information by international organizations to NGOs should be promoted in order to guarantee equal participation. Both NGOs and the public in developing countries have little access to information, even regarding their own domestic affairs. In many countries, information sources and mass communication are limited or controlled by the government, creating a clear obstacle to the growth of NGOs. It is therefore desirable for international organizations to provide as much information as possible to NGOs, especially in developing countries. A system to accomodate this should be devised.

(4) Review System

One weakness of treaty law is its tendency, due to its fixed text, to fall behind social progress over time. Because of this defect, the resolutions of international organizations are important in a changing world. There is also merit in devising a review system for treaty law.

In UNCLOS III, the review clause (Article 155) was a controversial issue in the final stage of negotiation. Review was necessary because complete provisions were not able to be finalized at that time, due to limited scientific knowledge and business experience. Developed countries feared future fundamental changes in the treaty text by majority vote, which would undermine the compromise packages. The problem was solved by the introduction of a safeguard clause, which stipulated that certain provisions were exempt from future review. While the clause was an effective method for promoting agreement, it would not have been necessary had there been confidence among the parties.

II. CONCLUSION

UNCLOS III finally adopted the Convention on the Law of the Sea after ten years of negotiation; however, its active role in the seabed regime was easily changed by the private consultations sponsored by the U.N. Secretary-General. While this change may have been inevitable to secure participation by developed countries, it may have also engendered a feeling of powerlessness among the diplomats of the developing nations. Although the diplomats may have left the negotiations frustrated, the changes may have provided a valuable lesson for them as well: no viable regime will emerge without a substantial agreement. No substantial agreement can be achieved only by the majority.

UNCLOS III should be highly regarded in that it persevered in trying to conclude a substantial agreement until the final hours. It may be the last big international conference in which all participants united to negotiate the future of the world's oceans. It endeavored to maintain the traditional lawmaking instrument, treaty law.

UNCLOS III differed from other recent conferences, in which negotiations ended quickly by a majority vote and diplomats left ill-tempered. Another problem is that a majority of nations tends to force its opinion on the minority. Leading nations should be more tolerant and pursue compromise. However, the improvement of the treatymaking process should be pursued before it is abandoned, in line with a Confucian saying "[s]tudying old is to know new wisdom."

INTERNATIONAL ENVIRONMENTAL AND HUMAN RIGHTS LAW: THE ROLE OF SOFT LAW IN THE EVOLUTION OF PROCEDURAL RIGHTS TO INFORMATION, PARTICIPATION IN DECISIONMAKING, AND ACCESS TO DOMESTIC REMEDIES IN ENVIRONMENTAL MATTERS

Linda C. Reif

As the corpus of international environmental law matures in terms of both volume and content, the concerns of international lawyers and policymakers have started to move beyond first stage problems, such as the preservation of wildlife or the regulation of transboundary pollution, toward broader and interrelated socioeconomic concerns which implicate protection of the environment. Topics such as the relationship of the environment and development, the connections between international trade and environmental protection, methods to improve implementation of international treaty obligations, and the interaction of human rights and the environment are currently under consideration.[1]

At the same time, the interest of international lawyers has been piqued by potential alternatives to environmental treaties which create new international norms or quasi-norms and which have risen despite the considerable number, speed of negotiation, and sophistication of environment-related treaties in recent years. The concept of "soft law," as discussed further below, is under scrutiny for its role as a normative medium and an alternative vehicle for achieving cooperative behavior on the international plane.

In addition to the negative impacts on nature caused by the deterioration of the environment, human life and health are also increasingly being harmed.

---

1. *See, e.g.*, Edith Brown Weiss, *International Environmental Law: Contemporary Issues and the Emergence of a New World Order*, 81 GEO. L.J. 675 (1993).

Destruction of the ozone layer, atmospheric and water pollution, desertification, flooding of land, and a decline in the quality and quantity of fresh water are some of the environmental problems implicating human rights issues. For a growing number of persons in the world, these consequences include threats to human health or life, forced movement of populations due to large international development projects or other factors destroying the lifesupporting capacity of the local environments, and threats to the existence or cultural identities of indigenous peoples caused by damage to traditional environments.

Given the broad connections between international human rights and the environment, this chapter focuses on the role of soft law in the formation of legal norms in one area: the procedural rights of members of the public to receive information on the environment, to participate in environmental decisionmaking and to have effective access to domestic remedies through judicial and administrative avenues. First, however, the nature of soft law and its function in contemporary international lawmaking on the environment will be reviewed, followed by a survey of the evolving elements of international human rights and the environment.

I. SOFT LAW DEFINED

The notion of soft law has developed over the past fifteen years as a metaphor for the phenomenon observed particularly by international economic law lawyers whereby states (and sometimes nonstate actors) reach agreement on international cooperative action that is limited in its substantive legal content. Soft law has been given wide and sometimes ambiguous definition by publicists, who have examined it extensively.[2] More recently, the existence and role of soft law in the environmental sector has been scrutinized by scholars.[3]

---

2. From a considerable body of literature, *see, e.g.*, C.M. Chinkin, *The Challenge of Soft Law: Development and Change in International Law*, 38 I.C.L.Q. 850 (1989); American Society of International Law, *A Hard Look at Soft Law*, 82 A.S.I.L. PROC. 371 (1988); T. Gruchalla-Wesierski, *A Framework for Understanding "Soft Law,"* 30 McGILL L.J. 37 (1984); J. Gold, *Strengthening the Soft International Law of Exchange Agreements*, 77 A.J.I.L. 443 (1983); M. Bothe, *Legal and Non-Legal Norms–A Meaningful Distinction in International Relations?* 11 NETH. YRBK. INT'L L. 65 (1980); I. Seidl-Hohenveldern, *International Economic "Soft Law,"* 163 REC. DES COURS 164 (1979).

3. *See e.g.*, M.A. Levy, *Remarks*, 87 A.S.I.L. PROC. 389 (1993) (session on *Environmental Law: When Does It Make Sense to Negotiate International Agreements?*); P. Sand, *International Environmental Law after Rio*, 4 EUR. J. INT'L L. 377 (1993); J. Brunnée, *Toward Effective International Environmental Law—Trends and Developments* (unpublished paper presented to 6th CIRL Conference on Natural Resources Law, Ottawa, May 13–14, 1993); P.W. BIRNIE & A.E. BOYLE, INTERNATIONAL LAW AND THE ENVIRONMENT, 26–30 (1992); G. Palmer, *New Ways to Make International Environmental Law*, 86 A.J.I.L. 259, 269–270 (1992); P.-M. Dupuy, *Soft Law and the International Law*

Soft law is often analyzed as an emanation of state agreement or consensus, wherein states attempt "to achieve the goals of collective action and limited constraint"[4] through direct or indirect interstate consensus (the latter through their representatives at intergovernmental organizations). In addition, documents drafted by nonstate actors, such as nongovernmental organizations (NGOs), "which purport to lay down international principles"[5] have been included by some publicists within the flexible notion of soft law.

Categorized differently, soft law can be divided into two streams. The first may include legal norms—principally treaty provisions—which have weak or indeterminate substantive obligations (sometimes called "legal soft law").[6] This type of soft treaty law is often found in human rights treaties and, increasingly, in environmental treaties. Legal soft law is often in framework treaties that serve as the foundation for later protocols which establish specific legal obligations.[7] Weak monitoring and enforcement provisions in treaties can also be called legal soft law. Again, it is often human rights treaties that contain such loose mechanisms.

The second stream contains instruments that are incapable of constituting innate legal norms ("nonlegal soft law"). This version of soft law encompasses a range of instruments, including codes of conduct, guidelines, intergovernmental conference declarations, United Nations General Assembly resolutions, resolutions of the organs of other international organizations, memoranda of understanding between states and, more controversially, documents created by nongovernmental actors containing subject matter with an international dimension.[8]

In the realm of international environmental law, the body of nonlegal soft law has grown considerably over the past twenty years. The 1972 Stockholm Declaration on the Human Environment,[9] the 1982 World Charter for Nature,[10] the 1991 Arctic Environmental Protection Strategy[11] and various instruments created

---

of the Environment, 12 MICH J. INT'L L. 420 (1991).

4. Gruchalla-Wesierski, *supra* note 2, at 39.

5. Chinkin, *supra* note 2, at 851.

6. Dupuy, *supra* note 3, at 429. Resolutions of international organizations that are legally binding on Member states can also be included under this category.

7. Dupuy, *id.*, at 429–30. *See, e.g.*, the framework convention-protocol format in the ECE Long Range Transboundary Air Pollution Convention and Protocols, the Vienna Convention-Montreal Protocol on the Ozone Layer, as amended and adjusted, and the U.N. Framework Convention on Climate Change.

8. *See generally* Chinkin, *supra* note 2. On the legal status of G.A. Resolutions, *see, e.g.*, B. Sloan, *General Assembly Resolutions Revisited (Forty Years After)*, 58 B.Y.I.L. 39 (1987).

9. 11 I.L.M. 1416 (1972) (international conference declaration).

10. G.A. Res. 37/7, U.N. GAOR Supp. No. 51 at 17, U.N. Doc. A/37/51 (1982).

11. 30 I.L.M. 1624 (1991) (environmental strategy, including protection of indigenous peoples, developed by the eight Arctic states and assisted by observers, including indigenous peoples organizations).

under the auspices of the OECD and United Nations Environment Programme[12] are some examples of international environmental soft law. State commitment to soft law has deepened since the 1992 United Nations Conference on Environment and Development (UNCED). Various international instruments concluded at UNCED were clearly in soft law form—the Rio Declaration on Environment and Development,[13] Agenda 21,[14] and the Non-Legally Binding Authoritative Statement of Principles for a Global Consensus on the Management, Conservation and Sustainable Development of All Types of Forests.[15]

Clearly, some aspects of these instruments are prenormative, having an extant or catalytic effect on state behavior. Even the treaties adopted at UNCED have been described as being, in essence, legal soft law.[16] Moreover, for a variety of functional reasons, some maintain that the creation of environmental nonlegal soft law will probably increase more quickly than will negotiation of treaties.[17] Further, the widening intersection between international human rights and the environment produces a number of references to soft law instruments. These instruments, although predominantly in the environmental area, may be found in both sectors. This is indicative of the multidisciplinary nature of the issues and is itself another reason for the use of soft law as governments explore with caution the implications of the increasing interaction between the two areas.

Nonlegal soft law can thus be further cataloged as being prenormative in two ways. First, soft instruments are indicative of movement toward interstate consensus. As Geoffrey Palmer stated:

> Soft law solutions change the political thinking on an issue. They alter the circumstances in which an issue is considered; they cause opinion to coalesce. These changes can be a very important catalyst in securing an agreement with a harder edge later. Soft law solutions can thus be useful steps on a longer journey. Soft law is where international law and

---

12. *See, e.g.*, C.A. Petsonk, *The Role of the United Nations Environment Programme (UNEP) in the Development of International Environmental Law*, 5 AM. U.J. INT'L L. & POL. 351 (1990); on the OECD, *see infra* notes 66–67.

13. 31 I.L.M. 876 (1992).

14. U.N. Doc. A/CONF. 151/4 (1992), *reprinted in* IV AGENDA 21 & THE UNCED PROCEEDINGS 1 (N.A. Robinson ed., 1993).

15. 31 I.L.M. 882 (1992) [hereinafter *Statement of Principles for Forests*].

16. Sand, *supra* note 3, at 380 (the Climate Change and Biodiversity Conventions are, at present, "largely aspirational").

17. *Supra* note 1, at 708 (for nonbinding instruments agreement is typically easier to obtain, transaction costs are lower, and there is greater opportunity to include complex strategies, and better capability for responding to changes in scientific knowledge of the environment and development relationships). *But cf.* J. Charney ch. 1.

international politics combine to build new norms.[18]

Accordingly, nonlegal soft law can be used either (1) as a template for the negotiation of a treaty on the same subject or (2) as material evidence of the development of state practice and *opinio juris* acting as a catalyst for the development of customary international law. In the latter case, the aggregate of the repetition of soft instruments' content within other soft or hard laws may lead to the establishment of sufficient state practice and *opinio juris* to form a customary norm.[19] Examples of each model of prenormativity in the environmental protection area are: (1) the assorted documents on the atmosphere and global climate change, influential both in the initiative and content of the 1992 U.N. Framework Convention on Climate Change,[20] and (2) the precautionary principle or approach, appearing in various hard and soft law instruments, and potentially emerging in the future as a customary norm.[21]

From another perspective, nonlegal soft law can have an immediate influence on state behavior irrespective of its potential to become a formal legal norm. For example, it may establish standards which are respected at once by a "well-governed State" even though the practice may not yet have attained—or may never attain—the status of a customary norm.[22] The same can hold true for the practice of international organizations. In addition, states may use soft law as the prototype for the design of national law, and domestic courts may be influenced by international soft law as interpretive guidance elucidating internal law or policy.[23] In this capacity, soft law can become directly applicable to individuals.[24]

The common thread running through these distinctions is that nonlegal soft law, although only a political expression, may have an immediate influence on state behavior. The notion that soft law can have a compelling influence on state conduct in the absence of normative prescription implies that there is some convergence between the affective possibilities of soft law and the concepts

---

18. G. Palmer, *New Ways to Make International Environmental Law*, 86 A.J.I.L. 259, 269 (1992).

19. Dupuy, *supra* note 3, at 432; Chinkin, *supra* note 2, at 857 (but also cautioning that there must be sufficient state practice and *opinio juris dehors* the soft instrument itself).

20. 31 I.L.M. 851 (1992). For the earlier soft instruments, *see, e.g., Selected International Legal Materials on Global Warming and Climate Change* 5 AM. U.J. INT'L L. & POL'Y 513 (1990); Dupuy, *supra*, note 3, at 427–28.

21. *See, e.g.,* Maastricht Treaty on European Union, 31 I.L.M. 253, art. 130(r)(2) (1992); Rio Declaration on Environment and Development, *supra* note 13, para. 15; Framework Convention on Climate Change, *supra*, note 20, art. 3(3); E. Hey, *The Precautionary Concept in Environmental Policy and Law: Institutionalizing Caution*, 4 GEO. INT'L ENV. REV. L. 303 (1992).

22. The term "well-governed State" is used by Dupuy, *supra* note 3, at 432.

23. Chinkin, *supra* note 2, at 858–59; Dupuy, *supra*., note 3, at 434–35.

24. Seidl-Hohenveldern, *supra* note 2, at 199.

developed by international relations scholars to explain cooperative behavior between states on the international level. The school of international organization[25] encompasses interfacing fields of research activity, including regime theory and the study of international institutionalism. It may be possible to position soft law within the concept of a regime which is utilized to explain cooperative behavior in a particular area of international relations.[26] Alternatively, a recent study of institutional behavior has cited the role of international institutions in promoting state cooperation through both formal and informal (or soft) vehicles.[27]

The reasons for preferring the creation of soft law over treaty or custom have been surveyed by publicists. Most cite the relative speed of negotiating soft instruments compared to treaty or custom formation[28] and the ability of soft law to realize some interstate consensus when extant political or economic differences make it impossible to conclude a treaty.[29] From the international relations perspective, Marc A. Levy has listed five ways soft law can improve interstate relationships: (1) providing the "home" for subsequent hard law; (2) helping expectations of states to converge, changing current behavior based on expectations regarding the future; (3) providing a focus for implicit agreement; (4) acting as an instrument for the dissemination of information to members of the public; and

---

25. *See* Friedrich Kratochwil and John G. Ruggie, *International Organization: A State of the Art on an Art of the State*, 40 INT'L ORG. 753 (1986); Anne-Marie Slaughter Burley, *International Law and International Relations Theory: A Dual Agenda*, 87 A.J.I.L. 205, 217–18 (1993).

26. "Regimes can be defined as sets of implicit or explicit principles, norms, rules and decisionmaking procedures around which actors' expectations converge in a given area of international relations." S.D. Krasner, *Structural Causes and Regime Consequences: Regimes as Intervening Variables*, *in* INTERNATIONAL REGIMES 2 (S.D. Krasner, ed., 1983).

27. INSTITUTIONS FOR THE EARTH: SOURCES OF ENVIRONMENTAL PROTECTION (P.M. Haas, R.O. Keohane and M.A. Levy, eds., 1993). For a discussion of how the study found three areas where international institutional cooperation can play an affirmative role (in international concern over subject matter, the international contractual environment and national capacity), *see* Levy, *Remarks*, *supra* note 3. Levy indicated how soft law is operative in these three areas: "A common obstacle with the problem of 'concern' is the ability of laggard countries to slow down the entire community. . . . Soft law creates a situation that discourages laggard countries—they can be pressured to stop slowing things down. As for 'capacity,' many countries want to increase their capacity-building functions through soft law, for example, through standard-setting organizations . . . . The intrusiveness is less direct, and countries are more willing to accept it. On the 'contractual environment,' sometimes you need to move very fast. Because hard law often takes too long, the soft-law route can be a vehicle for moving faster." *Id.*, at 389.

28. *Cf.* Chinkin, *supra* note 2, at 860.

29. Seidl-Hohenveldern, *supra* note 2, at 192–3; Chinkin, *supra*, note 2, at 861 (the compromissory function).

(5) assisting in the consensual validation of information, making it more inclusive of public participation.[30]

There are, however, some perceived negative aspects to soft law. It is clearly hampered by its nonlegal status, and sometimes by the vagueness of its contents and its weak or nonexistent enforcement capacity. In addition, treaty law is preferable to soft law in situations where states will incur material financial or competitive costs in implementing agreements, since treaty commitments help prevent free-rider or laggard states from exploiting the overt absence of obligation in soft law.[31] A "backlash" against soft law has also been observed as governments paradoxically credit soft law with some normative influence and consequently make disclaimers to soft law provisions denying that they have any legal effect—even when hortatory language was used.[32]

II. HUMAN RIGHTS AND THE ENVIRONMENT

As delineated earlier, deterioration of the environment—caused typically by human-source activities—has added human rights issues to concerns over the natural environment.[33] Considerable scholarly attention has been paid to the status of a right to a safe or healthy environment,[34] which is often propounded as a derivative right based on existing rights to life and health. This argument is evidenced in a variety of global and regional treaties and other international instruments.[35] Explicit human rights references to the environment exist in two

---

30. Levy, *supra* note 3, at 390.

31. Brunnée, *supra* note 3, at 24–25.

32. Sand, *supra* note 3, at 382.

33. *See, e.g.*, M. Leighton Schwartz, *International Legal Protection for Victims of Environmental Abuse*, 18 YALE J. INT'L L. 355 (1993).

34. *See, e.g.*, Schwartz, *id.*, at 359–375; A. Kiss, *Concept and Possible Implications of the Right to Environment, in* HUMAN RIGHTS IN THE TWENTY-FIRST CENTURY: A GLOBAL CHALLENGE 551 (K.E. Mahoney and P. Mahoney, eds., 1993); A. A. Cançado Trindade, ENVIRONMENTAL PROTECTION AND THE ABSENCE OF RESTRICTIONS ON HUMAN RIGHTS, *id.*, at 561; M. Déjeant-Pons, *The Right to Environment in Regional Human Rights Systems, id.*, at 595; R.S. Pathak, *The Human Rights System as a Conceptual Framework for Environmental Law*, ENVIRONMENTAL CHANGE AND INTERNATIONAL LAW: NEW CHALLENGES AND DIMENSIONS 205 (Edith Brown Weiss, ed., 1992); D. Shelton, *Human Rights, Environmental Rights, and the Right to Environment*, 28 STANFORD J. INT'L L. 103 (1991); M. Thorme, *Establishing Environment as a Human Right*, 19 DEN. J. INT'L L. & POL'Y 301 (1991); W.P. Gormley, *The Legal Obligation of the International Community to Guarantee a Pure and Decent Environment: The Expansion of Human Rights Norms*, 3 GEO. INT'L L. REV. 85 (1990).

35. *E.g.*, International Covenant on Civil and Political Rights, art. 6(1); International Covenant on Economic, Social and Cultural Rights, art. 12(1) and (2)(b); Universal Declaration of Human Rights, arts. 3 and 25; European Convention for the Protection of

regional treaties[36] and in a number of domestic constitutions,[37] and some relevant
jurisprudence emanates from the regional human rights regimes.[38] However, a
contemporary example of human rights soft law, the 1993 Vienna Declaration and
Programme of Action, contains no express reference to such a right and makes little
mention of environmental matters.[39]

There has been little support for the right to a healthy environment even within
the environmental sector and what does exist—contained in soft law—has grown
relatively more conservative over time. Whereas Principle 1 of the 1972
Stockholm Declaration employed rights discourse in relation to the environment,[40]
by contrast, the 1992 Rio Declaration on the Environment and Development avoids
specific reference to human rights to the environment in favor of the language of
entitlement and needs.[41] A critical view of the human rights aspects of UNCED is

---

Human Rights and Fundamental Freedoms, art. 2.

36. "All peoples shall have the right to a general satisfactory environment favorable to their
development." African Charter on Human and Peoples' Rights, art. 24, June 18, 1981, 21
I.L.M. 58.

"1. Everyone shall have the right to live in a healthy environment and to have access
to basic public services.
"2. The States parties shall promote the protection, preservation and
improvement of the environment."

Additional Protocol to the American Convention on Human Rights in the Area of Economic,
Social and Cultural Rights (Protocol of San Salvador), art. 11, Nov. 18, 1988, 28 I.L.M. 156.

37. See EDITH BROWN WEISS, IN FAIRNESS TO FUTURE GENERATIONS: INTERNATIONAL
LAW, COMMON PATRIMONY, AND INTERGENERATIONAL EQUITY, app. B (1989); Minors
Oposa v. Secretary of the Dep't of Environment and Natural Resources (Philippines
Supreme Court decision, July 30, 1993, on the Philippine Constitution clause protecting
"...the right of the people to a balanced and healthful ecology in accord with the rhythm and
harmony of nature.") 33 I.L.M. 173.

38. See Trindade, supra note 34, at 571 ff.

39. June 25, 1993, reprinted in 14 H.R.L.J. 352 (1993). But see para. 11 ("The right to
development should be fulfilled so as to meet equitably the developmental and
environmental needs of present and future generations. The World Conference on Human
Rights recognizes that illicit dumping of toxic and dangerous substances and waste
potentially constitutes a serious threat to the human rights to life and health of . . .
everyone").

40. Supra note 9, para. 1: "Man has the fundamental right to freedom, equality and
adequate conditions of life, in an environment of a quality that permits a life of dignity and
well-being, and he bears a solemn responsibility to protect and improve the environment for
present and future generations . . . ."

41. Supra note 13, para. 1: "Human beings are at the centre of concerns for sustainable
development. They are entitled to a healthy and productive life in harmony with nature.";
para. 3: "The right to development must be fulfilled so as to equitably meet developmental
and environmental needs of present and future generations."

taken by Pallemaerts, who notes the reluctance of both industrialized states and lesser developed countries at UNCED to recognize the environment-human rights nexus and the subjecthood of individuals under international human rights law:

> [m]any governments, both from the First and Third World, are confronted from within and without by environmental groups and other popular movements, opposing their environmentally destructive development policies. These governments have obvious reasons to fear the legal implications of the establishment of a direct relationship between international environmental law and the existing international legal mechanisms for the protection of human rights.[42]

Difficult to support is the argument that a right to a safe or healthy environment has crystallized into either a customary or general principle of international law. Soft law can, however, be seen to be acting in some prenormative capacity within the human rights-environment interface, fashioning some concordance in an area fraught with state concerns over the political and economic ramifications of recognizing such rights.

This soft law progression can be observed in a number of related aspects. Indigenous peoples, for example, have a multifaceted relationship with the environment. Although this relationship is vitally connected to their cultures—through their spiritual, historical, linguistic, artistic, and economic traditions[43]—recognition of the rights of the indigenous peoples of the world is only just beginning. While part of the evolving international law on the rights of indigenous peoples is in the form of treaty law,[44] much of the progress has been and will be in soft law form.[45] This configuration is carried through with respect to

---

42. M. Pallemaerts, *International Environmental Law from Stockholm to Rio: Back to the Future?, in* GREENING INTERNATIONAL LAW 1 at 10 (P. Sands ed., 1993).

43. M. Simon, *The Integration and Interdependence of Culture and the Environment, in* HUMAN RIGHTS IN THE TWENTY-FIRST CENTURY: A GLOBAL CHALLENGE, *supra* note 34, at 521–22.

44. *E.g.*, 1989 ILO Convention Concerning Indigenous and Tribal Peoples in Independent Countries (No. 169) (1989), 28 I.L.M. 1382 (in force 1991); International Covenant on Civil and Political Rights, art. 27 (minority rights protection). For a critical view of Convention 169, *see, e.g.*, D. Sambo, *Indigenous Peoples and International Standard-Setting Processes: Are State Governments Listening?*, 3 TRANSNAT'L L. & CONTEMP. PROBS. 13, at 30–32 (1993).

45. Draft United Nations Declaration on the Rights of Indigenous Peoples, approved by the Working Group on Indigenous Populations and accepted by Sub-commission on Prevention of Discrimination and Protection of Minorities, Aug. 1994, Doc. E/CN.4/Sub.2/1993/29; Vienna Declaration and Programme of Action, *supra* note 39, art. 20.

indigenous peoples' rights to their environment.[46] The 1992 UNCED soft law instruments, including Principle 22 of the Rio Declaration on Environment and Development,[47] various Principles of the Statement of Principles for Forests,[48] and Chapter 26 of Agenda 21,[49] contain numerous references to the interests, roles, and rights of indigenous peoples in environmental protection.

Other human rights-environment concepts with evolving normative value, often through the soft law medium, include sustainable development;[50] intergenerational equity;[51] the human rights and environmental implications of international financial institution projects (often interfacing with indigenous peoples' concerns);[52] a right to water; [53] the role of human rights (including women's rights) in population control policies designed, *inter alia*, to reduce environmental degradation attributed to excessive population growth;[54] and the

---

46. *See* A. Wiggins, *Indian Rights and the Environment*, 18 YALE J. INT'L L. 345 (1993); W.A. Shutkin, *International Human Rights Law and the Earth: The Protection of Indigenous Peoples and the Environment*, 31 VA. J. INT'L L. 479 (1991); Draft Declaration, *supra*, note 45, arts. 25–30; Vienna Declaration and Programme of Action, *supra*, note 39, para. 20, Programme paras. 28–32 (no explicit mention of the environment; reference to full and free participation); ILO Convention No. 169, *supra*, note 44, art. 7; UNCED Convention on Biological Diversity, 31 I.L.M. 822, pmbl. and art. 8(j) (1992).

47. *Supra* note 13.

48. Statement of Principles for Forests, *supra* note 15, paras. 2(b) and (d), 5(a), 7(f), 8(f) and 12(d).

49. *Supra* note 14.

50. *See, e.g.*, WORLD COMMISSION ON ENVIRONMENT AND DEVELOPMENT, OUR COMMON FUTURE (1987).

51. *See, e.g.*, Weiss, *supra* note 37.

52. *See, e.g.*, Conference Issue on Human Rights, Public Finance, and the Development Process 8 AM. U. J. INT'L L. & POL'Y 1 1988; *Symposium—International Development Agencies, Human Rights and Environmental Considerations*, 17 DEN. J. INT'L L. & POL'Y 29 (1988); T. Berger, *The World Bank's Independent Review of India's Sardar Sarovar Projects*, 9 AM. U.J. INT'L L. & POL'Y 33 (1993).

53. *See* S.C. McCaffrey, *A Human Right to Water: Domestic and International Implications*, 5 GEO. INT'L ENV. L. REV. 1 (1992).

54. *See, e.g.*, UNITED NATIONS POPULATION FUND, POPULATION AND THE ENVIRONMENT: THE CHALLENGES AHEAD (1991); OUR COMMON FUTURE, *supra* note 50; R. GARDNER, NEGOTIATING SURVIVAL: FOUR PRIORITIES AFTER RIO (1992); R. Houseman, *The Muted Voice: The Role of Women in Sustainable Development*, 4 GEO. INT'L ENV. L. REV. 361 (1992); B. Crane, *International Population Institutions: Adaptation to a Changing World Order*, *in* INSTITUTIONS FOR THE EARTH, *supra* note 27, at 351; 1994 U.N. INTERNATIONAL CONFERENCE ON POPULATION AND DEVELOPMENT, PROGRAMME OF ACTION, U.N. Doc. A/Conf.171/13, Annex (Oct. 18, 1994).

status and rights of environmental refugees.[55]

III. THE RIGHTS OF MEMBERS OF THE PUBLIC TO RECEIVE ENVIRONMENTAL INFORMATION, PARTICIPATE IN ENVIRONMENTAL DECISIONMAKING, AND HAVE EFFECTIVE ACCESS TO DOMESTIC JUDICIAL AND ADMINISTRATIVE REMEDIES

As threats to the environment and related dangers to human health and life have increased, so has parallel public concern over receiving from public authorities information on the environment. It is increasingly evident as well that many environmental disputes cannot be resolved successfully without involving affected local communities, whether the constituency comprises a relatively small geographic area or is the nation's public body in its entirety.[56] Persons in neighboring countries may also be affected. Public participation increases the knowledge base for dealing successfully with an environmental problem (including project design), assists in the resolution of conflicts over resource use or allocation, and increases both the chances of implementing the chosen response plan and obtaining public compliance with it.[57] In this respect, public participation takes a variety of forms, ranging from inclusion in environmental impact assessment procedures to consultation during public inquiries on general environmental issues. Further, as members of the public are harmed by environmentally damaging conduct or see threats to their environment, those affected desire effective preventative or remedial action by available judicial or administrative forces.

Over the past two decades, the human rights aspects of these procedural issues have become clearer. The procedural avenues are often the preventive and remedial complements to or substitutes for a substantive right to a safe environment.[58] As Professor Kiss states:

> [t]he practical means of exercising this right . . . will require that citizens
> be informed of the state of the environment in general and in particular of

---

55. *E.g.*, Pathak, *supra* note 34, at 235–238; G. Dirks, *The Intensification of International Migration Pressures: Causes, Consequences, and Responses*, 5 ACUNS, THE STATE OF THE UNITED NATIONS, 1993: NORTH-SOUTH PERSPECTIVES REPORTS AND PAPERS 65 (1993); G. McCue, Note, *Environmental Refugees: Applying International Environmental Law to Involuntary Migration*, 6 GEO. INT'L ENV. L. REV. 151 (1993).

56. *See* WORLD BANK, WORLD DEVELOPMENT REPORT 1992: DEVELOPMENT AND THE ENVIRONMENT 93–97 (1992); Berger, *supra* note 52.

57. World Bank, *supra* note 56, at 93. *See also* M. L. Becker, *The International Joint Commission and Public Participation: Past Experiences, Present Challenges, Future Tasks*, 33 NAT. RES. J. 235 (1993).

58. *See* Kiss, *supra* note 34, at 557–58; Shelton, *supra* note 34, at 117; Birnie and Boyle, *supra* note 3, at 194–97; N. Popovic, *The Right to Participate in Decisions That Affect the Environment*, 10 PACE ENV. L. REV. 683 (1993).

projects or events which threaten their environment. They must also be able to participate in the decisionmaking process and dispose of means of redress for non-observance of due process as well as, if necessary, for obtaining compensation for any damage their environment may have suffered.

. . .[T]he exercise of the right to environment thus implies a co-operation between the State and its citizens.[59]

The inclusion of indigenous peoples' rights adds another dimension. Further, the implementation of all three procedural rights—information, participation, and access to domestic remedies—requires the existence of satisfactory public procedures and institutions to act as a conduit between the state and members of the public.

The general international human rights law framework provides support for the development of more specific environmental procedural rights, based on the rights of freedom of expression, information, and participation in public affairs.[60] In the regional treaty system fora, particularly the European Human Rights Convention system, some jurisprudence has fleshed out foundational norms which are directly applicable to the environmental sphere.[61] Moreover, concepts loosely grouped around notions of or rights to democratic development, good governance, and political participation provide some additional support, which indicates the general trend toward a popular-sovereignty approach to state governance.[62]

a. Soft Law and the Evolution of Procedural Human Rights in Environmental Matters

The role of soft law is clear when one focusses on the evolution of these procedural environmental rights, since the relevant soft law has usually emanated from the environmental sector. In particular, soft law has served in its prenormative role through the creation of nonlegal soft law instruments over the past twenty years, leading to the recent adoption of a growing number of treaties on the environment that incorporate these procedural rights. On the national level, some states are also concurrently creating novel domestic mechanisms, such as

---

59. Kiss, *supra* note 34 at 557.

60. Schwartz, *supra* note 33, at 369–370. *See, e.g.*, International Covenant on Civil and Political Rights, arts. 19, 21, 22, 25; Universal Declaration of Human Rights, arts. 19–21; European Convention on Human Rights, arts. 10–11; African Charter of Human and Peoples' Rights, arts. 9, 10, 13; American Convention on Human Rights, arts. 13, 23.

61. *See* S. Weber, *Environmental Information and the European Convention on Human Rights* 12 H.R.L.J. 177 (1991).

62. *See, e.g.*, G. Fox, *The Right to Political Participation*, 17 YALE J. INT'L L. 539 (1992).

establishing environmental commissioners or ombudsman offices, to increase public information, participation, and access to domestic remedies in environmental matters.[63] Nongovernmental organizations and individuals also have developed effective machinery to achieve the same purpose. Some examples are the lobbying and educational activities of environmental NGOs. Another is the establishment of environmental public interest litigation groups that afford individuals and groups with an interest in an environmental matter access to the domestic litigation process relatively free of the usual financial barriers to entry.

The 1972 Stockholm Declaration on the Human Environment did not itself contain express reference to these procedural rights. However, the accompanying Action Plan for the Human Environment did recognize that persons required information on the environment for individual autonomy of action. Containing recommendations for implementation of the Conference consensus, the Action Plan also advocated that public participation should be "stimulated"—not because of the human rights aspect but rather as a means to further environmental protection.[64] By 1982, the World Charter for Nature, another example of oft-overlooked environmental soft law, contained a number of provisions which called on states to give environment-related information to the public, to permit effective public consultation and participation in decisions directly affecting the environment and to provide public access to means of redress.[65] With the World Charter for Nature, the focus had shifted: no longer was public involvement merely the means to the

---

63. *See, e.g.*, the jurisdiction of the Namibian ombudsman; the New Zealand and Ontario, Canada, commissioners for the environment; and the British Columbia, Canada Commission on Resources and the Environment.

64. Action Plan for the Human Environment, 1972, 11 I.L.M. 1416. Rec. 7(a): "That Governments and the Secretary-General provide equal possibilities for everybody, both by training and by ensuring access to relevant means and information, to influence their own environment by themselves." Rec. 97(1): "It is recommended that the Secretary-General make arrangements: (a) To establish an information programme designed to create the awareness which individuals should have of environmental issues and to associate the public with environmental management and control . . . . the programme must provide means of stimulating active participation by the citizens, and of eliciting interest and contributions from non-governmental organizations for the preservation and development of the environment."

65. *Supra* note 10, para. 16: "All planning shall include, among its essential elements, the formulation of strategies for the conservation of nature, the establishment of inventories of ecosystems and assessments of the effects on nature of proposed policies and activities; all of these elements shall be disclosed to the public by appropriate means in time to permit effective consultation and participation." Para. 23: "All persons, in accordance with their national legislation, shall have the opportunity to participate, individually or with others, in the formulation of decisions of direct concern to their environment, and shall have access to means of redress when their environment has suffered damage or degradation." Further, para. 24 imposed a duty on persons to act in accordance with the Charter and to strive to ensure that its aims and requirements are met.

end of improved environmental protection, in the political eyes of the international community it had become an end in itself.

The OECD has produced several decisions and recommendations, i.e., both hard and soft law within the context of that international organization, on public information, participation and access to dispute resolution procedures in environmental matters, and on the involvement of populations affected by development project proposals.[66] In particular, the 1988 OECD Decision-Recommendation Concerning Provision of Information to the Public and Public Participation in Decisionmaking Processes Related to Accidents Involving Hazardous Substances, although circumscribed in its jurisdiction, is detailed in its terms.[67] Other regional soft law developments include human rights references in some of the recent Conference on Security and Cooperation in Europe (CSCE)

---

66. OECD, Council Recommendation on Implementing a Regime of Equal Right of Access and Non-discrimination in Relation to Transfrontier Pollution, OECD Doc. C(77) 28 (Final) May 17, 1977, 16 I.L.M. 977; OECD, Council Decision-Recommendation Concerning Provision of Information to the Public and Public Participation in Decision-making Processes Related to the Prevention of, and Response to, Accidents Involving Hazardous Substances, OECD Doc. C(88) 85 (Final) July 8, 1988, 28 I.L.M. 279; OECD, Council Recommendation Concerning an Environmental Checklist for Development Assistance, OECD Doc. C(89) 2 (Final) Feb. 22, 1989, 28 I.L.M. 1314 (for possible use by high-level decisionmakers in bilateral and multilateral development assistance institutions, Annex I (the Checklist) includes under mitigation measures, para. 6: "Have concerned populations and groups been involved and have their interests been adequately taken into consideration in project preparations?. . ." and in Annex 2, which contains explanatory information on the Checklist, the counterpart to para. 6 states: "Affected populations should participate in defining and understanding the problems in planning and implementing the solutions associated with development projects. . . . This should be accompanied by efforts which help foster sustainable development and full participation on the part of the rural populations."

67. *Supra* note 66. For example, the Preamble includes a clause stating that the potentially affected public has a right to be informed about the hazards to human health or the environment which could arise from the defined accidents. The OECD Council Decision states that the member states ". . . shall ensure, through the legal and procedural means they deem appropriate" that the potentially affected public is provided with specific information on the safety measures they should adopt in the event of an accident, is provided with general information on the particulars of the off-site effects of possible major accidents, and has access to other information needed to understand the possible effects of an accident "and to be able to contribute effectively, as appropriate, to decisions concerning hazardous installations and the development of community emergency preparedness plans." The Recommendations urge members states to: ". . . take action to facilitate, as appropriate, opportunities for the public to comment prior to decisions being made by public authorities on siting/licensing of hazardous installations and the development of preparedness plans; and to take guiding principles (in Appendix) into account when implementing the Decision-Recommendation." The principles include those on provision of information to the public and on public participation.

meeting final documents;[68] provisions on the participation of Arctic Region indigenous peoples in the 1991 Arctic Environmental Protection Strategy;[69] and material arising out of the meetings of the U.N. Economic Commission for Europe (ECE).[70]

On a United Nations-wide basis, personal rights to notification, access and due process were recognized in the 1987 Brundtland Report.[71] In 1992, the UNCED incorporated procedural rights of the public to information, participation and access throughout its adopted soft law instruments. Principle 10 of the Rio Declaration on Environment and Development focuses on access to information and public participation—but without using rights language—as follows:

> Environmental issues are best handled with the participation of all concerned citizens, at the relevant level. At the national level, each individual shall have appropriate access to information concerning the environment that is held by public authorities, including information on hazardous materials and activities in their communities, and the

---

68. *See* evolution of attitude: CSCE, Helsinki Accords (1975), 14 I.L.M. 1292 (also includes the environment); CSCE, Third Meeting of 1989, 28 I.L.M. 527 (para. 35: "The participating States acknowledge the importance of the contribution of persons and organizations dedicated to the protection and improvement of the environment, and will allow them to express their concerns. . ."); CSCE, Charter of Paris for a New Europe and Supplementary Document, Nov. 21, 1990, 30 I.L.M. 190 (at 203, "We emphasize the significant role of a well-informed society in enabling the public and individuals to take initiatives to improve the environment. To this end, we commit ourselves to promoting public awareness and education on the environment as well as the public reporting of the environmental impact of policies, projects and programmes."); CSCE, Document of the Moscow Meeting on the Human Dimension, Emphasizing Respect for Human Rights, Pluralistic Democracy, the Rule of Law, and Procedures for Fact-Finding, Oct. 3, 1991, 30 I.L.M. 1670 (para. 26: affirmation of right to freedom of expression, but nothing expressly on right to information, participation, etc. in environmental matters); CSCE, Declaration and Decisions from the Helsinki Summit, July 10, 1992, 31 I.L.M. 1385 (VIII, para. 11: ". . .The participating States will take appropriate steps to enhance public participation in environmental planning and decision making.").

69. *See supra* note 11, Introduction, paras. 2.1 (objectives), 2.2(iii)(a)&(e), (vi)&(vii) (guiding principles). Para. 8 (emergency prevention, preparedness and response) is relatively weak: "States will take steps to convene a meeting of experts to consider and recommend the necessary system of cooperation which could include the following elements: . . .(ix) Measures for providing information to the public and public participation . . ."

70. *E.g.*, Bergen Ministerial Declaration on Sustainable Development in the ECE Region, Report of the ECE on the Bergen Conference, para. 16, U.N. Doc. A/CONF.151/PC/10 (1991) (ECE preparatory meeting for UNCED, Bergen, May 1990), *reprinted in* 20 ENV. POL'Y & L. 100 (1990).

71. OUR COMMON FUTURE, *supra* note 50, Annex 1, *Summary of Proposed Legal Principles for Environmental Protection and Sustainable Development Adopted by the WCED Experts Group on Environmental Law*, para. 6.

opportunity to participate in decisionmaking processes. States shall facilitate and encourage public awareness and participation by making information widely available. Effective access to judicial and administrative proceedings, including redress and remedy, shall be provided.[72]

The inclusion of Principle 10 was supported by the Western European nations, Canada and the United States and was bolstered by preceding developments in the ECE and the CSCE. A stronger ECE project for a Charter of Environmental Rights and Obligations was, however, unsuccessful, both at the internal ECE level and during the UNCED PrepCom process.[73] Moreover, Principle 10 does use some permissive and indeterminate language in the passages pertaining to public information and participation.[74] The Rio Declaration refers to the participation of women, youth, indigenous peoples and local communities in environmental management and development, and to the use of environmental impact assessment procedures.[75] Provisions on public participation in environmental decisionmaking, including environmental impact assessments, are also contained in the other UNCED instruments in both treaty and nonbinding form, although the treaty provisions are largely in soft language.[76] Further, despite its soft character, Agenda 21 provides detailed guidelines to governments,[77] on public participation in de-

---

72. *Supra* note 13.

73. J. Kovar, *A Short Guide to the Rio Declaration*, 4 COLO. J. INT'L ENV. L. & POL'Y 119, 130–31 (1993). On the ECE Charter initiative see Pallemaerts, *supra* note 42, at 11; Charter on Environmental Rights and Obligations—Draft, *reprinted in* 21 ENV. POL'Y & LAW 81 (1991).

74. *But see* Pallemaerts, *supra* note 42, at 11–12 (critical of para. 10).

75. Rio Declaration, *supra* note 13, paras. 20–21 (participation of women and youth); para. 22 (participation of indigenous people/local communities); para. 17 (environmental impact assessments).

76. Convention on Biological Diversity, *supra* note 46, preamble; art. 14(1)(a) (as far as possible and appropriate require environmental impact assessments of proposed projects that are likely to have significant adverse effects on biological diversity ". . . and, where appropriate, allow for public participation in such procedures"). U.N. Framework Convention on Climate Change, *supra* note 20, arts. 4(1)(i) & 6 (in carrying out the commitment to promote and cooperate in, *inter alia*, public awareness related to climate change and to encourage the widest participation in this process, promote and facilitate, *inter alia*, "public access to information on climate change and its effects" (art. 6(a)(ii)) and "public participation in addressing climate change and its effects and developing adequate responses" (art. 6(a)(iii)). Statement of Principles for Forests, *supra* note 15, para. 2(c) ("The provision of timely, reliable and accurate information on forests and forest ecosystems is essential for public understanding and informed decisionmaking and should be ensured.").

77. Ch. 23, para. 23.2.

cision-making and access to information on the environment in order to achieve sustainable development.[78]

b. The Development of Treaty Provisions on Public Access to Information, Participation in Decisionmaking, and Access to Avenues of Redress in Environmental Matters

Some limited treaty movement on a regional basis existed early in the 1974 Nordic Convention on the Protection of the Environment, with treaty enshrinement of public access to effective remedies in transboundary environmental pollution matters and on the publication of information.[79] More recently, negotiation of environmental treaty law has yielded provisions on public information, participation in environmental processes and rights of redress. Such treaty law has typically arisen on a regional basis, predominantly in the European and North American contexts.

The ECE has been active in this respect. The 1991 ECE Convention on Environmental Impact Assessment in a Transboundary Context (Espoo Convention)[80] created an environmental impact assessment procedure which must be followed for proposed activities likely to cause significant adverse transboundary impact.[81] Included in the Espoo Convention are requirements for notification of affected members of the public and public participation in the environmental impact assessment process.[82] The 1992 ECE Convention on the

---

78. *Supra* note 14. Cl. 23.2 states: "One of the fundamental prerequisites for the achievement of sustainable development is broad public participation in decision-making. Furthermore, in the more specific context of environment and development, the need for new forms of participation has emerged. This includes the needs of individuals, groups and organizations to participate in environmental impact assessment procedures and to know about and participate in decisions, particularly those that potentially affect the communities in which they live and work. Individuals, groups and organizations should have access to information relevant to environment and development held by national authorities, including information on products and activities that have or are likely to have a significant impact on the environment, and information on environmental protection measures."

79. Stockholm, Feb. 19, 1974, 13 I.L.M. 591, arts. 3 (right of access of persons affected by nuisance caused by environmentally harmful activities in another contracting state to have access to the courts/administrative tribunals of that state on an equal basis with persons of that state) and 7 (supervisory authority of a contracting state, if it finds it necessary on account of public or private interests, shall publish communications from the courts/tribunals hearing the environmental matters in local newspapers, etc.).

80. Espoo, February 25, 1991, 30 I.L.M. 802.

81. *Id.*, arts. 2(2)&(3). Appendix I lists activities that include crude oil refineries, nuclear facilities, toxic waste disposal facilities, and large dams.

82. *Id.* arts. 1(x), 2(2)&(6), 3(i), 3(8), 4(2), 6(1).

Transboundary Effects of Industrial Accidents[83] requires state parties to give adequate information to the public in places capable of being affected by an industrial accident.[84] Likewise, the 1992 ECE Convention on the Protection and Use of Transboundary Watercourses and International Lakes[85] obligates contracting parties to give information to the public.[86]

The European Union (EU) has acted similarly to develop EU supranational "hard law" and has established directives mandating dissemination of environmental and health-related information to members of the public. Its Directive 313 of 1990 is particularly broad in scope and has been influential in the drafting approach of the instruments in the wider European trend.[87] The Council of Europe also included treaty obligations in its 1993 Convention on Civil Liability for Damage Resulting From Activities Dangerous to the Environment, which gives persons the right of access to information held by public authorities and to improved access to judicial avenues of redress.[88]

---

83. Helsinki, March 17, 1992, 31 I.L.M. 1330.

84. *Id.* arts. 1(a)&(j) (definitions); art. 9 (information to, and participation of the public): art. 9(1) "The Parties shall ensure that adequate information is given to the public in the areas capable of being affected by an industrial accident arising out of a hazardous activity. This information shall be transmitted through such channels as the Parties deem appropriate, shall include the elements contained in Annex VIII . . . and should take into account matters set out in Annex V, para. 2, subparas. (1) to (4)&(9)." *See also* arts. 9(2)-(3); 22 (limitations on the supply of information); Annex VII, para. 2 (emergency preparedness measures pursuant to art. 8 should include provisions for warning people).

85. Helsinki, March 17, 1992, 31 I.L.M. 1312.

86. *Id.* art. 16, Annex II, art. 1(a)&(c). There is no provision for public participation.

87. EEC Council Directive 313 (June 7, 1990), 90/313/EEC, O.J. No. L 158, 23.06.90 at 56 (requires member states' public authorities to make information relating to the environment available to any person at his request and without having to prove an interest); Euratom Council Directive 618 (Nov. 27, 1989), 89/618/Euratom, O.J. No. L 357, 07.12.89 at 31 (information to the general public on health protection measures and action in the event of a radiological emergency); EEC Council Directive 610 (Nov. 24, 1988), 88/610/EEC, O.J. No. L 336, 07.12.88 at 14 (amending EEC Dir. 82/501/EEC to strengthen requirements on information to be given to the public re: industrial accidents); EEC Council Directive 337 (1985), 85/337/EEC, O.J. No. L 175 at 40 (environmental impact assessments).

88. Lugano, June 21, 1993, 32 I.L.M. 1228. For example, art. 14(1), on access to information held by public authorities, states: "Any person shall, at his request and without his having to prove an interest, have access to information relating to the environment held by public authorities. The Parties shall define the practical arrangements under which such information is effectively made available." Art. 14(2) lists situations where the right of access may be restricted, *e.g.* public security; commercial/industrial and personal data confidentiality, and art. 15 discusses access to information held by bodies with public responsibilities for the environment, on the same terms as art. 14. *See also* art. 19 (jurisdiction to bring actions in the courts different member states as defined) and art. 23 (recognition and enforcement of judgments in member states).

A recent incorporation of rights of the public to information, participation, and means of redress in formal treaty law in the environment and international business nexus is in the North American Agreement on Environmental Cooperation,[89] a side agreement to the North American Free Trade Agreement (NAFTA).[90] The NAFTA Environment Side Agreement has a complex structure which, *inter alia*, provides for increased public participation. It achieves this by permitting persons to lodge submissions with the Side Agreement Secretariat alleging that a state party has failed to enforce its environmental law effectively and by establishing a Joint Public Advisory Committee to provide information and advice to the Side Agreement Council on any matter within the ambit of the Agreement.[91]

In this respect, the NAFTA Environment Side Agreement is novel because it provides international procedural mechanisms to implement the duties of the state parties concerning public information and participation in decisionmaking. To a limited extent, it also involves members of the public in the treaty dispute settlement machinery, albeit involving the issue of the enforcement of a state party's domestic environment laws. Public access to government-held information concerning the environment and the opportunity to participate in decisionmaking processes related to such public access is addressed indirectly because the Council

---

89. 32 I.L.M. 1480 (1993). *See* C. Thomas and G. Tereposky, *The NAFTA and the Side Agreement on Environmental Co-operation*, 27 J.W.T.L. 5 (1993). *See, e.g.*, preamble; arts. 5 (state parties to enforce their environmental laws through appropriate government action and must ensure that judicial, quasi-judicial or administrative enforcement proceedings are available to handle violations); 6 (private access to remedies, minimum standards listed, persons with legally recognized interest must be granted appropriate access to domestic proceedings); 7 (procedural guarantees for domestic judicial, etc., proceedings); 10(5)–(7) (Side Agreement Council to promote and, as appropriate, develop recommendations re: public access to information on the environment held by public authorities of each party, including information on hazardous materials and activities, and participation in decisionmaking processes concerning access and impact assessments; function of the Council as a clearinghouse for comments from persons on NAFTA environmental goals); 9(5) (Council can use advice submitted by NGOs and persons); 13(2) (Secretariat Reports to the Council may include information submitted by NGOs, persons and the Joint Public Advisory Committee); 15(4) (same for the preparation of a factual record by the Secretariat for use by the Council in complaint resolution); 15(7) (factual record will be made available to the public if two-thirds of Council members agree); 14 (NGOs and persons can make "submissions," *i.e.* complaints, to the Secretariat alleging that a state party is failing to enforce effectively its environmental laws); 16 (joint public advisory committee which provides advice to the Side Agreement Council, the forum for discussion and dispute resolution on environmental matters); 17 (national advisory committee).

90. Dec. 17, 1992, 32 I.L.M. 289, 605 (entered into force Jan. 1, 1994). The NAFTA, in Ch. 20 on general dispute settlement process, includes environmental experts in the process to provide information and technical advice (art. 2014) and establishes a scientific review board (art. 2015).

91. *Supra* note 89. However, there is no legal obligation to follow through on all complaints.

is empowered to promote and develop recommendations on these issues. In addition, the access of persons to private remedies is enhanced through treaty clauses on domestic judicial or administrative procedures, minimum standards for private access to remedies, limited inscription of rights of persons to appropriate access to domestic proceedings for the enforcement of a state party's environmental laws, and listing of procedural guarantees for these proceedings.[92]

In the Asian region, through the Association of South East Asian Nations (ASEAN), there has been limited treaty development of rights to public participation in environmental matters.[93] Finally, there has been some treaty development at the global U.N. level since, as noted above, both the UNCED Framework Convention on Climate Change and the Convention on Biological Diversity refer to procedural rights of the public, but impose very weak obligations therein.[94]

IV. CONCLUSION

Ultimately, the categorization of soft law as a discrete source of norm-like or quasi-normative obligation can be questioned. Is soft law really only part of the customary law development process or simply a trial run for a subsequent treaty? Is state compliance with soft law an example merely of state usage or practice unaccompanied by *opinio juris*, such that it has been sustained by political, moral, or utilitarian imperatives but not by legal obligation?

An attempt to pigeonhole the status and role of soft law may be overly theoretical. Soft law, from a pragmatic view, fulfills a number of valuable purposes in the contemporary international politico-legal system. These functions are demonstrated in current developments emanating from international environment and human rights. A combination of political and financial concerns over state recognition of these rights resulted in a quite limited creation of soft law on a variety of environmental-human rights fronts. By contrast, there has been relatively more movement in the procedural rights area.

Over the past two decades there has been a growing body of soft law on the procedural rights of members of the public to information on the environment,

---

92. *Supra* note 89, arts. 5–7.

93. ASEAN Agreement on the Conservation of Nature and Natural Resources, art. 16(2), *rep. in* 3 BASIC DOCUMENTS OF INTERNATIONAL ENVIRONMENTAL LAW 1552 (H. Hohmann ed., 1992) (the contracting parties ". . . shall circulate as widely as possible information on the significance of conservation measures and their relationship with sustainable development objectives, and shall, as far as possible, organize participation of the public in the planning and implementation of conservation measures."). For a critical view, *see* R. Mushkat, *Environmental Sustainability: A Perspective From the Asia-Pacific Region* 27 U.B.C.L. REV. 153, 177 (1993).

94. *Supra* note 76.

participation in environmental decisionmaking and effective access to domestic procedures for the resolution of environmental disputes. Soft law has derived from both the European region and the U.N. system. Nonlegal soft law instruments have been used in a prenormative capacity by catalyzing development of other soft law instruments and treaty law. This is predominantly seen in the European region but recently is visible in the North American free trade regime and in the UNCED treaties. Although some of the treaty provisions can be criticized for being "legal soft law" and/or being limited in their subject coverage, others are relatively strong.

The relative success of soft law in this area may be due to containment of political and financial costs of governmental acceptance of procedural rights obligations in contrast to the unknown costs involved in recognizing broader substantive rights (e.g., to a healthy environment). Norms involving public access to environmental information, participation in decisions on the environment and access to domestic remedies are accommodated relatively easily by democratic states within their existing structures of governance. The implementation or maintenance of supportive mechanisms does require the expenditure of government resources however, making it more difficult for developing states to support these structures financially.

Cross-fertilization is also an interesting phenomenon. Much of the soft law and subsequent treaty norms on procedural rights have come from Europe and North America, where strong domestic environmental NGOs exist. Their repeated calls for improved procedural rights have been accompanied by the parallel development of domestic laws and procedures such as environmental impact assessment legislation, and the environment ombudsman or commissioner.

One feature of the modern international system is the influence that NGOs have on governments and international lawmaking. In addition, international soft law on procedural rights may have buttressed some domestic and international developments by providing a framework of legitimacy, facilitating the politico-legal progress. Furthermore, the tradition of liberalism and individual rights underlying European and North American legal systems provides another source of and support for these domestic legal developments. In contrast, the different philosophies and political histories of other regions may militate against the adoption or rapid recognition of procedural human rights in environmental matters in such areas.

Room for criticism of the current state of international law on procedural rights of members of the public in environmental matters still exists. The treaties that have been adopted are mainly regional—with some not yet in force—and the terms relating to procedural rights are often weak or indeterminate. At the global U.N. level, the UNCED developments are both predominantly in soft law form and soft in their terms. This state of international affairs will likely not improve materially in the near future based on the current state of domestic and international attitudes.

The relative utility of treaty law as opposed to soft instruments for effectiveness in spurring state action is certainly debatable. Despite this, the implementation of procedural environmental rights norms is dependant upon the existence of sufficient levels of state democratic governance, structures, institutions, and the financial means to achieve a procedural interaction between a citizen and a state furthering environmental and human health. These compliance factors will be crucial to whether extant international law is "hard" or "soft."

INTERNATIONAL ENVIRONMENTAL LAW IN TRANSITION

Edith Brown Weiss

I. INTRODUCTION

The two decades since the United Nations Stockholm Conference on the Human Environment have seen extraordinary change. In 1972, there were only about three dozen multilateral treaties pertaining to the environment. Today over nine hundred legal instruments are fully concerned with environment or contain important environmental provisions.

Contrary to popular myth, the international community has become very skilled at negotiating international agreements. Countries now conclude complex agreements in less than two years: the Climate Framework Convention, the Environmental Protocol to the Antarctic Treaty (which includes four detailed annexes), the Biological Diversity Convention, and the complex agreements on industrial accidents and volatile organic chemicals under the auspices of the United Nations Economic Commission for Europe. It is now rare for countries to need more than two years to negotiate even complicated, detailed international agreements, although it routinely takes more than two years for them to go into effect.

The scope of these instruments has expanded. Where once environmental treaties dealt mainly with oil pollution or species conservation, today they address the ozone layer, climate change, biological diversity, hazardous wastes, toxic chemicals, industrial accidents, environmental impact assessments, and maintenance of a level playing field in international trading relationships. The number and variety of environmental agreements has increased to the point that some critics ask whether they severely strain the physical and organizational capacity of the countries handling them. Moreover, there are signs of treaty congestion, in the form of separate negotiating fora; separate secretariats and funding mechanisms; overlapping provisions and inconsistencies between agreements; and severe demands on local capacity to participate in negotiations, meetings of parties, and associated activities.[1]

At the same time, the intergovernmental system of making, implementing, and complying with international environmental law has been changing. It has been moving from a state-centered, static, closed model to a dynamic, more open, porous, and complex one in which states are necessary, but by no means the only important, actors.

From a theoretical perspective, there has been a transition from a model that includes important features of the realist view of international law to one that shares important features of the liberal view.[2] While the notion of a transition is arguably inconsistent with either viewpoint, evidence nonetheless suggests that fundamental changes in the system of international environmental law may be taking place.

The inherited model of international law was state-centered in that it assumed that sovereign, independent states are the only significant actors. These states are in control and wish to remain so. They therefore are careful to avoid restricting their own freedom of action. They hold information close, retain their own counsel, confine decisionmaking to a small group, keep much of the international community at bay, avoid creating new international bureaucracies when they can—and when they cannot, try to keep them on a tight rope. When such states make agreements, they may be intentionally general in the obligations they assume.

Second, the model is static because it assumes that international instruments provide fixed solutions to clearly defined problems in a world that changes relatively slowly, particularly in regard to the degree of scientific understanding. Governments ask scientists for advice, and scientists advise governments, but the public is not significantly involved in the scientific debates. Treaties drafted under this assumption do not provide for regular scientific assessment or facilitate adjustment to changes in scientific understanding of environmental issues, other than by the traditional method of ratification of amendments. Moreover, there is little expectation that the regime itself may need to evolve in response to new conditions.

Third, the model is closed in that states are assumed to comply with their treaty obligations almost all of the time. The effectiveness of agreements is rarely questioned. Failure to comply is considered sufficiently unusual that an offended state may reasonably be expected to rely on formal dispute settlement provisions and sanctions. There is no recognition that compliance at the national level may change over time. States assume that other states will have the capacity to comply

---

1.   Edith Brown Weiss, *International Environmental Law: Contemporary Issues and the Emergence of a New World Order*, 81 GEO. L. J. 675, at 684–702 (1993).

2.   *See* Anne-Marie Slaughter Burley, *International Law and International Relations Theory: A Dual Agenda*, 87 A.J.I.L. 205 (1993) (distinguishing Neo-Realism and Neo-Liberal Institutionalism and setting forth the core assumptions of the Liberal concept of law).

with treaty obligations and do not consider it a primary purpose of the treaty to build the local capacity of member states to comply, or to encourage nongovernmental participation in the discharge of international obligations. Compliance itself is viewed as hierarchical: governments agree to the treaty and then pass implementing legislation, with which domestic units comply.

These assumptions prevailed in the diplomacy of twenty or even fifteen years ago. But international environmental law has changed. To be sure, states are still key actors and will remain so. But new actors are assuming important roles in setting agenda, in proposing alternative resolution of important issues, and in influencing the ultimate outcome. Transnational corporations, international industrial associations, and *ad hoc* groups are increasingly developing transnational environmental standards and practices, which effectively substitute for international legal instruments that might otherwise be negotiated by states. Nongovernmental organizations play an important role in the negotiation, implementation, and compliance with international agreements that states negotiate. This new model is a network of states, transnational corporations, industry associations, nongovernmental environmental organizations, and *ad hoc* associations, intricately connected through international legal instruments and associated institutions.

In the new model, parties recognize that scientific understanding about human environment is constantly changing and devise methods for countries to flexibly respond to these changes. Moreover, the regimes generated by the agreements change over time, so that issues that were once primary now cede the spotlight to newer issues, as in the London Convention of 1972 on marine disposal of wastes, in which parties are considering a Protocol to cover new priorities.

There are also renewed efforts to induce nonparty states to join the agreement, for they can either provide pollution havens and undercut the effectiveness of an agreement or operate as free riders by receiving the benefits of controlled pollution without incurring cost.

Finally, the concept of environment as a separate, isolated phenomenon, divorced from economic development, trading relationships, or human aspirations, is obsolete. Environment is closely interwoven with economics, as evidenced in the sweeping concept of sustainable development proclaimed at the Rio de Janeiro Conference on Environment and Development in 1992, and in such new legal areas as environment and trade.

The next century's most pivotal development may be the interaction of international intergovernmental environmental law with transnational environmental law as developed primarily by the private sector and nongovernmental institutions. International environmental law developed by states traditionally focused on transboundary pollution, conservation of species, and marine pollution. In the early 1970s, only a few agreements focused on protecting natural resources within national boundaries, e.g., the World Heritage Convention[3] and the Wetlands Convention.[4] The rationale for these agreements was a desire to protect the environment as an end in itself.

With today's shift in focus toward protecting environment while furthering economic development, there is increasing concern about the effects of environmental protection on economic competitiveness at both the national and individual firm level. This concern results in greater attention to differences in environmental standards at the national level. Currently, the focus is largely on pollution standards, but in the future will undoubtedly encompass natural resource exploitation and conservation. As a result, both governments and nongovernmental actors are actively engaged in encouraging a level playing field through the development of transnational environmental standards and practices. It is no longer possible to draw a sharp line between practices that are international and those that are local. Nor is it possible to distinguish clearly between legal standards that are the provinces of governments and those that may be appropriately developed by the nongovernmental sector.

II. INTERGOVERNMENTAL ENVIRONMENTAL LAW

Since 1972, there have been significant changes in the process of negotiating international legal instruments, in the content of the agreements, in implementation processes and compliance, and in the attention given to nonparties to the agreements.

a. Nongovernmental Organizations as Essential Participants

Nongovernmental organizations (NGOs) have assumed an increasingly central role in the negotiation, ratification, implementation, and enforcement of international environmental instruments. They provide links between the public and national governments and between the public and international treaty secretariats and other international organizations. They thrive on transparency and on having formal access to government deliberations. While most pronounced in developed Western countries, NGOs are gaining potency in all parts of the world. Some are international, others are nationally or locally based, and still others emerge only in response to a given issue, disappearing when the issue is no longer compelling.

Nongovernmental organizations have become routinely present at official negotiations of international environmental agreements. At the Climate Conven-

---

3.   Convention for the Protection of World Cultural and Natural Heritage, Nov. 23, 1972, 27 U.S.T. 37, 1037 U.N.T.S. 151.

4.   Convention on Wetlands of International Importance, Especially as Waterfowl Habitat, Feb. 2, 1971, 11 I.L.M. 963.

tion negotiations, for example, a wide array of nongovernmental organizations monitored the negotiations, distributed material, lobbied delegations, and otherwise tried to influence the negotiators. Representatives of nongovernmental organizations also appear on official country delegations, as in the negotiations for the Environmental Protocol to the Antarctic Treaty or the Climate Convention negotiations. Interactions among NGOs, governments, and intergovernmental organizations are complicated. NGOs attempt to influence national governments directly through ministries and indirectly through increased public awareness and public pressures on national legislatures. Governments use NGOs to convey their positions to the public. Ministries or agencies within governments may use NGOs to strengthen their views in relation to other parts of the bureaucracy. NGOs provide intergovernmental organizations with vital, independent communication links to national governments, and NGOs rely on intergovernmental organizations for information and insights useful in influencing national governments.[5]

In a few instances, NGOs have been integrated into the international institutional implementation structure. Two decades ago in the World Heritage Convention, for example, states gave three nongovernmental organizations official status in the agreement as advisors and provided that the World Heritage Committee could call upon these organizations "for the implementation of its programmes and projects."[6] The organizations have evaluated proposed sites for inclusion on the World Heritage List and, recently, monitored protection of listed sites.

For the Convention on International Trade in Endangered Species (CITES),[7] a nongovernmental organization, the World Conserving Monitoring Center (WCMC), with headquarters in Cambridge, England, maintains the primary data base on parties' implementation of the Convention. The WCMC maintains computerized files on country export and import permits for controlled species under CITES. The nongovernmental organization TRAFFIC, also in Cambridge, monitors trade in particular endangered species. In recent meetings of parties to CITES, nongovernmental organizations have outnumbered government participants.

---

5.   *See* Brown Weiss, *supra* note 1, at 69–94, and PETER HAAS et al., INSTITUTIONS FOR THE EARTH (1993).

6.   Convention for the Protection of World Cultural and Natural Heritage, Nov. 23, 1972, art. 13(7), 27 U.S.T. 37, 1037 U.N.T.S. 151. *See also* arts. 8(3) and 14(2), which provide for the participation of the International Centre for the Study of the Preservation and the Restoration of Cultural Property (the Rome Center), the International Council of Monuments and Sites (ICOMOS) and the International Union for Conservation of Nature and Natural Resources (IUCN).

7.   Convention on International Trade in Endnagered Species of Wild Fauna and Flora, Mar. 3, 1973, 27 U.S.T. 1087, 993 U.N.T.S. 243.

b. The Role of Scientific Uncertainty

While countries have long recognized that scientific understanding of environmental problems is essential to international environmental negotiations, there is a new awareness of the role that scientific uncertainty plays in determining the legal regimes that ought to be created.   There are several aspects to this issue.

First is the change in the model that relates science to governments. Traditionally, governments asked scientists for advice, and scientists initiated interactions with governments.   Today, however, the public has become a prominent actor in a new triangular relationship.   Scientists now influence governments through the public, as in the nongovernmental interest group assessments provided to negotiators, just as the public relates directly to scientists, as in the expressions of public fear about DNA experiments or the effect of oceanic climate sensors on whales. The public increasingly interprets science for representative governmental bodies, causing governments perhaps to seek international scientific consensus before embarking upon particular treaty negotiations or in implementing agreements. The Intergovernmental Panel on Climate Change (IPCC) report, which set forth a consensus on the likely range of human-induced climate change, was a necessary prelude to the opening of negotiations for the Framework Convention on Climate Change.[8]

Scientific uncertainty is inherent in all international environmental law. Drafters of international agreements must be careful to design instruments and implementation mechanisms with sufficient flexibility for parties to adapt to changes in scientific understanding and technological abilities.

Early agreements were inadequate for rapid adjustment to changes in scientific understanding of a problem.   Improved later agreements provide for periodic meetings of parties, for formulation of technical changes by experts or international secretariats subject to confirmation by the parties, and for entry into force of changes by agreement of the parties without resorting to the ratification process.[9] The new Climate Framework Convention provides for a standing body to provide

---

8.   WORLD METEOROLOGICAL ASSOCIATION AND UNITED NATIONS ENVIRONMENT PROGRAMME, REPORTS OF WORKING GROUPS TO THE INTERGOVERNMENTAL PANEL ON CLIMATE CHANGE, (June 1990) (on file with author).

9.   For example, the Montreal Protocol on Substances That Deplete the Ozone Layer, Sept. 16, 1987, 26 I.L.M. 1529 [hereinafter Montreal Protocol] provides for parties to meet on a biennial basis so that parties can respond to new scientific findings, for regular technical assessments to be made available to parties before a meeting, and for simplified adjustment procedures by which parties can agree to reduce consumption of listed chemicals faster and further than provided in the text without having to use formal and time consuming amendment procedures.

scientific and technological advice on a timely basis and to build local scientific and technical capacity.[10]

c. Attention to Nonparties

Since the global environmental system ignores political boundaries, nonparty countries that can either defeat the agreement's purpose or receive benefits from the agreement without incurring costs are of concern.

Most environmental agreements traditionally have not provided explicit incentives to join, but more recent multilateral agreements offer incentives such as technical assistance, special funds, differential standards, or other positive inducements. The Montreal Protocol, Climate Convention, and Biological Diversity Convention provide for technical assistance, technology transfer, or national capacity building and, in the case of the Montreal Protocol, for differential compliance.[11]

Countries are also resorting more frequently to negative inducements to join the treaty by banning trade with nonparties in regulated materials, as in agreements controlling international trade in endangered species, transboundary movements of hazardous wastes, and consumption of ozone-depleting chemicals. Parties to the General Agreement on Tariffs and Trade (GATT) are currently considering whether the practice is consistent with the GATT.[12] The North American Free Trade Agreement (NAFTA) provides in Article 104 that specified agreements containing such provisions will prevail even if otherwise inconsistent with the NAFTA.[13]

d. Compliance with International Legal Instruments

Since countries continue to devote considerable resources to negotiating new agreements and nonbinding legal instruments, it is relevant to ask whether these agreements are implemented and complied with, and whether they are effective in achieving their goals. While some have argued that most states comply with most international agreements most of the time,[14] there is now "reason to believe that

---

10. Framework Convention on Climate Change, May 9, 1992, 31 I.L.M. 849.

11. *See* Montreal Protocol, *supra* note 9, at art. 10; Climate Framework Convention, 1992, art. 4(c), 31 I.L.M. 855; Biological Diversity Convention, 1992, arts. 16 and 18, 31 I.L.M. 829.

12. General Agreement on Tariffs and Trade, Oct. 30, 1947, T.I.A.S. No. 1700, 55 U.M.T.S. 187.

13. North American Free Trade Agreement, Dec. 17, 1992, 32 I.L.M. 289, 32 I.L.M. 612.

14. Louis Henkin, for example, has commented that for public international law generally, "almost all nations observe almost all principles of international law and almost all of their obligations almost all of the time." LOUIS HENKIN, HOW NATIONS BEHAVE 47 (1979).

national implementation of and compliance with international agreements is not only imperfect, but often inadequate, and that such implementation as takes place varies significantly among countries" and over time.[15]

There are still few studies on implementation of and compliance with international environmental accords. Two notable governmental efforts address this question: the United States Government Accounting Office study,[16] which concluded that compliance with eight agreements was low, and the intergovernmental report prepared for the United Nations Conference on Environment and Development, which surveyed implementation of certain international environmental agreements and set forth general concerns about compliance.[17] Additional available literature has been limited.[18] Several international research efforts are now under way to address implementation, compliance, and effectiveness.[19]

It is useful to distinguish between implementation, compliance, and effectiveness.[20] Implementation refers to measures parties take to make international agreements effective in their domestic law. Compliance refers to whether countries adhere to implementing measures and whether the targeted actors change their behavior to comply with these measures. International agreements contain a variety of specific obligations. Some of these are procedural, such as reporting requirements, while others are substantive, such as phasing out certain chemicals by a targeted date. Effectiveness differs from compliance in that even if a country complies with a treaty, the agreement may be ineffective in achieving its stated purposes. For example, CITES is intended to control trade in endangered species

---

15.   Edith Brown Weiss and Harold K. Jacobson, *Strengthening Compliance with International Environmental Accords: Some Preliminary Observations from a Collaborative Project*, 2, 35th Convention of the International Studies Association, (Mar. 31, 1994) (available from the authors or from I.S.A.).

16.   U.S. Gov't. Acct. Off., International Agreements Are Not Well Monitored, GAO/RCED-92-43 (1992); U.S. Gov't. Acct. Off., Strengthening the Implementation of Environmental Agreements, GAO/RCED-92-188 (1992).

17.   For the summary and the background papers, *see* THE EFFECTIVENESS OF INTERNATIONAL ENVIRONMENTAL AGREEMENTS (Peter Sand ed., 1992).

18.   *See, e.g.*, HAROLD K. JACOBSON AND EDITH BROWN WEISS, IMPLEMENTING AND COMPLYING WITH INTERNATIONAL ENVIRONMENTAL ACCORDS: A FRAMEWORK FOR RESEARCH (1990); Arild Underdal, *Explaining Compliance and Defection: Three Models*, (A.A.A.S. Meeting, Feb. 1994, mimeo, available from author); Abram Chayes and Antonia H. Chayes, *On Compliance*, 47 INT'L. ORG. 175 (1993); Ronald B. Mitchell, INTENTIONAL OIL POLLUTION AT SEA (1994) (study of compliance with the London International Convention for the Prevention of Pollution by Ships (MARPOL)). *See generally*, ORAN R. YOUNG, COMPLIANCE AND PUBLIC AUTHORITY: A THEORY WITH INTERNATIONAL APPLICATIONS (1979).

19.   These include efforts by university scholars under the auspices of the U.S. Social Science Research Council, the International Institute for Applied Systems Analysis in Vienna, and the European Union.

20.   Brown Weiss and Jacobson, *supra* note 15, at 4–6.

for the purpose of protecting species, but even if all trade were controlled among countries, domestic consumption of the species could still cause species extinction.

Implementation and compliance with agreements at the national level involves a dynamic process between governments, secretariats, international organizations, subnational units, nongovernmental organizations, and entities or individuals whose behavior is the target of the agreement. There are feedback loops in this process that link the many actors.

Moreover, compliance with international agreements changes over time, both within and among countries party to the agreement. The preliminary results from an international study of five environmental and natural resource agreements in nine countries indicate that, in general, there is a secular trend toward improved implementation and compliance.[21] There appear to be many reasons for this, but one of the most important is international momentum, i.e., the collective force of states, secretariats, nongovernmental organizations, and individuals as is brought to bear upon the behavior of a state party. Preparations for the Rio conference, for example, appear to have enhanced countries' efforts to secure compliance with the obligations contained in various environmental agreements.

> Nongovernmental organizations significantly affect compliance. They mobilize public opinion and set political agendas. They make information about problems available, sometimes provide information that governments do not have or would prefer to keep confidential. Often the information they make available is essential to monitoring. They bring pressure on governments directly and indirectly. Because [of] connections with NGOs in other countries and international NGOs, they are a means of insuring a uniformity of concern throughout the world. There are also significant transfers of funds among NGOs, so NGOs in poorer countries may have surprisingly extensive resources at their disposal.[22]

While not all NGOs necessarily promote compliance, it is nonetheless impossible to explain the intergovernmental process of compliance with international agreements without taking them into account.

III. TRANSNATIONAL ENVIRONMENTAL LAW

Concerns about competitiveness and a level playing field in trade drive the international attention to differences among countries in national environmental standards and their enforcement. Both governments and the private sector are actively involved in addressing the issues.

---

21. *Id.* at 17.
22. *Id.* at 20–21.

The European Union has long been concerned with differences in environmental standards among its member states. While member countries have harmonized some standards, the new approach to regulation includes as a key element the strategy of "mutual recognition," which means "equivalence of the various basic requirements laid down under national law."[23] The Organization for Economic Cooperation and Development has developed many test guidelines and fostered a number of agreements concerning good laboratory practices. The North American Free Trade Agreement provides in Article 906 that the parties "shall to the greatest extent practicable, make compatible their respective standards-related measures, so as to facilitate trade in a good or service between the Parties."[24] The North American Agreement on Environmental Cooperation, which accompanies the NAFTA, aims to raise environmental standards among member countries and ensure a level playing field among the member countries in compliance.

The most important forces behind equality in national environmental standards and business practices may be associations in the business community, coalitions of interest groups from the business community and environmental nongovernmental organizations, and multinational corporations.[25] Their actions will profoundly affect not only the behavior of the private sector but also the activities of the public sector. Yet, there has been little exploration of either the dynamics of this interaction or of the implications for national sovereignty.

Increasingly, multinational corporations apply common standards and environmental practices to their plants, whatever their location. They do so partially because it is easier and cheaper to initially construct environmentally sound plants than to retrofit later or to cope with diverse environmental standards sporadically enforced by host governments.[26] Such standardization also reflects an awareness of the worldwide public concern for the environment and a recognition of multinationals' need to demonstrate to communities that they are environmentally sound.

---

23.   Giandomenico Majone, *Market Integration and Regulation: Europe After 1992*, METROECONOMICA 131, 141 (1992).

24.   North American Free Trade Agreement, Dec. 17, 1992, 32 I.L.M. 289, 32 I.L.M. 612, at art. 906.

25.   *See* BEYOND COMPLIANCE: A NEW INDUSTRY VIEW OF THE ENVIRONMENT (Bruce Smart ed., 1992) (describing a grass roots environmental consciousness); STEPHEN SCHMIDHEINY, CHANGING COURSE: A GLOBAL BUSINESS PERSPECTIVE ON DEVELOPMENT AND THE ENVIRONMENT (1992) (prepared in connection with the 1992 United Nations Conference on Environment and Development).

26.   The extent to which the parent company ensures that the standards are maintained is unclear. In developing countries, with scarce resources available for enforcement, the industries that initially meet standards higher than the national one may not be targeted for frequent monitoring or enforcement visits. *See generally* Edith Brown Weiss, *Environmentally Sustainable Competitiveness*, 102 YALE L. J. 2123, 2131–36 (1993).

Within the last few years, industry associations have assumed a central role in formulating common environmental standards across industries. The most prominent of these organizations is the International Standards Organization (ISO). Founded in 1947 to facilitate the exchange of goods and services, it now has ninety-seven members, 176 technical committees, and 2,698 subcommittees and working groups. The ISO is a hybrid governmental/private group. Each member country is represented by a national standards board. In Europe, the boards are quasi-governmental bodies; in the United States, the board member is the American Standards National Institute (ANSI), a voluntary nonprofit group.

While historically the ISO has been concerned with developing technical and manufacturing standards for products, it began in 1979 to develop global quality standards, known as the ISO 9000 series. As of January 1993, ISO quality standards in this series became mandatory for any company manufacturing or exporting products to the European Union.

As concern for the environment grew, the ISO formed the Strategic Advisory Group on the Environment (SAGE) to consider the need for standard environmental management practices. The ISO subsequently formed TC 207 and directed it to establish environmental standards in five areas: management systems, audits, life-cycle assessments to determine environmental impacts, environmental performance evaluations, and labeling. The subgroups for these five areas are now addressing industry-wide standards.

The development of these standards may greatly influence governmental control of business behavior. For example, standards may be set for practices that governments may never address; or that precede government action or provide greater specificity; or that are inconsistent with national standards, particularly if the representatives in the ISO are nongovernmental entities. Within countries, the standards could be used by federal and state authorities to determine appropriate responses to noncompliance with governmental standards, or even to decide whether to bring criminal actions for violations of environmental law. If companies follow ISO standards but are in violation of a national law, it may be difficult to bring criminal actions against the company. Moreover, compliance with ISO standards could influence sentencing for criminal behavior.[27]

One of the SAGE subcommittees is trying to develop criteria to measure a company's environmental performance. It may thus be possible to create new, more stringent environmental standards, which in turn might influence any standard of reasonable care invoked in common law claims for damage.[28] Some countries want the results of this evaluation to be publicly available, which would mean that nongovernmental organizations, in particular, could press for adherence to the higher industry association standard.

---

27. Karl S. Bourdeau and Paul E. Hagen, *Courts Examine U.S. Environmental Laws' Extraterritorial Reach*, NAT'L. L. J. at S5, S7 (Sept. 6, 1993).

28. *Id.* at S9.

Efforts to develop common standards or processes outside the intergovernmental framework may also take place informally. For example, at the end of April 1994, three major auto companies (France's Renault, Italy's Fiat, and Germany's BMW) promised to establish recycling programs in their countries and to allow cars produced in any of the three firms to be recycled through national programs. While the auto producers have called for the European Union to adopt a European strategy on automobile recycling, the European Commission has not yet issued any directive or regulation governing auto recycling.[29] The arrangements negotiated by the three companies could provide a basis for draft European legislation, or could alternatively cause the European Union to defer regulation.

In general, private sector firms recognize that promoting common standards of environmentally sound operation is in their own interest. In preparation for the Rio Conference on Environment and Development, the International Chamber of Commerce (ICC) drafted a Business Charter for Sustainable Development for the daily operations of firms. The Charter contains sixteen principles of environment management, which among other things call for: assessing environmental impacts of proposed projects and decommissioning of facilities, developing and maintaining emergency hazard preparedness plans, fostering public dialogue about potential hazards and environment impacts, measuring environmental performance, conducting regular environmental audits and assessing compliance, and providing information to the public. In Japan, the Keidanren Global Environment Charter, which is similar to the ICC document, has been circulated to the most influential Japanese business associations (comparable to the Fortune 100 list in the United States).[30]

The World Industry Council for the Environment (WICE), a group of more than ninety international companies, plays a similar role. Founded by the International Chamber of Commerce to ensure a strong voice for industry in setting governmental environmental standards, WICE has targeted the development of self-regulatory guidelines and an inventory of life-cycle analyses.

As the private sector increasingly self-regulates to ensure a level playing field and to preempt or modify governmental regulation, countries must face the question of accountability by the private sector. The ultimate client of environmental protection is the public worldwide. Under this scenario, the market serves as the primary instrument of accountability. It is assumed that consumers will reflect their preference for environmental protection through their purchases and will refrain from buying products or materials they find environmentally unsatisfactory.

There is some evidence that the market may be an effective instrument of accountability. A 1991 Wall Street Journal/NBC poll indicated that forty-six

---

29.   *Three European Automakers Agree to Establish Joint Recycling Network*, INT'L. ENVT. REP., 395–96 (May 4, 1994).

30.   *Corporate Environmental Reporting: Embraced or Resisted?* INT'L ENVTL. REP. (BNA), 330 (Apr. 6, 1994).

percent of those surveyed had purchased a product during the previous six months because either the product or manufacturer had a good reputation for protecting the environment. Fifty-three percent avoided purchasing a product because of concerns that it was harmful to the environment or that its manufacturer was not environmentally sound.[31]

But there are problems with relying largely on this system of accountability to ensure adequate environmental standards. It assumes that the market works perfectly and that prices adequately reflect environmental costs and benefits. Neither assumption is true. This means that we must also rely on the interaction of these private actors with governments to ensure greater accountability in the protection of the environment.

In the next decade, more discussions must take place at the national and international level between governments and the private sector to ensure this accountability.

IV. CONCLUSION

Several global developments contribute to the transition in international environmental law: the linkage of environmental protection with economic development and competitiveness; the blurring of the clear distinction between international and national or local occurrences; the rise of nonstate actors—both corporate and environmental; and the increasingly rapid rate of change in many aspects of society, including in our scientific understanding of problems. The result is a dynamic, porous, complex, and rapidly changing system of international environmental law which is no longer state-centered, static, and closed. Moreover, transnational environmental standards and practices formulated by nongovernmental actors are an increasingly important component. These developments will likely continue as international environmental issues become critical to countries' central concerns.

---

31. Jackie S. Prince and Richard A. Denison, *Launching a New Business Ethic: The Environment as a Standard Operating Procedure; Environmental Policies*, 34 INDUS. MGMT. 15 (1992).

Part II
Extraterritorial Application of Domestic Law in the Field of Trade and Economic Regulation and the Effect of Responses by the International Legal Community

| SUMMARY

H. Stuart Irvin, Jr.

Although comment on and criticism of extraterritorial assertion of jurisdiction have typically focused on U.S. policies, the papers submitted and the panel discussions at the Symposium made it clear that extraterritorial application of domestic law is not limited to U.S. judicial, executive and legislative action. Canada, a frequent critic of the extraterritorial application of U.S. antitrust law, has nevertheless resorted to laws that reach far beyond its borders to prohibit the introduction of pollutants into the Arctic Sea and to protect migratory fish stocks.[1] Similarly, the government of Japan has been quick to criticize U.S. antitrust enforcement policy,[2] but the Japanese Penal Code makes extensive use of the active personality principle, and also relies on the passive personality principle in a limited number of cases.[3]

The Symposium participants recognized and agreed that states generally reserve the right to apply domestic law extraterritorially when important national interests are at stake. As international trade increases, markets become more interconnected and communications technology criss-crosses national borders, the frequency with which domestic interests will be affected by conduct occurring outside national boundaries is likely to increase. In addition, the end of the cold

---

1. See H.S. Fairley and J.H. Currie, *Projecting Beyond the Boundaries: A Canadian Perspective on the Double-Edged Sword of Extraterritorial Acts*, *infra* ch. 7 [hereinafter Fairley & Currie].

2. See A. Kotera, *Extraterritorial Jurisdiction of Antitrust Law in International Law*, *infra* ch. 9 [hereinafter Kotera].

3. Japan's Anti-Monopoly Act is silent on the question of extraterritorial application and there is no case law that addresses the question directly. A 1990 report by a study group organized by the Kousei Torihiki Iinkai (Fair Trade Commission or "FTC") concludes that conduct which impedes competition in Japan's domestic market violates the Anti-Monopoly Act, even if the offending foreign companies do not have a presence in Japan. *See id.* at ch. 9. It will be interesting to watch developments in this area. If Japan opens its markets to manufactured goods in response to pressure from its trading partners, there may be more opportunities to test the extraterritorial reach of the Anti-Monopoly Act.

war has made agreement on nonproliferation, technology transfer and other global security issues more difficult as the more or less united front against Soviet expansionism is replaced with vigorous competition for business in emerging markets. The dissolution of COCOM,[4] and the failure of its member states to agree on a system to replace it, may lead to an increase in unilateral attempts to control the end use of high technology products after they have been exported from their place of manufacture.

Given the fact that extraterritorial application of domestic law is now a permanent feature of international legal practice, the Symposium avoided a catalogue and critique of past cases and focused instead on identifying general principles that can be used to classify extraterritorial acts. The participants also attempted to identify procedures that might be employed to avoid future conflicts and resolve disputes once they occur. Although the discussion ranged broadly over a number of important issues, several major themes emerged.

I. UNILATERAL ACTION—A POSITIVE SOURCE OF RULEMAKING OR THE UNWELCOME IMPOSITION OF VALUES IN AN ALIEN ENVIRONMENT?

Extraterritorial application of domestic law tends to be viewed as an evil. Academic treatises and government policy statements are sharply critical of U.S. antitrust decisions and export control regulations that have an international reach.[5] As extraterritorial application becomes increasingly common and is no longer limited to U.S. policy, new ways of approaching the issue are required. Scott H. Fairley, of Lang Michener in Toronto, argued that extraterritoriality should be viewed as a constructive source of rulemaking, rather than a disruption of international order. According to Mr. Fairley, states act unilaterally to protect what they perceive to be vital national interests. This unilateral extension of jurisdiction is typically followed by criticism, dialogue, and sometimes new international agreements. Thus, unilateralism begets internationalism in the sense that unilateral

---

4.   The Coordinating Committee for Multilateral Export Controls (COCOM) was an informal intergovernmental agency composed of North Atlantic Treaty Organization members (except Iceland and Spain). COCOM's goal was to restrict strategic and military exports to communist countries. *See, e.g.*, Philip H. Oettinger, *National Discretion: Choosing COCOM's Successor and the New Export Administration Act,* 9 AM. U.J. INT'L L. & POL'Y 557 (1994); Detlev F. Vagts, *Comment: Repealing the Cold War,* 88 AM. J. INT'L LAW 506 (1994). COCOM was dissolved at the end of March 1994. *U.S. Ends Cold War Controls on Telecommunications,* 14 COMM. DAILY 3, Apr. 1, 1994.

5.   *See, e.g.*, Thomas W. Dunfee and Aryeh S. Friedman, *The Extraterritorial Application of U.S. Antitrust Laws: A Proposal for an Interim Solution,* 45 OHIO ST. L.J. 883 (1984); Barry E. Hawk, *International Antitrust Policy and the 1982 Acts: the Continuing Need for Reassessment,* 51 FORDHAM L. REV. 201 (1982).

extraterritorial acts tend to promote dialogue and focus attention on the underlying problem.

Jonathan I. Charney, of Vanderbilt University, took exception to the cases cited by Mr. Fairley as examples of positive international rulemaking. Professor Charney stated his view that unilateral extraterritorial acts should only take place after efforts to resolve the underlying issue through international consultations have been exhausted. According to Professor Charney, Canada's extraterritorial fisheries claims off Newfoundland failed in this regard because the U.N. Conference on Straddling Fish Stocks and Highly Migratory Fish Stocks was ongoing at the time of Canada's unilateral acts.[6] Canada's extraterritorial assertion of jurisdiction was not, therefore, a positive development moving toward solutions, but rather a negative development moving toward controversy.

Mr. Fairley replied that Canada's action involved a question of timing. The fish were almost gone. Exhaustion of efforts to solve the problem by multilateral negotiations might have occurred only after the exhaustion of the fish stocks. Canada's action accelerated international procedures and thus was a positive source of international law.

The Chair of the session, Peter D. Trooboff of Covington & Burling in Washington, D.C., pointed out that exhaustion of multilateral negotiations alone does not legitimize a unilateral assertion of jurisdiction. For example, in the Soviet gas pipeline controversy of 1982, the United States acted unilaterally only after it failed to convince its allies to join in efforts to block construction of the pipeline.[7]

Detlev F. Vagts, of Harvard University, noted that the reaction of the target state to the claims of jurisdiction by the enacting state is an important way to assess the validity of the extraterritorial act. For example, the U.S. Congress has provided that the Equal Employment Opportunity Act applies to U.S. corporations doing business overseas.[8] If female employees of a U.S. subsidiary chartered in Japan bring suit, the Japanese government is not likely to protest.

---

6. On the Conference generally, *see* Secretariat, *Report on the Third Session of the United Nations Conference on Straddling Fish Stocks and Highly Migratory Fish Stocks*, U.N. Doc. A/CONF.164/20 (1994); Bryan Walters, *Reports of ASIL Programs:* ASIL Briefing Discusses U.N. Conference on Straddling Fish Stocks and Highly Migratory Fish Stocks, 1994 AM. SOC'Y INT'L L. 1, Sept. 1994.

7. For a detailed discussion of the Soviet pipeline case, *see* P. Trooboff, *Extraterritoriality and U.S. Foreign Trade Controls — Lessons from Old Disputes and Sources of Potential New Problems*, *infra* at ch. 10.

8. The Supreme Court ruled in 1991 that Title VII did not apply extraterritorially to regulate employment practices of U.S. employers who employ U.S. citizens abroad. EEOC v. Arabian Am. Oil Co., 499 U.S. 244 (1991). In response, Congress redefined the term "employee" as used in Title VII to include certain U.S. citizens working in foreign countries for U.S. employers. *Civil Rights Act of 1991*, Pub. L. No. 102–166, 105 Stat. 1071, 1077–78 (1991). *See* Lendgraf v. U.S.I Film Prods., 114 S. Ct. 1483, 1490 (1994).

Akira Kotera, of the University of Tokyo, discussed the civil law doctrine of opposability. Opposability is a contract law concept that provides a useful analogy because international law still retains a predominantly contractual character, rather than a legislative character.[9] Under the doctrine of opposability, it is not necessary to declare a contract (or an assertion of jurisdiction) invalid on its face. Rather, the inquiry is limited to whether or not a unilateral act is valid vis-a-vis the party in question. Professor Kotera used as an example the Icelandic Fisheries Jurisdiction case, in which the International Court of Justice (*ICJ*) refused to declare Iceland's claim to exclusive jurisdiction invalid; it decided instead that the claim was not valid vis-a-vis the United Kingdom.[10]

Yasuaki Onuma, of the University of Tokyo, agreed with Ambassador Owada that the problem with extraterritoriality is the unilateral application of values that are not shared in the target state. In the fields of human rights or the environment, the arguments for extraterritorial application of domestic laws are easier because there is a rough agreement on the basic values being enforced. But as far as U.S. enforcement of its antitrust law is concerned, it is not clear that the public policy that underlies the U.S. statute represents a universal value applicable in other states. Professor Onuma noted that the *Timberlane* case established a justification of U.S. public order objectives, not world public order principles.[11]

II. *LOTUS* LIVES—SANCTIONS IMPOSED INSIDE THE TERRITORY FOR CONDUCT OCCURRING OUTSIDE THE TERRITORY

Jun Yokoyama, of Hitotsubashi University, pointed out that the response of a government, and the Japanese government in particular, to a unilateral assertion of jurisdiction depends in part upon the sanction that is employed by the state claiming jurisdiction. Elaborating on this point, John H. Jackson, of the University of Michigan, outlined a hypothetical case for discussion purposes. Professor Jackson's example assumed that a U.S. law applied to subsidiaries of U.S. corporations, including subsidiaries chartered outside the United States. The law at issue purports to regulate conduct occurring outside the territory of the United States, but the sanctions for a violation of the law take place entirely inside the United States. Thus, the hypothetical assumes an assertion of extraterritorial jurisdiction, but there is no remedial extraterritoriality because the United States is acting entirely within its own borders. After sketching this hypothetical, Professor Jackson raised the following question: is there an international norm that would

---

9.   On "opposability," see Prosper Weil, *Towards Relative Normativity in International Law?*, 77 AMER. J. INT'L L. 413, 433 (1983); J. CHARPENTIER, LA RECONNAISSANCE EN DROIT INTERNATIONAL ET L'EVOLUTION DU DROIT DES GENS, 1956.

10.   *See* Kotera, *infra* ch. 9.

11.   For a discussion of the Timberlane case, see Fairley & Currie, *infra* ch. 7.

constrain a state from attempting to apply its law outside its borders with sanctions imposed entirely inside its borders?

Professor Vagts noted that, under *Lotus*,[12] if an assertion of jurisdiction is not prohibited by a specific rule of international law, then extraterritorial assertion is allowed. Thomas Franck, of New York University, observed that the law of state responsibility, which governs state treatment of aliens, constrains a state's right to impose penalties on aliens, including corporate aliens, regardless of whether the penalties are intra- or extraterritorial in reach. The imposition of arbitrary, confiscatory or unequal sanctions on aliens thus violates a specific rule of international law.

Professor Jackson acknowledged this point and conceded that if a sanction imposed inside the territory violates another norm of international law, the sanction is itself invalid. For example, in the *Tuna/Dolphin* case[13] the United States tried to regulate the conduct of fishermen operating in international waters, but the sanction employed by the United States—an embargo—violated the General Agreement on Tariffs and Trade (GATT). However, there are many sanctions that could be used domestically that would not violate international law, especially if the enacting state claims a national security exception to GATT. Professor Jackson expressed the view that there is no international norm that prohibits the use of sanctions inside national borders to regulate conduct that occurs outside national borders and, therefore, under *Lotus*, a state can use national sanctions to control international actions.[14] The European Community argued in the *Soviet Pipeline* case[15] that international law prohibits the use of domestic sanctions to control conduct outside national boundaries, but the argument was unconvincing.

---

12. 1927 PCIJ, ser.A, No. 10 at 18.

13. *United States — Restrictions on Imports of Tuna: Report of the Panel*, GATT Doc. DS21/R (Sept. 3, 1991), 30 I.L.M. 1594 (1991). *See generally* Matthew Hunter Hurlock, *The GATT, U.S. Law and the Environment: A Proposal to Amend the GATT in Light of the Tuna/Dolphin Decision*, 92 COLUM. L. REV. 2098 (1992); Robert Housman & Durwood Zaelke, *The Collision of the Environment and Trade: The GATT Tuna/Dolphin Decision*, 22 ENVTL. L. REP. (Envtl. L. Inst.) 10268 (1992).

14. Professor Jackson's thesis has interesting ramifications in the field of global environmental policy. Attempts to control or direct the environmental policies of developing countries by means of trade sanctions imposed by developed countries are likely to become an increasingly common form of extraterritoriality, as the Tuna/Dolphin case suggests.

15. *See generally* Comment, *Extraterritorial Application of U.S. Law: the Case of Export Controls*, 132 U. PA. L. REV. 355 (1984).

III. TAXONOMY OF EXTRATERRITORIALITY

The participants at the Symposium discussed various ways to classify extraterritorial acts and to distinguish between legitimate and illegitimate assertions of jurisdiction. Kazuhiro Nakatani, of the University of Tokyo, argued that in order to determine whether an assertion of extraterritorial jurisdiction is valid, a *prima facie* case must be established. The elements of a *prima facie* case would include (1) whether the assertion of extraterritorial jurisdiction is in accordance with the basic principles of international law, such as respect for state sovereignty, territorial integrity and nonintervention, and (2) whether the particular claim of jurisdiction has been previously asserted and recognized as valid under general international law. According to Professor Nakatani, the United States failed to establish a *prima facie* case of jurisdiction in the Soviet pipeline controversy because the claimed basis of jurisdiction had not been asserted previously and recognized as valid.

Professor Yokoyama drew a distinction between public law rules with an extraterritorial reach and private law rules that apply outside national boundaries. The extraterritorial application of private law rules does not generally produce a strong negative reaction from other states because these rules may be selected by parties to a contract and typically only have an impact when they are applied by courts in the target state pursuant to domestic choice of law principles. In contrast, the extraterritorial application of public law rules creates conflict because these rules apply automatically, without the consent of the parties to a contract or an affirmative act by the courts of the target state. Professor Yokoyama suggested that public law rules of the enacting state could be used by courts in the target state as factors in the traditional contract law analysis to determine whether a particular agreement which violates the public law rules of the enacting state is impossible to perform or tainted with immorality.

Mr. Fairley outlined a two-part test to be used to determine whether a claim of extraterritorial jurisdiction is valid. The first part of the test is derived from the American Restatement and examines the substantive reasonability of the extraterritorial act in question.[16] This is essentially a rule-of-reason-type analysis. The second part of the test examines the reaction of the target state. If the target state responds positively to the unilateral claim of jurisdiction, the extraterritorial act is legitimized and this adds to the international law creation process.

Shinya Murase, of Sophia University, asked whether and to what extent the legal theories and principles formed in U.S. domestic case law constitute precedents relevant to the development of international law. Mr. Fairley replied

---

16. *See generally* Marialuisa S. Gallozzi, *Jurisdiction - Extraterritorial Application of U.S. Statute Proscribing Employment Discrimination - Congressional Intent*, 83 AM. J. INT'L L. 375 (1989); Elanor M. Fox, *Extraterritoriality, Antitrust, and the New Restatement: Is "Reasonableness" the Answer?*, 19 N.Y.U.J. INT'L L. & POL. 565 (1987).

that *Alcoa*,[17] *Timberlane*, and other U.S. cases provide important guidelines that can help focus the debate. He suggested that these guidelines could prove useful in settling disputes: if the guidelines attract international consensus, there can then be authoritative settlements of disputes.

IV. CONFLICT AVOIDANCE AND DISPUTE RESOLUTION

The participants discussed various methods of conflict avoidance and dispute resolution in the context of extraterritorial jurisdiction. Professor Charney noted that there is an important distinction between procedures that precede extraterritorial action and procedures that follow it. He argued that consultation procedures are appropriate prior to unilateral actions as well as subsequent to them. According to Professor Charney, Canada's decision to take unilateral action to protect its east coast fisheries, combined with its withdrawal of consent to ICJ jurisdiction, was contrary to its objective of avoiding and resolving international disputes.

Several participants discussed guidelines for the resolution of disputes. Professor Vagts' paper raised the possibility of seeking guidance from the ICJ in the form of an advisory opinion on extraterritoriality. Woonsang Choi, of Tokyo International University, argued that an advisory opinion was not a viable solution given the difficulty of framing the issues for the court and the probability that a single advisory opinion would be unable to address all of the problems raised by extraterritorial jurisdiction claims.

Yoshio Ohara, of Kanagawa University, noted that some progress toward formulating guidelines for the resolution of disputes has been made in the area of antitrust cooperation agreements. These agreements emphasize the need for consultation and the role of comity in extraterritorial jurisdiction cases. However, antitrust cooperation agreements do not represent a definitive solution to the problem because they cannot prevent private parties from filing treble damage claims in the United States. Professor Ohara also noted that antitrust cooperation agreements are less than effective when there is disagreement over whether conduct occurring in the territory of a contracting state violates the antitrust law of that state. For example, the U.S. government argued that bid-rigging by Japanese construction companies in connection with construction at the U.S. military base in Atsugi constituted a violation of the Japanese Anti-Monopoly Act. However, the Japanese FTC investigated the matter and concluded that there had been no violation of domestic law.

Professor Choi argued that the issue of extraterritorial application of domestic law has become important enough—with enough diverse national laws and contradictory court cases—for the United Nations to pass a resolution calling for

---

17. United States v. Aluminum Co. of Am., 148 F.2d 416 (2d Cir. 1945).

an international conference to sort things out. The final work product of the conference, hopefully, would be an international convention on extraterritoriality.

Mr. Trooboff pointed out that the U.N. General Assembly is not viewed as a neutral forum by the United States when it comes to questions of extraterritoriality, particularly in light of the recent resolution condemning U.S. sanctions against Cuba.[18] Mr. Trooboff expressed the view that attempts to create "soft law," i.e., nonbinding standards similar to those used in the nonproliferation area, would probably be the most effective way to proceed.

V. CONCLUSION

The problems of extraterritoriality are created by a fundamental lack of agreement among states as to the substantive provisions of underlying law, and in particular the substantive content of antitrust, export control and environmental law. Many states have begun the long and arduous process of harmonizing the substantive provisions of domestic law. This process is fairly well advanced in the European Union and has just begun among the member states of the North American Free Trade Agreement. It remains to be seen whether the new World Trade Organization will be able to accelerate the process and spread the benefits of harmonization to other parts of the world. For some, the process of harmonization is not occurring fast enough. Edith Brown Weiss, of Georgetown University, noted that many multinational companies have begun their own in-house harmonization of environmental laws.[19] Multinationals from developed countries take domestic environmental standards, which tend to be more strict, and apply them in less developed countries where they do business in order to cut the cost of complying with a myriad of different regulations.

Despite these moves toward the harmonization of substantive law, it is clear that extraterritorial action will be a feature of international law for many years to come.   The challenge for scholars, practitioners, jurists, legislators, and administrators will be to find a way to make extraterritorial action a remedy of last resort and a remedy that minimizes the impact of an assertion of jurisdiction on other states. The discussions of the Trilateral Symposium helped identify ways to meet these important goals.

---

18. *See* Frank J. Prial, *U.N. Votes to Urge U.S. to Dismantle Embargo on Cuba*, N.Y. TIMES, Nov. 25, 1992, at A1.

19. *See, e.g.,* Richard B. Stewart, *Environmental Regulation and International Competitiveness*, 102 YALE L.J. 2039, 2070 (1993).

PROJECTING BEYOND THE BOUNDARIES: A CANADIAN PERSPECTIVE ON THE DOUBLE-EDGED SWORD OF EXTRATERRITORIAL ACTS

H. Scott Fairley and John H. Currie

I. INTRODUCTION

Canadian history and its predominantly British legal heritage have left a strong imprimatur of territoriality on Canadian notions of jurisdictional authority. Canada's highest court has recently observed that Canada's colonial legacy and initially uncertain status as a sovereign state have strengthened its inherited British tendency to view authority as necessarily linked to defined territory.[1]

Neither Canada nor the United Kingdom have been alone in considering territory to be the primary basis of jurisdiction. The notion is well-embedded in international law as a necessary corollary to the concepts of state sovereignty and the formal equality of nation-states as primary constituents of an international community.[2] The classic enunciation of the principle of territorial jurisdiction still belongs to the Permanent Court of International Justice in the *Lotus*:

> [t]he first and foremost restriction imposed by international law upon a State is that—failing the existence of a permissive rule to the contrary—it may not exercise its power in any form in the territory of another State. In this sense, jurisdiction is certainly territorial; it cannot be exercised by a State outside its territory except by virtue of a persuasive rule derived from international custom or convention.[3]

---

1. *See* Libman v. The Queen, [1985] 2 S.C.R. 178, 183–184 (1985).

2. I. BROWNLIE, PRINCIPLES OF PUBLIC INTERNATIONAL LAW 298 (4th ed. 1990).

3. The Steamship Lotus (France v. Turkey), 1927 P.C.I.J. (ser. A) No. 10, at 18–19 (September 7).

In a world where law and economics play as central a role as armies once did, the prohibition of the exercise of "power in any form" in the territory of another state brings two questions to the fore: whether national laws may purport to extend their effect beyond state boundaries and whether the extraterritorial enforcement of such laws can be countenanced.

It is a well-accepted common law presumption governing statutory interpretation in Canada that legislation does not apply extraterritorially unless such intent is clearly expressed in the relevant statutory language.[4] It is not doubted, however, that Parliament has the constitutional power to enact legislation with an extraterritorial effect:

> [i]t is hereby declared and enacted that the Parliament of a Dominion has full power to make laws having extra-territorial operation.[5]

The exercise of this power has been exceptional in Canada, however; the licence would appear not to extend to provincial governments or legislatures,[6] and the circumstances under which the federal Parliament and governments have exercised their extraterritorial reach have been seen as critical. Moreover, such exercises have usually, but as will be seen, not exclusively, been premised upon corollary qualifying principles of international law, such as the nationality, passive personality, protective and universal principles of jurisdiction.[7]

On the more fundamental question of the extraterritorial enforcement of national laws, "[t]he governing principle is that a state cannot take measures on the territory of another state by way of enforcement of national laws without the consent of the latter."[8] Canada has generally considered itself an offended jurisdiction under this principle and remains particularly sensitive to the long reach of its

---

4.   A.G. Ontario v. Reciprocal Insurers, [1924] A.C. 328, 345 (P.C. 1924); Cox v. Army Council, [1963] A.C. 48 (H.L. 1963); Air India v. Wiggins, [1980] 2 All E.R. 593 at 597 (H.L. 1980); see also, E.A. DRIEDGER, THE CONSTRUCTION OF STATUTES 218 (2nd ed. 1983).

5.   Statute of Westminster, 1931, 33 Geo. V, § 3 (UK), incorporated into the Constitution of Canada by virtue of s.52(2)(b) of the Canadian Constitution Act, 1982, Schedule B of the Canada Act 1982 (UK), 1982, c. 11. See also Croft v. Dunphy, [1933] A.C. 156 (P.C. 1933).

6.   See Interprovincial Cooperatives Ltd. v. Regina, [1976] 1 S.C.R. 477 (1976), reversing 38 D.L.R. 3d 367 (Man. C.A. 1975). See also G.V. La Forest, May the Provinces Legislate in Violation of International Law? 39 CAN. BAR REV. 78 (1961).

7.   See BROWNLIE, supra note 2, at 300–305; KINDRED et al, INTERNATIONAL LAW CHIEFLY AS INTERPRETED AND APPLIED IN CANADA 467–70 (4th ed. 1987); WILLIAMS AND CASTEL, CANADIAN CRIMINAL LAW: INTERNATIONAL AND TRANSNATIONAL ASPECTS 133–37 (1981); see also generally Akehurst, Jurisdiction in International Law 46 B.Y.I.L. 145 (1972–73); Mann, The Doctrine of Jurisdiction in International Law, in 111 REC. DES COURS 1 (1964–I).

8.   BROWNLIE, supra note 2, at 307.

prominent neighbor to the south. At the same time, however, Canada has also turned a conveniently blind eye to consent requirements when it has deemed it a matter of vital national interest to unilaterally extend its authority. We address both seemingly contrary themes.

This chapter explores the Canadian experience in seeking to reconcile traditional notions of territoriality with an evolving world order. It offers a dual approach, examining, first, Canadian reactive postures when foreign states seek to exercise authority in perceived breach of Canadian territorial sovereignty. It then examines Canadian assertions of authority beyond its territorial boundaries to demonstrate that departures from traditional notions of territoriality, at least while the nation-state persists as the principal building block of the international community, have both negative and positive potential. Our analysis will suggest that the impact of an extraterritorial assertion of authority on and its legitimacy within the international legal system depend not only on the circumstances in which it is invoked, but also on its substantive objective, in particular as the end in view relates to the growth and development of international law.

II. CANADIAN RESPONSES TO FOREIGN ASSERTIONS OF EXTRATERRITORIAL JURISDICTION

a. Early Cases and Diplomatic Best Efforts

In the last three decades, principally in response to American assertions of extraterritorial jurisdiction, Canada has shifted from relying on diplomatic channels of informal notification, consultation and cooperative conflict resolution towards resort to a unilateral legislated regime of "hard" defensive measures to defined encroachments on Canadian sovereignty, together with assertions (presumably on the theory that the best defense is a strong offense) of extraterritorial jurisdiction on its own behalf. This progressive hardening of stance has played itself out against a backdrop of highly assertive—some would say aggressive—American legislative and judicial developments in the field of competition ("antitrust") laws and their application to activities undertaken abroad through and with American controlled multinational corporations.

The catalyst for this Canadian reaction can be traced to the decision of the U.S. Court of Appeals for the Second Circuit in the *Alcoa*[9] case of 1945, which decisively articulated the American "effects" doctrine of (extra)territoriality in the context of applying the U.S. Sherman Act of 1890 to alleged anticompetitive conduct occurring outside the United States. In that case, Chief Justice Learned Hand declared in sweeping terms that:

---

9.   United States v. Aluminium Company of America, 148 F. 2d 416 (2d Cir. 1945) (hereinafter Alcoa).

[a]ny state may impose liabilities, even upon persons not within its allegiance for conduct outside its borders that has consequences within its borders which the state reprehends; and these liabilities other states will recognize.[10]

With this somewhat brazen assertion of jurisdictional competence, and its distressingly enthusiastic subsequent reception by the American judiciary, the Sherman Act's provisions were catapulted well beyond the traditional boundaries of territorial jurisdiction. Antitrust prosecutions by U.S. public authorities against foreign interests burgeoned at first instance following *Alcoa.*[11] While some of the earliest and most dramatic exchanges in the ensuing jurisdictional battles were fought across the Atlantic,[12] Canada was soon drawn into the fray.

The *Canadian Radio Patents* cases[13] brought into sharp focus the need for some new equilibrium between governments with respect to the extraterritorial application of U.S. antitrust laws to lawful commercial activity occurring within Canada. In these cases, it was alleged that a Canadian company, incorporated by American-owned Canadian subsidiaries, had effectively closed the Canadian market to other U.S. producers of home entertainment equipment by systematically denying licences and restricting patent infringement lawsuits.[14]

The *Canadian Radio Patents Cases* prompted private sector accommodation by way of consent decrees prohibiting the defendants from directly or indirectly restricting the export of American products into the Canadian market. Canadian governmental authorities, however, were not so readily placated. They correctly perceived the American prosecutions as direct incursions into Canadian economic sovereignty, since the American prosecutions were related to activity which was in complete conformity with Canadian law. Canada accordingly pressed the United

---

10. *Id.* at 443.

11. *See, e.g.*, United States v. National Lead, 63 F. Supp. 513 (S.D.N.Y. 1945), *aff'd*, 332 U.S. 319, 67 S.Ct. 1634, 91 L.Ed. 1077 (1947); United States v. General Electric Co., 82 F. Supp. 753 (D.N.J. 1949), *final decree*, 115 F. Supp. 835 (1953).

12. *See, e.g.*, United States v. Imperial Chemical Industries, 100 F. Supp. 215 (S.D.N.Y. 1952), and the countervailing British decision in British Nylon Spinners Ltd. v. Imperial Chemical Industries Ltd., [1953] Ch. 19 (Eng. C.A.), *made permanent*, [1955] 1 Ch. 37 (Eng. C.A.).

13. United States v. General Electric Co., 1962 CCH T.C. para. 70,342 (S.D.N.Y. June 25, 1962); United States v. Allen-Bradley Co., 1962 CCH T.C. para. 70,420 (E.D. Pa. July 31, 1962); United States v. General Electric Co., 1962 CCH T.C. para. 70,546 (S.D.N.Y. Nov. 1, 1962); *cf.* United States v. Singer Mfg. Co., 374 U.S. 174, 83 S.Ct. 1773, 10 L.Ed.2d 823 (1963).

14. *See,* Nathan Lane, *American Antitrust Law and Canadian Patent Rights*, 118 U. PA. L. REV. 983 (1970); Henderson, *Foreign Courts and the National Interest: The Effect of Foreign Judgments on Activities in Canada*, 17 C.P.R. (2d) 130, 131–33 (1974); B.R. Campbell, *The Canada-United States Antitrust Notification and Consultation Procedure: A Study in Bilateral Conflict Resolution*, 56 CAN. BAR REV. 459, 461–62 (1978).

States for, and obtained, a somewhat informal and very optimistically phrased emanation of good faith in the form of an Antitrust Notification and Consultation Procedure between the two countries.[15]

According to the then Canadian Minister of Justice, the Procedure was to be invoked

> when it becomes apparent that the interests of one of our countries are likely to be affected by the enforcement of the antitrust laws of the other. Such discussions would be designed to explore means of avoiding the sort of situation which would give rise to objections or misunderstandings in the other country.[16]

However, the fate of the Procedure was perhaps preordained by both the perception and the reality that it did not purport to enjoin any offensive conduct on the part of either government. It ultimately proved completely ineffective in containing the powerful economic forces at play and further failed to prevent an escalation of the jurisdictional tensions between the two countries. Rather, courts in the United States, Canada, and the United Kingdom continued to serve as polarizing battlegrounds for American assertions of extraterritorial antitrust claims with respect to commodities ranging from potash to uranium.[17]

Canada responded to this escalation by pressing for a more rigid consultation procedure. The Americans eventually agreed to a formalized antitrust notification procedure in 1984, contained in a Memorandum of Understanding between the Government of Canada and the Government of the United States of America as to Notification, Consultation and Cooperation with Respect to the Application of National Antitrust Laws.[18] Notification, at least, was thereby made mandatory in cases where, *inter alia*, antitrust investigations were likely to inquire into activity carried out wholly or partially outside the territory of the investigating state, or might be expected to lead to a prosecution affecting the national interest of the other

---

15. For a thorough review of the Antitrust Notification and Consultation Procedure, see CAMPBELL, *supra* note 14.

16. The Hon. D.E. Fulton, Minister of Justice of Canada in HOUSE OF COMMONS DEBATES (Feb. 3, 1959) at 619.

17. *See, e.g.*, Central Canada Potash v. Gov't of Saskatchewan, [1979] 1 S.C.R. 42 (1979); In Re Uranium Antitrust Litigation, 480 F. Supp. 1138 (N.D. Ill., 1979), 617 F. 2d 1248 (7th Cir. 1980); In Re Westinghouse Electric Corp. and Duquesne Light Co., 16 O.R.2d 273 (1977); Rio Tinto Zinc Corp. v. Westinghouse Electric Corp., [1978] 2 W.L.R. 81 (1978); Burmah Oil Co. Ltd. v. Bank of England, [1979] 3 All E.R. 700 (1979); Gulf Oil Corp. v. Gulf Canada Ltd., 111 D.L.R.3d 74 (1980).

18. Mar. 9, 1984, 23 I.L.M. 275 (Memorandum of Understanding); *see also,* Dyal, *The Canadian-United States Memorandum of Understanding Regarding Application of National Antitrust Law: New Guidelines for Resolution of Multinational Antitrust Enforcement Disputes*, 6 NW. J. INT'L L. & BUS. 1065 (1984–85).

party.[19]   Again, the procedures remained inadequate, especially with respect to private antitrust lawsuits, because notification and consultation remained discretionary on the part of the state in whose territory such private lawsuits were brought.[20] This shortcoming was exacerbated by the fact that in contemporary American antitrust litigation, private enforcement through treble damages suits has eclipsed public enforcement of U.S. antitrust laws.[21] The latter presumably would have been more amenable to intergovernmental consultation and review than private actors independently exercising their discretion to seek relief from the U.S. court system.

While Canada continued to pursue such cooperative measures, and further relied on other consultative frameworks[22] such as the Organization for Economic Cooperation and Development's (OECD) purely voluntary criteria for cooperation between member states,[23] it became increasingly clear that Canada would have to resort to unilateral defensive measures of its own.

b. Legislative Measures: The Blocking Statutes

Canada's first attempt to draw the sabre in preference to its demonstrably ineffectual rattling through diplomatic efforts involved amendments in 1976 to the (then) Combines Investigation Act.[24] These amendments empowered the Canadian Restrictive Trade Practices Commission to issue orders concerning the implementation of foreign judgments, laws, and directives.[25]

By far the most significant step taken by Canada, however, was the subsequent enactment in 1985 of the Foreign Extraterritorial Measures Act (FEMA).[26]   A Government news release accompanying the introduction of the Bill in Parliament

---

19. Memorandum of Understanding, *id*, at para. 2(2).

20. *Id.,* at para. 11.

21. *See*, W.L. FUGATE, FOREIGN COMMERCE AND THE ANTITRUST LAWS, Vol. 1, at 35 (4th ed. 1991).

22. *See*, A.L.C. DE MESTRAL AND T. GRUCHALLA-WESIERSKI, EXTRATERRITORIAL APPLICATION OF EXPORT CONTROL LEGISLATION: CANADA AND THE U.S.A. 106–113, 116–119 (1990); J.G. CASTEL, EXTRATERRITORIALITY IN INTERNATIONAL TRADE: CANADA AND UNITED STATES OF AMERICA PRACTICE COMPARED 96–98 (1988).

23. Guidelines were drafted as early as 1967, and later replaced by the Recommendations of The Committee of Experts on Restrictive Business Practices in 1979 (revised in 1986).

24. R.S.C. 1970, c. C-23.

25. S.C. 1974–75–76, c. 76; *see also*, Davidson, *The Canadian Response to the Overseas Reach of United States Antitrust Law: Stage I and Stage II Amendments to the Combines Investigation Act* (1979), 2 Canada–U.S. L.J. 166. In 1986, wholesale changes were made to the Act, which was also renamed the *Competition Act; see,* S.C. 1986, c.26. A review of the provisions of the *Competition Act* as it pertains to extraterritoriality issues in competition law may be found in CASTEL, *supra* note 22, at 30–48.

26. R.S.C. 1985, c. F–29.

used unusually frank language to describe the Act's intent, revealing the Canadian government's frustration with prior bilateral and multilateral efforts. FEMA's stated purpose was to "protect Canadian citizens and corporations from measures taken by foreign governments or foreign tribunals with *unacceptable* extraterritorial scope."[27]   Scholarly commentary at the time suggested that the Act was "a remarkable piece of legislation, the culmination point of an often-expressed frustration which Canadians have experienced through the extraterritorial application of American laws in Canada."[28]

FEMA gives the Attorney General of Canada comprehensive powers to prohibit the production of documents or records where the Attorney General believes that a foreign tribunal is purporting to exercise jurisdiction over Canadian commercial interests in such a way as to infringe Canadian sovereignty.[29] In similar circumstances and with the concurrence of the Secretary of State for External Affairs, the Attorney General may prohibit compliance with foreign judicial or governmental measures or directives within Canada.[30] Failure to adhere to such orders of the Attorney General constitutes an indictable offense.[31]

Perhaps the sharpest and most potent provisions of FEMA, however, are those which permit the Attorney General to declare foreign antitrust judgments, even when obtained by private litigants, unenforceable "in any manner in Canada."[32] Alternatively, the Attorney General may order that a money judgment be enforced, but only in an amount specified by the Attorney General.[33] The potential for defeating U.S. treble damage lawsuits is apparent. Further, where a foreign litigant in fact recovers damages against a Canadian entity pursuant to a foreign judgment which is the subject of an order of the Attorney General, the Canadian entity may in turn recover such damages in a Canadian action.[34]

To date, two orders have been made by the Attorney General under FEMA, both in response to American attempts to regulate Cuban trading activities of Canadian companies which are owned or controlled by U.S. parent companies. The first such attempt, the Mack Amendment enacting the U.S. Cuban Asset Control Regulations, prompted the Canadian Attorney General to promulgate the Foreign

---

27. Government of Canada News Release, "Government Introduces Foreign Extraterritorial Measures Bill" (May 28, 1984) quoted in DE MESTRAL AND GRUCHALLA-WESIERSKI, *supra* note 22 (emphasis added).

28. William Graham, *The Foreign Extraterritorial Measures Act*, 11 CAN. BUS. L.J. 410 (1986).

29. FEMA, *supra* note 26, § 3.

30. *Id.* § 5.

31. *Id.* § 7.

32. *Id.* § 8(1)(a).

33. *Id.* § 8(1)(b).

34. *Id.* § 9(1).

Extraterritorial Measures (United States) Order (1990).[35] The Order, which the
Government of Canada stated to be in response to an American infringement of
Canadian sovereignty over the regulation of Canadian-Cuban trade, imposed two
substantive obligations on Canadian companies. First, it prohibited such companies
from complying with the amended American regulations respecting trade with
Cuba. Second, it compelled persons who, by their positions in American-owned
subsidiaries within Canada, could influence compliance with the American
regulations by such subsidiaries, to report to the Attorney General any directions
given pursuant to the Mack Amendment. Congress was prorogued before the Mack
Amendment could be implemented by the U.S. Administration, however, and the
effectiveness of this first FEMA Order was accordingly never tested.

The Americans furnished Canadian authorities with another opportunity to test
the mettle of FEMA, however. In 1992, Congress enacted the Cuban Democracy
Act, (CDA),[36] which the Canadian government deemed to be an exercise of
extraterritorial jurisdiction with respect to Canadian-Cuban trade and commerce
policy. While the objective of the CDA was to modify existing U.S. trade sanctions
against Cuba to encourage a peaceful transition to democracy in Cuba,[37] the CDA
purported to extend applicable sanctions for noncompliance to U.S. subsidiaries
operating outside of the United States.[38]

Willing to take up the challenge, the Canadian government responded pursuant
to Section 5 of FEMA with the Foreign Extraterritorial Measures Act (United
States) Order, 1992.[39] Mirroring the 1990 Order, the 1992 Order imposes two
obligations on Canadian corporations which carry on business in whole or in part
in Canada. First, every such corporation or any of its officers who receives
directives or communications relating to an extraterritorial measure of the United
States from a person who is in a position to influence the corporation's policies
must report such communications to the Attorney General of Canada.[40] Second,
corporations are forbidden from complying with U.S. extraterritorial policy
affecting commerce between Canada and Cuba.[41]

The obvious conundrum for the relevant corporations operating under these
conditions is that compliance with one law necessarily entails violation of the other.
Questions might be raised about the wisdom of placing private economic actors in
an irreconcilable conflict of duties to national sovereigns in an interdependent world
economy. The difficulty for the Canadian government, however, is that, failing
countervailing unilateral measures of its own, which themselves suggest strain on

---

35. SOR/90–751.
36. H.R. 5383, 102nd Congress, 2nd Sess., 106 Stat. 2315 (1992).
37. CDA § 3.
38. *CDA* § 6.
39. SOR/92–584.
40. *Id.* § 3.
41. *Id.* § 4.

the limits of its own sovereignty, Canada would be forfeiting at least partial economic sovereignty to whatever foreign actor was sufficiently brash to try to assume it. It is no new axiom of international relations that extremes beget extremes. The question for both actors who have reached such a state of unilateral offensive and defensive measures is whether anything can be gained by legislated standoffs.

c.   Judicial Constraints on Extraterritorial Acts: Dialogues on Comity

It appeared for a period that the American courts were prepared to recognize these difficulties, as well as the sharp and escalating foreign responses to unbridled extraterritorial assertion of American antitrust jurisdiction, by mitigating the extreme nature of the "effects" doctrine articulated in *Alcoa*. In the *Timberlane* and *Mannington Mills* decisions[42] of the mid-1970s, the Ninth Circuit retreated substantially from the harsh insularity of *Alcoa*, observing that "at some point the interests of the United States are too weak and the foreign harmony incentive for restraint too strong to justify an extraterritorial assertion of jurisdiction."[43]   In response to this perceived reality, the Ninth Circuit elaborated at first instance in *Timberlane I* a doctrine of international comity, which required consideration of various factors before assuming jurisdiction over acts having connections to foreign jurisdictions:

[1] the degree of conflict with foreign law or policy; [2] the nationality or allegiance of the parties and the locations or principal places of business of corporations; [3] the extent to which enforcement by either state can be expected to achieve compliance; [4] the relative significance of effects on the United States as compared with those elsewhere; [5] the extent to which there is explicit purpose to harm or affect American commerce; [6] the foreseeability of such effect; and [7] the relative importance to the violations charged of conduct within the United States as compared with conduct abroad.[44]

---

42.   Timberlane Lumber Co. v. Bank of America Nat. Trust and Sav. Ass'n., 549 F. 2d 597 (9th Cir. 1976) [hereinafter Timberlane I]; Mannington Mills, Inc. v. Congoleum Corp., 595 F. 2d 1287 (3rd Cir. 1979) [hereinafter Mannington Mills]; Timberlane Lumber Co. v. Bank of America Nat. Trust and Sav. Ass'n., 574 F. Supp. 1453 (N.D. Calif., 1983), *aff'd*, 749 F.2d 1378 (1984), *cert. denied*, 472 U.S. 1032, 105 S.Ct. 3514, 87 L.Ed.2d 643 (1985).

43.   Timberlane I, 549 F.2d at 609. *But see* the more heavyhanded approach of the 11th Circuit in In re Grand Jury Proceedings the Bank of Nova Scotia, 740 F. 2d 817 (11th Cir. 1984), and the commentary by Lee Paikin, *Bank of Nova Scotia II: The American Subpoena and the Multinational Enterprise*, 9 CAN. BUS. L.J. 497 (1984).

44.   Timberlane I, 549 F.2d at 614.

Of course, the real question was whether the U.S. Supreme Court would ever endorse this new "rule of reason," or would instead opt to affirm the *Alcoa* approach. The 1991 decision of the Court in *Equal Employment Opportunity Commission v. Arabian American Oil Company (ARAMCO)*[45] suggested an affinity with, if not an affirmation of, *Timberlane I* in its conscientious application of the presumption that "legislation of Congress, unless a contrary intent appears, is meant to apply only within the territorial jurisdiction of the United States."[46] Thus, in the interests of avoiding "unintended clashes between our laws and those of other nations which could result in international discord,"[47] the Court signalled its unwillingness to assume extraterritorial jurisdiction unless expressly mandated to do so by Congress.

While these expressions of restraint might have presaged a harmonization of U.S. and foreign interests in regulating anticompetitive conduct, there are new and disturbing signs that the American judiciary is moving back to its traditionally rigorous pursuit of American policies and interests as represented by *Alcoa*, even where doing so trespasses on the sovereignty of otherwise friendly nations. Whereas the *Timberlane* and *ARAMCO* decisions suggested a substantial tempering of the *Alcoa* doctrine with considerations of international comity, thereby resiling from the full force of Learned Hand C.J.'s formula of strict deference to unilateralism, the U.S. Supreme Court's subsequent pronouncements in *Hartford Fire*[48] appear to have scotched any such trend.

Hartford Fire addressed preliminary motions to dismiss claims by nineteen states and several private plaintiffs. In these claims, it was alleged that a conspiracy existed between domestic insurers and, *inter alia*, English reinsurers to force other domestic insurers to change the terms of their standard domestic commercial liability insurance policies so as to conform with the policies the defendant insurers wanted to sell. Both the United Kingdom and Canada filed *amicus curiae* briefs stating that the application of U.S. antitrust laws to foreign private actors outside the United States in such circumstances would constitute substantial interference with the respective insurance laws of the United Kingdom and Canada.[49] As both states maintained comprehensive and sophisticated regulatory regimes governing insurance practices within their respective jurisdictions, each argued that any

---

45.   499 U.S. 244, 111 S.Ct. 1227, 113 L.Ed.2d 274 (1991).

46.   *Id.*, at 1230.

47.   *Id. See also generally*, on the implications of the ARAMCO approach, J.M. Spears, Address (Canadian Bar Association, International Law Section, Toronto, Sept. 15, 1992).

48.   Hartford Fire Insurance Co. v. California, — U.S. —, 113 S.Ct. 2891, 125 L.Ed.2d 612 (1993) [hereinafter Hartford Fire].

49.   Brief of the Government of the United Kingdom of Great Britain and Northern Ireland as Amicus Curiae in Support of Petitioners, Hartford Fire, *ibid* (No. 91–1128) [hereinafter UK Amicus Brief]; Brief of the Government of Canada as Amicus Curiae in Support of Certain Petitioners (Nov. 19, 1992), Hartford Fire, *id.* (Nos. 91–1111, 91–1128) [hereinafter Canadian Amicus Brief].

extension of American regulatory jurisdiction to cover these same activities would necessarily conflict with its existing domestic law regime.[50]

Canada and the United Kingdom emphasized, respectively, that American judicial assumption of jurisdiction with respect to insurance activities taking place within their respective territories would constitute an "offensive interference" with their sovereign rights and interests.[51] Significantly, both states advanced the further proposition that such interference could in fact imperil American interests, in that it might invite retaliatory measures necessary to safeguard such sovereign rights.[52] In contrast, the *amicus brief* filed on behalf of the U.S. Attorney General evidenced an alarming lack of concern for international comity by stating baldly that: "We believe that courts should not engage in any comity analysis in antitrust actions brought by the United States."[53]

The majority of the U.S. Supreme Court did not accept the arguments of the United Kingdom or Canada. Justice Souter's majority opinion concluded that "even assuming that in a proper case a court may decline to exercise Sherman Act jurisdiction over foreign conduct . . ., international comity would not counsel against exercising jurisdiction in the circumstances alleged here."[54] Justice Souter viewed the only substantial question governing the assumption of jurisdiction to be whether there is in fact a true conflict between domestic and foreign law.[55] Rejecting what might be called the "occupied field" arguments of the United Kingdom and Canada, Justice Souter found that there would be no conflict with foreign law in applying U.S. antitrust law unless foreign law specifically required the foreign actor to act in some fashion contrary to the law of the United States.[56]

In a strong dissenting opinion, Justice Scalia took issue with the majority holding, warning that:

[t]hat breathtakingly broad proposition, which contradicts the many cases discussed earlier, will bring the Sherman Act and other laws into sharp and unnecessary conflict with the legitimate interests of other countries

---

50. UK Amicus Brief at 7–10.

51. *Id.* at 10.

52. Canadian Amicus Brief at 17–18.

53. Brief for the United States as Amicus Curiae Supporting Respondents at 27, Hartford Fire, *supra* note 48.

54 Hartford Fire, *supra* note 48, at 2910.

55. *Id.*

56. *Id.* at 2910–2911. The result is a test curiously analogous to the Canadian constitutional doctrine of paramountcy in situations of federal and provincial legislation which falls within the respective spheres of legislative competence of both orders of government, but which also overlaps. Such overlapping is permissible if there is no direct conflict between the federal and provincial legislation. *See*, Multiple Access Ltd. v. McCutcheon, [1982] 2 S.C.R. 161 (1982).

—particularly our closest trading partners.[57]

While the resulting scope and ultimate impact of *Hartford Fire* remains unclear,[58] the U.S. Federal Trade Commission and the U.S. Department of Justice have cited the decision in serving notice that their policies regarding international and extraterritorial antitrust enforcement will be strengthened. Draft Guidelines released in October 1994[59] include a discussion of relevant U.S. federal antitrust and related statutes, as well as of the factors various enforcement agencies will consider in deciding whether to assert jurisdiction over alleged anticompetitive conduct. The guiding jurisdictional principle with respect to foreign conduct is set forth thus:

> [t]he reach of the U.S. antitrust laws is not limited, however, to conduct and transactions that occur within the boundaries of the United States. Anticompetitive conduct that affects U.S. domestic or foreign commerce may violate the U.S. antitrust laws regardless of where such conduct occurs or the nationality of the parties involved. In a world in which economic transactions observe no boundaries, international recognition of the "effects doctrine" of jurisdiction has become widespread.[60]

With respect to comity, the Draft Guidelines rely on the majority judgment's position in *Hartford Fire* that no conflict will exist between U.S. assertion of antitrust jurisdiction and the legislative or enforcement jurisdiction of the foreign sovereign unless it is not possible for a person subject to the jurisdiction of both

---

57.   Hartford Fire, *supra* note 48, at 2922, apparently referring to decisions in ARAMCO, *supra* note 45; Romero v. International Terminal Operating Co, 358 U.S. 354, 79 S.Ct. 468, 3 L.Ed.2d 368 (1959); American Banana Co. v. United Fruit Co., 213 U.S. 347, 29 S.Ct. 511, 53 L.Ed. 2d 826 (1909); Lauritzen v. Larsen, 345 U.S. 571, 73 S.Ct. 921, 97 L.Ed. 1254 (1953); Alcoa, *supra* note 9; Timberlane I, *supra* note 42; Mannington Mills, *supra* note 42; Montreal Trading Ltd. v. Amax Inc., 661 F. 2d 864 (10th Cir. 1981), *cert. denied*, 455 U.S. 1001, 102 S.Ct. 1634, 71 L.Ed. 2d 868 (1982); Laker Airways v. Sabena, Belgian World Airlines, 731 F. 2d 909 (D.C. Cir. 1984).

58.   For more detailed commentary, *see* J. H. Currie, *Extraterritoriality, Antitrust Law and the U.S. Supreme Court's Decision in Hartford Fire Insurance Company et al. v. California et al., 113 S. Ct. 2891 (1993)*, 1 CAN. INT'L LAWYER 25 (1994); R.C. Renland, *Hartford Fire Insurance Co., Comity and the Extra-territorial Reach of U.S. Antitrust Laws*, 29 Tex. Int. L.J. 159 (1994); S.A. Burr, *The Application of U.S. Antitrust Law to Foreign Conduct: Has Hartford Fire Extinguished Considerations of Comity?*, 15 U. Penn. J. Int'l Bus. L. 221 (1994).

59.   Draft Antitrust Enforcement Guidelines for International Operations, 59 Fed. Reg. 52810-03 (1994) [hereinafter Draft Guidelines]. The Draft Guidelines were released for public comment and are expected to be released in final form in 1995.

60.   *Id.*, at 13.

states to comply with the laws of both.[61] Further, the Draft Guidelines state that comity evaluations are properly performed within the context of the exercise of the prosecutorial discretion of the various U.S. enforcement agencies. The U.S. Department of Justice accordingly "does not believe that it is the role of the courts to second-guess the executive branch's judgment as to the proper role of comity concerns" in antitrust enforcement actions.[62]

The Draft Guidelines confirm the new thrust of U.S. government policy in the wake of *Hartford Fire*, announced in the spring of 1994, "to take enforcement action against foreign conduct that falls within the jurisdictional reach of the Sherman Act, even where the restraints do not have a direct impact on U.S. consumers."[63] To the extent these developments augur a new era of increased extraterritorial unilateralism on the part of the United States, the result is unfortunate and will ultimately prove to be counterproductive for not only the United States but also for its principal trading partners.

At the very time Clinton Administration policy and contemporary U.S. judicial doctrine signal a general resiliation from notions of comity, it is somewhat ironic that Canadian courts are moving to embrace it. Recently, Canadian law applicable to the recognition and enforcement of foreign money judgments has shifted quite dramatically as a result of the recent seminal ruling of the Canadian Supreme Court in *Morguard Investments Ltd.* v. *De Savoye*.[64] In that case the Court repudiated the nineteenth century English common law rule restricting direct enforcement of foreign judgments to situations where the defendant had in some way attorned to the foreign jurisdiction.[65] While *Morguard* is more fundamentally a federalism case which liberalizes jurisdiction to enforce judgments as between provinces under a

---

61. *Id.,* at 21.

62. *Id.,* at 22.

63. *See [Assistant Attorney General] Bingaman Pledges to Expand Civil Enforcement in [Antitrust] Division*, 66 INT'L DEV'PTS. 280, at 281 (Mar. 10, 1994).

64. [1990] 3 S.C.R. 1077 (1990).

65. *See* Emanuel v. Symon, [1908] 1 K.B. 302, 309 (C.A. 1908), (per Buckley, L.J.):

In actions in personam there are five cases in which the Courts of this country will enforce a foreign judgment:
(1) Where the defendant is a subject of the foreign country in which the judgment has been obtained; (2) where he was resident in the foreign country when the action began; (3) where the defendant in the character of plaintiff has selected the forum in which he is afterwards sued; (4) where he has voluntarily appeared; and (5) where he has contracted to submit himself to the forum in which the judgment was obtained.

For critical comment on the pre-Morguard state of the law, *see* V. Black, *Enforcement of Judgments and Judicial Jurisdiction in Canada*, 9 OXFORD J. LEG. ST. 547 (1989); R.J. Sharpe, *The Enforcement of Foreign Judgments*, in DEBTOR–CREDITOR LAW: PRACTICE AND DOCTRINE 641 (1985).

Canadian judicially implied constitutional equivalent of "full faith and credit,"[66] the Court also emphasized the need for comity in light of the exigencies of modern international commerce, leaving open the possibility for its application to foreign judgments.[67]

Justice LaForest, speaking for a unanimous Court, explicitly adopted, *inter alia*, the U.S. Supreme Court formulation of comity in *Hilton v. Guyot*.[68] In setting out his principal justification for applying the principle, Justice LaForest wrote:

> Accommodating the flow of wealth, skills and people across state lines has now become imperative. Under the circumstances, our approach to the recognition and enforcement of foreign judgments would appear ripe for reappraisal. Certainly, other countries, notably the United States and members of the European Economic Community, have adopted more generous rules for the recognition and enforcement of foreign judgments to the general advantage of litigants.[69]

In underscoring the importance of comity to changes in Canadian private international law rules to facilitate the enforcement of foreign judicial decrees, the Supreme Court of Canada effectively endorsed as a judicial tool of a receiving state,

---

66.   Morguard, *supra* note 64, at 1096, 1099: "[T]he English rules seem to me to fly in the face of the obvious intention of the Constitution to create a single country." *See* U.S. CONST. ARTICLE IV, §1: "Full faith and Credit shall be given in each State to the . . . judicial proceedings of every other State."

67.   Provincial superior courts have extended the Morguard principle thus far to judgments of various state jurisdictions and the United Kingdom with relative consistency to date, although there is inconsistent authority in Ontario. *See and compare*, Fabrelle Wallcoverings and Textiles Ltd. v. North American Decorative Products Inc., 6 C.P.C. 3d 170 (Ont. Gen. Div. 1992) (applying Morguard principle to UK judgment); Re Evans Dodd and Gambin Associates, 17 O.R. 3d 803 (Ont. Gen. Div. 1994) (rejecting application of Morguard principle to foreign judgments generally, here a UK judgment). For affirmation of applicability of Morguard to foreign judgments generally, see Clarke v. LoBianco, 84 D.L.R. 4th 244 (B.C.S.C., 1991) (California judgment); Minkler & Kirschbaum v. Sheppard, 60 B.C.L.R. 2d 360 (S.C., 1991) (Arizona judgment); Moses v. Shore Boat Builders Ltd., 83 B.C.L.R. 2d 177 (C.A., 1993), *leave to appeal refused* 23 C.P.C. 3d 294n (Can. Sup. Ct. 1994).

68.   Morguard, *supra* note 64, at 1096, *quoting* Hilton v. Guyot, 159 U.S. 113, 163-164, 16 S.Ct. 139, 40 L.Ed. 95 (1895):

> [c]omity" in the legal sense, is neither a matter of absolute obligation, on the one hand, nor of mere courtesy and good will, upon the other. But it is the recognition which one nation allows within its territory to the legislative, executive or judicial acts of another nation, having due regard both to international duty and convenience, and to the rights of its own citizens or of other persons who are under the protection of its laws. . . .

69.   *Id.,* at 1098.

allowing responsiveness to *appropriate* exercises of jurisdiction by judicial organs of originating states. However, the same considerations should prompt courts of originating states to decline jurisdiction at first instance in cases of clear interference with another jurisdiction. In that respect, *Morguard* asserts a prerequisite to enforcement—for the benefit of Canadian defendants—that the Canadian court must be satisfied under its own rules as to the existence of a "real and substantial connection" between the subject matter of the action and the originating jurisdiction[70] before principles of comity can come into play. Accordingly, it does not appear that comity as applied in *Morguard* would or could extend to any egregious assumptions of extraterritorial jurisdiction by a foreign court, irrespective of supervening statutory constraints such as FEMA.

The Supreme Court of Canada has since adapted the doctrine of comity introduced in *Morguard* to other procedural issues. In *Amchem Products Inc.* v. *British Columbia (Workers' Compensation Board),*[71] the Court recast judicial standards for the issuance of anti-suit injunctions to restrain parties from litigating in foreign jurisdictions. Most recently in *Hunt* v. *T&N PLC,*[72] the Court further extended the *Morguard* doctrine to constrain the application of provincial blocking statutes with respect to litigation in other provinces.

Hunt, even more fundamentally than *Morguard,* must be viewed as a decision resting primarily on constitutional principle,[73] not sensitivity to the legitimate interests of competing sovereigns in the international sphere. Nevertheless, Justice LaForest, again speaking for a unanimous Court, also acknowledges the point we wish to make here:

> Everybody realizes that the whole point of blocking statutes is not to keep documents in the province, but rather to prevent compliance, and so the success of litigation outside the province that that province finds objectionable. This is no doubt part of sovereign right, but it certainly runs counter to comity. In the political realm it leads to strict retaliatory laws and power struggles. And it discourages international commerce and

---

70. *Id.*, at 1104–1107, *citing* Moran v. Pyle National (Canada) Ltd., [1975] 1 S.C.R. 393, 408–09 (1975) (per Dickson J.); *see also,* Indyka v. Indyka, [1969]1 A.C. 33 (H.L. 1969).

71. Amchem Products, Inc. v. British Columbia (Workers' Compensation Board), [1993] 1 S.C.R. 897 1993 (jurisdiction and venue found by Texas Court over suit by Canadian asbestos workers); *see and compare,* SNI Aerospatiale v. Lee Kui Jak [1987] 3 All E.R. 510 (H.L. 1987); Laker Airways v. Sabena, Belgian World Airlines, *supra* note 57; *see generally,* E.L. Hayes, *Forum Non Conveniens in England, Australia and Japan: The Allocation of Jurisdiction in Transnational Litigation,* 26 U.B.C.L. Rev. 41 (1992).

72. Hunt v. T&N PLC, [1993] 4 S.C.R. 289 (1993) (ruling that the Province of Quebec's Business Concerns Records Act, R.S.Q., c. D–12 [am. 1988, S.Q. 1988, c.21, s.66] is constitutionally inapplicable to the blocking of production of documents in British Columbia proceeding).

73. *Id.,* at 329–331 (constitutionally mandated unitary court structure within the Canadian federal state).

efficient allocation and conduct of litigation. It has similar effects on the interprovincial level, effects that offend against the basic structure of the Canadian federation.

As a matter of legislative history, we were told, the Ontario and Quebec statutes were precipitated by the aggressively extraterritorial, "long arm" antitrust statutes of the United States. Unfortunately, these blocking statutes are a blunt response, and themselves have become like long arm statutes that haphazardly end up harming individuals who were not in the jurisdiction and are not pursuing the actions against which the blocking statutes were allegedly originally aimed.[74]

Placed in a global context, the observations of the Supreme Court strike to the heart of the extraterritorial dilemma. Unilateral action, even in the guise of an extended effects doctrine as espoused in the U.S. Draft Guidelines,[75] does not effectively resolve the conflicting interests of sovereign powers in a world where economic currents flow across traditional state boundaries. It merely serves to exacerbate them. The increased porosity of national borders in international commerce mandates greater, certainly not less, sensitivity in extraterritorial projections of sovereign will. It clearly cannot legitimately serve as a justification for any state purporting to unilaterally *internationalize* its national system of law.

Canada's experience in particular illustrates that one state, even one initially willing to negotiate, cooperate and accommodate, will ultimately have no choice but to respond to unilateral trespasses against its sovereignty by resorting to hardline unilateral action of its own. Unilateralism begets conduct in kind that—assuming interdependence applies as a functional limitation on outcomes—serves the interests of no one.

III. CANADA'S ASSERTION OF EXTRATERRITORIAL JURISDICTION AS A TOOL OF INTERNATIONAL LAWMAKING IN ITS OWN INTERESTS

By way of contrast to Canada's principally defensive posture in the duel over extraterritorial application of U.S. competition law, Canada has itself, on occasion, elbowed its way into areas beyond the traditionally and internationally recognized bounds of its territorial jurisdiction. This has been true notwithstanding the controversial nature of its position or assertions by others that its actions have been in violation of the strict letter of international law. Where deemed necessary in its own national interest, and where such self-interest has been linked to broader global interests, Canada has not shied from extending its jurisdictional reach beyond its borders, either through unilateral action, multilateral negotiation, or an effective

---

74. *Id.*, at 327–328.
75. *See supra* note 59; text accompanying notes 60, 63.

combination of both. Canada's peculiar success in such forays may demonstrate the constructive potential of judiciously asserted extraterritorial acts.

There is perhaps no better illustration of this phenomenon than Canada's assertion of sovereignty over the Arctic regions to the north of Canada. For many years, through a policy which has (perhaps not very flatteringly) been described as one of "creeping jurisdiction,"[76] Canada appears to have quietly assumed the *de facto* if not *de jure* existence of such sovereignty. However, the Canadian approach to its interests in the Far North underwent a fundamental transformation in the 1970s.[77] The unauthorized passage of the American oil tanker *Manhattan* through the Northwest Passage in September of 1969 caused considerable consternation in Canada over the international impact of this symbolic act, as well as speculation as to whether Canada's hitherto assumed sovereignty over the Arctic was being deliberately challenged.

The official Canadian response to this perceived throwing down of the territorial gauntlet was both swift—to the extent that any government can so move—and unprecedentedly assertive. In 1970 Parliament enacted the Arctic Waters Pollution Prevention Act[78] (AWPPA), which asserted a sweeping, if functionally defined, jurisdiction over all "Arctic waters . . . in a liquid or frozen state."[79] The area of claimed jurisdiction included all such waters "adjacent to the mainland and islands of the Canadian Arctic within the area . . . measured seaward from the nearest Canadian land [to] a distance of one hundred nautical miles."[80] This was obviously a novel and highly controversial departure from then-existing international law with respect to the extent to which coastal states were entitled to regulate activity in their coastal waters. Canada was suddenly and quite unilaterally extending a very long arm over the sea to its north.

In addition to the vast area to which the operation of the AWPPA was thereby extended, the substantive provisions of the Act were similarly broad. The AWPPA

---

76. D. JOHNSTON, CANADA AND THE NEW INTERNATIONAL LAW OF THE SEA 18 (1985).

77. The new approach appears to have been part of a general reorientation of Canadian foreign policy at the time towards recognizing the primacy of Canada's national interests over those of an international community which had proved persistently reluctant to put the common interest first. This new Canadian policy was evidenced in the 1970 White Paper of the Government of Canada entitled "Foreign Policy for Canadians"; for commentary, *see* Allan Gotlieb and Charles Dalfen, *National Jurisdiction and International Responsibility: New Canadian Approaches to International Law*, 67 A.J.I.L. 229 (1973). For a thorough review of the antecedents to Canada's new foreign policy position on the Arctic, *see* L.C. Green, *Canada and Arctic Sovereignty*, 48 CAN. BAR REV. 740, 741–760 (1970).

78. S.C. 1969–70, c.47. Although enacted in 1970, the Act was not proclaimed in force until Aug. 2, 1972: SI 72–76. Upon Proclamation, a number of regulations were promulgated in order to give effect to the detailed provisions of the Act: SOR/72–253, SOR/72–303, SOR/72–426. The regulations drew heavily on the provisions of the Canada Shipping Act, R.S.C. 1970, c. S-9 (now R.S.C. 1985, c. S-9).

79. *Id.* § 3(2).

80. *Id.* § 3(1).

prohibited the introduction of pollutants of any type into Arctic waters[81] and imposed heavy penalties on violators of this prohibition.[82] Power was conferred on the Canadian executive branch to designate certain areas as "shipping safety control zones" and to prohibit passage through such designated zones by any ship which did not meet certain safety and construction requirements.[83] Compliance with these provisions was to be ensured by "pollution prevention officers," who were empowered to board ships, order them to leave certain zones, and require their assistance in clean-up procedures.[84]

In tacit recognition of having unilaterally overstepped the bounds of its internationally recognized jurisdiction, Canada concomitantly sought to protect its legal position. It amended its acceptance of the compulsory jurisdiction of the International Court of Justice[85] under Article 36(2) of the Statute of that Court,[86] removing from the Court's jurisdiction issues arising from enactment of the AWPPA.[87]

Not at all surprisingly, the sharpest and most immediate reaction came from the Americans, who publicly castigated Canada for acting unilaterally rather than pursuing change of the international legal regime through negotiated agreement.[88] The Americans officially protested that Canada's actions set a dangerous precedent which invited other states to act unilaterally in their own interests, which might not always be as benign as protection of the Arctic marine environment.[89] The Americans were apparently unabashed by the irony of the fact that they had themselves engaged in a very similar exercise in 1945 with the Truman Proclamation, which unilaterally asserted American jurisdiction over the resources of the American continental shelf.[90]

Canada responded by justifying its position on a number of different bases. In addition to pointing out past American practices of the very sort which were now

---

81. *Id.* § 4(1).

82. *Id.* § 18.

83. *Id.* §§ 11, 12.

84. *Id.* §§ 14, 15.

85. Canada first accepted the compulsory jurisdiction of the World Court in 1929 (1968–69 I.C.J. Y.B. 46), but replaced this declaration with a declaration under Article 36(2) of the Statute of the International Court of Justice at the time of enactment of the *AWPPA. See* L.C. GREEN, INTERNATIONAL LAW: A CANADIAN PERSPECTIVE 321–322 (1984).

86. Statute of the International Court of Justice, June 26, 1945, 1945 C.T.S. 7, 59 Stat. 1055, T.S. No. 993, 1983 Y.B.U.N. 133 (entered into force for Canada Nov. 9, 1945).

87. *Canadian Instrument of Notification*, 9 I.L.M. 598 (1970).

88. *See, e.g.*, Louis Henkin, *Arctic Anti-Pollution: Does Canada Make or Break International Law?*, 65 A.J.I.L. 131 (1971).

89. Note of the United States of America to Canada, 9 I.L.M. 605, 605–606 (1970).

90. *See* 4 WHITEMAN DIGEST, at 756–757; *see also* Green, *supra* note 77, at 767–68.

being criticized,[91] Canada invoked an extended concept of self-defense, one which included protection of national environmental concerns:

> [i]t is the further view of the Canadian Government that a danger to the environment of a state constitutes a threat to its security. . . .
>
> . . . .
>
> The proposed anti-pollution legislation is based on the over-riding right of self-defense of coastal states to protect themselves against grave threats to their environment.[92]

The Canadian position went further, however, by implicitly acknowledging the dubious legality of asserting a 100-mile zone of even limited sovereign jurisdiction, functionally defined. Because it had failed to secure international agreement to a regime of absolute liability for pollution of the high and territorial seas by means of multilateral negotiations at the 1969 conference of the International Maritime Consultative Organization[93] Canada defended its unilateral action in terms of development of international law on the matter:

> [i]t is a well established principle of international law that customary international law is developed by state practice.[94]

In the Canadian view, international law on the question of a coastal nation's right to manage the marine environment along its coasts was "either inadequate or non-existent."[95] While the Third U.N. Conference on the Law of the Sea had not yet been convened, the Canadian government clearly had an eye to these eventual negotiations and obviously felt that some proactive groundwork in anticipation of the Canadian negotiating position would be highly useful.

While the Americans were protesting the Canadian initiative, some Canadian critics were worried that the Canadian government had not gone far enough. It was argued that Canada should have asserted outright sovereignty over the entire Arctic sea around and beyond the Arctic archipelago.[96] The concern was that mere

---

91.   Canadian Reply to U.S. Government, 9 I.L.M. 607, 608 (April 16, 1970) .

92.   *Id.* at 608, 610.

93.   *See* R. M. M'Gonigle, *Unilateralism and International Law: The Arctic Waters Pollution Prevention Act*, 34 U.T. FAC. L. REV. 180, 188 (1976); *see also* statements made in the House of Commons at the time of introduction of the Arctic Waters Pollution Prevention Bill. HOUSE OF COMMONS DEBATES (Apr. 16, 1970) at 5964.

94.   Canadian Reply, *supra* note 91, at 608.

95.   The Honourable Mitchell Sharp, Secretary of State for External Affairs, HOUSE OF COMMONS DEBATES (April 16, 1970) at 5951.

96.   *See* F. Griffiths, *Canadian Sovereignty and Arctic International Relations* in THE

assertion of limited sovereignty in terms of pollution management was an implicit waiver of longstanding Canadian claims to absolute sovereignty in the Arctic. This concern was particularly apparent from the Parliamentary debates which accompanied passage of the AWPPA. The Leader of the Opposition in the Commons expressed the fear that the Act's failure to explicitly claim full sovereignty over the Arctic would in fact weaken Canada's ultimate position with respect to such sovereignty.[97]

The government's response revealed the true intended scope of Canada's unilateral extension of its jurisdiction:

> [w]e claim these to be Canadian 'internal' waters. We regard the waters between the islands as our waters, and we always have.[98]

As we shall see presently, Canada bided its time before formalizing this more radical claim. Meanwhile, Canada set about shoring up its position and ensuring that its unilateral assertion of functional jurisdiction took on international lawmaking significance.

Canada parlayed its negotiating position at the Third U.N. Conference on the Law of the Sea with considerable success as measured by the contents of the 1982 Convention.[99] Consensus emerged at the Conference in a number of important areas, all of which were crucial to the entrenchment in international law of the Canadian position with respect to environmental jurisdiction in the Arctic.[100] In particular, agreement was reached on (1) a uniform 12-mile territorial sea;[101] (2) methods of delineation of the territorial sea;[102] (3) a regime of mid-oceanic archipelagic states;[103] (4) the restriction of the right of transit passage through international straits to "straits used for international navigation;"[104] (5) the 200-mile exclusive economic zone extending from baselines of the territorial sea;[105] and (6) the concept of the continental shelf.[106] Of most obvious direct relevance to the

---

ARCTIC IN QUESTION 1571 (E. Dosman, ed., 976); *see also*, Green, *supra* note 77, at 760, 771, 775.

97. House of Commons Debates (Apr. 16, 1970) at 5941–43.

98. *Id.* at 5953.

99. United Nations Convention on the Law of the Sea, Oct. 7, 1982, U.N. Doc. A/Conf. 62/122 (1982), 21 I.L.M. 1261 [hereinafter UNCLOS]; *see generally*, U.N. Conference on the Law of the Sea, Official Records, Vols. I-XVII (1973–1984).

100. *See* M. Killas, *The Legality of Canada's Claims to the Waters of its Arctic Archipelago*, 19 OTT. L. REV. 95, 98–99 (1987).

101. UNCLOS, *supra* note 99, art. 3.

102. *Id.* arts. 4–16.

103. *Id.* arts. 46–54.

104. *Id.* arts. 34–45.

105. *Id.* arts. 55–75.

106. *Id.* arts. 76–85.

validity of the AWPPA, however, was the acceptance of special rights for Arctic states in UNCLOS Article 234, which provides:

> Coastal States have the right to adopt and enforce nondiscriminatory laws and regulations for the prevention, reduction and control of marine pollution from vessels in ice-covered areas within the limits of the exclusive economic zone, where particularly severe climatic conditions and the presence of ice covering such areas for most of the year create obstructions or exceptional hazards to navigation, and pollution of the marine environment could cause major harm to or irreversible disturbance of the ecological balance. Such laws and regulations shall have due regard to navigation and the protection and preservation of the marine environment based on the best available scientific evidence.

Although the Convention has not yet come into force and the United States, significantly, has failed to ratify it, the inclusion of such a provision in an instrument which, in large part, has been authoritatively acknowledged as reflective of customary international law[107] is a significant vindication of Canada's sortie onto what was widely believed at the time to be forbidden ground.

Perhaps emboldened by this success, the Canadians went further, again in response to prodding by their ever restless neighbor to the south. In August 1985, without seeking permission from Canadian authorities, the U.S. Coast Guard icebreaker *Polar Sea* passed through waters of the Arctic archipelago directly to Canada's north from Baffin Bay to the Beaufort Sea on its way to Alaska. In Canada's view, these were internal waters within its sovereign jurisdiction, or so it had been assumed.[108]

The resulting furor in Canadian political circles[109] prompted the Canadian government to once again act unilaterally, this time to establish a system of baselines enclosing the Arctic archipelago to Canada's north, effective January 1,

---

107. *Id.* art. 234. The UNCLOS regime governing the deep-sea bed as part of the "common heritage of mankind" has been persistently objected to by the United States and other developed states. For discussion, *see* Brownlie, *supra* note 2, at 253–257. *See also,* Johnston, *supra* note 76, *passim;* H. KINDRED *et al., supra* note 7, at 702–704.

108. Interestingly, however, on Aug. 1, 1985, the Americans assured Canadian officials that the *Polar Sea* would be in compliance with the provisions of the AWPPA, apparently acknowledging Canada's right to manage the Arctic marine environment. *See* Killas, *supra* note 100, at 96 n.10.

109. *See, e.g.,* the comments of Mr. Chrétien of the Official Opposition, *House of Commons Debates* (September 10, 1985) at 6465; the statement of Mr. Clark, Secretary of State for External Affairs, *id.* at 6461–6463; the Statement issued by the Ministers of External Affairs, Transport and Indian and Northern Affairs, Aug. 1, 1985; and statements made by then Prime Minister Brian Mulroney, *P.M.'s Stand on Arctic Toughest Yet,* THE GLOBE AND MAIL, August 23, 1985, at 5.

1986.[110] The baselines, drawn around the outer perimeter of the archipelago, purported to enclose as internal waters that part of the Arctic sea to their landward side and established a basis for measuring the territorial sea and exclusive economic zone on their outward side. As has been pointed out elsewhere,[111] this represented at the very least an extension of existing international law with respect to the use of straight baselines,[112] particularly with respect to a coastal as opposed to a mid-oceanic archipelago.

Notwithstanding the opposition that the measure was likely to meet, particularly from the Americans who had continuously insisted that the Northwest Passage is an international strait and therefore part of the high seas, Canada felt justified in its position by both necessity and history:

> The exercise of functional jurisdiction in Arctic waters is essential to Canadian interests. But it can never serve as a substitute for the exercise of Canada's full sovereignty over the waters of the Arctic archipelago. Only full sovereignty protects the full range of Canada's interests. This full sovereignty is vital to Canadian security. It is vital to Canada's Inuit people. And it is vital to Canada's nationhood. The policy of this government is to exercise Canada's full sovereignty in and over the Arctic archipelago. We will accept no substitutes.[113]

While the ultimate outcome of this further assertion of extraterritorial jurisdiction in Canada's Far North remains to be seen, Canada is at it again, this time reaching beyond the internationally recognized limits of its jurisdiction off its east coast. Responding to overfishing by foreign fleets just beyond Canada's 200-mile exclusive economic zone, which seriously jeopardizes the continued existence of Atlantic fish stocks and undermines Canadian stock management strategies, the Canadian government has served notice that it intends to take whatever steps are necessary to "correct the situation."[114] In January of 1994, for instance, Canada's Fisheries Minister indicated that, if necessary, Canada was prepared to intercept foreign fishing vessels suspected of overfishing on the high seas and that Canada's Department of National Defence had already been given

---

110. Territorial Sea Geographical Co-ordinates (Area 7) Order, P.C. 1985–2739, SOR/85–872, C. Gaz. 1985.II. 3996.

111. *See* Killas, *supra* note 100, at 95, 105.

112. As articulated by the International Court of Justice in the Anglo-Norwegian Fisheries Case (United Kingdom v. Norway), 1951 I.C.J. 116 (Dec. 18); and the Convention on the Territorial Sea and the Contiguous Zone, Apr. 29, 1958, 516 U.N.T.S. 205, Articles 3–4.

113. The Hon. Joe Clark, Secretary of State for External Affairs, HOUSE OF COMMONS DEBATES, (Sept. 10, 1985) at 6463.

114. *See, e.g.,* the terse statement of intent contained in the new government's Speech from the Throne, Jan. 18, 1994: "The Government will take the action required to ensure that foreign overfishing of East Coast stocks comes to an end."

instructions to develop a strategy for such interceptions.[115]

In fact, in early April 1994, Canadian coast guard officials intercepted and boarded, in international waters some 228 nautical miles east of the Canadian coastline, the *Kristina Logos*, a fishing trawler flying the Panamanian flag found taking cod in contravention of a Northwest Atlantic Fisheries Organization (NAFO) moratorium[116] on such fishing.[117] Although a technicality meant that the action was not a clear precedent in terms of exercising purely extraterritorial jurisdiction,[118] it did illustrate the Canadian government's determination to "intercept . . . vessels on the high seas even though this would be beyond its territorial waters and, as such, illegal under the United Nations Convention on the Law of the Sea."[119]

In May 1994, moreover, the Canadian Parliament passed legislation which makes it an offense for anyone to fish for straddling fish stocks on defined sections of the high seas in contravention of prescribed conservation measures. The legislation empowers Canadian fisheries officers to use force in intercepting offending vessels in international waters and bring them to Canadian ports for prosecution.[120] In July 1994, Canadian fisheries officers flexed this new legislative

---

115. *See* CCH, OTTAWA LETTER, Feb. 1, 1994, at 473 (a weekly newsletter on Canadian legislative developments published by CCH Canadian Ltd.).

116. *See infra* text accompanying note 122.

117. *See Canada vows to stop 'pirates,'* THE GLOBE AND MAIL, Apr. 4, 1994, at A1–A2.

118. It appeared that, while the *Kristina Logos* was sailing under the Panamian flag at the time of its arrest by Canadian officials, the ship had previously been registered in Canada, which registration had not been properly removed by the vessel's owner. This oversight permitted Canadian officials to seize the ship without, strictly speaking, exercising jurisdiction on a purely extraterritorial basis.

119. *See* CCH, OTTAWA LETTER, Jan. 18, 1994, at 459.

120. Bill C-29, An Act to Amend the Coastal Fisheries Protection Act, S.C. 1994, c. 14, passed by the House of Commons May 11, 1994; Royal Assent May 12, 1994; in force May 25, 1994 by Order in Council P.C. 1994-835 (May 25, 1994), SI/94-74. *See also* the amendments to the Coastal Fisheries Protection Regulations consequent on the amendments to the Act, P.C. 1994-836 (May 25, 1994), SOR/94-362. The purpose of the Act is stated in § 2 thereof:
2.   The [Coastal Fisheries Protection] Act is amended by adding the following after section 5:
"5.1 Parliament, recognizing
(a)   that straddling stocks on the Grand Banks of Newfoundland are a major renewable world food source having provided a livelihood for centuries to fishers,
(b)   that those stocks are threatened with extinction,
(c)   that there is an urgent need for all fishing vessels to comply in both Canadian fisheries waters and the NAFO Regulatory Area with sound conservation and management measures for those stocks, notably those measures that are taken under the *Convention on Future Multilateral Cooperation in the Northwest Atlantic Fisheries*, done at Ottawa on Oct. 24, 1978, Canada Treaty Series 1979 No. 11, and

muscle and arrested two U.S. vessels and their crews for allegedly fishing for Icelandic scallops on the edge of the Grand Banks just outside Canada's 200-mile exclusive economic zone.[121]

The Canadian approach is not one of simple belligerence, however. Behind the scenes and in spite of the tough rhetoric of unilateral action, an intense diplomatic effort is underway to legitimate and gain international acceptance for unilateral acts of marine conservation beyond a state's 200-mile exclusive economic zone. Canada has chosen to meld its own obvious self-interest in preserving a crucial economic resource with the broader global interest in preserving natural resources, in order to create an impetus for change in the international law relating to a coastal state's right, if not obligation, to take such steps as are necessary to manage properly the resources off its coasts. This diplomatic effort has begun to bear fruit. In early February 1994, the fourteen members of the Northwest Atlantic Fisheries Organization agreed, at Canada's virtual insistence, to impose a ban on all fishing of southern Grand Banks cod in international waters.[122]

Further diplomatic efforts have been undertaken at the United Nations Conference on Straddling Fish Stocks and Highly Migratory Fish Stocks. The Canadian Fisheries Minister, addressing the Conference at the opening session of its March 14–31, 1994 negotiating round, stressed the critical role which the Conference could play in helping Canada and other coastal states end high seas overfishing.[123] The Minister's address also emphasized the need to be practical and not overly legalistic in addressing modern world problems:

> International law should be based on experience. It should recognize serious problems. It should provide practical means to solve them. *This conference should find practical means to solve the serious problems we face globally* in high seas fisheries with respect to both straddling stocks and highly migratory species.[124]

(d) that some foreign fishing vessels continue to fish for those stocks in the NAFO Regulatory Area in a manner that undermines the effectiveness of sound conservation and management measures, declares that the purpose of section 5.2 is to enable Canada to take urgent action necessary to prevent further destruction of those stocks and to permit their rebuilding, while continuing to seek effective international solutions to the situation referred to in paragraph (d)."

121. *See* CCH, OTTAWA LETTER, Aug. 2, 1994, at 636.

122. Fisheries and Oceans Canada, News Release, 94/10E, Feb. 10, 1994. NAFO's membership includes Bulgaria, Canada, Cuba, Denmark (for the Faroe Islands and Greenland), Estonia, the European Union, Iceland, Japan, Latvia, Lithuania, Norway, Poland, Romania, and Russia. Its resolutions bind only the members of the Organization.

123. Government of Canada News Release, 94/18E, Mar. 11, 1994.

124. Honourable Brian Tobin, Canada's Minister of Fisheries and Oceans, *Notes for an Address* (United Nations Conference on Straddling Fish Stocks and Highly Migratory Fish Stocks, New York, Mar. 14, 1994) (emphasis added).

Significantly, while the balance of the Minister's address naturally focused on Canada's concerns over its east coast fisheries, several references were made to similar situations elsewhere and to the need for change to international law in the *global* interest.

On August 23, 1994, the Conference Chair tabled a thirty-one page draft convention, and Canada has served notice that it will be pursuing its objectives during the Conference's two planned 1995 sessions with a view to finalizing the discussions and the draft convention.[125]

While the success or failure of Canada's dual approach of threatened unilateral action supported by diplomatic pressure in extending coastal states' management rights over their coastal resources has yet to be determined, a pattern is being repeated here. For present purposes, however, the interesting question is whether there is anything peculiar to the Canadian approach which makes it particularly well-adapted to securing Canadian interests without catalysing international disapproval or reprisals. Even more fundamentally, it may reveal the creative role that can be played by exercises of extraterritorial jurisdiction when such exercises are carefully aimed and even more carefully delivered.

IV. LEGITIMATING EXTRATERRITORIAL ASSERTIONS OF JURISDICTION

Rigid foreclosures of extraterritorial competence and legitimacy in international law have little more explanatory value than the pragmatic assertions of extraterritorial reach by various state actors which the law of nations seeks to enjoin. States reach out under their own law, sometimes successfully and sometimes not. The one certainty is that such claims will always be made as nationally-determined necessity demands. The role for international law is not to prohibit the inevitable, but to appropriately channel, constrain and thereby legitimate such practice. We suggest that legitimacy—beyond the success or failure of the individual case—requires a prescriptive rules-based rather than power-based justification for resort to such action. Of course, in this, we may also state the obvious. A framework of neutral principles does and will provide a basis for the recognition and acceptance of extraterritorial acts by other states. In turn, any state that seeks to embark on such a course may use such a framework as a measuring stick.

It is submitted that Canadian practice, both in terms of the extraterritorial reach of Canada's laws as well as Canadian responses to the extraterritorial incursions of other sovereigns, has remained sensitive to and generally supportive of a rules-based approach. The issues of environmental protection for Arctic waters and coastal state fisheries jurisdiction on the high seas each highlight extraterritorial claims premised on an appreciation of the possibility of reconfiguring an

---

125. *See* CCH, OTTAWA LETTER, Sept. 13, 1994, at 672.

international political consensus—at least among the most affected state actors—on the applicable law that will ultimately support and legitimate the claims that have been made. On the other hand, the "effects doctrine" *per se* contrasts sharply with an international lawmaking or "consensus building" approach. It reflects neither a concern for, nor posits the necessity of, a legitimating function in terms of law-making beyond the domestic legal priorities of the state invoking it. Rather, the effects doctrine requires only a finding of adverse impact on domestic interests at home or abroad[126] of conduct which, if committed within the state would be contrary to its law, notwithstanding the lawfulness of such conduct in the jurisdiction where it actually occurred. In short, under the effects doctrine, the resulting interference with the laws and jurisdiction of other state actors and possible conflict with international law standards simply do not form part of the internal calculus of legitimacy.

By way of contrast, the rule of reason advanced in part through the *Timberlane* doctrine of comity,[127] arguably codified in Section 403 of the American Law Institute's Restatement (Third) of the Foreign Relations Law of the United States,[128] does specifically incorporate the legitimating function of referencing international legal considerations to balance domestic interests with those of other states. In our view, such an approach is to be commended, while the majority opinion of the U.S. Supreme Court in the *Hartford Fire* case,[129] together with recent adjustments to U.S. antitrust policy reflective of that opinion, must be viewed as damaging to the international legal order and practically unproductive for all states concerned.

Several of the criteria advanced by the U.S. Court of Appeals for the Ninth Circuit in *Timberlane I*[130] identify exogenous variables from the international domain to inform the domestic legal determination of whether extraterritorial jurisdiction should be exercised or declined. Three of those particularly underscore our argument:

[1]   the degree of conflict with foreign law or policy. . .

[3]   the extent to which enforcement by either state can be
        expected to achieve compliance;

[4]   the relative significance of effects on the United States
        as compared with those elsewhere; . . .

---

126. *See* Alcoa, *supra* note 9.

127. *See infra* text accompanying notes 42–44.

128. *See* RESTATEMENT (THIRD) OF FOREIGN RELATIONS LAW § 403 (1987) and Comment, with Reporters' Notes at 245–254 [hereinafter Restatement (Third)].

129. *See supra* note 48.

130. *See supra* note 42.

In *Mannington Mills*,[131] the U.S. Court of Appeals for the Third Circuit partially reformulated and extended the original eight factors in *Timberlane I* into a ten-factor balancing test. Significantly, for our purposes, it added consideration of "[p]ossible effect upon foreign relations if the court exercises jurisdiction and grants relief. . . ."[132]

It is also significant that consideration of the first of the *Timberlane I/Mannington Mills* factors is consistent with the presumption—commonplace in the domestic legal rules of major state actors—that legislators do not intend to mandate violation of international law unless clear and express statutory language compels a contrary conclusion.[133]

More fundamentally, the rule of reason articulated in Section 403 of the latest American Restatement on the Foreign Relations Law of the United States highlights principles which limit domestic jurisdiction to prescribe by direct reference to foreign state interests and the international system. Subsection 403(2) is comprehensive in this respect, providing that the issue of "[w]hether exercise of jurisdiction over a person or activity is unreasonable is determined by evaluating *all relevant factors*, including, where appropriate . . ." eight factors to be considered, three of which emphasize the point we wish to make here:[134]

(1) the existence of justified expectations that might be protected or hurt by the regulation;

(2) the *importance* of the regulation *to the international* political, legal, or economic *system*;

---

131. *See supra* note 42, at 1297–1298.

132. *Id.* The remaining nine factors as restated and elaborated by the *Mannington* Court are: (1) Degree of conflict with foreign law or policy; (2) Nationality of the parties; (3) Relative importance of the alleged violation of conduct [in the United States] compared to that abroad; (4) Availability of a remedy abroad including the pendency of litigation there; (5) Existence of intent to harm or affect American commerce and its foreseeability; (6) [text quoted, *supra*]; (7) Whether a party will be . . . forced to perform an act illegal in either country or be under conflicting requirements . . . if relief is granted; (8) Whether the court can make its order effective; (9) Whether an order for relief would be acceptable in [the United States] if made by the foreign national under similar circumstances; and (10) Whether a treaty with the affected nation has addressed the issue.

133. The presumption exists, *e.g.*, in American law. *See* ARAMCO, *supra* note 45; Alexander Murray v. Schooner Charming Betsy, 2 Cranch 64, 6 U.S. 64, 116, 2 L.Ed. 208 (1804) (opinion of Marshall, C.J.). In Canadian law *see* Reference re Powers of Ottawa Rockcliffe Park to Levy Rates on Foreign Legations' and High Commissioners' Residences, [1943] S.C.R. 208, 231 (1943); Daniels v. White and The Queen, [1968] S.C.R. 517, 541 (1968); Ernewein v. Minister of Employment & Immigration, [1980] 1 S.C.R. 639, 662 (1980), Pigeon J. dissenting on another point. And in British law see Salomon v. Commissioners of Customs and Excise, [1967] 2 Q.B. 116 (C.A. 1967); Post Office v. Estuary Radio Ltd., [1968] 2 Q.B. 740 at 757 (C.A. 1968).

134. Restatement (Third) § 403(2) (1987), at 244–245 (emphasis added).

(3) the extent to which the regulation is *consistent with* the traditions of *the international system;.* . . .

The Commentary to Section 403 elaborates, *inter alia* that "[n]o priority or other significance is implied in the order in which the factors are listed"[135] and the Reporters' Notes add that a condition of reciprocity is not in itself a criterion for applying the rule of reason.[136]

We are left with the question whether Section 403 actually restates a rule of international law or merely propounds one. The claim for a rule does appear at odds with the current thinking of a majority of U.S. Supreme Court Justices and the U.S. Attorney General, not to mention a recent, important competition law ruling of the European Court of Justice.[137] Moreover, on its merits, the rule of reason manifested in both Section 403 of the American Restatement and its underlying jurisprudence has been characterized as nothing more than a modified version of the effects doctrine.[138] Some American scholars also find it troublesome for its excessive vagueness, particularly with respect to the absence of any prioritization of the factors to be considered,[139] and for possible U.S. constitutional disabilities arising from allegedly nonjusticiable aspects of interest balancing under the test.[140]

---

135. *Id.,* at 246.

136. But, there is the caveat that "in making the evaluation called for by this section, it is useful to consider whether the regulating state would regard it as reasonable were the other state to exercise regulatory jurisdiction if the situation were reversed." *Id.,* at 251.

137. *See* In Re Wood Pulp Cartel v. E.C. Commission, [1984] C.M.L.R. 901 (Eur. Ct. Justice 1984), *aff'g in part and voiding in part,* 54 C.M.L.R. 474 (E.C. Comm'n 1985); *see also* J.J. Friedberg, *The Convergence of Law in an Era of Political Integration: The Wood Pulp Case and the Alcoa Effects Doctrine,* 52 U. PITTSBURGH L. REV. 289 (1991). *But see contra,* Note, *European Community Law: The Territorial Scope of Application of ECC Antitrust Law,* 30 HARV. INT'L L.J. 195 (1989).

138. Friedberg, *supra* note 37, at 304 ("The Restatement (Third) of Foreign Relations Law exemplifies the retrenchment of the American effects doctrine. . . ."); *see generally,* C. Olmstead, *Restatement: Jurisdiction,* 14 YALE J. INT'L. L. 468 (1989).

139. *See* R. J. Weintraub, *The Extraterritorial Application of Antitrust and Securities Laws: An Inquiry into the Utility of a 'Choice-of-Law' Approach,* 70 TEXAS L. REV. 1799 (1992); L. Weinberg, *Against Comity,* 80 GEO. L.J. 53 (1991).

140. The argument here is a concern for justiciability based on the "political questions" doctrine to the extent that interest-balancing between domestic and foreign interests are executive and legislative rather than judicial functions. *See, e.g.,* R. P. Alford, *The Extraterritorial Application of Antitrust Laws: The United States and European Community Approaches,* 33 VA. J. INT'L L. 1, 13–14 (1992); P. M. Roth, *Reasonable Extraterritoriality: Correcting the 'Balance of Interests',* 41 INT'L. & COMP. L.Q. 245, 278 (1992).

While it has been affirmed by the U.S. Supreme Court in Baker v. Carr, 369 U.S. 186, 82 S.Ct. 691, 7 L.Ed.2d 663 (1962), the "political question" doctrine remains a confused and unsatisfactory aspect of American constitutional theory and practice. *See* Louis Henkin, *Is There a 'Political Question' Doctrine?,* 85 YALE L.J. 597 (1976); LAURENCE TRIBE, AMERICAN CONSTITUTIONAL LAW § 3–13 (2nd ed. 1988). For a recent revisionist critique,

In our view, if Section 403 is only a modification of the effects doctrine, the difference is of such a degree as to constitute a difference in kind that may be ultimately decisive for the question of legitimacy at the international level. We suggest that it is reflective of international law or, at minimum, a ripe candidate for international law status. The incorporation of analogous rules of reason and explicit reference to comity in the 1991 Agreement Between the United States and the Commission of the European Community Regarding the Application of their Competition Laws,[141] provides significant evidence in support of legal validity. This view is strengthened by an appreciation of the counterproposition that the *Alcoa* version of the effects doctrine is itself fundamentally at odds with international law.[142] More to the point, we agree with the recent scholarly observation that the jurisdictional rule of reason is and "will remain a lasting fixture on the legal landscape precisely because it represents the only genuine, though inexact, attempt by courts to fashion a jurisdictional test which incorporates the legitimate sovereign interests of foreign nations."[143]

V. CONCLUSION

Extraterritorial acts stem from perceptions of necessity on the part of interests the invoking state decides it is obligated by its own law to protect. External legitimacy for extraterritorial acts must, however, derive from a principled basis upon which to recognize that the priorities of the invoking state should be accepted and given preferential or controlling status. Cognizance of the international lawmaking purposes and potential of specific extraterritorial acts suggests a compelling justification for unilateral acts that can ultimately support shared expectations, interests and goals of the international community.

Canadian responses to extraterritorial incursions from other jurisdictions illustrate the limitations of real and perceived unilateralism, assuming that there is

---

see T. M. FRANCK, POLITICAL QUESTIONS/JUDICIAL ANSWERS: DOES THE RULE OF LAW APPLY TO FOREIGN AFFAIRS? (1992), arguing for a "rule of evidence" in place of the political questions doctrine: "Constitutionality . . . is for courts to détermine." *Id.* at 136. The Supreme Court of Canada has explicitly rejected a "political question" doctrine under the Canadian Constitution. *See, e.g.,* Operation Dismantle Inc. v. The Queen, [1985] 1 S.C.R. 441 (1985) ; H.S. Fairley, *Developments in Constitutional Law: The 1984–85 Term*, 8 SUP. CT. REV. 53, 82–91 (1986).

141.   Concluded Sept. 23, 1991, reprinted in 30 I.L.M. 1487. *See* in particular Articles V ("positive comity") and VI(3) ("rule of reason" factors).

142.   *See* Mann, *supra* note 7, at 104 (1964-I) ("from the point of view of public international law the Alcoa decision cannot be justified. . . ."); *cf.* E. M. Fox, *Extraterritoriality and Antitrust—Is 'Reasonableness' the Answer?*, FORDHAM CORP. L. INST. 49, 54 (B. Hawk ed., 1987) (Alcoa doctrine founds jurisdiction on U.S. interests and does "not give way in the face of even weighty foreign interests.").

143.   Alford, *supra* note 140, at 16.

some degree of interdependence between the invoking and the target state(s). Even where the invoking state may enjoy *carte blanche* because of its ability to enforce its extraterrritorial conduct in a particular case (a political, economic, military, or other calculus essentially outside the law), the attitude and practice of affected states becomes that much worse when the balance of power shifts back to one of mutual dependence. By that point, however, the international legal system may be less able to supply appropriate boundaries and guidelines and simple retaliation is the order of the day.

For most members of the international community most of the time, rules of reason, whatever their precise content, provide a principled and practically more viable alternative to the vagaries of the power equation. The content itself can remain elastic. Canadian practice in asserting extraterritorial competence may suggest that approaches geared to the development of new perceptions of common interest capable of subsequent legal recognition—the law-making function—are additional sources of legitimation for extraterritorial acts. Self-serving exercises which nevertheless advance the prospect of necessary revisions to international law, subject to ultimate acceptance by other state actors, may also be to that extent retrospectively justified.

Critiques premised only on the potential indeterminacy of judicial interest-balancing do not justify a refusal to invite international and domestic courts to apply a rule of reason where, absent constitutionally valid executive or legislative limitations on such a rule, the application of that option lies open. Assuming we do indeed have a rule of international law to work with, nonjudicial lawmakers and enforcers will do well to appreciate and factor these same considerations into their decisions regarding extraterritorial assertions of authority.

EXTRATERRITORIALITY AND INTERNATIONAL LAW

Shigeo Kawagishi

I. INTRODUCTION

The problem of extraterritoriality—the extraterritorial application of domestic law—is one of the most complex issues in international law, for it involves not only legal disputes but also conflicts of foreign, economic and social policies between states.

Under international law, a sovereign nation has the exclusive jurisdiction to impose its own laws and policies within its territory without interference from other states. The extraterritorial application of such laws and policies therefore inevitably clashes with the legitimate interests of other states. That being so, the question arises as to whether and to what extent a state is authorized under international law to enact and enforce law and regulations with respect to the persons and activities located within the territory of other states. The international community has become more economically interdependent so that the importance and scope of the extraterritoriality problem has grown in recent years.

The present chapter is an attempt to examine briefly the extraterritorial reach of domestic law in international law, with particular reference to competition laws and export control laws. First, a review of the jurisdictional principles of international law, that is, the territoriality principle and exceptions, will be made. Then, the extraterritorial jurisdiction in United States antitrust laws and export control laws under international law will be examined. A variety of approaches of restraint and moderation for the resolution of conflicting claims of jurisdiction between states will follow. The conclusion will stress the desirability of concluding international agreements for the allocation of jurisdiction in this field.

II. JURISDICTIONAL PRINCIPLES OF INTERNATIONAL LAW

Jurisdiction is a manifestation of state sovereignty. It means the right of a state to exert its authority through the instrumentality of its legislative, administrative or judicial branches. It is generally accepted in international law that a state has exclusive jurisdiction over a defined territory, including the persons and activities within that territory, which is free from intervention. The territorial principle of jurisdiction is, therefore, of primary importance in international law. However, international law recognizes other bases of jurisdiction which provide exceptions to exclusive territorial jurisdiction: these are the nationality principle, the protective principle and the universality principle.[1]

a.   The Principle of Territoriality

The principle of territoriality is the most fundamental of all the jurisdictional principles of international law. Under territoriality, a state has jurisdiction to prescribe law with respect to persons and property or conduct taking place within its territory, to the exclusion of the jurisdiction of other states, so that, in principle, no state can infringe on the sovereignty of other states by way of its legislation.

This principle has been extended to deal with the quite different situation in which prohibited conduct transcends the boundaries of a particular state. In this context, in response to the two possible situations, a distinction is made between the subjective territoriality principle and the objective territoriality principle. Under the former, a state may prescribe a rule of law with respect to an offense that is committed within its territory but completed abroad. Under the latter, a state may prescribe a rule of law with respect to conduct that, while taking place outside its territory, produces some effects within its territory, but only if at least one constituent element of the conduct takes place within the territory of the prescribing state.

b.   Exceptions to the Principle of Territoriality

As already indicated, the territoriality principle does not exclude other bases of jurisdiction in international law. It is widely accepted in international law that a state has jurisdiction over its nationals wherever they may be for offenses that they commit abroad. The nationality principle is therefore the most generally recognized exception to the principle of territoriality. Nevertheless, although a state may prescribe the conduct of its nationals abroad, it is not authorized to enforce that jurisdiction by requiring conduct which is illegal under the law of other states.

---

1.   RESTATEMENT (THIRD) OF FOREIGN RELATIONS 237 (1987) [hereinafter RESTATEMENT (THIRD)].

The principle is applicable to juridical persons as well. Under international law, therefore, a state likewise has jurisdiction over its companies wherever their economic activities take place. Generally speaking, a company is considered as a national of the state where it is incorporated, although there is no universally accepted test for the nationality of a company. In this connection, although a state may subject to its law the domestic subsidiaries of a foreign parent company, the question remains whether a state is authorized to prescribe the conduct of foreign subsidiaries of a domestic parent company by applying the nationality principle on the basis of a corporate or personal link between them.

Furthermore, under the passive personality principle, a state may exercise jurisdiction over foreign nationals who commit specific crimes against its own nationals outside its territory. In recent years, the principle has been increasingly accepted as applied to terrorist and other attacks on a state's nationals, including its diplomatic representatives.[2] For instance, the International Convention against the Taking of Hostages[3] authorizes a state to exercise jurisdiction over all acts of hostage-taking when the victim is a national of the state if that state considers it appropriate. The principle accordingly has substantial support in contemporary national legislation in order to domestically implement such treaty obligations.[4]

Second, it is also fully accepted in international law that a state protects its security by means of the exercise of its jurisdiction. In such a manner, under the protective principle, a state has jurisdiction over persons with respect to attacks on its security, territorial integrity or political independence. The principle is justified on the ground of self-defense in international law so that a state has the right to protect itself from any attack originating abroad, including a threat to a state's economy, such as the counterfeiting of currency abroad.

Third, under the universality principle, a state is authorized to exercise jurisdiction over a certain number of universally recognized offenses, such as piracy, regardless of where they are committed and on the sole basis of the presence of the offenders. It does not matter whether such offenses are international crimes or merely a matter of international concern. In effect, it is important that states condemn and cooperate to suppress such offenses in the interest of the international community as a whole. For instance, in conformity with the principle of *aut dedere aut judicare*[5] purported to supplement primary jurisdiction, the Convention for the Suppression of Unlawful Seizure of Aircraft obliges a state to prosecute and punish the offender in cases where he is present in its territory and it does not extradite him to any of other states concerned.[6]

---

2.   RESTATEMENT (THIRD), *id.* at 240.

3.   18 I.L.M. 1456, 1458 (1979).

4.   Jōta Yamamoto, *Current Treaty Systems to Combat International Terrorism—Features and Domestic Implementation*, 32 JAPAN ANN. INT'L L. 34, 45 (1989).

5.   Literally, "extradite or prosecute and punish the offender."

6.   Sōji Yamamoto, *The Japanese Enactment for the Suppression of Unlawful Seizure of Aircraft and International Law*, 15 JAPAN ANN. INT'L L. 70, 78 (1972).

III. ASSERTION OF EXTRATERRITORIAL JURISDICTION— CONFLICTS OF JURISDICTION

In recent years, states have sought to apply their domestic laws extraterritorially so as to regulate economic activities taking place outside their territory on the basis of either the effects doctrine or the nationality principle. A conflict of extraterritorial jurisdiction has occurred as a result, specifically in the economic field such as competition laws and export control laws.

a. Competition Laws

A great number of states, including Japan, have adopted competition laws prohibiting restrictive business practices such as private monopolization, unreasonable restraint of trade and unfair business practices. These laws have been applied traditionally to conduct taking place within a national territory. In recent years, states have sought to apply their domestic competition laws even to conduct taking place principally or wholly outside their territory.

In particular, the United States justifies such extraterritorial application of competition laws on the basis of the so-called effects doctrine. Under U.S. legislation, regardless of whether referred to as a wholly distinct basis of jurisdiction or an extension of the objective territoriality principle, the effect has been formulated now as a direct, substantial and reasonably foreseeable effect. In this respect, the Foreign Trade Antitrust Improvement Act of 1982 provides that the Sherman Act shall not apply to conduct involving trade or commerce with foreign nations unless such conduct has a direct, substantial and reasonably foreseeable effect in the United States.[7] Moreover, the Restatement (Third) of the American Law Institute takes the same position, allowing a state to exercise jurisdiction over a person or activity having connection with another state, among others, when the activity has substantial, direct and foreseeable effect in the territory.[8]

The validity of jurisdiction on this basis has often been justified through its adoption by the European Community. In fact, the European Community has applied EEC treaty competition rules to foreign conduct which restricts competition within the Community.[9] Indeed, in the *Beguelin Import Co.* case, the Community Court obliquely supported the effects doctrine. It ruled that the fact that one of the undertakings involved was established in a nonmember country does not bar the application of Article 85 provided the exclusive distribution agreement, concluded by a Japanese producer with a Franco-Belgian firm for sales in Belgium and France, produced its effects in Community territory.[10] In subsequent cases, however, the

---

7.   Foreign Trade Antitrust Improvement Act of 1982, 96 Stat. § 1246 (1982).

8.   RESTATEMENT (THIRD), *supra* note 1, at 244.

9.   EUROPEAN COMMUNITY, SIXTH REPORT ON COMPETITION POLICY 32 (1977).

10.   Case 22/71, Beguelin Import Co. v. S.A.G.L. Import Export, 1971 E.C.R. 949.

Court developed the theory of enterprise unity which, to some extent, supplements the effects doctrine. It held that a foreign company and the European Community subsidiary which it controls constitute a single economic enterprise that is subjected to European Community jurisdiction, regardless of the fact that the two companies have, respectively, separate legal personalities. In the Community, therefore, concerted conduct within the Common Market by a subsidiary is attributed to the parent company on the basis of control.[11]

There is, as a result, considerable disagreement between states as to whether economic effect alone is enough to support jurisdiction. Generally speaking, states have required a closer jurisdictional link between regulated conduct and national territory. In particular, the United Kingdom has consistently taken the position that the extraterritorial application of domestic law is permitted only when a constituent element of an offense takes place within national territory.[12] Likewise, the International Law Association concludes that a state has jurisdiction to prescribe rules governing conduct that takes place outside its territory and causes an effect within the territory only in cases where the conduct and its effect are constituent elements of an activity to which the rule applies.[13]

In this connection, the Japanese Antimonopoly Act is essentially territorial in purpose and scope.[14] The Act generally prohibits international agreements or contracts involving unreasonable restraint of trade or unfair business practices. In international agreements or contracts, usually one of the parties is a Japanese company and the other is a foreign company. In practice, therefore, the Foreign Trade Commission (FTC) usually challenges the Japanese party to the agreement or contract and orders it to delete the provisions which are held to be unreasonable restraint of trade or unfair business practices. Such restrictive provisions, thereby, can effectively be eliminated without involving the foreign party.[15]

In the *Novo Industri* case, the FTC formally intervened in the international contract concerning the exclusive distribution rights in Japan between a Danish company and a Japanese company, Amano Pharmaceutical Co.[16] The FTC held that the three restrictive provisions incorporated in the contract were in violation of the Act, and issued a formal recommendation to Amano to delete the said provisions from the contract. Novo responded by filing a lawsuit against the FTC in the Tokyo High Court to quash the FTC order. The Court held, however, that Novo had no standing to bring this action. Although Novo appealed to the Supreme Court, the

---

11. *See, e.g.,* Case 48/69, Imperial Chemical Industries Ltd. v. Commission, 1972 E.C.R. 619, 625; Case 7/73, Commercial Solvents Corp. v. Commission, 1974 E.C.R. 223.

12. A.V. LOWE, EXTRATERRITORIAL JURISDICTION 145 (1983).

13. INTERNATIONAL LAW ASSOCIATION. NEW YORK REPORT xx (1972). *See also* INSTITUT DE DROIT INTERNATIONAL, 57 ANNUAIRE, TOME II 343 (1977).

14. Makoto Yazawa, *International Transactions and the Japanese Antimonopoly Act*, 4 LAW ASIA 169, 171 (1973).

15. MITSUO MATSUSHITA, INTRODUCTION TO JAPANESE ANTIMONOPOLY LAW 70-71 (1990).

16. State of Japan v. Toshiba Machine Co., 16 JAPAN ANN. INT'L L. 97–102 (1972).

Court denied Novo's standing in the same manner, holding that Novo, being a third party, was not bound by the FTC recommendation order.

The Antimonopoly Act, therefore, does not apply to foreign companies unless they do business in Japan and commit therein the acts which are illegal under the Act. In April 1992, the United States announced a new antitrust enforcement policy to apply its antitrust laws to foreign restrictive business practices, such as boycotts and other exclusionary activities that hinder the export of American goods or services to foreign markets. Japan strongly objected to the U.S. policy, stating that any restrictive business practices, in principle, should be dealt with by the antitrust authorities of the state concerned.[17]

Furthermore, any person injured may bring an action for indemnification of damages sustained by conduct in violation of the Act. In this suit, the FTC holding is evidence of its illegality, so that the plaintiff can sue only after the FTC's decision on the matter is made final and conclusive.[18] To date, the United States has acted against a number of collusive business practices by Japanese companies with respect to construction projects at American military bases in Japan, and has recovered about $72 million from settlements involving bidrigging cases since the end of 1989.[19] In fact, in 1989, the United States filed a complaint against dozens of Japanese companies in connection with construction projects at the American naval base in Yokosuka, Kanagawa Prefecture. In this case, the FTC fined these companies a total of ¥289 million for violating the Antimonopoly Act on the ground that they had established a study group in 1984 to negotiate among contractors for U.S. Navy projects in advance of the bidding. Then the companies agreed to a court-mediated compromise and paid ¥4.7 billion to the United States.[20] More recently, in 1993, twenty-seven Japanese construction companies likewise paid the United States more than $1 million to settle claims of bidrigging on contracts during the 1980s at the U.S. naval base in Sasebo, Nagasaki Prefecture. It should be noted, however, that in this case, although the companies agreed to a settlement out of court, the FTC had not accused them of bidrigging.[21]

---

17. Antitrust Laws in U.S. Will be Applied Overseas, JAPAN TIMES, Apr. 5, 1992, at 1.

18. Yazawa, *supra* note 14, at 171.

19. *Firms Pay Up over Contracts: U.S. Gets $1 Million over Alleged Rigging of Tenders,* JAPAN TIMES, Aug. 1, 1993, at 2.

20. *140 Builders Rebuked for Bid-Fixing,* JAPAN TIMES, Dec. 9, 1988, at 2.

21. *Firms Pay Up over Contracts: U.S. Gets $1 Million over Alleged Rigging of Tenders,* *supra* note 19, at 2.

In March 1994, the United States government demanded a total of 70 Japanese construction companies pay more than ¥1.1 billion in penalties for alleged bidrigging on the projects at the U.S. naval station in Atsugi, Kanagawa Prefecture. It should be noted in this connection that the FTC could not find any evidence for bidrigging. *U.S. Eyes ¥1.1 billion 'Dango' Suit,* JAPAN TIMES, Mar. 16, 1994, at 1.

Between 1979 and 1993 there were fifty-five FTC decisions against bidrigging cases, whereas there were thirty-two decisions against bidrigging cases from 1992–93. The FTC therefore now has finalized the *Antimonopoly Act Guidelines Concerning the Activities of*

By contrast, in United States legislation, a private antitrust treble damage action has been regarded as the primary cause of extraterritorial jurisdictional conflicts. In fact, American courts, under discovery rules, have sought to obtain documents located within the territory of other states. As a result, a number of states, including Canada, have enacted so-called blocking legislation, specifically to prohibit compliance with American discovery requests. Therefore, as will be examined later, American courts have adopted an interest-balancing approach as a matter of international comity and fairness so as to cope with the problem.

b. Export Control Laws

Export control laws present another type of extraterritoriality problem. Generally speaking, such control measures are often a response to the policies of foreign countries and therefore usually implemented by governmental pressure in the form of refusal of permission to import or export goods to or from specified countries. To date, the United States, in particular, has administered a variety of export controls.

One of the major types of such export controls is the Trading with the Enemy Act of 1917. Under Section 5(b) of the Act, the president is authorized to prohibit any kind of economic activity with designated countries by any person, or with respect to any kind of property, subject to the jurisdiction of the United States.[22] Although the extraterritorial reach of such restriction is not the same, thus, the United States traditionally has prohibited trade with a number of states and their nationals.

In 1963, for instance, the United States prohibited all transactions with Cuba or its nationals by any person subject to the jurisdiction of the United States, including foreign subsidiaries of American companies. An exception, however, allowed licensing for certain transactions of foreign subsidiaries of American companies if the law or policy of the third country required or favored trade with Cuba. As a result, American companies traded with Cuba through their subsidiaries beyond the reach of American law by taking advantage of this loophole in the law. In 1991 alone, these U.S. companies did more than $700 million of trade with Cuba.[23]

In an attempt to promote democratic change in Cuba, the Cuban Democracy Act of 1992 revoked this exception to tighten further the trade embargo against

---

Firms and Trade Associations in Relation to Public Bids.   FTC, REGARDING THE PUBLICATION OF THE ANTIMONOPOLY ACT GUIDELINES CONCERNING THE ACTIVITIES OF FIRMS AND TRADE ASSOCIATIONS IN RELATION TO PUBLIC BIDS 1 (July 5, 1994).

22. The Trading with the Enemy Act, 50 U.S.C.A. 415 (1917).

23. Dean Baquet, *Companies Evade Sanctions by Use of Foreign Units,* N.Y. TIMES, Dec. 27, 1993, at A1. For instance, Cargill Inc., one of the world's largest agricultural companies, took advantage of a loophole in the law which made it virtually impossible to enforce U.S. sanctions against multinational corporations.

Cuba and effectively prohibited transactions with Cuba or its nationals by companies, wherever organized or doing business, which are owned or controlled by American residents or nationals. In so far as it extends national jurisdiction beyond the boundaries of the United States, the Act generated vigorous protest by other countries. By virtue of their blocking legislation, they issued orders blocking the United States attempt to ban trade with Cuba by American-owned subsidiaries based in their countries. For example, the United Kingdom invoked the Protection of Trading Interests Act to prohibit British companies owned by American interests from complying with United States legislation banning them from trading with Cuba, saying that the British government, not the United States Congress, would determine the United Kingdom trade policy with Cuba. Under the Foreign Extraterritorial Measures Act, Canada likewise issued an order blocking compliance by Canadian based companies with the American ban in order to block measures that infringe on Canadian sovereignty.[24]

In this context, the General Assembly of the United Nations adopted a resolution in November 1992 concerning the necessity of ending the economic, commercial and financial embargo imposed by the United States against Cuba. The United Kingdom asserted that the European Community and its member states could not accept unilateral determination and restriction by the United States of European Community economic and commercial relations with any foreign country which has not been collectively determined by the United Nations Security Council to be a threat to international peace and security.[25]

The most basic and comprehensive American export control law is the Export Administration Act of 1979. Section 6(a)(1) of the Act authorizes the president to prohibit the exportation of any goods, technology, or other information subject to the jurisdiction of the United States, or exported by any person subject to the jurisdiction of the United States, to the extent necessary to further the foreign policy of the United States or to fulfill its declared international obligation. The Act itself defines the term "United States person" to include not only any United States resident or national, and any domestic concern, but also foreign subsidiaries or affiliates of any domestic concern which are controlled in fact by such domestic concern.[26] For instance, in June 1982, in response to the role allegedly played by the Soviet Union in Poland, export controls were promulgated under the Export Administration Act, so as to prevent American companies and even foreign companies using American goods and technology from delivering pipeline

---

24. David Owen, *U.K. Rejects Trade Ban on Cuba by U.S.*, FINANCIAL TIMES, Oct. 21, 1992, at 7; *Canadian Government Issues Order Blocking Cuban Democracy Act Expansion*, 9 Int'l Trade Rep. 1758 (1992).

25. G.A. Res. 47/19, U.N. GAOR, 47th Sess., Supp. No. 49, at 20, U.N. Doc. A/47/49 (Vol. I) (1993); U.N. Doc. A/47/PV.70 81 (Dec. 9, 1992). The United Kingdom and Japan abstained, whereas Canada voted in favor of the resolution.

26. The Export Administration Act of 1979, 18 I.L.M. 1508, 1513 (1979).

equipment to the Soviet Union.[27]

As mentioned above, for jurisdictional purposes—to apply domestic law to the foreign conduct of companies incorporated under the laws of other states—the phrase "any person subject to the jurisdiction of the United States" has consistently been defined in U.S. legislation so as to include companies incorporated, doing business in foreign countries and owned or controlled by American natural or juridical persons. Accordingly, the Restatement (Third) also concludes that although a state may not ordinarily regulate activities of companies incorporated under the law of a foreign state on the basis that they are owned or controlled by nationals of the regulating state, a state may reasonably exercise jurisdiction over such affiliated entities for certain purposes.[28]

Such American attempts to control activities of foreign subsidiaries of American companies on the basis of corporate affiliation have generated much controversy. Indeed, there is no wide agreement as to whether the fact that a foreign company is owned or controlled by nationals of the regulating state can justify asserting export controls over the foreign company. Many states have protested such use by the United States of the nationality principle to justify application of its export control laws to foreign subsidiaries of American companies. In the British view, for example, it is not consistent with the principles of international law for a state to assert that a company has the nationality of that state merely by virtue of the nationality of its shareholders or managers, because the nationality of a company is determined by its place of incorporation. Thus, in the pipeline dispute, the European Community likewise asserted that the claim to regard companies incorporated and having their registered offices in member states of the Community as instead having United States nationality is not in conformity with recognized principles of international law.[29]

As early as 1970, the International Court of Justice ruled in the *Barcelona Traction* case that a company is traditionally a national of the state under the law of which it is incorporated and in whose territory it has its registered office.[30] In this respect, the Restatement (Third) itself affirms that for the purpose of international law, a company has the nationality of the state under the laws of which the company is incorporated.[31] Furthermore, even if links of ownership or control of a foreign company justify in certain cases the exercise of prescriptive jurisdiction over such a company, a state should not require such a foreign subsidiary to engage in conduct inconsistent with the law and policies of the state in which the conduct will take place. The Restatement (Third) also maintains that a state, in principle, may not require a person, even one of its nationals, to do abroad what that territorial

---

27. *Export of Oil and Gas Equipment to the Soviet Union*, 21 I.L.M. 864, 866 (1982).
28. RESTATEMENT (THIRD), *supra* note 1, at 269.
29. LOWE, *supra* note 12, at 216.
30. Barcelona Traction Light & Power Co., Ltd. (Belg. v. Spain), 1970 I.C.J. 42 (Feb. 5).
31. RESTATEMENT (THIRD), *supra* note 1, at 124.

state prohibits.[32] Even if jurisdiction on the basis of nationality were to be exercised over foreign subsidiaries, it would be restricted by the primacy of the territorial jurisdiction.

Moreover, by extending the active nationality principle to include, on a different basis, the nationality of goods or technology, the United States has asserted jurisdiction over goods and technology located abroad on the basis of their origin in the United States. Other states have lodged strong protests with the United States, stating that the American ban on sales of European made, United States licensed, equipment for the pipeline flouts international law. In the British view it is not acceptable that American jurisdiction could legitimately extend to the control of foreign companies with respect to their exports manufactured in other countries by incorporating parts or technology of American origin even after the goods or technology have been sold from the United States.[33] The same is true of the European Community's position: goods and technology do not have any nationality. There are also no rules of international law allowing a state to use goods or technology situated abroad as a basis of establishing jurisdiction over the persons controlling them.[34]

In this context as well, the United States claimed to apply its laws and regulations to foreign companies which had agreed in a contract made with American companies for the supply of goods or technology to observe American laws and regulations. As mentioned above, however, other states refused to cooperate with such an American trade embargo against the Soviet Union and even instructed their domestic companies to fulfill the contracts to produce American licensed components for the Soviet pipeline. In August 1982, the United Kingdom joined France and Italy in specifically ordering four British companies with contracts aiding the Soviet pipeline to ignore the United States ban which applies both in America and to its technology licensed to foreign companies in Europe.[35] In the British view, not only is the embargo an attempt to interfere with existing contracts and an unacceptable extension of American extraterritorial jurisdiction, but the provision in a contract between two private parties is not capable of replacing or overruling the domestic law of the state concerned.[36]

The European Community likewise concludes that such a submission clause can not confer a valid jurisdictional reach on the United States export controls

---

32. *Id.* at 341.

33. LOWE, *supra* note 12, at 214.

34. *European Communities: Comments on the U.S. Regulations Concerning Trade with the U.S.S.R.*, 21 I.L.M. 891, 894 (1982).

35. *Britain Joins France, Italy in Ignoring Pipeline Embargo*, JAPAN TIMES, Aug. 4, 1982, at 1. West Germany likewise decided to follow other European countries in defining the United States sanctions on the export of European goods made under American license for use in the pipeline construction. *Schmidt Supports U.S.S.R. Pipeline*, JAPAN TIMES, July 30, 1982, at 1.

36. LOWE, *supra* note 12, at 214.

which they would not otherwise have.[37] In this connection, Japan, likewise, filed a strong protest with the United States and urged it to lift the ban on the use of United States-made equipment in a Japan-Soviet joint project for oil and natural gas development off Sakhalin, saying that economic sanctions against the Soviet Union run counter to international law. Among others, the protest made the point that the sanctions, unilaterally expanding U.S. administrative authority beyond its territory, cannot be justified in the light of international law.[38] Under these circumstances, American extraterritorial jurisdictional claims are not likely to be supported by state practice.

In addition, Japan has not used export controls and other economic sanctions as primary instruments of foreign policy. Since August 1952, however, Japan, as a member of the Coordinating Committee for Export Control (COCOM), has restricted the export of COCOM strategic items to prevent the flow of strategic Western technological products to the Soviet Union and its allies. As a system, each member state is itself responsible for implementing multilaterally agreed controls by imposing domestic penalties in cases of infractions of its domestic export control law because COCOM has no multilateral control or enforcement mechanism.

In Japan, in almost all instances, such export controls have been imposed under the Foreign Exchange and Foreign Trade Control Law, which is a statutory framework for economic controls in general.[39] Under Article 25 of the Law, all exports from Japan have required the approval of the Minister of International Trade and Industry for such types of export of goods or areas of destination and/or method of transactions or payment as provided by Cabinet Order. For instance, in the *Toshiba Machine Co.* case, the Tokyo District Court fined the company ¥2 million and gave suspended jail terms to two of its employees for illegally exporting a computer program and parts for propeller milling machines to the Soviet Union in 1984.[40] During the trial, the prosecution did not touch on the relationship between the milling machines in question and the lowering of the noise of Soviet submarines. The defense attorney insisted, however, that the milling machines had nothing to do with the lowering of the noise of Soviet submarines, and that Toshiba only violated procedural matters. In its judgment, the Court found Toshiba and the two employees guilty of exporting twelve cutter heads for the milling machines and a computer program to operate the cutter heads, without receiving the approval of the Ministry of International Trade and Industry (MITI), but did not make any judgment on the question of whether the milling machines in question were actually responsible, as the United States charged, for reducing the noise of Soviet

---

37. *Id.* at 217.

38. *Japan Urges Washington to Ease Soviet Sanctions*, JAPAN TIMES, July 22, 1982, at 1.

39. Shinya Murase, *Trade versus Security: The COCOM Regulation in Japan*, 31 JAPAN ANN. INT'L L. 1 (1988). *Id.* at 206–211.

40. *Tokyo Court Fines Toshiba Machine for Illegal Exports*, JAPAN TIMES, Mar. 23, 1988, at 1.

submarines. It is noted in this connection, therefore, that what is important is the moral implication.[41]

In March 1988, when the United States included in its omnibus trade bill a call for sanctions not only against Toshiba Machine Co. but also against its parent company, Toshiba Corp., Japan officially expressed regret over the decision, maintaining that Japan has penalized Toshiba Machine Co. for its illegal sales of sophisticated high-tech machine tools to the Soviet Union in accordance with Japanese laws.[42]

IV. RESOLUTION OF JURISDICTIONAL CONFLICTS

As mentioned above, economic activities are not limited to one state's territory in today's interdependent world. Especially in the case of multinational enterprises, an economic transaction or a course of conduct usually takes place in two or more states. Where states assert jurisdiction beyond their territory, extraterritoriality is inevitable. Certain procedures must be created to deal with the conflicts of jurisdiction between states which arise out of such an extraterritorial application of domestic laws. In this connection, an approach of moderation and restraint has been recommended in recent years so as to avoid, minimize, or resolve such conflicting claims of jurisdiction over transnational economic activities.

a.   Unilateral Conflict Resolution

Although originally developed in antitrust actions involving foreign parties, the balancing of interests between states has become a standard used in the United States as moderator or restraint on the assertion of jurisdiction by a state over economic activities taking place in or outside its territory. By virtue of the interest balancing approach, in determining whether a state may exercise jurisdiction over transnational economic activity, in each case a court must consider not only the effect on the foreign commerce of the state, but also the type and magnitude of the alleged illegal behavior, and the appropriateness of exercising extraterritorial jurisdiction in accordance with international comity and fairness. Thus, in determining whether to exercise extraterritorial jurisdiction, a court must balance the interests of the countries concerned in the light of a jurisdictional rule of reason, and, eventually refrain from exercising jurisdiction in cases where the interests of

---

41. *Toshiba Decision's Implications*, JAPAN TIMES, Mar. 24, 1988, at 20.

42. *Tokyo Court Fines Toshiba Machine for Illegal Exports, supra* note 40, at 2. COCOM was dissolved as of Apr. 1, 1994. The United States therefore decided to ease controls on most exports to the former Soviet states and to China, effective Apr. 4. *New Agency Emerges with COCOM's Demise*, ASAHI EVENING NEWS, Mar. 31, 1994, at 6.

the forum are not sufficiently strong enough to justify such an assertion of jurisdiction.[43]

The Restatement (Third) likewise declares that whether the exercise of prescriptive jurisdiction over a person or his activity abroad is reasonable is determined as a matter of international law, in light of all relevant factors including legal and other factors, such as the link of the activity to the territory of the regulating state, the nationality of the person responsible for the activity to be regulated, the importance of the regulations to the international political, legal, or economic system, the likelihood of conflict with regulation by another state, and so forth.[44]

The question remains as to whether this approach will resolve adequately conflicts of interests over jurisdictional competence between sovereign states. Regardless of whether the approach is referred to as a jurisdictional rule of reason or a principle of reasonableness, it is noted that there are a number of difficulties inherent in the balancing of interests being undertaken by the courts of one state.[45] Above all, when the courts are forced to choose between a domestic law designed to protect domestic interests and a foreign law that is calculated to prevent the implementation of the domestic law in order to protect foreign interests allegedly threatened by the domestic law, there are substantial limitations on the courts' ability to conduct a neutral balancing of the competing interests.

When one state exercises its jurisdiction and another attempts to prevent such exercise of jurisdiction to protect its own interests, it is impossible for the courts to balance such mutually negating actions. Moreover, the courts, being domestic courts, can not refuse to enforce a law that its political branches have already determined as necessary.[46] The balancing of interests, therefore, would not be a suitable approach in so far as it leaves to domestic courts the matter of jurisdictional conflicts between sovereign states.

b. Bilateral or Multilateral Conflict Resolution

No general agreement has been reached on the limits of domestic laws to be applied to transnational economic activities, but efforts have been made to seek a reasonable accommodation of the interests of the states in the field of competition laws, in particular.

First, as early as October 1967, the Council of the Organization for Economic Cooperation and Development (OECD) adopted a recommendation concerning cooperation between member countries on restrictive business practices affecting

---

43. Timberlane Lumber. Co. v. Bank of America, 549 F.2d 597, 613 (1976); Timberlane Lumber Co. v. Bank of America, 749 F.2d 1378, 1383–84 (1984).

44. RESTATEMENT (THIRD), *supra* note 1, at 244–45.

45. D. W. Bowett, *Jurisdiction: Changing Patterns of Authority over Activities and Resources*, 53 BRIT. Y.B. INT'L L. 1, 21 (1982).

46. Laker Airways v. Sabena, Belgian World Airlines, 731 F.2d 909, 948 (1984).

international trade, largely in response to concerns that the extraterritorial application of United States antitrust laws was infringing unduly the interests of other member countries. In its recommendation, the Council recognized that the unilateral application of domestic laws in cases where business operations in other member countries are involved raises questions as to the state sovereignty of the other member countries. The Council therefore stressed the need for closer cooperation between member countries in the form of consultations, exchanges of information and cooperation of efforts on a voluntary basis. The recommendation to the member countries was that when they undertake an investigation or proceeding involving important interests of another member country under their restrictive business practice laws they should notify that member country in advance so that it may express its view on the matter.[47]

Moreover, in September 1979, the Council likewise recommended to the member countries that when a restrictive business practice investigation or proceeding conducted by a member country affects important interests of another member country, the latter country should transmit its views on the matter to, or request consultation with, the former. It also suggested that in cases where satisfactory solution cannot be reached between the member countries concerned, they should submit the case to the Committee of Experts on Restrictive Business Practices with a view to conciliation.[48] More recently, in May 1984, the Council adopted the revised recommendation and particularly stressed the need for giving effect to the principles of international law and comity and for using moderation and self-restraint in the interests of cooperation in the field of restrictive business practices affecting international trade.[49]

The OECD Committee on International Investment and Multinational Enterprises states in its report that, in respect to conflicting requirements imposed on multinational enterprises, member countries should not only have regard to the principles of international law to avoid and minimize such conflicts by following an approach of moderation and restraint, but also take fully into account the sovereignty and the legitimate economic, law enforcement and other interests of other member countries.[50]

Second, progress has also been made in the area of notification and consultation, with a number of bilateral agreements for consultation and cooperation entered into between the United States and other states. For instance, in 1984, the United States and Canada entered into a cooperation agreement in order to eliminate

47. OECD: Recommendation of the Council Concerning Cooperation between Member Countries on Restrictive Business Practices Affecting International Trade, 8 I.L.M. 1309, 1310 (1969).

48. OECD, COMPETITION LAW ENFORCEMENT 78–81 (1984).

49. OECD: Council Recommendation Concerning Restrictive Business Practices Affecting International Trade, 25 I.L.M. 1929, 1930 (1986).

50. OECD, INTERNATIONAL INVESTMENT AND MULTINATIONAL ENTERPRISES: THE 1984 REVIEW OF THE 1976 DECLARATION AND DECISIONS 26 (1984).

differences between the two countries on the appropriate application of domestic antitrust laws to conduct taking place wholly or partly outside the territory of the applying party. Under this agreement, both the United States and Canada will notify each other whenever their antitrust investigation or proceeding involves the national interests of the other country, and requires the seeking of information located in the territory of the other country. Moreover, either country may request consultation when it believes that an antitrust investigation or proceeding is likely to affect its significant national interests.[51]

Furthermore, in 1991, the United States entered into a bilateral antitrust cooperation agreement with the European Community as well. This agreement, however, is quite different from the earlier cooperation agreements. It is intended, among other things, to coordinate the enforcement activities of both the United States and the European Community, rather than primarily to protect the sovereign interests of one state against encroachment by another state. In this respect, Article V of the Agreement formalizes the concept of "positive comity," by providing that if one party believes anticompetitive activities carried out in the territory of another party adversely affect the first party's important interests, the first party may notify the second, and may even request its competition authorities to initiate appropriate enforcement activities. The Agreement thus formally recognizes the right of a party to make such a request, and formally obligates the other side to consider and, if possible, to act favorably upon the request.[52]

States cooperate, therefore, as an alternative to unilateral action in order to avoid, reduce or resolve conflicting claims of jurisdiction between them. Interests can only be met through cooperation.

V. CONCLUSION

International law has, as its primary object, the reasonable allocation of jurisdiction between sovereign states. In general, by virtue of the international law of jurisdiction, states can freely adopt their own laws and policies within their own territory, but they are not authorized to enforce these laws and policies within the territory of other states. To do otherwise would be in violation of such principles of international law as state sovereignty or the prohibition of intervention in the domestic affairs of other states. Therefore, in the absence of an international agreement, territoriality is still jurisdictionally important in international law.

In practice, however, a state's laws that have extraterritorial reach do come into conflict with the law and policies of other states. When they do, a cooperative

---

51. Memorandum of Understanding between the Government of the United States of America and the Government of Canada as to Notification, Consultation and Cooperation with Respect to the Application of National Antitrust Laws, 23 I.L.M. 275 (1984).

52. Agreement between the Government of the United States of America and the Commission of the European Communities Regarding the Application of their Competition Laws, 30 I.L.M. 1487, 1497 (1991).

rather than confrontational approach should be encouraged in order to resolve such conflict over extraterritotiality. Prior consultation has been advocated as the most appropriate procedure. States have so far developed both formal and informal practical cooperative arrangements for notification to and consultation with other states in the field of competition laws.

The jurisdictional reach of domestic laws should be tempered by way of international agreements such as treaties or other international instruments like memoranda of understanding. It then would be desirable also for states to enter into international agreements for the allocation of jurisdiction in order to prevent jurisdictional conflicts on the one hand, and to harmonize applicable rules of domestic laws at the international level on the other.[53]

---

53. INSTITUT DE DROIT INTERNATIONAL, *supra* note 13, at 343. From the very nature of things, there may be cases where the multilateral approach could be more effective than the bilateral approach.

EXTRATERRITORIAL JURISDICTION OF ANTITRUST LAW IN INTERNATIONAL LAW

Akira Kotera

I. INTRODUCTION

The main fields in which extraterritorial application of national law has been the subject of controversy are antitrust, export control, disclosure of documents in judicial or administrative proceedings, and tax.[1] This paper discusses the substantive aspects of antitrust law from an international law perspective. Up to this time, U.S. courts or the U.S. government have pursued a policy of extraterritorial application of antitrust law and in turn the Japanese government, as well as the governments of European States, have protested or complained against the United States.

One important recent example is the U.S. Department of Justice (DOJ) Antitrust Enforcement Policy Statement of 1992 and the resulting complaints of many states, including Japan. The main part of the DOJ Statement is as follows:

The Department of Justice will, in appropriate cases, take antitrust enforcement action against conduct occurring overseas that restrains United States Exports whether or not there is direct harm to U.S. consumers, where it is clear that:

(1) The conduct has a direct, substantial, and reasonably foreseeable effect on exports of goods or services from the United States; (2) The conduct involves anticompetitive activities which violate the U.S. Antitrust Laws—in most cases, group boycotts, collusive pricing, and other exclusionary activities; and

---

1. OSCAR SCHACHTER, INTERNATIONAL LAW IN THEORY AND PRACTICE 253 (1991).

(3) U.S. courts have jurisdiction over foreign persons or corporations engaged in such conduct.[2]

Upon issuance of this statement, the Ministry of Foreign Affairs of Japan immediately criticized it, stating:

> such application of the U.S. Antitrust Law would constitute extraterritorial application of domestic laws which is not permissible under international law. . . . The Government of Japan expects prudent handling hereafter by the Department of Justice in the application of the law.[3]

As indicated by this statement, the Japanese government considered the U.S. policy impermissible under international law—a position which the DOJ most likely did not agree with. From an international law viewpoint, the attitudes of the two governments were contradictory. What attitude should international lawyers take between two conflicting positions?

II. THE JAPANESE POSITION

It has been said that the Japanese courts and the Japanese government generally take a rigidly conservative position toward the extraterritorial application of national law. However, Japanese courts have not yet had an opportunity to examine the extraterritorial application of law in the Antimonopoly Law.[4] The Fair Trade Commission (FTC) *(Kōsei Torihiki Iinkai)* has, however, made several determinations in specific cases that reveal its policy on the jurisdictional issue.

a. Cases before the FTC

The *Triple Fares*[5] case of 1972 involved the terms of a contract that had been agreed upon by seventeen shipowners and consigners. Those terms had been adopted in the assembly of a shipping conference held in London which was organized by the shipowners, fifteen of which were foreign companies. The FTC declared those terms in violation of Article 19 of the Antimonopoly Law (Prohibition of Unfair Business Practices) after the conference had abolished the terms. In this case the original decision was adopted in London, but the FTC seized upon the contract, which was drafted in Japan, and based its proceeding on it. In form,

---

2.   U.S. Dep't of Justice, Pub. No. 92–117, Justice Department Will Challenge Foreign Restraints on U.S. Exports Under Antitrust Laws 1 (1992).

3.   Japan Foreign Press Center, F.P.C. Press Release No. 0194–09, Apr. 4, 1992.

4.   For the Antimonopoly Law, *see* MITSUO MATSUSHITA, INTRODUCTION TO JAPANESE ANTIMONOPOLY LAW (1990).

5.   FTC Decision of Aug. 18, 1972 (FTC v. Nippon Yusen et al.), 19 Shinketsushu [Fair Trade Commission Decisions Reporter] 57 (Japan).

therefore, extraterritorial application of the Antimonopoly Law was not an issue, but in substance, the FTC proceeded against action taken outside Japan. It would thus make sense to assume that the FTC's declaration had some impact upon activities outside Japan.

The second case was the *Chemical Fiber International Cartel*[6] case of 1974, in which Japanese and European producers of chemical fiber entered into cartel agreements on export trade. The FTC declared that the international cartel agreement as a whole was in violation of Article 6, Paragraph 1 of the Antimonopoly Law, which Article could be entitled Prohibition of International Agreement Containing Unreasonable Restraint of Trade or Unfair Business Practices, and ordered the Japanese producers to cancel it. In this case, the FTC order applied only to the Japanese producers that were restricted to exporting chemical fiber to European countries by the agreement, but not to the European producers that were restricted to exporting fiber to Japan.

This case's characterization of the international agreement under the Antimonopoly Law shows that the FTC's adjudication contains some element of extraterritoriality. As long as the addressees of the order were Japanese companies, though, the element of compulsion of the foreign producers was weak. It was not probable that the extraterritorial application of Antimonopoly Law would have become an international issue. The FTC's policy was seriously criticized as missing the true mark by not ordering the European producers to cancel the cartel agreement that harmed the Japanese market.[7] This would have been a real extraterritorial application of the Antimonopoly Law, but one must add that, in this case, the German Cartel Office (*Bundeskartellamt*) proceeded against the German participants to the agreement and heavily fined them.[8] The Japanese proceeding was the result of the notification by the German Cartel Office. Considering the whole story, this case was an example of good international cooperation in antitrust matters.

b. The Japanese Government Policy

The complaints that have been made by the Japanese government are among the main information sources of its policy, though. Few complaints, including that of 1992 stated above, have been available. One case that did not involve antitrust concerns involved the Toyota Corporation of Japan for the submission of

---

6.   FTC Decision of Dec. 27, 1972 (FTC v. Mitsubishi Rayon et al.), 19 Shinketsushu [Fair Trade Commission Decisions Reporter] 140 (Japan).

7.   Mitsuo Matsushita, *Kokunai Jigyōsha to Gaikoku Jigyōsha tono Yūshutsu Chiiki, Yushutsu Suryo, Saiteihanbai Kakaku no Kokusai Kyotei* [*International Agreement between Domestic Producers and Foreign Producers on the Export Area, the Export Quantity and Lowest Sales Price*], DOKKINHŌ SHINKETSU/HANREI HYAKUSEN [ONE HUNDRED IMPORTANT CASES OF FTC DECISIONS AND COURT JUDGMENTS] 74, 75 (1991).

8.   *Id.*

documents related to the transfer pricing issued in 1992 by the U.S. Internal Revenue Service. The Japanese government complained to the United States that:

> [t]o compel the submission of the documents directly to the parties on a matter which involves international judicial procedure, without going through the process of resorting to judicial assistance or of obtaining the prior consent of Japan is nothing else than an exercise of public power of the United States in Japan.[9]

The Ministry of Foreign Affairs of Japan noted that "this order for the submission of documents by the U.S. side is in our view inconsistent with the principles of international law."[10]   This statement, made by an official of the Ministry of Foreign Affairs in the Diet, indicates that the Japanese government would consider a certain extraterritorial application of national laws to be inconsistent with international law, depending upon the exercise of a state's public power in another state's territory. On this point, an officer of the Foreign Ministry wrote an interesting article analyzing the Japanese position on the domestic application of the Agreement on Technical Barriers to Trade (General Agreement on Tariffs and Trade Standard Agreement).[11] In order to apply the agreement, the Japanese Diet amended the Consumer Product Safety Law (*Shohi-seikatsuyōseihin-anzen-hō*) to the effect that the Minister of International Trade and Industry may permit type approval to manufacturers in foreign territories. The article discusses the legal justification of the system from the viewpoint of the limit of prescriptive jurisdiction. The author stated that, though the effects theory was not established under international law, this system was implicitly permissible under international law in considering the purpose of the GATT Standard Agreement. This view, on the one hand, reflects the very restricted attitude of the Japanese government toward the extraterritorial jurisdiction of a state; on the other hand, it indicates the need for extraterritorial application of national law.

A rather progressive movement toward extraterritoriality recently appeared in a 1990 report of extraterritorial application of antimonopoly law by a study group organized by the FTC.[12] This report, analyzing recent state practices including judgments of foreign states, concludes that Antimonopoly Law should be applied to an act that restricts competition in the national market while considering foreign

---

9.   Shigeru Oda and Hisashi Owada, *Annual Review of Japanese Practice in International Law*, 31 JAPANESE ANN. INT'L L. 138, 145 (1988).

10.   *Id.*

11.   Haruhisa Takeuchi, *Rippo Kankatsuken no Ikigaitekiyo* [*Extraterritorial Exercise of Legislative Jurisdiction*], 86 KOKUSAIHŌ GAIKŌ ZASSHI 407 (1987).

12.   KŌSEI TORIHIKI IINKAI [FAIR TRADE COMMISSION], REGULATION OF DUMPING REGULA-TIONS AND COMPETITION POLICY: EXTRATERRITORIAL APPLICATION OF ANTIMONOPOLY LAW (1990). For the report in detail, *see generally* Jiro Tamura, *U.S. Extraterritorial Application of Antitrust Law*, 25 N.Y.U.J. INT'L L. & POL. 385, 392-396 (1993).

state compulsion or other similar state interference, even though the actor is an enterprise in a foreign territory having neither a branch nor a subsidiary in Japan. This report says that jurisdictions are defined by international law, but that the international legal rule defining the limits of states' jurisdiction is uncertain.

It is not clear that this report's opinion has prevailed over the old conservative one. One presumes that this opinion has not garnered strong support from other branches of the Japanese government. One thus concludes that the Japanese government still maintains a conservative attitude toward extraterritoriality. Despite such a restrictive attitude, however, the FTC decisions, as analyzed above, substantially tried to regulate action taken outside Japan. The FTC's report, proceeding further, even claimed typical extraterritorial application of the Antimonopoly Law. These incidents show that the Japanese government cannot disregard actions taken outside Japan in the contemporary interdependent world where international cartels, for example, are often concluded by producers of various nationalities.

III. LEGAL POLICIES OF GOVERNMENTS OTHER THAN JAPAN

a.   The U.S. Position

The U.S. courts' position on extraterritorial application of antitrust law has been generally considered to be consistently positive. Their view on its international legal validity has not been so completely established. In the famous *Alcoa* case,[13] the court stated, "it is settled law. . . that any state may impose liabilities, even upon persons not within its allegiance, for conduct outside its borders that has consequence within its borders which the state reprehends; and these liabilities other states will ordinarily recognize."[14] The court took a clear positive position regarding extraterritorial application of antitrust law based upon the effects principle. This position's validity under international law was changed by the *Timberlane* case.[15] In *Timberlane* the court criticized the *Alcoa* judgment, saying that "despite its description as 'settled law,' *Alcoa's* assertion has been roundly disputed by many foreign commentators as being in conflict with international law, comity, and good judgment."[16] The court took the following position:

> [e]xtraterritorial application is understandably a matter of concern for the other countries involved. . . .[I]t is evident that at some point the interests of the United States are too weak and the foreign harmony incentive for restraint too strong to justify an extraterritorial assertion of jurisdiction.

---

13.   U.S. v. Aluminium Co. of America, 148 F.2d 416 (1945).

14.   *Id.* at 443.

15.   Timberlane Lumber Co. v. Bank of America, 549 F.2d 597 (1976).

16.   *Id.* at 610.

What that point is or how it is determined is not defined by international law.[17]

The frame of reference of the court was not clear from this statement. Did the problem reside in how to decide the sole legally proper bases for state jurisdiction, or in how to select the most appropriate jurisdictional basis among the legally permissible ones? The court recognized that international law did not provide a decisive standard.

The frame of reference for the extraterritoriality of antitrust law was clearly indicated by the court in the *Laker* case.[18] In *Laker*, the court said:

[n]o rule of international law or national law precludes an exercise of jurisdiction solely because another state has jurisdiction. In fact, international law recognizes that a state with a territorial basis for its prescriptive jurisdiction may establish laws intended to prevent compliance with legislation established under authority of nationality-based jurisdiction.[19]

This judgment shows that with respect to certain antitrust matters, more than two state jurisdictions may be legally established and that the focal point is which jurisdiction should prevail over the others. The famous "jurisdictional rule of reason," adopted for the first time in *Timberlane*, was interpreted in this context. The jurisdictional rule of reason is the test of "comity and fairness" that justifies the contacts and interests of the United States as sufficient to support the exercise of extraterritorial jurisdiction. The courts regard this rule as the prevailing test.

From an international viewpoint, one must consider that in *Timberlane* the court discussed the jurisdictional rule of reason by referring to Kingman Brewster, Jr.'s 1958 book, *Antitrust Law and American Business Abroad*. In this book Brewster proposed the jurisdictional rule of reason to improve antitrust policy,[20] proving that the court did not think that the jurisdictional rule of reason was a principle of international law. Further, the court in the *Laker* case said, "there is no evidence that interest balancing [by which the jurisdictional rule of reason was realized in concrete form] represents a rule of international law."[21]

Concerning the legal character of the effects principle, one must refer to the judgment of *Laker*. In *Laker*, the court said that the effects principle was characterized as a mode of authoritative territorial principle. This position coincides with that of the Restatement (Third) of Foreign Relations Law, Section 402.[22] Thus the

---

17. *Id.* at 608–09.

18. Laker Airways v. Sabena, Belgian World Airlines, 731 F.2d 909 (1984).

19. *Id.* at 950.

20. KINGMAN BREWSTER, JR., ANTITRUST AND AMERICAN BUSINESS ABROAD 446 (1958).

21. *Id.* at 950.

22. *See* 1 RESTATEMENT (THIRD) OF FOREIGN RELATIONS LAW 239 (1987).

U.S. courts recognize that (1) the jurisdictional reach of antitrust law is confined by international law; (2) the effects principle is characterized as a mode of territorial principle; (3) in regard to certain matters, jurisdictions of more than two states can be legally established upon international law; and (4) no international law resolves the conflict of more than two legally established state jurisdictions. How should one evaluate such U.S. court positions from an international law viewpoint? Before proceeding to this point, the policies of the United Kingdom and the EC will be examined in brief.

b. Positions of the United Kingdom and the EC

The attitude of the U.K. government toward the extraterritorial application of antitrust laws has been extremely conservative. The representative U.K. position on the international legal validity of extraterritorial application of antitrust law is expressed in an *amicus curiae* brief submitted by the U.K. government during the *Uranium* antitrust litigation:

> the 'effects' test is inconsistent with international law. This is so in relation to civil antitrust treble damage cases brought by private persons, as well as criminal or civil antitrust litigation instituted by the U.S. Government, since the former are to be deemed to be 'penal' actions for the purposes of international law.[23]

That is, the U.K. government categorically denies the international legal validity of the effects principle of antitrust law because penal law does not recognize the effects principle. The position regarding the penal nature of antitrust law is too extreme, however. How can one divide all laws between penal and private laws and then characterize antitrust as a penal law? There is not enough evidence to justify the conclusions of the U.K. government.

It is said that the European Court of Justice (ECJ), which previously took a conservative attitude, has changed its policy. The alleged turning point is the *Dyestuffs* case.[24] In this case, the applicability of Article 85, Paragraph 1 of the Treaty of Rome to Imperial Chemical Industries Ltd. (ICI) residing in the U.K.— then a nonmember state of the EEC—was a central issue. The ECJ, avoiding the effects principle, argued that since the actions of ICI's subsidiary, which resided in the EC, were attributable to ICI as its parent company, then Article 85, Paragraph 1 was applicable to ICI.

---

23. A.V. LOWE, EXTRATERRITORIAL JURISDICTION 159 (1983).
24. Case 48/69, Imperial Chemical Industries Ltd. v. Commission, 1972 E.C.R. 619 [hereinafter *Dyestuffs*].

Further, in the *Wood Pulp* case,[25] regarding the applicability of Article 85 to a cartel of producers—all of which had their registered offices outside the Community—the ECJ divided the alleged acts into two parts: "the formation of the agreements" and "implementation thereof," and concluded that "the decisive factor is. . . the place where it is implemented."[26] Therefore the applicability of Article 85 allegedly was justified by the territoriality principle. On the one hand, it is certain that the arguments, especially in the *Wood Pulp* case, were very similar to U.S. arguments, since both jurisdictions had the same need to apply the antitrust law in an extraterritorial manner. On the other hand, the ECJ was also unable to resist justifying its jurisdictional policy by referring to the traditional territorial principle.

IV. STATE JURISDICTION UNDER INTERNATIONAL LAW

Can one find international law rules or principles that solve the jurisdictional dispute concerning antitrust matters? There has been no case in an international court in which extraterritorial application of antitrust law was directly discussed. The judgment by the World Court in the famous *Lotus*[27] case, which concerned criminal matters, described the general rule of state jurisdiction as follows: "[international law] leaves [the states]. . . a wide measure of discretion [in the extension of application of their laws] which is only limited in certain case by prohibitive rules."[28]   The U.S. attitude toward extraterritorial application of antitrust law, examined in section III.A. of this chapter, is justified by this *Lotus* statement, though whether this *Lotus* theory really goes so far as to justify the U.S. position in the present situation remains uncertain. In this respect, one must bear in mind that the needs of effective regulation of the worldwide activities of multinational enterprises could justify such U.S. antitrust law policy to an extent. Even the conservative Japanese policy, as analyzed in section II, includes the attempt to regulate activities that substantially took place abroad. Because this need is universally recognized, whether extraterritorial jurisdiction itself is valid is not central to this issue; rather, as an international law specialist, one has to consider why the U.S. courts introduced the jurisdictional rule of reason.

The following two situations in which more than two jurisdictions could conflict with each other must be distinguished. The first is a case in which a jurisdiction makes a claim for exclusivity while denying the legality of competing claims. The other is a case in which more than two jurisdictions make legally legitimate claims. In contemporary international society, one is usually faced with the the latter, not former situation, though it was the latter that concerned the U.S. court in the *Timberlane* and *Laker* cases.

---

25.   Joined Cases 89, 104, 114, 116, 117 & 125–129/85, 1988 E.C.R. 5193 [hereinafter *Wood Pulp*].

26.   *Id.* at 941.

27.   The Case of the S.S. "Lotus" (Fr. v. Turkey), 1927 P.C.I.J. (ser. A) No. 9 (Sep. 7).

28.   *Id.* at 19.

This latter situation is the core of the jurisdictional problem in contemporary international law.[29]   In this respect, the *Fisheries Jurisdiction*[30] case of 1974 provides a useful reference. The ICJ judged that the Icelandic claim to exclusive fisheries jurisdiction that went beyond the preferential rights that had been generally established was not opposable to the United Kingdom, as the Icelandic jurisdiction disregarded the U.K. rights. But the court proceeded further to seek an equitable, non-adversarial solution to the differences between the two states. The court, establishing the preferential rights of Iceland (a coastal state) and the established rights of the United Kingdom (a fishing state) in the same waters, declared that the two states were "under mutual obligations to undertake negotiations in good faith for the equitable solution of their differences."[31]

From this *Fisheries Jurisdiction* case one may conclude two things. First, one presumes that the Court hesitated to adjudge the invalidity of the Icelandic exclusive fisheries jurisdiction for which the United Kingdom had asked and instead declared nonopposability of the Icelandic claim. The term "opposability" has been used in various senses.[32]   In the judgment, the term opposability means that the Icelandic jurisdiction cannot be validly claimed against the United Kingdom under special circumstances. Therefore the judgment does not mean that the Icelandic jurisdiction is not validly established against other states or *erga omnes*. This fact shows that to declare the invalidity of the application of national jurisdiction is a difficult or impossible matter if "practice is contradictory and lacks precision."[33]

Second, the Court, as well as the United Kingdom, considered that merely to declare the invalidity or non-opposability of the Icelandic claim did not suffice to solve the existing differences between the two countries. Disputation in a court is distinguished from the true existing substantive differences between the two countries.   Disputation is therefore distinct from the underlying substantive differences, and strict application of the legal rules does not necessarily resolve the existing differences behind the dispute. The fishing jurisdiction as claimed by Iceland was not recognized as generally established under international law; rather, a certain special position in favor of coastal states called "preferential rights" was explicitly recognized. Following the court's reasoning, it is natural that to obtain a genuine solution to the differences the parties should construct a relationship that respects both the preferential rights of Iceland and the established rights of the

---

29.   *See* Maarten Bos, *The Extraterritorial Jurisdiction of States: Preliminary Report*, 65-I ANNUAIRE DE l'INSTITUT DE DROIT INTERNATIONAL 13, 33–36 (1993); D. W. Bowett, *Jurisdiction: Changing Patterns of Authority over Activities and Resources*, 53 BRIT. Y.B. INT'L L. 1, 14–18 (1982).

30.   Fisheries Jurisdiction Case (U.K. v. Iceland), 1974 I.C.J. 3 (July 25).

31.   *Id.* at 34 (Joint Separate Opinion of Judges Forster, Bengzon, Jimenez de Arechaga, Nagendra Singh, and Ruda).

32.   For opposability in general, *see* J. G. Starke, *The Concept of Opposability in International Law*, 4 AUSTR. Y.B. INT'L L. 1 (1968-1969); PIERRE-MARIE DUPUY, DROIT INTERNATIONAL PUBLIC 251 (2d ed. 1993).

33.   Fisheries Jurisdiction Case (U.K. v. Iceland), 1974 I.C.J. 3, 49 (July 25).

U.K.. This is why the Court declared an obligation to negotiate, which the United Kingdom had requested.

Applying this analysis to the jurisdictional problem of antitrust law when more than two jurisdictions are claimed to be legally established, it is very difficult to decide which jurisdiction prevails by referring to international law. The best method is to determine whether the alleged jurisdiction is opposable. If the extraterritorial application of jurisdiction is opposable to another state, for instance because the state formerly acquiesced, the state cannot complain about this extraterritoriality and the dispute is completely solved.

In almost all the cases in which the extraterritorial application of antitrust law is claimed, however, the jurisdiction is not opposable to a complaining state. This situation is the same as that of the *Fisheries Jurisdiction* case. In such situations, the ICJ could not only declare an obligation to negotiate, but also identify the legal situation underlying the differences. Concerning jurisdictional disputes on antitrust matters, an international lawyer can say to the parties concerned that they should negotiate with each other, while also explaining the rights and interests of the parties concerned. It is therefore rational that the OECD recommended to its member states the following procedures for avoiding or solving jurisdictional conflicts: notification, exchange of information and coordination of action, consultation, and conciliation.[34]

Moreover, efforts to harmonize antitrust laws have been recognized as vitally important, and cooperative agreements on antitrust matters have contributed to a decrease in jurisdictional disputes. As the failure of the negotiation between the United Kingdom and Iceland[35] indicate, however, there is no guarantee that the parties will be able to solve their differences by negotiation. Rules cannot lead to a real resolution of differences; they only provide materials for consideration during negotiations. The functions of international law in the solution of the jurisdictional disputes have been very limited.[36]

A lacuna exists in international law. In regard to antitrust law, one must recognize two important factors to be considered in negotiating a solution. First, the interests of states are slightly more easily reconciled in the antitrust area than in the export control law area, as antitrust acts are generally prohibitive.[37] Further, a state generally cannot effectively regulate antitrust matters occurring outside its

---

34.   Organization for Economic Cooperation and Development, Council Recommendation Concerning Restrictive Business Practices Affecting International Trade, May 21, 1986, 25 I.L.M. 1629 (1986).

35.   Gunther Jaenicke, *Fisheries Jurisdiction Cases*, *in* 2 ENCYCLOPEDIA OF PUBLIC INTERNATIONAL LAW 97 (R. Bernhardt ed. 1981).

36.   *See* Joseph P. Griffin, *EC and U.S. Extraterritoriality: Activism and Cooperation*, 17 FORDHAM INT'L L.J. 353 (1994).

37.   *See* A. H. HERMANN, CONFLICTS OF NATIONAL LAWS WITH INTERNATIONAL BUSINESS ACTIVITIES: ISSUES OF EXTRATERRITORIALITY 56 (1982).

territory if it neither adopts extraterritorial application of antitrust law nor takes some cooperative measures with a foreign country.

Second, the nonintervention principle by which a state should not infringe upon other states' sovereign autonomy has been firmly established. The rule of reason is partially based on respect for autonomy of another state. The Restatement (Third) of Foreign Relations Law of the United States admits a territorial preference in Section 441 in effect that "prohibitions by the state in whose territory the act is to be carried out ordinarily prevail over orders of other states."[38]

---

38.   1 RESTATEMENT (THIRD) OF FOREIGN RELATIONS LAW 342 (1987).

EXTRATERRITORIALITY AND U.S. FOREIGN TRADE CONTROLS: LESSONS FROM OLD DISPUTES AND SOURCES OF POTENTIAL NEW PROBLEMS

Peter D. Trooboff

I. INTRODUCTION

Several of the chapters in this volume provide valuable summaries of the international legal principles that relate to extraterritoriality. They also identify recent developments that have led to intergovernmental disagreements and to controversy in the literature.

For this reason, in this chapter I will focus on certain details regarding United States actions, past and proposed. My purpose is to raise the question of whether we need to recognize new distinctions in discussing the international law of extraterritoriality, specifically in reference to foreign trade controls. I hope that this focus on particular circumstances will help to enrich the dialogue among the participants by causing us to consider the application of general legal principles in specific, and often controversial, situations which raise difficult policy issues.

In particular, I will consider whether U.S. sanctions should be regarded as extraterritorial and arguably not in compliance with international law when they are directed at conduct of foreign individuals or legal entities that occurs entirely outside national jurisdiction (no U.S. product, technology, or person involved) and when the U.S.-imposed penalty is confined to denying U.S. government contracts, U.S. export financing, exports to the U.S. market, imports of U.S.-origin goods or technology, or other such benefits. The authority to impose such far-reaching sanctions appears in recent proposed U.S. legislation; hence, its status needs to be considered so that imposition does not result in foreign policy disputes.

a. Background: The Soviet Gas Pipeline Controversy

It is important to recall why the Soviet gas pipeline controversy in 1982 was a watershed. Let us review the three claimed jurisdictional nexuses that gave rise to that dispute and examine some of the issues that emerged. This will allow us to study with greater understanding the trade controls that the United States has imposed since 1982 and their implications on a definition of the jurisdictional limits under international law. It will also permit consideration of pending U.S. legislation that raises new issues.

(1) Person Subject to the Jurisdiction of the United States

In 1982, the United States invoked, for only the second time, the authority that Congress had included in a 1977 amendment of the Export Administration Act of 1969 (EAA). The 1977 EAA amendment permitted the president to impose export controls on goods or technology "exported by any person subject to the jurisdiction of the United States."[1]

The first reliance on this provision in March 1980 drew little but scholarly attention. It related solely to the U.S. refusal to participate in the 1980 Summer Olympics and the resulting prohibition on U.S. "persons subject" from furnishing products or technical data to assist with those games.[2] This restriction affected few U.S. commercial interests and was only effective for a short period.

In 1982, President Reagan relied on this same EAA authority in prohibiting "persons subject" from exporting or reexporting certain designated U.S. products or technical data which were used in oil and gas exploration, production, transmission, or refinement to the U.S.S.R. without prior authorization. These restrictions were expressly stated for purposes of foreign policy and not national security.[3] The Commerce Department defined "person subject" not only to be companies organized under U.S. law and their branches; in addition, the Department's definition of "person subject" included any foreign corporation that was "owned or controlled" by a U.S. corporation. Thus, Dresser France, a wholly owned French subsidiary of the U.S. company Dresser Industries, was prohibited—solely because of the ownership of that French subsidiary by its U.S. parent—from exporting French-manufactured oil and gas equipment to the U.S.S.R.[4]

---

1.   Pub. L. No. 95-233, tit. III, 91 Stat. 1625, 1629 (1977).

2.   45 Fed. Reg. 21, 612 (Apr. 2, 1980).

3.   Statement of Extension of U.S. Sanctions, 18 Weekly Comp. Pres. Doc. 820 (June 18, 1982); 47 Fed. Reg. 27, 250 (1982)(amending 15 C.F.R. § 385)(implementation of Executive Order by U.S. Commerce Department).

4.   *In re* Dresser (France) S.A., No. 632, 47 Fed. Reg. 28,170, *mdf'd*, 47 Fed. Reg. 39,708 (U.S. Dep't of Commerce, Int'l Trade Admin., 1982); for court challenge, *see* Dresser Indus. v. Baldridge, 549 F. Supp. 108 (D.D.C. 1982).

The "person subject" language was not new: it had appeared for many years in the regulations that the U.S. Treasury Department imposed, for example, under the Trading with the Enemy Act against North Korea (Foreign Assets Control Regulations)[5] and Cuba (Cuban Assets Control Regulatiorṡ). The Treasury Department had originally included owned or controlled foreign subsidiaries in the definition of "person subject" in the early 1950s, thus rendering these subsidiaries subject to the U.S. postwar trade embargo against the People's Republic of China. The same "person subject" provision applied under the U.S. Treasury embargo against Cambodia until January 1992, Vietnam until 1994, and currently applies against North Korea and Cuba.

The Treasury definition gave rise to the *Fruehauf*[7] and other well-known *causes célèbres*. In 1982, the Commerce Department adopted that Treasury Department definition in its regulations implementing the 1977 EAA amendment.[8] Commerce did so in an attempt to defeat the supply by European companies of equipment for the Soviet pipeline. In *Compagnie Européenne des Pétroles S.A. v. Sensor Nederland B.V.*, the Dutch District Court in The Hague held that the assertion of U.S. jurisdiction on the basis of the "person subject" definition did not provide a defense for the refusal of a Dutch subsidiary of a U.S. company to deliver goods for the Soviet pipeline.[9] The Dutch court could find no basis in international law for the U.S. "person subject" provisions, at least when the foreign subsidiary had not been established solely for the purpose of evading the U.S. regulations and when the U.S. controls were imposed for foreign policy and not national security purposes. Although there were allusions by U.S. policymakers to the benefits to the Soviet Union arising from the pipeline, the United States based the pipeline controls on foreign policy purposes and never claimed that they were imposed to achieve national security objectives. This "person subject" jurisdiction also gave rise to the decision of the French court in *Fruehauf* to order the appointment of an administrator to cause a French subsidiary, owned and controlled by a U.S. company, to perform the subsidiary's contract with the People's Republic of China.

In protesting the Soviet pipeline sanctions, the European Communities maintained that the "person subject" definition was contrary to a general principle

---

5.   31 C.F.R. pt. 500 (1994) prohibiting in section 201(b) "persons subject to the jurisdiction of the United States" from transactions involving any dealings in property in which the government of North Korea or one of its nationals has any interest and defining in section 329(d) "person subject" to include foreign corporations "wherever located" if "owned or controlled" by U.S.-organized corporations.

6.   31 C.F.R. pt. 515.

7.   Fruehauf v. Massardy, 1968 D.S. Jur. 147, 1965 J.C.P. II 14, 274 bis, 1965 Gaz. Pal. Cour d'appel, Paris.

8.   47 Fed. Reg. 27, 251 (1982).

9.   Compagnie Europeene des Petroles S.A. v. Sensor Nederland B.V., 22 I.L.M. 66 (Dist. Ct., The Hague 1982).

of international law reflected in the ICJ decision in *Barcelona Traction*.[10] (The EC conceded that the Barcelona Traction holding concerned diplomatic protection but correctly noted that the decision is widely viewed as precedent with respect to the assertion of national jurisdiction.[11]) *Barcelona Traction*, the EC argued, stood for the proposition that place of incorporation and place of a registered office were the accepted bases of jurisdiction for a legal entity. The Court rejected other purported bases, the EC added.

These same arguments are the basis for the strong EC protest against the Cuban Democracy Act, which, in 1992, removed the authority of the U.S. Treasury Department to issue licenses for U.S.-owned or U.S.-controlled foreign subsidiaries to engage in the sales to and purchase of goods from Cuba. The European Parliament resolution on the Cuban Democracy Act labeled the statute "a flagrant violation of international law on free trade and freedom of transit."[12] As is well known, this U.S. legislation has also given rise to the invocation of blocking statutes by the United Kingdom and Canada. To date, no case under the Cuban legislation has led to a major diplomatic confrontation between the United States and its allies. This is probably because the United States has adopted a narrow construction of the statute, when possible, and other sanctions programs have occupied the attention of U.S. Treasury officials (notably Iraq, Yugoslavia, and Haiti), and possibly also because vigorous pursuit of violations has not been a high enforcement priority.

Despite these significant occurrences during the dispute over the Soviet gas pipeline, the Restatement (Third) would allow extraterritorial jurisdiction over foreign-owned or foreign-controlled subsidiaries of U.S. companies "in exceptional cases." Under Section 414 of the Restatement (Third), the lawfulness under international law of jurisdiction to prescribe for a corporation organized under a host country's laws but owned or controlled by a foreign parent company depends upon the degree to which such regulation:

> [is] essential to implementation of a program to further a major national interest . . . can be carried out effectively only if applied also to foreign subsidiaries . . . and the regulation conflicts or is likely to conflict with the law or policy . . . [of the host country].[13]

---

10. Barcelona Traction, 1970 I.C.J. 3.

11. European Communities, Comments on the U.S. Regulations Concerning Trade with the U.S.S.R., 21 I.L.M. 891 (1982).

12. 1993 O.J. (C 21) 156 (Jan. 25, 1993); *see also* Eur. Parl. Res. (A3-0243/93), 1993 O.J. (C 268) 153 (Oct. 4, 1993) and Report of the Committee on External Economic Relations on the Embargo against Cuba and the Torricelli Act, Eur. Parl. Doc. (EN\RR\232\232726, July 26, 1993 and EN\RR\232958, July 29, 1993).

13. RESTATEMENT (THIRD) OF THE FOREIGN RELATIONS LAW OF THE UNITED STATES, § 414(2)(b)(I)–(iii)(1987).

The Restatement authors cite little support for this proposition and concede that incorporation of a subsidiary in another state "limits the jurisdiction to prescribe of the state of the parent [company]."[14] They seem to base the black-letter rule, at least in part, on the proposition that "a host state cannot, by requiring a foreign-owned enterprise to incorporate under its laws, deprive the state of the parent corporation of all authority over the enterprise."[15] They add that "[t]he enterprise itself cannot, by incorporating in a foreign state, escape all regulatory authority of the state of the parent corporation."

This analysis explains little in the usual case of parent companies that establish foreign subsidiaries for entirely appropriate business reasons having nothing to do with "escape" from home-country regulatory authority. For example, Dresser France was established years before issues of the Soviet pipeline were even discussed. The Restatement avoids coming to grips with the ultimate issue of jurisdiction and articulating a rationale for its position on this important subject.

The Restatement (Third) acknowledges that "orders issued directly to a foreign corporation are regarded as particularly intrusive and can be justified only by a clear showing of necessity in light of [the] factors" previously mentioned.[16] In addition, the Restatement (Third) suggests that the burden for making such a showing may be greater when a substantial portion of the shares of the host-state corporation are owned locally and traded in the local financial markets.[17] Having mentioned these qualifications, the Restatement (Third) takes the position that the exercise of jurisdiction "may be unreasonable" when a host-country corporation is asked to take action within the territory of the host country that is contrary to the policy of the host-country government (or to refrain from acts that are encouraged under the host-country government policy).

In light of the outcome of the Soviet pipeline controversy and subsequent U.S. state practice in avoiding application of new sanctions programs to owned or controlled foreign subsidiaries (e.g., Libya, Iraq, and Yugoslavia[18]), this Restatement (Third) position seems—if not flatly incorrect, as many nations would argue (including those of the European Union)—excessively protective of a position that today the United States would have considerable difficulty sustaining before any international tribunal. It is difficult to understand the benefit that the United States would gain by causing its closest allies to believe that the U.S. government wishes to preserve the legal authority to instigate another controversy based on the legal theory that led to the Soviet pipeline controversy. There is reason to believe that this inclination to protect the legal "foundation" of unilaterally asserted extraterritorial jurisdiction undermines the very multilateral cooperation that the

---

14. *Id.* § 414, Comment b.

15. *Id.*

16. *Id.* at Comment c.

17. *Id.* at Comment e.

18. 31 C.F.R. pt. 550 (Libya); 31 C.F.R. pt. 575 (Iraq); 31 C.F.R. pt. 585 (Yugoslavia (Serbia and Montenegro)).

United States would require in order that economic sanctions might succeed in the post–Cold War world.

There is ample evidence that the ideas reflected in the Restatement (Third) continue to be held by some U.S. government officials; thus, there is danger of further extraterritorial action. The Clinton Administration's proposed legislation to revise the Export Administration, which expires on June 30, 1994, would continue to permit U.S. export controls to be applied to "any item subject to the jurisdiction of the United States or exported by any person subject to the jurisdiction of the United States."[19] No definition of "item subject" or "person subject" appears in the draft legislation or is proposed. While this legislation failed in the Congress for other reasons, these provisions remained without change in the bills that emerged from the legislative process.

The Administration bill would in this same provision also add another ground for asserting jurisdiction: the proposed statute would permit the president to "regulate domestic and foreign conduct, consistent with the policies of this Act." Here we have what would be a new head of authority for asserting jurisdiction to apply U.S. export controls without any clear explanation of its purpose or, more important for our study, the extent of its extraterritorial reach.

It is evident that the new provision is intended to permit actions reaching outside the United States. In its bill, the Administration proposes the following elaboration of its authority to impose controls on exports and to regulate domestic and foreign conduct:

> [s]uch authority shall include, but not be limited to, the authority to prohibit activity such as financing, contracting, servicing or employment, to deny access to items in the United States *and abroad*, to conduct audits of reports and inspections of facilities, to compel reports, and to implement international commitments of the United States with respect to the control of exports.[20] (Emphasis added.)

Elements of this continued extraterritorialism appear in the alternative bill that leading members of the Congress have prepared in an effort to bring about more comprehensive revision of U.S. export control legislation.[21] Specifically, so-called "emergency controls" (effective for only six months unless extended by Congress) could be applied to "persons subject to the jurisdiction of the United States." As originally formulated, the proposal of these members of Congress avoided the use of the "person subject" authority in defining "normal" multinational export controls.[22] However, when their bill was introduced, the "person subject" language

---

19. Administration Proposal, The Export Administration Act of 1994 § 5(a)(1) (Feb. 24, 1994) (copy on file with the author).

20. *Id.*

21. H.R. 4663, 103d Cong., 2d Sess. § 106(a)(1).

22. Discussion Draft § 105(a), March 2, 1994 (on file with the author).

comprehensive revision of U.S. export control legislation.[21] Specifically, so-called "emergency controls" (effective for only six months unless extended by Congress) could be applied to "persons subject to the jurisdiction of the United States." As originally formulated, the proposal of these members of Congress avoided the use of the "person subject" authority in defining "normal" multinational export controls.[22] However, when their bill was introduced, the "person subject" language appeared in the provision governing so-called "multilateral controls" which would be the nonemergency export controls under the bill introduced.[23]

By mid-1994, the House Committee on Foreign Affairs had reported out a new Export Administration Act.[24] Four other House committees have jurisdiction over some provisions of this same legislation: the Armed Services, the Judiciary, Public Works & Transportation, Ways & Means and the Permanent Select Committee on Intelligence.

In the bill reported by the House Committee on Foreign Affairs, section 104(b) provides, *inter alia*, that:

> no person may export any item which such person knows will materially contribute to a program or activity for the design, development, or manufacture of a weapon of mass destruction or missile in a country that is not a member of, or a cooperating country with respect to, an export control regime controlling such weapon or missile.

"Person" is defined in the bill to include "any individual, partnership, corporation, or other form of association."[25] Since the bill uses the terms "United States person" and "foreign person" when it wishes to draw a distinction in treatment, as discussed below, it would seem that section 104(b) applies to foreign nationals and foreign incorporated legal entities. Further, the Committee report on this provision makes it clear that the provision is intended to prohibit exports "when on a control list or not."[26] In other words, this would be a new, broad-based end-use export control provision which applies to export by any person of any product, regardless of its character, if the material contribution test is met.

There were some efforts in the 103d Congress to have the legislative history to a new EAA make clear that the "person subject" is intended to apply to owned

---

21. H.R. 4663, 103d Cong., 2d Sess. § 106(a)(1).

22. Discussion Draft § 105(a), March 2, 1994 (on file with the author).

23. H.R. 4663, 103d Cong., 2d Sess. § 105(a)(1).

24. H.R. 3937, 103d Cong., 2d Sess. § 104(b); H.R. Rep. No. 531, 103d Cong., 2d Sess., pt. 1 (May 25, 1994)(Foreign Affairs), pt. 2 (June 16, 1994)(Intelligence), pt. 3 (June 7, 1994)(Ways and Means) and pt. 4 (June 17, 1994)(Armed Services).

25. H.R. 3937, 103d Cong., 2d Sess. § 116(22)("person"), (29) ("United States person") and (13)("foreign person").

26. H.R. Rep. No. 531, 103d Cong., 2d Sess. 90 (1994).

alteration. While the efforts in the 103d Congress to pass new export control legislation failed, there was no real dispute over the "person subject" or similar provisions that seem likely to appear in the new Export Administration Act and that would have the potential of creating new problems of extraterritoriality.

(2) Reexport of U.S.-Origin Products

Under the EAA, the United States had for many years imposed restrictions on the reexport of U.S.-origin products. Further, the relevant regulatory provision makes it clear that whether U.S.-origin products may be reexported without prior U.S. governmental authorization is to be determined at the time of proposed reexport, not at the time of initial export from the United States. Foreign recipients of high-technology U.S. products have been asked for many years to furnish written undertakings that they would not reexport them contrary to U.S. law and regulation. Further, the exporter of the goods is required to notify the recipient of these reexport restrictions by a Destination Control Statement on the commercial invoice and shipping documents.

In January 1980, the United States imposed controls on the reexport of grain sales to the U.S.S.R. These controls applied even to grain that was exported from the United States prior to the imposition of the sanctions. Similarly, the 1982 Soviet gas pipeline controls applied to U.S.-origin machinery that was located abroad at the time of the new U.S. sanctions. These actions were, of course, inconsistent with the holding of the Hong Kong court in 1953 in *American President Lines Ltd. v. China Mutual Trade Co.* that after goods are discharged they "ceased to be subject to the jurisdiction of the United States." [27]

When the Soviet gas pipeline sanctions appeared, the EC submitted that this attempt to assert retroactive control over U.S. products located abroad also contravened international law. In brief, the EC maintained that "goods and technology do not have any nationality and there are no known rules under international law for using goods or technology situated abroad as a basis for establishing jurisdiction over the persons controlling them." [28] The EC relied on the principle that jurisdiction over goods ends when they are discharged and relied upon *American President Lines* and also *Moen v. Ahlers North German Lloyd*, the latter a significant 1966 decision of the Tribunal of Commerce of Antwerp that has not been widely available. [29]

The Clinton Administration's proposal for the new EAA would continue to authorize controls over "items subject" to U.S. jurisdiction. [30] Similarly, the

---

27. 1953 A.M.C. 1510, 1526 (Hong Kong Sup. Ct.).

28. European Communities, Comments on the U.S. Regulations Concerning Trade with the U.S.S.R., 21 I.L.M. 891, 894 (1982).

29. 30 R.W. 360 (Tribunal of Commerce Antwerp 1966).

30. Administration Proposal, The Export Administration Act of 1994 § 5(a)(1) (Feb. 24, 1994) (copy on file with the author).

alternative bill proposed by leading members of Congress would apply its authority for "normal" and "emergency" export controls to "any commodity or technology subject to" U.S. jurisdiction.[31] Finally, section 105(a) of the bill reported by the House Committee on Foreign Affairs would apply multilateral controls, the new term for national security and nonproliferation controls, to "commodities or technology subject to the jurisdiction of the United States."[32]

(3) Foreign-Manufactured Products of U.S.-Origin Technical Data

For many years, United States export regulations have imposed restrictions on the export from third countries of the direct products of U.S.-origin technical data. If the data related to a high-technology product, the overseas recipient of U.S. data would, as a condition to receiving the data, be required to undertake not to reexport the data or its direct product to the Soviet Bloc countries. The United States carried such direct-product controls one step further in 1982: the Soviet pipeline sanctions applied direct-products controls to U.S. data located abroad that was not subject to such controls at the time of its export from the United States. In other words, the United States took the position that *European* licensees of U.S. data could not utilize such previously exported data to make *European* direct product equipment with *European* raw materials for export to the Soviet pipeline even if no such restriction on the direct product existed at the time of the U.S. export of the data.

What was the nexus for such direct-product controls? The Soviet pipeline controls applied when either a "person subject" had licensed the data or was to receive royalties or compensation for use of the data or when the foreign recipient of the data had agreed to comply with U.S. export control regulations. It mattered not at all that the no U.S. restrictions on supplying the Soviet pipeline existed at the time of such a license, royalty arrangement, or undertaking—or that the undertaking was limited to existing regulatory provisions.

Dresser Industries challenged this far-reaching, retroactive provision in litigation against the United States. The defense of the United States was almost as troubling as the provision itself. Lawyers for the Justice Department took the position in briefs filed in the Commerce Department administrative proceedings that each use of U.S.-origin technical data abroad under a licensing agreement involves a new export from the United States of the data subject to U.S. export controls. In effect, the United States argued that the licensee's exercise of its contractual right to use the technology was deemed to be a new U.S. export of the data itself. Under this theory, if the United States changed the rules applicable to the data after export, then the metaphysical "new export" of the data was allowed to occur only if the European licensee was using the data in compliance with the new restrictions. The written undertakings by the licensee were viewed by the Justice Department lawyers as a voluntary acceptance of this ever-changing U.S. control regime. The European

---

31. H.R. 4663, 103d Cong., 2d Sess. §§ 105(a)(1) and 106(a)(1).
32. H.R. 3937, 103d Cong., 2d Sess. § 105(a) (1994).

Communities termed "reprehensible" the U.S. reliance for this theory on such so-called "voluntary" submissions to U.S. jurisdiction by non-U.S. companies.[33] Noting that U.S. policy strongly opposed submission to foreign-nation boycotts, the EC took the position that "[p]rivate agreement should not be used . . . as instruments of foreign policy." In any event, such an undertaking could not provide a U.S. jurisdictional basis under international law that otherwise did not exist, the EC argued. Foreign nations were free to protest U.S. infringement of jurisdiction even if private companies organized under the laws of those nations entered into such undertakings. This position appears analogous to the U.S. view regarding the ineffectiveness of waivers by U.S. companies of diplomatic protection in nations that required acceptance of the Calvo Clause in investment contracts.[34]

(4) Protective Principle and Effects Doctrine

With respect to each of the three previously discussed nexuses for jurisdiction, the EC saw no basis for the United States to base its jurisdiction on either the protective principle or the effects doctrine. The former was inapplicable, the EC maintained, because the United States did not contend that the pipeline sanctions were necessary to "proscribe [generally recognized illegal] acts done outside its territory but threatening its security or the operating of its governmental functions."[35] Rather, the U.S. controls were, as noted above, expressly based under U.S. law on "foreign policy" grounds. This raises the interesting question of what position the EC would take under the new U.S. export administration legislation, which will blur or eliminate the distinction between national security and foreign policy controls and allow for export controls based on nonproliferation concerns, antiterrorism and human rights enforcement.

As for the "effects doctrine," the EC could not find any basis for concluding that the EC exports to the U.S.S.R. had "direct, foreseeable and substantial effects," which "constitute an element of a crime or tort proscribed by U.S. law." Indeed, the EC argued that "[i]t is more than likely that they [the EC exports to the Soviet gas pipeline] have no direct effects on U.S. trade."[36]

---

33. European Communities, Comments on the U.S. Regulations Concerning Trade with the U.S.S.R., 21 I.L.M. 891, 895 (1982).

34. For a discussion of the Calvo Clause and the United States position that U.S. private interests could not by private contract waive the right of the United States for diplomatic espousal of claims based on injury to its citizens *see* Restatement (Third) § 713 and Comment (g)("The United States regards companies that sign such clauses or submit to such laws [that purport to waive the protection of their state of nationality] as waiving rights that are not theirs to waive, since, in principle, the injury is to the state."). *See also id.* at Reporters' Note 6.

35. European Communities, Comments on the U.S. Regulations Concerning Trade with the U.S.S.R., 21 I.L.M. 891, 896 (1982).

36. *Id.* at 897.

b.   Post-Pipeline Experience: New U.S. Moderation in U.S. Trade Sanctions Against Libya, Iraq, and Yugoslavia

Following the Soviet gas pipeline incident in 1982, United States policy makers acknowledged tacitly that attempts to apply such U.S. controls unilaterally encountered two difficulties: they were often ineffective and they gave rise to foreign policy disputes with our allies. The pipeline affair had shown that the dispute could overshadow the original purpose of the controls.

This logic had, in fact, received some recognition before the Soviet pipeline controversy. For example, the U.S. trade sanctions against Iran in 1979 and 1980 did not apply to U.S.-owned or U.S.-controlled foreign subsidiaries. Rather, U.S. parent companies were obligated to notify the Treasury Department several days in advance if a foreign subsidiary intended to carry out a transaction with Iran that would be prohibited if performed by the U.S. parent.[37] I had occasion to ask the Director of the Office of Foreign Assets Control, U.S. Department of Treasury, what would happen if one of my clients filed such notice. The Director said that he would call the parent company's general counsel and urge that its foreign subsidiary not perform the transaction. "And if the foreign subsidiary ignored the request?" I asked. Then, the OFAC Director said, "the Secretary of the Treasury will call the president of the company with the same request." The OFAC Director added, "you know who next calls the company chairman if the Secretary also receives 'no' for an answer."

What is interesting is that this U.S. moderation worked in the case of Iran. There was little controversy with our allies under the Iranian sanctions even though many of them continued to have some normal trade relations with Iran during the hostage crisis from November 1979 until January 1981. It is regrettable that the lessons of that experience were lost when the Soviet pipeline sanctions were imposed.

After the pipeline sanctions were removed, it was a State Department lawyer who informed me on the first day of the effectiveness of our Libyan Sanctions Regulations in 1986 that there would be "no ET—no extraterritoriality."[38] And there has been no extraterritoriality under the Treasury Department sanctions against Libya. U.S.-owned or U.S.-controlled foreign subsidiaries are not subjected to the U.S. foreign trade sanctions against Libya.[39] The situation with respect to U.S. products is more complicated. Exports of U.S. products to Libya (other than food and medicines) are prohibited; reexports require prior U.S. governmental

---

37. 31 C.F.R. § 535.207(b) (1981)) (Although U.S.-owned or controlled foreign subsidiary not subject to the implementing U.S. regulations prohibiting trade with Iran, U.S. parent required to report to U.S. Treasury any proposed foreign subsidiary transaction with Iran ten days before the subsidiary enters into such transaction).

38. 31 C.F.R. pt. 550 (1994).

39. 31 C.F.R. § 550.308 defining "U.S. person" and not using the term employed in extraterritorial controls, "person subject to the jurisdiction of the United States."

authorization and, as a policy matter, are generally granted for nonstrategic products that are generally available from foreign sources, provided that the recipient is a civilian end-user in Libya. The U.S. goods to be reexported must be drawn from bona fide inventories in a third country; they cannot be transhipped upon receipt from the United States. Also, U.S. components may not be exported to third countries for use in manufacturing foreign products that are destined for the Libyan oil and gas industry.[40]

The United States did not apply its trade controls against Iraq and Yugoslavia to U.S.-owned or U.S.-controlled foreign subsidiaries. Rather, the controls apply only to U.S. nationals, U.S. corporations and the foreign branches of U.S. companies that are the same legal entity.[41] This U.S. moderation resulted, of course, from the international consensus in the United Nations that gave rise to these mandatory sanctions under Chapter VII of the U.N. Charter. Because of that consensus, there has been less controversy over the reach of the Iraq and Yugoslav sanctions. Thus, there has been little attention to the U.S. Executive Orders for Iraq and Yugoslavia that prohibit the exportation to those countries of "any goods, technology (including technical data or information), or services (1) from the United States, or (2) requiring the issuance of a license by a Federal agency."[42]

The latter phrase—"goods . . . requiring issuance of a license by a Federal agency"—had never before appeared in U.S. trade sanctions. When the Treasury Department issued regulations implementing those orders, the Iraqi Sanctions Regulations did not clarify its meaning. Section 205 of the Iraqi Sanctions Regulations prohibits the unauthorized export to Iraq of "goods, technology (including technical data or other information), or services . . . from the United States, or, *if subject to U.S. jurisdiction*."[43] "Goods . . . subject to U.S. jurisdiction" was also a new and not previously defined term under the Treasury Department regulations. Interpreting the same phrase, the Treasury Department Yugoslavia Sanctions Regulations repeated the language of the Executive Order by referring to "goods requiring the issuance of a license by a Federal agency."[44] The Yugoslav regulations did not define the term "goods . . . subject to U.S. jurisdiction."

Section 411 of the Iraqi and Yugoslav regulations prohibits the export from the United States to third countries if the U.S. exporter "knows or had reason to know" that the goods will be reexported or transhipped to Iraq or Yugoslavia as the case may be. Further, exportation to third countries is prohibited if the U.S. item will be incorporated or transformed by a foreign manufacturer into a third-country product that "is to be used in Iraq/Yugoslavia, is being specifically manufactured to fill an

---

40. 31 C.F.R. § 550.409 (1994) (Export to third countries; transhipments).
41. 31 C.F.R. § 575.321 and 322 (1994) (defining "U.S. person" and "U.S. national" under the Iraqi Sanctions Regulations) and 31 C.F.R. § 585.317 (1994) (defining "U.S. person").
42. Exec. Order No. 12,724 § 2(b), 3 C.F.R. 297 (1991) (Iraq); Exec. Order No. 12,810 § 2(b), 3 C.F.R. 308 (1993) (Yugoslavia (Serbia and Montenegro)).
43. 31 C.F.R. § 575.205 (1994)(emphasis added).
44. 31 C.F.R. § 585.205 (1994).

order from" Iraq/Yugoslavia or "if the manufacturer's sales of the particular product are predominantly to" Iraq/Yugoslavia.[45]

The term "goods requiring a license by a Federal agency" has received virtually no definitive interpretation by U.S. officials who concede its ambiguity. Further, there is little doubt that the use of the phrase "goods . . . subject to U.S. jurisdiction" in the Iraqi Sanctions Regulations was intended to avoid clarifying the meaning of the Executive Order. The difficulty with the terminology is that prior to the Kuwait invasion most U.S.-origin goods did not require a Federal agency license for export to Iraq; similarly, no prior Federal agency specific authorization was needed to export most U.S. goods to Yugoslavia prior to the imposition of the U.N.-mandated sanctions. Further, after the imposition of U.S. sanctions, the Commerce Department did not issue new regulations under the Export Administration Regulations requiring licenses, i.e., specific authorization, for the export to Iraq or Yugoslavia of goods that previously could be exported without securing such approval.

There is to date no published ruling by the U.S. Treasury Department regarding the meaning of this highly ambiguous terminology—"goods requiring a license by a Federal agency" and "goods . . . subject to U.S. jurisdiction." In the case of Iraq, the Treasury Department position was from August 2, 1992, through late 1994 that no reexport of U.S.-origin goods is permissible without prior U.S. authorization. Further, foreign-manufactured products with any U.S. content, however minimal, are apparently viewed by U.S. Treasury officials as potentially "subject to U.S. jurisdiction" and, consequently, require a license for export to Iraq. It is unclear but doubtful that any other U.N. member nation took such an expansive view of its export control sanctions against Iraq.

For the Yugoslavia regulations, the situation until the end of 1994 was not much clearer. At one point, the responsible Treasury officials appeared to take the view that the phrase applied if the U.S. content exceeded twenty-five percent by value of foreign-manufactured goods. Thus, the reexport of U.S.-origin goods that had undergone no further manufacture would not be permitted; nor would the United States permit the export to Yugoslavia of foreign-made goods with greater than twenty-five percent U.S. content. A test along these lines would be drawn from the provisions of the Export Administration Regulations which establish a twenty-five percent by value threshold for requiring prior U.S. authorization to export high-technology foreign-manufactured goods with U.S. content.[46]

These same Treasury officials have at times taken a more extreme position regarding the Yugoslav sanctions. They contended that, as in the case of Iraq, any U.S. content in a foreign-manufactured product subjected that product to a required U.S. authorization for export to Yugoslavia. They also may have taken the view that such authorization was necessary for the export of any foreign-manufactured product which was based on U.S.-origin technology. In both instances (with the

---

45. 31 C.F.R. § 575.411 and § 585.411 (1994).
46. Export Administration Regulations, 15 C.F.R. § 776.12. (1994).

exception of food and medical products), the United States would generally deny such approval and refuse to submit the case for clearance by the U.N. Sanctions Committee.

By late 1994, these U.S. Treasury officials abandoned this extreme position and issued rulings that suggested that they had adhered to the interpretation that U.S. authorization is required under the Yugoslav Sanctions Regulations only when a foreign-manufactured product destined for Yugoslavia contains more than twenty-five percent U.S. content. These officials also adopted a similar position under the Iraqi Sanctions Regulations. However, U.S. approval would be required if the U.S. exporter knows (or has reason to know) at the time of export that the U.S. materials or parts will be used in foreign-manufactured products destined for Yugoslavia or Iraq, specifically manufactured to fill an order for either country or sent to a manufacturer whose manufacture of the particular product is predominantly for either of those countries. At the same time, U.S. Treasury officials made clear that prior U.S. governmental authorization would be required to reexport to Iraq or Yugoslavia any U.S.-origin product even if shipped from a non-U.S. inventory and even if authorized for shipment by the U.N. member country in whose territory such inventory is located. It seems reasonably clear that the European Union countries would regard the position articulated at the time of the Soviet pipeline controversy to preclude U.S. jurisdiction, at least in this last situation, and possibly even when U.S. licensing is occasioned by the twenty-five percent threshold.

As previously noted, the Cuban Democracy Act, by prohibiting U.S. Treasury licensing of foreign subsidiary product sales to or purchases from Cuba, presents a stark contrast to the moderation evident in the U.S. sanctions against Libya, Iraq, and Yugoslavia. For present purposes, it may be sufficient to note the absence of any major controversy between the United States and any nation regarding the application of this statute, even countries that have invoked their blocking statute. This suggests that either other governments are accepting the effectiveness of the U.S. provisions—a most unlikely conclusion—or that the United States is taking a low-profile attitude towards enforcement. In addition, the United States may have authorized activities by U.S.-owned or U.S.-controlled foreign subsidiaries that can be viewed as not expressly prohibited under the Cuban Assets Control Regulations as amended by the Cuban Democracy Act. Such state practice may, of course, be significant in defining the content of international law in this field.

c. Sanctions Against Foreign Persons for Violation of COCOM and Nonproliferation Regimes

When foreign companies in two nations diverted advanced milling machinery to the Soviet Union, the United States viewed the action as a violation of the COCOM understandings and a direct threat to U.S. and Western national security interests.[47] In its legislative response to this incident, Congress found that:

> [i]n order to protect United States national security, the United States must take steps to ensure the compliance of foreign companies with COCOM controls, including, where necessary conditions have been met, the imposition of sanctions against violators of controls commensurate with the severity of the violation.[48]

As is well known, this same legislation imposed specific U.S. sanctions against the two concerned companies, notably a three-year prohibition of U.S. government procurement of goods and services and a three-year prohibition on importation into the United States of products of those companies. In addition, and subject to certain exceptions for preexisting contracts, sole source suppliers, and national security requirements, the legislation imposed a three-year prohibition on U.S. government procurement of products from the parent company of each of the subsidiaries involved in the machinery sales.

It is significant that Congress at the same time included in the Export Administration Act a provision requiring the president to impose sanctions of between two and five years against any foreign person found to have violated the COCOM controls issued by any country for national security purposes. Such sanctions were permitted if the violation resulted in "substantial enhancement" of Soviet and East bloc capabilities in certain critical technologies, e.g., submarines and antisubmarine equipment, ballistic missiles, etc. This mandatory provision requires imposition of the sanctions against the person or entity violating the COCOM regime, as well as against any parent, subsidiary, affiliate or successor. The sanctions included not only a prohibition on U.S. government contracting but also a prohibition on the importation of products into the United States.

Under the legislation, the president is permitted to forego sanctions against the parent, subsidiary, affiliate, or successor if he determines it "has not knowingly violated the export control regulation," and if the government of the country with jurisdiction over the parent, subsidiary, or affiliate had "an effective export control system" under COCOM which meets certain criteria specified by Congress in the legislation (e.g., national laws and regulations, licensing system, enforcement mechanism, etc.).[49] The president may relax the sanctions after two years if he makes a number of specific findings, including improvement by the foreign government of its export control system under the congressionally mandated criteria and improvement in the internal controls of the sanctioned entity so that violations are less likely to occur in the future. Congress also required the president, as a

---

47. For a review of the origins and role of the Coordinating Committee (COCOM) of the Consultative Group and its functions during the Cold War *see* Berman & Garson, *United States Export Controls—Past, Present, and Future,* 67 COLUM. L. REV. 791 (1967).

48. Omnibus Trade Act of 1988, Pub. L. No. 100–418, § 2442, 102 Stat. 1107 (1988).

49. 50 USC. § 2410a(d)(2).

condition for relaxing the controls, to find that the impact of the sanctions on the parent, subsidiary, or affiliate "is proportionate to the increased defense expenditures imposed on the United States" by the violation giving rise to the sanctions. Congress also specified that the president seek compensation from the concerned foreign person or government "in an amount proportionate to the costs of research and development and procurement of new defensive systems by the United States" and U.S. allies as a result of the COCOM controls violation by the foreign entity.[50]

The amended EAA also gives the Attorney-General authority to bring a damage action in U.S. courts seeking recovery for "the costs of restoring the military preparedness of the United States" as a result of the violation. This action may be brought against the foreign entity violating the COCOM control, "any person that is owned or controlled" by the violating entity or "any person who owns and controls" the violating entity. Thus, the parent company of a violating entity may be subjected to such a legal action for recovery of losses by the United States.

Beginning in the late 1980s, the United States began to enact legislation and promulgate regulations to limit the spread of weapons of mass destruction (nuclear, chemical, and biological) and missile delivery systems. These actions were coordinated with nations that are members of the Nuclear Suppliers Group, the Australia Group (chemical and biological weapons) and the Missile Technology Control Regime (MTCR). Unlike COCOM, which expired on March 31, 1994, none of these nonproliferation groups has a formal structure requiring, as COCOM did, unanimous approval for exceptions to the control regimes. Further, none has an established administrative structure such as COCOM maintained in Paris or a unified enforcement mechanism, the latter also never having existed for COCOM.

When Congress sought a legislative framework for sanctions against foreign persons who violate the nonproliferation regimes, it turned to the precedent established in the previously mentioned incident involving the sale of advanced machinery to the Soviet Union. As a result, the EAA includes far-reaching provisions mandating sanctions against foreign persons who violate the Missile Technology Control Regime or the Australia Group provisions. Further, the Foreign Relations Authorization Act for Fiscal Years 1994 and 1995 included a new Nuclear Proliferation Prevention Act which will almost certainly be incorporated in the revised Export Administration Act.

In brief, U.S. import prohibitions and a denial of U.S. government procurement must be imposed if a foreign person has knowingly and materially contributed to a foreign country that has used chemical/biological weapons in violation of international law or against its own citizens (or has made substantial preparations to do so), any foreign country designated as supporting international terrorism or any other country identified by the president. A parent or subsidiary company of the violating entity is also subjected to sanctions if it knowingly assisted in the violating activity. To date, neither the Bush nor Clinton Administration has

---

50.   50 USC. 2410a(I)(1).

imposed sanctions under this provision, which the Bush Administration opposed because of its inflexibility. Similar sanctions may be imposed under the newly enacted Nuclear Proliferation Prevention Act against any foreign person who has "materially and with requisite knowledge" contributed to the acquisition of unsafeguarded special nuclear material or the use or development of a nuclear explosive device as a result of exports from the United States or any other country of any goods or technology.

While the broad chemical/biological sanctions have not yet been imposed, the United States has imposed sanctions against a number of foreign entities for the supply of missile equipment or technology to countries that do not adhere to the MTCR. Under these provisions, the level of the sanctions depends upon the type of equipment or technology furnished. If the foreign persons furnish rockets, long-range (over 500 kg. payload to a range of 300 km.) unmanned air vehicle systems, complete subsystems or specially designed production facilities for such systems or subsystems, then the sanctions include denial of U.S. export licenses for products on the Munitions List and for products controlled under the Export Administration Regulations, denial of U.S. government contracts and a prohibition on imports into the United States. For furnishing components and technology relating to missile production to non-MTCR parties, narrower import and export sanctions are to be applied.

To date, MTCR sanctions have been imposed against a number of important foreign national agencies, including the Indian Space Research Organization, Glavcosmos in the Soviet Union, ARMSCOR in South Africa, the Iranian Ministry of Defense, the Pakistan Ministry of Defense and Space Research Commission, the Chinese Ministry of Aerospace Industry, China Great Wall Industry Corporation, China Precision Machinery Import-Export Corporation (CPMIEC), and the Syrian Ministry of Defense and Scientific Research Center. In each instance, the entity has been denied validated licenses for U.S. products that are controlled for missile proliferation purposes. The State Department maintains that they should also be denied access to all U.S. products requiring specific authorization for export. In any event, the Commerce Department has, under existing EAA authority, notified some U.S. exporters that they may not supply some products to these entities that would otherwise not be subject to any export license restriction.

d. Proposed Legislation to Prevent Nonproliferation—New Extraterritorial Concerns

The pending EAA amendment legislation includes two provisions, among others, that are likely to give rise to new disagreements over extraterritorial assertion of U.S. foreign trade sanctions. In brief, the new legislation would require the president to impose certain mandatory sanctions against any foreign person (and allow certain discretionary sanctions) if the president finds such person has engaged in, facilitated, or solicited the unauthorized export or transfer of MTCR items (whether of U.S. or foreign origin), any chemicals, biological agents, or equipment contributing to chemical or biological weapons production, unsafeguarded special nuclear material or nuclear explosive devices, or participated in a transaction involving financing any of these actions. The president would also have authority to impose actions "on other persons as the President determines should be subject to sanctions because they are related to that person [who engaged in the conduct breaking non-proliferation controls]."

The sanctions in question are quite broad and may be imposed to up to two years. They could severely impact the foreign persons and the U.S. subsidiaries and affiliates because they potentially include not only denial of U.S. government contracts and financing but, perhaps more seriously, mandatory prohibitions on imports into the United States and denial of all U.S. export privileges.

The mood of Congress regarding such provisions and their prospective extraterritorial reach is reflected in recent comments that were made by leading Senators in support of similar far-reaching sanctions against foreign countries and persons who transfer goods or technology that permit Iraq or Iran to acquire advanced conventional weapons. (The sanctions did not include import restrictions but were otherwise comparable.) The proposed provision was approved by the Senate in its foreign relations authorization bill for fiscal years 1994 and 1995. The provision was dropped by the Conference Committee when the House bill had no comparable provision.

On the Senate floor, Senator McCain with support from Senators Kerry and Lieberman stated the following in favor of their amendment authorizing so-called "third-party" sanctions against foreign governments and persons that furnish advanced conventional weapons to Iran or Iraq:

> [o]ur amendment does not mandate action by the United States when foreign governments are willing to take real and decisive action on their own. The legislation offers traditional incentives for foreign governments to join in international arms control efforts and to pass and enforce national legislation that parallels the non-proliferation legislation adopted by the United States.

> . . .We believe that every effort should be made to reach international and regional agreements and to persuade foreign governments to establish sanctions on the actions of their own companies and citizens. . . . Our bill reinforces the seriousness we attach to the threat posed by Iran and Iraq.[51]

As is well known, the failure of the COCOM members to agree upon a successor regime has occurred precisely because of the reluctance of other nations to join in imposing controls on conventional arms transfers to states considered terrorist by the United States, particularly Iran. The Senate action reflected the wil-

---

51. 140 Cong. Rec. S346 (daily ed., Jan. 28, 1994).

lingness of the Senate to impose sanctions unilaterally and extraterritorially if consensus cannot be achieved with our allies.

When the leading members of Congress proposed their alternative bill for the new export administration legislation, they suggested a narrower standard than the administration for imposing sanctions on such third parties. Specifically, the alternative bill provides that a parent or subsidiary of the violating party may be subjected to nonproliferation sanctions "if that parent or subsidiary materially and with requisite knowledge assisted in the activities which are the basis of that determination."[52] This narrower version of the sanctions provision imposing sanctions only if the parent with "requisite knowledge assisted" in the violations appears in the bill that emerged from the House Committee on Foreign Affairs.[53]

In formal comments to the Congress on the alternative bill, the Assistant Secretary of Commerce for Export Administration opposed this narrower provision. She argued that the more "rigorous provisions [of the Administration bill] could be used to guard against evasion of the impact of sanctions." She added that the broader standard, requiring no showing of assistance by a related party, "could also strengthen sanctions, if limiting sanctions to the particular operating unit identified as involved would have inadequate economic impact."[54] These comments are not only interesting for what they reveal about the Clinton Administration's views regarding extraterritoriality; they suggest the mistakes of the Soviet gas pipeline controversy may well be repeated in the name of sanctions for nonproliferation violations.

If there were any doubt about the need for concern regarding the current views toward extraterritoriality, a second disagreement between the Administration and the Congress over the EAA draft legislation should make the point even clearer. In their alternative bill, the Congressmen proposed that the United States would not impose nonproliferation sanctions against a U.S. or foreign person:

> if the government of a regime adherent, other than the United States, is taking judicial or other enforcement action against that person with respect to such acts, or that person has been found by the government of a regime adherent to be innocent of wrongdoing with respect to such acts.

This provision is embodied in the bill approved by the House Committee on Foreign Affairs.[55]

---

52.   H.R. 4663, 103d Cong., 2d Sess. § 111(c)(3)(C) (1994).

53.   H.R. 3937, 103d Cong., 2d Sess. §§ 111(c)(3)(C) and (D) (1994).

54.   Letter from Assistant Secretary for Export Administration Sue Eckert to Chairman Lee H. Hamilton, House Committee on Foreign Affairs, Summary at 7 (commenting on Section 111(a)(3) of House members Discussion Draft)(Mar. 24, 1994) (letter on file with the author).

55.   H.R. 3937, 103d Cong., 2d Sess. § 111(c)(7) (1994).

The Clinton Administration has also opposed this provision on the ground that, again in the words of the Assistant Secretary of Commerce for Export Administration, U.S. sanctions should be permitted "if it [the United States] deems foreign action inadequate."[56] In other words, the United States will review whether the courts and administrative agencies of foreign governments in a cooperative export control regime—the TCR, Australia Group, and Nuclear Suppliers—are exercising their sanctions authority with sufficient vigor. If not, the United States will do the job for them.

It is respectfully submitted that this newly proposed EAA authority will, if exercised, undermine the very nonproliferation regime whose purposes it is intended to serve. Or, these provisions will give rise to another multinational controversy that will make the dispute over the Soviet gas pipeline seem, in retrospect, to be only a warm-up. That would be a most regrettable outcome and suggests why international lawyers need to devote more thinking to the principles governing extraterritorial assertions of jurisdiction with respect to foreign trade controls.

e.   Need for International Legal Principles Supporting Multilateral Approach to Nonproliferation and Other Foreign Trade Controls

When governments become involved in disputes over extraterritoriality, the dialogue often occurs at a high level of abstraction. In this paper, I have attempted to identify some of the specific legal theories that have given rise to disputes with the United States over the extraterritorial application of foreign trade controls. Further, I have endeavored to show that in the post-COCOM world, there are new U.S. proposals in the field of nonproliferation and antiterrorism controls that may serve as the basis for further disputes with our allies concerning extraterritorial reach of U.S. law and regulations. Even more ominous, the advocates in Congress and in the Administration of these U.S. legal measures sometimes seem to ignore the lessons of prior conflicts over just such U.S. unilateral provisions.

In the post–Cold War world, the focus of foreign trade controls will be on preventing proliferation of weapons of mass destruction—nuclear, chemical, biological, and missile delivery systems—and denying support to state-sponsored terrorism. In the case of COCOM, there was a reasonable basis for contending, especially in the decade or so following World War II, that the United States could unilaterally implement effective strategic trade controls even if our allies did not cooperate. The Soviet gas pipeline controversy should have marked the end of such thinking although some U.S. policymakers simply ignored its lessons. By the 1980s after the Soviet pipeline controversy, the United States recognized that unilateral

---

56.   Letter from Assistant Secretary for Export Administration Sue Eckert to Chairman Lee H. Hamilton, House Committee on Foreign Affairs, Summary at 8 (commenting on Section 111(7)(A) of House members Discussion Draft)(Mar. 24, 1994)(letter on file with the author).

action would achieve little in the field of foreign policy or strategic controls. In the contemporary cases of nonproliferation controls and prevention of state-sponsored terrorism, the point is even more clear—success is possible only through multilateral action.

For international lawyers, the challenge is to articulate principles that will provide guidance for policymakers seeking to implement antiproliferation, antiterrorism policies through foreign trade sanctions. I suggest that those principles will provide for greater restraint on extraterritorial action than is apparent in past actions or current proposals of the U.S. Executive and Congress. Those principles will probably extend beyond the Restatement (Third) by establishing a nearly irrefutable presumption against extraterritorial sanctions in the absence of express acquiescence by the state whose corporate citizens would be subjected to restraints not applicable under their local law or on whose territory are located the goods or technology not otherwise subject to control. Perhaps a small exception to those principles will have to remain under such principles for extraterritorial actions vital to preserving national security. It is unlikely that such an exception would find much scope for application, given the need for multilateral cooperation for most sanctions to be effective in today's global economy.

Finally, the new U.S. proposals for sanctions against foreign persons for violating nonproliferation and state terrorism controls risk reopening old controversies on a new terrain. It is true that these U.S. sanctions would involve the denial of only U.S. legal privileges and in that sense they may be regarded as only semi-extraterritorial—i.e., they apply U.S.-based sanctions for conduct outside of the United States. There may well be a reasonable argument that such sanctions should not give rise to the same level of controversy as those that gave rise to the Soviet pipeline controversy.

In my judgment, that approach based on nice theoretical distinctions is not viable in the post–Cold War world in which the United States is participating. Based on prior experience, there is ample reason to doubt whether that distinction alone will avoid protest and controversy when the first such penalties are imposed on a non-U.S. company or non-U.S. citizens by a U.S. Administration. Differences among governments are almost certain to arise, especially if an allied government has decided to mete out a less severe penalty against one of its citizens or domestic companies than the United States believes appropriate or to pursue a different enforcement strategy in implementing multilateral controls against a target state. In short, sanctions for violations of foreign trade controls may become a new battleground for extraterritoriality in the 1990s if governments fail to cooperate in multilateral action and fail to avoid unilateral action based on extraterritorial application of substantive rules or enforcement action.[57]

---

57.   For evidence that concerns about extraterritoriality in new Congressional legislation have not diminished in the new 104th Congress, *see* Senator D'Amato's S. 277, 141 Cong. Rec. S1540 (Jan. 25, 1995) (proposing sweeping extraterritorial application of a new United States embargo of all economic relations with Iran, including a specific section titled *Extraterritorial Application* (Section 3(c)) and a definition of "United States national" that would possibly for the first time in U.S. law include within that term any foreign corporation in which U.S. interests hold more than 50 percent of the outstanding capital stock or other beneficial interest (Section 7(5)).

RETHINKING THE CONCEPTUAL FRAMEWORK OF EXTRATERRITORIAL ISSUES AND THE METHODS FOR RESOLVING CONFLICTS

Detlev F. Vagts

I. INTRODUCTION

In the last forty years American practice regarding extraterritoriality has seemed to be out of step with the rest of the world; the United States has consistently asserted the right to regulate matters that others consider beyond its jurisdiction. This chapter will attempt to explain American extraterritoriality theory, describe how it reached its present posture, and explore the means that could mitigate its tendency to bring the United States into conflict with other countries. During these four decades, the U.S. position on extraterritoriality has led to collisions that painfully affect U.S. foreign policy, as well as causing disputes with the allies most crucial to creation of a peaceful and balanced world order; these disputes often result in isolation and estrangement. As we are well into the post-Cold War period, 1994 seems a suitable year in which to reexamine these matters: this is a time when the felt imperative of blocking the Soviet Union at every turn has ceased to justify extension of American legal power to the remote corners of the world. The United States currently is faced with the task of building coalitions for common enterprises in the Security Council, in the realm of international economic law, and in the struggle against the remaining enemies of civilized society—such as the drug trade, terrorism, and international financial fraud. The United States must learn to cope with these problems in the role of being the first among equals rather than the military suzerain of the Western world. And these tasks must be carried out in a world of incredible interconnectedness and complexity; they will require much adjustment on the part of policymakers as well as academic theoreticians.

II. HISTORY OF AMERICAN POLICY AND SCHOLARSHIP ON EXTRATERRITORIALITY

It is now largely forgotten that the United States originally was quite averse to assertions of extraterritoriality. The predominant theory was one of rigid territorial sovereignty that divided the world sharply into nation-states, each surrounded by walls. As Chief Justice Marshall explained in *The Schooner Exchange*,[1] a foreign sovereign could only penetrate that space by complying with the terms imposed by the local ruler—although it could be assumed that the local ruler would impose only such terms as were customary among civilized states. Private traders could penetrate that space only in conformity with the locally imposed rules. Physical presence within the walls subjected one to seizure by the sovereign's minions, which in turn exposed one to the possibilty of being sued in the sovereign's courts. The same principle was applicable if one left property within the sovereign's grasp. This strict geographical view of sovereignty cast into sharp relief the practice by some Western states of wresting a set of concessions from some less-developed countries that exempted their citizens from local sovereignty; Japan and China in particular were recipients of such treatment.[2]

It was in this context that the first great American opinions on jurisdiction took shape. In the *American Banana*[3] case, Justice Holmes enunciated a doctrine of strict territorial limits. He found that the behavior of the United Fruit Company, a basically American firm operating in Central America, was not subject to the restrictions of the Sherman Act—even though it was quite apparent that the principal and indeed only significant effect of United Fruit's activities was upon American consumers of bananas, and even though the language of the Sherman Act was open to the interpretation that it covered a restraint on a stream of trade that concluded by delivering goods in the United States. Grudgingly, Justice Holmes conceded that Congress *could*, if it wanted to, extend the reach of U.S. law beyond its frontiers. But that great nationalist was clearly thinking of limited cases in which American expatriates might betray their allegiance to their country by trafficking with its enemies or frustrating its policies.

John Bassett Moore, the leading American international lawyer of his time, affirmed the converse proposition that foreign nations could not project their power within the United States. His prime vehicle was the *Cutting*[4] case, in which Mexico sought to punish an American newspaperman who had set into circulation copies of newspapers from the northern side of the Rio Grande river. These newspapers contained articles that offended the dignity of an important citizen of Mexico. On behalf of the Department of State, Moore asserted that this action transgressed the basic principles of the relations between sovereign states; Mexico was attempting

---

1.   The Schooner Exchange v. McFadden, 11 U.S. (7 Cranch) 116 (1812).

2.   *See generally* EBB, REGULATION AND PROTECTION OF INTERNATIONAL BUSINESS 1–19 (1964).

3.   American Banana Co. v. United Fruit Co., 213 U.S. 347 (1909).

4.   The Cutting Case, 2 Moore, DIG. INT'L L. 228–269 (1906).

to govern transactions—the setting of type and the rolling of presses—that took place on American soil.

Moore adhered to these principles even when he sat on the Permanent Court of International Justice. In the *Lotus*[5] case, he maintained in his separate opinion the most restrictive view of any of the judges in regard to Turkey's capacity to impose penalties on Lieutenant Demons for negligently sailing the Lotus into the unfortunate Boz-Kourt. Many less illustrious American judges and publicists who held the same restrictive view could be cited. For instance, a Georgia judge struggled to reconcile territoriality with the facts of an interstate shooting case. In doing so he maintained the position that, in contemplation of law, a man who fired in South Carolina accompanied his leaden messenger into Georgia long enough to complete the act of attempted murder within Georgia's jurisdiction.[6]

What, then, converted the United States into the world's most aggressive extraterritorialist? The development can be traced through a series of antitrust cases, primarily ones in which the United States, rather than a private party like American Banana, was the moving party. Concurrently with *Ford v. United States*,[7] a case under the uniquely American prohibition laws, the Supreme Court reconsidered antitrust extraterritoriality in the *Sisal*[8] case of 1924. The Court there distinguished the *Banana* case as one in which all the illegal activity took place abroad, whereas in *Sisal* the activity was distributed between the United States and abroad.

The culmination of the series of antitrust cases is the *United States v. Aluminum Company of America* (*Alcoa*) case,[9] decided in 1945 (the year that World War II ended), by America's most famous court of appeals judge of the day. *Alcoa* stated the "effects" doctrine in crisp and categorical tones. It is an expression of mature American power on the world scene. This doctrine made it evident that it was important for the United States to be able to reach out and prevent or undo the type of cartel behavior that had built up German industrial power and sustained the Nazi war effort.

Although some factors existed that linked extraterritoriality to U.S. policy, Judge Learned Hand chose to sweep past them and enounce an almost pure theory of extraterritoriality. He ignored the fact that the same two families owned controlling interests in both the American defendant corporation and the Canadian firm that was a party to the conspiracy based in Switzerland. He also ignored the fact that the Canadian firm's principal administrative office was in New York. He bequeathed to posterity a case which enunciated that the parties who conspired in Switzerland to restrain imports into the United States were within the reach of U.S. authorities (even if it could not be proved that they had succeeded in their effort to restrain).

---

5.   The S.S. Lotus, 1927 P.C.I.J. (ser.A) No. 10.
6.   Simpson v. State, 92 Ga. 41 (1893).
7.   Ford v. United States, 273 U.S. 593 (1927).
8.   United States v. Sisal Sales Corp., 274 U.S. 268 (1927).
9.   148 F.2d 416 (2d Cir. 1945).

A number of cartel cases, all of which attacked pre-World War II arrangements designed to restrict competition during the depression years, generalized the doctrine of the *Alcoa* case and caused quite intense friction between the United States and some of its closest allies during the Cold War, particularly Great Britain.[10] British animosity escalated to the point that blocking legislation was passed which authorized the British government to take steps to frustrate American antitrust activities—even to the extent that defendants in American antitrust suits were allowed to retrieve ("claw back") two-thirds of American treble damage judgments.[11]

The other major branch of U.S. extraterritorial aggressiveness after 1945 was the Cold War front itself. Here the crusading quality of American anti-Communism drew upon a British tradition: in two world wars Britain had conducted economic warfare with Germany on a worldwide front. It had blacklisted neutrals who traded with Germany and penalized traders who were not careful about seeing to it that goods approved for sale to one party were not transshipped for use to further the Kaiser's or the Fuehrer's war efforts. The United States followed suit during World War II and then transferred the effort to fight the undeclared cold war against Moscow. In so doing it had partial concurrence from the nations that belonged to NATO. These nations, for the most part, also were its partners in the Coordinating Committee (COCOM) which sought to negotiate agreed-upon lists as to what goods could not be sold to the Soviet Union or its allies. This cooperation achieved some success; but it also experienced failure, for the different nations varied in their judgment as to what constituted an appropriate subject of trade across the Iron Curtain.

Major breakdowns in the system include: (1) differences over trade with Beijing, which the United States sought to keep in complete isolation—until the sudden demarche of Henry Kissinger in 1973—while France and other countries sought to develop connections beginning in the early 1960s; (2) a continuous gap between the perceptions of the United States and other countries, particularly in Latin America, in regard to Cuba and Castro's government: a discrepancy that has grown even larger since the United States, through the so-called Cuban Democracy Act,[12] has tightened the screws on intercourse with Havana; meanwhile, a majority of countries in the U.N. General Assembly has condemned the continuing boycott of a state in grave political and economic difficulty; (3) striking differences between the position of the United States and its allies in Western Europe over the institution of a denial to Russia of technology necessary to develop the natural gas pipeline to Europe. This denial was to be used as a weapon in connection with the imposition of martial law in Poland in order to thwart the march of *Solidarnosc*, an action that

---

10. The American and British cases in this controversy are excerpted in STEINER, VAGTS & KOH, TRANSNATIONAL LEGAL PROBLEMS 968–77 (4th ed. 1994).

11. Lowe, *Blocking Extraterritorial Jurisdiction: The British Protection of Trading Interests Act, 1980*, 75 AM. J. INT'L L. 257 (1981).

12. 22 U.S.C. §§ 6001–6010 (Supp. V 1993).

Americans blamed on the leaders in the Kremlin; (4) the Toshiba episode, which was particularly significant in regard to relations with Japan. In this incident, Toshiba transferred technology to the Soviet Union which related to the ul-tra-precise milling of propeller blades for submarines. The action was clearly in violation of the Japanese version of export control legislation and Toshiba was duly punished. The technology in question was wholly Japanese and Toshiba was in no sense an American firm. Nonetheless, the U.S. Congress became highly incensed and passed legislation that imposed penalties by way of restrictions on the Japanese firm's right to import and sell to the United States.[13]

Alongside these two major aspects of extraterritoriality—antitrust and Cold War—there has been a steady trickle of activity from other fields. The United States is the most enthusiastic of all countries in the pursuit of inside traders and others who take advantage of more naive participants in the securities markets. Thus there has been a periodic flurry of Securities and Exchange Act prosecutions and civil suits that seek to envelop securities transactions that are more or less foreign in their location within the United States sphere of legal influence. There has been a sprinkling of cases involving such matters as U.S. antidiscrimination in employment legislation,[14] environmental quality statutes, and the like. There has also been one category of cases that involves outreach in a way that is usually applauded by rightminded commentators, namely, human rights cases. While these cases have immensely appealing histories, they do involve application of rules by American courts that are said to be universal, i.e., derived from public international law. The targets of such suits, however, may be justified in their sense that American courts do not apply these rules in the same spirit as do international tribunals.

Yet it would be a mistake to view the American position as being simply and directly aggressive. While the United States has stubbornly refused to concede that there are weaknesses in its conceptual justifications of its actions, it often has been willing to address the practical details of its approaches realistically. For instance, as a result of vehement foreign protests, it has been willing to stay its hand in particular antitrust cases. It also has been willing to enter into agreements that envisage the notification of antitrust initiatives to other antitrust agencies before any irrevocable steps have been taken, in order that representations can be made and accommodations reached.[15] Bringing restraint to the antitrust field might have progressed further if the U.S. authorities had been able to deter private parties from initiating expensive suits in order to recover three times the amount allegedly lost through antitrust violations. The pipeline controversy culminated in U.S. termina-

---

13. Pub. L. No. 100–418, 102 Stat. 1107 (1988) (expired 1992).

14. EEOC v. Arabian American Oil Co., 499 U.S. 244 (1991), partly overruled by Congress in 42 U.S.C.A. § 2000e-1 (1991).

15. *Symposium, Antitrust: Minimizing Friction between the Trading Blocks*, 24 L. & POL'Y INT. BUS. 1035 (1993); Chang, *Extraterritorial Application of U.S. Antitrust Law to other Pacific Countries*, 18 HASTINGS INT'L & COMP. L. REV. 295 (1993).

tion of its boycott attempt—even though it proclaimed that it was doing so because victory had been achieved. Administrators of securities regulation laws have a tendency to understand each others' problems and to avert collisions before matters become too tense. Nonetheless, a looming shadow of danger surrounds controversies over extraterritoriality; genuine trouble conceivably could ensue in the realm of already sensitive interstate relations.

III. THE AMERICAN CODIFICATIONS

There have been three major attempts by groups of American scholars to lay a conceptual foundation for extraterritorial practice. The first of these took place from 1932 to 1935, under the auspices of the so-called Harvard Research; a draft convention was produced on jurisdiction regarding crime.[16] The American scholars who made up that party swept their research nets across prior attempts in Europe and Latin America to codify the topic as well as the practice of the states that at the time played a role in making international law. About ninety percent of the citations in their bibliography were non-American. They found a wide variety of outreach episodes among those states. They lined up the justifications used and pronounced each of them to be acceptable. These became a classic catalogue of bases for jurisdiction.

That methodology seemed to be mandated by the almost contemporaneous judgment of the Permanent Court in the *Lotus* case: restrictions on states were not to be presumed and thus any basis of jurisdiction that had not been authoritatively condemned by state practice was licit. The first basis approved in the convention was the unquestioned foundation of territoriality—the locus of the action to be regulated. The comments to that section make it apparent that the drafters accepted an "objective" territoriality component, that is, cases in which the activity took place outside the country although its effects were to be realized within it. Next they presented a sprinkling of cases in which states had applied some of their criminal law to their nationals while abroad. Some states made extensive use of this principle, subjecting their citizens, at least in theory, to more or less all of their penal codes, even while out of the country. Others made sparing use of the link, restricting it to cases in which the national was violating some duty of loyalty to the home government. Third, the researchers included a narrow type of effects test-cases that threatened the territorial integrity or political independence of the nation (or counterfeited its currency). The draft recognized that precedent existed for the prosecution of pirates and perhaps slave traders wherever they were captured—usually on the high seas—by whomever seized them. Their crimes were universally condemned and the inconveniences of dragging them to their home country for trial and punishment seemed manifest. Finally, the codifiers paid their respects to the *Lotus* case by indicating their disdain for the so-called "passive personality" principle, that is, the assertion of power by the state whose citizen is

---

16.   29 AM. J. INT'L L. (SUPP.) 435 (1935).

hurt. That principle had constituted the foundation for the Turkish statute on the basis of which Lieutenant Demons had been prosecuted.

The Permanent Court carefully avoided reliance on that ground, focusing instead on the effect of the prow of the French vessel crashing into the Turkish collier, which it regarded as being for these purposes essentially a little floating piece of Turkish territory. It is evident that most of the cases cited in the Harvard project condemned criminal behavior that each of the states involved regarded as reprehensible—at the time of the convention, the more subtle questions of economic regulation were not yet in the foreground. Also, the incidence of assertions was fairly evenly distributed among the major commercial and imperial powers of the time. Indeed, the most extravagant extraterritorial assertion recorded was the German prosecution of a French citizen for shouting *"vive la France!"* loud enough that it could be heard within the Reich.

The American Law Institute (ALI) turned its attention to the "foreign relations law of the United States" in a project that began in 1956 and concluded with publication of the Restatement (Second) (there never was a first) in 1965. The ALI, it should be noted, is a private institution that is dedicated to rendering U.S. law, particularly common law, more logical and comprehensible. Its processes begin as reporters who are specialists in the field in question compose a draft; then it is reviewed by a larger panel of lawyers familiar with the field. Subsequently, the generalists on the council of the Institute revise the draft; discussion and approval by a plenary session of the whole membership follows. For the purposes of this Restatement, a panel of European advisers was introduced to the process. The process brings to bear a wide variety of expertise and tends to produce assurance that the result is "sound," that is, conservative and free from idiosyncratic or erratic creativity.

The Restatement of Foreign Relations Law, as other restatements, was an essentially American-based operation—more so than was the Harvard Research. By the 1960s circumstances had altered in the outside world. The proliferation of American episodes of extraterritorial aggression was well under way; thus, the burden seemed to fall on the United States to justify practices that were not followed by the rest of the world. More so than the Harvard Research, the Restatement relied upon such episodes in order to justify an expanded scope of jurisdiction. The structure of the relevant paragraphs of the Restatement paralleled that of the Harvard Research. While the Restatement did not limit itself to criminal law cases, it did focus on public law doctrines and did not particularly heed the Institute's own Restatement of Conflict of Laws, promulgated in 1934. Comments by the Reporters in effect footnoted the "black letter" sections and presented justifications for them. More so than the Harvard version, the Restatement had to rely on episodes that involved U.S. assertions of power.

After an unusually short cycle the ALI authorized another restatement that commenced in 1979. This restatement began under the leadership of Richard Baxter, who resigned in order to take a seat on the International Court of Justice, and then under that of Professor Louis Henkin of Columbia, who was assisted by three other academics, of which this author was one. This team was assisted by an international—this time not exclusively European—advisory panel that included Judges Shigeru Oda and Jimenez de Arechaga, who provided non-American perspectives. By the 1970s there had been a great deal more practice in the field of extraterritoriality that illuminated the problem, even if it also confused it. It had been necessary that U.S. courts deliberate over whether they should find limitations on the sweeping scope of statutes and regulation. There even had been some episodes in which European institutions, particularly the Commission of the European Communities, had found themselves confronted with the need to give extraterritorial effect to their rules if they were to have an effect on conditions that violated their policies.[17]

The progress of the sections that addressed extraterritoriality proved tempestuous at times. It was controversial in complicated ways. American business representatives who feared being caught in the middle of interstate confrontations, or being unable to compete with unregulated foreign businesses, tended to appreciate the merits of restricting U.S. assertions of power. On the other hand, government officials suspected indications that there was any restraint other than sound executive appraisal of the international situation.

One of the major novelties in the Restatement (Third) was the addition of section 403, which asserted the existence of a rule that jurisdiction could not be asserted if the outcome were unreasonable—even if one of the traditional bases was present. This rule was found to be one of international law as well as domestic American law. The Restatement then provided a list of circumstances in which an exercise might be unreasonable, including such considerations as the degree of conflict between the assertion of jurisdiction and the policies of the other state or states involved. This addition was unpopular in various circles that feared interference with American initiatives abroad but, with various modifications, it ultimately appeared in the final version.

Another feature of the 1987 version was the more explicit division of jurisdiction into three parts. The one that concerns us here was termed "jurisdiction to prescribe," that is, jurisdiction to lay down rules that must be obeyed. It was distinguished from "jurisdiction to adjudicate"—the power of courts to take to themselves an item of civil or criminal litigation because the defendant is sufficiently closely connected with the forum. Finally, "jurisdiction to enforce" was addressed, which is the right of a state to take police measures in order to ascertain that its rules are followed and that those who disobey them are punished. Extraterritorial exercises of American enforcement jurisdiction, in Panama and in Mexico,[18] have defied the consensus of the international community most strikingly in recent years. For, as early as the *Lotus* case, the court considered the rule against exercising police functions in the territory of another sovereign the most basic prohibition in international law. The Restatement (Third) paid tribute to the

---

17. THE RESTATEMENT (THIRD) FOREIGN RELATIONS LAW OF THE UNITED STATES cites some of these cases in § 415, Reporters' Note 9.

18. *See* United States v. Alvarez-Machain, 112 S. Ct. 2188 (1992).

diversity of contexts in the general field of extraterritoriality by devoting separate sections to jurisdiction to prescribe taxation, regulation of anti-competitive activities, and securities regulation. Finally, it recognized the relevance of the work of other authors who had produced the Restatement (Second) of Conflicts of Law in 1971—to which it frequently referred.

IV. THE CONCEPTUAL FRAMEWORK

It would be beneficial to examine the edifice that the Restatement has erected and test it against the views of other international lawyers. First is the listing of bases as stated in section 402, which generally seems to win consensus. There is no dispute about the right to regulate activity within a state's own territory. There is dispute about the "substantial effects" test. Publicists are likely to agree that a bullet winging its way into the nation's territory or a blackmail letter addressed to a specific person or persons within the state entails such effects. But they find the reverberations of indirect effects can be too weak to support an exercise of extraterritorial power. For example, the Europeans were skeptical of the idea that the effects of a Netherlands firm's sales of pipeline equipment to the Soviet Union had such an impact on the United States as to provide it with a right to interfere in the transaction.

A second source of disagreement has been the propensity of the United States to extend its entitlement to regulate the conduct of its nationals abroad to include the conduct of corporations:[19] its export control rules classify corporations—as well as individuals born or naturalized in the United States—as "U.S. nationals." This leap could conceivably be tolerated by others, but the next one definitely arouses discord: we classify corporations that are owned or controlled by individual or corporate American nationals as American. A Netherlands court found it unsupportable that an American rule should forbid the execution of a contract between a Dutch firm and a Dutch subsidiary of an American firm that envisaged the ultimate delivery of U.S.-type equipment to the Soviet Union—for it seemed to be a wholly internal Dutch matter.[20] In fact there is a good deal of treaty practice and a sprinkling of international case law, most conspicuously the *Barcelona Traction* case,[21] which supports the idea that the nationality of corporations in international law is judged by the location in which its constitutive papers are filed or by the law of its principal seat of administration. Curiously, in the last few years the United States even has come to flirt with the "passive personality" princi-ple—chiefly in regard to legislation that is designed to protect Americans from terrorist attacks abroad. Some of these actions might be defended as supportable under some other concept. For, as the purpose of terrorist attacks against

---

19. RESTATEMENT (THIRD) § 414.

20. For a review of the pipeline controversy, *see* RESTATEMENT (THIRD) § 414, Reporters' Note 8.

21. Barcelona Traction, (Belgium v. Spain) 1970 I.C.J. 3 (February 5).

Americans abroad is apt to be to sway the policies of the United States government, some of these laws may be justified on the basis that the terrorist activity in question was condemned by international law and could be addressed under the universality principle.[22]   One may question why the passive personality principle is the disfavored stepchild of the jurisdictional base family. Perhaps it is because an actor in country X may be subject to the rules of X as well as of her or his home country but knows nothing about the rules that prevail in the victim's home state. It is by no means a simple reciprocal of the rule under which the nationality of the actor is a basis for exercising regulatory power.

Finally one must determine whether such bases for jurisdiction ought to be regarded as a closed category. Why, for example, should not the origination of an item of technology in an American laboratory be a basis for U.S. pursuance of it abroad and regulation of the conditions under which it may be sold? Why should the United States be limited to categories that were evolved fifty years ago? Why should the fact that the technology was made possible by the national education, intellectual property protection, and scientific subsidization policy of the United States not be an adequate basis for jurisdiction? It would not be difficult to produce arguments to the contrary, but an uneasy sense remains that there has been no resolution of the problem. One should note that the United States has approached these situations through a somewhat different technique. It clearly has the right to control the original export of the technology or its product and insists, as a condition to allowing its export, that the foreign importer agree to observe certain conditions regarding its resale or the resale of its products. As a result of the pipeline controversy, the United States altered its rules regarding Soviet-bloc trade after the Netherlands importer had received the technology and signed up to limit its resales; but the clause the importer signed was not formulated to address the issues that later arose.[23]

V. RESOLUTION OF CLAIMS

In what forum might this type of international dispute be resolved? Is it justiciable; that is, would it be useful to submit the parties' claims to the International Court of Justice, a panel of that court, or some other tribunal? In order to be susceptible to adjudication the subject matter must possess a certain amount of consistency and stability. The parties must be able to agree on starting points upon which they can vigorously argue their respective cases and hope to be able to predict their reception by the court. In national court systems, judges occasionally have constructed a coherent body of case law from initially unpromising materials. The U.S. courts constructed an elaborate antitrust law on the basis of terse statutory provisions that vaguely referred to "restraints of trade" or "monopolization."

22. RESTATEMENT (THIRD) § 402, Reporters' Note 3, *supra* note 17.

23. Compagnie Européenne des Pétroles S.A. v. Sensor Nederland B.V., 22 I.L.M. 66 (Hague Dist Ct. Neth. 1982).

Doubtless, business leaders and their legal advisors would prefer more certainty and predictability than exists, yet the current situation is generally considered tolerable. Some provisions of the great civil law codes were similarly stated in an open-ended fashion and thus called for a significant amount of creative-interpretive effort on the part of judges. But the personnel who sat on those courts shared a great deal of common background and culture and possessed the confidence of lawyers who worked in the system. Surely the United States would not want the fifteen judges of the ICJ to pass judgment on its extraterritorial practices—particularly in light of its grievance regarding the Court's treatment of the *Nicaragua* case.

Constitution of a special *ad hoc* panel, as in the *Gulf of Maine* case, might be a little more amenable to the United States, but the United States would likely be outnumbered by European and Japanese judges who would view the case unsympathetically. On the whole one suspects that it will not be until more progress has been made in stating generally acceptable concepts regarding the reach of regulatory jurisdiction that one can think seriously about adjudicating these questions.

Could a more informal dispute resolution device prove effective? Alternative Dispute Resolution (ADR) is extremely popular in the United States and its popularity is growing in other countries. Such devices appear to be less threatening to countries that fear being on the minority side of international controversies. The outcome of the process need not be published and a state that finds its position in disfavor can dig in its heels and refuse to follow the mediator's recommendation. In effect, the groundwork for such a process has been laid in various arrangements that relate to antitrust questions. Issues of the appropriateness of state actions can be discussed in the Organization for Economic Cooperation and Development among experts in the field, all of whom take their area of specialty seriously. The bilateral agreements that currently join the United States to Germany, the European Community, Canada, and Australia are designed to allow vigorous discussion of antitrust enforcement actions to take place before any one country is publicly committed to a position and the media have inflamed the issue.[24] Of course, there are holes in the system; it is difficult to include private American plaintiffs in the process or prevent them from playing their independent game of reaching as far as possible. Also, the views of experts in the administration, who have become sensitized to the reactions provoked by far-reaching extraterritorialism, may be overwhelmed by political powers who only consider the short-term consequences of the action they are pressing. Still, this seems the most promising method of alleviating pressure on this front.

What type of substantive rule could achieve a degree of acceptability in such a process? In the case of a direct clash between a rule laid down by a state acting on a nationality or effects principle and a rule laid down by the state in whose territory the action takes place, a rule that provided for the latter to prevail would

---

24. *See* articles on cooperation agreements cited note 13 *supra*.

be found attractive.[25] For it is entirely unsympathetic to expose a private party to a situation in which it is condemned and punished by state A if it fails to commit a given act, but is punished by state B if it yields to that pressure and commits the act. Lawyers intrinsically believe that this situation is a form of double jeopardy to which parties ought not to be subjected by any sort of legal system that seeks the name of "law." There does seem to be a residual preference for the law of the territorial state. Despite the spread of other jurisdictional bases, they are all auxiliary to the persistent idea of territorial primacy. Only at the fringes might there be attacks on this tie-breaking principle. There may be cases in which the connection of the territorial state to the transaction is so questionable that one would be tempted to disregard such primacy as the governing principle. This disregard would be particularly pertinent in connection with states such as tax havens that have a reputation for being excessively helpful to parties who have come to establish themselves under their aegis and who pay handsomely for the privilege. Even in the case of more powerful states, it occasionally has become apparent that parties were begging the government to forbid them to do things that they considered contrary to their interests.

An alternative tie-breaking rule would be to assign primacy to the law of the state that had maintained the more important interest at stake in the matter. This solution appears plausible but problems suggest themselves very quickly. For instance, suppose that there is controversy surrounding an export of goods from country X to country Y. Country Z wishes to prevent the export, relying on the fact that they originally were exported from Z or were made with technology of Z origin. It asserts that its national security would be threatened if Y came into possession of the items. Country X claims that it is important to the survival of that branch of its industry that it be allowed to fulfill its commitment to make the goods and export them. Alternatively, suppose that a party is accused of reaping illicit profits through the use of inside information in relation to a given stock. Country X is interested because the stock is issued by one of "its" corporations. Country Y would like to pursue the matter because the stock in question was traded on its national securities exchange. Country Z is interested because the insider is its national and set the purchase in motion by phone calls made from Z to a broker doing business in Y. This is a matter in which national interests run more parallel than in the first hypothetical situation. Yet a heated contest may take place between the prosecuting authorities of the three states, for they each covet the glory of successfully prosecuting the case and will attempt to portray the other prosecutors as being slack and overly sympathetic to the accused. Still, one could imagine the development of guidelines that would assign priority to one or the other government, ones that would function among states that had a reasonable degree of respect for the integrity and vigor of the others' legal systems.

It is also possible to borrow from the accumulation of experience in private international law or, as the Americans call it, "conflicts of law." There is an

---

25. Hartford Fire Ins. Co. v. California, 113 S. Ct. 2891 (1993).

abundance of case law, scholarly writing, and some statutory material in this field. But this input does not seem to advance the process to any remarkable degree. National systems vary widely in their approaches to private international law. Some of them still employ relatively rigid approaches that first entail classification of the question and then selection of a "connecting factor" that assigns the question to the law of one particular state.[26] Others, particularly the United States, have sought solutions that are directly concerned with the end result. They enquire as to which country's solution is more modern, more important, or more just. They enquire into the legislative purposes that underlie the different rules that state X and state Y have laid down. The difficulty with these approaches is that they allow so many factors into play that the outcome becomes very tenuous, particularly in an international setting where courts are under intense pressure to ensure that their own country's legislative purpose is given full effect.

VI. CONCLUSION

The matter of extraterritoriality is a long-standing irritant to relations among states that in other respects share common goals and points of departure. As the world becomes more complex and relations between national economies more intricate and crucial, the stress on legal concepts will increase. The minimum requirement for a modern legal theory of extraterritoriality is that it make policy-makers and adjudicators aware that the matter is complex and not susceptible to simple solutions. It also should make a strong appeal to national authorities to exercise restraint, rather than being overly eager to enforce a particularly cherished policy. Modern regime theory accomplishes this much more effectively than did the classical sovereignties through their "walled boxes" theory. It recognizes that boundaries are porous, that communications do not occur only between foreign ministries but between many government entities and even more private ones and their counterparts abroad. Alliances may be formed between persons in state X and state Y that set them into opposition with other persons in both countries. Regime theory recognizes that allocation of jurisdictions between different countries is by no means the only conceivable solution to this class of problems, that it might be preferable to work out a common substantive solution to the matter at hand and entrust the administration of that solution to either cooperative agencies or a supranational authority. After all, neither the American states nor the European nations had created wholly satisfactory jurisdiction-allocating rules before agreeing to entrust major regulatory powers to the United States and to the European Community. Solutions to the persistent problems here discussed will not be tidy and universally satisfactory but will involve mutual concessions and sometimes reluctant cooperation. Fortunately, the gaps between the economic policies pursued

---

26. Hay, *Flexibility versus Predictability and Uniformity in Choice of Law: Reflections on Current European and United States Conflicts Law*, 226 HAGUE ACADEMY, RECEUIL DES COURS 280 (1991).

by the major trading powers can be bridged, for these countries share a common vision of a world in which economic entities are free to compete with each other and operate without private or public constraints. Scholarship has a role to play in keeping these complications before the eyes of those who make policy.

PRIVATE LAW EFFECTS OF FOREIGN EXPORT CONTROL LAWS WITH EXTRATERRITORIAL REACH

Jun Yokoyama

Japanese courts have apparently never been faced with such problems caused by foreign export prohibitions as the Rechtsbank at the Hague had to deal with on September 17, 1982.[1] In this chapter, I shall suggest the attitude which Japanese courts are likely to take in litigation between private persons whose transactions are affected by foreign export regulations with extraterritorial ambit.

I. INTRODUCTION

It is best to start by explaining the dichotomy between public and private law in their scope of application. It is true that the increasing role of public law in the form of a state's interference in relations between private persons has blurred the line of demarcation between the two. This division has long been accepted in Japan, however, and it would be useful if maintained when dealing with the problems relevant to this report.

While, in the light of their scope of application, private law rules are spatially unlimited, other states apparently have not protested against a state's exercising its legislative jurisdiction. The spatial ambit of public law rules, in principle, is demarked by the rules' purpose and content, though certain rules have raised questions of jurisdiction.

---

1. The Netherlands: District Court at the Hague Judgment in Compagnie Européene des Pétroles S.A. v. Sensor Nederland, 22 I.L.M. 66 (1983).

a. Private Law

The rules classified as private law are thought to enjoy potentially unlimited application. In the late nineteenth century, the drafter of the Japanese Civil Code, for example, almost exclusively bore in mind the purely domestic relations between private parties. The rules embodied in the Civil Code, however, regulate relations which take place in a remote country. Did they not, no one could explain a situation in which the court applies Japanese law as *lex fori* instead of applying foreign rules which would cause results contrary to Japanese *ordre public* or whose content is not established even where Japanese law has no other connection with the situation in dispute other than the fact that it is the law of the court before which the dispute was brought.[2]

Apart from this subsidiary scope of application, choice of law rules allocate extraterritoriality to private law rules, normally in respect to family matters. According to Japanese private international law, divorce shall be governed by the national law which the spouses have in common.[3] This choice of law rule enables Japanese rules, which allow divorce by agreement, to govern the divorce of Japanese spouses domiciled in Manila, where divorce is prohibited.

In 1808 Lord Ellenborough posed the well-known question: "Can the island of Tobago pass a law to bind the rights of the whole world? Would the world submit to such an assumed jurisdiction?"[4] As far as private law rules are concerned, we would not hesitate to answer in the affirmative. It may thus frequently happen that, in the sphere of private law, the same matter is within the ranges of the private laws of more than one state. This convergence, however, has apparently not been the subject of animated controversy. For example, the Philippines, whose law prohibits divorce, has never raised any objection to the extraterritorial application of Japanese divorce law. The principal reason is that private law rules only have some impact on the foreign territory when they are applied by the foreign authorities in accordance with choice of law rules at their disposal.[5] The courts in the Philippines will presumably not apply Japanese divorce law on the ground of public policy; even if they did, it would be because the Philippine choice of law rule allows them to apply Japanese law. The Philippines can control the impact which Japanese law might have on Philippine soil.

---

2.   *See* Pierre Mayer, *Droit international privé et droit international public sous l'angle de la notion de compétence*, 68 R.C.D.I.P. 555–556 (1979).

3.   Hōrei Zensho, Application of Laws (General) Act, No. 10 (1898) art. 16 (*as amended in 1989*) (Japan).

4.   Buchanan v. Ryder, 9 East 192 (1808) (England).

5.   *See* Jean-Michel Jacquet, *La norme juridique extraterritoriale dans le commerce international*, 112 Journal du Droit International 383 (1985).

b.   Public Law

Public law rules are spatially limited in their scope of application. Whether explicitly or implicitly, their spatial reach is dictated by their purpose and content. The Japanese export control law cannot apply as a substitute for foreign export control laws whose application is excluded because of their contrariety to Japanese *ordre public*. Public law rules are legally indifferent to matters outside their range.

Although spatially conditioned in their scope of application, their application has, from time to time, evoked much controversy, particularly when a state has tried to extend its regulation to facts situated within the foreign territory. As mentioned above, it is not until foreign authorities apply a particular rule that the private law rule of a state may have effects in that foreign territory. On the contrary, some public law rules of a state may have effects upon a foreign state without their being applied by the latter's authorities. If a state, for example, ousts from its market foreign companies which have violated the re-export prohibition, the measure is capable of adversely affecting the industry of that foreign state. The latter state would have great difficulty in preventing by effective means such a situation from taking place.[6]

II. EXPORT CONTROL LAW AS PUBLIC LAW

The scope of application of public law rules is determined unilaterally. To apply foreign counterparts by means of a bilateral conflict rule is hardly conceivable. The export control law is a typical example of public law and its scope of application varies with the policy of the enacting state.

a.   Unilateral Character of Public Law

The legislative purpose of public law rules requires they apply to situations which, according to the ordinary choice of law rules, are not subject to the *lex fori*; their application is not determined by the ordinary (usually bilateral or multilateral) conflict rules, but by their proper (usually one-sided or unilateral) conflict rules. The court of the emanating state is bound to apply them whenever the situation falls under the scope of application dictated by their legislative purpose. The anti-trust law would be such public law rule. While the Japanese anti-trust law has no explicit conflict rule, it is said that it applies to all restrictions of competition that have an effect within the Japanese territory.

In private international law, to "bilateralize" one-sided conflict rules is a usual technique which enables courts to apply foreign private law rules. It may be questioned whether public law rules are susceptible to being bilateralized. For example, are Japanese courts expected to formulate the following bilateral conflict

---

6.   *Id.* at 387.

rule in the sphere of anti-trust law: "[c]laims based upon restrictions on competition shall be governed by the law of the state in whose market the restrictions have effects upon the injured"?[7] The answer would be negative. While it is crucial to bilateralization that rules of forum and the foreign counterparts are thought to be interchangeable, it seems that the anti-trust law of each state is designed to protect only its own market, excluding the possibility that a foreign anti-trust law will be applicable for the protection of the "domestic market" in lieu of the *lex fori*.[8]

b. Scope of Application of Export Control Law

Export regulations are typically public law. Article 25(1) of the Japanese Foreign Exchange and Foreign Trade Control Law, as amended immediately after the *Toshiba Machine* episodes,[9] provides that residents desiring to engage in a transaction with non-residents may be required to procure the approval of the Minister of International Trade and Industry (MITI) for exporting technologies designated by Cabinet Order to be for designing, manufacturing or using designated commodities likely to endanger international peace and security. Japanese courts should apply this provision, when the intended transaction requires the activities of the parties which fall under the scope of application as indicated by the provision, i.e., the transfer of certain technologies from residents in Japan to non-residents.

The legislative purpose of public law rules sometimes requires a more far-reaching scope of application. The Cuban Democracy Act of 1992, § 1706(a), for example, prohibits third-country companies substantially owned or controlled by U.S. nationals from engaging in any transactions with Cuba or Cuban nationals. A court sitting in the United States is bound to apply this provision when the intended transactions may lead to the transfer of goods or technologies from third countries to Cuba.

The question is whether and when a public law rule with extraterritorial reach such as this may be applied or taken into consideration by the courts of countries other than the emanating one.

---

7.   The Swiss Private International Law has such a bilateral conflict rule in its antitrust law. Article 137(1) reads: "Les prétentions fondées sur une entrave à la concurrence sont régiés par le droit de l'État sur le marché duquel l'entrave a produit directement ses effets sur le lésé." ["Claims based on an impediment to competition are governed by the law of the state in whose market the impediment directly produces its effects on the injured party."] (translation provided by the author).

8.   Paolo Picone, *L'applicazione extraterritoriale delle regole sulla concorrenza e il diritto internazionale, in* IL FENOMENO DELLE CONCENATRAZIONI DI IMPRESE NEL DIRITTO INTERNO E INTERNAZIONALE 199 (1989).

9.   *See, e.g.*, Gordon B. Smith, *The Politics of East-West Trade: An Analysis of Cyclical Trends, in* LAW AND POLITICS OF WEST-EAST TECHNOLOGY TRANSFER 58 (Hirosha Oda ed. 1991).

III. FOREIGN EXPORT RESTRICTIONS AND THE PROPER LAW OF CONTRACT

In Japan, the general principle of party autonomy is recognized as the basis of choice of law in contract. A contract is governed by the law which the parties have chosen or which they are presumed to have chosen. The parties cannot, however, refer to a legal system on the whole. In addition, reference to public law rules should be excluded.

Under Japanese private international law, a contract is governed by its proper law with respect to its essential validity and effects. The proper law of the contract is the law by which the parties, explicitly or implicitly, intend their contract to be governed (article 7(1) of *Hōrei*). In the absence of an express or tacit choice of law, the provision of article 7, paragraph 2 objectively determines the law applicable to the contract: the *lex loci contractus*. Before applying this rule, however, the courts have tried quite often to find a legal system which the parties presumably would have chosen if they had determined the question of the applicable law as reasonable men. In presuming this hypothetical intention of the parties, the courts, in fact, appear to search the law of the state with which the contract is most closely connected.

Fortunately, there have been no reported decisions which affirm that the application of foreign rules of public law inspired by economic guidance should be rejected only on the ground of their public law nature even when they have effects upon private relations. There are some decisions which seem to assume that, when the rules of public law are the proper law of contract, their nature does not prevent the courts from applying them. The Japanese Supreme Court,[10] in its decision of October 6, 1920, allowed the English Trading with the Enemy Act to make a payment by a German debtor impossible under English law as the *lex causae*. A decision of the Tokyo District Court (July 11, 1967) affirms the supremacy of the *lex causae* in a negative way. It had to decide a case in which the plaintiff, a Japanese resident who was the assignee of a deposit, demanded payment from the defendant, the Tokyo branch of a Korean bank. The defendant bank alleged that the assignment of the deposit in question had been prohibited by the Minister of Finance of the Republic of Korea. The court, after finding that the assignment of the deposit was governed by Japanese law, held that the Korean ministerial order would give no legal ground for the defendant bank to derogate from the principle recognized under the Japanese Civil Code that claims are assignable.

It should be noted that, in spite of these sporadically found decisions, the application of foreign public law, which represents the state's interference with relations between private individuals particularly in the economic field, is still uncertain. The case law does not seem to establish that all the relevant rules belonging to the proper law, whether of private or public law, should be subject to the ordinary conflict rules. The author does not believe that it should be so,

---

10. Judgment of Aug. 6, 1920, Daishin'in [Great Court of Judicature], 1694 Shinbun 21 (Japan).

because, if the view were upheld that all legislations and enactments of the proper law of contract, irrespective of their nature, are applied, it would lead to an unsatisfactory result. As mentioned above, in the absence of an explicit choice of law by the parties, the court has to apply the law of the country with which the contract is most closely connected. When the court tries to find out such a law, e.g., in the contract of sale, great importance will be given to the law of the seller's place of business, because the choice of that law enables the seller to make all the contracts with customers coming from different countries subject to the same law. Since, according to the view in question, foreign public law rules are to be applied when and only when they belong to the proper law of the contract, the export control law would be applied as a part of the law of the seller's place of business. On the other hand, in the absence of a choice of law by the parties, the related public law rules forming part of the law of the buyer's place of business, e.g., import control regulations and exchange control regulations, would almost always be disregarded.[11]

The application of a foreign public law whose principal object is not to regulate the conflicting interests between the private parties is to be determined in a different way. Thus, the parties' choice of the law of a state of the United States does not automatically lead to the application of, e.g., the Cuban Democracy Act. The "submission clause" will not be regarded as the parties' choice of law.[12]

IV. FOREIGN EXPORT CONTROL LAW AS A DATUM

Before referring to the conditions of application of foreign public enactments, it should be noted that, even if their application were totally denied, certain legal significance, it is said, should be given to them as a datum to be evaluated within the framework of the proper law of contract. They might be taken into account as facts which taint a contract with immorality or which cause impossibility of performance.

---

11. KARL KREUZER, AUSLÄNDISCHES WIRTSCHAFTSRECHT VOR DEUTSCHEN GERICHTEN 85 (1986); Frank Vischer, *General Course on Private International Law*, 232 RECUEIL DES COURS DE L'ACADÉMIE DE DROIT INTERNATIONAL 166 (1992).

12. This does not mean that the submission clause is legally meaningless. It may be understood as a clause designed to incorporate the U.S. export control regulations in a contract as a contractual term. Thus, for example, an American exporter could claim certain contractual rights against a foreign importer, when the latter did not abide by the U.S. export control regulations. The validity of such clause depends upon the *lex contractus*. It seems that, whatever the *lex contractus* may be, no one could argue that a foreign party is forced to accept the said clause with the result that it is null and void due to duress. When the forum state adopts a "blocking statute," however, its validity will be negated irrespective of the attitude of the *lex contractus*.

a. Immorality

The Japanese Civil Code declares transactions *contra bonos mores* as void in its article 90. For example, when Japanese law is the proper law, the extensive interpretation of the said provision will allow courts to declare a contract purporting to smuggle opium into a foreign country void as a contract *contra bonos mores*. Would then a contract whose object is to violate the export control law of a foreign country be void as well? While there appear to be no decisions rendered by Japanese courts on this point, the German Federal High Court has made an analogous ruling. In *Fa.W.R. v. S.G.B. AG*[13] (the *Borax* case), which involved a contract purporting to have brought borax into the eastern bloc in violation of the U.S. export ban, the contract was declared void in accordance with Article 138 of the German Civil Code. The Court held:

> [d]oubtless the American embargo regulations were supposed to prevent the increase of the eastern war potential by means of western goods; the embargo regulations were therefore meant to maintain the peace and the liberty of the West. The measures were therefore not only in the American interest but in the interest of the entire free West and thus also in the interest of the Federal Republic of Germany. The embargo regulations therefore served vital interests of the general public. Whoever frustrates the maintenance of these interests out of self-interest by misleading the institutions which work for this purpose, acts against public policy.[14]

b. Impossibility

Such concepts as "impossibility of performance" or "frustration" ostensibly exist in every legal system.   In a contract case involving "impossibility of performance," a court may take into account the factual situation caused by the foreign export ban as a datum constituting the impossibility of performance under the proper law of contract. The debtor may be relieved from performing his contractual obligations, not because the foreign export control prohibits the debtor from performing but since the debtor's performance will entail penal or administrative sanctions, thereby causing no one to expect him to do so.

c. Appraisal

It can be argued that taking foreign public law rules into consideration as data

---

13. Judgment of Dec. 21, 1960, Budesgerichtshof, 34 B.G.H.Z. 169 (F.R.G.).

14. Gerhard Kegel, *The Role of Public Law in Private International Law: German Report*, *in* BASLE SYMPOSIUM ON THE ROLE OF PUBLIC LAW IN PRIVATE INTERNATIONAL LAW 45 (Frederic-Edouard Klein ed., 1991).

is not more than to apply them in a roundabout way.[15] A contract purporting to infringe or evade them is regarded as immoral by the proper law of contract, because the parties purport to perform the act evaluated "illegal" by the legal system to which relevant public law rules belong. A factual situation which entails the impossibility of performance derives from the very fact that the performance is "illegal" in the enacting state.

The evaluation of illegality as such by the enacting state should be respected: a contract should be void, because, for example, in addition to penal or administrative effects, a foreign export control law invalidates a contract as a private law sanction; a performance should be regarded as impossible simply because it is prohibited.

It is true that in some situations it might be only a matter of theoretical preference whether the foreign public law should be directly applied or taken into consideration as a datum. When specific goods such as cultural properties are situated within the boundary of the state which prohibits their export, there seems to be nothing to choose between the two. The impossibility of performance appears to be readily recognized under any law. On the other hand, this is not the case where goods of inspecific nature are situated within a country other than the enacting state, e.g., goods produced by foreign subsidiaries. Do certain penal or administrative sanctions suffice in constituting the factual situation which leads to the impossibility of performance? Courts in most countries would probably answer in the negative.[16] It may happen, however, that, regardless of the proper law of contract, the state of forum which concurs under certain international agreements with the policy of the foreign state's export ban has interests in making the performance impossible.

V. THE CONDITIONS OF APPLICATION OF FOREIGN EXPORT CONTROL LAW

While the door should be opened for the direct application of foreign public law rules, courts here are likely to apply them to a very limited extent, i.e., when Japan is "the disinterested third state."   The theory of special connections (*Sonderanknüpfung*) seems to offer a guideline for the direct application of foreign public law rules in general, although the door for their application seems only narrowly opened.

a.   Export from the Forum State

As suggested above, foreign public enactments are to be applied independently of the proper law of contract. It should be noted that there would be no room for

---

15. Wilhelm Wengler, *Die Anknupfung des zwingenden Schuldrechts im internationalen Privatrecht*, 54 ZEITSCHRIFT FUR VERGLEICHENDE RECHTSWISSENSCHAFT 202–206 (1941).

16. *See* Jürgen Basedow, *Private Law Effects of Foreign Export Controls,* GER. YB. INT'L L. 134 (1984).

the application of foreign public law rules to a situation which falls under the spatial ambit of the forum's equivalents. As far as exports from Japanese territory are concerned, the court is bound to apply only the Japanese export control law, even where the Japanese rules are enacted in close coordination with, e.g., United States policy.[17] The same is true where the Japanese export control law does not prohibit the export in question. The lack of prohibition does not mean that Japan is legally "indifferent" to the export in question, however, but should rather be understood to connote "permission" which reflects the policy of the promotion of freetrade.

It follows that the export control law of the United States may be applicable when Japan is "the disinterested third state," i.e., when goods or technologies are exported from the United States and from other foreign countries.

b.   Exports from a Foreign State

In 1941 Wilhelm Wengler advocated the theory of special connection (*Sonderanknüpfung*) for mandatory rules which interfere with contractual relations.[18] It may be safely said that the idea of special connection has culminated in article 7(1) of the EC Rome Convention on the Law Applicable to Contractual Obligations of 16 June 1980. It reads:

> [w]hen applying under this Convention the law of a country, effect may be given to the mandatory rules of the law of another country with which the situation has a close connection, if and in so far as, under the law of the latter country, those rules must be applied whatever the law applicable to the contract. In considering whether to give effect to these mandatory rules, regard shall be had to their nature and purpose and to the consequences of their applications or non-applications.

As to this provision, Kegel says: "[s]uch a provision does not provide the guidance required by a legal rule. It does not, therefore, assist the good judge and could lead the bad one to indulge in adventures. Lawyers do not know how to advise their clients."[19] As the Giuliano-Lagarde Report[20] points out, however, it can hardly be denied that the provision reflects practices prevailing in certain countries.

It is observed that the academic writers' views as well as the said provision commonly enumerate the following three conditions under which foreign public law rules are to be applied or taken into account: (a) the foreign public law rules claim to apply to the situation; (b) the situation has a close connection with the enacting

---

17. Von Oliver Remien, *Aussenwirtschaftsrecht in kollisionsrechtlicher Sicht*, 54 ZEITSCHRIFT FÜR AUSLÄNDISCHES UND INTERNATIONALES PRIVATRECHT 457–458 (1990).

18. Wengler, *supra* note 15, at 169.

19. Kegel, *supra* note 14, at 60.

20. Mario Giuliano & Paul Lagarde, *The Rome Convention on the Law Applicable to Contractual Obligations*, CONTRACT CONFLICTS 355 (P.M. North ed., 1982).

state; and (c) the policy which underlies the public enactments is acceptable to the state of forum. While the *Hōrei* has no explicit provision designed to refer to foreign public enactments, the court will regard these conditions as useful guidelines in developing the case law on the matter dealt with in this report. In the light of Japanese private international law, these conditions should be understood as follows.

(1) The Public Enactment's Claim to Apply

It seems that the first condition would pose no serious problem here. When the spatial ambit of the public enactment is implicit, the judge would have much difficulty in deducing it from the legislative purpose of the rule. It may be safely said, however, that in most cases the legislator, wishing to extend the restrictions to exports from a foreign country, explicitly stipulates the extraterritorial ambit in the relevant provisions.

(2) The Close Connection

The understanding of the second condition varies with the author. Why is a "close connection" with the enacting state required for the application of the foreign public enactments? Is this condition necessary to ensure that the enacting state has lawfully exercised its legislative "jurisdiction" in the sense of public international law?[21] It may be true that no state will foster the foreign measures enacted in violation of international law, but the well-established bases of jurisdiction do not seem to exist in the field of the export control. While it is admitted, as mentioned below, that international law may have some relevance to the problem of the application of foreign export regulations, it must be emphasized that civil courts do not seek to solve the conflict of governmental interests, but to settle the dispute between the (private) parties. The second condition should be understood in the light of the function of civil courts to find a just solution for private disputes.

It is observed that, whether cases may be international or purely domestic, the party who alleges either the impossibility of performance or the nullity of contract with recourse to the public law enactments is almost always a debtor whose contract yields little or no profit to him, or results in a loss. Quite often, a prohibitory rule which was once intended to infringe is invoked by the debtor as a pretext for being liberated from his obligations. Dealing with purely domestic cases, the Japanese courts, which understand the true intentions of these debtors, apparently have the tendency to stick to the principle of *pacta sunt servanda* by means of denying, in some way or other, private law effects of state interference. The same attitude is likely to be taken in international cases, too. The judge will undoubtedly have difficulty in doing so in international cases, however, because the debtor may take

---

21. For the legal writings which understand the second condition in the light of jurisdiction, *see, e.g.*, KREUZER, *supra* note 11, at 90–92.

advantage of invoking more than one state interference. Without a reasonable limit, the cumulative applications of public enactments would work only in the direction of negating the (quite often shameless) debtors' obligations.

How closely the situation should be connected with the enacting state will vary with the facts of each case and the type of related public law rules.[22] It follows that the conditions are hardly susceptible to being crystallized into more specific criteria. Foreign measures, however, will not meet this condition, which the parties could not be expected to predict because of their remoteness from the situation.

As far as the export of goods or technical data from the territory of the enacting state is concerned, the "close connection" will be readily recognized. The state can enforce its will in its territory and force the parties to respect public enactments including the export prohibition. On the other hand, the "close connection" does not necessarily connote "territoriality." On condition that they are able to be foreseen by the parties, the export restrictions of the state which extend to exports from third states will not be excluded from the application.

(3) Acceptability of the Foreign Export Ban

This is not to say that all foreign public enactments which satisfy the first and the second conditions should be applicable. To apply a foreign public law by recognizing its private law effects would be tantamount to promoting the interests of the enacting state. In principle, Japanese courts are not obliged to do so, at the sacrifice of the claimant's contractual rights. One should concede, however, the fact that the state can enforce its will in its territory. As far as the foreign state's export regulations prohibit the export of goods which still remain within its own boundary, they, in principle, should be applied here. The same result would be substantially obtained if that foreign export ban were taken into consideration only as a datum constituting a factual situation which, for example, entails the impossibility of performance. One should not, however, compare a state which lawfully exercises its power with a gang of highwaymen who rob a debtor of all he needs to fulfill his obligations.

Where the foreign export control restriction extends to the export from the third state, the domestic courts, in principle, have no reason to promote the interests of the former state in applying its export restriction. It may happen, however, that the foreign state and Japan are so strongly bound together in political and economic interests that to make the debtor's performance impossible or to invalidate a contract, for example, would promote the interests of Japan, too. Do such shared interests override the private parties' interests? As mentioned above, the function of the civil court is to find a just solution for private disputes. It is beyond its power to evaluate the political or economic interests of the state, as the German Federal

---

22. For example, in the sphere of antitrust law, the "market" would have great importance in this context. It should be noted that courts have rarely faced the problem of the application of foreign antitrust laws. *See* Picone, *supra* note 8, at 195–196.

High Court did in the *Borax* case.[23] It may safely be said that the Japanese court will not apply the foreign export restrictions with extraterritorial ambit, unless, for example, a contract is related to the object whose transfer is regulated by an international agreement to which the enacting state and Japan are parties (for instance, a Security Council decision under article 41 of the U.N. Charter).

---

23. *Supra* note 13.

PART III
INTERNATIONAL LEGAL PERSPECTIVES ON JAPAN—NORTH AMERICAN (U.S./CANADA) ECONOMIC FRICTIONS

|SUMMARY

Geoffrey A. Wexler

I.   INTRODUCTION

In the discussion on international legal perspectives on Japan–North American economic frictions, chaired by Professor Armand de Mestral, panelists and members of the audience explored the causes of and possible solutions to economic frictions between Japan and North America. The benefits and disadvantages of rule-based versus results-oriented methods of trade regulation were of particular interest, as was the constitutionality under the GATT of U.S. Section 301 legislation. Whether countries can even begin to understand definitions of fairness, let alone agree upon them, was also debated, and a number of participants asked whether Japan and its market truly are different and thus require entirely new philosophies of trade negotiation and regulation.

In preparation for the discussion, each panelist prepared a paper exploring a particular aspect of international trade regulation. Professor John H. Jackson of the University of Michigan Law School considered in particular the upcoming WTO charter, attorney Susan L. Karamanian, Esq., of Lock, Purnell, Rain and Harrell (Dallas, Texas) reviewed the interaction of economics and policy and the dangers of threats presented by unilateral sanctions, Keio University Professor Masao Sakurai discussed the problems of harmonizing the variety of laws, legal systems and policies of the world's trading nations; Professor Masato Dogauchi of the University of Tokyo assessed the use of the Structural Impediments Initiative (SII) talks as a model for dealing with international economic frictions; Professor Hyuck-Soo Yoo of Yokohama National University examined the role of Section 301 in the era of the WTO; and Panel Chair Professor A.L.C. de Mestral of the Institute of Comparative Law at McGill University identified and proposed procedures for dispute avoidance, using the experiences of the United States and Canada as examples.

Professor de Mestral opened the panel with broad questions, asking whether both Japan and North America are benefitting from the current liberal world trade order, whether general principles of international law are adequate for the resolution of trade issues, and whether the recently concluded Uruguay Round of the GATT will reduce or aggravate economic frictions. We must assess the current regime of unilateral, bilateral and multilateral approaches to trade regulation, especially in light of the potential for coercion, commented Professor de Mestral. Professor de Mestral noted that the area of Japan–North American trade relations is one particularly characterized by finger pointing, tension and a constant flow of adrenaline, though trade tensions and accusations of GATT violations are not unique to the Japan - North American relationship. Recent trade relations history includes many cases of unilateral or bilateral action followed by retaliation between other trading partners. Why, then, is the Japan relationship given so much attention?

II. IS JAPAN DIFFERENT?

A threshold question for the panel was whether Japan is different, or, more particularly, whether Japan and its markets present unique challenges to trade negotiators.

Professor Jackson called this a puzzle, asking why there is trade friction between Japan and the U.S. Some of the problems faced by the two nations are unique, but more often the issues are systemic worldwide. Jackson opined that, given the overall quality of the U.S.-Japan relationship, there is more friction than one would expect and that the vigor and bitterness seen on trade issues reflects the depth of the complex relationship between the two trading superpowers. We should ask, said Jackson, how the U.S. should respond to a persistent trade surplus country.

The emotional nature of the U.S.-Japan relationship makes it both a popular area for debate and a useful political tool, said Ms. Karamanian, in considering the obsession Americans have with Japan. Both sides share the same goal of economic gain, but Ms. Karamanian suggested this may not be a completely appropriate goal. Rather, more attention should be paid to increasing consumer welfare, but current liberalization activities are inimical to that goal.

Professor Yoo agreed, arguing that the Japanese consumer sees barriers and that this perception raises special concerns. Japan, he asserted, must endeavor to dismantle barriers that cause misunderstanding and emotional reactions. However, globalization of markets can lead to an unacceptable hollowing out of domestic markets, combined with an increase in imports, noted Professor Sakurai. The internal aspects of Japan must be examined when considering globalization activities. Such aspects include the nature of Japan's industrial society, the growing interdependency of global economics, and worldwide expansion of Japan's economic activities.

Unique or not, Professor Michael K. Young of Columbia Law School reminded the panel of the cold hard fact that statistically Japan remains the least penetrated of all major industrial countries. Still, noted Professor Detlev Vagts of Harvard Law School, Japan is headed for trying times, and negotiators must bear in mind concerns regarding domestic prosperity while trying to eliminate trade impediments.

III. FAIRNESS

Panel members briefly addressed the stubborn question of defining "fairness" in the context of fair trade and fair trade regulation. Ms. Karamanian noted that while the U.S. has sometimes argued a definition of fairness that is closer to equivalency of opportunity or reciprocity, Japan has responded by offering "equal opportunity" or natural treatment. Better to ask, she suggests, what "unfair" conditions justify unilateral actions? Professor Yoo agreed that the situation in Japan is very close to one of equal opportunity and praised the stance taken by Japan's Ministry of International Trade and Industry (MITI). But he also called the Ministry too passive and its definition of fairness too narrow.

IV. MARKET FAILURE

Deepening economic interdependencies lead to a loss of control and an increase in fraudulent activities, said Professor Jackson, and thus make it harder to regulate trade that crosses borders. Such results challenge traditional notions of "market failure." When do markets fail, and how do we justify intervention to slow or stop trade? Furthermore, the nature of "market failure," and thus the appropriate solutions, varies when we consider international, as opposed to domestic, problems. Professor Edwin M. Smith of the University of Southern California asked Professor Jackson to explain further the distinctiveness of international market failure, and to provide some examples. Professor Jackson highlighted the problem of securities fraud and varying approaches taken toward securities regulation, and to different meanings given to "monopolization" in domestic arenas as compared to the interpretation used in the international market. We must ask, said Jackson, which is the relevant market? What are common structures in all markets? What aspects are country specific? And how can we give coherent and consistent meaning to the term "market" in the international setting?

Professor Jackson addressed actions often taken to alleviate market failure. One domestic tool is tax policy, but this approach is difficult on an international level given limits on extraterritorial reach. More common in the multinational context have been efforts at promoting harmonization of competition policy. Citing game theory and the "prisoners' dilemma," Jackson noted the risks inherent in attempts at competitive "downward" regulation, the so-called "race to the bottom" to attract business and capital. This may result in unilateral actions, such as those embedded in U.S. Section 301-type activities, or bilateral efforts, such as the Structural Impediments Initiative (SII) talks. Multilaterally, regional agreements such as the European Union and the North American Free Trade Agreement and multilateral treaties such as the newly created World Trade Organization (WTO) may attempt to address these concerns. Whether the multilateral approaches can deal effectively with many of these vague bilateral problems, however, still remains to be seen, said Jackson.

V. RULES OR RESULTS

Central to the development of regulatory schemes is the fundamental selection of the basic orientation of the method to be adopted, and panel members vigorously debated the pros and cons of rule-oriented approaches versus results-oriented approaches.

Professor Yoo asserted that negotiating countries must respond to three problems when addressing a trade conflict: (1) gaps in perception; (2) selection of criteria to be used in deciding when a specific act is unfair; and (3) the approach taken to solve the problem. He characterizes the Japanese view as one in which current trade imbalances have little or no correlation to market access, and where the focus is on macroeconomics. The rationale is that Japan's culture cannot support rule-based solutions, and thus results-oriented solutions must be employed. Presently Japan is inflexible, especially given Japan's global superpower status, and must move away from its use of rule-oriented criteria based upon international standards. This view is in line with the U.S. results-based criteria, noted Professor Yoo.

In marked disagreement was Professor Jackson, who claimed that more rule stability is needed in economic affairs. Market players want to know the rules so they can make the proper investments, especially in light of the decentralized nature of modern economic structures. More rigor and strict rules will provide more certainty and more predictability. The result of the Uruguay Round of GATT, for example, provides investors with increased certainty, thereby reducing transaction costs and risk premiums.

In response, Professor Jonathan I. Charney of Vanderbilt University commented that while industry does want rules to a degree, there is also a desire to balance the rigidity of such rules against our lack of knowledge of the future. In an environment of great uncertainty, the international community cannot be expected to legislate strict, rigid rules.

While there are powerful conceptual arguments for and against numerical targets, noted Professor Young, we should at least consider them as tools to force market openings. U.S. trade negotiators might, for example, concede to Japanese assertions of uniqueness and inscrutability and simply ask the Japanese to fix the problem themselves in whatever way they think best, consistent with their own cultural sensibilities and economic uniqueness. This accepts the Japanese entirely at their word (e.g., they want open markets, but must accomplish that goal in a Japanese way) and deeply acknowledges Japanese sovereignty. At the same time, U.S. negotiators will "know" the problem has been "fixed" when Japan's degree of import penetration is equivalent to that of other similarly situated major, industrialized countries. In other words, numerical market share goals are merely barometers of the degree to which the Japanese have fixed the problem of artificially imposed market barriers. Such results-oriented approaches thus serve not as a managed trade system, but as instrumentalities to reach other goals.

VI. U.S. SECTION 301

The most spirited discussion centered around the methodology, constitutionality, and GATT consistency of U.S. Section 301 and its progeny, and the potential for 301-type legislation in other countries.

a. The Method of 301

Professor Yasuaki Onuma of the University of Tokyo asked Professors Jackson and Yoo to discuss the conditions under which Section 301 would be legitimate and lawful under the newly established WTO.

An author of the original Section 301 legislation, Professor Jackson responded that Section 301 enhances the tools available to the president to provide protection abroad of the interests of U.S. citizens. An individual brings a complaint against the trade practices of another country, especially a complaint involving the violation of a right protected under a treaty. The government can then proceed with the complaint and negotiate with foreign governments on behalf of the individual and others with similar concerns. Section 301, said Jackson, serves as a "stick in the closet" that gives the president the power to act in trade negotiations.

It is important to note, stressed Jackson, that Section 301 requires that a complaint first be taken to an established international dispute resolution forum, if such exists. The president is not required to wait until the complaint is fully resolved in the international forum, a process that can take years under the old GATT procedures, if it is ever resolved at all. But the president must first go to the international forum. In the end, Section 301 also gives the president authority to take action inconsistent with international practices, but does not require it. The statute itself does not violate international obligations. In the vast majority of cases, the president has used Section 301 only after first obtaining at least a preliminary ruling from the international forum that U.S. treaty rights had been violated. Jackson noted that since the beginning of the Bush administration there has been no use of 301-granted power in violation of international obligations.

Regarding the time limits imposed by Section 301, Jackson said that they were a reaction to the dilatory practices of the GATT. However, now that the WTO procedures are designed to operate on a much stricter time schedule, Section 301 should be altered accordingly.

Section 301 is inevitable on a political level, argued Professor Yoo, for international trading countries and trade liberalization. After the Second World War, the GATT was created and led mainly by the U.S. with the idea that international trade should become *freer* trade, though not entirely free trade. Although only a domestic statute, Section 301 furthers the liberalization of trade among developed countries. Section 301 also results in the imposition of U.S.-developed standards on the international community, resulting in a type of lawmaking, often through GATT. From a legal perspective, explained Yoo, mandatory Section 301 action covers issues within the scope of GATT, while discretionary Section 301 actions may deal with practices of foreign nations deemed "unreasonable" by the U.S., even though such practices are not covered by GATT disciplines. The question still remains, however, whether the exercise of power under Section 301 is legitimate for issues not covered by GATT.

b. The Constitutionality of Section 301

The panelists also considered the role of Section 301 in light of the powers granted and limits imposed by the U.S. Constitution.

Professor Jackson explained that without such statutory authority from Congress, under Section 301, the president would have no constitutional authority to impose "retaliatory" measures, even where such measures would be acceptable under GATT. While under EC law all actions must be consistent with international obligations, Jackson noted that the U.S. Congress did not impose this limitation on the president in the exercise of his statutory authority under Section 301.

When asked if it is appropriate to have statutes that leave open the possibility of violation of the international system, Professor Jackson responded in the affirmative, pointing to inadequacies in the international legal system and stating that governments have a moral obligation to act even if such actions are illegal internationally. However, he continued, refined dispute settlement procedures in GATT always permit the president to act in a manner consistent with GATT rules and practices, despite the fact that there are forces in the U.S. market that desire actions that violate international obligations.

If the president, asked Professor Woon Sang Choi of Tokyo International University, acting on Section 301 powers, clearly violates international law, would U.S. courts find such action unconstitutional? Jackson responded that any such challenges in the U.S. courts would be quickly denied, because treaties are handled in a last-in-time fashion, that is, domestic statutes prevail where they are enacted after conflicting treaties were adopted. Professor Vagts agreed, offering as one example the U.S. cancellation of South African airlines' flying rights.

Professor Charney offered a different view of the power held by the president, disagreeing with Jackson's assertion that the president lacks the ability to act in this area without legislation, and indicating that he believes that the president is not weak as regards foreign trade affairs.

c.   Section 301 as a Threat

Moving beyond the constitutional question, Professor Onuma expressed his concern regarding not only the use of 301, but even the mere threat of its use. Will such use or the threat thereof violate the WTO system, Onuma asked Professor Jackson.

There is no inevitable clash between 301 and the proposed WTO procedures, answered Jackson. If an international panel, such as a GATT or WTO panel, rules against a U.S. complaint, the president is not mandated to act further. The appropriate response at that point would be to do nothing.

But if the threat of Section 301 retaliation affects the flow of trade, then there is a GATT problem, suggested Osaka City University Professor Yuji Iwasawa. The question of Section 301 ought to be considered in the broader context of state responsibility and countermeasures. Professor Iwasawa noted that the International Law Commission is currently addressing this issue, and that we should consider whether retaliatory actions by the U.S. can be justified by the principle of state responsibility even if such actions are illegal under the GATT, with the U.S.-Brazil pharmaceutical and U.S.-Japan semiconductors cases as examples.

Calling the WTO dispute settlement procedure a "self-contained regime," Professor Iwasawa stated that the WTO does not allow a state to take a GATT-inconsistent retaliatory measure without the prior authorization of the Contracting Parties. Iwasawa continued, however, that such a restriction does not mean that the resort to a retaliatory measure cannot be justified by the principle of state responsibility in cases where the other party does not cooperate in the dispute settlement procedures, citing the *Oilseeds* case as an example for the potential application of this position.

Professor Jackson agreed, stating that the threat of use is an inconsistent measure, and that the preferred course of action is utilization of the dispute resolution procedures provided in the WTO.

More difficult, however, are the complaints in "nonviolation cases" brought to the GATT, explained Professor Jackson. For cases where a violation of GATT or other applicable rules is found, the violating party has an obligation under international law to conform to the panel report, and must reform its domestic law to conform to the rule, or compensate injured parties for its failure to do so. However, the initiation of a non-violation complaint, where a country's trade policies nullify or impair a contracting party's benefits under the Agreement, but do not comprise a violation of international obligations or domestic law, presents only a starting point for the bargaining for compensation. The fundamental premise of such a case is that reasonable expectations have been violated. Jackson proposed that if a contracting party perceives a threat in the policies or legislation of another country, it can file a nullification/impairment complaint, and call for examination as to whether the alleged threat is affecting trade.

d. Section 301-type Legislation in Other Countries

Should other countries enact Section 301-type legislation, Mr. Ichiro Araki of Japan's Ministry of International Trade and Industry asked, could it not be used against the U.S.

Professor Onuma elaborated, commenting that if many nations had their own Section 301-type statutes, such nations would be acting unilaterally, and thereby undermining the stability of the multilateral system. These are potentially high costs to be paid, he warned. Still, even if enacted, most nations do not have the power to carry out Section 301-type actions.

Professor Onuma also noted that while the U.S. argued for revision of the GATT dispute settlement procedures, with resulting revisions incorporated into the procedures of the WTO, the U.S. still maintains that there is a need for Section 301, perhaps to ensure the continued existence of a threat for compliance. Maintaining Section 301 at this point is unfair, contended Onuma.

VII. ISSUES FOR FUTURE DEBATE—A "REALITY CHECK"

As the third session drew to a close, audience members offered comments as to issues for future debate, with a notable emphasis on the importance of keeping in mind the true conditions of the world's markets and the desires of its various players.

Professor Shinya Murase of Sophia University called on scholars and practitioners in this area not to lose sight of reality by focusing on legality and national responsibility as we deal with "gray areas of normativity." Ms. Karamanian noted that the challenges presented by such "gray areas" have led governments to use objective criteria instead of rules for insuring adequate market access.

Citing similar concerns, Peter D. Trooboff, Esq., of Covington & Burling warned that international lawyers are in danger of being marginalized in this area. Mr. Trooboff asserted that as we utilize available procedures we must strive to develop new procedures with the needs of affected parties in mind, whether those parties are consumers in Japan or members of industry in the U.S. Echoing Professor Murase, Mr. Trooboff called on players in this field to be aware of the true state of affairs in the world's markets and not to lose sight of today's changing reality.

THE RESOLUTION OF DISPUTES BETWEEN JAPAN AND CANADA AND THE UNITED STATES: A MODEST PROPOSAL

Armand L. C. de Mestral

I. INTRODUCTION

Trade disputes between Japan and its North American[1] trading partners have arisen from a multitude of causes and will, no doubt, continue to arise in the future. No trading relationship, however close, seems immune from tensions: witness the many trade disputes that have accompanied the relationship of Canada and the United States. Indeed, the greater the intensity of the relationship, the greater appears to be the likelihood of trade disputes. Problems, which initially arise between private parties, often escalate to the point that companies, unions, and other interest groups call for government intervention, which governments eventually find impossible to resist. Just as frequently, problems arise as a result of legislative or administrative intervention and governments must then intervene to defend their own policies.

The trade relationship between Japan and North America is especially complex and crucial to both sides, given the fact Japan is the second most important trading partner of both Canada and the United States. Unlike the relationship between Canada and the United States—two countries that share many commercial and political values and much common geography and history—the relationship between North America and Japan is one that began in trauma scarcely 125 years ago. However enthusiastically Japan has embraced the commercial culture of North America, the trauma of the Black Ships lurks in the background. From the North American perspective, what began as an act of force against a largely alien culture

---

1.   With apologies to Mexico, the expression "North American" will be restricted to Canada and the United States in this paper.

and society continues to be marked by a high degree of ignorance and insensitivity: despite the intensity of the relationship at the end of the twentieth century, few North Americans are well versed in Japan's language or history. It is no small wonder, then, that the relationship has been marked by aggressivity and even war.

Given the many obstacles, it is nearly miraculous that Japan and North America trade well over U.S.$200 billion in goods and services each year. Trade remains the central dimension of a relationship that is vital to all parties to maintain and improve. This chapter sets out a proposal for dispute avoidance and resolution applicable to trade matters. Arguably, any improvement in the management of the trading relationship improves overall relations between the parties. The proposal made here is of a legal and procedural nature and is intended to adapt to the legal cultures of both Japan and North America.

I. THE RANGE OF DISPUTES, PAST AND PRESENT

a. Dumping of Goods

Major trade disputes between North America and Japan have resulted from allegations of dumping of goods. Among the most significant charges have been the proceedings in the United States concerning imports of steel[2] and silicon chips.[3] Despite the fact that antidumping procedures are authorized under the General Agreement on Tariffs and Trade (GATT) Anti-Dumping Code of 1979,[4] considerable commercial and political controversy attended the U.S. actions. This is not surprising. One need only consider the degree of animosity that succeeded a number of similar proceedings involving imports from Canada, including imports of steel, to understand the sensitivity of the issues raised.

The simplest way to avoid future disputes concerning allegations of dumping would be to do away with these laws. It has become difficult to find any credible intellectual justification for them; Canada and the United States once attempted (and failed) to abolish them *inter se*[5] but did not formally commit to try again under the aegis of the North American Free Trade Agreement (NAFTA).[6] There may well be further efforts, at least between Canada and the United States. On the assumption,

---

2.   The most recent of a very long series at time of writing (May 24, 1994) being *Certain Steel Wire Rod from Brazil and Japan*, Investigations Nos. 731-TA-646 and 686 (Final), U.S.I.T.C. Pub. 2761, March (1994).

3.   Reviewed in *Global Competitiveness of U.S. Advanced-Technology Industries: Computers*, Investigation Bo. 332-339, U.S.I.T.C. Pub. 2705, December (1993).

4.   GATT B.I.S.D., 26th Supp. 171 (1980).

5.   The Canada–United States Free Trade Agreement, S.C. 1988 c. 65, Schedule A Canada–United States Free Trade Agreement art. 1906; 27 I.L.M. 281 (1988) [hereinafter CFTA].

6.   Decision taken pursuant to the North American Free Trade Agreement, 1992, S.C. 1993, c. 44; 32 I.L.M. 296 & 605 (1993) [hereinafter NAFTA].

however, that the hardest thing for governments to do is that which is rational, one must expect that these laws will continue to plague relations between Japan and North America in the foreseeable future. One must note that recently Japan adopted an antidumping procedure and has begun to use it.[7]

b. Subsidies

Allegations of subsidized production have seldom been formally made between Japan and North America in either direction. This is thus one area of trade law in which future disputes do not appear to be a major concern. Furthermore, to the extent that such issues might arise, it is hoped that the new GATT Subsidies Code[8] will provide the basis for a reasonable solution.

This situation could conceivably change significantly if all forms of voluntary restraint agreements are removed and replaced by safeguards, as required by the Uruguay Round Final Act.[9] Only then will it be possible to determine the full effect of these agreements; it is possible that governments will formulate arguments to compensate their losses.

c. Other U.S. Trade Remedies

From the Japanese perspective, the most grave concerns stem from U.S. trade remedy legislation designed to deal with situations not obviously covered by the GATT-sanctioned codes arising out of the 1979 Tokyo Round of Multilateral Trade Negotiations (MTN). These U.S. laws either cover matters that were not dealt with in the Tokyo Round or in earlier GATT agreements, or create remedies that arguably go beyond those envisaged by the various GATT articles or codes. Many of these laws date from the 1980s and are codified in the Trade and Competitiveness Act of 1988. Others date from much earlier times and were adopted in a very different context. Finally, some of these remedies deal explicitly with trade between Japan and the United States.

Among the laws of the United States that have caused particular concern are, *inter alia*:

---

7.   *See* S. Hagiwara, Y. Noguchi, K. Masui, *Anti-Dumping Laws in Japan*, 22 J. OF WORLD TRADE 35 (1988); S. Hagiwara, *First Application of Japanese Anti-Dumping Law*, 21 INT'L BUS. LAWYER 21 (1993); N. Komuro, *Japan's First Anti-Dumping Measures in the Ferro-Silico-Manganese Case*, 27 J.W.T.5 (1993).

8.   Adopted in the Final Act of the Uruguay Round of Multilateral Trade Negotiations, GATT Doc. MTN/FA, Dec. 15, 1993, Agreement on Subsidies and Countervailing Measures, pt. II, annex 1A, 13.

9.   *Id.* Agreement on Safeguards, pt. II, annex 1A, 14.

1) Section 301 of the Trade Act of 1974;[10]
2) Super 301;[11]
3) Special 301;[12]
4) Telecommunications Trade Act of 1988;[13]
5) Section 337 of the Tariff Act of 1930, dealing with intellectual property.[14]

Canadian legislation designed to back up safeguards action[15] has not been regularly invoked against Japanese goods but is of potential concern, as is antidumping legislation in both countries.[16] Both Japanese and Canadian substantive prohibitions and specific procedural remedies have been variously singled out.[17]

The most significant aspect of these laws for the purposes of this chapters is that they all appear to deal with matters or to create procedures not explicitly envisaged by the GATT or related Tokyo Round codes. The United States has chosen to deal with a perceived problem directly without prior international sanction. The multilateral rule was perceived to be inadequate or nonexistent and a legislative decision was taken to supplement it with domestic legislation. Whether this decision was taken after repeated attempts to secure international agreement on a common international standard is not discussed here, but would surely be a question for analysis should the justification of such measures be subject to impartial analysis. Similarly, the compatibility of these measures with American and Canadian international commitments, particularly the GATT, has seldom been referred to impartial bodies for decision.[18]

---

10. Trade Act of 1974, § 301, 88 Stat. 1978, 2041–43 (1975) (current version at 19 U.S.C. § 2411 (1988)).

11. 19 U.S.C. § 2411 (1988) (originally enacted as Omnibus Trade and Competitiveness Act of 1974, § 301, 102 Stat. 1988, 1108, 1176-1179 (1988)) (Super 301).

12. 19 U.S.C. § 2242 (1988) (originally enacted as Omnibus Trade and Competitiveness Act of 1974, § 301, 102 Stat. 1988, 1108, 1179–1181 (1988)) (Special 301).

13. Telecommunications Trade Act of 1988, 19 U.S.C. § 3101 (1988).

14. 19 U.S.C. § 1337 (1988 & Supp. 1993) (originally enacted as Tariff Act of 1930, c. 497, Title III, § 337, 46 Stat. 703 (1930)).

15. Canadian International Trade Tribunal Act, R.S.C., c. 47, § 22 (1985), *amended by* c. 47 1994 S.C. §§ 27–47 (Can.); The Customs Tariff Act, R.S.C., c. 41, §§ 60, 61, 62 (1988), *amended by* c. 47 1994 S.C. §§ 74–100 (Can.).

16. *Id.* §§ 1311–40 (U.S.); Special Import Measures Act, R.S.C., c. S-15 (1985), *amended by* c. 47 1994 S.C. §§ 145–190 (Can.).

17. *See* M. Matsushita, *Report on Unfair Trade Policies and Trade Practices*, FAIR TRADE CENTER —TOKYO, June (1991).

18. This was done with respect to the United States Japan Arrangement concerning Trade in Semi-conductor Products. *See* Japan—Trade in Semi-Conductors, Report of the Panel, GATT B.I.S.D, 35th Supp. 116 (1987–88). Similarly, having entered into the Cellular Phones Agreement, Japan is not likely to wish to contest its legality under the GATT but the question can be raised by an academic commentator.

There have been successful complaints against U.S. trade legislation, perhaps most notably concerning section 337 of the Tariff Act of 1937.[19] This complaint by the European Community (EC), in which Japan intervened, involved the allegation that American patent legislation treated foreign patents differently from domestic ones and hence provided discriminatory protection to the United States patent. The complaint was successful. This experience suggests that Japan might continue to make successful use of the GATT dispute settlement process, as it did against the EC in the challenge to the EC antidumping regulation involving so-called "screwdriver" auto plants in Great Britain.[20] Certain types of unilateral retaliation by way of higher import duties without prior GATT approval would seem open to challenge under the GATT. This is an avenue that Japan might be well advised to explore, both as a result of the broader ambit of the 1994 GATT and of the new GATT dispute settlement system, which will enter into force in July 1995.

Some of the laws in question, however, do not lend themselves to challenge under the GATT. This is because some purport to deal with procedural or substantive matters not explicitly covered by the GATT (or at least the pre-Uruguay Round GATT), when the nontariff barriers most fully covered were dumping and subsidies. Section 301 of the Omnibus Trade and Competitiveness Act of 1988 not only purports to deal with alleged "unfair trade practices" not covered by the GATT, but also creates remedies more draconian than those provided by the GATT and related GATT Codes. Some of these measures are aimed at situations of a structural nature, based on the assumption in the United States that the trading environment in the foreign country is deliberately maintained in a fashion that denies American goods fair competition in the foreign market.[21]

These measures raise issues of principle that can be debated either in function of the GATT or in function of the general principles of public international law. Does the existence of the GATT imply a duty to attempt to resolve all trade disputes, or at least those involving the trade in goods, by negotiations under the GATT and using GATT procedures to the full, or is there a general right of self-help that is not restrained by the GATT? Such measures as Section 301 and Super 301 are generally defended as handling practices which are not covered explicitly by the GATT. This puts the argument on the level of general principles of public international law by maintaining that what is not covered by treaty law remains within the discretion of sovereign states. This is a most serious assertion and must be carefully considered. It does not, however, address the legality under the GATT

---

19. GATT B.I.S.D., 36th Supp. 345 (1988–89).

20. E.C. Regulation on the Import of Parts and Components, GATT B.I.S.D, 37th Supp. 132 (1989–90).

21. See the exhaustive presentation of these arguments by the International Trade Commission in Phase II: Japan's Distribution System and Options for Improving U.S. Access, Report to the House Comm. on Ways and Means on Investigation No. 332–383 Under Section 332(g) of the Tariff Act of 1930, U.S.I.T.C. Pub. 2327, October 1990.

of the retaliatory measures themselves. Here a case can be made that denying market access or imposing higher tariffs or retaliatory charges of any kind requires GATT scrutiny before implementation. This issue is not one which has been fully considered and few governments have wished to make it the subject of a GATT panel complaint. The GATT 1947 has proven to be a surprisingly rich document and the 1994 GATT will doubtless prove to be equally rich: governments may be well advised to press this matter more aggressively against the United States.

The broader issue raised by these trade remedies of the United States, and to a lesser extent of Canada, regards the right of any state to legislate over matters not explicitly covered by existing international agreements. Of parallel salience is the basis of obligations under international law, which was at the heart of the differing positions of the judges in the *Lotus* case.[22] Does international law exist solely by virtue of the consent of states? If so, states should be free to deal with any issue and to adopt any policy they wish, unless they have agreed to be limited by specific commitments. The evidence remains strong that this is the position from which most governments operate, or that at the very least most governments insist on reading their treaty commitments narrowly, to guarantee themselves the maximum freedom of maneuver. Furthermore, it is tenable that other principles of international law, such as territorial sovereignty, reinforce the authority of a state to regulate the conditions under which its nationals trade with other states. It is probable that not only the government of the United States but also the governments of Japan and Canada would be comfortable with this interpretation of their rights and obligations under international law.

Intimately related is the relationship of international and domestic legal orders. Some constitutions, such as that of the Netherlands, grant unequivocal primacy to international law. Yet many, such as those of the United States and Canada, clearly allow their legislatures to violate international law, should that be the express desire of the elected representatives of the people.[23] If anything, this power is even more clearly enshrined in Canadian constitutional law than American.[24] The Japanese Constitution is somewhat less dualist, but in the final analysis the Diet also appears capable of acting contrary to international law.[25] For this reason, it is unlikely that arguing for the absolute primacy of international law over domestic law will yield

---

22.   1923 P.C.I.J. (ser. A) No.10.

23.   Many of these issues are canvassed in J. Jackson, *The Status of Treaties in Domestic Legal Systems*, 86 AM. J. INT'L LAW 310 (1992).

24.   *See* National Corn Growers Federation v. Canadian Import Tribunal, 2 S.C.R. 1324 (S.C.C.) (1990).

25.   *See* S. Murase *Reception of International Law into the Domestic Law of Japan, in Canada, Japan and International Law*, PROCEEDINGS OF THE 1990 CONFERENCE OF THE CANADIAN COUNCIL ON INTERNATIONAL LAW (1990).

absolute respect for the rules of the GATT and the other general principles of public international law.[26]

An alternative position to that set out above may be maintained as regards the rights and obligations of states with respect to international trade. This posits the existence of more than restrictively interpreted specific international trade treaty commitments. It can be argued that international trade is governed by a host of general principles and standards as well as by limited treaty commitments, and that these have the effect of requiring states to take the interests of other states into account before they adopt measures that restrain the flow of trade between them. One need not go this far, but surely a serious argument can be made that there is a right to trade, at least between market economy countries, and that this right should not be unreasonably fettered. Some scholars argue that it is essential to the maintenance of a liberal and competitive international trading order that the general principles governing international trade should enjoy constitutional or quasi-constitutional status in each GATT member state.[27] The consequence of any of these positions is to place greater restraints on the right of states to impose certain conditions on the entry of goods into their territory.

d. Restrictions of a "Structural" or "Cultural" Nature

It is sometimes alleged that commercial relations in Japan are structured so as to exclude any reasonable possibility of access by foreign goods to Japanese markets. The United States has responded to this perceived exclusion by the so-called "structural impediments initiatives."[28] Examples given to justify this legislation initially pointed to the difficulty of American traders to sell to Japanese companies that were already linked to other Japanese companies by a variety of arrangements, some formal, others informal; others included refusal to open up distributorship systems or the refusal of Japanese law to allow certain types of retail selling.[29] Sometimes this complaint focuses on Japanese regulation or administrative procedures, such as those governing product standards.[30] Another argument relates to the very close relationship between industry and government, especially the role of the MITI. These arguments reflect the frustration of one culture dealing with another. Many could be made by the Japanese in their dealings with the

---

26.   The policies militating against the absolute primacy of international law are studied by Jackson in his article, *supra* note 23.

27.   *See generally* E.U. PETERSMAN, CONSTITUTIONAL FUNCTIONS AND CONSTITUTIONAL PROBLEMS OF INTERNATIONAL ECONOMIC LAW (1991).

28.   The legislative basis for retaliatory measures underlying these initiatives is Section 1301 of the Omnibus Trade and Competitiveness Act of 1988, *supra* note 10.

29.   *See* U.S.I.T.C. Pub. 2327, *supra* note 21.

30.   *See, inter alia*, D. Cohen & K. Martin, *Western Ideology, Japanese Product Safety Regulation and International Trade*, 19 U.B.C.L. REV. 315 (1985)

United States.[31] Surely many such arguments would be made with respect to access to the French-speaking market of the Province of Québec, or the Spanish-speaking market of Puerto Rico, if these markets were sufficiently large to cause concern to Japanese and American traders.

There is no end to these arguments. They could be levelled by virtually any trader against any area where the culture and even the language is different. Such arguments become harder to reject out of hand with respect to the charge that open markets, subject to the disciplines of the GATT, are easier to penetrate than relatively closed markets. In the United States and Canada, which have by general acceptance among the most open markets in the world, it is not difficult to see why the political representatives of North American producers express their discontent in the form of legislated structural initiatives. The fact that virtually all international economists maintain that even the unilateral removal of trade barriers operates to the advantage of the country removing them does not seem to have convinced legislators of the wisdom of this view; nor is this view openly espoused by Japanese legislators and policymakers.

e. Conclusion

The cultural trade barrier is the hardest of the four to deal with, though all barriers demonstrate the advantage to reaching and respecting a multilateral consensus under the aegis of the GATT. It is to be expected that the reinforcement of the GATT 1994—by the expansion of its rules, the creation of the International Trade Organization and the strengthening of its dispute settlement procedures—will do much to assist in this process. This should not be minimized; it should be the source of considerable confidence for the future. On the other hand, there remains a variety of issues that will continue to plague North American-Japanese trading relations. Part II of this chapter is devoted to the proposal of a system of dispute avoidance and dispute resolution designed to deal with issues which have so far proven intractable.

II. PROPOSAL FOR DISPUTE SETTLEMENT AND AVOIDANCE

International lawyers have long criticized each other and been criticized for undue reliance on procedural devices, in particular those procedures used for the resolution of international disputes. While international lawyers may have moderated their expectations as to the potential impact of international dispute settlement procedures, such as judicial and arbitral settlement, they have quietly continued to experiment with other forms of dispute avoidance and dispute settlement. During the last two decades many new and old forms of dispute settlement have been used successfully. Major disputes over territory and economic

---

31.   *See* M. Matsushita, *Report on Unfair Trade Policies and Practices: Trade Barriers and GATT Obligations in the U.S., EC and Canada, supra* note 17.

concessions have been resolved by arbitration;[32] investment disputes have been submitted to the ICSID procedure;[33] and major disputes between Iran and the United States have been resolved by the Iran-United States Claims Tribunal.[34]

After a period of disuse in the late 1970s, GATT dispute settlement panels were increasingly used throughout the 1980s, and the GATT 1994 will be reinforced by an expanded procedure, including a standing appeal tribunal in 1995.[35] Canada and the United States adopted a procedure based on the GATT and a second, even more novel procedure, in the Free Trade Agreement of 1988;[36] they have joined with Mexico in doing the same and more in the North American Free Trade Agreement of 1992.[37] Even the International Court of Justice, which some gave up as a lost cause in the 1970s, currently has more cases on its docket than ever in its long history. In the admittedly supranational context of the European Union, the European Court of Justice has played a central role in the promotion of Europe's economic integration.[38] The picture for international dispute avoidance and settlement procedures is thus far from bleak at the present time. One can therefore envisage the possibility of establishing a useful dispute avoidance and settlement procedure in 1994 between Japan and North America with more confidence than might have been possible even a few years ago.

Dispute avoidance and settlement procedures should be carefully designed to fit their cultural, political, and economic contexts. In this case we are faced with the challenge of designing a procedure for two highly different contexts. American and, to a lesser extent, Canadian society are accustomed to resolving disputes by contentious and contradictory legal processes, while Japanese society has traditionally solved problems through negotiation and compromise and generally avoided displays of contradiction. It is therefore unlikely that a proposal based on conflictual models would find favor or function well in the Japanese context. From the North American perspective, it is equally necessary to design a procedure that would instill public confidence. This would unlikely result if a procedure regarded

---

32. *Inter alia* English Channel Arbitration (Fr. v. U.K.), 18 I.L.M. 379 (1979); *La Bretagne Arbitration*, 90 REV. GEN. DR. INT'L PUB. 713 (1986); Texaco v. Libya, 17 I.L.M. 1 (1978).

33. International Centre for the Settlement of Investment Disputes, Washington, *Annual Report* (1966-67).

34. Claims Settlement Agreement (Declaration of the Government of Algeria) 20 I.L.M. 230 (1980). *See generally* TOOPE, MIXED INTERNATIONAL ARBITRATION: STUDIES IN ARBITRATION BETWEEN STATES AND PRIVATE PARTIES (1990).

35. Subsidies Code, *supra* note 8.

36. Canada-United States Free Trade Implementation Act, S.C. 1988, c. 65, Schedule, pt. A., Chapters 18, 19, 27 I.L.M. 281 (1988).

37. North American Free Trade Agreement Implementation Act, S.C. 1993, c. 44, chapters 19, 20 and others, 32 I.L.M. 605 (1993).

38. *See, inter alia,* D. LASOK AND BRIDGE, LAW AND INSTITUTIONS OF THE EUROPEAN COMMUNITIES, (5th Ed., 1991); SCHERMERS, JUDICIAL REVIEW OF EUROPEAN COMUNITY LAW (5th Ed., 1993).

as based entirely on negotiation and discretion and not conducted by persons perceived to be neutral and independent of governments were proposed.

For the reasons set out above it would not seem useful to propose judicial settlement, arbitration, or other types of highly formalized judicial or arbitral procedure. This would not seem appropriate to the Japanese situation or the context of trade relations. Nor would it be appropriate simply to reproduce the GATT panel procedure. This procedure already exists and will shortly be strengthened. Furthermore, the GATT panel procedure is designed to assist in the enforcement of GATT rules, while the purpose of a Japanese–North American dispute avoidance and settlement procedure would be to deal with a more open-ended and undefined range of future problems. The recurring common concern of the three governments appears to center on fair treatment, openness of markets, and the manner in which trade remedy laws are applied. At the limit, there is also an issue of compatibility of legislation or administrative decisions with the GATT, but it must be remembered that the GATT processes exist precisely to make such determinations and arguably have been doing so more and more effectively. If there is an analogy to the GATT, it is with nonviolation nullification and impairment claims rather than with allegations of violation of the formal provisions of the GATT and its related codes.

What is needed, therefore, is a procedure that speaks with authority, that supplements but does not replace the GATT process, and that commands support from two very different legal cultures. Is there any existing procedure that can provide guidance either as a model or at least by way of analogy? In terms of conceptual analysis, the nonviolation nullification and impairment procedure does provide a framework worthy of further study. A number of panel proceedings under the GATT[39] and lately under the Canada–United States Free Trade Agreement [40] (CFTA) indicate that this concept can usefully supplement the more traditional concept of violation of the terms of a treaty by allowing the panel to consider a wider range of concerns that go beyond the letter of the law. While it can be argued that GATT or CFTA nonviolation nullification and impairment arguments must be made with reference to a specific legal text, using nullification and impairment allows the parties to raise wider issues of fairness and legitimate expectations central to many trade disputes between Japan and North America. It is in this sense that the analogy is drawn.

If the concept of nonviolation nullification and impairment does provide a useful approach to dispute avoidance and settlement, it does not necessarily provide the model for the most appropriate procedure to be adopted. What type of

---

39. *See, inter alia,* EEC—Payments and Subsidies Paid to Professors and Producers of Oilseeds and Related Animal-Feed Proteins, GATT B.I.S.D., 37th Supp. 86 (1989–90); U.S.A.—Restrictions on the Importation of Sugar and Sugar-Containing Products Applied under the 1955 Waiver, GATT B.I.S.D., 37th Supp. 228 (1989– 90).

40. *In the Matter of Puerto Rico Regulations on the Import, Sale and Distribution of UHT Milk from Québec,* USA–93–1807–01, Final Report of the Panel, June 3, 1993, 5 World Trade Materials 53 (1993).

procedure, then, would be most appropriate? Two elements seem paramount: flexibility and authority. A system structured too much like a judicial proceeding would be unlikely to command support in Japan, while an open-ended negotiation would add nothing to existing bilateral relations. Some degree of formality and authority would seem essential. The answer may lie in the purpose of the procedure. Fact finding should be the first objective. Few issues bedevil Japanese–North American trade relations more than a proper determination and understanding of the facts. Is the Japanese bureaucracy biased in its approach to the licensing of a particular product? Are Japanese industrial groups concerting to impede the entry of foreign products and services in certain sectors? Are some foreign marketing techniques unfairly excluded from Japan? These are in very large measure questions of fact, which should benefit from being aired before an impartial and authoritative group of experts. Is the NAFTA being used to inhibit the entry or expansion of Japanese firms into Canada or the United States? Are the rules of origin of the NAFTA more restrictive for Japanese automotive products than those of the CFTA? Surely such questions, often posed in Japan, could be aired in the same way.

If factfinding seems to be the most significant function of a dispute avoidance and resolution procedure, authoritative appraisal and comment are also extremely important. A mechanism for the temporary removal of an issue from the arena of public dispute and negotiation could provide an avenue for reducing tensions while allowing for progress toward resolving the dispute. What is needed is a process that falls short of judicial or arbitral settlement but which allows those charged with its direction to make a serious appraisal of the situation and to give their reasoned comments toward reaching a solution for the parties.

In summary, what is required is an authoritative but noncontentious procedure directed towards establishing the facts and allowing the panel to make an assessment of the reasonability of the complaints that they have heard, in light of the reasonable expectations of both parties. What should such a hybrid procedure look like? Are there any analogies to assist in framing it?

A useful analogy would seem to lie close at hand, at least in the Canada–United States context. It is to be found in the principal chapters of the CFTA devoted to dispute settlement, namely Chapters 18 and 19. Chapter 18 is a process based on the GATT panel review model but which has been adapted to the bilateral context. Chapter 19 is a more original and special process, in that it is applicable only to disputes arising out of antidumping and countervailing duty decisions. Domestic decisions in these matters may be appealed to a special binational panel, which then stands in lieu of the normal courts of appeal. The binational panel reviews the administrative or quasi-judicial decision and renders a binding ruling as to whether the original decision was made in accordance with applicable domestic law. Central to the process of review in both countries is the issue of whether the original decision was made in light of all the relevant evidence. These models have been carried forward with some embellishment into the trilateral context of the NAFTA.[41] The NAFTA Parallel Agreements on Environmental Protection and Labor Standards[42] provide an additional avenue of dispute settlement when one of the NAFTA governments is alleged to have persisted in failing to enforce its environmental or labor legislation and where this failure results in harm to another party.

It is not suggested that either the Chapter 18 or 19 models could or should be carried over to the Japanese–North American context. What is suggested below is that some of the principal features of these models could be used to create an appropriate procedure.

If central to the problem of approaching disputes between Japan and North America is the absence of an independent review of the domestic administrative and legislative process underlying the dispute in question, it would seem that the Chapter 19 process provides a useful model with respect to the object of the proposed procedure. Chapter 19 is designed to allow review of the domestic decision, not by subjecting it to an external standard, but by reviewing it in its own administrative and legislative terms. The binational review produces a result declaring the decision to have been fairly and openly reached and removing any taint of manipulation or of favoring domestic over foreign interest. During the life of the CFTA over forty such decisions have been, or are in process of being, rendered.[43] They have not stopped recourse to antidumping and countervailing duty laws between Canada and the United States. Despite this potentially serious problem, commentators have been cautiously positive in their overall assessment of the CFTA dispute settlement procedures.[44] At least it can be said that these decisions have helped to clear the air in a number of vexed disputes where politicians and regulators were under intense pressure from producer interests to take more protectionist steps. Clearly a formal appeal process would not be appropriate to the Japanese–North American context, but what can be taken from the Chapter 19 model is a method of scrutiny of domestic decisions.

What is proposed is a process, forged by mixing the Chapter 18 and 19 panel processes, whose object is not to render a binding decision but rather to give advice. The decisions should be based on a full review of the domestic regulatory and legislative situation and inform the parties that the domestic measures that have

---

41.   NAFTA chs. 19 and 20, *supra* note 37 (reference the other principal dispute settlement provisions, especially the financial services roster).

42.   North American Agreement on Environmental Cooperation, 32 I.L.M. 1480 (1993); North American Agreement on Labor Cooperation, 32 I.L.M. 1499 (1993).

43.   All disputes arising after Jan. 1, 1994 will be heard under the NAFTA procedures.

44.   *See, inter alia,* W.C. Graham, *Dispute Resolution under the Canada–United States Free Trade Agreement: One Element in a Complex Relationship,* 37 McGILL L.J. 544 (1992); G.N. Horlick & F.A. DeBusk, *Dispute Resolution Panels under the U.S.-Canada Free Trade Agreement: The First Two and a Half Years,* 37 McGILL L.J. 574 (1992); A.F. Lowenfeld, *The Free Trade Agreement Meets its First Challenge: Dispute Settlement and the Pork Case,* 37 McGILL L.J. 597 (1992).

been appealed have been taken in strict conformity with the domestic law of one party and with the legitimate commercial expectations of the nationals of the other party. This process would have as its primary focus fact-finding with respect to the domestic administrative and legislative situation. It would also allow for an informed and authoritative opinion as to the legitimate commercial expectations of the nationals of the complaining party in the light of the determination of the panel.

The authority of the panel's opinion would come essentially from the standing of the panelists and the quality of their reasoning. The creation of the panel would thus require careful consideration. The CFTA model involves separate national rosters and a process of negotiation for the selection of a panel in a particular case. More appropriate here might be the formation of a single Japanese–North American roster (perhaps "college" would be the more appropriate characterization), on the model of Chapter 20 of the NAFTA. A single roster of some twenty-five Japanese and North American former cabinet members, judges, senior trade officials, senior business people, or respected academics (if such there may be) would seem to be ideal. A panel of five roster members should be subject to rules of procedure, thus affording an opportunity to all parties to make submissions and to be heard orally. The rules of procedure should also empower the panel to ask for all information, including expert opinion, that it deems necessary to answer the question before it. The process could be initiated either unilaterally or pursuant to negotiations between the parties. It would seem that the latter approach should be preferred, since it allows the parties the time and the discretion to frame the question the panel is to answer.

This process is envisaged as part of a continuum of relations between the parties leading to the resolution or avoidance of disputes; therefore, it must be flexible and assist the parties. It should not be perceived by them as source of annoyance or embarrassment. One question to be resolved is the proper role of private commercial interests in the process. Should private parties be allowed to participate directly in the process? Their initiation of the process would seem to be out of the question, but allowing participation in the hearings, either by way of submissions or response to requests for information, should be seriously considered.

The proposed procedure is not an end in itself, nor will it constitute a final determination of the particular dispute. What is envisaged is a panel report enabling the parties to clarify issues and to reach a rapid settlement. The final determination of matters should continue to remain in the hands of the parties.

III. CONCLUSION

This proposal, admittedly of a theoretical and somewhat abstract character, is made with a view to bridging as much the cultural as the legal space dividing Japan and North America. Our trade relations demand, especially when disputes inevitably arise, a search for a common understanding and a search for the common interest that surely exists between such important trading partners. In cultural and legal terms, what is needed is a stronger sense of the common interest and community which binds Japan and North America in the global village. It is to this end that the proposal is advanced.[45]

---

45. Similar questions are discussed from the Australian perspective by R. Field, *Japanese Cultural Trade Barriers and the Search for an Appropriate Dispute Settlement Forum*, 21 AUSTRALIAN BUS. L. REV. 173 (1993).

THE STRUCTURAL IMPEDIMENTS INITIATIVES: A MODEL FOR DEALING WITH INTERNATIONAL ECONOMIC FRICTIONS[*]

Masato Dogauchi

I. INTRODUCTION

Societal differences are the motivation for international trade and investment. Were every society identical, no movement of people, goods, or money would occur. The uniqueness of social structure itself is not to be blamed, but advantages in international economic competition derived from the uniqueness are sometimes deemed unfair by the competitors. The structure of society—including legal frameworks—may be a *de facto* export subsidy, unregulated by international treaties. For example, because of a relatively loose antitrust policy in its domestic market, a company may have large profits to spend on the development of new technologies for future export to foreign markets. Societal structure may also cause a *de facto* barrier to investment of foreign capital. For example, regulations on land and house leases that excessively protect existing lessees may block foreign companies that plan on direct investment, since lessors who cannot earn enough from the existing lessees must increase the initial rent for new lessees. These matters traditionally have been deemed domestic matters, into which foreign countries have not intervened. Due to modern international interdependence, however, purely domestic matters no longer exist.

The Structural Impediments Initiative (SII) conducted between Japan and the United States from 1989 to 1990 was a unique opportunity to discuss each society's domestic affairs. Such an approach towards problems in international trade and

---

*This chapter is based on Masato Dogauchi, *Nichibei Kōzō Mondai Kyōgi no Hōteki Ichizuke* [*Legal Standing of U.S.–Japan Structural Impediments Initiative*], 1258 SHŌJIHŌMU 25 (1991).

investment is indispensable in this interdependent world. The SII has been analyzed and evaluated from various standpoints, including the political, economic, and diplomatic. While some of these analyses are rather emotional, there are some valuable research papers written in the context of the history of U.S.-Japan trade frictions and the strategic significance of U.S. trade diplomacy, which provide a broad view of the SII.[1] Compared with those analyses given from the standpoint of international political science, a legal analysis of the SII is inevitably limited to confirmation of the fundamental matters.

Given that the methodology of legal analysis on international trade has not yet been established, it is not clear on what basis a legal analysis of the SII should be made. The legal nature of the SII will be examined in section II of this chapter, with attention to the formal aspects of the SII. In section III, its position within the legal framework of international trade will be discussed in consideration of the essential background of the SII. An evaluation will be made from two angles: the negative being the undeniable relation to "Super 301" of the U.S. Trade Act,[2] and the positive being the model for coordination of legislative policies between closely related countries.[3]

---

1.   For example, according to Professor Heizo Takenaka, the SII was a strategy devised by the White House which aimed at the successful conclusion of the GATT Uruguay Round negotiations, checking the protectionists of Congress. Professor Takenaka also explained that the SII was designed to urge Japan to adopt an American-style market mechanism about which the United States became confident through the collapse of Eastern Europe, while restraining the export from Japan of the Japanese-style "philosophy of poverty" which was represented by high land prices and low consumption. HEIZO TAKENAKA, NICHIBEI MASATSU NO KEIZAIGAKU [ECONOMICS OF JAPAN-U.S. TRADE FRICTIONS] at 285 (1991).

     See also HIDEO SATO, NICHIBEI KEIZAI MASATSU [JAPAN-U.S. ECONOMIC FRICTIONS], 164 (1991) (a comprehensive summary of the history of the SII); Gary R. Saxonhouse, *Japan, SII and the International Harmonization of Domestic Economic Practices*, 12 MICH. J. INT'L L. 450 (1991) (an economic analysis of the SII).

2.   Section 301 of the Trade Act of 1974, *amended by* the Omnibus Trade and Competitiveness Act of 1988, 19 U.S.C.A. §§ 2411 *et seq*. (Supp. 1994).

3.   The structural impediments pointed out in the SII were:

    Japan:

        (1) saving and investment patterns, (2) land policy, (3) distribution system, (4) exclusionary business practices, (5) *Keiretsu* relationships, (6) pricing mechanisms;

    United States:

        (1) saving and investment patterns, (2) corporate investment and supply capacity, (3) corporate behavior, (4) government regulations, (5) research and development, (6) export promotion, (7) workforce education and training.

    This chapter does not intend to study these items in detail. For greater detail, *see* articles in *Nichibei Kōzō Mondai Kyōgi—Hōteki Kadai no Kentō [Japan-U.S. SII: Study of Legal Issues]* 965 JURISUTO (1990).

II. THE LEGAL NATURE OF THE JOINT FINAL REPORT OF THE SII

a. A Superficial History of the SII

The formal aspects of the SII are decisive in identifying its legal nature and therefore a brief history of the SII will first be presented. In May 1989 President Bush proposed "negotiations" with Japan concerning the structural problems in the Japanese economy, including Japanese practices that impede fair competition in Japanese markets.[4] Japan responded that it would not "negotiate" its domestic affairs with any foreign country but would welcome "talks" on mutual structural problems.[5] "Negotiations" are different from "talks": in the former, the aim is to reach promises by one country to another concerning matters discussed; in the latter, each country presents its idea and discusses the problems of both countries, but then decides by itself what shall be done about its particular problems.

Talks on the SII formerly began according to the following agreement reached between two countries at the time of the Arche Economic Summit[6] in July 1989:

> Both Heads of Government agree to complement the economic policy coordination efforts which have been hitherto made, by launching the Structural Impediments Initiative to identify and solve structural problems in both countries that stand as impediments to trade and to balance of payments adjustments, with the goal of contributing to the reduction of payment imbalances. Both Heads agree to set up a working group consisting of officials representing various governmental agencies from each Government in order to start talks between two countries. Both Heads appointed three joint chairmen respectively. The joint chairmen will preside over the conference on a vice-minister level.
>
> These talks will take place outside Section 301 of the United States Trade Act. An interim report will be issued in spring 1990 and a joint final report will be submitted within a year.[7]

---

4.   This proposal was made on the initiative of the Treasury Department. [1989] Facts on File Y.B. at 397. It is important to note that the SII was proposed simultaneously with the announcement of the identification of Japan as a foreign priority country under Super 301, but the United States made it clear that the SII had nothing to do with Super 301. *See* Gaiko Seisho [Diplomatic Blue Paper] 190 (1990).

5.   *See* Mitoji Yabunaka, *Nichibei Kōzō Mondai Kyōgi: Sono Konnichiteki Igi, Tokushoku oyobi Hōteki Ichizuke [Japan-U.S. SII: Its Significance, Characteristics and Legal Standing]* 965 JURISUTO, 46 (1990).

6.   This summit meeting was held in Arche, Paris among the heads of seven industrial countries to discuss matters such as macroeconomic policies, international trade, and global environmental problems.

7.   Joint communiqué by President Bush and Prime Minister Uno on economic problems of July 14, 1985.

Thereafter, five plenary sessions of the Working Group were held between September 1989 and June 1990, under the joint chairmanship of the representatives of the Ministries of Foreign Affairs, Finance, and International Trade and Industry on the Japanese side, and those of the Departments of State and Treasury, and the United States Trade Representative (USTR) on the American side, and with the participation of representatives of various governmental agencies on both sides. An Interim Report on the progress of the SII talks was issued on April 5, 1990, and a Joint Final Report was submitted on June 28, 1990.[8] It is worthy of note that the report was submitted to Prime Minister Kaifu and President Bush from the chairmen of both governments.[9] On the cover letter of the Final Report was the following:

> Pursuant to the decision made by the U.S. and Japanese Heads of Government at the Economic Summit in July 1989, the U.S.-Japan Working Group on the Structural Impediments Initiative (SII) presents herein the attached Final Report on the SII talks.

This indicates that the SII were not "negotiations" but from beginning to end merely "talks." In the Final Report, the SII Working Group agreed to meet three times in the first year and twice a year thereafter to review progress achieved in regard to issues identified in the Final Report; to discuss matters relevant to problem areas already identified in the SII and the need for action to address them; and to produce in the spring of each year a written report on the progress made by each country toward solving structural problems. The aim was to reduce external imbalances, review reports together, and issue reports with a joint press release. It was also agreed that the SII Working Group would review follow-up progress after three years, taking into account measures in the Final Report that extend beyond three years. The follow-up talks were held as scheduled based on this agreement.

b. Legal Appraisal

As delineated above, the Final Report of the SII was not designed to describe agreements between Japan and the United States. Nor was it a treaty or administra-

---

8.   TSŪSHŌ SANGYŌ CHŌSAKAI ED., NICHIBEI KŌZŌ MONDAI KYŌGI SAISHŪ HŌKOKUSHO [FINAL REPORT OF THE STRUCTURAL IMPEDIMENTS INITIATIVES] (1990) (contains the Japanese text and the English text of the final report and other related documents).

Incidentally, measures to be taken by the Japanese government which were contained in the Interim Report were approved by the Cabinet on Apr. 4, 1990. On June 28 the Cabinet also gave its approval to those measures incorporated in the Final Report, declaring that "the Government of Japan will steadily implement those measures."

9.   On the Japanese side was the Deputy Minister for Foreign Affairs, the Vice Minister for International Affairs, the Minister of Finance, and the Vice Minister for International Affairs, Ministry of International Trade and Industry; on the U.S. side was the Under Secretary of State, the Assistant Secretary of the Treasury, and the Deputy U.S. Trade Representative.

tive or other kind of agreement between the two countries.[10] It was merely a study report on the policies made by the officials of each government to aid heads of government in making decisions. In essence it was nothing more than a public expression of intention by the respective governments.[11] Since the Working Group was formed by a Heads Conference, and the results of the study by the Working Group were adopted by the respective governments as their own policies, the SII practices could never constitute an infringement on the sovereignty of each country or an interference in domestic affairs. The SII talks were instructive opportunities for government officials in charge of domestic affairs to hear opinions of closely related countries and to understand that even a nation's decisions on domestic matters can significantly affect conditions in another country.

With respect to the commitment given to the contents of the report, it was important to note that the measures to be taken on Japanese problems contained in the Report were approved by the Japanese Cabinet. The Report otherwise would have merely been an elaborate statement of the study results by those in charge of making policy. The commitment of the Japanese government was made by Cabinet approval on its own initiative to implement the measures contained in the report.

This commitment would be by and large politically significant. If the government did not sufficiently implement the measures contained in the report, it would lead to a serious diplomatic problem. This, however, would never constitute breach of treaty under international law. The policies in the Report would not have a binding effect on the Diet of Japan under Japanese law, since they were simply policies determined by administrative power. Accordingly, it is possible that the budget plan to implement the policies stated in the SII Report could be rejected by the Diet.[12]

---

10. The word "treaty" is defined in Article 2(1)(a) of the Vienna Convention on the Law of Treaties of 1969, 1155 U.N.T.S. 331, 8 I.L.M. 679.

11. SeeMitoji Yabunaka, *supra* note 5, at 49. Note, *International Trade: Joint Report of the United States–Japan Working Group on the Structural Impediments Initiative, June 28, 1990*, 32 HARV. INT'L L.J. 245, 247 (1991).

12. For instance, with respect to the Japanese "commitment" to the public investment of ¥430 trillion over a decade from FY 1991 to FY 2000, there was a difference in understanding as to its meaning between Japan and the United States right after the Final Report was issued. The Japanese government understood it as a "guideline," while the United States seemed to have deemed it to be a "firm commitment" instead of a mere blueprint. 7 INT'L TRADE REP. (BNA) at 982 (July 4, 1990).

The Final Report stated that "the Government of Japan has newly launched the 'Basic Plan for Public Investment,' which serves *as guiding principles* for steady accumulation of the social overhead capital toward the twenty-first century," and further stated that "the Plan includes the aggregate investment expenditure of about 430 trillion yen for the decade." (Emphasis added) In any case, it would not be meaningless to contest the interpretation of the plan because it was not a promise between two countries. Even if this plan were a firm commitment to the public by the Government of Japan, the Diet would not necessarily approve the implementation of the commitment.

The SII has outwardly had no connection with Section 301 of the Trade Act, as both the joint communiqué made in July 1989 at the Heads Conference and the SII Final Report of June 1990 clearly state that the SII talks took place outside the ambit of Section 301 of the U.S. Trade Act.[13]

III. SIGNIFICANCE OF THE SII: LEGISLATIVE POLICY COORDINATION IN AN INTERDEPENDENT AGE

The previous section examined the legal character of the SII in terms of its formal aspects. This section will provide an appraisal of the SII by taking its background into account. First, the relationship of the SII with Super 301 of the Trade Act will be examined; second, the policy coordination of the two countries will be evaluated.

a. Background

The SII talks appears to have been conducted outside the scope of Section 301 of the Trade Act, but it goes without saying that the United States placed emphasis on Japanese unfair practices as a target for remedying external payment imbalances, as a huge trade imbalance existed between the two countries. The essential link between the SII talks and Super 301 of the Trade Act cannot be disregarded.

(1) Super 301

After the U.S.-Japan trade friction regarding semiconductors,[14] the United States amended the Trade Act of 1974 in August 1988,[15] in which the so-called

---

13. Though the official understanding on the administrative level is that the SII had no relation to Section 301, the relationship between the SII and Section 301 or Super 301 could not be denied from the standpoint of the Trade Act because the results of the SII were to be subject to evaluation under the Trade Act. In fact, the progress of the SII was referred to in the annual report under Super 301 submitted by the USTR to Congress on Apr. 27, 1990. 55 Fed. Reg. 18693 (1990).

14. In June 1985 the United States Semiconductor Industry Association filed a petition under Section 301 alleging that Japan was restricting access to the domestic semiconductor market for United States producers. In September 1986 Japan and the United States formally concluded an Arrangement concerning Trade in Semiconductor Products. In March 1987 the United States imposed a sanction on the exports of Japanese products to the United States. In June 1991, both countries entered into a renewed agreement, and upon initiation of the agreement in August the unilateral retaliatory duties were withdrawn.

15. Omnibus Trade and Competitiveness Act of 1988. *See generally*, Mitsuo Matsushita, *1998 nen Hōkatsu Bōeki Kyōsōryoku Kyokahō no Kenkyū* [*Study of Omnibus Trade and Competitiveness Act of 1988*] 16 KOKUSAI SHŌJIHŌMU, No. 10, at 835 and No.11, at 957 (1988).

"Super 301" was stipulated in addition to an amendment to Section 301 of the Trade Act aimed at coping with unfair trade practices ("Super 301" was in force only for a limited period during 1989 and 1990).

Super 301 is the provision of Article 310 of the Trade Act[16] entitled "Identification of Trade Liberalization Priorities." The USTR has submitted to Congress an annual report on the trade barriers of foreign countries known as the National Trade Estimates (NTE) Report every year since 1988.[17] According to Section 310, during the two-year period from 1989 to 1990 the USTR is required to identify U.S. trade liberalization priorities on the basis of the report within thirty days following submission of the annual report to Congress. A Report submitted to Congress[18] includes priority practices[19] and priority foreign countries, taking into account various factors,[20] and an estimation of the total amount by which United States exports of goods and services to each country so identified would have increased during the preceding calendar year had the priority practices of such countries not existed.

Further, within twenty-one days following submission of this report to Congress, the USTR shall initiate investigations with respect to all of those priority practices identified for each of the priority foreign countries.[21] In connection with these investigations, the USTR shall request consultations with the priority foreign country.[22] In this consultation the USTR shall seek to negotiate an agreement that provides for the "elimination of, or compensation for, the priority practices" within three years following the initiation of the investigation, and "the reduction of such practices over a three-year period with the expectation that United States exports to the foreign country will, as a result, increase incrementally during each year within such three-year period."[23] If such agreement is entered into with the foreign country before a prescribed date, the investigation will be suspended.[24] Otherwise,

---

16. 19 U.S.C. § 2420.

17. *Id.*, § 181.

18. *Id.*, § 301(a)(1)(D).

19. Section 310(a)(1)(A) reads, "priority practices, including major barriers and trade distorting practices, the elimination of which are likely to have the most significant potential to increase United States exports, either directly or through the establishment of a beneficial precedent."

20. *Id.*, § 310(a)(2) and (3).

21. *Id.*, § 302(b)(1); § 310(b).

22. *Id.*, § 303(a).

23. *Id.*, § 310(c)(1).

24. *Id.*, § 310(c)(2). According to § 310(c)(3), if the USTR determines that the foreign country is not in compliance with such an agreement, the USTR shall continue the investigation that was suspended by reason of such agreement as though such an investigation had not been suspended.

the USTR shall determine whether the foreign practices are fair within twelve months following the initiation of the investigation.[25]

If the practices of the foreign country are determined to be unfair, the USTR shall take action under Section 301, which is so devised as to affect the goods or services of the foreign country to an amount equivalent in value to the burden being imposed by that country on United States commerce. For the purpose of retaliation, the USTR is authorized to suspend or withdraw trade benefits, to impose duties or other import restrictions on goods and services, or to carry out such actions as the USTR determines to be appropriate.[26] The USTR is also required to monitor increased U.S. exports to foreign countries with which an agreement entered into has been concluded, and to submit a report on such progress for a period from the submission of the annual report identifying priority foreign countries up to at least 1993.[27]

(2) Identification of Japan as a Priority Country under Super 301 and Japan's Response

In April 1989 the USTR made an annual report in which trade barriers in thirty-four countries and two regional groups were listed. As for Japan, thirty-four trade barriers were enumerated including communication, supercomputers, semiconductors, construction, agriculture, automobile parts, and distribution systems. On May 25, 1989, the USTR identified Japan as a priority foreign country under the Super 301, together with Brazil (for restrictions on imports) and India (for restrictions on trade related to investment and insurance market practices), and identified as priority practices such items as government procurement of supercomputers and satellites, and technical barriers related to forestry products.[28]

---

25. *Id.*, § 304(a)(2)(B). According to § 304 (a)(2)(A), in the case of an investigation involving a trade agreement, the USTR shall determine whether the foreign practices are fair on or before (1) the date that is 30 days after the date on which the dispute settlement procedure is concluded, or (2) the date that is 18 months after the date on which the investigation is initiated. Further, according to § 304 (a)(3)(A), in the case of an investigation involving alleged infringement of intellectual property rights, the USTR shall make such determinations no later than the date that is six months after the date on which such investigation is initiated.

26. Section 301(a)(2) provides for cases in which the taking of retaliatory actions are not required.

27. *Id.*, § 310(d).

28. For an annual report under Section 310(a)(1)(D), *see* 54 Federal Register, No.108, at 24438 (1989). According to this annual report, there is not enough information to make an estimation of the amount by which United States' exports to the identified priority foreign country would have increased if the priority practices did not exist.

Taiwan was excluded from identification as a priority country by making a commitment to increase domestic demand from 86.3% of its GNP to 93.7% by 1992; Korea was also excluded from identification by making a commitment that it would implement before 1993

Japan expressed regret at such unilateral identification as a priority country with priority practices, and made it clear that Japan would not comply with the U.S. request for negotiations on the basis of potential invocation of unilateral sanctions.[29] Japan argued, at the GATT Council meeting in June 1989, that such unilateral measures as those under Super 301 were inconsistent with the GATT dispute settlement mechanism based upon mutual equality of the contracting parties.[30]

Since the USTR was required to initiate investigations with respect to identified priority practices of priority foreign countries within twenty-one days following submission of its annual report to Congress, the investigation under section 302(b)(1) commenced on June 16, the twenty-first day from the date of submission of the annual report.[31] Although Japan refused to negotiate under Super 301, negotiations were conducted on the basis of "talks without anticipating any sanctions."[32] Eventually this investigation as to the three priority practices of Japan was suspended on June 15.[33]

---

such measures as the liberalization of foreign investment into Korea, the lifting of restrictions on imports of pharmaceutical and cosmetics, the lifting of restrictions on activities of foreign travel agents and advertising agents, and the opening of the market to bean oils and other agricultural products. *See* Note, *International Trade—the Implementation of 'Super 301,' Omnibus Trade and Competitiveness Act, sec.301, 19 U.S.C. 2411 (Supp. VII 1989)*, 31 HARV. INT'L L.J. 359, 362 (1990).

29. *See Talk of Foreign Minister*, Gaiko Seisho [Diplomatic Blue Paper] 189 (1990); Keizai Hakusho [Economic White Paper], 241 (1989); 6 Int'l Trade Rep. (BNA) at 686–87 (May 31, 1989). Brazil and India also raised objections against the United States unilateral actions. The EC also criticized the United States, saying that such unilateral actions would impair the world free trade system. *See supra* note 28, at 362–363. Japan expressed objections to unilateralism as seen in Super 301 at the meeting of the OECD Ministerial Council in May 1990 and at the Arche Economic Summit in July 1990 (*see supra* note 6). Finally, in a communiqué of the OECD, it was clearly stated that unilateralism as shown in the Super 301 clause would hinder the multilateral trade framework and ruin the GATT Uruguay Round negotiations.

30. At the meeting of the GATT Council, Canada, Mexico, Argentina and the Scandinavian countries also criticized the Super 301. *See* Note, *supra* note 28, at 363.

31. *See* 54 Fed. Reg. No. 118, at 26136–8 (1989).

32. While the Japanese Diplomatic Blue Paper of 1990 described "talks without anticipating any sanctions (at 190), the report of the USTR submitted to Congress regarding the suspension of an investigation under Section 302 stated that the USTR conducted negotiations with Japan under Section 310(c)(1) and would monitor Japan's compliance with the agreement. 55 Federal Register No. 121 at 25761–6 (1990). The report further stated that if the USTR determined Japan is not in compliance with the agreement, the USTR would resume the investigation. In addition, a report dated Apr. 27, 1990 stated measures accepted by Japan to remedy the identified three priority practices "as Super 301 Results." 55 Fed. Reg. No. 86 at 18693 (1990).

33. According to the report submitted by the USTR to Congress on the suspension of an investigation under Section 302 with regard to Japanese three priority practices (Federal Register, Vol. 55, No. 121, at 25761–6), the exchange note with Japan dated June 15, 1990 was regarded as an "agreement" under Section 310. *See also*, Tsūshō Hakusho [White Paper

In the annual report prepared by the USTR in March 1990 regarding Japan, amorphous metals, intellectual property rights, and automobile parts were identified as fields with existing trade barriers. On April 27 the USTR submitted to Congress the annual report identifying U.S. trade liberalization priorities for 1990.[34] In this report the USTR pointed out that it was a "key trade priority" for the world economy that the Japanese economy—which was the second largest in the world—should operate on the basis of an open and truly competitive market system. The USTR also conducted a survey of the progress of trade issues relating to Japan, referring to the Interim Report of the SII dated April 5, 1990; furthermore, it excluded Japan from its list of identified foreign priority countries, stating that a satisfactory solution was reached with respect to the three priority practices.[35]

(3) Relationship between Super 301 and the SII

Concurrent with the identification of Japan as a priority country, the United States proposed the SII to Japan, but clarified, as stated previously, that the talks under the SII took place outside Section 301 of the Trade Act.[36] It cannot be denied, however, that there was a substantial relationship between Super 301 and the SII. First, Super 301 was primarily aimed at enabling the USTR to proceed with necessary procedures automatically based on authorization by Congress, which has power over international trade under the U.S. Constitution.[37] The president is thereby precluded from intervening in an invocation of Section 301 through use of the presidential diplomatic power[38] and thus does not have authority to suspend a Super 301 procedure at his discretion. Second, the date of issue of an Interim Report of the SII, which showed the substantial results of the SII, coincided with the requirement of Section 304(a)(2)(B) that the USTR must determine the fairness of foreign practices within twelve months following the initiation of an investigation. Moreover, the Interim Report was issued only two months before the Final Report of the SII during the talks of the Working Group, which spanned one year. Third, the agreement in the Final Report of the SII that the Working Group review the follow-up progress of the measures after three years coincided with the requirement under Section 310(d) that the USTR monitor increased U.S. exports to each of the

---

on International Trade] at 76 (1990).

34. *See* 55 Fed. Reg. No. 86, at 18693.

35. India was again identified as a foreign priority country.

36. *See supra* note 4.

37. Article I, Section 8 (3) of the Constitution of the United States provides that the Congress has the power "(t)o regulate Commerce with foreign Nations, and among the several States. . . ."

38. As to the history of the establishment and power of the USTR, *see* Kiyoshi Aoki, *Beikoku no Tsusho Soshiki Taisei to USTR* [*U.S. Trade Organization and the USTR*] *in* KOKUSAI TORIHIKI TO HŌ [INTERNATIONAL TRANSACTIONS AND LAW] at 27 (Yoshio Matsui, et al., eds., 1988).

foreign countries through the submission of an annual report on the identification of foreign priority countries until at least 1993.[39]

Since the impediments pointed out in the SII were not regarded as priority practices identified by the USTR, the talks under the SII appear to have taken place outside the scope of Super 301. It is also true that the word "initiative" of the SII represented the intention of the U.S. administration to conduct talks of its own volition without any instruction from Congress. However, that was merely the intention of the administration. From the viewpoint of Congress, the SII would likely have appeared to have been conducted essentially along the lines of Super 301. It may have at any rate been necessary for the USTR to have arranged the content and schedule of the SII in such a manner as to convince Congress.[40]

(4) Unilateral Sanctions

Unilateral sanctions provided for in Section 301 of the Trade Act are not consistent with the dispute settlement procedure of the GATT, to which both the United States and Japan are Contracting Parties.[41] Should the United States invoke sanctions against Japan based on Section 301 despite the adoption by the Contracting Parties to the GATT of the panel report to the effect that U.S. allegations of unfair trade practices by Japan are groundless, such unilateral sanctions would be considered a breach of the GATT.[42] Before invoking Section 301 however, the United States cannot be deemed to have violated the provisions of the GATT.[43] Considering the aforementioned legal character of the SII as merely an exchange of views for information on making decisions on respective

---

39. The fact that Taiwan and Korea which were excluded from identification as priority countries (*see*, *supra* note 18) and promised to lift trade barriers by 1992 and 1993 also coincides with this three year monitoring requirement.

40. According to Professor Kazunori Ishiguro, the SII was described as a "procedure" by which the United States determined that Japan was an unfair country with respect to international trade. Kazunori Ishiguro, *Nichibei Bōeki Masatsu heno Hikakuhō Bunkateki Shiten*, [*Comparative Legal and Cultural Aspects of Japan-U.S. SII*] Bōeki-to-Kanzei, 22 (January 1992).

41. *See* Ichiro Komatsu, *GATT no Funsō Shōri Tetsuzuki to Ippōteki Sochi* [*GATT Dispute Settlement Procedure and Unilateral Measures*] 89 Kokusaihō-Gaikō-Zasshi, Nos.3&4, at 37 (1990).

42. Section 301(a)(2)(A) provides that the USTR is not required to take such action if the Contracting Parties to the GATT have determined that foreign practice is not a violation of, or inconsistent with, the rights of the United States and so on.

43. On May 26 the Foreign Minister of Japan spoke on the identification by the United States of priority practices, and it was stated that Japan sincerely hoped the United States would not take any action in violation of the rules of GATT. This seems to have indicated the view of the Japanese government that mere identification of priority practices did not constitute a violation of the GATT. *Talk of the Foreign Minister, supra* note 29, at 189.

policies at an administrative level, the SII is essentially irrelevant to the issue of unilateral sanctions.

b.   Coordination in Legislative Policy in an Interdependent Age

From a positive approach, the SII can be deemed to have disclosed new dimensions of international trade law. In light of the interdependent relationship between Japan and the United States, those in charge of policymaking in both governments ought to share a common view that one country cannot independently determine its domestic legislation regarding not only trade but also almost all other aspects. Indeed, although legislation *per se* is a part of the exercise of independent sovereign power, it is always necessary to consider the effect of such legislation on another country.[44]   The White Paper on International Trade by the Ministry of International Trade and Investment (MITI) described the SII talks as an "exchange of ideas between friendly nations" based upon the mutual understanding that those policy decisions can be made respectively.[45]

This kind of trend has of course already been seen. Border issues were the focus of discussion for many years following the end of World War II. With the progress of reductions in tariffs since approximately the time of the GATT Tokyo Round negotiations of 1974, world attention gradually shifted to issues of dumping, export subsidies, government procurement, standards, and certification. The Uruguay Round negotiations has extended the subject matter of the negotiations to include services and intellectual property rights.[46]   The scope of the GATT is primarily limited to the field of trade, but if the adjectival phrase "trade-related" is added, various issues could be treated in its framework. In this so-called globally borderless age in which countries are closely interwoven, it may not be inconceivable to append this phrase to almost all issues. In the next round of WTO negotiations, in fact, such issues as antitrust policy and trade-related environmental protection policy will be taken up as part of the formal agenda.

Despite the official position that the issues raised in the SII were only matters for each party to deal with by itself, substantially significant talks were conducted

---

44.   *See* Yabunaka, *supra* note 5, at 47–8. As to coordination of legislative policy in the age of interdependence, *see generally*, Masato Dogauchi, *Sōgoizon, Kokusaika to Hōkisei: Hō no Ikigaitekiyō to Gaijinhō* [*Interdependency, Internationalization and Legal Regulation—Extraterritorial Application of Law and Law Concerning Foreigners*] *in* SŌGOIZON JIDAI NO KOKUSAI MASATSU [INTERNATIONAL FRICTION IN THE AGE OF INTERDEPENDENCY] 75 (Susumu Yamakage ed., 1988).

45.   White Paper on International Trade, at 281 (1990).

46.   *See* Mitsuo Matsushita, *Nichibei Kōzō Mondai Kyōgi to Keizai Seido Chōsei* [*Japan-U.S. SII and Economic System Adjustment*] 965 JURISUTO 15 (1990) (discussion of the significance of the SII in comparison to the GATT multilateral system, the Regional Adjustment System of EC and the U.S.-Canada Free Trade Agreement). *See also* Matsushita, *The Structural Impediments Initiative: an Example of Bilateral Trade Negotiation*, 12 MICH. J. INT'L L. 436 (1991).

under circumstances where the opposing country's issues had a direct effect on each country. These kinds of bilateral talks are expected to increase, and more substantially significant talks with respect to legislative policy coordination are expected to take place even more frequently in the future. In this age of interdependence, close coordination is necessary between Japan and the United States in many fields of legislative policy. A positive and affirmative view of such talks between the two countries must thus be cultivated.[47]

IV. CONCLUSION

This chapter has attempted to make a legal evaluation of the SII. Its conclusion is quite simple. First, from the viewpoint of international law, the Final Report of the SII is not an agreement between two countries, but only a statement of each country's own policies. Second, from the viewpoint of domestic law, the measures written in the Final Report are not binding on the parliament. Third, accordingly, there could arise cases in which the measures written in the Final Report would not be implemented by the parliament. This could lead to political complications, but it would not cause any legal problems. Fourth, the essential relationship between Section 301 of the Trade Act and the SII is an undeniable fact, but it would be difficult to argue this point legally. Fifth, such bilateral talks as seen in the case of the SII are a necessary means for coordinating legislative policy between countries in this interdependent age. Therefore, such talks will be expected not only with the United States but also with other nations, including Canada, in the future. Thus, it is necessary to view such bilateral talks positively as an essential means to promote coordination between countries.

Finally, it seems necessary to mention more recent negotiations between Japan and the United States. After the SII, Japan and the United States began the "Framework" consultations. According to the Joint Statement on a Framework for a New Economic Partnership in July 1993, "Japan and the United States will engage in *negotiations and consultations* to expand international trade and investment flows and to remove sectoral and structural impediments that affect them." Further, "[t]he two Governments are committed to implement faithfully and expeditiously all *agreed on* measures taken pursuant to this Framework." (Emphasis added.) This means that in the Framework certain measures regarding some sectors are negotiated to be agreed upon. The difference between "talks" with a foreign country in the process of making up its own policy and "negotiations" to conclude" an agreement between countries is important. Such negotiations in areas of such deeply rooted social structures inevitably cause great difficulty, and in reality the Framework did cause great conflict between the two countries. It seems that

---

47. It is necessary to consider from this standpoint the meaning of the *Unfair Trade Policy Report: Trade Barriers in the United States, EC and Canada and GATT Rules* by the Fair Trade Center (1990), which is the report of the study on trade barriers to be remedied existing in countries from the Japanese perspectives.

bilateral talks such as the SII are more appropriate for coordinating domestic policies among interdependent countries.

REFLECTIONS ON PROBLEMS OF INTERNATIONAL ECONOMIC RELATIONS

John H. Jackson

I. INTRODUCTION

This section involves an exploration of economic frictions between Japan on the one hand and North America on the other (particularly the United States and Canada). For several decades, there has been a constant and somewhat depressing series of trade conflicts and "frictions," especially, but not limited to, those between the United States and Japan. Other countries, such as the European Community nation member states and many nations in Asia, have expressed concern over the "Japan problem." This chapter will try to come to grips with this problem, though recognizing that two decades of similar attempts by thousands of diplomats, politicians, entrepreneurs, and citizens have largely failed.

Some fundamental aspects of international economic relations in the world today and for the near future are explored here. While they can be variously described, I suggest that these aspects relate to the generalized problem of how governments can appropriately regulate economic behavior that crosses borders. These aspects, however, also relate to what can be called the "interface problem," referring to the difficulty that sometimes occurs even when two relatively similar economic systems trade extensively with one another. These difficulties arise from economic interdependence. This chapter does not elaborate in great detail; however, some of the text is drawn from longer works which are cited should readers be interested in further exploring these matters.[1]

---

1. *See, e.g.*, JOHN H. JACKSON, THE WORLD TRADING SYSTEM: LAW & POLICY OF INTERNATIONAL ECONOMIC RELATIONS, ch. 1 (1989). Concerning a number of matters discussed in this paper, the reader may wish to consult other works by this author, including: JOHN H. JACKSON, WORLD TRADE AND THE LAW OF GATT: A LEGAL ANALYSIS OF THE GENERAL AGREEMENT ON TARIFFS AND TRADE (1969); JOHN H. JACKSON, WILLIAM J.

In Part I, I examine some broad general problems of governmental regulation of international economic behavior. In Part II, I briefly inventory various categories of responses to these problems, such as unilateral, bilateral, regional, and multilateral actions. In Part III, I focus on the multilateral responses, particularly in the context of the developing multilateral institutions of the GATT/WTO and the results of the Uruguay Round. An obviously important question is what utility might these institutions have for the "trade frictions" between Japan and North America.

I do not attempt to go further into regional, bilateral, or unilateral approaches, partly because I perceive that other chapters will deal more extensively with these. In Part IV, however, I take a brief look at the relationship of the WTO and Uruguay Round texts and U.S. Section 301. Section 301 has very important implications for the trade frictions to be discussed here and there is undoubtedly a variety of perceptions about its appropriateness.

Finally, I draw a few conclusions.

I.   REFLECTIONS ON PROBLEMS OF REGULATING INTERNATIONAL ECONOMIC BEHAVIOR

a.   The Interface Problem[2]

Many of the unfair trading practices have been considered unfair because they interfere with or distort free market economy principles upon which, of course, the General Agreement on Tariffs and Trade (GATT) was largely based. It is not surprising, therefore, that it is often difficult to apply GATT's trading rules to nonmarket economies. In addition, even among the relatively similar Western industrial market economies, there are wide differences in the degree of government involvement in the economy, which takes the form of regulation or ownership of various industrial or other economic segments. As world economic interdependence has increased, it has become more difficult to manage relationships among numerous and varied economies. This problem is analogous to the difficulties involved in trying to get two computers of different design to work together. To do so, one needs an interface mechanism to mediate between the two computers. Likewise, in international economic relations, particularly in trade relations, some

---

DAVEY, AND ALAN SYKES, LEGAL PROBLEMS OF INTERNATIONAL ECONOMIC RELATIONS—CASES, MATERIALS AND TEXT ON THE NATIONAL & INTERNATIONAL REGULATION OF TRANSNATIONAL ECONOMIC RELATIONS (3d ed., 1995); JOHN H. JACKSON, JEAN-VICTOR LOUIS & MITSUO MATSUSHITA, IMPLEMENTING THE TOKYO ROUND: NATIONAL CONSTITUTIONS AND INTERNATIONAL ECONOMIC RULES (1984); JOHN H. JACKSON & EDWIN A. VERMULST, ANTIDUMPING LAW & PRACTICE: A COMPARATIVE STUDY (1989); JOHN H. JACKSON, RESTRUCTURING THE GATT SYSTEM (1990).
2.   JACKSON, THE WORLD TRADING SYSTEM, *supra,* note 1 at 218–221.

"interface mechanism" may be necessary to allow different economic systems to trade together harmoniously.

For example, part of the definition of dumping is selling for export at below-cost prices. But are there meaningful costs and prices in nonmarket economies? In the case of subsidies, it may be easy to identify cash payments to an exporter, but there are a myriad of government policies that affect the competitiveness of a business. If the goal is really to achieve a "level playing field," does that imply that all governments must adopt uniform policies? If not, how will it be possible to analyze the effect of different policies? Besides, isn't trade to some degree based on differences between countries?

In some cases, the problem involves preventing or inhibiting what are deemed unfair practices, such as dumping or export subsidies. As the subject of unfair practices develops, however, it becomes clear that it deeply touches matters of domestic concern to governments, so that questions of unfairness become more controversial. In many cases of subsidies, for example, the government providing such subsidies feels that they are an essential and praiseworthy tool, proving sometimes useful to correct disparities of income or to help disadvantaged groups or regions. With respect to dumping, it is argued that such a practice—a form of "price discrimination"—does have beneficial effects to world and national prosperity by encouraging competition. The rules for responding to some unfair trade practices allow the use of import restrictions, such as added duties (and quantitative measures applied pursuant to settlements of dumping or countervailing cases), which can be anticompetitive and detrimental to world welfare. In some cases, exporting nations feel bitterness toward these import restrictions, and argue that the rules on unfair trade are manipulated by special interests for protectionist reasons.

The "interface" problem and the difficulties of defining unfairness may arise in the context of two economies that differ only slightly in their acceptance of basic free-market economic principles. Even given such similarities, there may be differences between the ways respective economies operate over the course of the business cycle which may create situations that are considered unfair, even though these differences may not have resulted from any consciously unfair policies or practices. For example, differences in debt-equity ratios between corporations in two societies have an effect on "marginal cost," which can affect incentives to produce, especially during an economic downturn. Likewise, differences regarding worker "tenure" can affect the marginal cost calculation. (Firms generally have an incentive to sell at any price that exceeds short-term variable costs since fixed costs have to be paid anyway, which can induce pricing below average costs.)

Such problems have no easy answers and are indeed much more complicated than the foregoing discussion indicates. For example, whatever general rules exist, it is often argued that special considerations should apply to developing countries. In addition, it must be recognized that economic structural characteristics vary from sector to sector within a country, and that advantages that tilt one way for one sector might tilt in the opposite direction for another. Furthermore, these differences may alter across time or the direction of the tilt might reverse.

b. Market and Government "Failure" in an Interdependent World[3]

"Economic interdependence" is a phrase now common in describing the developing conditions of international economic relations. Manifestations of the gallop towards linking economies abound: enterprises must cope with competition and developments from abroad; national governments find it increasingly difficult to regulate their economies; democratic political leaders find it hard to fulfill election promises and to satisfy constituents because of forces beyond their control; and resentment against foreign competition and influences stirs the electorate, possibly even endangering democratic governments.

Since the 1940s, world economic relations have been guided, but not governed, by a set of institutions nobly put in place by visionary leaders during the immediate post–World War II years: The Bretton Woods system (the International Monetary Fund, the World Bank, the GATT), the United Nations complex of organizations and agencies, the OECD, and others. Subsequently, many thousands of treaty instruments and organizations have been designed for commodity regulation, transport regulation, taxation, and many other subjects. The 1948 draft International Trade Organization (ITO) charter failed, but the GATT uneasily took its place.[4] In addition, a number of regional arrangements have developed,[5] yet the operation of this system has not kept pace with actual economic changes.[6]

As the decades passed, it has become increasingly clear that the world is growing smaller and economies more difficult to manage[7]—at least without

---

3.   *See* John H. Jackson, *Alternative Approaches for Implementing Competition Rules In International Economic Relations*, 2/94 AUSSENWIRTSCHAFT—SWISS REV. INT'L ECON. REL. 2–25 (1994).

4.   *See, e.g.*, JACKSON, THE WORLD TRADING SYSTEM, *supra* note 1, at 30–39; WORLD TRADE AND THE LAW OF GATT, *supra* note 1, at 49–53; RESTRUCTURING THE GATT SYSTEM, *supra* note 1, ch. 2.

5.   For a list of regional arrangements, *see* GATT, Analytical Index, Notes on the Drafting, Interpretation and Application of the Articles of the General Agreement (Geneva: GATT, looseleaf) article XXIV, point 22. *See also* JACKSON, THE WORLD TRADING SYSTEM, *supra* note 1, at 141 & 145–148; JACKSON, WORLD TRADE AND THE LAW OF GATT, *supra* note 1, at 575–621; Jackson, *Regional Trade Blocs and GATT*, 16 WORLD ECONOMY, 121–131 (1993); Jagdish N. Bhagwati, *Regionalism versus Multilateralism*, 15 WORLD ECONOMY 1, at 535 (1992); BHAGWATI, THE WORLD TRADING SYSTEM AT RISK, ch. 5 (1991).

6.   *See* Lester C. Thurow, *GATT Is Dead; The World Economy as We Know It Is Coming to an End, Taking the General Agreement on Tariffs and Trade with It*, J. OF ACCOUNTANCY 36 (September 1990). *See also General Agreement on Tariffs and Trade: Report of Eminent Persons on Problems Facing the International Trading System: Trade Policies for a Better Future*, 24 I.L.M. 716 (1985).

7.   FRED C. BERGSTEN, MANAGING INTERNATIONAL ECONOMIC INTERDEPENDENCE: SELECTED PAPERS OF C. FRED BERGSTEN 1975–1976, (1977); JOHN H. JACKSON, THE WORLD TRADING SYSTEM, *supra* note 1, ch. 14.4; JOHN H. JACKSON & WILLIAM J. DAVEY, LEGAL PROBLEMS OF INTERNATIONAL ECONOMIC RELATIONS, *supra* note 1, ch. 22.

important elements of international cooperation. In every direction they turned, leaders discovered trends that were hard to control without important multilateral coordination, be it informal, such as the Group of Seven,[8] or more formal, as under the web of bilateral, regional, and multilateral treaties. The seventh major GATT trade negotiation, the Tokyo Round of the 1970s, was an ambitious effort to develop additional rules for the trading system.[9] The subsequent Uruguay Round was an even more ambitious attempt to enlarge and improve the system and was aimed at covering complex and multilayered new subjects, such as trade in services and trade related intellectual property.[10]

It has thus become more apparent that the existing rule and institutional system is inadequate. Various suggestions for priority post–Uruguay Round attention[11] have already been made, with environment and trade[12] concerns often topping the list but with competition policy[13] not far behind. These particular subjects have perplexed informed participants in the world economic system. Although intense exploration of the relationship of environmental protection policies with trade rules and policies is relatively new, even within the last few years this exploration has led down intricate, serpentine paths. These issues are intertwined with many government issues,[14] such as:

whether rulemaking at the international level adequately considers some of the scientific and moral concerns involved in the subjects linked to trade;

---

8.   The member nations of the Group of Seven are Canada, France, Germany, Italy, Japan, the United Kingdom, and the United States.

9.   JACKSON, LOUIS & MATSUSHITA, IMPLEMENTING THE TOKYO ROUND, *supra* note 1; GILBERT R. WINHAM, INTERNATIONAL TRADE AND THE TOKYO ROUND NEGOTIATION (1986).

10. *See The Dunkel Draft, Draft Final Act Embodying the Result of the Uruguay Round of Multilateral Trade Negotiations* [hereinafter *The Dunkel Draft*] GATT Doc. MTN.TNC/W/FA (Dec. 20, 1991).

11. John H. Jackson, *GATT and the Future of International Trade Institutions, Symposium: The Uruguay Round and the Future of World Trade,* 18 BROOKLYN J. INT'L L. 11 (1992); *Panel Discussion: What's Needed for the GATT After the Uruguay Round?* Proceedings of the Annual Meeting, Am. Soc'y Int'l L. Annual '92, 69–87 (1992).

12. John H. Jackson, *World Trade Rules and Environmental Policies: Congruence or Conflict?*, 49 WASH. & LEE L. REV. 1227 (1992). Steve Charnovitz, *Environmentalism Confronts GATT Rules—Recent Developments and New Opportunities*, J. WORLD TRADE 37 (April 1993); Ernst-Ulrich Petersmann, *International Trade Law and International Environmental Law: Prevention and Settlement of International Disputes in GATT*, J. WORLD TRADE 43 (Feb. 1993).

13. John H. Jackson, *Statement on Competition and Trade Policy Before the U.S. Senate Committee on the Judiciary*, 26 J. WORLD TRADE 111 (October 1992).

14. *Id.* Several of these issues have also been raised in *Symposium: Environmental Implications of International Trade*, 7 J. ENVTL. L. & LITIG. 1–99 (1992).

to what extent international dispute settlement procedures adequately consider opposing policy goals or provide for appropriate advocacy from interested authorities and citizen groups;

whether international procedures incorporate adequate democratic processes, including transparency and the right to be heard;

the relation of international rules to domestic constitutional and other laws;[15]

the operation and procedures of national constitutional bodies and how these promote or inhibit international cooperation;[16] and

activity of interest groups, both those broadly oriented and those concerned with specific interests or single issues, and how it relates to international institutions and procedures.

While environmental issues have suddenly pushed the frontiers of thinking on these and other various issues, such thinking can be viewed as a forerunner for comparable activity concerning a number of different "regulatory issues," including:

- competition policy;
- labor standards;
- commodity agreements and regulation;
- product standards (food, pharmaceutical, safety of goods, etc.);
- insurance;
- banking and fiduciary institutions;
- investment protection;
- securities regulation and institutions;
- government procurement procedures and preferences;
- shipping and transport (including air transport);
- intellectual property protection and regulation;
- taxation.

---

15. JACKSON, THE WORLD TRADING SYSTEM, *supra* note 1, at 75–76; JACKSON & DAVEY, LEGAL PROBLEMS, *supra* note 1, ch. 3; Jackson, *Status of Treaties in Domestic Legal Systems: A Policy Analysis*, 86 AM. J. INT'L L. 310 (1992); Jackson, *The General Agreement on Tariffs and Trade in United States Domestic Law*, 66 MICH. L. REV. 249 (1967).

16. JACKSON, LOUIS & MATSUSHITA, IMPLEMENTING THE TOKYO ROUND, *supra* note 1, ch. 2, 3 and 5; JACKSON, THE WORLD TRADING SYSTEM, *supra* note 1, ch. 3; JACKSON, RESTRUCTURING THE GATT SYSTEM, *supra* note 1, ch. 3.3.

Many of the regulatory "interdependence" questions which arise in these seemingly disparate subjects are similar. For example:

Problems of regulatory competition, wherein governments employ lower standards of regulation in order to attract economic activity to their societies (sometimes called the "race to the bottom," or, in the United States, the "Delaware Corporation" problem);[17]

Procedural requirements, "due process," avoiding abuse of power and process, and as previously mentioned, democracy principles including transparency;[18]

Questions of appropriate allocation of powers of regulation among national government bodies, sub-national bodies, and international bodies (a subject sometimes referred to as "subsidiarity").[19] To some extent the currently criticized concept of "sovereignty" relates to these questions;

Management of the transnational problems and tensions which arise in the context of different regulatory goals and procedures. Suggested methods include "harmonization," "reciprocity," "interface mechanisms," "cooperation agreements" (at least for procedure), extraterritorial unilateral measures, etc.[20]

Fundamental differences among societies and governmental structures obviously affect some, if not all, of the above. When, for example, a society's economy is organized by "market economics," many of these questions, particularly as to competition policy, are answered differently than in the situation of a nonmarket economy.[21]

---

17. *See* Joel P. Trachtman, *International Regulatory Competition, Externalization and Jurisdiction*, 34 HARV. INT'L L.J. 47 (1993).

18. Environmentalists have stressed the need for increased transparency and public participation in the international decisionmaking process and dispute settlement. *See* Robert F. Housman and Durwood J. Zaelke, *Making Trade and Environmental Policies Mutually Reinforcing: Forging Competitive Sustainability*, 23 ENVT'L L.545, 569–571 (1993).

19. For an analysis of the role of subsidiarity in economic integration in general, *see* Joel P. Trachtman, *L'Etat C'est Nous: Sovereignty, Economic Integration and Subsidiarity*, 33 HARV. INT'L L.J. 459 (1992). For an account of the subsidiarity concept in the context of the European Community, as well as its origins in various political systems, *see* Marc Wilke & Helen Wallace, *Subsidiarity: Approaches to Power-Sharing in the European Community* (Royal Institute of Int'l Aff. Discussion Paper No. 27, 1990).

20. JACKSON & DAVEY, LEGAL PROBLEMS, *supra* note 1, ch. 23, section 23.3.

21. JACKSON, THE WORLD TRADING SYSTEM, *supra* note 1, ch. 10.1 and 13.2.

Likewise, the governmental and institutional structures of a society, such as the degrees to which a government is democratic; protects human rights; has social cohesion; is corrupt either in the government or in nongovernmental structures; and has social hierarchies, all relate to these various questions. These differences among societies hinder the potential for international cooperation and coordination of economic regulation (increasingly essential in the face of interdependence).[22] The advocacy efforts of environmentalists with respect to the coordination efforts represented in the North American Free Trade Agreement (NAFTA) and its supplements are a particularly interesting example of these problems.[23] The NAFTA also demonstrates how far into national sovereignty some international regulatory treaty clauses may delve.[24]

Various theories and models of economics aid in understanding the problems mentioned. Obviously, the doctrines of comparative advantage are relevant,[25] as is the "prisoner's dilemma," which often suggests the need for cooperation among government or other actors.[26] The increasing attention to public choice theories illuminates how governments regulate economic matters.[27]

II. VARIOUS RESPONSES

The issue of how governments can respond to the problems posed above can be approached in a number of different ways, which can be roughly grouped under the subtopics of "unilateral," "bilateral," "regional," and "multilateral." Running vertically through each level are certain general questions:

---

22. The United Nations World Conference on Human Rights: Vienna Declaration and Program of Action, adopted June 25, 1993, 32 I.L.M. 1661 (1993).

23. Marc Hammarlund, *NAFTA Put Our Environmental Laws at Risk*, 10 ENVTL FORUM 31 (1993); Michael S. Barr, Robert Honeywell, Scott A. Stofel, *Labor and Environmental Rights in the Proposed Mexico-U.S. Free Trade Agreement*, 14 HOUSTON J. INT'L L. 1 (1991).

24. *See* NAFTA, Chapter 11, Investment. *See also* EEC Provisions on Sex Discrimination: Article 119 EEC (equal pay for equal work); Directive 75/117/EEC of Feb. 10, 1975, in 45 O.J. EUR. COMM. 19 (1975) (equal pay for work of equal value); Directive 75/207/EEC of Feb 9, 1976 in 39 O.J. EUR. COMM. 40 (1976) (equal treatment in hiring, promotion and work conditions); Directive 79/7/EEC of Dec. 19, 1978, in 6 O.J. EUR. COMM. 24 (1979) (equal treatment to matters of social security).

25. In particular, PETER KENEN, THE INTERNATIONAL ECONOMY, ch. 2–6 (1989); PAUL R. KRUGMAN & MAURICE OBSTFELD, INTERNATIONAL ECONOMICS—THEORY AND POLICY 2nd ed. (1991).

26. ROBERT AXELROD, THE EVOLUTION OF COOPERATION (1984); WILLIAM POUNDSTONE, PRISONER'S DILEMMA (1993). *See also* AVINASH K. DIXIT & BARRY J. NALEBUFF, THINKING STRATEGICALLY: THE COMPETITIVE EDGE IN BUSINESS, POLITICS AND EVERYDAY LIFE (1991).

27. DENNIS C. MUELLER, PUBLIC CHOICE (1979); GLEN O. ROBINSON, AMERICAN BUREAUCRACY: PUBLIC CHOICE AND PUBLIC LAW (1991).

(i) Should cooperative approaches be voluntary or binding under international law? If binding, should violators be sanctioned?

(ii) Should the emphasis on cooperation be procedural or relate more substantively to the rules applied?

(iii) With respect to substantive rules, should the approach be that of national treatment (nondiscrimination between domestic and imported goods), most-favored-nation (nondiscrimination among imported goods and exporting countries), or based on a minimum standards rule?

a. Unilateral Approaches

One response to the problem has been for a nation, such as the United States, to attempt to apply its own policy rules and principles on private or governmental actors operating outside its borders. This "extraterritorial reach" has been utilized in the application of U.S. antitrust law to foreign-based cartels and other collusion[28] by certain U.S. environmental statutes (such as the well-known case of the recent Tuna embargo),[29] and by such statutes as the U.S. Section 301 of the trade laws.[30] There is no question that some of these unilateral actions by the United States have been effective. There is also no question that many of these unilateral actions have evoked great criticism from trading partners, and in some cases retaliatory action (such as "claw-back statutes" in the antitrust area, or retaliatory trade actions).[31]

---

28. There are numerous articles on the extraterritorial application of antitrust laws. For a comparative study *see* Royer P. Alford, *The Extraterritorial Application of Antitrust Laws: The United States and the European Community Approaches*, 33 VA J. INT'L L. 1 (1992).

29. In 1990, the U.S. government banned Yellowfin Tuna imports from Mexico, because fishing was not in compliance with the U.S. Marine Mammal Protection Act. MMPA, Pub. L. No. 95–552, 86 Stat. 1027—codified with subsequent amendments at 16 U.S.C. §§ 1361–1362, 1371–1384, 1401–1407 (1988 & Supp. III 1991). A GATT Panel found the MMPA's embargo provisions to be inconsistent with GATT (dispute settlement Panel Report on United States Restrictions on Tuna, 30 I.L.M. 1594 (1991)).

30. Alan D. Sykes, *Constructive Unilateral Threats in International Commercial Relations: The Limited Case for Section 301*, 23 L. & POL'Y INT'L BUS. 263 (1992).

31. *Id. See also Trading Partners' Reaction to 301* in AGGRESSIVE UNILATERALISM: AMERICA'S 301 TRADE POLICY AND THE WORLD TRADING SYSTEM (Jagdish Bhagwati and Hugh T. Patrick eds. 1990). Section 301 has also met with U.S. domestic criticism. *See* Jagdish Bhagwati, *Aggressive Unilateralism: An Overview, id*; and Robert E. Hudec, *Thinking About the New Section 301: Beyond Good and Evil, in* AGGRESSIVE UNILATERALISM, *id* at 113–160. On the foreign reaction to the U.S. extraterritorial application of antitrust laws, *see* Pettit and Sykes, *The International Response to the Extraterritorial Application of U.S. Antitrust Law*, 37 BUS. LAWYER 697 (1989); Carl A. Cira, *The Challenge of Foreign Laws to Block American Antitrust Actions*, 18 STAN. J. INT'L L. 247 (1982).

The degree to which such unilateral action will continue to be successful in the future is debated, and the extent to which it is appropriate for a large power like the United States to utilize such measures can also be debated.

b. Bilateral Approaches

Sometimes sets of countries enter into bilateral agreements, such as the U.S.-EC Cooperation Agreement on antitrust matters.[32] It appears that so far most of these agreements are procedural in nature.

Another bilateral approach is that of the U.S.-Japan Structural Impediments Initiative (SII), which consists of in-depth discussions (with much focus on competition policies) about societal structures which impede trade. Likewise, a plethora of other bilateral discussions and pressures has been tried in the U.S.-Japan relationship.

c. Regional Approaches

A slightly broader approach would be to act through regional agreements. Clearly the treaty rules of the European Community go very far indeed in trying to harmonize and rationalize policy within the European Community.[33] Certain bilateral or trilateral free trade agreements, such as the U.S.-Canada Free Trade Agreement (CFTA) and the NAFTA, have some similar measures.[34]

---

32. Agreement between the Commission of the European Communities and the Government of the United States Regarding the Application of Their Competition Laws, 30 I.L.M. 1487 (1991). For a comment on the agreement, *see* William K. Walker, *Extraterritorial Application of U.S. Antitrust Laws: The Effect of the EC-U.S. Agreement*, 33 HARV. INT'L L.J. 583 (1992). A similar bilateral treaty is the Australia-United States Agreement Relating to Cooperation on Antitrust Matters, 21 I.L.M. 702 (1982). *See* James W. King, *A Comparative Analysis of the Efficacy of Bilateral Agreements in Resolving Disputes Between Sovereigns Arising from Extraterritorial Application of Antitrust Law: The Australian Agreement*, 13 GA. J. INT'L & COMP. L. 49 (1983). The U.S. has also signed bilateral treaties with Canada (23 I.L.M. 275 (1984)) and Germany (27 United States Treaties 1976 T.I.A.S. no. 8291). On other calls for bilateral cooperation, *see* Seing Wha Chang, *Extraterritorial Application of U.S. Antitrust Laws to Other Pacific Countries: Proposed Bilateral Agreements for Resolving International Conflicts Within the Pacific Community*, 16 HASTINGS INT'L & COMP. L. REV. 295 (1993).

33. For an introduction to EEC Competition law, see the chapter on Competition Policy in P.J.G. KAPTEYN AND P. VERLOREN VAN THEMMAT, INTRODUCTION TO THE LAW OF THE EUROPEAN COMMUNITIES 467–587 (1990); VALENTINE KORAH, AN INTRODUCTORY GUIDE TO EEC COMPETITION LAW AND PRACTICE (1990).

34. *See* NAFTA, Chapter 15: Competition Policy, Monopolies and State Enterprises and Art. 2010 of the U.S.-Canada Free Trade Agreement. The Australian–New Zealand Free Trade Agreement also includes antitrust provisions: *Closer Economic Relations Agreement* art. 12 in 22 I.L.M. 948 (1983). *See* Rex J. Ahdar, *The Role of Antitrust Policy in the*

The danger, of course, is creating tensions between regional blocs.[35] Another problem is that often important trading relationships (like that of U.S.-Japan or Canada-Japan) are not embraced within an adequate regional treaty framework.

d. Multilateral Approaches

Over the decades since World War II, there have been a number of multilateral efforts to develop some harmonization or cooperative rules for various regulatory policies. In particular, the Organization for Economic Cooperation and Development (OECD), the United Nations, and the United Nations Conference on Trade and Development (UNCTAD) have worked on a variety of proposals and voluntary rule guidelines,[36] particularly concerning competition policy. Finally, of course, the GATT, with its uneasy origins, and now the World Trade Organization (WTO) Charter, must be considered.

III. MULTILATERAL INSTITUTIONS: THE GATT/WTO AND URUGUAY ROUND PROSPECTS[37]

a. The World Trade Organization Charter

The Uruguay Round, the eighth broad trade negotiation round under the auspices of the General Agreement on Tariffs and Trade, is clearly the most extensive undertaken by the GATT system, and possibly by any similar endeavor in history. The goals of the September 1986 Ministerial Meeting at Punta del Este, which set forth the agenda for the Uruguay Round, were extremely ambitious. If half of the objectives are achieved, the Uruguay Round would still be the most extensive and successful trade negotiation ever. In fact, despite the many years of delay and negotiating impasses, the Uruguay Round has achieved considerably more than half its objectives.[38]

Development of Australian–New Zealand Free Trade, 12 NW. J. INT'L L. & BUS. 317 (1991).

35. Jackson, *Regional Trade Blocs and GATT*, *in* 16 THE WORLD ECONOMY 121–131 (March 1993).

36. For a comment on the U.N. Codes, *see* Miller & Davidow, *Antitrust and the U.N.: A Tale of Two Codes*, 18 STAN. J. INT'L L. 347 (1982). On the OECD Guidelines, *see* Joel Davidow, *Some Reflections on the OECD Competition Guidelines*, 22 ANTITRUST BULLETIN 441 (1977).

37. *See* John H. Jackson, Testimony prepared for the U.S. Senate Finance Committee Hearing on Uruguay Round Legislation, Mar. 23, 1994.

38. Final Act Embodying the Result of the Uruguay Round of Multilateral Trade Negotiations, MTN/FA, Dec. 13, 1993 (Draft Text).

One of the interesting achievements of the Uruguay Round is the development of a new institutional charter for an organization to facilitate international cooperation concerning trade and economic relations. Some have said that this may be the most important element of the Uruguay Round.

It is well known that the GATT was never intended to be an organization. Negotiated in the 1947–1948 period, the same time when negotiators prepared a charter for an International Trade Organization (ITO), the GATT was to be a multilateral trade and tariff agreement, depending on the ITO for its organizational context and secretariat services. The ITO, however, never came into being, because in the late 1940s the United States Congress did not approve it. The GATT, on the other hand, was negotiated under advance authority granted to the president in the 1945 extension of the Reciprocal Trade Agreements Act.[39] Compounding the anomalies of that period, the GATT treaty instrument was and is applied to this day only provisionally. At the time, it was contemplated that the GATT would be applied provisionally for several years until the ITO came into force, at which time it would be put under the umbrella of and conformed to the ITO Charter. However, because the ITO was stillborn, the GATT gradually became the focus for international government cooperation on trade matters.[40]

Despite this inauspicious beginning, the GATT has been remarkably successful over its nearly five decades of history. Partly this is because of ingenious and pragmatic leadership in the GATT, particularly in its early years, as the GATT struggled to fill the gap left by the ITO failure.

With a new WTO Charter in effect, the Uruguay Round results, when implemented, should offer a better institutional structure to fill the "Bretton Woods Gap."[41] The WTO is not an ITO. The WTO Charter itself is entirely institutional and procedural, but it incorporates the substantive agreements resulting from the Uruguay Round into annexes.

The WTO also facilitates the extension of a GATT-like institutional structure to the new subjects negotiated in the Uruguay Round, particularly services and intellectual property. The WTO will similarly be able to apply a unified dispute settlement mechanism and the Trade Policy Review Mechanism to all of the subjects of the Uruguay Round for all nations who become members.

Finally, the WTO Charter offers considerably better opportunities for the future evolution and development of the institutional structure for international trade cooperation. Even though the WTO Charter is minimalist, the fact that there is provision for explicit legal status coupled with the traditional organizational privileges and immunities to improve the efficiency of an organization helps in this regard. With the WTO focusing on the institutional side, it also offers more

---

39. The first such Act was in 1934.

40. *See supra* note 1.

41. The 1944 Bretton Woods Conference prepared the charters for the IMF and the World Bank and noted that a trade organization would be needed also. The ITO failure left this "gap" in the conceptual plan of the Bretton Woods System.

flexibility for future inclusion of new negotiated rules or measures that can assist nations in facing the constantly emerging problems of world economics, such as environmental and competition policies.

b.   The WTO Dispute Settlement Procedures

One of the many achievements of the GATT has been the development of a reasonably sophisticated dispute settlement process. The original GATT treaty contained very little on this, although it did specifically provide (in Article 22 and 23) for consultation and then submission of issues to the GATT Contracting Parties. As time went on, however, the practice began to evolve more towards a "rule-oriented" system. In the late 1950s, for example, the practice introduced a "panel" of individuals to make determinations and findings and recommend them to the Contracting Parties. Before that, disputes had been considered by much broader working parties comprised of representatives of governments.

During the next several decades, the Contracting Parties increasingly utilized the panel process. Reports gradually began to focus on more precise and concrete questions of "violation" of treaty obligations. At the conclusion of the Tokyo Round in 1979, the GATT Contracting Parties adopted an understanding on dispute settlement that embraced some of these concepts, and restated the practice concerning dispute settlement procedures that had developed during the previous decades.

As might be expected given the history of GATT, however, there were a number of defects and problems in the dispute settlement process, some of which were gradually overcome through practice. But the Uruguay Round December 1993 text includes an "Understanding on Rules and Procedures Governing the Settlement of Disputes." This new text solves many, though not all, of the issues which have plagued the GATT dispute settlement system, by accomplishing the following:

1)   It establishes a unified dispute settlement system for all parts of the GATT/WTO system, including the new subjects of services and intellectual property. Thus, controversies over which procedure to use will occur less frequently, if at all.

2)   It reaffirms the right of a complaining government to have a panel process initiated, which prevents blocking at that stage.

3)   It more carefully outlines the steps of the procedure, first requiring consultation and allowing the parties to utilize "good offices" to help them achieve a settlement. If there is a failure to agree, then a panel can be requested. The panel is usually comprised of three persons, and if agreement on its composition fails, the Director General can impose a panel. The panel proceeds, as before, to receive oral and written advocacy

and express provision is made for third country advocacy (by nondisputants with a legitimate interest). The panel then drafts its report. The rules call for certain consultation about it with the disputing parties and the first panel examination normally is supposed to take no more than six months.

4)   The WTO rules establish a new appellate procedure to substitute for some of the Council approval process of a panel report and overcome blocking. Thus, a panel report will automatically be deemed adopted by the Council, unless it is appealed by one of the parties to the dispute. If appealed, the dispute will go to an appellate panel. After the appellate body has ruled, its report will go to the Council, though it will be deemed adopted unless there is a consensus *against* adoption, and presumably that negative consensus can be defeated by any major objector. The presumption is thus reversed, as compared with the previous procedures, and the ultimate result is that the appellate report will in virtually every case come into force as a matter of international law.

5)   The Uruguay Round dispute settlement text explicitly addresses the question of implementation of a panel report, and provides for added procedures to reinforce such implementation through possibilities of compensatory or retaliatory type action.

6)   The WTO rules clarify the general international law obligation that the disputants should fulfill the recommendation of an adopted panel report. (Compensation should be resorted to only if withdrawal of a measure that is inconsistent with a covered agreement is impractical.)

7)   A very interesting additional provision of the dispute settlement procedures deals with so-called "nonviolation cases." The GATT language on disputes (Article 23) has always contained the phrase "nullification or impairment" as the grounds for a complaint, although it is very vague. Through practice under the GATT, a *"prima facie* nullification or impairment" concept developed whereby a violation of treaty obligations would be considered a *prima facie* nullification or impairment. Thus, most disputes have focused in fact on "violation." Nevertheless, there have been a certain number of disputes involving "nullification or impairment" even when there is no violation. This is most commonly the situation when there has been a relatively recent tariff concession and then a later action, such as a domestic subsidy, which tends to undermine the reasonable expectations of the exporting country which negotiated for the tariff concession.

As the procedures for dispute settlement evolved, particularly in the1980s, it became clear that there was a question of how to handle "nonviolation cases." Some precedents established that nonviolation cases would not result in a mandatory international obligation to conform to international obligations (partly because it would be unclear what the international obligation was). Rather, the idea developed that nonviolation cases would be treated more as a "negotiating concept" calling for compensatory measures. The new text of the Uruguay Round has a segment dealing separately with nonviolation cases, with certain separate procedures that follow this general trend. Interestingly, the result of a panel in a nonviolation case is not to mandate "conformance" within an international rule, but instead to enter into negotiations for compensation.

8)   The Uruguay Round dispute settlement procedures include a measure continuing a certain "preference" for developing country complaints.

It should also be understood that the international legal system does not embrace the common law jurisprudence calling for courts to operate under a stricter precedent or *stare decisis* rule. Most nations do not have *stare decisis* as part of their legal systems, nor does the international law. This means that technically a GATT panel report is not strict precedent, although there is certainly some tendency for subsequent GATT panels to follow what they deem to be the "wisdom" of prior panel reports. Nevertheless, a GATT panel has the option to refrain from following a previous panel report, as has occurred in several cases.[42] In addition, although an adopted panel report will generally provide an international law obligation on the participant in the dispute to follow the report, the GATT Contracting Parties acting in a Council or the Ministerial Conference can make interpretive rulings or other resolutions that depart from that GATT panel ruling or can even establish a waiver to relieve a particular obligation.
There is often misunderstanding about international law procedures and how they affect domestic law. The results of a GATT dispute settlement procedure (and a WTO panel report) are not automatically part of most nations' domestic law; they must instead be accepted and implemented into domestic law, which is often done by a parliamentary enactment or, in some cases, by authority of the executive. This allows a nation that considers the issue significant enough to resist implementing a GATT ruling to do so, although such action is, of course, usually a violation of its international obligations.

c.   Trade Policy Review Mechanisms

One of the innovations for the GATT system was developed at the Uruguay Round meeting in Montreal in December 1988. This is the Trade Policy Review Mechanism (TPRM). The basic idea of this procedure is to establish a regular

---

42. GATT Dispute Panel Report, EEC Restriction on Imports of Dessert Apples, Complain by Chile, Doc. L/6491, June 22, 1989, 36 B.I.S.D. 93, 127, para. 12.10.

process of general review of trading nations' trade policies. The potential agenda is quite broad and clearly goes beyond the question of rule consistency or "legality." The GATT has now had five or six years of experience with this system, and while there certainly is room for satisfaction, some problems are becoming clear.

Since the TPRM explores matters not necessarily covered by the rules, it has the opportunity to push the forefront of policy analysis in an increasingly interdependent world fraught with the difficulties of regulating international economic behavior. To some extent the bilateral SII enterprise could be part of the TPRM. The TPRM could offer an opportunity for a general probing analysis of "structural impediments," including cultural problems, economic structures, and other societal impediments.

d. The WTO and Japan—North American Trade Frictions

It would be folly to expect the new WTO system to solve the Japan-U.S. and Japan-Canada "trade frictions," particularly because the dispute settlement process is oriented towards a "rule system" and many of the intractable problems of Japan-North American trade frictions are not covered by appropriate rules. Whether in the future the rules will be expanded and enhanced to cover some of these issues is hard to predict at the moment. The vast area of services trade, now embraced in the trading system under the WTO, will of course approach a number of issues heretofore not covered by the GATT system with some relating to the trade frictions that we are worried about.

It would appear plausible, however, that the WTO institutional reform will potentially modestly contribute to reducing the trade frictions between Japan, the United States, Canada, and others. The TPRM offers an opportunity for the policy analysis to "get out in front" of the more precise rules. If constructively used, it could be a format to deflate some of the bilateral slug matches that have captured newspaper headlines in recent years. Still, the multilateral system (which is more important to perhaps Japan than any other major trading nation) will be unable to handle many of the subtle and sometimes intricate trade friction problems.

The procedures of the new dispute settlement understanding will apply more pressure on all governments in the WTO to conform to the results of a dispute settlement process. This is in part because the new dispute settlement procedures deal explicitly with responses available to a complaining state when a defending member of the WTO does not conform to its obligations after a dispute settlement procedure.

A critical provision in the Uruguay Round text of December 1993 concerning dispute settlement in this regard is Article 23. Article 23.1 requires members of the WTO to use the dispute settlement procedures whenever they seek redress of a violation of obligations or other nullification or impairment. It also states that members shall "abide by the rules and procedures of this understanding." Thus, the several instances in the 1980s when the United States took unilateral and independent action without proceeding through the GATT would be inconsistent with the new rules. However, those instances were also inconsistent with the old rules, to the extent that actual trade restraining measures, such as an increase in tariffs, were applied at the border, in violation of the GATT.

There is certainly room for further developments of the GATT dispute settlement process. For example, the process has been criticized for being too secretive. The Uruguay Round December Understanding does provide for a small measure of transparency, enabling national governments to inform the public of its arguments before a dispute panel.[43] It would be wise to increase this transparency, perhaps by allowing more disclosures by parties and some careful additional opportunities for nongovernmental parties to address the panels orally or in writing.

Likewise there has been some concern over whether panels have the appropriate expertise regarding certain technical issues, such as product standards and environmental policy. The procedures make it clear that the panels may call upon various expert bodies to assist them, though more is needed to ensure the appropriate expertise on the panels. Following the analogous provisions of the NAFTA dispute settlement procedures may perhaps facilitate this.

One of the major problems for nations of the world in connection with their relations is the question of government regulation of international economic behavior. Governments find themselves frustrated by trying to regulate appropriately in situations where international economic behavior crosses borders, because the perpetrators of such behavior can sometimes play one nation off against another and develop rival or competitive "reductions in regulation rigor" (the "race to the bottom"). Thus, an institutional structure with the potential to meet and deal with these problems in an appropriate and balanced way through mutual cooperation is important.

With respect to the dispute settlement provisions, many policies suggest the value and importance of a creditable, rule-oriented system that results in relatively effective implementation of treaty obligations. If the treaty obligations are not creditable, one may ask why the trouble should be taken to negotiate them. The treaty rules provide a framework that is particularly important for market structures that rely heavily on decentralized decision making, i.e., individual enterprises. It is these enterprises that need the modicum of stability and predictability, often essential for investment decisions, provided by a rule structure.

---

43. *See, e.g.,* WTO Charter: Article V:2, which authorizes arrangements for consultation and cooperation with nongovernmental organizations; Article 13 (Dispute Settlement Understanding (DSU)), regarding panel authority to seek information and questions of confidentiality; and Appendix 3, paragraph 3 of the DSU, allowing members to disclose their own statements to the public.

IV. U.S. SECTION 301

One of the controversial techniques utilized by the United States in its trade friction management is U.S. Section 301.[44] Outside the United States, Section 301 is much maligned, while domestically Section 301 has many staunch defenders and considerable political support, particularly in Congress. My own view is that Section 301, if appropriately used, can be an important and useful tool in some situations. It can also be constructive from a world policy viewpoint, and not just for that of a single nation like the United States. This is in part because Section 301 (at least the regular Section 301) requires the United States to take a disputed issue to the appropriate dispute settlement procedures at the international level if they exist for the subject concerned. With the greatly expanded subject matter of the GATT system in the new WTO, there should be many more referrals to the WTO dispute settlement system covering a much broader range of issues than before. To a large degree, this supports and enhances the international WTO and its dispute settlement procedures, at least if the disputing parties finally accept the recommendations of panel rulings.

Some have raised the question of whether the new GATT/WTO dispute settlement procedures of the Uruguay Round results will require fundamental changes in the Section 301 statutes of the United States. Section 301 provides a procedure for individual U.S. enterprises to direct U.S. government attention to foreign government practices that allegedly harm U.S. commerce. This is mostly targeted to U.S. exports, but is also applicable to matters such as intellectual property, subsidized imports, and service trade.

A preliminary but incomplete examination of Section 301 compatibility with the WTO rules suggests that very few statutory changes will be needed to Section 301, or at least the "regular 301" (as compared to Special 301 and other similar statutory provisions, such as those on telecommunications). There may need to be some alterations to time limits or transition measures, but the basic structure of 301 is not necessarily inconsistent with the Uruguay Round results. Section 301 calls for cases presented under the 301 procedural framework to be taken to the international dispute settlement process that pertains to the case. Likewise, in its present formulation Section 301 does not *require* the Executive Branch to ignore the results of the international dispute settlement process. Thus, the Executive appears to have the discretion to apply actions under Section 301 in a manner consistent with the proposed new rules of the Uruguay Round dispute settlement understanding.

Although there are plausible ways to interpret the statutory provisions of regular Section 301 so as to give the president discretion to act consistently with the Uruguay Round dispute settlement rules, in a few cases, particularly in Section 301(a) (the mandatory provision) the interpretations allowing this are a bit strained.

---

44. *See supra* notes 30 and 31.

It would be better if the statute were amended to give the president and the trade representative the discretion in all cases under the statute to act consistently with U.S. international obligations. Alternatively, the Statement of Administrative Action by the president, along with other legislative history, could clarify this position.

One of the important aspects to watch in how the United States continues to use its Section 301 is whether the United States in fact will abide by the results of the international dispute settlement procedures under the WTO or, when they exist, other treaty frameworks.

V. CONCLUDING PERSPECTIVES

In sum, the subject we are addressing is part of a vastly broader question of how governments can regulate cross-border economic behavior in the interdependent economies we face now and in the future. A series of perplexing institutional questions, as well as other policy questions, is part of this general subject. Approaches can be considered in different groupings, such as unilateral actions, bilateral activity, regional and multilateral activity, and institutions. The new WTO charter and dispute settlement procedures offer an important step forward for the multilateral institutions related to international economic matters. Certainly, these multilateral institutions should be part of an overall framework for trying to address the question of "trade frictions," and for some international relationships they should be the principal part. Whether the multilateral system can successfully provide the major approach for dealing with the trade friction problem between Japan and North America, is, however, an unresolved question.

ECONOMIC RELATIONS BETWEEN JAPAN AND NORTH AMERICA: A CHALLENGE TO THE INTERNATIONAL LEGAL SYSTEM

Susan L. Karamanian

I. INTRODUCTION

An air of optimism abounded in early 1994 regarding trade relations among the major economic powers and the system of rules and agreements which attempts to manage these relations. After nearly eight years of contentious negotiation and three years after its original completion date, an agreement was reached on the Uruguay Round of the General Agreement on Tariffs and Trade (GATT). The United States, Canada, and Mexico had recently signed the North American Free Trade Agreement (NAFTA) and thereby recognized that cooperation served their mutual economic, political and social interests. The Fall 1993 conference of the Asian-Pacific Economic Cooperation (APEC) was heralded as improving trans-Pacific trade and investment. In the words of United States Treasury Secretary Lloyd Bentsen, the APEC brought promises of "cooperation, consultation and commitment" among APEC nations, including Japan, Canada, and the United States.

The optimism and lofty rhetoric abruptly abated with the spring thaw. The precipitous event was the breakdown in the bilateral talks between two formidable economic forces, the United States and Japan. Without assurance from Japan as to a measurable improvement in four priority Japanese market sectors,[1] President

---

1.   The four sectors are (1) automobiles and automobile parts; (2) insurance; (3) telecommunications equipment procurement; and (4) medical equipment procurement. *See* Nakamoto and Abrahams, *Little Progress in Market Access Discussions*, FINANCIAL TIMES, Feb. 10, 1994, at 4. In particular, as to automobiles and automobile parts, the United States sought numerical targets for all imports and an opening of the Japanese distribution system

Clinton swiftly reinstated the United States "crowbar for levering open foreign markets,"[2] Super 301. Japan denounced the United States for engaging in "unilateral retaliation" or "coercion," possibly violating the principles of the GATT, or the World Trade Organization (WTO). European Union and GATT officials quickly joined Japan in criticizing the United States.[3]

The intensity of the current dispute highlights the need to reexamine the issues relating to trade between North America and Japan, and possible solutions to the problem. What are the reasons for the current dispute? Must the differences between North America and Japan necessarily lead to tension? How can international trade law best manage what appears to be an intractable conflict? What is the role of the new multilateral system in this persistent conflict? In an era of increased influence of multinational corporations and increased alliances among and between North American and Japanese companies, is the significance of the apparent conflict between Japan and the United States overstated?

This chapter analyzes these and other issues to conclude that although the differences between the economies of Japan and North America are considerable, the current U.S. approach of threatening unilateral sanctions and/or urging a form of "managed trade" with Japan is inimical to long-run economic liberalization.

---

to American automobiles. The automobile and automobile parts sector accounted for 62 percent of the U.S. $59 billion trade deficit with Japan in 1993. Regarding insurance, the United States has demanded that foreign insurers be able to attain a share of the Japanese life insurance market comparable to that which foreign companies can obtain in other markets. As to both telecommunications and medical equipment, the United States sought the Japanese government's purchase of these items. For a more detailed discussion of the United States position, *see* Sterngold, *The Men Who Really Run Fortress Japan*, N.Y. TIMES, Apr. 10, 1994, at 1, 8.

2. *Trade Warriors Ride Again*, THE ECONOMIST, Feb. 19, 1994, at 14.

3. Nakamoto, *U.S. Warns Japan on Surplus*, FINANCIAL TIMES, Mar. 11, 1994, at 6, (officials of the European Union criticized the United States decision to revive Super 301 as "going against the trend of multilateralising trade issues"); Dunne and Dawkins, *Clinton Moves Against Japan*, FINANCIAL TIMES, Mar. 4, 1994, at 1, (Peter Sutherland, director-general of the GATT, stated that the United States trade policy towards Japan is "misguided and dangerous" and is a risk to the multilateral system).

II. FRICTION BETWEEN JAPAN AND NORTH AMERICA

a.   Reasons for and Nature of the Dispute

(1) The United States Perspective

The trade relationship between the United States and Japan has been described as one of trade friction.[4] Economists, journalists and a host of others have written at length about the reasons for and the nature of the friction.[5] From the United States perspective, the dispute raises the perennial and sometimes popular themes of (1) Japan's global trade surplus;[6] (2) Japan's industrial policy, which has allegedly subsidized Japanese corporations in high-technology and other capital intensive industries, and afforded protection to these businesses;[7] (3) Japan's internal regulatory and legal system, which allegedly encourages what the United States

---

4.   Yachi, *Beyond Trade Frictions—A New Horizon for U.S.-Japan Economic Relations*, 22 CORNELL INT'L L.J. 389 (1989).

5.   *See, e.g.*, C. PRESTOWITZ, TRADING PLACES: HOW WE ALLOWED JAPAN TO TAKE THE LEAD (1988) (discussing Japan's emphasis on production as opposed to consumption); E. LINCOLN, JAPAN'S UNEQUAL TRADE (1990) (documenting the Japanese market-access problem); L. THUROW, HEAD TO HEAD: THE COMING ECONOMIC BATTLE AMONG JAPAN, EUROPE, AND AMERICA (1992) (describing the "empire-building firms of Japan" and Japan's "communitarian capitalism"); F. BERGSTEN & M. NOLAND, RECONCILABLE DIFFERENCES? UNITED STATES-JAPAN ECONOMIC CONFLICT (1993) (analyzing the United States–Japan trade dispute primarily in macroeconomic terms); J. FALLOWS, LOOKING AT THE SUN: THE RISE OF THE NEW EAST ASIA ECONOMIC AND POLITICAL SYSTEM 17 (1994) (the Occupation caused Japan's economic institutions to grow stronger while the political system atrophied: "[t]his legacy of the Occupation is the fundamental source of the endless 'trade friction' between Japan and the rest of the world").

6.   *Bill Aimed at Getting Japan to Open Its Markets Introduced*, INT'L TRADE DAILY (BNA) (Feb. 25, 1994) (in introducing the "Fair Market Access Act of 1994," House Majority Leader Richard A. Gephardt (D. Mo.) cited the U.S.$60 billion trade deficit with Japan and noted that "our relationship with Japan is so important—our common goals and commitments are so important—that we can no longer live with an economic Grand Canyon between us"); BERGSTEN & NOLAND, *supra* note 5, at 28–29 (between 1985 and 1992, due to the already high level of imports from Japan, U.S. exports had to grow more than three times as fast as U.S. imports to keep the trade deficit from widening in absolute terms); LINCOLN, *supra* note 5, at 2 ("[f]rom a deficit of $11 billion in 1980, Japan's current account exploded to an unprecedented surplus of $87 billion in 1987").

7.   L. TYSON, WHO'S BASHING WHOM? TRADE CONFLICT IN HIGH-TECHNOLOGY INDUSTRIES 98 (1992) ("[p]rotection allowed Japanese producers to reach minimum scale; promotion reduced their risk in making the big capital investments necessary to enter").

perceives as anticompetitive behavior to enhance market power;[8] (4) nontariff impediments restricting access to Japanese markets, including cultural and social factors that promote extensive networks of businesses, and lack of an efficient distribution system;[9] and (5) the lack of a strong macroeconomic growth policy.[10] In the minds of many Americans, the United States has been the persistent loser to Japan in a zero-sum game, and a major change is needed to level the playing field.[11]

Many of these common reasons for, or manifestations of, the trade dispute, however, have been challenged, from either the North American or Japanese perspective, as hollow. For instance, the MITI's practice of "attempting to select and support 'winning' business sectors" has been characterized as a "failure."[12] Professor Drucker has noted that the MITI ignored or opposed the major Japanese business successes, such as Sony and the automobile companies.[13] The notion that

---

8.   The Japanese Ministry of International Trade and Industry (MITI) "encouraged cartels and other collective means of reducing 'excessive' competition and the risks of economic expansion and attempted to restrain entry and to induce greater concentration." Haley, *Luck, Law, Culture and Trade: The Intractability of United States-Japan Trade Conflict*, 22 CORNELL INT'L L.J. 403, 411 (1989) (citing Iyori, *Antitrust and Industrial Policy in Japan, in* LAW AND TRADE ISSUES OF THE JAPANESE ECONOMY 56, 57 (1986)); *see also USTR Report Takes Aim at Japan in Foreign Trade Barriers Inventory*, INT'L TRADE REP. (BNA) 534–35 (Apr. 6, 1994) (quoting Rep. Sander M. Levin (D. Mich.): Japan's "'complex web of restrictive regulations and private business arrangements has backed competitive U.S. companies out of any key markets'"); Yamamura, *Caveat Emptor: The Industrial Policy of Japan, in* P. KRUGMAN, STRATEGIC TRADE POLICY AND THE NEW INTERNATIONAL ECONOMICS 169 (1992).

9.   Yachi, *supra* note 4, at 395–97.

10.   Okawara, *Restructuring the Japanese Economy from a Global Perspective, in* TRADE FRICTION AND ECONOMIC POLICY: PROBLEMS AND PROSPECTS FOR JAPAN AND THE UNITED STATES 13 (R. Sato and D. Wachtel eds. 1987).

11.   Hoagland, *Pushing Japan to the Brink*, WASHINGTON POST NATIONAL WEEKLY EDITION, Feb. 28–Mar. 6, 1994, at 29 (quoting pollster Daniel Yankelovich: "The [American] public is persuaded . . . that the American-Japanese relationship is zero-sum, with Japan the winner and the United States the loser . . . . The only vision of future American-Japanese relations acceptable to the public is one that creates a new pattern of competition and cooperation."). Given the American public's simple view of United States–Japan trade relations, it should come as no surprise that the United States has resorted to unilateral threats to attempt to resolve complex matters, the resolution of which will have consequences beyond the bilateral relationship.

12.   Drucker, *Trade Lessons from the World Economy*, 73 FOREIGN AFF. 99, 105–06 (Jan./Feb. 1994).

13.   *Id.* at 106. *See also* Haley, *supra* note 8, at 411 ("without most stringent licensing controls or coercion powers, the MITI and Japan's other economic bureaucracies failed to achieve their primary objectives in nearly all 'targeted' industries"); *MITI's Identity Crisis*, THE ECONOMIST, Jan. 22, 1994, at 65 (criticizing the MITI's strategy on semiconductor chips as the cause of the depressed price of chips; noting the MITI's failure in the development of an all-Japanese commercial aircraft; and discussing the MITI's failure in petrochemicals).

American companies cannot compete and gain a significant market share is defied by the success of Schick (70 percent share of Japanese safety razor market), Polaroid (70 percent share of Japanese instant photography market), Coca-Cola (62 percent share of Japanese soft-drink market), and IBM (27 percent share of the Japanese computer market).[14] The United States trade deficit with Japan is said to inaccurately measure United States competitiveness because it does not consider the equally large surplus in capital flow into the United States.[15] Further, the deficit does not take into account that "approximately one-quarter of so-called Japanese exports to the United States are structurally linked to the production and marketing activities of United States firms on their home territory."[16]

Professor Paul Krugman of the Massachusetts Institute of Technology has provided a powerful critique of some of the trade "myths," including attacking the concept that a trade surplus signals national weakness.[17] In Krugman's view, corporations, not countries, compete. To charge that "Japanese growth diminishes U.S. status is very different from saying that it reduces the U.S. standard of living— and it is the latter that the rhetoric of competitiveness asserts."[18]

Nevertheless, even assuming Krugman's hypothesis that companies, not nations, compete, strong evidence suggests that many North American companies simply cannot gain a meaningful foothold in the Japanese market. Bergsten and Noland have presented evidence that "a combination of economy-wide structural and sector-specific practices in Japan reduces U.S. exports to that country by U.S.$9 billion to $18 billion annually from what they would otherwise be," and

---

But see Borrus, Tyson & Zysman, *Creating Advantage: How Government Policies Shape International Trade in the Semiconductor Industry*, in P. KRUGMAN, STRATEGIC TRADE POLICY AND THE NEW INTERNATIONAL ECONOMICS 91, 97–101 (1992) (documenting the success of the MITI's involvement, and indeed, the Japanese state's involvement, in the development of Japan's semiconductor industry).

14. *Roundtable Discussion,* 22 CORNELL INT'L L.J. 517, 528 (1989) (statement of Shotaro Yachi, Economic Counselor, Embassy of Japan).

15. Wallis, *Economics, Foreign Policy, and United States–Japanese Trade Disputes,* 22 CORNELL INT'L L.J. 381, 384 (1989).

16. Pempel, *The Trade Balance Isn't the Problem,* 22 CORNELL INT'L L.J. 435, 442 (1989). Professor Pempel discusses the effect of corporate mergers and other alliances in possibly overstating the significance of the deficit as a measure of competitiveness. As an example, he notes that Merck's acquisition of two Japanese companies, Banyu and Torii, increased Merck sales in Japan but reduced Merck's exports to Japan. As another example, by 1982, "Texas Instruments–Japan exported, principally to its parent, one-half of the estimated $300 million worth of memory chips it produced," and IBM-Japan exported 100 percent of its XT model disk drives to its United States parent. *Id.* (citing Encarnation, *Cross-Investment: A Second Front of Economic Rivalry,* in AMERICA VERSUS JAPAN 141 (T. McCraw ed. 1986)).

17. Krugman, *Competitiveness: A Dangerous Obsession,* 73 FOREIGN AFF. 28, 31 (Mar./Apr. 1994).

18. *Id.* at 35.

more than half of that gap is in manufactured products.[19] Given that the Japanese market is the second largest in the world, the denial of access has repercussions beyond the mere dollar loss in exports. Denial of market access means the loss of potential economies of scale and possible denial of access to other markets, including the emerging Asian market.

The economy-wide structural barriers include government involvement well beyond the MITI's preferential treatment of a few industries and imposition of measures to protect domestic markets.[20] The widespread involvement of Japan's Ministry of Finance (MOF) and other agencies, including the MITI, in spurring Japan's economic growth since World War II cannot be understated. The central bureaucracy's industrial policy encouraged an "investment race," which caused a surge in exports and "prompted firms to adopt successively newer technology and invest rapidly while inducing firms to compete fiercely for market share in improving quality and services."[21] At the heart of the policy was the MOF's direction of capital to selected large firms, the MITI's restrictions on imports into Japan, which enabled the MITI to significantly affect the investment and marketing decisions of private companies, and the MITI's allocation of resources to select companies.[22] These activities created a protected Japanese market and cartels, *de jure* and *de facto*, among oligopolistic firms in key growth areas, such as the steel, chemical and other industries.[23]

Government control and influence have persisted despite Japan's increased liberalization.[24] Japan imposes rigid standards, testing and certification processes; burdensome customs procedures; and exercises control over procurement to benefit domestic suppliers.[25] Many of these controls, or nontariff "barriers," exist in the "concentrated or cartelized industries."[26] The Japanese agencies still maintain an important influence over investment and policy decisions, as evidenced by their control over capital and their current ability to "co-opt new entrants" in the Japanese markets into existing cartels.[27]

---

19. BERGSTEN & NOLAND, *supra* note 5, at 210.

20. As anecdotal evidence of this involvement, a relatively low-level MITI employee was recently quoted in *The New York Times* about how he became astonished when his Harvard Business School classmates erupted in applause upon learning that the subject of a case study, a failed airline, had never sought government help. The MITI employee stated that he was "shocked" because there are so many stakeholders in the company, and the decision not to have any government intervention was so "coldhearted." *Sterngold, supra* note 1.

21. Yamamura, *supra* note 8, at 202.

22. *Id.* at 172–73.

23. *Id.* at 176.

24. Bergsten and Noland have concluded that the restrictive effect of Japan's barriers is 25 percent of what it was in the 1980s. BERGSTEN & NOLAND, *supra* note 5, at 220.

25. LINCOLN, *supra* note 5, at 14–16.

26. BERGSTEN & NOLAND, *supra* note 5, at 74.

27. *Id.* at 178.

The behavior of Japanese business has also served to limit access to the Japanese market. The *keiretsu* system is a prime example of both concentration and cooperation in the Japanese economic system to the detriment of non-Japanese competitors. *Keiretsu* is "interlocking family relations that Japanese companies have developed with their suppliers and distributors and with large manufacturers in other industries."[28] It is a network which consists of a core group of firms linked horizontally across markets and vertically with input suppliers.[29] The networking, which generally includes access to finance through banks and insurance companies, is argued to be "inherently exclusionary."[30] As Tyson has noted, "preferential arrangements both within and between the Japanese suppliers and their *keiretsu* partners acted as an opaque but nonetheless powerful barrier to foreign suppliers."[31] The absence of any meaningful antitrust laws or enforcement mechanism and the presence of other laws, such as the Large-Scale Retail Store Law,[32] have further enhanced the anticompetitive effects of the *keiretsu*.

Jeffrey Garten, the current Undersecretary of Commerce for International Trade, perhaps has best summarized the United States' perception of trade relations with Japan: "[i]n no country are the barriers to entry so widespread and so deeply rooted as they are in Japan. In no country have we been negotiating so long and so hard without sufficient success."[33] While his remarks are hyperbolic—in that Garten neglects the many areas in which Japanese markets and other foreign markets are converging, the changes that Japan has made since the 1980s, and that Japan has been in a deep recession—they reflect a perception, correct or not, which Japan must address when dealing with the United States.

(2) The Japanese Perspective[34]

From Japan's perspective, the trade dispute raises issues concerning the United States' macro- and microeconomic policies, such as (1) the United States budget deficit as manifesting low savings and high consumption without sufficient

---

28. Note, *Free Trade Area Agreements as the Economic and Legal Solution to Bilateral Trade Relationships: The Case of Japan*, 28 COL. J. TRANSNAT'L L. 499, 519 (1990).

29. BERGSTEN & NOLAND, *supra* note 5, at 74–75.

30. *Id.* at 75.

31. TYSON, *supra* note 7, at 192.

32. Enacted in 1974, the Large-Scale Retail Store Law limited the expansion of major retail chains. In response to the Structural Impediments Initiative, however, Japan amended this law to allow various retailers to enter its market.

33. *Super 301 Renewal Said Designed to Send Message to Japan to Open Markets*, INT'L TRADE DAILY (BNA) (Mar. 7, 1994).

34. This section is deliberately abbreviated, with the expectation that the Japanese contributors to this volume will provide greater insight to this subject.

allocation to long-term investment;[35] (2) the inability of U.S. corporations to compete in all respects, including as to productivity, quality, innovation, marketing, and technology;[36] and (3) domestic practices that favor United States business. As many commentators have noted, even if Japan were a completely open market, the United States would still require major structural changes in its macroeconomic policies so as to take advantage of market access.[37]

These common criticisms, however, may not hold the importance that they once did. Terumasa Nakanishi of Shizuoka University was recently quoted in *The Washington Post* as stating that "Japan's mood toward America has reversed . . . [t]here's a sense that American industry has really changed in the last few years. The Japanese now understand that America is the toughest competitor in markets around the world."[38] By way of illustration, Japan's two leading video-game companies, Nintendo and Sega, recently selected American companies as allies on software.[39] The 1994 U.S. budget reduction measures and other attempts to restructure the American economy no doubt will continue to improve the ability of American business to allocate more resources to improving their competitive posture.

Perhaps of greater concern to Japan is the manner in which the United States has addressed trade imbalances. Among other things, Japan objects to (1) U.S. insistence on "managed trade," with its emphasis on outcome rather than a set of defined rules for dispute resolution;[40] and (2) the ready willingness of the United

---

35. *Japan: View that SII Will Correct U.S.-Japan Deficit Is Against Economic Logic, Japan's Akao Says*, 7 INT'L TRADE REP. (BNA) 193 (1990); S. COHEN, UNEASY PARTNERSHIP: COMPETITION AND CONFLICT IN U.S.-JAPANESE TRADE RELATIONS 212 (1985).

36. Note, *The Feasibility of a United States–Japan Free Trade Agreement*, 26 TEX. INT'L L.J. 275, 294–95 and n. 105 (1991) (quoting K. OGURA, TRADE CONFLICT: A VIEW FROM JAPAN 25 (1984)).

37. Farnsworth, *Caution Urged in Battle Against Unfair Trading*, N.Y. TIMES, May 4, 1989, at 6, col. 3 (quoting then-U.S. Trade Representative Carla Hills that the "trade deficit is the product of broader economic factors"); *see also White House Maintains Its Hard-Line Approach to Japan, Despite Ongoing Political Turmoil*, WALL ST. J., Apr. 14, 1994, at A16 (noting that Paula Stern, a Clinton trade adviser, has urged that the United States "should emphasize broad deregulation and tax cuts . . . instead of individual trade disputes").

38. Reid, *In Japan, the Sun Shines on 'Rising Sam,'* THE WASHINGTON POST NATIONAL WEEKLY EDITION, Feb. 28–Mar. 6, 1994, at 21; *see also* Ohmae, *For Japan's Economy, a Call to Arms*, WALL ST. J., Jan. 13, 1994, at A18, (observing that Japan's high labor costs result in 30 percent cost savings if goods are produced in the United States).

39. *MITI's Identity Crisis*, *supra* note 13, at 66.

40. *Japan's Panel Criticizes U.S. Trade Weapons*; Report, Agence France Presse, Apr. 1, 1994, *available* in LEXIS, Nexis Library, CURNEWS File (the draft of the Japanese government's Annual Report on Unfair Trade Policies by Major Trading Partners "strongly criticized U.S. trade policies that aim to set up so-called numerical targets for sales, describing it as a breach of 'the spirit' of the General Agreement on Tariffs and Trade"); *see*

States to use antidumping and countervailing provisions, such as Super 301,[41] unilateral measures to promote the American concept of "fair" trade.[42] In particular, the U.S. demand for quantitative measures of progress cannot be reconciled with Japan's recent efforts, also at the request of the United States, "to reduce bureaucratic red tape and allow free market forces to play a bigger part in Japanese economic life."[43] In other words, by advocating a policy that the Japanese government should and could force Japan's businesses to meet import targets, the United States has encouraged, not deterred, the Japanese government's control over business.

Unilateral efforts by the United States are also under attack for lack of any clearly defined objectives and finality.[44] The recent threat of punitive action under Super 301 was initiated despite Japan's package of trade liberalization measures to reduce the approximate $60 billion trade surplus.[45] In sum, Japan is argued to be at the mercy of the United States, while the United States has failed to adopt a clear and consistent policy of what constitutes fair trade.

b. Attempts at Managing the Dispute

(1) Bilateral Efforts

Despite serious differences regarding substantive economic policy and methods of resolving trade imbalances, Japan and the United States have had extensive and, at times, productive bilateral negotiations on trade. Bilateral talks have ranged from the current framework negotiations, which address specific products or practices in an industry with the aim of establishing a measure of progress, to market-oriented, sector-specific talks (MOSS), to discussions on a broader level about structural differences, as launched by the Structural Impediment Initiative (SII) in 1989–1990.

---

describing it as a breach of 'the spirit' of the General Agreement on Tariffs and Trade"); *see also* Bhagwati, *International Trade Issues for the 90's*, 8 BOSTON UNIV. INT'L L.J. 199, 199–201 (1990) ("[t]rade should be conducted by rules, not by preset quantities").

41. 19 U.S.C. § 2411 (1988) (originally enacted as Omnibus Trade and Competitiveness Act of 1974, § 301, 102 Stat. 1988, at 1108, 1176–1179 (1975)).

42. BERGSTEN & NOLAND, *supra* note 5, at 70 ("Between 1979 and 1991, U.S. firms filed a total of 5 countervailing duty and 58 dumping suits against Japanese exporters, 43 of these (69 percent) resulting in restrictions on trade") (citing I.M. DESTLER, AMERICAN TRADE POLITICS (1992)).

43. Nakamoto, *Japan Resists U.S. Pressure on Trade*, FINANCIAL TIMES, Feb. 10, 1994, at 4.

44. *Id*("neither the semiconductor agreement and [sic] the announcement by Japanese car makers of their procurement plans for foreign car parts were intended as government commitments but have been treated as such by the U.S.").

45. *Japan Tops List of Unfair Traders*, Agence France Presse, Mar. 31, 1994, *available* in LEXIS, Nexis Library, CURNEWS File.

such as the High-Technology Working Group, the Industrial Policy Dialogue, and the Trade Committee, designed to educate both sides and institutionalize trade meetings.[46]

Recognizing that any policy that would attempt to dismantle Japan's trade barriers in a single effort would either destabilize the trade relationship or be totally ineffective, the United States has focused on the sector-specific approach.[47] Another reason for this method, arguably, is that key American businesses have effectively lobbied the current and two preceding administrations to use numerical targets, presumably to promote Japanese imports of *their* goods.[48] A third reason is that a focus on specific sectors, with a goal of promoting a quantifiable result, creates an objective criteria that cannot be readily circumvented.[49]

Efforts at targeting sectors began in 1986 when, after numerous dumping complaints were lodged against Japanese producers of semiconductors and the U.S. Semiconductor Industry Association filed a Section 301 petition against Japan for unfair trading practices, Japanese and U.S. trade officials announced the Semiconductor Trade Agreement (STA). A side-letter to that agreement provided that foreign firms would be allowed a 20 percent share of the semiconductor industry.[50] In 1991, the STA was amended with a specific target of 20 percent set for foreign market share.[51]

Other forms of results-oriented measures have been used, such as voluntary import expansions (VIE) or voluntary export restraints (VER) of exports from Japan to the United States. Noting that VIE and VER were important to the Reagan and Bush administrations' dealings with Japan, Bergsten and Noland have documented the numerous results-oriented bilateral arrangements in automobiles, automobile parts, and steel.[52] The recent agreement between the United States and Japan that requires a Japanese company, Nippon Idou Tsushin Corporation (IDO), to purchase equipment from the U.S.-based corporation Motorola, Inc., in constructing a mobile

---

46. LINCOLN, *supra* note 5, at 144.

47. Friedman, *U.S. Approach to Japan: 'Economic Acupuncture,'* N.Y. TIMES, Mar. 18, 1994, at C1.

48. Dunne, *Impasse Threatens Japan and U.S. Trade Summit*, FINANCIAL TIMES, Feb. 10, 1994, at 1 (observing that the Economic Strategy Institute, a think-tank with close ties to the U.S. car industry, sent a letter to the president, signed by 81 business leaders, economists, and academics, supporting "a pragmatic results-oriented strategy" with numerical targets).

49. Prestowitz, *Getting Japan to Say Yes*, THE WASHINGTON POST NATIONAL WEEKLY EDITION, Jan. 31–Feb. 6, 1994, at 24 ("experience has taught us that agreements on procedural issues can be circumvented so that nothing really changes").

50. *Mismanaged Trade*, THE ECONOMIST, Jan. 22, 1994, at 17.

51. BERGSTEN & NOLAND, *supra* note 5, at 129–32.

52. *Id.* at 225.

phone system in the corridor between Tokyo and Nagoya further exemplifies the ability of the nations to reach agreement on a sector-specific basis.[53]

At the same time, both nations have, under the guise of the SII, continued to work toward their respective commitments to alleviate structural impediments. Under the SII, the United States identified six areas of concern in Japan's economy: savings and investment, land use, the distribution system, pricing mechanisms, exclusionary business practices, and *keiretsu*.[54] On the other hand, Japan targeted U.S. macroeconomic shortcomings.[55] In the SII Joint Report issued on June 28, 1990, both countries agreed to undertake reforms in these areas. Indeed, Japan committed to spend 430 trillion yen from 1991 to 2000 on social infrastructure, aimed to stimulate domestic demand.[56] While Japan has been praised for implementing its obligations under the SII, the United States had been less than aggressive, until the recent budget reforms, in implementing its commitments.

(2) Unilateral Action

The administration's unilateral strong-arm is Section 301 of the Trade Act of 1974, as amended by the Omnibus Trade and Competitiveness Act of 1988 (the 1988 Trade Act).[57] Under Section 301, private parties in the U.S. may petition the United States Trade Representative (USTR) to investigate a foreign government's acts, policies and practices that violate a trade agreement or that are unjustifiable and burden or restrict United States commerce.[58] If the USTR determines under Section 2414(a)(1) that a violation occurred, certain actions as set forth in 28 U.S.C. Section 2411(c) automatically ensue.[59] Although criticized as retaliatory, Section 301 has been heralded by U.S. trade officials because it has provided a "credible threat of retaliation," which, when coupled with the opening of the U.S. market, could "pry open foreign markets" and thus further liberalize trade.[60] In other words,

---

53. Pollack, *America as Trade Micro-Manager*, N.Y. TIMES, Mar. 13, 1994, at C1.

54. *See Destination Japan: A Business Guide for the 90's*, 48 U.S. DEPT. OF COMMERCE, INTERNATIONAL TRADE ADMINISTRATION (1991).

55. In addition to those items listed at *supra*, text accompanying notes 47–56, the Japanese complained about American business practice of corporate raiding (a common occurrence in the late 1980s) and America's short-term focus. BERGSTEN & NOLAND, *supra* note 5, at 211.

56. *Destination Japan, supra* note 54, at 49.

57. *See supra* note 41.

58. *Id.* at § 2412.

59. Under section 2411(c), the USTR may "suspend, withdraw, or prevent the application of, benefits of trade agreement concession;" impose duties or other restrictions; or enter into a binding agreement with a foreign country to eliminate the practice or burden on U.S. commerce. *Id.* at § 2411(c).

60. Holmer & Bello, *U.S. Trade Law & Policy Series No. 14, The 1988 Trade Bill: Savior or Scourge of the International Trading System?*, 23 INT'L LAW. 523, 527 (1988).

the United States has urged that Section 301 complements, rather than derogates, the principles and policies of the GATT because it is the threat of retaliation that is significant.[61] As Bello and Holmer have noted, Section 301 has been used effectively and "arguably was more successful in opening markets— generally on a most-favored-nation basis, benefiting third-country producers, exporters and consumers as well as Americans—than any developments at GATT headquarters in Geneva."[62]

The United States has relied on unilateral measures, or threat thereof, in attempting to improve its trading posture with Japan. Unilateral action under Section 301 has heightened the tension between the two countries because Section 301 action may violate multilateral rules and because of serious consequences if Japan does not succumb to U.S. demands. Unilateral action alone, however, cannot reasonably be considered an attempt to *resolve* a trade dispute because of the inherent nonconciliatory posture of the parties and the dominant position of the United States. Nevertheless, given U.S. insistence on its right to act unilaterally and its contention that unilateral measures are used only to enhance liberalization, unilateral mechanisms must be considered as a factor in the trade relationship.

While President Reagan used the pre-1988 version of Section 301, his enforcement measures were not enough to stymie what appeared in the mid-1980s to be a plethora of trade bills in the Congress.[63] With the adoption of the 1988 Trade Act, the administration has access to a procedure to identify "priority foreign countries" and "trade liberalization priorities" for Section 301 negotiations.[64] It imposes a rigid timetable so that the administration cannot conveniently neglect the issue.[65]

Super 301 has been heralded in the United States as a means to "open markets and liberalize trade, not to protect U.S. business and workers or to close the American market."[66] Critics have charged, however, that Super 301 is a "crowbar" and an example of a unilateral measure that "will result in a shrinkage of world

---

61. Bello & Holmer, *U.S. Trade Law & Policy Series No. 13, Unilateral Action to Open Foreign Markets: The Mechanics of Retaliation Exercises*, 22 INT'L LAW. 1197, 1205–06 (1988).

62. Bello & Holmer, *The Post-Uruguay Round Future of Section 301*, GEO. J.L. & POL'Y INT'L BUS. (forthcoming); *compare Gunboat Diplomacy*, THE ECONOMIST, Mar. 12, 1994, at 71 (citing the recent work of Patrick Low analyzing all Section 301 investigations and concluding that liberalization occurred in only a third of cases and retaliation in a tenth of the cases).

63. Holmer & Bello, *supra* note 60, at 523–24 (noting that in 1985 over three hundred trade bills were introduced in Congress and that the trade bills passed in either the House or Senate in 1986 and 1987 could not withstand a presidential veto).

64. Bello & Holmer, *supra* note 61.

65. 28 U.S.C. § 2420.

66. Holmer & Bello, *supra* note 60, at 532.

trade."[67] Of significance to the United States–Japan relationship is that Super 301 has been perceived as being "written for Japan."[68] Republican Senator John C. Danforth of Missouri has candidly acknowledged that Super 301 "'was not meant to single out Japan . . . [b]ut we had no less than Japan in mind.'"[69]

The effectiveness of Super 301 is now being tested. The breakdown in February 1994 of the bilateral trade talks between the United States and Japan prompted the president to sign an executive order on March 3, 1994, styled *Identification of Trade Expansion Priorities*, which revived Super 301.[70] The pronouncements made when the order was signed and the administration's subsequent conduct in implementing the order indicate that the administration is using the threat of sanctions flexibly (and perhaps haphazardly) to maximize trade concessions from Japan. Mickey Kantor, the current USTR, emphasized that with the reinstatement of Super 301 the United States was not "designating or identifying any practice of any country" but it was identifying those "'priority foreign country practices' the elimination of which have the greatest potential for the expansion of U.S. exports."[71] Reinstating Super 301 is part of the Clinton administration's effort to "complement our market-opening efforts around the world and to help establish trade priorities."[72] Secretary of Commerce Ron Brown remarked that initiation of Super 301 was "just another step along a consistent path of convincing the Japanese and others with closed markets that we're serious about having those [markets] open."[73]

Under the order, the USTR must identify by September 30, 1994, unfair trade practices of "priority" countries.[74] The National Trade Estimate Report (NTE) on Foreign Trade Barriers, issued on March 31, 1994, foreshadows the U.S. position on Japanese practices currently under scrutiny. The NTE report devoted 44 of its 281 pages to Japan and listed 43 Japanese trade barriers under seven industry categories. In issuing the report, the USTR's general counsel remarked that the section on Japan documents "how the barriers in Japan to the imports of manufactured goods and services far exceed the barriers of other G-7 nations and place an unacceptable burden on the global trading system."[75] While the

---

67. *Clinton Moves Against Japan, supra* note 3, at 1 (remarks of Mr. Hideaki Kumano, Japan's Vice-Minister of International Trade and Industry).

68. *Roundtable Discussion*, 22 CORNELL INT'L L.J. 517, 520 (1989) (remarks of Professor Victor Koschmann).

69. Farnsworth, *supra* note 37.

70. Exec. Order No. 12,901, 59 Fed. Reg. 10,727 (1994).

71. *U.S. Statement on Executive Order Reinstating Super* 301, JAPAN ECONOMIC NEWSWIRE (Mar. 4, 1994).

72. *Id.*

73. *Super 301 Renewal Said Designed to Send Message to Japan, supra* note 33.

74. *Supra* note 70.

75. The Group of Seven is comprised of Canada, France, Germany, Italy, Japan, the United States, and the United Kingdom.

administration will attempt to negotiate an agreement to eliminate the practices, with compensation if appropriate, it will continue investigations and act under Super 301 if the practices are not eliminated. Thus, even with the advances made in a particular sector, such as that between Motorola and IDO, Super 301 investigations will continue.

III. MANAGING THE FRICTION—SOME THOUGHTS

a. Does the Friction Matter?

Recent comments by Professor Krugman suggest that the outcome of the dispute between Japan and the United States may not be material to the overall well-being of Japanese and American citizens.[76] Krugman maintains that it is not relevant whether the United States can compete with Japan if the American standard of living is increasing at a growth rate equal to the growth in domestic productivity. If true, the current state of affairs—in which each nation routinely attacks the other for being either a unilateralist or protectionist—reflects political posturing more than a serious concern about improving the economic welfare of each nation's citizens.

In a similar vein, the transnational ties between and among corporations make it increasingly difficult for a corporation to be identified as a United States or Japanese corporation. For example, increased efficiency and productivity at Honda (Japan) due to improved technology can be readily transferred to Honda (United States). Both entities will realize economic gains, and these gains, in turn, are ultimately reflected in the respective country's economic indicators.

Nevertheless, the history of the United States–Japan trade dispute demonstrates that government policies influence whether a particular business can compete. A government that subsidizes research, creates opportunities for companies to enjoy economies of scale, and eases access to capital can at least, in the short run, enhance the competitiveness of companies benefiting from these measures. Likewise, a government that encourages allocation of resources for education and worker-training to corporations within its boundaries will improve the likelihood of creating a workforce capable of adapting to competitive demands.

Recognizing that the United States and Japanese governments each has a stake in the trade issue does not necessarily mean that either should negotiate trade agreements based on the assumption that trade is a zero-sum game.[77] Instead, negotiations should be tempered to addressing both macro- and microeconomic solutions which promote liberalization. Focus on macroeconomic policies which deal with trade and current account balances should continue. The SII talks are a

---

76. The allocation of valuable resources to unproductive trade negotiations, however, is an unnecessary burden which reduces an individual's welfare.

77. Krugman, *supra* note 17, at 34.

step in this direction, as are continued efforts to remove market impediments. Efforts directed at broad-scale investment through the activities of the APEC should also be encouraged.

Thus, friction matters to the extent that it manifests an unwillingness or inability of both governments to reach an agreement on issues that could lead to further liberalization. It also matters because of its likely negative repercussions on other aspects of the United States–Japan relationship and of the increased possibilities that such friction could lead to a global trade war.

The goal of any sanction should be to open markets and strengthen Japan's economy. Threatened use of a unilateral measure, such as Super 301, without intent to follow through with its remedy will, in the long run, be counterproductive. Unilateral measures should be tolerated only under extreme circumstances and only if they do not cause Japan to retreat and reinstate protective measures. Although the fall of Prime Minister Morihiro Hosokawa cannot be directly attributed to the American decision to reinstate Super 301, the timing suggests that the administration's actions could not have had a more perverse effect.

b. Managing the Friction v. Managed Trade

There remain significant differences between the economies of the United States and Japan, and such differences will not suddenly disappear in light of a U.S. test of brinkmanship. Both countries, however, must assure that these differences do not impede growth. Further, both share other strategic interests, including geopolitical and political concerns, which define and expand the overall relationship beyond economic concerns. Managing the friction entails establishing lines of communication, discussing matters of mutual economic interest, resolving trade disputes within mutually-agreeable institutions, such as the GATT/WTO, bilaterally addressing policies which hamper imports, and working to eliminate those policies.[78]

Managed trade, with an emphasis on Japan's importing certain goods in specified quantities or at a desired general level, is inconsistent with "managing the friction." The administration's recent announcement that it intends to address the problem on a "piecemeal" basis is not a solution. If successful, managed trade means little more than newly gained access to Japan for a few, select sectors, or even a few, select companies in a select sector. The costs associated with imposing quantified targets are significant: the American company becomes entitled "to share the [oligopoly] rents—and typically finds that their Japanese operations are among the most profitable in the world" due to the protected market but other American companies do not benefit.[79] In the meantime, the Japanese government will have expanded its controls and established administrative agencies to maintain

---

78. BERGSTEN & NOLAND, *supra* note 5, at 210–18.
79. BERGSTEN & NOLAND, *supra* note 5, at 226–27.

compliance with the targets. If targets are not met, the Japanese will be accused of breaking their promises. The managed trade proposal is anything but liberalizing and is more likely a mechanism for increasing friction.

c. In the Shadow of Section 301: The GATT/WTO

The irony of the current United States–Japan dispute is that it began shortly after the completion of the negotiation of the world's most important multilateral trading agreement. Throughout the Uruguay Round, questions were raised regarding the validity and effectiveness of Section 301 and unilateral market/opening legislative measures.[80] USTR Kantor has subsequently claimed that the Uruguay Round "d[id] not settle everything," suggesting that certain Super 301 targets are not covered by the Round.[81] The European Union, on the other hand, has charged that the United States must use multilateral mechanisms before using unilateral measures.[82]

As a matter of policy, however, the swift reinstatement of Super 301 without serious deference to the multilateral system raises grave questions about U.S. commitment to the WTO. Given the ability within the context of the GATT/WTO for the United States to attract other exporting countries to its side and the political benefits of taking the dispute to the GATT,[83] a logical conclusion to draw is that the United States may have forsaken its commitment to the vision of a rules-based trading system.

IV. CONCLUSION

The current dispute between the United States and Japan on trade issues has raised considerable doubts about the commitment of each to economic liberalization and about United States willingness to use reasonable measures and restraint in attempting to resolve a complex matter. Considering the importance of the issues and the serious consequences that the dispute raises for economic stability and growth, however, reconsideration of substantive policy and procedural issues is imperative. A meaningful, nonthreatening dialogue on these matters with the goal of a long-term solution will better serve all interests.

---

80. *Private Sector Advisors Broadly Support GATT Accord But Cite Some Serious Flaws,* INT'L TRADE DAILY (BNA) (Jan. 26, 1994). For cogent arguments on the validity of unilateral action, *see* JACKSON, INTERNATIONAL LEGAL PERSPECTIVES ON JAPAN–NORTH AMERICAN ECONOMIC FRICTIONS (Mar. 31, 1994) and Bello & Holmer, *supra* note 61.

81. *Super 301 Renewal Said Designed to Send Message to Japan, supra* note 33.

82. *Id.*

83. BERGSTEN & NOLAND, *supra* note 5, at 224.

JAPANESE LAW AND POLICY FOR GLOBALIZATION OF INDUSTRY AND THE CORPORATION: MEASURES FOR RELIEF FROM INVESTMENT AND TRADE FRICTIONS

Masao Sakurai

I. INTRODUCTION

Globalization of Japanese industry and corporations is proceeding steadily while progress is being made in structural adjustments. However, Japan is concerned about investment friction and about the hollowing-out of domestic industry because of imports and foreign direct investment in Japan. There is also a need for improved integration of the policies of different nations in order to promote stable development of the world economy. Japan's industrial society will continue to be an influence on the world. The following examination of the legal and policy aspects of the globalization of industry and corporations is based on such concerns.[1]

---

1.   This chapter relies mainly on the following materials: MINISTRY OF INTERNATIONAL TRADE AND INDUSTRY, INDUSTRIAL POLICY BUREAU, KYOZON TEKI KYOSO ENO MICHI [WAY TO INTERDEPENDENT COMPETITION: JAPAN'S INDUSTRIAL ACTIVITIES AND INDUSTRIAL POLICY UNDER GLOBALIZATION] 247 (1989); TOKYO INDUSTRIAL STRUCTURE RESEARCH COUNCIL, INDUSTRIAL STRUCTURE IN 2000 at 50–64 (1990); MINISTRY OF INTERNATIONAL TRADE AND INDUSTRY, OVERSEAS DIRECT INVESTMENT STUDY COMMITTEE, JAPAN'S OVERSEAS DIRECT INVESTMENT TOWARD MULTIFACIAL INTERNATIONALIZATION 92 (1985); Masao Sakurai, *Globalization of Industry and Enterprise: Law and Policy*, 1000 JURIST 312–317 (1992); MINISTRY OF INTERNATIONAL TRADE AND INDUSTRY, HEISEI ROKU NENDO TSUSHO SANGYO SEISAKU NO JUTEN (KEY POINTS IN INTERNATIONAL TRADE AND INDUSTRIAL POLICY IN FISCAL YEAR 1994) 32 (1994); MINISTRY OF INTERNATIONAL TRADE AND INDUSTRY, INDUSTRIAL STRUCTURE COUNCIL. GENERAL COMMITTEE, FUNDAMENTAL

II. LEGAL SYSTEM OF INDUSTRIAL ACTIVITIES AND INDUSTRIAL POLICY

a. Globalization

The foreign and domestic activities of business corporations currently take place against a backdrop of a volatile foreign exchange rate, intensified protectionism in some countries, regional integration movements, the development of the Association of South East Asian Nations (ASEAN), and other broad changes. These conditions create strong pressure to deepen the interdependency now emerging in the global economy and to strengthen the policy ties between nations and legal systems. Such ties can be achieved through the use of trade and investment dispute resolution mechanisms and through a system that coordinates policy on behalf of the global economy.[2]

b. Present Conditions and Issues of Industrial Activities

(1) Direct Foreign Investment by Japanese Interests

Subsequent to the Plaza Accord,[3] Japanese corporations, benefiting from appreciation in the value of the yen, increased their overseas investments and

---

(1994); MINISTRY OF INTERNATIONAL TRADE AND INDUSTRY, INDUSTRIAL STRUCTURE COUNCIL. GENERAL COMMITTEE, FUNDAMENTAL PROBLEMS SUBCOMMITTEE, REPORT 92 (1994).

2.   "Industrial policy" is defined here as policy intended to supplement market mechanisms and to arrive at the optimum overall solution(s) without intervening in the decisionmaking process at the firm level. *See* TSUSHO SANGYO [INTERNATIONAL INDUSTRY] 21 (Tsusho Sangyo Gyosei Kenkyu Kai [International Trade and Industry Administration Study Group] ed., 1983). Professor Ryutaro Komiya and Keiichi Yokobori use this term to indicate "economic policies intended to affect inter-industrial resource allocation and to regulate, restrain or stimulate certain economic activities by private firms in response to 'market failures' or for other purposes." Ryutaro Komiya and Keiichi Yokobori, *Japan's Industrial Policies in the 1980s*, at 7 (1991). *See also* Fumihiro Gotō and Kazutomo Irie, *Theoretical Basis of Industrial Policy*, 8 (1989).

3.   The Plaza Accord, so named because it was concluded at a conference held at the Plaza Hotel in New York City on Sept. 22, 1985, is formally known as "Announcement of the Ministers of Finance and Central Bank Governors of France, Germany, Japan, the United Kingdom, and the United States." Paragraph 18, section 2 provides: "[t]hey (Ministers and Governors) believed that agreed policy actions must be implemented and reinforced to improve the fundamentals further, and that, in view of the present and prospective changes in fundamentals, some further orderly appreciation of the main non-dollar currencies against the dollar is desirable."

continued to deploy "managerial resources"[4] on a global scale. Japanese foreign subsidiaries currently experience a buildup in production capacity as off-shore production ratios are raised. This creates jobs in the host countries while contributing both to growth of those countries' exports and to Japanese increases in imports. Among those corporations are those that seek to become transnational corporations (TNCs) by implementing a multifaceted strategy that links centers of business activity, and those that have established regional headquarters as a means of organizing overseas subsidiaries.

Regarding their overseas firms, Japanese corporations are striving to fade out their proportional shares of capital, increase the percentage of directors and officers that are from the host country, use more materials produced in the host countries, promote local staffing, and enhance the localization process through technology-transfer and research, and through development activities. In comparison to the presence of the Japanese-owned corporations, however, progress in achieving the *performance requirements* for localization has nevertheless been slow and there has not been sufficient appreciation of the importance of the subsidiaries' non-business activities that constitute contributions to the host societies.

Direct foreign investment may involve conflict with the host countries. Increasingly evident is "investment friction,"[5] which has in some instances given rise to movements for legislation to limit investment.[6] In order to solve or prevent such conflict, it is necessary for the Japanese-affiliated company to assimilate into the economy and society of the host country. To avert a "hollowing-out"[7] of industry over the long term in Japan, Japanese corporations must improve the technology used in Japan. The Japanese government should also provide appropriate legislative measures to promote local and specialized industries, to create more jobs, and to further foster technological development.

---

4. The term "managerial resources" encompasses skills necessary for the efficient running of a firm, such as managerial, technological, marketing and organizational expertise. Ryutaro Komiya, *Japan's Foreign Direct Investment: Facts and Theoretical Considerations*, in INTERNATIONAL FINANCE AND TRADE IN A POLYCENTRIC WORLD: PROCEEDINGS OF THE BASEL CONFERENCE OF THE INTERNATIONAL ECONOMIC ASSOCIATION 276, 240–289 (Silvio Borner, ed., 1988).

5. Masao Sakurai, *Toshi Masatsu [Investment Friction]* 211 (1988).

6. For information on Japan's ambivalence to foreign capital and related laws, *see* MASAO SAKURAI, KOKUSAI KEIZAI HŌ [INTERNATIONAL ECONOMIC LAW] (1992), especially chapter 21, which discusses the national legal system of inward foreign investment.

7. The future effects of the "hollowing-out" phenomenon are uncertain.

(2) Direct Investment in Japan by Non-Japanese Interests

Foreign investment in Japan helps maintain industrial activities, raises the standard of industrial structure, promotes the globalization process within Japan, rectifies external imbalances, and advances investment inflows and outflows. The Foreign Exchange Control Law places no legal restrictions on direct investment in Japan. Despite the absence of legal restrictions, the scale of inward foreign investment has been small due to the perception that the Japanese market is closed. Low foreign investment is also due to difficulties in collecting information and in hiring personnel, increasing financial obligations in the initial stage of investing in Japan, the underdeveloped state of acquisition business, inadequate medical facilities, and differences in the manner of entering into business transactions and using distribution mechanisms.

The instability of the world economy demands that Japan open its domestic economy, especially because Japan has benefited from the trade system. An open Japanese market would also significantly improve the daily life of Japanese and would promote structural adjustments. Because there are almost no laws in Japan that create barriers to imports, the proper role of the government is to support and facilitate the efforts of each domestic economic entity.

(3) Liaison with Other Nations' Policies

Each country can strengthen coordination and cooperation with other nations through their own economic policies, though the reverse result is also possible. External imbalances hinder the stable growth of the world economy. The United States is one such nation with a large external balance which, if appropriate policies are not adopted, will only increase. Other industrialized countries need to adopt policies that will offset the deflationary effects of a reduction of America's external deficit. Those especially influenced by a reduction of the United States trade deficit would be the High-Performing Asian Economies[8] (HPAEs), including the Newly Industrializing Economies[9] (NIEs) and ASEAN members in the course of developing intra-regional division of production. To accomplish this, a multilateral body of an institutionalized or legal framework may have to be created.

The cumulative debt of the developing countries is an increasing problem which industrialized creditor countries must try to solve from a long-term

---

8.   HPAE's are identified by several common characteristics, such as very rapid economic growth. HPAE's are subclassified roughly according to the duration of their successful record of economic growth: The Four Tigers—Hong Kong, the Republic of Korea, Singapore, and Taiwan (China); and NIEs—Indonesia, Malaysia, and Thailand. INTERNATIONAL BANK FOR RECONSTRUCTION AND DEVELOPMENT, THE EAST ASIAN MIRACLE xvi (1993).

9.   See supra note 8.

viewpoint. Some action has already been taken. Most significantly, the Paris Club[10] postponed the maturation of obligations (officially guaranteed export credits, government lending, loan by the Export-Import Bank of Japan, etc.). Club members reduced outstanding debts, which lead to advocacy, at the Toronto Summit, of debt-reduction measures on behalf of Lower-Income Countries[11] (LICs). At the Houston Summit maturations were extended beyond the Paris Club's September 1990 deadline. The extensions—formally known as the Brady Plan[12]—where granted to those countries which were neither the poorest developing countries nor the Upper-Middle-Income Countries[13] (UMICs), namely the Lower-Middle-Income Countries[14] (LMICs). Club members reduced the debts of Egypt and Poland. Finally, then-British Finance Minister John Major advocated the Trinidad terms, which were intended to reduce the obligation and to extend payment schedules of the LICs that were objects of the Toronto scheme.

Although the possibility that the cumulative debt problem will lead to an upheaval in the international financial system has been somewhat reduced, it nevertheless contributes to the destablization of the international relationships upon which interdependency rests.

---

10. The Paris Club is an unofficial conference where creditors countries negotiate on rescheduling and refinancing. The number of creditors countries is fifty-two.

11 The List of ODA (Official Development Assistance) recipients classifies "developing countries" as follows:

    1) Developing Countries and Territories

- LLDCs		
- Other LICs	- per capita GNP	< $675 in 1992
- LMICs	- per capita GNP	$676 – $2695 in 1992
- UMICs	- per capita GNP	$2696 – $8355 in 1992
- HICs	- per capita GNP	> $8355 in 1992

    2) Countries and Territories in Transition

        - CEECs/NIS (Central and Eastern European Countrie / New Independent States)

        - More Advanced Developing Countries and Territories

ORGANISATION FOR ECONOMIC CO-OPERATION AND DEVELOPMENT, DEVELOPMENT CO-OPERATION 12–13 (1993). *See also* Masao Sakurai, *Kokusai Kaihatsu Kyoryoku Hō [Law of International Development Co-operation]* 12-15 (1994).

12. This was proposed by Nicholas F. Brady, Secretary of Treasury of the United States. City banks were required to opt for relief measures to reduce the capital, interest, new money and debt buy-backs in transactions involving Mexico, the Philippines, Costa Rica, Venezuela, and Uruguay. Japan adopted the proposed measures of reducing capital, interest, and buy-backs with all recommended nations except the Philippines.

13. *See supra,* note 11.

14. *See supra,* note 12.

II. INTERNATIONAL HARMONIZATION IN LEGAL SYSTEMS

a. Background

As industrial activities become more globalized, the scope of legislation related to those activities has expanded to encompass certain domestic affairs. Moreover, in many legislative areas, international organizations and bilateral arrangements for there to be international coordination. The Treaty on European Union (Maastricht Treaty) and the North American Free Trade Agreement (NAFTA), both provide a basis for member countries to reduce and eliminate their own legislative restrictions in order to create a more vigorous environment for all member countries of the region. Japan must contribute to the construction and maintenance of these evolving international frameworks and activities contrary to the framework must be corrected on the basis of international rules.

b. Investment and Trade Law

Protectionist activities, such as opposition to interdependence and "unfair" trade, are evident even today.   In the European Community, for example, international law is commonly used to restrain trade, notably through antidumping taxes for parts and components[15] in response to an alleged GATT infraction, or through antidumping regulations.   In the United States, when an "unfair" trade practice has been identified, unilateral remedial measures are provided for by the Omnibus Trade and Competitiveness Act.[16] Efforts to restrict trade are also evident through the combined use of country-of-origin rules, antidumping measures, and import quotas. There is also a large body of protectionist legislation that applies to inward foreign investment. In both the EC and the United States, there have been efforts to increase limitations on investment by foreign interests.[17] Judgments in cases which impose punitive tarrifs regarding parts dumping also distort investment.

Because of the expansion of trade in high-tech goods and services, a goal of the GATT Uruguay Round was to establish a new framework of international economic law which covers fields hitherto not within the scope of international trade agreements, trade-related investment measures (TRIMs),[18] trade-related aspects of intellectual property rights (TRIPs), or the trade in services. Individual

---

15. MASAO SAKURAI, KOKUSAI KEIZAI HŌ [INTERNATIONAL ECONOMIC LAW], ch. 8, sec. 1 (EC Antidumping Tax on Parts and Components) (1992).

16. Pub. L. No. 100–418, 102 Stat. 1176, 1176–1179 (1988).

17. SAKURAI, *supra,* note 15, at ch. 21 (national legal systems of inward foreign investment in the United States).

18. *Id.* at ch. 15 (trade-related investment measures).

groups have also been working to prevent abuse of schemes to offset subsidies and to formulate new antidumping regulations and rules for certification of country-of-origin. For example, with regard to parts-dumping duties, disputes between Japan and the EC have been brought before the GATT. Moreover, the Committee on International Investment and Multinational Enterprises (CIME), a subgroup of the OECD, provides a forum for discussion by member countries of investment regulation, based on the "Guidelines for Multinational Enterprises."[19]

c. Intellectual Property Law

In the area of intellectual property, there is still a great need to ensure compatibility of national legal systems, to establish systems to protect intellectual property in developing countries, and to create legal measures to prevent international commerce in counterfeit merchandise. A number of new proposals and arrangements have been examined by the TRIPs group, which was established in connection with the Uruguay Round, the World Intellectual Property Organization (WIPO), the Trilateral Conference among the European Patent Office (EPO), the U.S. Patent and Trademark Office, the Japanese Patent Office, and private-industry organizations. There have also been bilateral conferences convened to improve mutual understanding of the legal system of each participating country.

d. Standardization

The adoption and use of standards on an international scale is promoted by the International Organization for Standardization (ISO), the International Electrotechnical Committee (IES) and other bodies. The GATT Standard Code is designed to encourage greater transparency of each nation's standards and certification systems. Following the integration of the European Community based on the Maastricht Treaty, the lowering of trade barriers through changes in the manner by which nations use standards and by adopting a reciprocal certification of standards system may lead to a European bloc with regard to standards.

e. Tax Law

In order to prevent excessive taxation of overseas business activities, countries use various means of providing credit for taxes paid abroad. For indirect tax credits, Japanese corporate tax law provides only for an exemption from tax applicable to dividend payments by means of an overseas subsidiary tax paid overseas by that subsidiary. Bilateral tax treaties exist in great number, and in

---

19. *Id.* at ch. 9, sec. 2, item 8-2 (OECD guidelines for multinational enterprises).

Japan's treaties with some developing countries, a tax sparing credit is employed.[20]

Application of the unitary tax of the United States to foreign-owned companies has been identified as a major issue because it includes income of the parent company in the calculations. Corporations normally make efforts to minimize their total tax. All nations adopt legal measures of some kind to limit the use of "tax havens," which tend to distort determination of the appropriate taxation of each country. Japan's Special Tax Measures Law provides for inclusion of retained earnings by certain subsidiaries in the taxable income of parent companies.[21]

Regarding transfer pricing, major industrialized countries have adjusted their legislation to improve control. In Japan this was done on the occasion of the 1986 amendment of the Special Tax Measures Law.[22] Unless there have been appropriate adjustments on a bilateral or multilateral basis regarding taxation, it is possible for double taxation to occur or for there to be "tax friction" between the countries involved.

Because all nations' tax laws are highly complex, international coordination is exceedingly difficult. Japan has been criticized for having a high effective tax rate on corporate earnings. The amendment of Japan's Corporate Tax Law[23] in 1989 has fueled expectations that the rate would be brought closer to the level of other countries.

f. Product Liability

In the United States, the problem of product liability has been so great as to place a strain on the insurance system, yet there has been no enactment of a Federal law to remedy this serious problem. However, among the EC and EFTA[24] countries progress has been made in the passing of such legislation, . In Japan, the Product Liability Act was enacted in July 1994 and will go into effect on July 1, 1995. The act is well-balanced so that the development of new products is not hindered, and the provisions are internationally harmonized. The act is therefore

---

20. According to the provisions of tax treaties that have been concluded between Japan and certain developing countries, Japanese residents, individuals and corporations can claim tax credits against Japanese taxes on income as if no special exemption or reduction was provided, even though the tax amount is exempted or reduced by special tax incentive measures in those developing countries. This foreign tax credit system is called "tax sparing."

21. SAKURAI, *supra* note 10, at ch. 7, sec. 4 (tax law havens).

22. SAKURAI, *supra* note 15, at ch. 6, sec. 3, item 3 (taxation of transfer pricing) & chap. 7, sec. 4, item 4 (transfer pricing).

23. For greater detail, *see* YUJI GOMI, GUIDE TO JAPANESE TAXES 410 (1995).

24. The founding members of EFTA were the United Kingdom, Denmark, Sweden, Norway, Austria, Switzerland, and Portugal. They were subsequently joined by Finland and Denmark, but the departure of Denmark, the United Kingdom and later Portugal, who left to join the European Community, reduced the total group membership.

not so harmful to foreign investment from abroad or to imports from developing countries.

g.   Antimonopoly Law

Because enforcement of Japan's Antimonopoly Act has been lax, foreigners have complained that it creates a barrier to entry. Accordingly, there have been demands for enforcement to be tightened. Extraterritorial application of the antimonopoly law could lead to an infringement of the sovereignty or autonomy of other nations and create further discord. For example, in 1986 the OECD Council warned that there must be improved international cooperation regarding voluntary export restraints (VERs), to ensure that contradictions between trade policy and competition policy are reduced or prevented. In Japan, the policy of permitting export cartels under the Export Transaction Law and the policy of using an export approval system under the Export Trade Control Regulation are both carried out to avoid complications regarding the Antimonopoly Act.

Unfortunately, there are no clear-cut international rules regarding associations formed by a nation's industries or communication of information from the standpoint of competition policy. As a link in the chain of limitations on mergers, host governments generally control inward foreign investment by acquisitions and joint ownership through domestic antimonopoly law. Moreover, domestic antimonopoly laws may be ineffectual when acquisitions, mergers and joint ventures traverse national markets, as is increasingly the case in modern global business.

Antimonopoly legislation is related to industrial policy and to issues concerning intellectual property. Regarding the former, there has been criticism, especially in Japan, that industry uses cartels that circumvent antimonopoly legislation, effectively imposing import restrictions and improving the competitive advantage of cartel members. As to intellectual property, antimonopoly legislation may not be suitable when disparities exist between the technological levels of transacting nations.

It is practically impossible to unify competition policy across borders. This does not mean, however, that international cooperation and coordination cannot be achieved to reduce disparities and frictions.

III. A LEGAL SYSTEM TO COPE WITH GLOBALIZATION AND TO RELIEVE FRICTION

a.   The Role of Industrial Policy

Japan improved her post-war competitiveness under the GATT and the IMF systems and improved the business environment through the support of law and government policy. Japan's rapid economic success has caused friction with other nations. It remains necessary to ensure that international industrial activities comply with international coordination; that a global system that supports free trade, investment and technology exchanges is developed and maintained, and that efforts are made to further develop the world economy and to lay the foundation for long-term autonomous development. The globalization policy of the Japanese government must improve the business environment to assure interdependent competition that will increase the benefits mutually enjoyed by each nation.

b. Coping with Globalization by Means of Law and Policy

Based on the above assessments, the following concrete approaches relying on law and policy should be considered.

(1) Direct Foreign Investment

The past fifteen years have seen some noteworthy changes regarding corporate conduct.   Beginning in 1976, the OECD formulated its *Guidelines for Multinational Enterprises*. In 1987, several Japanese business organizations developed and revised self-regulating codes of conduct. Thereafter, the Industrial Structure Council of the Ministry of International Trade and Industry (MITI) drafted *Desirable Corporate Behavior in Proceeding with Overseas Business Activities* in May 1989.[25]   While these standards and recommendations are generally regarded as "soft law" and are forceful only as exhortations of principle or suggested moral conduct,[26] it is hoped that they will have the legally binding character of legislation.[27]

To the promotion indigenization or localization, the government must improve the laws and policies that support the autonomous efforts of corporations. For example, tax laws may be modified in order to encourage charitable activity or public recognition may be given to companies acknowledged to be "good corporate citizens," though any practical, material effect of any such action is unlikely to be strong.[28] It should be noted that the only comprehensive sources of information on the true status of overseas business activities of Japanese domestic companies are

---

25. The MITI Committee on a Code of Conduct on Overseas Investment finished drafting its code of government-based conduct in March 1972, while the author was a member of the Committee. The five main business conferations (Keidanren [Japan Federation of Economic Organizations], Nihon Shoko Kaigisho [The Japan Chamber of Commerce and Industry], Keizai Doyukai [Japan Association of Corporate Executives], Nikkeiren [The Japan Federation of Employers' Association], and Nihon Boekikai [Japan Foreign Trade Council, Inc.]) accepted MITI's request for input by amending and publishing the Code.

26. SAKURAI, *supra* note 10, at ch. 9, sec. 2.

27. Some believe that Japanese-owned enterprises should be subject to Japanese law while others maintain that such an application would be both legally questionable and unfeasible.

28. The Japanese Chamber of Commerce and Industry is considering a "good corporate citizen" award for Japanese overseas enterprises (especially for those in the United States).

the tabulations of notifications submitted to the Ministry of Finance (MOF). These tabulations are based on the Foreign Exchange Control Law (MITI's annual benchmark survey of overseas business activities), studies by the Export-Import Bank of Japan, the Japan External Trade Organization (JETRO), and other similar organizations. The collection and dissemination of information must therefore be improved by establishing an "industrial information organization."[29]

(2) Direct Investment in Japan

Use of the legal system to modify foreign direct investment has not slowed growth of investment in Japan. It is therefore necessary to pursue policy measures which would encourage investment in Japan, such as offering financial support of such investment. Foreign companies cannot avail themselves fully of the financing that is obtainable from the Japan Development Bank, so limitations on industrial categories qualifying for preferential credit should be eliminated and the conditions for lending expanded.

Two Japanese laws can be sources of aid for foreign investors. The "technopolis law" (Law of Promoting Regional Development of High-Technology Industrial Districts) and what may be called the "private-sector participation law" (Temporary Measures Law Related to Promoting Improvement of Specific Facilities through Utilization of the Abilities of Private Sector Interests) should both be used by and on behalf of foreign corporations. Doing so would enable them to benefit from these laws at an early stage in their investment.

The government must promote imports from foreign companies and expand the base of potential investors that may enter Japan. On the other hand, existing controls based on law and administrative guidance[30] should be simplified, not merely to facilitate the entry of foreign companies into the Japanese market but also to promote the globalization process within Japan. Laws should be changed to conform to an environment which fosters international business and the standards benefiting such a legal system.

---

29. In 1989 the Institute of International Trade and Investment was established under the support of the Japan Trade Association. In 1991 the Japan Institute for Overseas Investment was established with the support of the Export-Import Bank of Japan.

30. Administrative Guidance (*Gyosei shido*) is generally defined as "that, without coercive force, which restricts the rights of nationals and puts them under obligations and induces them to make certain commissions or omissions so as to perform certain administrative objectives within the limits of function or competence endorsed by law based on which the administration was organized." Masao Sakurai, *Formulators and Legislators of International Trade and Industrial Policy in Japan and the United States*, in THE U.S.-JAPANESE ECONOMIC RELATIONSHIP: CAN IT BE IMPROVED? 160, 186, n. 13 (1989) (comment by M. Tsunoda, Director of the First Department of the Cabinet Legislation Bureau in the Standing Committee on Trade and Industry of the House of Councilors).

In order to expand imports, Japan must support industrial structure adjustments and a restructuring of the international horizontal division of labor. It must also try to change the business management system so that companies are less susceptible to the adverse effects of exchange rate fluctuations and more reliant on domestic demand. Surges in exports due to unfair and irrational acts are harmful to the exporting country in the long term. The Japanese Government must thus establish punitive laws and policies to protect domestic industry.[31]

Japan should further study issues regarding foreign workers to comply with the Law for Immigration Control and Refugee Recognition Act.[32] Japan must reappraise the existing situation, improve and restructure the legal framework, reconsider allocation of the cost of social services, and completely change attitudes towards living and working with non-Japanese.

(3) Policy Liaisons between Countries

Underlying the above suggestions is recognition that Japan must contribute to the international harmonization of legal systems. There is no doubt that the Marrakesh Agreement Establishing the World Trade Organization[33] stimulates the world economy to combat protectionist measures which distort freedom of trade and investment and technology flows. Among the important measures to be taken with regard to formulation of an international code for TRIMs is construction of a framework within which both industrially advanced home countries and developing host countries can grow.[34]

To protect intellectual property, a system for research and study of legal aspects of intellectual property must be established. This should occur while efforts to promote collaboration of public and private entities progress.

Changes in the tax law should be considered, including adding dividends paid by overseas subsidiaries' subsidiaries ("grandchild companies") to Japanese provisions for authorization of foreign tax credits, while simultaneously taking into account the tax structures of the United States and Europe. Tax authorities of the relevant nations must exchange information and adjust legal systems to ensure that

---

31. Although a new import insurance system to amend the Trade Insurance Law had been under review in government circles, it has not however been realized. For further details, *see* EXPORT INSURANCE ASSOCIATION, REPORT OF THE IMPORT INSURANCE STUDY COMMITTEE 12 (1985).

32. Shutsunyukoku Kanri oyobi Nanmin Ninteiho (Immigration Control and Refugees Recognition Act), 13 GENKO HOKI SORAN [COMPILATION OF EXISTING LAWS] 4181–4263.

33. Final Texts of the GATT Uruguay Round Agreements including the Agreement Establishing the World Trade Organization as Signed on Apr. 15, 1994, Marrakech, Morocco, 7–373 (1994).

34. MASAO SAKURAI, BOEKI KANREN TOSHI SOCHI NO HŌRITSU MONDAI [LEGAL PROBLEMS OF TRADE-RELATED INVESTMENT MEASURES] 67 (1990).

application of taxation with regard to transfer pricing is not arbitrary. Not to be overlooked, of course, is the influence of the Japanese corporate tax rate (including local government taxes) and the difference between that rate and the rates of other industrial countries.

With respect to standardization laws and regulations, product liability, and antimonopoly laws, Japan must study how to harmonize national legal systems to enable competitive coexistence of industrial activity without neglecting trends in international regulation.

Policy coordination among nations at both the macro and micro levels should be promoted. Macroeonomic policy should be implemented on the basis of the deeper awareness of macroeconomic conditions among the major industrial powers. Next, there must be structural adjustment within each nation, which is one aspect of policy coordination among OECD member countries. Japan has endeavored to adopt policies to realize structural change in accordance with the two *Maekawa* reports and the *Hiraiwa* report[35] and now must make considerable further changes
while the corporate sector continues to increase production, to raise the value added of manufactured goods, and to diversify.

To reduce their indebtedness, debtor nations must strive to develop their macroeconomic and structural adjustment policies. In addition to improving their debt repayment capabilities (with cooperation from the industrial powers) through measures that include promotion of direct investment from other countries, these developing countries will be able to reduce the burdens of debt service while receiving new loans and grants. Further, debtor countries must be developed through the transfer of "managerial resources" while maintaining the flow of private capital.

A greater role in solving the debt problem of developing nations should be given to trade and investment insurance based on the Trade Insurance Law.[36] Hopefully, Japan will more closely resemble other aid-donor countries by making more flexible efforts to encourage the economic development of debtor countries by supporting projects that will earn foreign exchange, contributing to import substitutions, and/or developing infrastructures which contribute to an enhanced industrial structure. Japan can achieve this in part by taking into account the activities of relevant international organizations, such as the Multilateral

---

35. For the full texts of each of the *Maekawa Reports*, *see* SHIN 'MAEKAWA REPORT' GA SHIMESU MICHI [NEW 'MAEKAWA REPORT' INDICATES JAPAN'S WAY] (1987). For the full text of the final *Hiraiwa Report* and the interim report on mitigation of government regulations, *see* NIKKAN KOGYO SHIMBUN, HIRAIWA RIPOTO [HIRAIWA REPORT] 189–213 (1994).

36. Boeki Hoken Ho [Trade Insurance Law], 68 GENKO HOKI SORAN [COMPILATION OF EXISTING LAWS] 2381–2433. The law covers trade and investment risks against (1) credit risk (bankruptcy and default); and (2) noncommercial risk (expropriation, war, incontrovertibility and nonperformance).

Investment Guarantee Agency (MIGA),[37] and by carrying out its plan within the framework of international cooperation. In order to accomplish this, insurance operations shall be managed and the Special Account for Trade Insurance shall be improved to alleviate user (insuree) burdens, and appropriate financial measures should be taken by the government to enhance these changes.[38]

Finally, to supply new funds to the developing countries, Japan must make use of its Official Development Assistance (ODA) and other official funds. Promotion of a comprehensive economic policy that links direct investment, export credits, and promotion of imports from developing countries is vital. If necessary, a law, perhaps entitled the "Basic Law for Foreign Assistance," should be enacted, and other relevant laws and institutions should all be appropriately amended. These would include the Law for the Overseas Economic Cooperation Fund, the Export-Import Bank of Japan Law, the Japan International Cooperation Agency Law.

IV. CONCLUSION

The globalization of the Japanese economy has generated many unprecedented experiences for Japan. Since the range of activities encompassed by the Japanese economy has expanded, Japan must modify its domestic legal system to better harmonize industrial activities with the international society. Japan must help to promote the economic development of other nations and of the world and must contribute to the creation and improvement of international legal systems to minimize friction and protectionism. In so doing, the government, corporations and people of Japan must have an awareness of law based on the international sensibility of competition in economic symbiosis.

37. Masao Sakurai, *Tasukokukan Toshi Hōsho Kikan: Hosho Gyomu no Genkyo* [*Multilateral Investment Guranatee Agency: Actual Operations*], KOKUSAI SHOJI HŌMU [INTERNATIONAL BUSINESS LAW] 269–73 (1991).

38. MITI TRADE INSURANCE COUNCIL, INTERIM REPORT, 1988 (1988); MITI, INTERIM REPORT, 1991 (1991).

FAIRNESS, RECIPROCITY, AND RETALIATION AFTER THE WTO: SECTION 301 OF THE U.S. TRADE ACT OF 1974

Hyuck Soo Yoo

I. INTRODUCTION

After seven long years of talks, the Uruguay Round was successfully concluded December 15, 1993, establishing the new World Trade Organization (WTO), which entered into force on January 1, 1995. The WTO Agreement not only considerably expands the subject matter of the General Agreement on Tariffs and Trade (GATT), but also strengthens international rules governing trade. The WTO also contains integrated dispute settlement mechanisms, which will repair many defects of past GATT procedures. It is expected, especially in Japan, that these enhanced procedures will render unnecessary many unilateral measures, like Section 301 of the U.S. Trade Act of 1974.

In contrast, there has been no change in the basic U.S. position regarding unilateral measures. Super 301 was already revived by executive order in March 1994 and the U.S. Trade Representative reportedly will not oppose any attempts by the U.S. Congress to maintain or strengthen Section 301 and Super 301 in the draft bill implementing the results of the Uruguay Round.[1] The United States does not believe that the new GATT/WTO dispute settlement procedures will require either the abolishment of Section 301 or any fundamental changes to U.S. statutes. Also, the United States still takes the position that it is entitled to invoke the threat of retaliatory measures under Section 301 concerning problems outside the scope of the WTO Agreement.[2]

The United States, creator of the GATT, has vigorously supported the Uruguay Round, sometimes by resorting to threats of retaliation through Section 301.[3] Therefore, it can be said that Section 301 has contributed, to some degree, to the

---

1.   NIHON KEIZAI SHINBUN, Aug. 3, 1994, at 2.

2.   INDUSTRIAL STRUCTURE COUNCIL, 1994 REPORT ON UNFAIR TRADE POLICIES BY MAJOR TRADING PARTNERS: TRADE POLICIES AND WTO at 240, 258–59 (1994).

3.   19 U.S.C. § 2411 (1988) (originally enacted as Omnibus Trade and Competitiveness Act of 1974, § 301, 102 Stat. 1988, 1108 (1975)).

successful completion of the Uruguay Round. On the other hand, Section 301 has been seen as the most notorious device the United States uses to pursue fairness claims against other trading partners, and Section 301 has garnered much criticism from irritated foreign nations, especially Japan.

Notwithstanding these criticisms, some American scholars praise the high profile role of Section 301,[4] while others defend the use of Section 301 by arguing that its use is "a lesser evil" than alternative means.[5] For example, Judith Bello stated:

> [n]onetheless, the track record of Section 301's use in the period from 1985 to the present demonstrates that the judicious application of such unilateral measures can have substantial trade liberalizing effects, to the benefits of governments, producers, exporters, and consumers around the globe.[6]

W.J. Davey said:

> I believe that Section 301 and the GATT multilateral trading system can and will be able to coexist. Indeed, I think that past judicious uses of Section 301 have actually strengthened the multilateral trading system. Admittedly, the mere existence of the broad 301 powers will always cause uneasiness for fear that they will be misused, but I do not believe that it is unreasonable to hope that they will generally be exercised responsibly.[7]

In contrast to the opinions above, others, both outside and inside the United States, insist that Section 301 represents a serious threat to the multilateral trading system established under the GATT. The Japanese government and many scholars have strongly criticized United States employment of Section 301. The most representative opinion of Japan is expressed in the *1994 Report on Unfair Trade Policies by Major Trading Partners: Trade Policies and WTO*, which is an inventory of alleged unfair trade policies and measures of Japan's twelve major trading partners, including the United States, and published by the Industrial Structure Council, the official advisory body to the Minister of International Trade and Industry:

---

4.   J. Bello, *Section 301 of the U.S. Trade Law: Champion of Market Liberalization*, in TRADE LAW OF THE EUROPEAN COMMUNITY AND THE UNITED STATES IN A COMPARATIVE PERSPECTIVE 111 (P. Demaret et al., eds. 1992); W.J. Davey, *Comment: Section 301 and its Effect on the Multilateral Trading System*, in Bello, *id.* at 167.

5.   R.E. Hudec, *Thinking About the New Section 301: Beyond Good and Evil*, in AGGRESSIVE UNILATERALISM 113 (J. Bhagwati ed. 1990). It should be noted that Professor Hudec considers that Section 301 is essentially inconsistent with GATT obligations of the U.S., but that it can be justified as "legitimate disobedience" in certain cases. His is a very different view from that of Bello and Davey, who argue that Section 301, as such, is a GATT legal policy tool.

6.   Bello, *supra* note 4, at 131.

7.   Davey, *supra* note 4, at 167.

[u]nilateral measures are fundamentally at odds with the basic principles of the GATT/WTO. The free trade system is based on the premise that each country obeys the existing international rules that regulate the system, even if those rules are not perfect. Disputes should not be resolved by unilateral threats. When there are problems, countries should use and work with the existing international rules, thereby enabling the further development of the free trade system.[8]

These points of view manifest strikingly contrasting opinions concerning Section 301. They raise the issue of the viability of the coexistence of Section 301 and the GATT multilateral trading system after WTO comes into effect. If coexistence is achieved, under what conditions can it occur? Moreover, is Section 301 a danger to the multilateral trading system, and should it be abolished unconditionally? These points will be explored briefly here.

a. Preliminary Observations

When considering unfair trade laws, it will be useful to distinguish at the outset between "offensive" and "defensive" unfairness claims, as has been done by Professor R.E. Hudec.[9] Although these two types of claims have many common elements and share the same problems as found in the fairness claim, it must be noted that they arise from completely different situations, and are made by a different set of actors for quite different purposes.[10]

The offensive unfairness claim deals primarily with claims against foreign firms allegedly employing unfair business practices, such as receiving subsidies or dumping. These are dealt with by antidumping duty (AD) and countervailing duty (CVD) laws. The core content of offensive unfairness claims derives from a concept known as fair competition. The normative assertion behind the idea of fair competition is that merit should determine business outcome. Competition will be fair if no competitors have advantages not based on their own merit.[11]

Due to both the misuse of AD/CVD laws and their "capture" by forces of protectionism,[12] offensive unfairness claims have been the subject of considerable controversy during the past two decades. If, as indicated by Professor Bhagwati,[13]

---

8.   Industrial Structure Council, *supra,* note 2, at 236.

9.   R.E. Hudec, *Mirror, Mirror on the Wall: The Concept of Fairness in United States Trade Policy* (Revised Text of a Paper Presented at the 1990 Annual Meeting of the Canadian Council of International Law, Oct. 19, 1990).

10.   *Id.* at 19.

11.   *Id.* at 5.

12.   *See* N.D. Palmeter, *The Capture of the Antidumping Law,* 14 YALE J. INT'L L. 182 (1989).

13.   J. BHAGWATI, PROTECTIONISM 33 (1988). On the other hand, J. Tumlir has insisted that one of the intellectual failures at the founding of GATT was that it has never fully and rigorously stated the case for free trade. Put another way, the premise of economic theory that free trade is the best policy for all countries, was reduced to free trade is a good policy *only* if all countries practice it. J. Tumlir, *International Economic Order and Democratic Constitutionalism,* 34 ORDO 75 (1983). Regardless of these opposing points of view, there

the GATT system is essentially based not on an economic theory of free trade for one country but on a cosmopolitan version of the theory of free trade requiring adherence to free trade everywhere, the idea of fair competition seems a precondition to an international trade system. Moreover, although outside the aim of this article, it should be noted that AD/CVD laws have depoliticized trade affairs in domestic politics.[14]

In contrast to the above, "defensive unfairness" claims pertain to actions which foreign governments take to protect their markets from U.S. competition.[15] These claims arise primarily in the context of Section 301, which provides two kinds of action. First, Section 301 orders the U.S. Trade Representative (USTR) to attack all foreign trade barriers which violate U.S. legal rights. Second, Section 301 then requires the USTR also to attack "unreasonable" trade barriers. Unreasonable trade barriers are defined as "foreign acts, policies, or practices which, while not necessarily in violation of, or inconsistent with, the international legal rights of the U.S., are otherwise unfair and inequitable."[16] Although not in violation of any U.S. legal right, these acts are nevertheless to be attacked simply because the United States considers them unfair. While the effects of AD/CVD laws are limited to the U.S. domestic market, Section 301 attempts to attack the root of foreign actions which the United States considers to be unfair.

This defensive unfairness claim rests mainly on the criteria of "unreasonableness" and seems to have a different normative basis than those of the offensive unfairness claim. The "unreasonable" standard has the appearance of a fairness claim, but the fundamental notion behind it is "reciprocity." It is evident that Section 301 (d)(3)(D) directs the USTR to consider reciprocal opportunities in the United States for foreign nationals and firms for the purpose of determining whether any act, policy, or practice is unreasonable.[17]

There is no doubt that underlying the defensive unfairness claim and Section 301 there exists a tension between two different notions of reciprocity, as indicated by Bhagwati.[18] These two types of reciprocity are GATT's "full-reciprocity" goal (i.e., a broad balance of market-access obligation by the contracting parties), and its procedural practice of "first-difference reciprocity" in negotiation (i.e., tariff cuts are to proceed via bargaining that reflects a balance of perceived advantages at the margin). In light of the huge U.S. trade deficit, the U.S. Congress calls for unilaterally reopening the question of overall market access balance.

The tension between these two kinds of reciprocity was expected to be managed by the concept of "nullification or impairment," in particular, the "nonviolation" complaint track in the dispute settlement procedure in the GATT. Whether the GATT could actually have accomplished this task depended upon the

---

is no doubt that, as Bhagwati has indicated, the GATT system has been based on the premise that free trade must apply to all.

14. Hyuck Soo Yoo, *Kokusai Tsusyōhō ni okeru Kōsei Fukōsei Bōeki no Kubun no Rezon-Detor* [*Raison d'Être of the Distinction Between Fair and Unfair Trade in International Trade Law*], 41 ECONOMIA 38 (1991).

15. Hudec, *supra* note 5, at 2.

16. 19 U.S.C. § 2411(a).

17. 19 U.S.C. § 2411(d)(3)(D).

18. Bhagwati, *supra* note 13 , at 35–36.

formation of a "community consensus" about cases where measures have a reciprocity-upsetting effect, based on the common law approach of case-by-case adjudication.[19] This needs two further conditions. First, the creation of "community consensus" requires enough cases to develop the substantive content of a "nullification or impairment" doctrine. Second, the GATT Contracting Parties must agree to hand over some kind of lawmaking authority to panels for them to judge cases in which measures have a reciprocity-upsetting effect.[20] The past history of the GATT, however, shows a reverse pattern. A common law approach regarding a "nonviolation" complaint has not been developed to any great extent, and the United States has adopted an increasingly aggressive attitude toward reciprocity-upsetting measures to U.S. interests. Moreover, Section 301 goes beyond reciprocity in that the United States attempts to limit access to its markets according to the reciprocal degree of access afforded to the markets of other countries. The United States pursues its domestic economic aims by reshaping foreign markets and inducing other countries to adopt the U.S. regulatory scheme.[21]

II. THE OUTCOME OF THE URUGUAY ROUND

In order to consider the possibility of coexistence between Section 301 and the multilateral trading system after the WTO comes into effect, it is necessary to examine the result of the Uruguay Round to the extent that it is related to Section 301.

a. U.S. Complaints About the GATT System

It is widely known that one of the principal motives of Section 301 is to strengthen the GATT as a multilateral trading system. Its main objective is, on the one hand, to contribute to trade liberalization by providing the U.S. executive with leverage in negotiations on the elimination of unfair practices of foreign countries and, on the other hand, to preserve domestic support for a free trade system through the elimination of unfair foreign trade practices which impede U.S. exports. To achieve this objective, the United States has assigned itself the role of a "world trade policeman," guarding and watching foreign practices in international trade.[22]

U.S. complaints about the GATT system can be clarified first by admitting that the content of the GATT's substantive rules of conduct are very narrow. The subject matter of the GATT is limited to the area of trade in goods, and, even within that area, there are many loopholes. From the early 1980s, the United States has strongly argued for beginning negotiations on an extention of the GATT rules to

---

19. R.E. Hudec, *Retaliation Against "Unreasonable" Foreign Trade Practices: The New Section 301 and GATT Nullification and Impairment*, 59 MINNESOTA L. REV. 500–02 (1975).

20. R.E. Hudec, *Dispute Settlement*, *in* COMPLETING THE URUGUAY ROUND: A RESULT-ORIENTED APPROACH TO THE GATT TRADE NEGOTIATIONS 200 (J.J. Schott ed. 1990).

21. U.S. TRADE BARRIERS: A LEGAL ANALYSIS 374 (R. Grabits & A. von Bogdandy eds.) (1991).

22. *Id.*

cover international transactions in trade in services, the regulation of foreign investment, and the protection of intellectual property.

Both the formation of rules to close many loopholes in the GATT and an extension of the GATT rules to cover the new issues require other countries consent. Due both to the nature of the new issue areas and to the various national philosophies and economic systems, it was difficult to find a compromise between the free market ideology of the United States and the ideology of other countries.[23] Moreover, the GATT amendment procedures largely have not been functioning. By using Section 301, the U.S. established both the agenda for trade liberalizing negotiations and the fairness standard based on "reciprocity" to assess unilaterally foreign countries' practices.

The second U.S. complaint pertains to the procedural mechanism for applying substantive rules to particular controversies, in particular the ineffectiveness of the GATT dispute settlement process. In practice, the Article 23 procedure has many defects, with the consensus principle in the GATT dispute settlement procedure at the core of the problem. The defendant must consent to the creation of a panel, the adoption of a panel's ruling and the decision of retaliation by the Council. In short, the consensus principle enables the country in error to block any GATT action at any stage of the dispute settlement process.

It should be noted that although the U.S. perception that the GATT dispute settlement procedure required a large revision and U.S. efforts to make the GATT dispute settlement procedures effective were both right and legitimate, Section 301 went beyond the issue of GATT adjudication. Section 301 does not require the USTR to respect U.S. obligations under the GATT, and the causes of action under Section 301 are so broad that it is probably beyond the causes of action permitted under the GATT, even in nonviolation cases. Consequently, as Professor R.E. Hudec argued, the only possible excuse for Section 301 was one of "justified disobedience" to make the existing dispute settlement mechanism function more effectively.[24]

b.   The Outcome of the Uruguay Round

As mentioned above, the Uruguay Round expanded and strengthened international rules governing trade. In its scale and comprehensiveness, the Uruguay Round is far different from the rounds of the past. Moreover, there were 125 participants in the final stage of the Uruguay Round, a large number of which had become Contracting Parties to the GATT since the start of the Round. Consequently, the WTO Agreement, the product of the Uruguay Round, will extend the expanded and strengthened international rules to more countries definitively and unconditionally, which is wholly different from the "Code Conditionality" of the Tokyo Round. It is unnecessary to repeat the details of the results of the Uruguay Round, but two points must be noted which relate to the question of the balance in overall market access which is the main background to the introduction of Section 301.

---

23. *Id.* at 391.
24. Hudec *supra* note 5.

The first question is to what extent the new text, *Understar.ding on Rules and Procedures Governing the Settlement of Disputes* (DSU), will contribute to achieving balance in overall market access. Certainly, the DSU not only repairs many past GATT dispute settlement procedural defects, but also has a broader scope of application, in comparison to the GATT.

In this regard, the following two points are important. First, the DSU concentrates on procedural, not substantive, aspects. As Professor Jackson pointed out, the "rule-oriented" direction of the GATT dispute settlement process is maintained, and many problems for which Section 301 attempts to correct are not covered by rules.[25] There is therefore no change in the "nullification or impairment" doctrine which was clearly confirmed by the panel report regarding the Uruguay Case. Its report said:

> [i]n its view impairment and nullification in the sense of Article 23 does not arise merely because of the existence of any measure; the nullification or impairment must relate to benefits accruing to the contracting party "under the Agreement."[26]

Moreover, a tendency in the "rule-oriented" direction was strengthened by the DSU. If we read through the new text of the DSU carefully, the DSU goes further toward "legalization" of the dispute settlement process, which gives weight to the violation cases.[27] This means that in the WTO, whether an act, policy or practice of a member is unfair or not will be judged mainly according to agreed pro-GATT rules. Therefore, one principal motive of Section 301, closing GATT loopholes, will remain.

Second, the DSU preserves the provisions which deal with nonviolation cases and elaborates on the practices of these cases.[28] As previously mentioned, the past history of the GATT dispute settlement procedure shows that there have been few cases of nonviolation, so jurisprudence regarding "nonviolation" complaints has not developed to any great extent. Although the possible field of application of the nonviolation procedures is extremely broad because of the wording of Article 23, in practice, nonviolation complaints have been successful only if the impairment of a tariff binding could be proved.[29] The nonviolation provision has contributed to situations in which reciprocity, in the sense of balance of trade concessions, cannot be ensured. After 1980, several cases appeared[30] and the panel began expanding nonviolation cases to a broader range of cases in which the tariff bindings are of little or no importance, but these are not yet recognized by the Contracting Parties.

---

25. JOHN H. JACKSON, INTERNATIONAL LEGAL PERSPECTIVES ON JAPAN–NORTH AMERICAN ECONOMIC FRICTIONS 12 (1994).

26. BISD, 11th Supp., 95.

27. Understanding on Rules and Procedures Governing the Settlement of Disputes in the Uruguay Round Final Act (Apr. 15, 1994).

28. *Id.* art. 26.

29. *See Bhagwati, supra* note 13, at 35–36.

30. *See* A. von Bogdandy, *The Non-Violation Procedure of Article XXIII:2, Its Operational Rationale*, 26 J. OF WORLD TRADE 95 (1992).

It would be premature to expect these provisions to function in the future, mainly because of dependence upon the capacity of the WTO to construct a "community consensus" regarding cases in which measures have a reciprocity-upsetting effect. Although the "reasonable" standard exceeds the range of the nonviolation case, the activation of latter cases in the future could affect the use of Section 301 by the United States.[31]

The introduction of the Trade Policy Review Mechanism (TPRM) in 1989 is also important to the present issue. The purpose of the TPRM, as stated in the Mid-Term Review agreement, is "to improve[d] adherence by all contracting parties to GATT rules, disciplines and commitments, and hence to the smoother functioning of the multilateral trading system," through "achieving greater transparency in, and understanding of, the trade policies and practices of contracting parties." To do so, contracting parties regularly appreciate and evaluate "the full range of individual contracting parties' trade policies and practices and their impact on the functioning of the multilateral trading system."[32]

The TPRM certainly is not intended "to serve as a basis for the enforcement of specific GATT obligations . . . or to impose new policy commitments on contracting parties."[33] On the other hand, the scope of the TRPM's review mechanism clearly goes beyond the question of rule consistency or legality.[34] To understand the expected role of this mechanism, it is useful to recall the 1982 EC challenge of the Japanese trading and economic structure. The EC wanted to increase its share of imported manufactured goods, but Japan's resistance and counterclaim blocked this case from making any progress.[35] Although it is not clear which direction the TRPM will take in the near future, first of all, it provides an arena where a number of complaints of trade barriers which are not regulated within the WTO system can be presented. Second, it can be expected to carry out three distinct, though perhaps incomplete, functions: a review function, a corrective function and a creative function.[36] Lastly, the "legitimizing effect" of the GATT report which notes criticism expressed by other parties, should not be underestimated.[37]

---

31. *Id.*

32. Function of the GATT System, Decisions of Apr. 12, 1989, arising from action taken by the Uruguay Round Trade Negotiations Committee, BISD, 36th Supp. 403.

33. *Id.*

34. JACKSON, *supra* note 25, at 12.

35. For details on this event, *see* Marco C.E.J. Bronckers, *A Legal Analysis of Protectionist Measures Affecting Japanese Imports into the Economic Community - Revisited, in* PROTECTIONISM AND THE EUROPEAN COMMUNITY 116 (E.L.M. Volker ed., 2nd ed. 1987).

36. For the three functions of supervision within the framework of international economic organizations, *see* G.J.H. van Hoof & K. de Vey Mestdagh, *Supervisory Mechanisms in International Economic Organization, in Supervisory Mechanisms, in* INTERNATIONAL ECONOMIC ORGANIZATIONS 3 (P. van Dijk et al., eds. 1984).

37.   Petros C. Mavroidis, *Surveillance Schemes: The GATT New Trade Policy Review Mechanism*, 13 MICH. J. INT'L L. 410 (1992).

III. SECTION 301 AFTER THE WTO

As mentioned above, Section 301 provides for two kinds of action, the first regarding enforcement of U.S. rights and the second a response to unreasonable trade practices. To explore the viablility of the coexistence of Section 301 and the new WTO system, it is important to bear in mind the distinction between these two facets. The former challenges the enforcement mechanism of the GATT/WTO, while the latter relates to the international trade system rule making process.

a. Section 301 and the Enforcement of U.S. Rights

In this case, the application of Section 301 takes place in an area where internationally agreed upon rules exist. Thus, the main problem is one of procedure. This facet of Section 301 has the potential to violate GATT/WTO in two ways. Under Section 301, the USTR shall make the determination whether a foreign practice violates the rights of the United States or otherwise denies benefits to the United States under any trade agreement within thirty days after the conclusion of the dispute settlement procedure, or eighteen months after the initiation of investigation, whichever is first.[38] These time limits are too tight for the WTO procedures to determine whether the foreign practice is actionable and if so, what action (if any) will be taken in response. Further, although Section 301 does not require the president and the USTR to ignore the ruling of the Dispute Settlement Body of the WTO, there is the possibility of retaliation by the United States without prior authorization by the Contracting Parties.

Whether retaliation without prior authorization by the Contracting Parties violates the GATT depends on concrete circumstances. According to prevailing opinion,[39] although the existence of multilateral control prevents its members from undertaking unilateral measures, this rule presupposes the normal function of the multilateral system. Certainly past GATT dispute settlement procedures have had serious defects in the ability of participating parties to block the establishment of a panel and/or block the adoption of panel reports.

The DSU of the WTO considerably improves these defects, however, especially under the "negative consensus" rule in which the panel process proceeds automatically unless a consensus to stop the proceeding is achieved. Consequently, only unanimous opposition can block establishment of panels, adoption of panel reports, and authorization of retaliatory measures for failure to implement Dispute Settlement Body recommendations. Moreover, the new text adds Article 23.1, which says:

> [w]hen members seek the redress of a violation of obligations or other nullification or impairment of benefits under the covered agreements or an impediment to the attainment of any objective of the covered agreements,

---

38. 19 U.S.C. § 2414 (a)(2)(A).

39. P. Pescatore, *The GATT Dispute Settlement Mechanism: Its Present Situation and its Prospects*, 27 J. WORLD TRADE 5 (1993).

322 Trilateral Perspectives on International Legal Issues

they shall have recourse to, and abide by, the rules and procedures of this Understanding.[40]

It should be further noted that it was none other than the United States which strongly supported the adoption of new text of the DSU, in particular the introduction of the "negative consensus" rule. It was even said that "agreement on the new text was reached on the assumption that the U.S. had agreed to resort to the Uruguay Round Understanding to deal with international trade disputes, and not rely on unilateral trade measures."[41]

Given the above mentioned improvements of the new text of the DSU and a sort of "estoppel" effect of the United States commitment in the Uruguay Round negotiation, it is doubtful that the United States can preserve Section 301 in this facet. If the United States preserves Section 301, the tight time limit should be loosened, and the potential for premature retaliation must be amended to provide the president and the USTR the discretion to act in a way that is consistent with U.S. international obligations. At the same time, the United States must remember that it will be more difficult in the future to justify "restor[ing] in a negative way the symmetry of the initial positions through the countermeasures."[42]

The critical point with Section 301 is that the U.S. Congress authorizes the executive to take action against foreign practices, regardless of the consistency of that action with the international obligations of the United States. For example, Article 19 of the Subsidies Code provides that no specific action can be taken except in accordance with international obligations of the U.S..[43] Put another way, the main U.S. defense of Section 301 is not the denial of the potential conflict between Section 301 and the WTO, but rather that market liberalization and the elimination of unfair foreign barriers will benefit all GATT parties.[44]

b. Section 301 and the Response to "Unreasonable" Trade Practices

Here the focus is on extension of Section 301's scope to trade practices beyond internationally agreed upon standards. The fairness standard under Section 301, which is essentially a reflection of the U.S. *de lege ferenda*, is likely to force its own free market ideology on other countries.[45] This relates directly to the inadequacy of the development of the international norms about the definition of "unfairness." This is therefore not a question of legality or lawfulness, but one of the dimensions of the "legitimacy" of the U.S. demand for fairness. That is to say, these measures try to change the *status quo* and plan the realization of "equity *praeter legem*" which exceeds the structure of positive international law. Faced with this situation,

---

40. *See supra* note 27.

41. *See* Palitha T.B. Kohona, *Dispute Resolution Under the World Trade Organization–An Overview*, 28 J. WORLD TRADE 39, 42 (1994).

42. *See* Zoller, *Self-Help in International Trade Disputes*, in PROCEEDINGS OF THE AMERICAN SOCIETY OF INTERNATIONAL LAW 39 (1991).

43. Agreement on Interpretation and Application of Articles 6, 16, and 23 of GATT, BISD 26 Supp. (1980).

44. E. Grabits & A. von Bogdandy, *supra* note 21, at 391.

45. *Id.* at 393.

the partner country, in the event it does not immediately confront U.S. measures or submit a persuasive and effective counter-plan, will face retaliation by the United States.[46]

The rule-creating function of Section 301 has two elements, the first of which is the formulation of rules to close GATT/WTO loopholes. The "unreasonable" standard goes beyond even the nonviolation cases, so retaliation of this kind is independent of the GATT/WTO dispute settlement process. Secondly, it has increasingly focused on trade barriers which are not regulated within the GATT system, e.g., the larger scope of the Structural Impediment Initiative between the United States and Japan.

In favor of this facet of Section 301, Davey argued:

[s]o long as the U.S. invokes it only to encourage other countries to follow open market, free trade policies that are followed by the U.S., Section 301 is unobjectionable. In the absence of an agreement, the U.S. should not have to open its markets to those that will not reciprocate. Indeed, to the extent that the U.S. goal is to promote a more open trading system, the use of Section 301 in these situations seems appropriate, and it is arguable that its use has in fact promoted more open markets. It would be nice if there were multilateral agreements on all aspects of trade, but since there are not, the U.S. use of Section 301 to promote reciprocal open markets can be viewed as desirable.[47]

As Davey said, in the absence of an agreement, the United States should not have to open its markets to those that will not reciprocate. Economic actions beyond legal limitations on sovereign freedom are still governed by the basic right of states to act unilaterally so long as those acts do not negatively affect other countries.[48] As long as the United States forces other countries to open their markets, however, she must have a legitimate basis for her demand. If the U.S. does not have such a basis, given the recognized value of diversity of domestic economic systems in contemporary international law, her demand may infringe on economic sovereignty of the partner country.

At the same time, all unilateral measures like Section 301 should not be condemned immediately and unconditionally as a violation of present law or charged as illegitimate. This is because even though various countries in a general sense recognize the need for interest by the entire international community, the multifaceted domestic situation makes the formation of legislation a difficult task. Now that a multilateral international institution like the WTO has been formed, however, "the reversed domain" theory, which allows a state to do anything not forbidden by international law, and the suppressive unilateral measures based on such a precept, should be limited. The issue remaining is which types of unilateral measures, as judged by either their purpose or their methods, promote the common interest of the international commercial community.

---

46.   Yamamoto Soji, *Ippōteki Kokunai sochi no Kokusaihō Keisei Kinō* [*The Law-Creating Function of Unilateral Measures in International Legal Order*], 33 SOPHIA HŌGAKU RONSHŪ 64 (1990); KOKUSAIHŌ [INTERNATIONAL LAW] 65 (1994)

47.   Davey, *supra* note 4, at 170.

48.   E. Grabits & A. von Bogdandy, *supra* note 21, at 394 n. 117.

The answer is neither obvious nor immediate. It may be tentatively said that the purpose of a unilateral measure should be to promote a more open trading system. Second, a demand should be equitable and applicable to almost all other countries. Last, a unilateral measure is not justified by a goal to eliminate unfair trade practices. As long as the use of Section 301 constitutes the extraterritorial application of U.S. domestic law, the United States is required to observe the principles and rules of international jurisdictional law.[49] If these conditions are satisfied, Section 301 can be a novel way to generate international norms or can act as a catalyst to form multilateral agreements. However, Section 301 may not be superior to the formation of a multilateral agreement by the parties directly concerned.

Because of U.S. concern over loss of competitiveness in locomotive industries and its demands for markets to be opened on a sector-by-sector basis, the utility of Section 301 in protecting U.S. economic interests in new issues may have frequently outweighed its significance as a tool to promote a more open trading system. Moreover, Section 301 is a product of a period in which U.S. enthusiasm for the benefits and advantages of multilateralism had faded. This is why Section 301 has been considered to be a tool available only to a country as economically strong as the United States.

IV. CONCLUSION

It is not the aim of this chapter to insist that Section 301 is a protectionist tool. Section 301 was and still is the byproduct of the GATT system's shortcomings and U.S. domestic politics.   U.S. trading partners should endeavor to raise the international minimum standard without demands by others,[50] for now is not the time to hide unjustified protectionist practices behind a shield of claimed sovereignty.

The question of how to achieve trade liberalization is another matter. The creation of international standards ultimately requires the consent of a number of countries wishing to liberalize trade barriers. Given the expansion of substantive law and the increase in the degree of commitment by other trading partners, especially the more advanced developing nations, it can be expected that the gap in the overall degree of market access among main Contracting Parties will be

---

49. *See* Note, *The Thai Copyright Case and Possible Limitations of Extraterritorial Jurisdiction in Actions Taken Under Section 301 of the Trade Act of 1974*, 23 L. & PUB. POL'Y INT'L BUS. 725 (1992).

50. From this perspective, the position of the Industrial Structure Council regarding the definition of "unfairness" seems to be a passive one. *See The Industrial Structure Council, supra* note 2. It approaches the question of "unfairness" from the perspective of "rule-based" criteria. Rule-based criteria means that a decision whether the policies and measures are fair or unfair should be based on existing international standards and rules. Regardless of Japan's praiseworthy attitude toward multiculturalism, it seems too passive and inflexible given that Japan has now become a global economic superpower. Japan has to provide the substance of the definition of unfairness and engage in talks with her trading partners, especially the United States, with confidence to create international minimum standards.

narrowed dramatically. The United States should address the function of trade policy politics in the multilateral trade system.

* * *

After this Conference ended, the Uruguay Round Agreement Act, which implements the final result of the Uruguay Round, was adopted by Congress on December 23 after extensive discussions.[51] The Act preserved both the tight time line of Section 301 procedures[52] and the potential for premature retaliation[53] It strengthened Section 301 by clarifying the scope of the president's authority to take action,[54] and added services to the provisions on the toleration of anticompetitive business practices.[55] It also added new language on the use of Section 301 to address intellectual property rights violations and on the ability of the USTR to address a country's failure to comply with an agreement.[56] Also, it provides a formal mechanism by which USTR is to enforce U.S. rights under the Subsidies Agreement.[57] Finally, the Uruguay Round Agreements Act codified the provisions of the Omnibus Trade and Competitiveness Act of 1988.[58]

After the enactment of Uruguay Round implementation legislation, USTR stated its opinion on the Section 301 in the *1995 Trade Policy Agenda and 1994 Annual Report* as follows:[59]

[s]ection 301 should be an even more effective tool as a result of the Uruguay Round agreements. The new rules under this multilateral agreement mean more foreign unfair practices can be challenged before WTO dispute settlement pannels.

From this statement, regarding the enforcement of U.S. rights, the U.S. government seems to be planning to use Section 301 in combination with WTO dispute settlement procedures more in the future than it has in the past. This means that Section 301 could be used as "domestic legal authority for WTO-authorized retaliation"[60] in many cases. However, it should be noted that the statutory provisions of Section 301 would force the president and the USTR to act in a way that is inconsistent with U.S. international obligations in some cases.

---

51. Uruguay Round Agreements Act, PL 103–465, Approved Dec. 8, 1994, 108 Stat. 4813.

52. 19 U.S.C. 2414(a)(2).

53. 19 U.S.C. 2411(a).

54. 19 U.S.C. 2411(a)(1) & (b)(2).

55. 19 U.S.C. 2411(d) 930(B)(i)(IV) & (F)(ii).

56. 19 U.S.C. 2411(d)(3)(B)(i)(II) & (III), and (F)(i).

57. 19 U.S.C. 3571(d).

58. 19 U.S.C. 2420.

59. USTR *1995 Trade Policy Agenda and 1994 Annual Report of the President of the United States on the Trade Agreements Program*, 95.

60. Judith H. Bello and Alan F. Holmer, "The Post-Uruguay Round Future of Section 301," 25 L. & Pol'y Int'l Bus.1307(1994).

Regardless of the broadened scope of the WTO, some of the issues that give rise to trade friction do not fall under the rules of the WTO. Among these are environmental issues, which have been considered to be the most important, as well as many other regulatory issues including competition policy and labor standards. Both globalization of production and the decreasing competitiveness of the U.S. in global markets will cause the U.S. to become more and more concerned about "competitive fairness" and "unreasonable" trade practices.[61] It is too early to judge whether the U.S. attempt to attack these issues through a combination of negotiation and threat of retaliatory measures under Section 301 will be as successful in the future as it has been in the past. This will depend not only on the legitimacy of U.S. demands and the satisfaction of the above–mentioned conditions as a way to generate international norms, but also on the effectiveness of the WTO. In any case, there will be no change in the fact that Section 301 is a tool which can only be used by a country which is as economically strong as the United States.

---

61. Gezefeketekuty, the new trade agenda (Group of Thirty, Occasional Papers 40, 1992) 1–5.

PART IV
ADJUSTMENT AND DEVELOPMENT OF PROCEDURES FOR THE SETTLEMENT OF INTERNATIONAL DISPUTES

| SUMMARY

Michael K. Young[*]

The fourth panel focussed on recent developments and trends in international dispute resolution with particular emphasis on designing dispute resolution institutions that states will actually use to resolve disagreements. The discussion ranged from relatively nonintrusive dispute resolution processes—and even steps states might take before a potential disagreement evolves into a dispute—to formal, binding adjudication, such as that undertaken by the International Court of Justice. The panelists also discussed a broad spectrum of potential disputes, from trade disputes to disagreements over actions that affect the environment to disputes over borders and territory.

At the outset, each panelist briefly summarized the salient points of his or her paper. Professor Young began by pointing out that the theory of international dispute resolution is woefully underdeveloped, especially when compared with the work that has been done on domestic dispute resolution, and that the international community might learn much from the work of scholars and practitioners on the domestic front.

Four aspects of international dispute resolution deserve particular analytical attention. First, most multilateral dispute resolution treaties focus principally on resolving disputes. In actual practice, however, countries spend considerable time avoiding disputes and, if disagreements are unavoidable, managing the consequences of those disputes in order to minimize any adverse political and economic effect. More attention must be directed towards regularizing and institutionalizing those avoidance and management devices and techniques.

Second, the international community must develop dispute resolution devices that are more often used than those that currently exist. Much evidence suggests that countries are more likely to resort to dispute resolution processes when they have some say in the design and selection of the particular process used to address their dispute, and when they have some role in devising the actual solution to the dispute.

Third, most multilateral dispute resolution agreements force a dispute through a series of processes, progressing from less intrusive techniques (e.g., mediation and

---

* The contribution of Jason Schwartz as Reporter for this session is gratefully acknowledged.

conciliation) to more intrusive mechanisms (e.g., binding arbitration and adjudication), until the dispute is resolved. However, the nature and characteristics of disputes vary dramatically, and not all disputes resolution processes are equally well suited to the resolution of all different kinds of disputes. The characteristics of the dispute must be well suited to the characteristics of the dispute resolution process in order to achieve meaningful, lasting, efficient, and effective solutions. Rigid, linear, lockstep procedures are highly unlikely to fit all the different kinds of disputes that arise among states, and thus are unlikely to commend themselves to disputants.

Fourth, under even the most optimistic scenario, international legal rules are unlikely to be developed with sufficient specificity and consensual agreement within the foreseeable future to allow coverage of all possible problems that can arise among countries. Accordingly, rather than focussing exclusively on the dispute at hand, it is important to consider how countries can develop patterns of mutual peaceful interaction that allow them to address the myriad problems certain to arise among them.

Professor Young concluded by suggesting that the Experts' Report on Dispute Resolution of the 1991 Experts Meeting of the Conference on Security and Cooperation in Europe (CSCE)—and the so-called Valletta Mechanism first developed in that report, both of which were adopted by the CSCE Ministers in Berlin that same year—are worth further study in this regard. That report appears to make at least some rudimentary attempt to address some of these concerns and to devise a mechanism that builds on these fundamental understandings.

Professor Irish also focussed on the need to devise dispute resolution mechanisms suited to the needs of the parties. She initially examined binding arbitration and adjudication, noting that they lead to a binding result, as opposed to conciliation, mediation and good offices, which do not. Even at that, however, adjudication at the international level is significantly different than at the domestic level, and can be made even more different by the parties themselves. For example, internationally, jurisdiction and enforcement depend on consent and are not automatic as in a domestic system. Moreover, while the parties can choose to make the results binding, in many cases they may prefer that the results be nonbinding. Advisory opinions of the International Court of Justice (ICJ), while authoritative and influential, are decidedly not binding. In other cases, the parties may want the decision to be "binding," but not actually enforceable, and thus may decide to omit any penalty mechanisms or agree that the penalty mechanisms will not be binding. Such is the case, for example, with the NAFTA side agreements on labor and environment.

In the case of binding arbitration or adjudication, the parties give up substantial control over both process and substance. Accordingly, they may prefer some other mechanism that allows them more input into the process and the subsequent decision. Mediation and conciliation may be appropriate choices in these circumstances. Such ongoing control may serve to reduce the tensions in the conflict. At the same time, law, even in the international sphere, is a public phenomenon—rules are social. Regardless of the interests of the disputing parties, the international community has an interest in a public record that establishes and clarifies international rules. These various needs must be balanced against each other when deciding how best to resolve disputes.

Professor Saiki then addressed the issue of dispute settlement in the context of trade. She focused on the current WTO dispute settlement mechanisms, particularly their most notable feature, the panel proceedings. The function of a panel is to assist the contracting parties or the Council in discharging their responsibilities in dispute settlement. In the past, panel reports had no legal force until adopted by the Council. This allowed the parties to the dispute to participate fully in all aspects of the decisionmaking process. Under the new mechanisms in the WTO, this has changed radically. Panel reports will be adopted automatically unless the contracting parties decided unanimously to the contrary. This, along with the standing appellate body that will hear appeals from panel cases, will give the proceedings a much more judicial flavor. The automaticity of adoption is particularly significant because it reduces the political dimension of the debate about adoption. Furthermore, the appellate body, unlike the panel, has no mediatory role to play. All these changes will create a much more adjudicatory style process and fundamentally alter the delicate combination of political and adjudicatory aspects under the old dispute settlement scheme.

Whether the new WTO dispute settlement procedures will function successfully depends largely on the political will of the contracting parties. Of course, under general principles of international law, sovereign nations are not obliged to solve their disputes at all. Nevertheless, the underlying premise of the WTO dispute resolution procedures is that parties will at least make good faith attempts to address seriously and resolve disputes, where possible. The system will operate best if the parties can reach agreement on the dispute resolution method to be used. Such agreement can be given in advance in a comprehensive manner—as stated in Article 36, paragraph 2 of the statute of the ICJ or the dispute settlement agreements of the GATT and WTO. In cases of adjudication, the parties to the dispute must be willing to implement the judgment. In short, once a state has entered into an agreement that either putatively resolves the dispute or that commits the dispute to some adjudicatory resolution, the state must have the political will to respect that agreement and abide by its terms.

Professor Iwasawa continued the discussion of dispute resolution under the multilateral GATT/WTO framework. He first noted that like many other disputes, trade disputes can be divided into two distinct groups. In the first type of dispute, the complaining party alleges a violation of law by the other party. This dispute might be characterized as a legal dispute. In the other type of dispute, more political in character, one party tries to create new legal rules or seek equitable changes in the existing law.

In a dispute of the first kind—legal disputes—there is no reason why the WTO dispute settlement mechanism should not be used. Japan has benefited most from the multilateral GATT/WTO framework and therefore has special responsibilities and interests in promoting multilateralism in the WTO. Although the WTO procedures have been judicialized to a great extent and have come very close to adjudication, Japan is likely to use the WTO procedures more vigorously in the future. In North America, while the NAFTA mechanisms may be used to resolve disputes involving GATT-related rights, it is doubtful that parties will choose this course once the adoption of WTO panel reports becomes virtually automatic.

WTO panel procedures, on the other hand, are not well suited for resolving political disputes in which the parties seek to change the law. There are nonviolation complaint procedures in the WTO, but they have been limited and are narrow in scope. It is also very difficult to succeed procedurally in these complaints.

The question is whether we can establish a bilateral mechanism to deal with these kinds of disputes, especially those involving the United States and Japan. Professor de Mestral has proposed that the establishment of dispute settlement procedures between Japan and North America be modeled after Chapters 18 and 19 of the U.S.-Canada Free Trade Agreement. A panel would be established to review the domestic administrative and legislative situations and give advice regarding changes necessary to facilitate trade.

The primary task of the panel would be fact finding. If the terms of reference of the panels are limited to fact finding, the proposed procedures may work since an examination of the facts by an independent body may be helpful to ease tension.

However, disputes between Japan and North America often relate to differences in the two societies' cultures and values. Setting up a panel in this context is more difficult than in the context of a dispute between the United States and Canada, which share many social and cultural values. Although panels under Chapter 19 have been successful and have not been divided by the nationalities of the panelists, bilateral panels between Japan and North America are more likely to be divided in such a way. One might appoint panelists who are not nationals of either party, but it is unlikely that Japan is prepared to accept a third party's assessment of matters relating to Japanese culture.

If the terms of reference of panels include policy recommendations, moreover, it is unlikely that bilateral panel procedures will work. North America and Japan are not prepared to entrust important policy considerations to panels consisting of three individuals. Conciliation in international law has not been successful as a means of dispute settlement because states have been reluctant to entrust politically sensitive disputes to such panels. But mediation-type dispute settlement procedures, such as the good offices of the director general of the GATT, may work. One example is the successful resolution of the copper dispute between the EC and Japan, which used the good offices.

Mr. Highet then turned the attention of the panel to the ICJ, noting first and foremost that the future of the ICJ is up to the states. The ICJ is powerless to direct itself. Its future depends entirely on the kind of cases that states are prepared to bring. Like most litigants, states are generally disinclined to bring cases unless they believe the dispute is likely to be resolved in their favor. States may also be reluctant to engage the Court if its decision might constrain their scope of action in foreign affairs.

The result of these constraints is that only one out of the twelve pending cases was brought by special agreement. The others were all commenced by application. There is not a single case before the court today involving chambers. A list of seven judges who theoretically comprise an environmental chamber exists, but no state is required to select them, and to date, no state has. Moreover, even though it was made legal three years ago, no state has sought intervention in any case pending before the Court. (At the same time, on the positive side, it is worth noting that no state has refused to appear before the Court in several years).

Because of these constraints, the range of issues and countries that have never been part of the Court's docket is considerable. Recent cases brought before the Court have involved matters of constitutional interpretation, protection, genocide, maritime issues, and use of force. Nevertheless, in its entire history, the Court has never had an international trade case and only one human rights case (and that was thirty years ago). It has only just had its first environmental case. Japan, China, and Russia have never had cases before the court. Only if attitudes of nations around the world change will the range and extent of the Court's docket increase sufficiently to fulfill its initial promise.

Following the panelists' presentations, Professor Brown Weiss inquired whether international law scholars could develop a typology of international disagreements based on subject matter (e.g., environment, trade, human rights, labor, arms control) and then map that against the type of dispute resolution process to which states are willing to commit the dispute (e.g., dispute management, conciliation, mediation, adjudication). From this we might be able to identify the characteristics of a dispute that make it well-suited or ill-suited for a particular type of dispute resolution process.

The trade regime has headed towards adjudicatory mechanisms, for example, and the environmental field rarely has compulsory dispute settlement procedures. What do we learn from this? Is this because of the characteristics of the problem? Is there a maturation process? Or is it culturally determined? What factors can explain the differences and can we indeed think of a matrix for these kinds of issues?

Professor Irish responded that much may be determined by the state of development of the law in a particular area and the political dynamic underlying international relations in that area. In the case of the Law of the Sea Treaty, for example, there were reasons why the parties wanted a complex system with many alternatives in many situations.

Professor Iwasawa added that while international lawyers tend to adopt a linear approach to dispute settlement and tend to think that judicial settlement is the ultimate form of dispute resolution, we should instead recognize that there are two different types of disputes and thus different methods of dispute settlement should be employed in each of these two cases. In the case of legal or justiciable disputes, in which one party invokes the law and the third party is expected to apply the existing law, adjudication is certainly appropriate.

However, all this assumes the existence of hard law that can be applied. If the law is "soft" in the particular area, then other means of dispute settlement may be more appropriate. Such is also the case for political or nonjusticiable disputes in which a party wants changes in the law. For these kinds of dispute, a dynamic means of dispute settlement is necessary. The third party is not expected just to apply the law, but to come up with new policy recommendations and adjust the argument of the parties. So what needs to be distinguished is the difference between static means of dispute settlement in which the third party applies the law and dynamic means of dispute settlement in which the third party proposes equitable terms of settlement. Thus, we should not simply distinguish between adjudicatory and nonadjudicatory means. Conciliation is often considered as a nonadjudicatory means, but when we think of dispute settlement in this way, conciliation is similar to arbitration because the conciliation commission consists of three individuals, and tends to be static. Although it is a nonadjudicatory means of dispute settlement, it is not very appropriate for political disputes in which a state party seeks equitable changes in the law. For this kind of dispute, a softer dispute settlement means such as mediation by a third party that has political influence perhaps might be more appropriate.

Professor Young added that while the idea of trying to categorize disputes based on a range of variables was intriguing, it was, based on his experience in the U.S. Government and his involvement in many disputes, very hard to do honestly and accurately. Moreover, at a minimum, one must add another matrix to the grid, that of what the parties desire to achieve by submitting the dispute to some resolution process. Sometimes the goal is to increase the certainty of the body of law; other times simply to stop the parties from shooting at each other; and still other times the aim is to create a relationship where the parties develop habits, a culture, and institutions that facilitate continued interaction of a much broader array of issues. It is clear that different dispute resolution processes are not only suitable for resolving different kinds of disputes, but different processes also lead to different kinds of subsequent patterns and dynamics of interaction between the disputing parties.

Finally, Mr. Highet opined that the scope of action of states, when viewed from the perspective of their international legal obligations, was often circumscribed, and that it was necessary to consider this factor when evaluating the methods selected for resolving disputes. The world is filled with existing legal obligations to go before a court in many existing treaties, which do not comprehend or forecast every kind of dispute that can arise later. Just because a dispute becomes deeply political does not mean it is not a legal dispute. What needs to be considered is not whether the dispute is political, but rather what are the concerned governments likely to negotiate toward in terms of settling hot political disputes and, more important, whether they are bound by previous treaty commitments to resolve the dispute in a particular way. Examination of the surrounding legal regime is as important as examining the nature of the dispute.

Following upon Professor Young's presentation, Professor Koga asked whether it might be possible to create a mechanism in multilateral treaties which prevents disputes. Professor Iwasawa noted the existence of many provisions about consultation in the GATT. He also noted that the NAFTA, unlike the GATT and

WTO, also requires prior review and notification of amendments to law in certain circumstances. All this suggests that dispute avoidance techniques can be developed through treaties and that this idea should receive considerably more attention.

Panelists and audience then turned their attention to the WTO dispute settlement procedures, focusing particularly on the extent to which the processes had been made much more judicial in character. Mr. Trooboff first questioned when, if ever, the appellate procedure would be desirable and whether the new process would be workable in practice. Ms. Saiki responded first with an appeal to history. She noted that the GATT dispute settlement mechanism has evolved over the years as necessary, benefiting from experiences with individual cases. In this respect, the creation of the appellate body as stipulated in the WTO charter is quite revolutionary. But, she opined, the relevant question is not whether a two-tier system or one-tier system is more desirable, but rather whether the system would maintain its credibility. If so, then the parties would use it, if not, they would not.

Professor Iwasawa added that while some believe it was not a good idea to extensively judicialize the procedures, it was a political necessity. The U.S. agreed to a provision restraining unilateral measures on the condition that dispute settlement procedures were streamlined and judicialized. He also added that he believed it was, in principle, a good idea to make the procedures more predictable and the results more certain. Positive changes include the clear establishment of the right to a panel, the introduction in the panel of procedures of a stricter time frame, and the virtually automatic adoption of panel reports.

He questioned the wisdom of automatically authorizing countermeasures, however. Though this too was a political necessity, countermeasures are problematic from both economic and political perspectives. Economic theory asserts that the economic welfare of a state is reduced by taking countermeasures. Countermeasures also usually affect sectors other than the target sector and do not necessarily bring about an increase in exports in the target sector. Accordingly, we should not aim for the automatic authorization of countermeasures, but rather for the strengthening of the surveillance of implementation.

Professor Iwasawa also questioned the wisdom of establishing an appellate process within the WTO. While appellate review in itself is not objectionable, the extremely broad basis on which appeals are allowed may well result in virtually all cases being appealed. Professor Young added that domestic political imperatives might require governments to appeal virtually all adverse rulings. If the prediction holds true that most, if not all, cases will be appealed, then one might legitimately question the wisdom of establishing an appellate body.

Professor Jackson agreed that appellate review is not necessarily the optimal procedure and may be somewhat cumbersome, but that it is nevertheless a worthwhile tradeoff for eliminating the blocking of panel reports. If every case is indeed appealed, it may be prudent for the members to reevaluate the appellate process and collapse the two procedures into one, as long as the prohibition against blocking panel reports remains intact.

On the other hand, the appeal process may have other advantages in the long run. The appellate body panel is composed differently than the initial panel. Most important, there is more continuity—a group of seven that sits in panels of three and has four-year terms on a staggered basis. This may aid in the development of a coherent, consistent WTO jurisprudence that will expand free trade.

Professor Ida questioned whether, with the increasing shift to adjudication and automatic adoption, the political will of the states to resolve trade disputes will become increasingly less important. Ms. Saiki responded that while the roles of adjudication and legal rules are closely linked, they are not identical. It is not necessarily true that the more automatic, judicial, and precise the dispute settlement mechanism we institute, the more likely the dispute will be solved. Sovereign states act—and will continue to act—with their individual benefit in mind. Although we may pretend to "impose" something on a country which is apparently unwilling to implement a decision, nevertheless the international community does not have any means to enforce its will. In the end, the political will or intent of the party concerned is critical. Even a beautifully organized judicial system will not obviate the need for countries to possess the political will to comply with the agreed upon rules.

Mr. Fairley turned attention to the International Court of Justice again and questioned its efficacy as a dispute resolution forum. He noted that eleven of the twelve cases currently before the World Court are by application, and therefore at least one party is involuntary before the Court. Moreover, at the moment, no great powers are before the court, save as unwilling respondents. Does all this suggest, he asked, that, while the Court may be the Rolls Royce of international dispute settlement in terms of image, it may lack the reliability in terms of efficacy and authoritativeness in the long term?

Mr. Highet responded that some of the involuntary cases are less involuntary than one might think, though some are very involuntary. Moreover, even reluctant defendants are brought to the Court pursuant to their own previous agreement. For example, the United States is party to approximately eighty existing treaties that contain jurisdictional provisions which, if invoked by the other state, would result in an involuntary, though consensual, appearance in the Court. Mr. Highet also opined that the fact that the medium-sized powers appear to be the aggressors at the moment has no real bearing on the value of Court's decisions—it only indicates that many medium states are now seeking redress in the Court. He also predicted that states will increasingly come to the Court to seek recourse for their disputes, though others disagreed.

RECENT DEVELOPMENTS IN THE INTERNATIONAL COURT OF JUSTICE

Keith Highet

I. INTRODUCTION

In order to assess correctly the state of international dispute resolution today, one must consider first and foremost the work of the International Court of Justice. Various other tribunals have made, and continue to make, substantial contributions. These include courts of arbitration, the U.S./Iran Claims Tribunal, mixed arbitral panels, specialized regional courts, or institutions such as the International Centre for Settlement of Investment Disputes (ICSID), the North American Free Trade Agreement (NAFTA), the European Free Trade Association (EFTA), or the World Trade Organization (WTO). At the same time, for a variety of reasons, each of the other tribunals' contribution to international law has been limited in important ways.

Most notably, the U.S./Iran Claims Tribunal in The Hague has produced an immense body of work over the past dozen years. The contribution that the Tribunal appears to have made to the field of international law, however, is uneven, and by its very nature—that of handling largely "mixed" claims—the Tribunal is not principally concerned with questions of public international law. The entire process is affected by the fact that the United States and Iran are conducting between them a carefully arranged bilateral dispute settlement procedure which is (if not *sui generis*) at least confinable to its unusual origins and its particular facts.

The special nature of the work of the Tribunal, and the uneven quality of its achievement, is further underscored by the fact that it has found it necessary to operate mainly through three chambers with different compositions. Thus the U.S./Iran Tribunal will likely be remembered for the uniqueness of its origin and the important role that it has served.

The U.S./Iran Tribunal has produced an enormous number of decisions. Yet, sadly, there are only a handful of current cases in the more general universe of public international arbitration. ICSID is still striving to live up to its promise. The two most recent cases (*Vacuum Salt Products Limited v. Ghana* and *Scimitar Exploration Limited v. Bangladesh*) have been dismissed for want of jurisdiction. The Canada/France arbitration of 1992 on the maritime boundary extending from St. Pierre and Miquelon has not met with wide acclaim. The controversial United Nations Tribunal for War Crimes in the former Yugoslavia has only recently[1] announced the institution of its first case. The new EFTA Court has not yet begun to function. The United Nations Tribunal on the Law of the Sea and the related adjudicatory bodies contemplated by Part XV of the United Nations Convention on the Law of the Sea have of course not yet commenced operations.

Although the work of the Court of Justice of the European Community proceeds on a solid and energetic basis, its relevance is limited to the steady development of the internal constitutional and administrative law of the European Community and does not as such subtend generally applicable rules of public international law. Further, although the general principles of human rights law that have been so ably elucidated by the regional human rights courts in Europe and in Latin America constitute perhaps the most interesting legal developments afoot outside the work of the International Court (indeed, the work of the International Court has scarcely ever involved human rights issues), the work of these tribunals—though concerned with general principles—is somewhat circumscribed in context to the underlying treaty partners. One might note here in passing that there has been little if no activity in multilateral dispute resolution on an institutional basis in the Far East. It forms a stark contrast to the lengthy and also uneven history of international tribunals in Europe and the Americas. States bearing the leadership role in the new East, one of the most effective and powerful of which is surely Japan, ought to create regional adjudicatory institutions that would parallel at least the human rights tribunals that have been agreed upon and functioning for many years in the Americas and in Europe.

The panels of arbitration contemplated by the NAFTA have not yet commenced operations. Their activity in the various important fields in which they will function will be watched with great interest by scholars and practitioners in the three countries involved and elsewhere. The NAFTA model is one that will certainly be folowed increasingly as other barriers to interdependency are slowly dissolved over the decades to come. The new WTO Dispute Settlement Body (DSB) is also coming into use. The usefulness of these institutions and mechanisms, and the predictability and consistency of their decisions, however, will only be assessable after years of experience.

It is therefore to the International Court of Justice that one turns almost instinctively in order to determine the nature of the international law issues being litigated today and any novelties in the manner in which they are brought before the third-party decisionmaker. If this seems unfair, one has only to reflect on a few basic elements. It is important to remember the difference between the International Court of Justice and its predecessor, the Permanent Court. The latter actually

---

1.   Nov. 8, 1994.

functioned for just seventeen years (1922–1939). The present Court has functioned continuously for forty-seven years (1947–1994), more than two and one-half times as long as the Permanent Court. (Some also tend to forget that the League of Nations had ended by the time when the United Nations had reached the ripe age of twenty, i.e., in 1965.)

The present Court has in addition inherited the benefits of the jurisprudence of its predecessor. Legal scholars and practitioners alike tend to assimilate the case law of the one with the case law of the other. And why not? Under the design of the Statute, whose design itself[2] has so substantially persevered since the 1930s, there is precious little difference between the decisions of one court and the other. Under Article 38 of the Statute, all such decisions are reserved to the universe of "judicial decisions."[3] Although no decision binds a state other than the parties to it,[4] all decisions flow from and are built upon one another.

It is insufficiently appreciated that the weight given by the Court to its own previous decisions in matters of legal principle, and the importance naturally attached by the judges to finding and applying international law consistently with the Court's prior decisions, are far more powerful elements guiding the development of international law than are the principles related to more narrow issues of the binding quality of a decision, or its *res judicata* effect. Too often scholars and commentators focus on the "binding force" established by Article 59 of the Statute; too seldom is the great size of the Court's achievements since 1922 recognized. What we are presented with when we contemplate the past jurisprudence and present practice of the Court is a judicial record spanning nothing less than sixty-five years, or three generations (1922–1939 and 1947–1994).

In the nineteen years from 1922 to 1940, the Permanent Court decided thirty-one contentious cases and rendered twenty-seven advisory opinions.[5] In the forty-seven years between 1948 and 1994, the International Court rendered fifty-five decisions in contentious cases and handed down twenty-one advisory opinions.[6] The total number of international law decisions by both the Permanent Court and its successor is eighty-six, and forty-eight advisory opinions—some 134 judicial

---

2. With the notable exception of the advisory jurisdiction, which was not expressly contained in the original Statute of the Permanent Court but was added in the 1929 Statute revision process; *see* S. ROSENNE, THE LAW AND PRACTICE OF THE INTERNATIONAL COURT 651–52 (1965).

3. Para. 1(d).

4. Statute, art. 59.

5. It also delivered 25 procedural or interlocutory Orders.

6. It has also rendered some 71 Orders. For the purposes of this calculation, the two separate cases in Nuclear Tests (Austl. v. Fr.; N.Z. v. Fr.), 1974 I.C.J. 253, 457 (Dec. 20) and in Fisheries Jurisdiction (U.K. v. Ice.; F.R.G. v. Ice.), 1973 I.C.J. 3, 49 (Feb. 2) (Jurisdiction of the Court) and 1974 I.C.J. 3, 175 (July 24) (Merits) are treated as if they had been one case (as has South West Africa (Eth. v. S. Afr.; Lib. v. S. Afr.), 1962 I.C.J. 319 (Dec. 21) (Preliminary Objections); 1966 I.C.J. 6 (July 18) (Second Phase)).

determinations of great complexity, and an average of more than two per year, year in and year out.

Moreover, the importance of the canon of the Court's principled decisions becomes more important with every passing year. Other tribunals or courts of arbitration may come and go, but the Court continues uninterruptedly. Arbitration tribunals are created, exist for a few years, and disappear, leaving their awards behind like the smile of the Cheshire cat.[7] This is even true of arbitration tribunals that function in an institutional context, such as ICSID.

The other courts that could vie for public acceptance or scholarly weight equivalent to those of the International Court—the European courts, or the international human rights courts —function in fields that are less centralized and less likely to pronounce general rules of international law and in more limited relationships than the International Court. Most important of all, their decisions and judgments do not appear to build upon themselves in the same manner that the decisions of the International Court have built upon those of the Permanent Court. They do not possess the same continuity and never will. Even if the new future Tribunal on the Law of the Sea can expect to establish a canon of judicial decision equivalent to that of the International Court, it will always be seventy years shorter in experience, and it will have to start from the beginning.

Is the nature of international dispute resolution altering? Where does the Court stand in 1994, and how have its present jurisprudence and case load changed over the past few years?

a. Cases Before the Court

The cases now before the Court include the following, listed in chronological order from the date of their commencement:

1) *Aerial Incident of July 3, 1988 (Islamic Republic of Iran v. U.S.)*, Application filed on May 17, 1989 [the *Airbus* case];[8]
2) East Timor *(Portugal v. Australia)*, Application filed on February 22, 1991 [the *East Timor* case];

---

7.   "' . . . I wish you wouldn't keep appearing and vanishing so suddenly [said Alice]: you make one feel quite giddy!' 'All right,' said the Cat; and this time it vanished quite slowly, beginning with the end of the tail, and ending with the grin, which remained some time after the rest of it had gone." CARROLL, ALICE'S ADVENTURES IN WONDERLAND 74–75 (1965 ed., 1867).

8.   Oral proceedings in this case have been, as of September 1994, postponed indefinitely. It is now hoped that the parties may be working toward an agreed settlement of liability and compensation in the matter and an ultimate withdrawal of the proceedings by Iran (in the same manner as that in which the Nicaragua (Compensation) case was withdrawn only a few years ago).

3) *Maritime Delimitation between Guinea-Bissau and Senegal (Guinea-Bissau v. Senegal)*, Application filed on March 12, 1991 [the *Guinea-Bissau* case];[9]

4) *Maritime Delimitation and Territorial Questions between Qatar and Bahrain (Qatar v. Bahrain)*, Application filed on July 8, 1991 [the *Qatar-Bahrain* case];[10]

5) *Questions of Interpretation and Application of the 1971 Montreal Convention Arising from the Aerial Incident at Lockerbie (Libyan Arab Jamahiriya v. U.K.)*, Application filed on March 3, 1992; and *Questions of Interpretation and Application of the 1971 Montreal Convention Arising from the Aerial Incident at Lockerbie (Libyan Arab Jamahiriya v. U.S.)*, Application filed on March 3, 1992 [referred to jointly as the *Lockerbie* cases];[11]

6) *Oil Platforms (Islamic Republic of Iran v. U.S.)*, Application filed on November 2, 1992 [the *Oil Platforms* case];

7) *Application of the Convention on the Prevention and Punishment of the Crime of Genocide (Bosnia and Herzegovina v. Yugoslavia (Serbia and Montenegro))*, Application filed on March 20, 1993 [the *Genocide* case];

8) *Gabcikovo-Nagymaros Project (Hungary/Slovakia)*, notified on July 2, 1993 [the *Danube* case]; and

9) *Land and Maritime Boundary between Cameroon and Nigeria (Cameroon v. Nigeria)*, Application filed on March 29, 1994 (and supplemented by

---

9. It should be noted that the Guinea-Bissau case is not active; indeed, the matter may be close to a pre-litigation settlement. "There is another case on the Court's list in which negotiations are active, the Court having been asked by both Parties to grant a delay in the procedures to enable the negotiations to continue in order to see whether it might be possible to reach a settlement." Report of President Sir Robert Jennings to the General Assembly, U.N. Doc. A/48/PV.31, 2–4 (1993), delivered on Oct. 15,1993, *reprinted in* 88 A.J.I.L. 421 (Apr. 1994), [hereinafter *Jennings Report*].

10. A decision in the Preliminary Objections and Admissibility phase of this case was rendered on July 1, 1994 (1994 I.C.J. 112), but was of an indeterminate nature; it did not, as such, decide one way or the other as to the court's jurisdiction. In accordance with the terms of the judgment the parties have until Nov. 30, 1994 "to take action" . . . "to submit to the Court the whole of the dispute." (*Id.* at 127, para. 41 (3) and (4) [*dispositif*]). The Court's Judgment of July 1 is therefore somewhat interlocutory in nature. Nevertheless one may well expect to see this case, probably transformed from its present form by the addition of Bahrain as a full party, in the court from the end of 1994 for the next several years. (The writer is Counsel to Bahrain in this case.)

11. For the purposes of this discussion, the two parallel Lockerbie cases will be considered as one case.

Application filed on June 6, 1994) [the *Land and Maritime Boundary* case].[12]

One request of great importance for an advisory opinion has been filed. Presented in the form of a resolution of the World Health Assembly of May 14, 1993, it is the *Legality of the Use by a State of Nuclear Weapons in Armed Conflict* (Request for Advisory Opinion), request transmitted on August 27, 1993 [the *Nuclear Weapons* case].   Resolution WHA46.40, adopted by the World Health Assembly on May 14, 1993, requested the court to render its advisory opinion on the following question: "In view of the health and environmental effects, would the use of nuclear weapons by a State in war or other armed conflict be a breach of its obligations under international law including the WHO [World Health Organization] Constitution?"

In addition, a contentious proceeding [the *NATO* case] was filed on March 16, 1994, by Yugoslavia (Serbia and Montenegro) against the member states of NATO, relying on acceptance of jurisdiction of the court under Article 38 (5) of the Rules of Court[13] and challenging the decision by NATO to employ armed force in the form of air strikes in the event that the Bosnian Serb forces did not put their heavy weapons around Sarajevo under U.N. control or remove them twenty kilometers from Sarajevo.[14]   No official announcement has been made that jurisdiction has been accepted and that the NATO case has been entered into the Court's list.[15]   It is to be expected that the case will not be accepted and thus will not see the light of day.

---

12.   *See* I.C.J. Communiqué No. 94/13 of June 20, 1994, reporting that the Additional Application was to be treated as an amendment to the initial Application "so that the Court could deal with the whole as one case."

13.   Stating as follows: "5) When the applicant State proposes to found the jurisdiction of the Court upon a consent thereto yet to be given or manifested by the State against which such application is made, the application shall be transmitted to that State.   It shall not however be entered in the General List, nor any action be taken in the proceeding, unless and until the State against which such application is made consents to the Court's jurisdiction for the purposes of the case."

14.   *See* I.C.J. Communique No. 94/11 of Mar. 21, 1994.   "Yugoslavia applies to the International Court of Justice in a dispute with the Member States of NATO in respect of the threat of use of force by NATO."

15.   This case is unusual in that it is the first instance of a "unilateral arraignment" or "come-on" application in a number of years.   (It is an *invitatio ad forum prorogatum*.)   *See* L. Gross, *Compulsory Jurisdiction Under the Optional Clause: History and Practice*, THE INTERNATIONAL COURT OF JUSTICE AT A CROSSROADS 19, 57 (L. Damrosch ed., 1987) (Table 12) [hereinafter CROSSROADS].

b. Cases Recently Decided

Six other cases that are important to this analysis have recently been decided by the Court. They are the following:

12) *Land, Island and Maritime Frontier Dispute (El Salvador/Honduras)*, Application by Nicaragua for Permission to Intervene [the *Nicaragua Intervention* case];[16]

13) *Arbitral Award of July 31, 1989 (Guinea-Bissau v. Senegal)* [the *Arbitral Award* case];[17]

14) *Land, Island and Maritime Frontier Dispute (El Salvador/ Honduras; Nicaragua intervening)* [the *El Salvador/Honduras* case];[18]

15) *Certain Phosphate Lands in Nauru (Nauru v. Australia)* [the *Nauru* case], Preliminary Objections, Judgment; [19]

16) *Maritime Delimitation in the Area between Greenland and Jan Mayen (Denmark v. Norway)* [the *Jan Mayen* case];[20] and

17) *Territorial Dispute (Libyan Arab Jamahiriya/Chad)* [the *Libya-Chad* case].[21]

A seventh case, *Maritime Delimitation and Territorial Questions between Qatar and Bahrain* (Jurisdiction and Admissibility),[22] was decided in July 1994 but is as yet indeterminate in its effect since it is actually not much more than a declaratory judgment on certain issues, but not one, as such, on jurisdiction. Its effect is (at the time of writing) merely to encourage the parties to complete the process by which the matters in dispute would be laid before the court.[23]

c. Cases Recently Settled

Two other cases have also been settled by the parties in the last year or two in an important manner and are therefore also of considerable significance. They are:

---

16. 1990 I.C.J. 92 (Sept. 13). The writer served as Counsel to El Salvador in this matter.

17. 1991 I.C.J. 53 (Nov. 12). The writer served as Counsel to Guinea-Bissau in this matter.

18. 1992 I.C.J. 351 (Sept. 11). The writer served as Counsel to El Salvador in this matter.

19. 1992 I.C.J. 240.

20. 1993 I.C.J. 38 (June 14). The writer served as Counsel to Norway in this matter.

21. 1994 I.C.J. 6 (Feb. 3). For a current general discussion of the case-load before the Court as it stood in the autumn of 1991, *see* Highet, *The Peace Palace Heats Up: The World Court in Business Again?* 85 A.J.I.L. 646 (1991) and, for a more current and more authoritative comment, the *Jennings Report, supra* note 9.

22. 1994 I.C.J. 112 (July 1). *See supra* note 10.

23. The writer has served as Counsel to Bahrain in this matter.

Passage Through the Great Belt (Finland v. Denmark), Application filed on May 17, 1991, discontinued by Order of July 29, 1991 [the *Great Belt* case]; and *Certain Phosphate Lands in Nauru (Nauru v. Australia)*, Application filed on May 19, 1989, discontinued by Order of September 13, 1993. This latter was the sequel to the *Nauru* (preliminary objections) case mentioned above. Both it and *Great Belt* were brought under optional clause declarations.

Prior to this, the case of *Border and Transborder Armed Actions (Nicaragua v. Honduras)*[24] had been withdrawn, but only after its initial phase on jurisdictional and admissibility had been fully litigated. Of course, *Military and Paramilitary Activities in and against Nicaragua (Nicaragua v. U.S.)* had, in its reparations phase, been withdrawn on September 12, 1991.[25] Finally, the *Airbus* case, as noted above, is on the verge of settlement—as may also be the *Guinea-Bissau* maritime delimitation case.

II. NEW TRENDS

The directions in which the Court now seems to be headed are of course governed solely by the states that seek to make use of it or are brought before it. The Court itself, it must always be recalled, has no independent role whatever in the formation of innovations in international law or the development of new rules. Its duty is to "decide in accordance with international law such disputes as are submitted to it";[26] it controls neither the type of disputes that are submitted to it nor the manner in which they are submitted.

This is why a current review of the Court's work is so rewarding: it can assist in identifying the trends and tendencies that are in essence given to the Court by the actions of the states that use its services. The disputes reveal, through their subject matter, the issues that states are now bringing before the Court. By examining the manner in which those disputes are brought, we can detect trends in the way in which the functioning of the Court's process is perceived by the members of the international community. The major trends are of two different sorts: procedural and substantive. It is well to consider procedural developments first, since they inform the substance of the cases being considered.

---

24. The case was discontinued by order of the Court on May 27,1992 (1992 I.C.J. 222) after renunciation of the claim by Nicaragua on May 11, 1992; this of course had followed the Court's Judgment of Dec. 20, 1988 (1988 I.C.J. 69) by which the Court found that it had jurisdiction to entertain Nicaragua's Application under Article XXXI of the American Treaty of Pacific Settlement (the Pact of Bogotá) and that the Application was admissible.

25. This was accepted by the President's Order of Sept. 26, 1991, recording the discontinuance of the proceedings and the case's removal from the list.

26. Statute, art. 38. The Court of course possesses other duties under the Charter and the Statute, such as to render advisory opinions when requested under Article 96 of the Charter (Statute, art. 65) although that duty is not unqualified and is, indeed, discretionary (*see* the Memorial of the United States in the pending WHO matter).

One general caveat should be kept in mind: because of the rule of confidentiality that now attaches to the submissions and written proceedings of the parties to a case right up to the commencement of oral proceedings,[27] it is never possible to comment reliably on the content of pending cases.

This point is deceptively narrow but highly significant. One reason that the work of the International Court is not sufficiently well-known, and neither covered adequately by the press nor appreciated by the public, is clearly related to the fact that, as a general rule, the written proceedings before the Court are shrouded in relative mystery and that no one can have much of an idea of the content of pending cases until the beginning of the oral proceedings in the case—by which time it is only practical to assume that whatever public interest might once have been focused on the dispute referred to the court has evaporated.

The rule of confidentiality was obviously inherited by the Court from its institutional forebear, the Permanent Court. Arbitration also impairs the functioning and practicality of the right of nontreaty intervention under Article 62 of the Statute. It is difficult for a state to determine whether or not it actually has ". . . an interest of a legal nature which may be affected by the decision in the case, [so that] it may submit a request to the Court to be permitted to intervene." In cases brought by special agreement, their substance is detectable only by the traditionally generalized formulation of the question agreed for presentation to the Court. In cases brought by application, the only clue as to the issues is the printed application of the applicant (and not the response of the respondent) as transmitted to other states under Article 42 of the Rules.

Although many of the difficulties previously encountered by states in seeking to intervene in current matters (most notably illustrated by the aborted attempts of Malta and Italy to intervene in the *Tunisia/Libya* and the *Libya Malta Continental Shelf* cases) have been resolved by the judgment in the successful effort in 1990 of Nicaragua to intervene in the *Land, Island and Maritime Frontier Dispute* case,[28] the deleterious effect of the anachronistic rule of confidentiality on the ability of other states to determine whether or not they should attempt to exercise the right of intervention remains unaffected.

---

27. Article 53 of the Rules provides that:

"1. The Court, or the President if the Court is not sitting, may at any time decide, after ascertaining the views of the parties, that copies of the pleadings and documents annexed shall be made available to a State entitled to appear before it which has asked to be furnished with such copies.

"2. The Court may, after ascertaining the views of the parties, decide that copies of the pleadings and documents annexed shall be made accessible to the public on or after the opening of the oral proceedings."

28. Continental Shelf (Tunis./Libyan Arab Jamahiriya), 1981 I.C.J. 3 (Application [Malta] for Permission to Intervene, Judgment); Continental Shelf (Libyan Arab Jamahiriya/Malta), 1984 I.C.J. 3 (Application [Italy] for Permission to Intervene, Judgment); Land, Island and Maritime Frontier Dispute case (El Salvador/Honduras), 1990 I.C.J. 92 (Application to Intervene).

a. New Procedural Trends

Returning to the major areas in which trends in the court's work can be identified, let us first consider the procedural aspects.

(1) Applications, Not Special Agreements

The first point to be noted is that all but one of the present cases pending before the court have been brought by application under the optional clause or under compromissory clauses in treaties. Surely this contradicts the related view, often expressed in the 1980s,[29] that cases brought by application would eventually be supplanted by fully consensual litigation[30] under special agreements. Moreover, it was then predicted that most states would carefully select chambers of the Court in preference to going before the full bench.[31] It is obvious that this supposition is related to the key assumption that the cases would have been brought by special agreement as opposed to application, since only one case brought by application has ever been confided to a chamber.[32]

A more emphatic contradiction of such predictions could hardly have been imagined. Indeed, the recent trend since the 1980s has been precisely in the other direction. Much of this tendency is owed to the use of bilateral treaty provisions in treaties of friendship, commerce, and navigation, as well as otherwise questionable jurisdictional provisions in multilateral conventions, to found general jurisdiction

---

29. *See, e.g., Statement Concerning U.S. Withdrawal from the Nicaragua case*, Jan. 18, 1985, *reproduced as* Annex E to CROSSROADS *supra* note 15, at 472, 474–75: "We will continue to support the International Court of Justice where it acts within its competence—as, for example, where specific disputes are brought before it by special agreement of the parties." XXIV I.L.M. No. 1, at 246, 249 (January 1985). *See also* Press Statement of Oct. 7, 1985 (accompanying Department of State's termination of acceptance of compulsory jurisdiction, XXIV I.L.M. No. 6, at 1743, 1745 (Nov. 1985)).

30. *See* A. Sofaer, *Adjudication in the International Court of Justice: Progress through Realism*, the second Coudert Lecture delivered at the Association of the Bar of the City of New York on Dec. 15, 1988, *reprinted in* 44 A.B.C.N.Y. REC. 462, 481–82 (1989): " . . . why in any event should parties be deprived of the opportunity to appear before a selection of judges with whom they are comfortable, merely because they are together unrepresentative of the world's legal systems?" *See also* J.R. Stevenson, *Conclusion*, CROSSROADS *supra* note 13, at 459, 461: "For the future, it will be important to deal with the difficulty in obtaining confidence in the Court. In addition to obtaining the genuine consent of all parties to the Court's adjudication of a particular matter, one of the most constructive developments is the possibility of use of smaller panels of the Court, consisting of judges who clearly enjoy the confidence of all the parties." (Emphasis added.)

31. *See generally* Sofaer, *id.*, at 478.

32. *See infra* note 49.

against the respondent. The United States is unhappily the respondent in three such actions. (This amounts to one-third of the cases now pending before the court.)

Thus, in the *Airbus* case, Iran was apparently[33] proceeding against the United States under the provisions of the Chicago Convention of 1944,[34] the 1971 Montreal Convention, and the 1955 Treaty of Amity, Economic, Relations, and Consular Rights between the United States and Iran.[35] Libya is also proceeding against the United Kingdom and the United States under the Montreal Convention in the *Lockerbie* cases. In addition, Iran is again apparently proceeding under the Treaty of Amity against the United States in *Oil Platforms*.

It may be noted that, just as the United States incomprehensibly left in effect the 1956 Treaty of Friendship, Commerce and Navigation with Nicaragua during the 1982–1986 period of conflict in Central America that became resolved in the International Court's finding of jurisdiction in the *Nicaragua Jurisdiction* case[36] (which was indeed assisted by the existence of that Treaty[37]), so has the United States left in place the 1955 Treaty of Amity and Economic Relations between the United States and Iran. Iran has apparently amended its application in *Oil Platforms* so as to include the treaty as a source of jurisdiction, just as Nicaragua introduced the 1956 Treaty in its memorial (but not in its application) in that case—but without prejudice to its success on jurisdiction.[38] It remains to be seen whether the court will restrict any such application of friendship treaties in the future, particularly in the light of its decision eight years ago in the merits phase of the *Nicaragua* case.[39]

One other pending case, the *Genocide* case, is based on a compromissory clause contained in a multilateral convention. By way of contrast, the current cases based on optional clause declarations include the *East Timor*, *Land and Maritime Boundary*, and *Guinea-Bissau* cases. Only one case, the *Danube* case, is based on a special agreement.

The ninth and last current or pending case, *Maritime Delimitation and Territorial Questions between Qatar and Bahrain*, was sought to be based by the

---

33. *See generally* discussion in text supported by note 27 *supra*, concerning the effect of the Court's rule of confidentiality on the ability of third persons to make intelligent comments on cases pending before the Court which have not, however, reached the oral proceedings phase.

34. 15 U.N.T.S. 295.

35. 8 U.S.T. 899, T.I.A.S. 3853.

36. Military and Paramilitary Activities In and Against Nicaragua (Nicar. v. U.S.) 1984 I.C.J. 392 (Jurisdiction of the Court and Admissibility of the Application, Judgment) [hereinafter the Nicaragua Jurisdiction case].

37. Nicaragua Jurisdiction, note 36, at 426–29, paras. 77–83.

38. Nicaragua Jurisdiction, *id.*, at 426–27, paras. 77–81.

39. *See and contrast* Military and Paramilitary Activities In and Against Nicaragua (Nicar. v. U.S.) 1986 I.C.J. 14, 135–42, paras. 270–52 [hereinafter Nicaragua (Merits)].

applicant (Qatar) on a series of statements and undertakings possessing together the character of a treaty compromissory clause, in a manner similar to that in which Greece sought to found the jurisdiction of the Court against Turkey in the *Aegean Sea* case in 1978.[40]

A brief review of recent cases reveals that two out of the three discontinued actions (*Great Belt* and *Nauru*) were brought under optional clause declarations and one (*Border* and *Transborder Armed Actions*) under a treaty compromissory clause. Of the cases that came to a decision, two were instituted by special agreement, *Libya-Chad* and *El Salvador/Honduras*,[41] and two by application under optional clause declarations, *Arbitral Award* and *Jan Mayen*.

Conclusions drawn by this author in 1991 as to the eight cases then pending before the Court are equally applicable to the nine substantially new cases now pending before it:

> The first and most obvious conclusion is that, with one exception, these are all cases brought by application. Titles of jurisdiction vary from assertions of commitments made in the course of mediation to straight-forward reliance on the optional clause. They include a variety of treaty compromissory clauses, including friendship, commerce and navigation treaties and the Chicago Convention. But the fact remains that seven out of the eight have not been brought by special agreement.[42]

(2) New Constituency

In 1991 it was noted that new parties before the Court included Bahrain, Chad, Finland, and Qatar,[43] and that the Court then faced two South Pacific cases, two Middle Eastern ones, three African cases, and two Scandinavian ones.[44] In the past three years the geographical palette of the Court has been broadened even further, as it now includes Eastern Europe and the Balkans (*Danube* and *Genocide*) and central West Africa (*Land and Maritime Boundary*). Moreover, it should be noted that two states with cases still pending before the Court have suffered decisive setbacks. Libya, "one of the Court's most persistent customers,"[45] has now suffered a stinging defeat in its border dispute with Chad as well as a decisive rejection of

---

40. Aegean Sea Continental Shelf, 1978 I.C.J. 3. For further discussion, *see supra* note 10.

41. In which one must consider that the Nicaraguan Intervention case (*see supra* note 16) is incorporated.

42. Highet, *supra* note 21, at 649.

43. *Id.* at 652.

44. *Id.* at 653.

45. *Id.* at 652.

requests for provisional measures in the *Lockerbie* cases.[46] Guinea-Bissau's claim to nullify the arbitral award with Senegal has also been decisively rejected.

Iran has brought a new case, *Oil Platforms*, based on the same 1955 Treaty of Amity, Economic, Relations, and Consular Rights as it had added to the jurisdictional basis for the *Airbus* Application. Cameroon has now reappeared as a litigant before the Court for the first time since 1963.[47] New states before the Court include Nigeria, Hungary, Slovakia, Bosnia-Herzegovina, and the former Yugoslavia (Serbia and Montenegro). These are not precisely "great powers;" they are, rather, "middle powers." Some conclusions will be ventured concerning this trend.

(3) Full Court, Not Chambers

The fact that these cases have almost all been brought by application under either optional clause declarations or treaty compromissory clauses also means that it is the full Court that will be concerned with these matters, not a chamber of the Court.[48] This of course continues to reflect a position that is inconsistent with what had been so widely heralded in the 1980s as the likely future trend for the International Court: the use of chambers. The only case in history that was placed before a chamber and brought by application was the *ELSI* case in 1989,[49] which, because of the friendly relations between the litigants and the long history of the dispute, must be treated as anomalous.

In fact there is no case now pending before a chamber of the Court. Yet, on March 14, 1994, the Court extended until February 6, 1995, the mandate of the Members of the Chamber for Environmental Matters established by it in July 1993.[50] In his report to the General Assembly, President Jennings stated that:

> All of the cases at present on the [Court's] list are cases brought before the full Court. The Court has, however, found time to establish a Chamber for Environmental Matters, in the belief that some litigants might prefer a Chamber composed of Judges who have expressed a special interest in such matters. It may be useful, however, to make it clear that the establishment of this Chamber for Environmental Matters is in no way intended to suggest that cases involving environmental matters should go to that Chamber, or any other Chamber, rather than the full Court.[51]

---

46. *See* 1992 I.C.J. 3, 114 (Apr. 14).

47. Northern Cameroons (Cameroon v. U.K.), 1963 I.C.J. 15.

48. *See* Highet, *supra* note 21, at 649.

49. Elettronica Sicula S.p.A. (ELSI) (U.S. v. Italy), 1989 I.C.J. 15.

50. *See* I.C.J. Press Communiqués Nos. 94/10 and 93/20 and the *Jennings Report*.

51. *Id.* at 423.

Sir Robert continued:

> The jurisdiction of the full Court obviously comprehends environmental
> matters, as indeed it comprehends any other question of international law.
> Furthermore, to take a contentious-jurisdiction case to a Chamber will
> normally require agreement of the parties to do so, whereas the full Court
> might have jurisdiction, whether under paragraph 2 of Article 36 of the
> Statute or under some treaty-jurisdiction clause, in a case brought by
> unilateral application.[52]

Thus the President of the Court has conceded, as indeed he must, that the
Chamber for Environmental Matters announced by the Court is purely voluntary
and that parties intending to use that chamber in any case would have in any event
to select it by common consent. What the Court's announcement of the chamber
does, however, is to suggest that there are seven judges of the Court who have a
particular interest in environmental matters.[53] The Court has only recently handed
down its first decision that touched on environmental questions: the *Jan Mayen*
case, in which the presence of pack ice, the effect of the seasons on fishing, and the
presence during the year of schools of fish were all factors relevant to the decision.
The Court is now charged (by special agreement) with the *Danube* case, in which
environmental considerations are at the heart of the matter.

It may well be helpful for the Court to state unequivocally that it stands
prepared to serve states in adjudicating environmental matters, and that almost half
of its judges have indicated a particular interest to consider them. Whether other
environmental cases emerge in the future remains to be seen. It also remains to be
seen whether states will bring those matters to the Court by special agreement and,
if they do, whether they can seek agreement on a chamber of the Court which will
be comprised of some if not all of the judges now listed as members of the Chamber
for Environmental Matters. At the very least, however, this announcement by the
Court, even if it never results in the selection of a chamber based on it, is a step in
the right direction. It is a step away from the ghost of "state arbitration" in its
pre–World War I configuration, which haunts the Court slightly from time to time
and casts its spell in the selection of chambers comprised of judges with whom the
parties feel "comfortable."[54]

This trend in the Court's functioning, one which had been heralded widely by
those who were suspicious of the Court in the 1980s (in particular, over its handling
of the *Nicaragua* case), has fortunately now been reversed. One says "fortunately"
simply because, as this author wrote in 1991:

---

52. *Id.*

53. President Bedjaoui, Vice-President Schwebel, and Judges Shahabuddeen, Weer-
amantry, Ranjeva, Herczegh and Fleischhauer. (*See* I.C.J. Communiqué No. 94/10 of Mar.
14, 1994.)

54. *See supra* note 30.

Too many of the same judges were being used for chambers assignments, to the obvious detriment of the functioning of the whole Court; other judges were left with little to do; and there was a responsible question as to whether such chambers could really be constituted at the direction of the parties without losing their quality as judicial institutions rather than arbitral panels, and without inconsistency under the Statute.[55]

It remains to be seen whether state litigants will revert to the heyday of the chamber, as in the 1980s, or whether they will stay with the whole Court *en banc*. No general rule can be suggested, since preference of a selected chamber to the full Court depends on a multitude of specific factors: the identity of the parties, the nature of the case, the issues presented in the case, the identity of the judges, the identity of the President of the Court, the busyness of the Court as a whole, the number of other chambers at work (if any), and so forth.

(4) Intervention

It is however ironic that there has been no attempt by any third state to intervene in any of the cases under discussion, even though the doctrinal impossibility of nontreaty intervention —once hopelessly tangled in a series of logical fallacies presented by ambiguities in the Statute and Rules—has now been resolved in the Nicaragua Intervention proceeding in the *El Salvador/Honduras* case.[56] It will be interesting to see whether any Article 62 interventions will be sought in future years. These are "interest" or "nontreaty" interventions, and may only be accomplished at the discretion of the Court. It cannot of course escape one's attention that there have been no Article 63 interventions for many years; these are "treaty" or "interpretative" interventions which are exercised as of right, and do not depend on the Court's permission.

(5) "Non-appearance" Technique

Nor has there been any recrudescence of the "non-appearance" technique which was popular in the 1970s and 1980s,[57] and which was given its most prominent

---

55. Highet, *supra* note 21, at 649. This comment continued: "A thoughtful examination and denial of the validity of chambers has been made by Judge Shahabuddeen in his Dissenting Opinion to the Order of the Court concerning the Nicaragua Intervention in the *El Salvador/Honduras Case*," and the footnote stated that "Judge Shahabuddeen is of the view that fully consensual chambers—in which the judges are handpicked by the parties—are inconsistent with the Statute."

56. *See supra* notes 16 and 28.

57. *See generally* K. Highet, *Nonappearance and Disappearance Before the International Court of Justice*, 81 A.J.I.L. 237 (1987).

expressions in the *Nuclear Tests*,[58] *Fisheries Jurisdiction*,[59] *Aegean Sea*,[60] *Hostages*,[61] and *Nicaragua (Merits)* cases. It must have by now become obvious that this is, at best, a losing tactic: France was well on the way to "losing" the *Nuclear Tests* case, had jurisdiction been found; Iceland suffered in *Fisheries Jurisdiction* by its absence; and Iran and the United States made strange bedfellows by failing to appear in *Hostages* and *Nicaragua (Merits)*, and suffered similar consequences only too vividly.

The United States now has indicated that it would appear in both proceedings brought by Iran; it has also appeared to contest the Libyan claims in *Lockerbie*.[62] Of course, as disappearance has waned, so have preliminary objections waxed. The Court has recently rendered a judgment on the preliminary jurisdictional objection in the *Qatar-Bahrain* case,[63] and would have heard jurisdictional arguments in the *Airbus* case in September 1994 had the oral proceedings not been postponed. In addition, the United States is contesting jurisdiction in the *Oil Platforms* case.

Yet this is a trend which is only to be expected. In particular, in a case that has been as fraught with sensitivity as *Qatar-Bahrain*, the examination of the giving of consent by a state to the jurisdiction of the Court and its seisin in a particular case is a fundamental exercise that is not only of great delicacy but is also immensely important for the future of consensual international adjudication.

b. New Substantive Trends

(1) "Protective" Cases

In one interesting way, the current workload of the Court demonstrates a new searching by states for protection against the actions of other states. This is even true in an unaccepted "come-on" case such as the *NATO* case filed by Yugoslavia.[64] The *Land and Maritime Boundary* case is also such a case, where Cameroon is seeking active current protection against the use of force by Nigeria.[65] The *Genocide* case is the very paradigm of a protective recourse to the Court.

---

58. Nuclear Tests (Austl. v. Fr.; N.Z. v. Fr.), 1974 I.C.J. 253, 457.

59. (U.K. v. Ice.; F.G.R. v. Ice.), 1973 I.C.J. 3, 49 (Jurisdiction of the Court) and 1974 I.C.J. 3, 175 (Merits).

60. *See supra* note 40.

61. United States Diplomatic and Consular Staff in Tehran (U.S. v. Iran), 1980 I.C.J. 3.

62. *See* Highet, *supra* note 21, at 650–51.

63. *See supra* note 10.

64. *See supra* note 14.

65. *See* Application of Cameroon, summarized in I.C.J. Communiqué No. 94/12 of Mar. 14, 1994 (paras. (c), (d), and (e)).

The difference is striking between this type of protective case and the other kinds of case with which the Court has been involved in the past few years. Territorial disputes not involving the use of force (as in *Land and Maritime Boundary*) are dispositive in nature. So are all the boundary cases, although indeed there had been wars antecedent to the actual claims for relief in both the *Libya-Chad* case and the *El Salvador/Honduras* case. But calmer disputes such as *Jan Mayen*, or the classic continental shelf and maritime cases of the 1980s,[66] or a dispute such as the *Frontier Dispute*,[67] did not involve the same type of "protective" element that seems to be more current today. Indeed, the *Lockerbie* cases are, of course, also protective in nature, seeking to enjoin collective action against Libya in connection with the two suspects in the Lockerbie tragedy.

Of the cases recently settled, the *Great Belt* case between Finland and Denmark was clearly protective, its goal being to preserve Finnish access to the North Sea through the Great Belt for its drilling rigs. The *Nauru* case, whose purpose was to hold Australia accountable for disposition of Nauruan phosphates during the trusteeship years, was clearly related to state responsibility. Indeed, state responsibility questions, brought before the Court by application under a general title of jurisdiction, appear to be on the rise. *Airbus*, *Oil Platforms*, the *Danube* case, and even *East Timor* seem to be of this kind, although the state responsibility[68] in the *East Timor* case is somewhat attenuated and indirect in contrast with the others.

(2) "Use of Force" Cases

It should not therefore be surprising that a good number of the current or recent cases before the Court involve the use of force somewhere in their background. *Airbus*, *Oil Platforms*, *Lockerbie*, *Genocide*, *Land and Maritime Boundary*, *Border and Transborder Armed Actions*, and *East Timor* are all of this type. At the time of the *Nicaragua* case there were substantial discussions on all sides of the issue whether the Court was equipped or intended to deal with questions that involved the use of force, and in particular "ongoing" conflicts. It would now appear that, as in the *Corfu Channel* case[69] or the *Hostages* case,[70] it will become more broadly acknowledged that the Court may, and sometimes must, provide a judicial

---

66. Concerning the Continental Shelf (Tunis/Libyan Arab Jamahiriya), 1982 I.C.J. 18; Continental Shelf (Libyan Arab Jamahiriya/Malta), 1985 I.C.J. 13; and Delimitation of the Maritime Boundary in the Gulf of Maine Area (Can./U.S.), 1984 I.C.J. 246.

67. (Burk. Faso/Mali), 1986 I.C.J. 554.

68. Allegedly for recognizing the validity of the Indonesian occupation of East Timor by virtue of concluding a maritime delimitation agreement with Indonesia in respect of maritime territory that would otherwise have accrued to the benefit of East Timor.

69. Corfu Channel (U.K. v. Alb.), 1949 I.C.J. 4 (Merits).

70. *Supra* note 61.

determination of legal principles applicable to given instances of armed conflict and the use of force. Indeed, this element is obviously also presented by the underlying issues in the *Nuclear Weapons* request for advisory opinion.[71]

(3) Genocide

The Court, in the *Genocide* case brought by Bosnia-Herzegovina against Yugoslavia (Serbia and Montenegro), now finds itself on wholly virgin territory. The applicability and scope of the jurisdictional provisions of Article IX of the Genocide Convention have never been tested, even though in this particular factual context, one which becomes more tortured and tragically confusing with each passing day, the issue of standing to initiate proceedings is not as clearly raised as it would be in the instance of a state seeking to accuse another of genocide of inhabitants of its territory who are not citizens of the applicant state. In that last instance, the Court would have to deal with the problems of standing, jurisdiction *erga omnes*, and the concept of *actio popularis* that were adumbrated in *South West Africa*[72] and in *Barcelona Traction.*[73] (The questions of standing, and of right and interest, are also raised in the *East Timor* case.)

Perhaps the Court will also be mindful of the first decision ever rendered in a contentious case by its predecessor the Permanent Court (in 1923) in the case of the *S.S. Wimbledon,*[74] where there were four applicants (Great Britain, France, Italy, and Japan) as well as one statutory intervenor (Poland). The case, brought against Germany, requested that Germany not deny passage through the Kiel Canal for a British-registered vessel carrying armaments to Poland. In dealing with the question of "standing," the Court stated that " . . . each of the four Applicant Powers has a clear interest in the execution of the provisions relating to the Kiel Canal, since they all possess fleets and merchant vessels flying their respective flags."[75]

Likewise, the court might also be mindful of the *Interpretation of the Statute of Memel* case,[76] brought in 1932 by the same four applicants against Lithuania. It is interesting to notice that this kind of "multi-party" litigation, almost an

---

71. *See* section I.a. (Cases Before the Court).

72. South West Africa (Eth. v. S. Afr.; Lib. v. S. Afr.), 1962 I.C.J. 319 (Preliminary Objections); 1966 I.C.J. 6 (Second Phase).

73. Barcelona Traction, Light and Power Company, Limited (Belg. v. Spain), 1964 I.C.J. 6 (Preliminary Objections); 1970 I.C.J. 3, especially at 32–33, paras. 34–36, and 47, para. 91 (Second Phase).

74. Series A, No. 1; Judgment No. 1, Aug. 17, 1923. HUDSON, I WORLD COURT REPORTS 163 (1934; Oceana repr. 1969).

75. Series A, No. 1, 20; HUDSON, *id.* at 172.

76. Series A/B, No. 47, 245–58 (Judgment (Preliminary Objection) of June 24, 1932); III HUDSON, WORLD COURT REPORTS 23 (1938; Oceana repr. 1969) and Series A/B., No. 49, 294-360 (Judgment (Merits) of Aug. 11, 1932); HUDSON, *id.* at 35.

international law form of class action, has not really been used since the War, with the possible exception of the *South West Africa* cases.[77]

(4) Jurisdiction

Comment has been made above on the importance of the Court's recent judgment in the *Qatar-Bahrain* case.[78] What constitutes an agreement to go to court? Haunted by the shades of the *Aegean Sea* case, the decision is of particular importance for any states who, in the future, may seek to negotiate or conclude special agreements either bilaterally or, as was the case in *Qatar-Bahrain*, may use the good offices of a third state as conciliator. When is an agreement an agreement, and at what time does it develop a full set of teeth, sufficient to bite into jurisdiction? These questions were only partially answered by the court in the summer of 1994.

(5) "Constitutional" Cases

It is also evident that there is a substantial number of matters up for resolution that can be characterized as "constitutional." The *Nuclear Weapons* advisory opinion request is a "constitutional" issue inasmuch as it raises basic questions about the use of the kinds of weapon that, ironically enough, provided an early termination to World War II and an early birth to the United Nations Organization. For this issue to be raised fifty years later is something that our friends and colleagues in Japan can understand with particular feeling. The question is one that must receive the most serious and intelligent consideration by the Court.

The *Lockerbie* cases, involving as they do the interplay between the actions of the Security Council and the role of states members of the council (and permanent members, at that), are evidently also of a "constitutional" nature. If one expands the concept of "constitutional" determination to embrace the ordering of rights and duties in the larger international community, and the relationships between states and the realities created by international treaties, it becomes clear that the *Genocide* and *East Timor* cases also share important elements of general application that are

---

77. The Nuclear Tests (Nuclear Tests (Austl. v. Fr.; N.Z. v. Fr.), 1974 I.C.J. 253, 457 (Dec. 20)) and Fisheries Jurisdiction (Fisheries Jurisdiction (U.K. v. Ice.; F.R.G. v. Ice.), 1973 I.C.J. 3, 49 (Feb. 2) (Jurisdiction of the Court); and 1974 I.C.J. 3, 175 (July 24) (Merits)) cases were really run as separate matters, and the North Sea Continental Shelf cases (North Sea Continental Shelf Cases (Den./F.R.G.; Neth./F.R.G.), 1969 I.C.J. 3 (Feb. 20)) were brought by special agreement, as had been the Territorial Jurisdiction of the International Commission of the River Oder in 1929 (1929 P.C.I.J. (ser. A) No. 23). HUDSON, 2 WORLD COURT REPORTS 609 (1935; Oceana repr. 1969), in which the parties were Czechoslovakia, Denmark, France, Germany, Great Britain, Sweden and Poland (although in substance the case was between the first six States and Poland).

78. *See supra* note 10.

"constitutional" to the extent that they will define the rights and obligations of states vis-a-vis one another in relation to recognition and treaty practice, and in relation to lawmaking treaties such as the 1948 Genocide Convention.

(6) Specialization of the Court

With the conclusion of the *El Salvador/Honduras* and *Jan Mayen* cases, and with the probable disappearance of the *Guinea-Bissau* case, there remain only two cases before the Court that speak in the context of maritime delimitations: the ultimate merits phase in *Qatar-Bahrain* (however that may be instituted by the parties) and *Land and Maritime Boundary*. Each case contains a request for delimitation of maritime areas by a single maritime boundary.

However it can still be maintained that:

> The Court is . . . now continuing full speed ahead on its productive and convincing path toward mastery of the law of the sea. It has already produced, from 1969 to the present day, the only single body of jurisprudence in the area. It will continue to do so and thus redouble and affirm its position.[79]

The question has been raised as to what competition may be expected from the prospective Law of the Sea Tribunal to be instituted under Part XV of the 1982 Convention on the Law of the Sea, of which Article 279 provides that "States Parties shall settle any dispute between them concerning the interpretation or application of this Convention by peaceful means. . . . "

It should be recalled that the Law of the Sea Convention has come into force as of November 1994, and that the signatories that will be bound by its provisions will include Japan and the component states of the former Soviet Union, principally Russia. This could possibly raise interesting prospects for compulsory adjudication of aspects of the "Northern Territories" problem (of the Kuril Islands)[80] between

---

79. Highet, *supra* note 21, at 653. *See also* J. Charney, *Progress in International Maritime Boundary Delimitation Law*, 88 A.J.I.L. 227, 256 (1994).

80. *See* BEYOND HOPPŌ RYŌDO, JAPANESE–SOVIET–AMERICAN RELATIONS IN THE 1990'S (Jacob ed., American Enterprise Institute, Washington, 1991); JAPAN'S NORTHERN TERRITORIES (Ministry of Foreign Affairs, Japan, 1980); JAPAN'S NORTHERN TERRITORIES (Northern Territories Issue Association, Tokyo 1974); J.J. STEPHAN, THE KURIL ISLANDS (Oxford 1974); and S.D. Thomsen, *Kuril Islands in* 12 ENCYCLOPAEDIA OF PUBLIC INTERNATIONAL LAW 208–13 (Max Planck Institute, North Holland, 1990). *See also* BEYOND COLD WAR TO TRILATERAL COOPERATION IN THE ASIA–PACIFIC REGION: SCE-NARIOS FOR NEW RELATIONSHIPS BETWEEN JAPAN, RUSSIA, AND THE UNITED STATES (Strengthening Democratic Institutions Project, Harvard 1992). *See also* K. Highet, *The Kurils Quandary, in* LIBER AMICORUM FOR EDUARDO JIMÉNEZ DE ARÉCHAGA (Fundación de Cultura Universitaria, Montevideo, Uruguay, 1995) and K. Highet, BEYOND COLD WAR TO TRILATERAL COOPERATION IN THE ASIA–PACIFIC REGION: SCENARIOS FOR NEW

Japan and Russia.[81]

Common sense, however, seems to suggest that the Law of the Sea Tribunal[82] "will likely find itself a more technical body [than the International Court] at the outset,"[83] and that the continuing work of the International Court will maintain its preeminence in the law of the sea and the law of maritime delimitation.[84]

(7) Environmental Cases

We have already discussed the fact that the Court is freshly embarking on environmental matters, both (although to a limited extent) in its 1993 decision in the *Jan Mayen* case and in the facts and law that are to be presented at length in the *Danube* case. This latter, being brought by special agreement, is likely to continue its course, and should prove a valuable contribution to the jurisprudence of the Court in this vital area of developing international law. Indeed, the Court has, by forming its Chamber on Environmental Matters, acknowledged the importance of this field, its own preparedness to handle matters of international environmental law, and the interest of almost one-half of its judges in participating in such cases.[85]

RELATIONSHIPS BETWEEN JAPAN, RUSSIA, AND THE UNITED STATES Vol. II, Appendix H, at 1–30, addendum to appendix I, 1–5 ("International Legal Issues Presented by the Kurils Dispute;" "Analogies from International Law and Practice;" "Sovereignty, Title, and Possession: Some Informal Observations on Difficult Subjects;" "Judicial and Quasi-Judicial Options;" and "Report of the International Boundaries Research Unit") (Strengthening Democratic Institutions Project, Harvard 1992).

81. *But see* art. 298, para. 1 (a) (i) [optional exceptions to applicability of section 2], which excludes "any dispute that *necessarily involves the concurrent consideration of any unsettled dispute* concerning sovereignty or other rights over continental or insular land territory" from submission to conciliation, where no agreement within a reasonable period of time is reached in negotiations between the parties—and thus from the overall "recapture" mechanism of art. 298, par. 1 (a) (i) and (ii). (Emphasis added.)

82. Which will now, apparently, be established in Hamburg owing to Germany's accession to the 1982 Law of the Sea Convention and the effectiveness of that treaty.

83. Highet, *supra* note 21, at 653.

84. *Id:* "[The Law of the Sea Tribunal] will probably be confronted with narrower and more specialist claims under the Convention than had been planned: activities such as those of its Sea-Bed Disputes Chamber under Article 197. . . . The chances are also that Hamburg will still never catch up to The Hague."

85. *See* discussion *supra* notes 50-53.

c. Settlement

It has been mentioned that two cases have recently been settled in a space of as many years.[86] This is a very interesting development, and indeed is one that does not appear to have any substantial precedent in either court. The settlements in both *Great Belt* and *Nauru* occurred before the commencement of oral proceedings. Neither one represented a discontinuation on other grounds, as was the case in *Border and Transborder Armed Actions* or *Military and Paramilitary Activities in and against Nicaragua*. In addition, negotiations have been continuing in the *Guinea-Bissau* case toward a similar resolution.

It was thus possible for Sir Robert Jennings to state in his final report to the General Assembly as President of the Court that these cases: " . . . illustrate a new role for the Court, unimagined by earlier commentators on the adjudication process in international matters." [87] President Jennings added that:

> In this way, the Court procedure is beginning to be seen as a resort to be employed in a closer relationship with normal diplomatic negotiation. No longer is resort to the International Court of Justice seen, to use the traditional phrase, as a `last resort' when all negotiation has finally failed. Rather, it is sometimes now to be seen as a recourse that might usefully be employed at an earlier stage of the dispute. . . . This tendency to use the Court, acting under its contentious jurisdiction, as a partner in preventive diplomacy rather than as a last-resort alternative is after all only to conform to the place that courts enjoy in any developed domestic system of law.[88]

III. CLOSING CONSIDERATIONS

It would not be fair to conclude this brief review of new developments in the practice of the Court without at least acknowledging an element that is as real and as important as it is difficult to document or describe. It is perhaps more of an impression than a conclusion; certainly, however, it is an impression gained over a direct experience of more than thirty years in practice before the Court. It relates to the smoothness with which the Court functions or appears to function as an institution, and in particular the mechanical, small, procedural elements that affect practitioner and counsel. Much of the improvement in the efficacy of practice before the Court has of course been affected and made possible by electronic

---

86. *See* Section I.c (Cases Recently Settled).

87. *Jennings Report, supra* note 9, at 421–22. The report continued: " . . . it was the intervention of some part of the procedures before the court which apparently not only made further negotiations in this new context possible but made it possible for them to succeed."

88. *Id.* (emphasis added).

progress: modern telephones, faxes, and above all, the ability to absorb and process large quantities of written materials with celerity, accuracy, and skill. Much of the improvement in the smoothness of the practice before the Court, however, has been the progressive development not merely of international law but of a modern international bar that serves it. This is not the ethereal body that Oscar Schachter has described in his graceful phrase, "the invisible college of international lawyers."[89] It is a different body, perhaps a smaller faculty within the mother house, consisting of those international lawyers who since at least the mid-1960s have practiced and continue to practice before the Court, who know the judges of the Court and the members of the Registrar's staff, who know how things work out in practice and what the difficulties and pitfalls and tricks of the trade might be.

This "bar" is the body of practicing international advocates who work in a number of cases for diverse governments before the Court. In effect, the litmus test must be: how many states, other than his or her own government, has an international advocate represented in cases before the Court? It is this "bar" to which the late lamented Eduardo Jiménez de Aréchaga, friend and mentor, referred so frequently when he counseled devoting energy and attention to it. He was proud of his membership in that bar and, being the kind of man that he was, gave little thought to his own preeminence in it.

The key point is that there exists today an efficient mechanism and apparatus for handling cases, and an informal but experienced bar of the Court that knows how those cases should be handled. The difference between the practice in The Hague today and in 1965 is, to this observer at least, far more marked than any differences in practice before municipal courts. The arguments are more condensed, although still tending to prolixity. Counsel appear to be more generally experienced in getting to the point and sparing the judges from repetition or hectoring on points of law. Procedural flexibility and skill appear to be growing, whether in the area of handling of written evidence or that of dealing with oral testimony, cross-examination, and even limited powers of discovery.[90]

At the same time, the ease with which the Court (and in particular the President) now handles questions of scheduling is a significant improvement from the dark days of the mid-1960s, when a beleaguered and intransigent South Africa refused to cooperate with the Court and insisted on spinning out the proceedings at great length so as to ensure that every bit of its legal arguments and evidence could be presented at its own pace.[91] The new activity and busyness of the Court combines to make it possible if not mandatory for the Court and its President to limit the arguments of parties to a reasonable length, to insist on reasonable

---

89. Schachter, *The Invisible College of International Lawyers*, 72 Nw. U.L. Rev. 217 (1977).

90. *See* Highet, *Evidence, the Court, and the Nicaragua Case*, 81 A.J.I.L. 1 (1987).

91. *See supra* note 72.

deadlines, and in general to act in a more efficient and professional manner than heretofore.

More important perhaps than one might think is that the construction, style, and standards for presentation of written pleadings before the court show an increasing degree of uniformity in style and appearance as a result of word processing programs. The written pleadings are becoming easier for the judges to deal with; it is easier for them to compare like with like and to match expectations.

It is now the normal practice for each side in cases before the court to exchange the texts of their oral pleadings immediately after they have delivered them, so that each side may benefit from studying the arguments of its opponent somewhat earlier than if they had to merely await the official court transcript. It is also the current expectation that litigants will deliver diskettes containing the word-processed versions of their speeches to the Registry at the outset of each morning's arguments. The effect on the accuracy, uniformity, and usefulness of the official transcripts is palpable—augmented, no doubt, by the excellent and continually improving effectiveness of the Registry.

Another element that deserves positive mention is the degree to which relations between different sides appear to have become improved and more clearly professional. In 1965 it was difficult for the South Africans to speak calmly to lawyers for Ethiopia and Liberia, and perhaps even more difficult the other way around. Relations have been strained in many a case. But now, perhaps, by virtue of the large number of cases in which a large number of members of the invisible bar of the International Court[92] participate and will continue to participate, and by virtue of the concomitant imperative that different counsel attend at different times on different sides of different cases, there has been a salutary effect on the conduct of courtroom proceedings. The bar is becoming increasingly professionalized, and perhaps therefore after the lapses and sadnesses of a number of highly charged political cases it is reverting to a more classical, antique, and well-mannered model.

One final observation, however, concerns the nature of the present states that are applicants or parties before the Court. There is not one "great power" amongst them, save as unwilling respondent. The list of applicants includes: Bosnia-Herzegovina, Cameroon, Guinea-Bissau, Iran, Libya, Portugal, and Qatar; the current consensual parties are Hungary and Slovakia.

Does this imply that the Court, which the major powers have long been sensitive to, is becoming a judicial institution that primarily serves "secondary" or "middle" powers?[93]

---

92. To paraphrase Oscar Schachter (*see supra* note 89).

93. *See* Highet, *supra* note 21, at 654: "The real work of the Court over the next decade will be the reconciliation of the interests of developing countries with those of the developed countries, and its real constituents a wide range of middle-level powers seeking to resolve or defuse critically important local problems, usually—although, of course, not always—concerning a boundary."

Will we learn by this experience—guaranteed to take us through 1995—that this constituency of states is perhaps the one that will most frequently use, and be directed by, the Court? Is this all that bad a result? Perhaps it is the correct one for the next decade. The greater powers could not be expected to abide by decisions of the Court in every instance; it is the lesser powers that by definition require the additional strength and protection of the Court, and it is by their participation and willingness to use the Court that new ground is broken, and past prejudices and fears set aside and allayed."[94]

Perhaps, indeed, the directions will be set by the middle-level and lesser states, only to be followed, at some point in the future, by the greater powers. One can hardly refrain from noting that neither China nor Russia has ever litigated a case before this institution or its predecessor.[95] Japan has been involved in only two cases.[96] France, the United Kingdom, and the United States have been involved (as two of them still are) more frequently as respondents than as applicants. The "Permanent Five Initiative" so enthusiastically advanced in the 1980s seems to have vanished without a trace.[97]

The impact on the business of the Court of the now-effective Convention on the Law of the Sea also remains to be seen. The effect on the Court's business of its handling of the new class of "protective" cases is unclear. It is an open question how the Court will deal with major, untried, ambiguous, and unclear conventions such as the Genocide Convention. The answers to all of these will in turn affect the Court's ability to draw business, either directly or indirectly, over the remaining years of this century.

It is only to be hoped that the confidence that will be reposed in the Court by states that can litigate before it will be on the same level as the skill and ability shown in the litigation of those matters before the Court by the invisible bar that has slowly but steadily come to serve it, and worthy of the skill and diligence displayed in the decision of those matters in recent years by members of the Court and the Court itself.

---

94. *Id.*

95. China was named as a respondent in the case concerning Denunciation of the Treaty of November 2, 1865, between China and Belgium (Belg. v. China) (proceedings terminated by order of May 25, 1929). "The Chinese Government appointed no agent in the case, nor did it at any time take part in the proceedings." HUDSON, II WORLD COURT REPORTS 3.

96. Wimbledon (*see supra* note 74) and Statute of Memel (*see supra* note 76).

97. Highet, *supra* note 21, at 654: "Perhaps the still-uncompleted initiative of the permanent five has been overtaken by events."

TRANSNATIONALISM AND THE SETTLEMENT OF DISPUTES: THE ROLE OF NONSTATE ACTORS

Maureen Irish*

I. INTRODUCTION

Public international law formed its roots in Europe—particularly since the rise of the territorial nation-state following the 1648 Peace of Westphalia. Much modern thinking is influenced by the European positivism of the nineteenth century, a period in which national governments became increasingly representative, powerful, and legitimate. People were more isolated than now in that they lived in a world without telephone, radio, television, fax, or airplane. The question I wish to discuss is whether or not it is helpful to look beyond the concept of the nation-state when examining procedures for global dispute management.

In our modern world, it is history that makes the territorial state a suitable political entity, since states do not necessarily reflect groups that are distinct by race, religion, language, culture, ethnicity, economic links, or general social ties. In our interconnected world, it is not only the state that is involved in global relations, but also its citizens and residents.[1] The porosity of the territorial state can be seen from many points of view. Some may welcome the new trends, which create room for movements of "grassroots globalism" such as feminism and environmentalism.[2] Others fear the end of the dream of the European Enlightenment: that a political state able to enforce democratic and humanist values will no

---

*   I wish to express my appreciation to my colleague Professor Marcia Valiante of the Faculty of Law, University of Windsor for her helpful comments.

1.   *See generally* YALE H. FERGUSON & RICHARD W. MANSBACH, THE STATE, CONCEPTUAL CHAOS AND THE FUTURE OF INTERNATIONAL RELATIONS THEORY (1989).

2.   RICHARD FALK, EXPLOPRATIONS AT THE EDGE OF TIME: THE PROSPECTS FOR WORLD ORDER (1992).

longer exist, and human society will degenerate to corruption, privatized violence, and loss of identity.[3]

Although a new transnational world is not yet upon us, we may nevertheless observe some leakage of authority from states to private entities and functional global organizations of various types. In this chapter, I do not discuss intergovernmental organizations but consider only the position of individuals, private corporations, and other nongovernmental agencies. I argue that participation by such nonstate actors can reduce international tensions, contribute to efficient dispute management, and increase the range of available settlement techniques.

The positivist view of law as legitimate command implies a power of enforcement in a defined territory. This notion is problematic for international lawyers, since even the strongest enforcement for judgments of the International Court of Justice under Article 94(2) of the U.N. Charter is subject to political decisions.[4] When neither jurisdiction nor enforcement is automatic, international law fails the positivist test.[5] There are, of course, many views of how to define law. If the power of compulsory enforcement is seen as important or helpful, I suggest that we should consider the links to domestic enforcement systems that are available to nonstate actors.

In the following sections I discuss first the position of nonstate actors in dispute settlement at the international level and then the question of the link to domestic systems of law.

II. INTERNATIONAL DISPUTE SETTLEMENT

International law may be defined in a preliminary way as that which we have agreed is binding. This is law for members of a community who will have future dealings with each other, who are not like passengers in a subway about to get off at the next stop.[6] Law, according to this model, spares us from having to renegotiate everything all the time. It could easily be called a regime of rules that

---

3.   JEAN-MARIE GUÉHENNO, LA FIN DE LA DÉMOCRATIE (1993).

4.   *See* OSCAR SCHACHTER, INTERNATIONAL LAW IN THEORY AND PRACTICE 233–35 (1991).

5.   To blunt this criticism and similar criticism from the realist school of international relations theory, some refer to international "rules" rather than international "law:" THOMAS M. FRANCK, THE POWER OF LEGITIMACY AMONG NATIONS (1990). For argument in favor of the term "law," *see* Anthony D'Amato, *Is International Law Really 'Law'?* 79 NW. U.L. REV. 1293 (1984-85). I use both terms here, without taking a stand in that debate.

6.   FRANCK, *id.* at 196–98.

promotes a pattern of behavior.[7] The rules enable us to navigate through situations because we have some idea of how we are all expected to behave.

But then who are "we," those who have agreed on the rules? Traditionally, only states qualify as subjects of international law, creating rules for themselves. Nonstate actors are mere objects, like mountains, lakes, and rivers; they do not participate in the formation of law.[8] A more transnational approach would consider whether important global understandings, such as the Incoterms from the International Chamber of Commerce,[9] could have some independent effect. In this short paper, I do not argue for expansion of the sources of law. I simply suggest that even if states are the subjects who agree on law, they may not intend to be the only participants in its application. When disputes arise, participation from nonstate actors can be helpful in dispute resolution on the basis of previously agreed upon rules and on other bases.

A dispute may be defined as a disagreement over specific facts or over what should be done about them. To decide what to do, one might look to rules previously agreed upon or proceed on some other basis. Some dispute settlement processes result in decisions that are binding or that carry compulsory penalty mechanisms. Other important procedures lead to rulings on questions of fact and law that are quite authoritative, although not strictly binding. Disputes may, in

---

7. ROBERT O. KEOHANE, AFTER HEGEMONY: COOPERATION AND DISCORD IN THE WORLD POLITICAL ECONOMY (1984). Many lawyers with common law training probably hear echoes of H.L.A. Hart in this book:

> [r]egimes contribute to cooperation not by implementing rules that states must follow, but by changing the context within which states make decisions based on self-interests. International regimes are valuable to governments not because they enforce binding rules on others (they do not), but because they render it possible for governments to enter into mutually beneficial agreements with one another. They *empower* governments rather than shackling them. (*Id.* at 13) (emphasis original).

The image of Ulysses tied to the mast (*id.* at 17) is perhaps not quite appropriate to express this notion. If we see law as facilitating action, then stars and instruments to guide the ship might be a more apt metaphor.

8. In some cases, nonstate actors participate in fact. *See, e.g.,* T.O. ELIAS, NEW HORIZONS IN INTERNATIONAL LAW 393–94 (Francis M. Ssekandi ed., 1992), concerning the Draft Code of Conduct for Transnational Corporations; Yogesh K. Tyagi, *Cooperation between the Human Rights Committee and Nongovernmental Organizations*, 18 TEXAS INT'L L.J. 273, 277–85 (1983); Edith Brown Weiss, *International Environmental Law: Contemporary Issues and the Emergence of a New World Order*, 81 GEORGETOWN L.J. 675, 693–94 (1993). On the advisability of including transnational corporations as participants, *see* Jonathan I. Charney, *Transnational Corporations and Developing Public International Law*, 1983 DUKE L.J. 748. On rejection of the subject/object division generally, *see* Rosalyn Higgins, *International Law and the Avoidance, Containment and Resolution of Disputes*, 230 RECUEIL DES COURS 9, 80–81 (1991).

9. International Chamber of Commerce, INCOTERMS, 1990.

addition, be addressed on some basis other than the application of legal rules. I list below a few examples of involvement by nonstate actors in binding decision-making, in other legal rulings, and in dispute settlement on bases other than law.

Sometimes nonstate actors play a major role in the process that leads to a binding decision. When the nonstate actor has power to force this sort of determination, the nonstate actor is particularly affected or injured in some way, and the complaint goes ahead directly, without need of state sponsorship. This procedure may be used to set compensation at the end of a war[10] or other major international confrontation, as in the case of the Iran–United States Claims Tribunal.[11] A commercial investment may provide the necessary direct interest. Under Article 1116 of the North American Free Trade Agreement (NAFTA), for example, arbitration is available to private investors for claims that a state is in breach of the relevant investment provisions of the Agreement.[12] Private investors also have standing for arbitrations against a state under the auspices of the International Centre for the Settlement of Investment Disputes: for determinations that are not necessarily based on international law, but may be based on domestic law or a mixture, in accordance with choice of law clauses.[13] When the injured private party has direct access, a dispute can be addressed without cumbersome diplomatic machinery and without defining the problem as a clash of national interests.

Filters may be imposed when the nonstate actor is less directly affected, but has a special interest or expertise. Under the North American Agreement on

---

10. Early examples were the Mixed Arbitral Tribunals set up after World War I: Hermann Mosler, *Supra-National Judicial Decisions and National Courts* 4 HASTINGS INT'L & COMP. L. REV. 425, 429 (1980–81). *See* Karl Strupp, *The Competence of the Mixed Arbitral Courts of the Treaty of Versailles* 17 AM. J. INT'L L. 661 (1923).

11. *See* STEPHEN J. TOOPE, MIXED INTERNATIONAL ARBITRATION: STUDIES IN ARBITRATION BETWEEN STATES AND PRIVATE PERSONS 263–383 (1990). The mechanism for claims against Iraq after the Gulf War is a more administrative, less adjudicative process: Charles N. Brower, *The Lessons of the Iran–United States Claims Tribunal: How May They Be Applied in the Case of Iraq?* 32 VA. J. INT'L L. 421 (1992).

12. North American Free Trade Agreement between Canada, Mexico and the United States, done Dec. 17, 1992, in force Jan. 1, 1994, 32 I.L.M. 289, 605 (1993). Under the Convention on the Law of the Sea, disputes involving private parties are referred to binding commercial arbitration, which may include application of an interpretive ruling from the Sea-Bed Disputes Chamber. U.N. Convention on the Law of the Sea, done Dec. 10, 1982, in force Nov. 16, 1994, 21 I.L.M. 126, arts. 187, 188; *see also* annex III, art. 5 and annex VI, art. 20(2) (1982).

13. Toope, *supra* note 11. Under the MIGA Convention, the Agency is subrogated to claims of a private investor on the payment of compensation and can pursue them through conciliation and arbitration: Convention Establishing the Multilateral Investment Guarantee Agency, done Oct. 11, 1985, in force Apr. 12, 1988, 24 I.L.M. 1605, arts. 17, 18, 56, 57, annex II (1985); *see* Linda C. Reif, *Conciliation as a Mechanism for the Resolution of International Economic and Business Disputes* 14 FORDHAM INT'L L.J. 578 (1990–91).

Environmental Cooperation, for example, nongovernmental organizations can submit complaints to the Secretariat, which then takes over the process. After several steps that are not subject to the discretion of the nongovernmental organization, an arbitral panel may rule on whether one of the three countries has breached its treaty obligation to enforce domestic environmental law.[14] Here, there is far greater distance between the nonstate actor and the legal ruling. The process nevertheless benefits from the information and expertise of the nongovernmental organization.

Participation by nonstate actors can also enhance coordination and management. The International Convention on the Harmonized Commodity Description and Coding System[15] contains the classification code used for customs and statistical purposes for most international trade in goods. Under Article 10, disputes may be settled by the Harmonized System Committee or by the Customs Co-operation Council, which administers the convention. The settlement can be binding if the states so agree. Private commercial entities are likely to be acutely aware of any discrepancies in interpretation when states do not classify goods under the same heading. Under Article 7, the Harmonized System Committee can respond to requests for guidance from "intergovernmental or other international organizations." There is no specific provision for direct inquiries from importers and exporters, but the Council reports that it regularly receives such communications from private firms.[16] In such instances, nonstate actors are quite directly affected and have information that can assist in early identification of potential problems. Their participation can facilitate cooperation and efficient communication in situations that would not necessarily involve a clash of national wills.

States may retain control of binding settlement mechanisms, requiring specific consents or other conditions before a dispute is submitted for a win/lose decision on the basis of established law. If they do not want to take this risk, they might still want a legal ruling to clarify a situation or to persuade themselves and others to keep their promises. In such a case, they might prefer a nonbinding decision, which could be quite authoritative but would not involve a penalty mechanism or an express undertaking to implement.

---

14. North American Agreement on Environmental Cooperation between Canada, Mexico, and the United States, done Sept. 13, 1993, in force Jan. 1, 1994, 32 I.L.M. 1480 (1993), art. 14—submissions from "any nongovernmental organization or person." Art. 34 allows a panel to impose monetary enforcement assessments, which may be collected through a suspension of benefits under art. 36.

15. Done June 14, 1983, amended June 24, 1986, in force Jan. 1, 1988, Can. T.S. 1988 No. 38.

16. Customs Co-operation Council, *The Activities of the Council*, Bulletin No. 34 at 14 (1988–89); Bulletin No. 35 at 15 (1989–90); Bulletin No. 36 at 9 (1990–91); Bulletin No. 37 at 10 (1991–92). *Compare* Bulletin No. 38 (1992–93) at 9. The Customs Co-operation Council was recently renamed the World Customs Organization.

In the human rights area, the petition procedure under the Optional Protocol to the International Covenant on Civil and Political Rights[17] produces rulings that are very authoritative although not explicitly binding. Individuals[18] can set the process in motion through a simple communication, which leads to a decision from the Human Rights Committee.[19] If the process is to be effective at all, making it subject to state supervision would be unrealistic, since petitioners complain about actions of their own governments. In the European[20] and American[21] Human Rights systems, a filtering mechanism is imposed. The petition goes to a Commission, which tries to arrange a settlement before the matter is referred to a Court for legal judgment. Here, the persons specially affected set the process into motion, but do not have control of subsequent steps. It should be noted, however,

---

17.   Done Dec. 16, 1966, in force Mar. 23, 1976, Can. T.S. 1976 No. 47, *reprinted in* BASIC DOCUMENTS IN HUMAN RIGHTS 144 (Ian Brownlie ed., 3d ed. 1992).

18.   Art. 2 only mentions "individuals" but individuals could claim rights as part of a group. This procedure may be somewhat awkward for the protection of certain group rights, in particular those of Indigenous peoples. *See* Mary Ellen Turpel, *Indigenous Peoples' Rights of Political Participation and Self-Determination: Recent International Legal Developments and the Continuing Struggle for Recognition* 25 CORNELL INT'L L.J. 579 (1992); Anne-Marie Wilson, *L'utilisation traditionnelle du territoire par les Autochtones et les instruments de droit international* 3 REVUE QUÉBÉCOISE DE DROIT INTERNATIONAL 231 (1986). Are indigenous peoples best described as nonstate actors? Former states? Quasi-states?

19.   Similar procedures are contained in the International Convention on the Elimination of All Forms of Racial Discrimination, adopted Dec. 21, 1965, in force Jan. 4, 1969, 660 U.N.T.S. 195 (Brownlie, *supra* note 17 at 148) for petitions from "individuals or groups of individuals" (art. 14(1)) and in the Convention Against Torture and Other Cruel, Inhuman or Degrading Treatment or Punishment, adopted Dec. 10, 1984, in force June 26, 1987, G.A. Res. 39/46, 39 U.N. GAOR, Supp. (No. 51), U.N. Doc. A/39/51, at 197 (1984) (Brownlie at 38) for communications "from or on behalf of individuals" (art. 22(1)). . *See* Siân Lewis-Anthony, *Treaty-based Procedures for Making Human Rights Complaints Within the U.N. System*, *in* GUIDE TO INTERNATIONAL HUMAN RIGHTS PRACTICE 41 (Hurst Hannum ed., 2d ed. 1992).

20.   European Convention for the Protection of Human Rights and Fundamental Freedoms, done Nov. 4, 1950, in force Sept. 3, 1953, 312 U.N.T.S. 222 (Brownlie *supra* note 17, at 326), art. 25—petitions from "any person, nongovernmental organization or group of individuals." *See further* Protocol 9, Concerning Access to the Court by Individuals, done Nov. 6, 1990 (Brownlie at 359); Markus G. Schmidt, *Individual Human Rights Complaints Procedures Based on U.N. Treaties and the Need for Reform* 41 INT'L & COMP. L.Q. 645, 647 (1992).

21.   American Convention on Human Rights, done Nov. 22, 1969, in force July 18, 1978 (Brownlie *supra* note 17, at 495), art. 44 (petitions from "[a]ny person or group of persons, or any nongovernmental entity legally recognized in one or more member states").

that in these latter two systems the legal decisions produced are binding[22] and that damage awards are possible.[23]

Authoritative legal rulings may also be obtained through various procedures of the International Labor Organization (ILO), a U.N. specialized agency. The ILO is a hybrid organization, one half consisting of government representatives and the other half of representatives of workers' and employers' associations from member countries. Under Article 26 of its Constitution,[24] the Governing Body of the ILO may set up a Commission of Inquiry to deal with a complaint that a state is not observing an ILO convention that it has ratified. Such a complaint may be filed by any delegate to the International Labor Conference during the Conference session.[25] An industrial association of workers or employers can make a representation to the ILO Governing Body concerning nonobservance of a ratified convention (Article 24). A similar, qualified association could also refer a complaint concerning freedom of association to the Governing Body's Committee on Freedom of Association.[26] Here, the nonstate actor is more or less directly affected, and is clearly the entity with information essential for the effective functioning of the processes.

Nonstate actors can take part in fact-finding and other international mechanisms that may or may not involve the application of legal rules. Perhaps the rules are not sufficiently precise, or they are out of date, or otherwise unsuitable. Perhaps it would be more effective to use less confrontational structures that do not produce win/lose outcomes. The ILO provides an example of a regular state reporting system that can assist in dispute management and avoidance (Article 22).

---

22. European Convention, art. 32(4) (decision of the Committee of Ministers); art. 53 (decision of the Eur. Ct. of H.R.); American Convention, art. 68(1) (decision of the Inter-Am. Ct. H.R.).

23. American Convention, art. 68(2): "That part of a judgment that stipulates compensatory damages may be executed in the country concerned in accordance with domestic procedure governing the execution of judgments against the state." *See* Barbra Fontana, *Damage Awards for Human Rights Violations in the European and Inter-American Courts of Human Rights* 31 SANTA CLARA L.R. 1127 (1991); Schmidt, *supra* note 20, at 651.

24. 15 U.N.T.S. 35, as amended, *reprinted in* BASIC DOCUMENTS IN INTERNATIONAL LAW 49, (Ian Brownlie ed., 3d ed. 1983).

25. *See* Lee Swepston, *Human Rights Complaint Procedures of the International Labour Organization,* in Hannum ed., *supra* note 19, 99, at 106–07. A government which does not accept the recommendations of a Commission of Inquiry may refer the complaint to the International Court of Justice for a final decision (arts. 29, 31, 32).

26. *See also id.* at 109–12; David Weissbrodt, *The Contribution of International Nongovernmental Organizations to the Protection of Human Rights, in* HUMAN RIGHTS IN INTERNATIONAL LAW: LEGAL AND POLICY ISSUES 2, 403, 423–24 (Theodor Meron ed., 1984); C. WILFRED JENKS, SOCIAL JUSTICE IN THE LAW OF NATIONS: THE ILO IMPACT AFTER FIFTY YEARS 45–68 (1970).

Other reporting systems are available and open to influence by nonstate actors.[27] Nonstate actors have been active in providing information to the U.N. Commission on Human Rights through the Resolution 1503 procedure concerning persistent patterns of human rights violations, as well as through the Commission's rapporteurs and working groups.[28] Nongovernmental organizations with observer status are, of course, involved in various U.N. activities, and in some cases have a certain ability to suggest items for the agenda.[29]

In contrast to individual and private commercial complainants, some nongovernmental organizations are able to do much of the dispute settlement work themselves. They have expertise and may be given responsibility for fact-finding and recommendations. A notable example is the International Committee of the Red Cross, which has some investigative powers under the Geneva Conventions of 1949 but undertakes much of its humanitarian work in situations outside the framework of those Conventions.[30] The ICRC uses its considerable experience and authority for fact-finding, reporting, and mediation on behalf of victims and prisoners, but avoids involvement in political mediation among parties to an armed conflict.[31] In the environmental field, nongovernmental organizations may possess the special expertise and technical information required for monitoring, standard-setting, policy development, and advice on implementation. Nongovernmental

---

27. For discussion of NGO involvement in the reporting systems of the Covenant on Civil and Political Rights, the Covenant on Economic, Social and Cultural Rights, the Convention on the Elimination of All Forms of Racial Discrimination, the Convention on the Elimination of all Forms of Discrimination against Women, the Convention against Torture and Other Cruel, Inhuman or Degrading Treatment or Punishment and the Convention on the Rights of the Child, *see* Sandra Coliver, *International Reporting Procedures in* Hannum ed., *supra* note 19, at 173.

28. For discussion of the work of the Commission on Human Rights, including the 1503 procedure, the Working Group on Enforced or Involuntary Disappearances, the Special Rapporteur on Summary or Arbitrary Executions, the Special Rapporteur on Torture, the Special Rapporteur on Religious Intolerance and the Working Group on Arbitrary Detention, *see* Nigel S. Rodley, *United Nations Non-Treaty Procedures for Dealing with Human Rights Violations, in* Hannum ed., *supra* note 19 at 60. ECOSOC Resolution 1503 appears in Brownlie, *supra* note 17, at 16. A similar procedure is available for communications from nonstate actors under art. 55 of the African Charter on Human and Peoples' Rights, adopted June 17, 1981, in force Oct. 21, 1986 (Brownlie, *supra* note 17 at 551).

29. Weissbrodt, *supra* note 26, at 417. *See generally* Erik Suy, *The Status of Observers in International Organizations* 160 RECUEIL DES COURS 75, 101–02, 137, 143–45 (1978: II); Maya Prasad, *The Role of Non-Governmental Organizations in the New United Nations Procedures for Human Rights Complaints* 5 DENVER J. INT'L L. & POL'Y 441, 460 (1975).

30. Captain George A.B. Peirce, *Humanitarian Protection for the Victims of War: The System of Protecting Powers and the Role of the ICRC* 90 MILITARY L. REV. 89 (1980).

31. David P. Forsythe, *Humanitarian Mediation by the International Committee of the Red Cross,* INTERNATIONAL MEDIATION IN THEORY AND PRACTICE 233 (Saadia Touval & I. William Zartman eds., 1985).

organizations with expertise can, on occasion, find themselves fulfilling quasi-public, bureaucratic roles and stretched to the limit of their resources by a crisis of "too much credibility."[32]

Nonstate actors might participate in international dispute settlement when their interests are specially affected, when their involvement will contribute to efficient dispute processing, and when they possess useful special expertise. They are usually closest to a binding ruling if their interests are directly affected. As the world becomes increasingly transnational, it is likely that there will be pressure for greater openness in international decisionmaking and demands for observer status and related procedures to recognize the involvement of nonstate actors.

Individuals and private commercial entities represent their own interests. Nongovernmental organizations offer a greater range of interests, expertise, and information. Yet as most nongovernmental organizations are located in the well-off nations of the world, there may be a risk of lack of representativeness—particularly if nongovernmental organizations are given quasi-public roles. It can be beneficial for a dispute to be handled without becoming a conflict of national wills. But we may still wonder who, if anyone, fulfills the balancing functions of the Enlightenment state.[33]

III. DOMESTIC SYSTEMS

Disputes can be resolved by negotiation with minimal reference to legal rules. Once lawyers are involved—in either international or domestic matters—law will have an influence on the definition of issues and the suggested solutions. If law serves its function of facilitating action, it should be no surprise that lawyers are

---

32. MICHAEL GRUBB ET AL., THE 'EARTH SUMMIT' AGREEMENTS: A GUIDE AND ASSESSMENT 45 (Energy and Environmental Programme, The Royal Institute of International Affairs 1993) (referring to a comment by Secretary General Boutros Ghali on increased demands for U.N. activities). *See generally* Günther Handl, *Environmental Security and Global Change: The Challenge to International Law*, in ENVIRONMENTAL PROTECTION AND INTERNATIONAL LAW 59, 73–75 (W. Lang et al. eds., 1991).

33. Venkata Raman, *The Emergence of Non-Sovereign and Non-Governmental Entities*, INTERNATIONAL LAW: CRITICAL CHOICES FOR CANADA 1985–2000 at 483 (1986). *See generally* Jerome J. Shestack, *Sisyphus Endures: The International Human Rights NGO* 24 N.Y.L.S.L. REV. 89 (1978); Thomas M. Franck & H. Scott Fairley, *Procedural Due Process in Human Rights Fact-Finding by International Agencies* 74 AM. J. INT'L L. 308 (1980); David Weissbrodt & James McCarthy, *Fact-Finding by International Nongovernmental Human Rights Organizations* 22:1 VA. J. INT'L L. 1 (1981); Karen J. Jason, *The Role of Non-Governmental Organizations in International Election Observing* 24 N.Y.U.J. INT'L L. & POL'Y 1795 (1992).

guided by legal rules even when a court procedure is unavailable or unlikely. Law without adjudication, thus, is the usual situation, rather than an aberration.[34]

Adjudication traditionally involves impartial judges who apply previously agreed upon rules in a rational, orderly way. Their decisions are normally binding for the disputes in question and serve as guidelines for the future.[35] This form of dispute settlement produces a win/lose outcome and can be risky for parties. The mechanism is ideal when a dispute is to be settled on the basis of existing legal rules but the parties are in disagreement as to what those rules require. The legal determination can have independent effect on the dispute in question and on future disputes even if official enforcement of a judgment would be difficult or impossible. Compulsory jurisdiction, in other words, has an effect even in the absence of compulsory enforcement.

While most disputes do not lead to court cases, disputes in domestic legal systems take place in a framework that offers compulsory jurisdiction and enforcement to a persistent plaintiff. Unless parties agree otherwise, the legal rules apply and compliance measures are available, at least in theory, even if practical difficulties make adjudication and enforcement unlikely in fact. For international dispute settlement to offer a similar choice of procedures, including fully "legal" mechanisms with compulsory compliance, one should consider the links to domestic enforcement systems that nonstate actors can provide.

Decisions from international arbitral tribunals are commonly recognized and enforced in domestic systems.[36] Chapter 19 of the NAFTA provides a trinational antidumping and countervailing duties dispute settlement process that gives extensive control to private parties. Decisions of the trinational panels are binding at both the international and domestic levels.[37] Under the related agreements on

---

34. Richard B. Bilder, *Some Limitations of Adjudication as an International Dispute Settlement Technique* 23:1 VA. J. INT'L L. 1 (1982).

35. J.G. MERRILLS, INTERNATIONAL DISPUTE SETTLEMENT 237–41 (1991).

36. U.N. Convention on the Recognition and Enforcement of Foreign Arbitral Awards, 330 U.N.T.S. 3 (1959); Convention on the Settlement of Investment Disputes between States and Nationals of other States, done Mar. 18, 1965, in force Oct. 14, 1966, 575 U.N.T.S. 159, 17 U.S.T. 1270; T.I.A.S. 6090; U.N. Convention on the Law of the Sea, *supra* note 12, annex VI, art. 39; North American Free Trade Agreement, *supra* note 12, art. 1136; Convention Establishing the Multilateral Investment Guarantee Agency, *supra* note 13, annex II, art. 4(j); UNCITRAL Model Law on International Commercial Arbitration, adopted June 21, 1985, 24 I.L.M. 1302 (1985). Can a successful state sue to enforce a judgment of the International Court of Justice in domestic law? *See* SCHACHTER, *supra* note 4 at 235.

37. North American Free Trade Agreement, *supra* note 12, art. 1904(9). *See* Special Import Measures Act, R.S.C. 1985, Chap. S-15, s.77.016, added by North American Free Trade Agreement Implementation Act, S.C. 1993, c.44, s.218; 19 U.S.C.A. s.1516a(g)(7), as amended by North American Free Trade Agreement Implementation Act, P.L. 103–182, 107 Stat. 2057.; United States International Trade Commission, Fresh, Chilled or Frozen Pork from Canada, Views on Second Remand, Feb. 1991, USITC Publication 2362; J.G. CASTEL, A.L.C. DE MESTRAL & W.C. GRAHAM, THE CANADIAN LAW AND PRACTICE OF INTERNA-

labor and environmental cooperation, arbitral awards against Canada can be recognized and enforced through Canadian domestic courts.[38]

Even if an international ruling is not recognized directly in domestic law, it can still have an effect at that level. Treaty obligations apply in the domestic systems of monist states and even strongly dualist states in the British tradition normally incorporate international custom automatically.[39] International law may be used under an interpretive presumption that statutes are to be construed as consistent with international obligations.[40] A domestic statute may even base a cause of action explicitly on international law.[41] It is difficult to maintain that the two realms are completely separate.

International law is not entirely state-centered, after all. It is not based solely on treaties and custom under Articles 38(1)(a) and 38(1)(b) of the Statute of the International Court of Justice. Article 38(1)(c) also lists general principles of law as an accepted source. There is controversy, of course, about the extent to which this negates the positivist emphasis on the state and recognizes the law of nations[42] or natural law. At a minimum, the provision implies some connection between domestic and international spheres. Certain principles may be drawn by analogy from domestic law, at least for technical procedural matters such as *res judicata*.[43] As international law expands its influence over domestic systems, there will be many instances in which domestic courts are required to interpret international obligations. If such decisions cannot be used to show general recognition under

---

TIONAL TRADE 469–80 (1991); THOMAS M. BODDEZ & MICHAEL J. TREBILCOCK, UNFINISHED BUSINESS: REFORMING TRADE REMEDY LAWS IN NORTH AMERICA (1993).

38. North American Agreement on Labor Cooperation, done Sept. 13, 1993, in force Jan. 1, 1994, 32 I.L.M. 1499 (1933), annex 41A; North American Agreement on Environmental Cooperation, *supra* note 14, annex 36A.

39. James Crawford, *General International Law and the Common Law: A Decade of Developments* 76 AM. SOC'Y INT'L L. PROC. 232 (1982).

40. PIERRE-ANDRÉ CÔTÉ, THE INTERPRETATION OF LEGISLATION IN CANADA 308–09 (2d ed. 1991); Ralph G. Steinhardt, *The Role of International Law as a Canon of Domestic Statutory Construction* 43 VAND. L. REV. 1103 (1990).

41. Jorge Cicero, *The Alien Tort Statute of 1789 as a Remedy for Injuries to Foreign Nationals Hosted by the United States* 23 COLUM. HUMAN RTS. L. REV. 315 (1991–92); Karen E. Holt, *Filartiga v. Peña-Irala After Ten Years: Major Breakthrough or Legal Oddity?* 20 GA. J. INT'L & COMP. L. 543 (1990); Anne-Marie Burley, *The Alien Tort Statute and the Judiciary Act of 1789: A Badge of Honour* 83 AM. J. INT'L L. 461 (1989); Cynthia C. Lichtenstein, *Does International Law Have Something to Teach Monetary Law?* 10 MICH. J. INT'L L. 225 (1989); Harold Hongju Koh, *Civil Remedies for Uncivil Wrongs: Combatting Terrorism Through Transnational Public Law Litigation* 22 TEXAS INT'L L.J. 169 (1987).

42. On returning to a prepositivist view of the law of nations derived from multinational sources, *see* M.W. Janis, *Individuals as Subjects of International Law* 17 CORNELL INT'L L.J. 61 (1984).

43. For full discussion, *see* SCHACHTER, *supra* note 4 at 49–60.

Article 38(1)(c), then they might be used as subsidiary evidence under Article 38(1)(d) or at least state practice subsumed under the state structure.   The traditional emphasis in public international law on the exhaustion of local remedies indicates that the link between the two levels is not new.[44]   As the world becomes increasingly transnational, the relationship between domestic courts and international law will assume added importance.

Some may be reluctant to rely on domestic courts, as the system lacks central authoritative determinations.   To encourage harmonization, it has been suggested that the International Court of Justice be given jurisdiction for references from domestic courts, similar to the jurisdiction for advisory opinions on references from organs and agencies of the U.N. under Article 96(2) of the Charter.[45] Within the European Union, the European Court of Justice has jurisdiction for interpretive rulings on references from domestic courts.[46] Article 2020 of the NAFTA provides another mechanism for coordination, allowing a domestic court or administrative body to solicit views from its own government which then refers the question to the Free Trade Commission for an agreed interpretation.[47]   Elaborate centralizing

---

44. Note also that in the environmental area, it is common to provide for reciprocal access to domestic legal remedies: North American Agreement on Environmental Cooperation, *supra* note 14, art.6; Treaty between the United States and Great Britain Respecting Boundary Waters between the United States and Canada, done Jan. 11, 1909, in force May 5, 1910, 36 Stat. 2448; T.S. 548; 12 Bevans 319, art. II; Stockholm Declaration on the Human Environment, U.N. Doc. A/Conf.48/14 (1972), 11 I.L.M. 1416, Principle 22. *See also* Catherine A. Cooper, *The Management of International Environmental Disputes in the Context of Canada–United States Relations: A Survey and Evaluation of Techniques and Mechanisms* 24 CAN. Y.B. INT'L L. 247, 278–81 (1986); Philippe J. Sands, *The Environment, Community and International Law* 30 HARV. INT'L L.J. 393, 412 (1989).

45. Louis B. Sohn, *Broadening the Advisory Jurisdiction of the International Court of Justice* 77 AM. J. INT'L L. 124 (1983); Stephen M. Schwebel, *International Court of Justice Advisory Opinions* 33 CATH. U. L. REV. 355 (1984); Stephen M. Schwebel, *Preliminary Rulings by the International Court of Justice at the Instance of National Courts* 28 VA. J. INT'L L. 495 (1988). For the opposing position, *see* Shabtai Rosenne, *Preliminary Rulings by the International Court of Justice at the Instance of National Courts: A Reply* 29 VA. J. INT'L L. 401 (1989). *See also* Stephen M. Schwebel, *Was the Capacity to Request an Advisory Opinion Wider in the Permanent Court of International Justice than it is in the International Court of Justice?* 62 BRIT. Y.B. INT'L L. 77 (1991).

46. Treaty Establishing the European Economic Community, done Mar. 25, 1957, Article 177, as amd. by Treaty on European Union, Title II, Art. G(56).

47. North American Free Trade Agreement, *supra* note 12, art. 2020. The provision appeared in a slightly different form as art. 1808 of the Canada–United States Free Trade Agreement, done Jan. 2, 1988, in force Jan. 1, 1989, Can. T.S. 1989 No. 3, 27 I.L.M. 281 (1988). *See also* art. XXVI of the Canada–United States Income Tax Convention, 1980, which permits a taxpayer to trigger a consultation procedure between the competent authorities of the two countries when the taxpayer alleges taxation in excess of the amount allowed under the treaty (Convention Between Canada and the United States of America with Respect to Taxes on Income and on Capital, done Sept. 26, 1980, as amended June 14,

procedures may not be necessary for general questions of international law. Legal interpretations can vary with circumstances and perspectives without losing legitimacy. Some diversity of opinion would be expected among national courts and, indeed, would evidence that international law was not dominated by any particular legal culture. If domestic courts are involved in the global system of interpretation, international law will continue to grow away from its European roots, ensuring more and more representativeness. If diverging interpretations were to lead to disputes or cause other harm, simple reference mechanisms or procedures for coordination could be designed.

In the literature on alternative dispute resolution in domestic systems, early enthusiasm has been tempered with criticism. Official, formal adjudicative procedures are considered more capable of delivering fairness in situations of power imbalances.[48] The relationship between law and power is, of course, a complicated one. It is legitimate to be skeptical of any claims about the law as an instrument of social change.[49] Neither domestic law nor international law can guarantee justice for the weak, whether the weak be states or nonstate actors. Not all nonstate actors, of course, are in a weak position, but those that are might benefit from a link to the enforcement powers of domestic systems.

Enforcement of international law through domestic courts is the exception rather than the rule, and depends on an existing base in the provisions of domestic law. States have not yet faded from view. Frictions among states are inevitable and many matters are most accurately described as conflicts of national interests. When nonstate actors are directly affected, however, the state structure makes settlement bulky and awkward, as various other interests will influence the formation of national positions. If the goals are to reduce the number of disputes that are treated as nation-to-nation conflicts and to develop dispute settlement that offers a full range of legal choices, it is worthwhile to consider whether an international obligation can be defined as owing to a nonstate actor and enforceable in domestic courts.

1983 and Mar. 28, 1984, in force Aug. 16, 1984, Can. T.S. 1984 No. 15). A similar cooperative measure is the Memorandum of Understanding between Canada and the United States as to Notification, Consultation and Co-operation with respect to the Application of National Antitrust Laws, 23 I.L.M. 275 (1984); see B.R. Campbell, *The Canada–United States Antitrust Notification and Consultation Procedure* 56 CAN. BAR REV. 459 (1978).

48. *See generally* Laura Nader, *The ADR Explosion—The Implications of Rhetoric in Legal Reform* 8 WINDSOR Y.B. ACCESS JUSTICE 269 (1988); HILARY ASTOR & CHRISTINE M. CHINKIN, DISPUTE RESOLUTION IN AUSTRALIA 11–76 (1992); Neil Gold, *Canadian Perspectives on Dispute Resolution*, paper presented at Going International conference, International Law Section, Michigan Bar Association, Dearborn, Michigan, Oct. 27, 1993.

49. W.A. BOGART, COURTS AND COUNTRY: THE LIMITS OF LITIGATION AND THE SOCIAL AND POLITICAL LIFE OF CANADA (1994).

IV. CONCLUSION

Nonstate actors have a function in dispute settlement at the international level and also within domestic legal systems. The territorial nation-state, of course, still exists, and national identities remain important. Geography, however, is less of a barrier than it was in the nineteenth century. Our technology now produces global effects on the environment. Economic decisions are in many ways made in global markets that are open twenty-four hours a day. Whether we like it or not, we are all interconnected in a web of telephone, radio, television, and fax communication. We cannot just get off at the next subway stop. Participation by nonstate actors in global dispute settlement is a reflection of their participation in world affairs.

SETTLEMENT OF DISPUTES CONCERNING THE WTO AGREEMENT: VARIOUS MEANS OTHER THAN PANEL PROCEDURES

Yuji Iwasawa

I.   INTRODUCTION

The Uruguay Round negotiations conducted under the auspices of the General Agreement on Tariffs and Trade (GATT or General Agreement) was concluded in 1994 with the signing of the Final Act Embodying the Results of the Uruguay Round of Multilateral Trade Negotiations. The Agreement Establishing the World Trade Organization (WTO Agreement), which forms the principal part of the Final Act, entered into force in January 1995.[1] The WTO has replaced the GATT as an organization and administers various agreements concluded in the Uruguay Round, including the revised GATT. One of the most important developments in the Uruguay Round was the adoption of the Understanding on Rules and Procedures Governing the Settlement of Disputes, which is annexed to the WTO Agreement and is made an integral part of the Agreement (1994 Understanding). The 1994 Understanding is designed to improve the dispute settlement procedures developed and applied under Articles 22 and 23 of the General Agreement.

The WTO/GATT dispute settlement procedures are among the most effective dispute settlement procedures in international law. More than 150 disputes have been referred to the Contracting Parties of the GATT and most have been settled as a result. The Contracting Parties have developed a practice of establishing panels for the settlement of disputes. A panel, a legal body consisting of independent experts, examines arguments of the parties from a legal point of view and presents its findings and recommendations to the Dispute Settlement Body

---

1.   Marrakesh Agreement Establishing the World Trade Organization, Apr. 15, 1994, 33 I.L.M. 1144.

(DSB) of the WTO in the form of a report. The DSB, a political body consisting of all the members of the WTO, then adopts the report. Thus, a unique feature of the WTO panel procedures is a combination of legal and political considerations, although, under the 1994 Understanding, adoption of panel reports by the DSB is a mere formality and thus legal consideration predominates. Proceedings of panels are quasi-judicial and their reports read like court judgments. In that sense, panel procedures are comparable to arbitration. Panel procedures, however, have other aspects which are more akin to conciliation than to arbitration. The report of the panel is not binding on the parties in itself; it has no legal value until adopted by the DSB. Moreover, the parties are encouraged to settle the dispute by an agreement. Devices to promote bilateral settlement are built into the panel procedures: for instance, before a panel finalizes its report, it issues an interim report to the parties, allowing them to develop mutually satisfactory solutions. The WTO panel procedures are thus a *sui generis* mode of dispute settlement, comprising elements of both arbitration and conciliation.[2]

Admittedly, panel procedures are perhaps the most well-known of all available means of dispute settlement in the WTO, and their contribution to making the WTO dispute settlement procedures effective is substantial. Available in the WTO, however, are other means of dispute settlement, which also form important parts of the entire WTO dispute settlement mechanism. In fact, a notable feature of the WTO dispute settlement mechanism is the availability of various means of settling disputes. The means of dispute settlement under international law—negotiation (consultations), good offices, mediation, conciliation, inquiry, arbitration, and judicial settlement—are also available in the WTO. This paper will analyze methods of dispute settlement which are less known than the panel procedures. First, nonadjudicatory or diplomatic means will be discussed, followed by an examination of adjudicatory or legal means. The nonadjudicatory means include negotiation (consultations), good offices, mediation, conciliation, and inquiry. Adjudicatory means consist of arbitration and judicial settlement.

Disputes concerning the various agreements annexed to the WTO Agreement, including the revised GATT, may be settled by domestic courts. Disputes concerning the WTO Agreement may also be referred to the dispute settlement mechanisms set up by regional free trade agreements—the North America Free Trade Agreement (NAFTA) and its predecessor, the U.S.-Canada Free Trade Agreement (CFTA). The settlement of disputes in these fora is not settlement of disputes *within* the WTO *stricto sensu*. Nevertheless, these are significant and

---

2.   *See generally* YUJI IWASAWA, WTO NO FUNSŌ SHORI [DISPUTE SETTLEMENT OF THE WTO] (1995). *See also* ERIC CANAL-FORGUES, L'INSTITUTION DE LA CONCILIATION DANS LE CADRE DU GATT: CONTRIBUTION À L'ÉTUDE DE LA STRUCTURATION D'UN MÉCANISME DE RÈGLEMENT DES DIFFÉRENDS (1993); ROBERT E. HUDEC, ENFORCING INTERNATIONAL TRADE LAW: GATT DISPUTE SETTLEMENT IN THE 1980S (1993); ROBERT E. HUDEC, THE GATT LEGAL SYSTEM AND WORLD TRADE DIPLOMACY (2d ed. 1990); Ernst-Ulrich Petersmann, *Strengthening GATT Procedures for Settling Trade Disputes*, 11 WORLD ECON. 55 (1988).

undeniable means of settling disputes *concerning* the WTO Agreement. Accordingly, they, too, will be analyzed.

II.   NONADJUDICATORY OR DIPLOMATIC MEANS

Various means of dispute settlement available under international law are commonly divided into adjudicatory (legal) means and nonadjudicatory (diplomatic) means. In adjudicatory means, a third party intervening in a dispute— normally an international tribunal—delivers a judgment binding on the parties to the dispute. In contrast, in nonadjudicatory means, a third party does not issue a binding decision. It is up to the parties of the dispute to agree on terms of settlement. The third party simply assists the parties in reaching an agreement. In this section nonadjudicatory means will be analyzed. In negotiation (consultations), a third party does not become involved; it is a *private* means of dispute settlement. In other nonadjudicatory means—good offices, mediation, conciliation, and inquiry—a third party intervenes in the dispute; these are *public* means of dispute settlement. The extent and manner of the third party's involvement in the dispute varies from one method to another.

a.   Negotiation (Consultations)

Negotiation is especially effective as a means to settle international economic disputes. The parties to an international economic dispute often genuinely wish to resolve the dispute swiftly and fairly, for it impairs their long-standing trade relationship.[3] Negotiations, however, have a serious weakness: the terms of settlement tend to reflect the bargaining positions of the disputing parties. Even a major economic power like Japan often has no alternative but to succumb to the demands of the United States and agree on "voluntary" export restraints (e.g., "voluntary" restraints on automobile exports).[4] The General Agreement does not use the term negotiation, providing instead for consultations in many places. The two major functions of consultations are prevention and settlement of disputes. In the latter function, consultations resemble negotiation as a means of dispute settlement.[5] Three kinds of consultations are available in the GATT: bilateral,

---

3.   For an author who stresses the importance of negotiation in the settlement of international economic disputes, *see* ROBERT KOVAR, LE RÈGLEMENT DES DIFFÉRENDS ÉCONOMIQUES INTERÉTATIQUES DANS LES ORGANISATIONS INTERNATIONALES 39–48 (1969–70).

4.   For details on "voluntary" restraint on automobile exports, *see, e.g.*, Michael William Lochmann, *The Japanese Voluntary Restraint on Automobile Exports: An Abandonment of the Free Trade Principles of the GATT and the Free Market Principles of United States Antitrust Laws*, 27 HARV. INT'L L.J. 99 (1986).

5.   On the distinction between negotiations and consultations, *see, e.g.*, Stephen L. Kass, *Obligatory Negotiation in International Organization*, 3 CAN. Y.B. INT'L L. 36, 43–46

plurilateral, and organizational consultations.

(1) Bilateral Consultations

The General Agreement provides for bilateral consultations of a general character in Articles 22(1) and 23(1). According to Article 22(1), a member of the WTO may request consultations with any other member with respect to any matter affecting the operation of the GATT. The responding member has only to accord "sympathetic consideration" to the complaints, though it cannot refuse consultations altogether.[6] Consultations provided for in Article 23(1) differ only slightly from consultations provided for in Article 22(1); under Article 23(1), the complaining member must allege that benefits accruing to it under the General Agreement are being nullified or impaired or that the attainment of an objective of the General Agreement is impeded.

Because negotiation is an effective means of settling international economic disputes, international economic organizations often attach special importance to consultations or negotiation.[7] The WTO is no exception. The WTO dispute settlement procedures are built upon a belief that disputes are best settled by an agreement of the parties, and therefore attach special importance to consultations. In fact, most disputes have been resolved by consultations in the GATT; far more disputes have been settled by consultations than by panels. Consultations, however, have limitations as a private means of dispute settlement. They will bring about equitable solutions only when public means of dispute settlement are available. In the WTO, consultations are indeed buttressed by effective panel procedures. Even after a panel is established, consultations continue and disputes are often settled by an agreement of the parties before the panel issues a report. In some instances, the parties reached an agreement after a report of the panel was issued to them but before it was circulated to other states.[8] Some panels even called on the parties for

---

(1965); Adrian Nastase, *Utilization of Negotiations and Consultations in the Process of Settlement of Disputes within International Economic Organizations*, 21 REVUE ROUMAINE D'ÉTUDES INTERNATIONALES 431, 434–37 (1987); Soji Yamamoto, *Kokusai Funsō ni okeru Kyōgi Seido no Henshitsu* [*The Change in the System of Consultation in International Disputes*], *in* MINAGAWA TAKESHI SENSEI KANREKI KINEN: FUNSŌ NO HEIWATEKI KAIKETSU TO KOKUSAI HŌ [COMMEMORATING THE SIXTIETH BIRTHDAY OF PROFESSOR TAKESHI MINAGAWA: PEACEFUL SETTLEMENT OF DISPUTES AND INTERNATIONAL LAW] 215 (1981).

6.   Some scholars believe that "an obligation to negotiate" exists also under customary international law. NGUYEN QUOC DINH ET AL., DROIT INTERNATIONAL PUBLIC 765–67 (4th ed. 1992).

7.   Kovar, *supra* note 3, at 39–48. Nastase, *supra* note 5, at 439.

8.   *E.g.,* Restraints on Imports of Manufactured Tobacco (U.S. v. Japan), BASIC INSTRUMENTS AND SELECTED DOCUMENTS [BISD], 28th Supp. 100 (panel report adopted on May 15, 1981). When a dispute is settled by an agreement of the parties, it is the practice of panels to simply indicate that fact in the report. Accordingly, the panel in the *Tobacco*

further consultations, thus avoiding passing upon difficult issues.[9] One weakness of bilateral consultations in the WTO is that the parties often "settle" disputes through "compensation," that is, reduction of tariffs on other products. Thus, the "settlement" does not signify a permanent resolution of the dispute but merely a temporary cease-fire, because the measure which contravenes the General Agreement and constituted the root cause of the dispute remains intact.

Because the consultation process is confidential and the terms of settlement are often not disclosed, the realities of consultations are scarcely known. The 1958 Decision of the GATT Contracting Parties obligated a contracting party seeking a consultation under Article 22 to so inform the GATT Director-General.[10] There was no obligation of a similar kind with regard to consultations under Article 23(1) until 1989, when a decision to improve the dispute settlement procedures adopted at the Mid-Term Review of the Uruguay Round (1989 Improvement) provided that requests for consultations under Articles 22(1) or 23(1) shall be notified to the GATT Council (this provision is incorporated in Article 4(4) of the 1994 Understanding).[11] Until that time, the parties were not obligated to notify the GATT whether the dispute had been settled by consultations or to inform the GATT of the terms of settlement. The parties sometimes notified the GATT on their own accord that the dispute had been settled by consultations, but they rarely disclosed the terms of settlement. The 1994 Understanding placed bilateral consultations under the control of the WTO by providing that mutually agreed solutions shall be notified to the DSB and relevant Councils and Committees of the WTO (Article 3(6)).

(2) Plurilateral Consultations

According to the 1958 Decision of the Contracting Parties, any contracting party seeking a consultation under Article 22 shall so inform the GATT Director-General for the information of all contracting parties. Any other contracting party asserting a substantial trade interest in the matter may advise the consulting countries and the Director-General of its desire to be joined in the consultations. There are more than twenty instances in which third parties have been joined in consultations in accordance with this provision.[12] Plurilateral consultations,

---

case rewrote the report, never disclosing the findings which it had reached in the original report.

9. *E.g.*, Dollar Area Quotas (U.S. v. U.K.), BISD, 20th Supp. 230, 236 (panel report adopted on July 20, 1973); Canadian Import Quotas on Eggs (U.S. v. Can.), BISD, 23d Supp. 91, 92–93 (report of the working party adopted on Feb. 17, 1976).

10. Procedures under Art. XXII on Questions Affecting the Interests of a Number of Contracting Parties, adopted on Nov. 10, 1958, BISD, 7th Supp. 24.

11. Improvements to the GATT Dispute Settlement Rules and Procedures, Decision of Apr. 12, 1989, Sec. C (3), BISD, 36th Supp. 61.

12. GATT, ANALYTICAL INDEX: GUIDE TO GATT LAW AND PRACTICE 577–82 (6th ed. 1994) [hereinafter *GATT, Analytical Index 1994*].

however, have not been used extensively.

(3) Organizational Consultations

Article 22(2) of the General Agreement, which was added in 1955, provides that the Ministerial Conference, at the request of a member, may consult with any member or members. These consultations may be called organizational consultations. Organizational consultations are usually carried out in the form of working parties. (See section b.(4), below.) As will become evident through further discussion, although referred to as *consultations*, the process is actually a *mediation* of the dispute by the WTO.

(4) Consultations as a Prerequisite to the Reference of Disputes to a Public Means of Dispute Settlement

A request for consultations by the Ministerial Conference under Article 22(2) of the General Agreement may be made only after bilateral consultations under Article 22(1) have proven fruitless. Similarly, establishment of a panel may be requested under Article 23(2) of the General Agreement only after bilateral consultations under Article 23(1) have failed to result in satisfactory adjustment.[13] In order to avoid sabotage, the 1994 Understanding sets time limits on various stages of consultations. It provides, *inter alia*, that if the consultations fail to settle a dispute within sixty days, the complaining party may request the establishment of a panel. Thus, in the WTO, *private* means of dispute settlement must be exhausted before recourse may be had to *public* means of dispute settlement, as is often the case with international economic organizations.[14] Some scholars and courts take the view that this principle is recognized by customary international law as well. They maintain that unless negotiations are exhausted, disputes may not be referred to public means of dispute settlement, including international adjudication. Other scholars and courts, however, repudiate such a theory.[15] The fact that treaties establishing international economic organizations, such as the WTO Agreement and the General Agreement, specifically require consultations to be exhausted before disputes may be referred to public means of dispute settlement seems to indicate that customary international law does not recognize such a principle.

---

13. *E.g.*, Uruguayan Recourse to art. XXIII (Uruguay v. Fifteen Developed Contracting States), BISD, 11th Supp. 95, 98 (panel report adopted on Nov. 16, 1962). Because consultations under art. 22(1) and under art. 23(1) are similar, it is established that if consultations have been tried under art. 22(1), the complaining party may request the establishment of a panel without seeking further consultations under art. 23(1).

14. KOVAR, *supra* note 3, at 39–48. GEORGES MALINVERNI, LE RÈGLEMENT DES DIFFÉRENDS DANS LES ORGANISATIONS INTERNATIONALES ÉCONOMIQUES 110–17 (1974).

15. *See generally* MALINVERNI, *supra* note 14, at 110–12.

as well. They maintain that unless negotiations are exhausted, disputes may not be referred to public means of dispute settlement, including international adjudication. Other scholars and courts, however, repudiate such a theory.[15] The fact that treaties establishing international economic organizations, such as the WTO Agreement and the General Agreement, specifically require consultations to be exhausted before disputes may be referred to public means of dispute settlement seems to indicate that customary international law does not recognize such a principle.

b. Good Offices, Mediation, and Conciliation

(1) Distinctions between Good Offices, Mediation, and Conciliation under International Law

Good offices, mediation, and conciliation are nonadjudicatory, public means of dispute settlement—a third party intervenes in a dispute but refrains from imposing specific terms of settlement on the parties to the dispute. How can these three modes of dispute settlement be distinguished? Good offices encompass assistance of a third party from outside in dispute settlement without examining the subject-matter of the dispute. The third party recommends to the parties to the dispute that the dispute be settled by negotiation or provides them with facilities for negotiation. Mediation, on the other hand, requires more positive involvement on the part of the third party. The third party examines the subject-matter of a dispute, modifies claims of the parties, and proposes specific terms by which the dispute may be settled. In the real world, a third party often engages in actions which have elements of both good offices and mediation. Consequently, the two terms are often used interchangeably.

Conciliation is similar to mediation in that a third party examines the subject-matter of the dispute and proposes specific terms of settlement to the parties of the dispute. A distinguishing feature of conciliation is that it is conducted by a commission consisting of individual experts. Accordingly, two ways of distinguishing mediation and conciliation have been suggested by scholars. Some scholars emphasize the identity of the intervening third party: while mediation is performed by states, conciliation is carried out by international organs.[16] In contrast, others stress the quality of the third party: while mediation relies on the *political influence* of the third party to settle the dispute, conciliation relies on the

---

15. *See generally* MALINVERNI, *supra* note 14, at 110–12.

16. *E.g.*, RAYMOND R. PROBST, "GOOD OFFICES" IN THE LIGHT OF SWISS INTERNATIONAL PRACTICE AND EXPERIENCE 6 (1989); ARNOLD DE SAINT SEINE, LA CONCILIATION INTERNATIONALE 11 (1930); 2 YUICHI TAKANO, EINFÜHRUNG IN DAS VÖLKERRECHT 224, 230–31 (1986); C. VULCAN, LA CONCILIATION DANS LE DROIT INTERNATIONAL ACTUEL 9 (1930).

Two different systems of dispute settlement are usually available in international organizations: one by its organs which are composed of states—General Assembly or Council—and the other by independent commissions made up of individual experts. According to the first view, both of these forms of dispute settlement will be characterized as conciliation because in both cases the intervening third party is an international organ. The settlement of disputes by the General Assembly or Council of an international organization, however, is more akin to mediation traditionally performed by states in its substance, because the political weight of the intervening third party is the key in the successful resolution of the dispute. It is superficial to consider this form of dispute settlement as conciliation simply because the intervening third party is not a state but an international organ. It is more accurate to regard it as mediation. On the other hand, the settlement of disputes by independent commissions composed of individual experts may be regarded rightly as conciliation. These commissions rely on the neutrality and expertise of its members for the successful settlement of disputes. In the real world, however, conciliation and mediation are often not distinguished and, consequently, the two terms are used interchangeably.

(2) "Good Offices" of the Director-General of the WTO

The 1994 Understanding has an article on "Good Offices, Conciliation and Mediation" (Article 5). These three modes of dispute settlement are lumped together and not distinguished and, as used in the WTO, apparently correspond to "mediation" as defined in the previous section.[19] The 1994 Understanding seems to assume that the Director-General will engage in these actions to assist members to settle a dispute. Although other entities, such as an organ of the WTO, a state, or a group of states, could act as the intermediary, normally it will be the Director-General who intervenes in the dispute.

The 1966 Decision of the GATT Contracting Parties gave developing countries a right to refer a dispute with a developed country to the "good offices" of the GATT Director-General.[20] The 1982 Ministerial Declaration recognized that any party to a dispute may seek the "good offices" of the Director-General, provided that the other party agrees. In spite of these provisions facilitating requests for the good offices of the Director-General, states have not sought his good offices very frequently. Even when they have, the dispute was often not solved by his good offices, but had eventually to be referred to the panel procedures.[21]

---

19. *Accord* Eric Canal-Forgues & Rudolf Ostrihansky, *New Developments in the GATT Dispute Settlement Procedures*, 24 (No. 2) J. WORLD TRADE 67, 70 (1990).

20. Procedures under art. XXIII, Decision of Apr. 5, 1966, BISD, 14th Supp. 18.

21. Developing countries have sought the good offices of the Director-General in the following cases: Export Refunds on Malted Barley (Chile v. EC), GATT Doc. L/4588 (Nov. 1977), GATT ACTIVITIES IN 1977, at 78 (withdrawn by Chile); Import Restriction of Leather

In the last decade, however, the good offices of the Director-General have proven useful and some disputes have actually been successfully settled by his good offices. The *Copper* case between the European Community (EC) and Japan is a good example.[22] In 1987, the EC and Japan agreed to jointly request the good offices of the Director-General to help resolve their disputes over copper ores and concentrates. The Director-General appointed Professor Gardner Patterson, former Deputy Director-General of GATT, as his personal representative for good offices. The EC copper smelting and refining industry had difficulties obtaining adequate supplies of copper concentrates on acceptable terms. The EC maintained that the high internal price of refined copper in Japan had distorted the world copper market. After presenting their positions in joint meetings, the parties requested that the Director-General offer an "advisory opinion." While concluding that Japan had not violated any of its GATT obligations, Professor Patterson advised the parties to enter into reciprocal and mutually advantageous negotiations with a view to substantially reducing or eliminating the Japanese tariff on cathode and wire bar (the form in which the bulk of refined copper is traded).[23] Both the EC and Japan expressed satisfaction with Professor Patterson's report.[24] Similarly, Canada and the EC settled their dispute over wet salted cod in 1988 with the help of an "advisory opinion" of the Director-General.[25] In these cases, the Director-General (or his personal representative) examined the subject-matter of the dispute and offered "advisory opinions." The activities of the Director-General may be characterized as mediation rather than good offices according to the distinctions made in the previous section. As demonstrated in these examples, the "good offices," "mediation," or "conciliation" of the Director-General, no matter how termed, will

---

(India v. Japan), BISD, 31st Supp. 94, 108 (the parties agreed to a mutually satisfactory solution in bilateral consultations); Taxes on Petroleum and Certain Imported Substances (Mexico v. U.S.), BISD, 34th Supp. 136 (referred to the panel procedures and a panel report adopted on June 17, 1987); Unilateral Retaliation in the Informatics Dispute (Brazil v. U.S.), GATT Doc.L/6274/Add.1 (Dec. 1987) (the parties reached an agreement following bilateral consultations); Import Restriction on Bananas (Columbia et al. v. EC) 97 GATT FOCUS 2 (1993) (referred to the panel procedures); Import Restriction on Wool Suits (Brazil v. U.S.) (the Director-General recommended further consultations and the parties reached an agreement), 99 GATT FOCUS 2 (1993). In only one case a developed country sought the good offices of the Director-General: Citrus from Certain Mediterranean Countries (U.S. v. EC), GATT Council, Minutes of Meeting, July 21, 1982, GATT Doc. C/M/160, at 17–22 (1982), Minutes of Meeting, Oct. 1, 1982, C/M/161, at 6 (1982) (referred to the panel procedure).

22. *See generally* GATT ACTIVITIES 1984, at 43; GATT ACTIVITIES 1986, at 52; GATT ACTIVITIES 1987, at 59; GATT ACTIVITIES 1988, at 74.

23. Note by the Director-General, BISD, 36th Supp. 199 (Jan. 31, 1989).

24. GATT Council, Minutes of Meetings, Feb. 21, 1989, at 5–6, GATT Doc. C/M/229 (1989) (the Council taking note of the report and the statements of the parties).

25. GATT Council, Minutes of Meetings, Oct. 19, 1988, at 2, GATT Doc. C/M/225 (1988).

actually correspond in substance to mediation in most cases.[26]

(3) "Conciliation" by the Committees Established under the Tokyo Round Agreements

Under some of the Tokyo Round agreements, a contracting party had to refer a dispute to the committee established under the agreement for its "conciliation" before the party could request the establishment of a panel.[27] At the conciliation meetings of the committee, any committee member state, including the parties to the dispute, could express an opinion. The "conciliation" by the committee was an attempt by an international organ composed of states to settle a dispute using its political influence. Such actions of the committee may be characterized as mediation rather than conciliation according to the distinctions made above. The parties to the dispute were to declare their views before the entire committee, thereby making their positions firm and inflexible. Some states usually simply read prepared statements. This exercise rarely led to a resolution of the dispute.[28] The 1994 Understanding eliminated the "conciliation" phase, which had proven mostly a waste of time and "worse than worthless."[29] The 1994 Understanding provides that if the consultations fail to settle a dispute within sixty days, the complaining party may proceed to a request for the establishment of a panel.

(4) Working Parties

A working party consists of five to twenty states, depending on the importance of the question and always includes parties to the dispute. A working party holds

---

26. In 1993 Brazil requested the good offices of the Director-General, complaining that the United States had not abided by recommendations of the Textiles Surveillance Body that Brazil should be treated with equity with respect to men's and boy's wool suits. The Director-General requested both parties, "as a first step," to intensify bilateral talks. As a result of the bilateral contacts, the matter was resolved. GATT Council, Minutes of Meeting, May 12–13, 1993, GATT Doc. C/M/263, 99 GATT FOCUS 2–3 (1993). The action of the Director-General in this case was limited indeed to good offices.

27. The Antidumping Agreement, art. 15(3). The Subsidies and Countervailing Measures Agreement, art. 17(1). Other agreements provide that the Committee shall meet to "investigate" the matter. The Customs Valuation Agreement, art. 20(1). The Standards Agreement, art. 14(4). The Government Procurement Agreement, art. 7(6).

28. "Conciliation" by the Committee was of use in the following cases: Homologation Requirements for Heating Radiators and Electrical Medical Equipment (EC v. Spain), BISD, 31st Supp. 236; Purchase of Computers under French "Computer Literacy Program" (U.S. v. EC), BISD, 32d Supp. 152, BISD, 33d Supp. 192, 196.

29. Robert E. Hudec, *Dispute Settlement, in* COMPLETING THE URUGUAY ROUND: A RESULTS-ORIENTED APPROACH TO THE GATT TRADE NEGOTIATIONS 180, 194 (Jeffrey J. Schott ed. 1990).

several meetings to examine a question and issues a report recording the different views of the states. It is a procedure in which an international organ consisting of states uses its political influence to assist the disputing parties in reaching an agreement and hence, the procedure may be characterized as mediation according to the distinctions made above.

Working parties may be established under either Article 22(2) or Article 23(2) of the General Agreement. Article 22(2) provides for organizational consultations. (See section II.(3), above.) Requests for the establishment of a working party have been made under Article 22(2) in around ten cases, with many requests made in the 1960s when calls for the establishment of a panel pursuant to Article 23(2) were regarded as a hostile act in the GATT circle. Since then, however, with only one exception, working parties have seldom been requested under Article 22(2).[30] The sole exception is the *Copper* dispute between the EC and Japan, in which the EC requested the establishment of a working party before the two parties agreed to request the good offices of the GATT Director-General.[31] Presumably the EC did not ask for the establishment of a panel because it was aware that the actions of Japan were not inconsistent with the General Agreement.

In the 1940s and early 1950s when the panel procedures had not yet been devised, working parties were often set up for the settlement of disputes referred to the Contracting Parties under Article 23(2). Nevertheless, since 1953, when the panel system was first introduced, the panel procedures have become a preferred mode of dispute settlement under Article 23(2). It is still possible for a complaining party to request the establishment of a working party instead of a panel under Article 23(2). But an overwhelming majority of states requests the establishment of a panel rather than a working party and there has been no request at all since the middle of the 1970s.[32] The 1989 Improvement made reference to working parties, stipulating that a working party could be established under Article 23(2).[33]

Because working parties are seldom requested pursuant to Article 23(2), the 1994 Understanding eliminated all the references to working parties. This does not necessarily mean, however, that a complaining state cannot request the establishment of a working party in lieu of a panel. An agreement of the responding state will be required, however. Under the 1994 Understanding, if a WTO member requests the establishment of a panel, a panel shall be established even if the responding member does not agree to its establishment. In that sense, a WTO

---

30. For the list of cases, *see* GATT, ANALYTICAL INDEX: NOTES ON THE DRAFTING, INTERPRETATION AND APPLICATION OF THE ARTICLES OF THE GENERAL AGREEMENT, art. XXII, at 6–8, GATT/LEG/2 (5th ed. 1989).

31 . *See* text accompanying *supra* note 23.

32. Working parties were requested in the following cases: Special Temporary Compensation Tax on Imports (Italy v. France), BISD, 3d Supp. 26 (decision of the Contracting Parties on Jan. 17, 1955); Import Quotas on Eggs (U.S. v. Canada), BISD, 23d Supp. 91 (report of the working party adopted on Feb. 17, 1976).

33. The 1989 Improvement, *supra* note 11, sec. F.

member has a "right to a panel." A WTO member has no comparable "right to a working party."

As we have seen, good offices, mediation, and conciliation are available in the WTO as well. No matter how named, however, in substance they will be characterized as mediation as defined in this article. The dispute settlement by working parties may also be regarded as a form of mediation. In the WTO, these nonadjudicatory means of dispute settlement are used infrequently. The panel procedures are admittedly the preferred and principal mode of dispute settlement. There are some instances, however, in which a dispute was successfully resolved by means of good offices, mediation, or conciliation. These modes of dispute settlement have proven useful for disputes in which the complaining party had difficulty in alleging violations of law on the part of the responding state (e.g., the *Copper* dispute between the EC and Japan).[34] Professor Abbott stressed the importance of rule-based decisions, and criticized the "ADR techniques" (good offices, mediation, and conciliation),[35] which are designed to promote compromise settlements.[36]

There is a tendency among international lawyers to adopt a linear approach to dispute settlement: they list various means of dispute settlement from negotiation to judicial settlement and espouse that judicial settlement is the highest form and the best way of settling any dispute. One should recognize, however, that there are two different types of disputes and that different methods of dispute settlement are to be employed in accordance with the different nature of the dispute. In some disputes, the parties may seek a resolution of the dispute by applying the existing law. For such *legal* disputes, *static* means of dispute settlement such as adjudication, are to be employed. When static means are employed, the existing law is applied. The WTO panel procedures can be considered a static means as far as "violation complaints" (complaints alleging violations of the WTO Agreement) are concerned. In other disputes, the parties may seek resolution of the dispute by changing the law

---

34. *See* text accompanying *supra* note 23.

35. It is doubtful that the concept of "ADR" (alternative dispute resolution) could be of meaningful use in international law. One may ask what they are alternative to. Adjudication in courts is by far not the primary means of dispute resolution in international law. Professor Abbott uses the term ADR in the sense of dispute resolution alternative to the GATT panel procedures, and refers to good offices, mediation, and conciliation—but excludes arbitration. However, if the term is used in the sense of dispute resolution alternative to adjudication in courts, not only arbitration but also the panel procedures are themselves "ADR." For the use of ADR in this sense, *see Symposium: Alternative Dispute Resolution in Canada-United States Trade Relations*, 40 ME. L. REV. 223 (1988); Jack R. Miller, *Alternative Dispute Resolution in Canada–U.S. Trade, in* THE CANADA–U.S. FREE TRADE AGREEMENT: IMPLICATIONS, OPPORTUNITIES, AND CHALLENGES 95 (Daniel E. Nolle ed. 1990); O. Thomas Johnson, Jr., *Alternative Dispute Resolution in the International Context: The North American Free Trade Agreement*, 46 SMU L. REV. 2175 (1993).

36. Kenneth W. Abbott, *The Uruguay Round and Dispute Resolution: Building a Private-Interests System of Justice*, 1 COLUM. BUS. L. REV. 111, 119–26.

in an equitable manner. For such *non-legal* disputes, *dynamic* means of dispute settlement, such as mediation, are more appropriately used. When dynamic means are employed, efforts are made to find a fair and equitable solution of the dispute rather than mechanically applying the preexisting law.[37]

c. Inquiry

Inquiry is a means of dispute settlement in which a commission of inquiry ascertains the facts in contention. In the WTO, the parties to a dispute may agree to establish a factfinding commission with such a mandate. It is also possible for them to refer a dispute to a panel but agree to restrict its terms of reference to an ascertainment of facts. In the *Copper* dispute between the EC and Japan, the EC asked the Council to establish a working party first. A working party was not established, but instead a Group of Governmental Experts on Measures Affecting the World Market for Copper was established in 1986 to "examine problems falling under the competence of the General Agreement relating to current trends in world trade in copper, including the supply and demand situation for copper." In their report, the governmental experts agreed that world trade in copper had been negatively affected by various factors, but was unable to agree on whether certain (in effect, Japan's) pricing and trade practices constituted a distortion in the supply and demand of copper.[38] The EC and Japan, unable to settle the dispute with the report of the Group of Governmental Experts, agreed to seek the "good offices" of the Director-General as previously explained. The activities of the Group of Governmental Experts in this case may be considered an example of inquiry. Inquiry has seldom been used in the WTO as a means of dispute settlement.[39]

The 1979 Standards Agreement allowed the Standards Committee to form a technical expert group, in lieu of a panel, and direct it to make findings on technical matters. In the *Hormone Beef* conflict, the United States requested the establishment of a technical expert group under the Standards Agreement to examine the EC directive prohibiting the import of beef treated with growth hormones. The request was blocked by the EC, however.[40] The 1994

---

37. *See* 4 TAKEO SOGAWA, INTERNATIONAL LAW 231–32 (1950) (criticizing the linear approach and advocating distinguishing static and dynamic means of dispute settlement).

38. Measures Affecting the World Market for Copper Ores and Concentrates, BISD, 34th Supp. 168 (report of the Group of Governmental Experts adopted on Dec. 2, 1987).

39. For another example, *see* the report of the Group of Experts in the Greek Increase in Bound Duty case, GATT Doc. L/580 (Nov. 9, 1956) (finding that newly developed "LP records" belonged in the generic tariff item of "gramophone records," and that Greece should not have imposed a higher duty on "LP records" without resorting to the procedures for modification of a bound rate).

40. *See* GATT ACTIVITIES 1987, at 80; GATT ACTIVITIES 1988, at 72; GATT ACTIVITIES 1989, at 123. For details on this case, *see, e.g.*, Holly Hammonds, *A U.S. Perspective on the EC Hormones Directive*, 11 MICH. J. INT'L L. 840 (1990); Werner P. Meng, *The Hormone*

Understanding contains explicit provisions on an "expert review group," which may be formed by a panel under any of the agreements annexed to the WTO Agreement. The 1994 Understanding has placed expert review groups under the panel's authority.[41] If activities of an expert review group may be separated from those of a panel, they may be considered a kind of inquiry.

III. ADJUDICATORY OR LEGAL MEANS

a.   Arbitration

There are two kinds of international adjudication: arbitration and judicial settlement. Arbitration refers to adjudication by an *ad hoc* tribunal set up by the parties themselves. Judicial settlement refers to adjudication by a standing tribunal. This section will examine whether these adjudicatory means of dispute settlement are available for the settlement of disputes concerning the WTO Agreement.

The stillborn International Trade Organization's (ITO) Charter had a provision explicitly allowing ITO members to submit disputes to arbitration. Although this provision has not been taken over either by the General Agreement or by the WTO Agreement, arbitration has always been available in the GATT as a means of dispute settlement if the parties decided to have recourse to it. The parties have rarely had recourse to arbitration, however. It is reported that in some cases, the GATT Director-General, another member of the GATT Secretariat, or independent outside experts have served as arbitrators, although most of them are not on public record.[42]

An example of a dispute which was settled by arbitration is the so-called "Chicken War" between the EC and the United States. In 1962 the EC imposed a variable levy on poultry and consequently U.S. exports of poultry to Germany contracted substantially. Accordingly, the United States decided to withdraw concessions on EC exports equivalent in value to the U.S. poultry exports affected by the EC action, invoking Article 28 of the General Agreement. The EC did not challenge the right of the United States to retaliate in accordance with Article 28, but it did challenge the valuation by the United States of the poultry exports. In the end, the EC and the United States reached an agreement to refer the dispute regarding the value of the poultry exports to an advisory opinion of an impartial

---

Conflict between the EEC and the United States within the Context of GATT, 11 MICH. J. INT'L L. 819 (1990).

41. The 1994 Understanding, art.13(2), Appendix 4. *See also* the Sanitary and Phytosanitary Measures Agreement, art. 11(2); the Standards Agreement, art. 14(2), Annex 2; the Custom Valuation Agreement, art. 19(3), (4); the Subsidy and Countervailing Measures Agreement, art. 4(5).

42. Ernst-Ulrich Petersmann, *Strengthening the GATT Dispute Settlement System: On the Use of Arbitration in GATT*, in THE NEW GATT ROUND OF MULTILATERAL TRADE NEGOTIATIONS 323, 339 (Ernst-Ulrich Petersmann et al. eds. 1988).

panel appointed by the Council. The value ascertained by the panel was $26 million.[43] The organ entrusted with the settlement of the dispute was named a "panel," but it was not an ordinary panel. The mandate of the panel was restricted to the valuation of the poultry trade. The report of the panel was not adopted by the Contracting Parties but was presented directly to the parties. Under the circumstances, some scholars have regarded the panel as performing an inquiry,[44] while others have considered it as conciliation.[45] This case, however, should be regarded as a case of arbitration. Although what was formally requested of the panel was its "advisory opinion," the parties were, in fact, under an agreement,[46] or at least a "silent understanding,"[47] to abide by the "advisory opinion." The "advisory opinion" was thus, in reality, a binding award which, it was asssumed, the parties were to accept. Moreover, what was assigned to the panel involved more than simple finding of facts.[48] The panel had to choose a reference period on the basis of which the value of U.S. poultry exports should be determined. Since poultry exports were rapidly increasing, the choice of the reference period could have made an enormous difference in calculating the value of trade. The panel also had to evaluate the market share the United States would have had in the absence of the quantitative restrictions. Both these tasks required more than a simple finding of facts; they forced the panel to make legal judgments.

The 1994 Understanding formally recognized arbitration as an alternative means of dispute settlement within the WTO, stressing that expeditious arbitration "can facilitate the solution of certain disputes." Resort to arbitration is subject to mutual agreement by the parties. With respect to certain disputes, such as a dispute over the level of suspension of concessions proposed, arbitration is required. The provisions on arbitration in the 1994 Understanding are simple. A great deal depends on an agreement between the parties of a dispute, who must agree on such details as the arbitrators, the procedures to be followed, and the applicable law. In July 1990, Canada and the EC agreed to have recourse to arbitration pursuant to the 1989 Improvement, which had provisions nearly identical to those of the 1994

---

43. GATT Doc. L/2088 (panel report of Nov. 21, 1963), *reproduced in* 3 I.L.M. 116 (1964).

44. *E.g.,* COT, *supra* note 17, at 335–36.

45. *E.g.,* Daniel Vigne, *Le fonctionnement d'une procédure de conciliation: A propos de la guerre de poulets,* 9 ANNUAIRE FRANÇAIS DE DROIT INTERNATIONAL 473 (1963).

46. Meinhard Hilf, *Settlement of Disputes in International Economic Organizations: Comparative Analysis and Proposals for Strengthening the GATT Dispute Settlement Procedures, in* THE NEW GATT ROUND OF MULTILATERAL TRADE NEGOTIATIONS 285, 305–06 (Ernst-Ulrich Petersmann et al. eds. 1988). Petersmann, *supra* note 42, at 338–39.

47. ROSS B. TALBOT, THE CHICKEN WAR: AN INTERNATIONAL TRADE CONFLICT BETWEEN THE UNITED STATES AND THE EUROPEAN ECONOMIC COMMUNITY, 1961-64, at 113–14 (1978).

48. Herman Walker, *The "Chicken War:" Steps Toward Arbitration,* 19 ARB. J. 38, 43–44 (1964).

Understanding. Professor Gardner Patterson was chosen as the sole arbitrator, to whom two questions were put: first, whether Canada maintained, through the bilateral agreement of March 29, 1962 with respect to quality wheat, all the negotiation rights provided for in Article 28 of the General Agreement; second, what kind of rights under the General Agreement Canada maintained through the bilateral agreement on ordinary wheat. An award by the arbitrator was transmitted to the parties in October 1990. The arbitrator concluded that with respect to quality wheat, Canada had maintained through the bilateral agreement all the negotiation rights provided for in Article 28 of the General Agreement, and that by maintaining silence on the bilateral agreement on ordinary wheat Canada had relinquished any rights under the General Agreement.[49]

Involvement of the WTO in the arbitration process is much more restricted than in the panel process. It is the parties who determine the arbitrators, the procedures to be followed, and the applicable law. The applicable law could include some rules other than the WTO Agreement. The award binds the parties directly; it does not need to be adopted by the DSB of the WTO. On the other hand, it would follow that the award has no binding force except between the parties concerned; it is binding neither on the WTO as the organization, nor on any other member which did not participate in the arbitration. The ITO Charter had an explicit provision to that effect (Article 93(2)). In reality, arbitral awards will have undeniable influence on the interpretation of the WTO Agreement. Accordingly, the 1994 Understanding required the parties to notify awards to the DSB where any member could raise any point relating thereto. Nevertheless, as long as awards are not adopted by the DSB, the possibility of inconsistency in jurisprudence cannot be eliminated. In the implementation phase, the WTO gets involved in the arbitration process to the same extent as in the panel process. The 1994 Understanding provides that Article 21 (Surveillance of Implementation of Recommendations and Rulings) and Article 22 (Compensation and the Suspension of Concessions) shall apply *mutatis mutandis* to arbitration awards (Article 25(4)).

Noting the unconditionally binding character of arbitral awards, Professor Petersmann has stressed that arbitration could bring about another salutary reform in the GATT dispute settlement process, no less important than the historical evolution from working parties to panels. Even though arbitration has always been available in the GATT, the panel procedures have been the preferred mode of dispute settlement. The main factors of states' preference for the panel procedures are as follows: panel reports are reviewed on adoption by the Contracting Parties and, once adopted, carry substantial political weight and may be considered to represent authoritative interpretations of the General Agreement. Although the 1994 Understanding has judicialized the panel procedures and, as a result, they have come very close to arbitration, the above features of the panel procedures have not been totally lost (under the 1994 Understanding, adoption of panel reports becomes

---

49. Art. XXVIII Rights (Can. v. EC), BISD, 37th Supp. 80 (arbitral award of Oct. 16, 1990).

virtually automatic; review of reports is carried out by the Appellate Body). On the other hand, the paramount feature of arbitration is the unconditionally binding character of the arbitral award. The regularity with which states will actually have recourse to arbitration depends upon which feature of the panel procedures and arbitration they consider to be most advantageous.

b. Judicial Settlement

(1) Recourse to the International Court of Justice

Judicial settlement involves the reference of a dispute to a standing tribunal. In this section, we will consider whether disputes concerning the WTO Agreement may be referred to the International Court of Justice (I.C.J.). The ITO Charter contained explicit provisions allowing the ITO to request advisory opinions of the I.C.J. on legal questions arising in the ITO (Article 96). Because these provisions were taken over neither by the General Agreement nor by the WTO Agreement, and because neither the GATT nor the WTO is a specialized agency authorized by the U.N. General Assembly to request advisory opinions of the I.C.J. under Article 96 of the United Nations Charter, it is impossible for the GATT or the WTO to request advisory opinions of the I.C.J.

As for the contentious jurisdiction of the I.C.J., it is possible for WTO members to refer a legal dispute concerning the WTO Agreement to the I.C.J., provided that the I.C.J. has jurisdiction over the case, for instance, under Article 36 (2) of the I.C.J. statute. Professor Jackson has suggested, however, that the internal GATT interpretative processes might be held to be exclusive and that the jurisdiction of the I.C.J. might be denied.[50] In 1949 the Chairman of the GATT Contracting Parties stated:

> [i]t was open to any government disagreeing with an interpretation [of the Contracting Parties] to take the dispute which had given rise to such an interpretation to the International Court [of Justice], although neither a government nor the Contracting Parties acting jointly could take a ruling of the Contracting Parties to the Court.

It is noteworthy that this statement was not contested.[51] In any case, if a panel report has been adopted in the WTO, it is doubtful that the I.C.J. will take up the same dispute and review the report in substance.[52] In one case, the I.C.J. refrained

---

50. JOHN H. JACKSON, THE WORLD TRADING SYSTEM: LAW AND POLICY OF INTERNATIONAL ECONOMIC RELATIONS 91 (1989).

51. GATT, ANALYTICAL INDEX 1994, *supra* note 12, at 670–71, 811.

52. Rudolf Ostrihansky, *Settlement of Interstate Trade Disputes: The Role of Law and Legal Procedures*, 22 NETH. Y.B. INT'L L. 163, 213 (1991).

from reviewing an arbitral award in substance.[53]

Even if one concludes that the I.C.J. has jurisdiction over a dispute concerning the WTO Agreement, one may still ask whether it is wise to refer such a dispute to the I.C.J.[54] International economic treaties rarely provide that disputes arising under the treaties should be referred to the I.C.J. A treaty establishing an international economic organization usually provides that a dispute should be referred to the political organs—General Assembly or Council—of the organization. Since rules of international economic law are often so vague, it may be assumed that the treaties' drafters believed that disputes arising under those treaties were unsuitable for inflexible application of rules by the I.C.J. Further, the subject-matter of the WTO Agreement is so specialized and detailed that the I.C.J. may not possess the expertise necessary for the adjudication of various cases arising under the Agreement.

(2) Establishment of Standing Tribunals

There have been several proposals to establish a separate standing tribunal to deal with GATT disputes.[55] The proposal put forward by Mr. de Lacharrière, then Vice President of the I.C.J., is particularly noteworthy. He proposed establishment of a standing GATT tribunal just as the 1982 Law of the Sea Convention established a tribunal for the law of the sea. He believed, however, that the tribunal's awards should be advisory opinions and be subject to a decision of the GATT Contracting Parties.[56] Other scholars have put forward proposals of establishing a standing panel or a superpanel (a group of ten or so legal experts from which panelists are to be selected).[57] The 1994 Understanding has adopted the idea of establishing a standing body. While the Understanding left the *ad hoc* nature of the panel procedures intact, it introduced a system of appellate review and established a standing Appellate Body consisting of seven individual experts. Three of them serve on a case in rotation. The Appellate Body is not a tribunal, for it issues only a report subject to adoption by the DSB, a political organ of the WTO.

---

53. Case Concerning the Arbitral Award Made by the King of Spain on Dec. 23, 1906 (Hond. v. Nicar.), 1960 I.C.J. Rep. 192 (Nov. 18).

54. *See* Hilf, *supra* note 46, at 307–08; Günther Jaenicke, *International Trade Conflicts before the Permanent Court of International Justice and the International Court of Justice, in* ADJUDICATION OF INTERNATIONAL TRADE DISPUTES IN INTERNATIONAL AND NATIONAL LAW 43, 56–57 (Ernst-Ulrich Petersmann & Günther Jaenicke eds. 1992).

55. *E.g.,* PANEL ON INTERNATIONAL TRADE POLICY AND INSTITUTIONS, AMERICAN SOCIETY OF INTERNATIONAL LAW, REMAKING THE SYSTEM OF WORLD TRADE: A PROPOSAL FOR INSTITUTIONAL REFORM 33–35 (1976).

56. Guy Ladreit de Lacharrière, *Case for a Tribunal to Assist in Settling Trade Disputes*, 8 WORLD ECON. 339, 350 (1985).

57. *E.g.,* William J. Davey, *Dispute Settlement in GATT*, 11 FORDHAM INT'L L.J. 51, 103–05 (1987).

Adoption of the report, however, is virtually automatic, because it will be adopted unless the DSB decides otherwise by consensus. Moreover, the adopted report of the Appellate Body arguably binds the parties concerned and thus, the standing Appellate Body comes very close to a standing international tribunal.

IV. DOMESTIC ADJUDICATION

Disputes on the WTO Agreement may also be settled by domestic courts.[58] Private individuals—nationals or aliens—may challenge government actions in domestic courts, invoking the WTO Agreement. Because the rule of exhaustion of local remedies does not apply in WTO dispute settlement procedures, other states can bring the matter to the attention of the WTO while the lawsuit is still pending. In such a case, if the domestic court applies the WTO Agreement, the dispute on the international plane is also settled. The *Hawaiian Regulations on Eggs* case is a case in point. In 1955 Australia complained before the GATT that the Hawaiian regulation requiring retailers to display signs stating "We sell foreign eggs" contravened the General Agreement. The GATT Contracting Parties agreed to defer pending the outcome of a legal action challenging the regulation in the Hawaiian courts. The regulation was invalidated by the Hawaiian Supreme Court on the ground that it violated Article 3(4) of the General Agreement,[59] and thus the international dispute between Australia and the United States was settled.

Even when a state has yet to bring a complaint into the WTO dispute settlement procedures, if a domestic court applies the WTO Agreement and disposes of the pending case in accordance with the obligations the government undertakes under the Agreement, it will prevent a domestic case from developing into a dispute between two states. Domestic courts therefore play an important role in settling and preventing international disputes relating to the WTO Agreement.

Although the General Agreement was applied in the *Hawaiian Regulations on Eggs* case and the dispute was settled accordingly, direct applicability of the General Agreement is often denied by domestic courts. The lack of the GATT's direct applicability becomes a significant obstacle to the successful resolution of disputes concerning the General Agreement in domestic courts. Many scholars in the United States believe that the General Agreement is not self-executing in the United States,[60] although the position of U.S. courts on this question is not entirely

---

58. Professor Petersmann includes domestic adjudication in the concept of "judicial settlement" which, according to him, involves the reference of a dispute to "a national or international standing tribunal." Ernst-Ulrich Petersmann, *Settlement of International and National Trade Disputes through the GATT: The Case of Anti-Dumping Law, in* ADJUDICATION OF INTERNATIONAL TRADE DISPUTES IN INTERNATIONAL AND NATIONAL LAW 77, 84–85 (Ernst-Ulrich Petersmann & Günther Jaenicke eds., 1992).

59. Territory v. Ho, 41 Hawaii 565 (Hawaii 1957).

60. *E.g.,* Robert E. Hudec, *The Legal Status of GATT in the Domestic Law of the United States, in* THE EUROPEAN COMMUNITY AND THE GATT 187, 197, 200–01 (Meinhard Hilf et

clear.[61] In the European Community, the Court of Justice denied the direct applicability of the General Agreement in the legal order of the European Community in 1972[62] and in the legal order of the member states in 1983[63] In Japan, the Kyoto District Court denied the direct applicability of the General Agreement in the *Kyoto Necktie* case in 1984 and the Japanese Supreme Court seems to have endorsed the decision of the Kyoto District Court in 1990.[64]

The WTO Agreement is more likely to be regarded as directly applicable than the original GATT (GATT 1947). Unlike GATT 1947, the WTO Agreement neither will be applied "provisionally" nor contain a "grandfather clause" allowing contracting parties to maintain legislation which is inconsistent with the agreement. In addition, the dispute settlement procedures are more judicialized and no longer as "flexible" as they were alleged to be under GATT 1947. In 1990 the Austrian Constitutional Court concluded that Article 2 of the Subsidies Agreement concluded in the Tokyo Round in 1979 was "directly applicable."[65] However, if a statute has an explicit provision excluding the direct applicability of trade agreements, such as Article 3 of the U.S. Trade Agreements Act of 1979 and Article 102(c) of the U.S. Uruguay Round Agreements Act of 1994, the direct applicability of the trade agreements has to be denied.

In the *Nakajima* case, the European Court of Justice held that an antidumping regulation of the European Community violated neither Article 2(4) nor Article 2(6) of the 1979 Antidumping Agreement. In doing so, the court emphasized that the

---

al. eds., 1986); John H. Jackson, *The General Agreement on Tariffs and Trade in United States Domestic Law*, 66 MICH. L. REV. 249, 280–90 (1967). *But cf.* Ronald A. Brand, *The Status of the General Agreement on Tariffs and Trade in United States Domestic Law*, 26 STAN. J. INT'L L. 479 (1990).

61. *See* Hudec, *supra* note 60, at 210–18, 221–25.

62. Cases 21 to 24/72, Int'l Fruit Company v. Produktschap voor Groenten en Fruit, 1972 ECR. 1219. *See also* Case 9/73, Schlüter v. Hauptzollamt Lörrach, 1973 ECR. 1135.

63. Case 266/81, SIOT v. Ministero delle Finanze, 1983 ECR. 731, Cases 267 to 269/81, Amministrazione delle Finanze dello Stato v. SPI & SAMI, 1983 ECR. 801. For details on the direct applicability of the General Agreement in the European Community, *see, e.g.*, THE EUROPEAN COMMUNITY AND THE GATT (Meinhard Hilf et al. eds., 1986).

64. Judgment of June 29, 1984, Kyoto District Court, 31 Shomu Geppo 207, *aff'd*, Judgment of Nov. 25, 1986, Osaka High Court, 634 Hanta 186, Judgment of Feb. 6, 1990, Supreme Court, 36 Shomu Geppo 2243. For details on this case and criticism of the court's reasoning, *see* Yuji Iwasawa, *Implementation of International Trade Agreements in Japan, in* NATIONAL CONSTITUTIONS AND INTERNATIONAL ECONOMIC LAW 299, 320–28 (Meinhard Hilf & Ernst-Ulrich Petersmann eds., 1993).

65. Judgment of Nov. 30, 1990, VfGH, 5 WIRTSCHAFTSRECHTLICHE BLÄTTER 230 (1991). For commentaries on this judgment, *see* Thomas Eilmansberger, *Zur unmittelbaren Anwendbarkeit des GATT-Subventionskodex*, 5 WIRTSCHAFTSRECHTLICHE BLÄTTER 214 (1991); Franz Zehetner, *Ist der GATT-Subventionskodex wirklich "unmittelbar anwendbar?,"* 18 ÖSTERREICHISCHE ZEITSCHRIFT FÜR WIRTSCHAFTSRECHT 81 (1991) (criticizing the conclusion of the court).

applicant had not urged the court to recognize the direct applicability of the said provisions.[66] Despite the court's caveat, it is important to note that the court recognized the competence of the court to exercise judicial review and scrutinize whether EC regulations were in conformity with the Antidumping Agreement.[67] In approving the conclusion of the WTO Agreement, the Council of the European Union stated: "by its nature, the Agreement establishing the World Trade Organization, including the Annexes thereto, is not susceptible to being directly invoked in Community or Member State courts."[68] The questions whether this statement of the Council binds the European Court and whether it excludes not only the direct applicability of the WTO Agreement but also the Court's competence to exercise judicial review in the light of the WTO Agreement remain to be decided by the Court.

Even if the WTO Agreement cannot be directly applied, domestic courts can still play an important role in settling disputes concerning the WTO Agreement. States implement the WTO Agreement in national laws and regulations. Adjudication by domestic courts of cases arising under those laws and regulations is a kind of settlement of disputes concerning the WTO Agreement. The General Agreement attaches great importance to domestic adjudication, providing that "[e]ach contracting party shall maintain . . . judicial, arbitral or administrative tribunals or procedures for the purpose . . . of the prompt review and correction of administrative action relating to custom duties" (Article 10(3)). Antidumping and countervailing duty determinations are often challenged before domestic courts and their correctness is scrutinized in the light of the national laws of the state concerned. Because the rule of exhaustion of local remedies does not apply in the WTO dispute settlement procedures, other states can file complaints with the WTO over the antidumping or countervailing duty determination while the domestic proceedings are still in progress. If domestic courts apply the national laws on antidumping and countervailing duty in conformity with the WTO Agreement, most international disputes will be prevented from occurring. Domestic courts sometimes expressly refer to the General Agreement and the related agreements in interpreting national laws.[69]

---

66. Case 69/89, Nakajima v. Council, 1991 I ECR. 2069, 2177–81. *See also* Case 188/88, NMB v. Commission, 1992 I ECR. 1689, 1735, 1739–41. *But cf.* Case 280/93, Germany v. Council, 1994 I ECR. 4973.

67. For an analysis of the role the General Agreement can play in the judicial review of the secondary law of the European Community, *see generally* Michael J. Hahn & Gunnar Schuster, *Zum Verstoß von gemeinschaftlichem Sekundärrecht gegen das GATT: Die gemeinsame Marktorganisation für Bananen vor dem EuGH*, 28 EUROPARECHT 261 (1993).

68. Council Decision 94/800/EC, 1994 O.J. (L 336) 1, preamble.

69. Even before the *Nakajima* case, the European Court of Justice had referred to the Antidumping Agreement in some cases. *E.g.,* Case 157/87, Electroimpex and Others v. Council, 1990 I ECR. 3021, 3022. For U.S. cases in which the court referred to the General Agreement and the related agreements, *see, e.g.,* Suramericana de Aleaciones Laminadas, C.A. v. U.S., 746 F. Supp. 139, 150 (Ct. Int'l Trade 1990). *But see* Mississippi Poultry Ass'n

The *Zenith* case demonstrates that domestic adjudication plays an important role in settling an international dispute concerning the WTO Agreement. The U.S. Customs Court held in 1977 that the Japanese law exempting exported electronic products from the commodity tax constituted a bounty.[70] Japan immediately raised the matter in the GATT and a working party was formed to examine the judgment of the U.S. court. In a report presented after three weeks, the working party expressed concern over the judgment, pointing out that the Japanese law was in conformity with the General Agreement.[71] Thereafter, the U.S. Court of Customs and Patent Appeals reversed the judgment of the Customs Court. The U.S. Supreme Court affirmed the reversal, pointing out that "[the General Agreement] is followed by every major trading nation in the world."[72] Thus, the international dispute between Japan and the United States was also settled.

V. SETTLEMENT OF DISPUTES CONCERNING THE WTO AGREEMENT IN REGIONAL DISPUTE SETTLEMENT MECHANISMS—NAFTA

Disputes concerning the WTO Agreement may be settled in the dispute settlement mechanisms set up by regional free trade agreements, i.e., the North American Free Trade Agreement (NAFTA) and its predecessor, the U.S.-Canada Free Trade Agreement (CFTA).[73] The NAFTA sets up general interstate dispute settlement procedures in Chapter 20 and procedures to settle disputes over antidumping and countervailing duties in Chapter 19, both of which can take up disputes concerning the WTO Agreement.

a. The General Procedures to Settle Interstate Disputes (Chapter 20)

The general procedures to settle interstate disputes set out in Chapter 20 of the NAFTA are modeled after the GATT panel procedures and similar procedures set out in Chapter 18 of the CFTA. The NAFTA panel procedures are very similar to the WTO panel procedures. The Free Trade Commission, a political body consisting of representatives of the parties to the NAFTA, establishes an arbitral panel and the panel presents a report to the parties of the dispute. There are some

---

v. Madigan, 992 F.2d. 1359, 1365–68 (5th Cir. 1993); Suramericana de Aleaciones Laminadas, C.A. v. U.S., 966 F.2d 660, 667–68 (Fed. Cir. 1992); Footwear Distrib. & Retailers of Am. v. U.S., 852 F.Supp. 1078, 1088–96 (Ct. Int'l Trade 1994).

70. Zenith Radio Corp. v. U.S., 430 F. Supp. 242 (Cust. Ct. 1977).

71. Report of the Working Party, BISD, 24th Supp. 134 (adopted on June 16, 1977).

72. U.S. v. Zenith Radio Corp., 562 F.2d 1209 (C.C.P.A. 1977), *appeal denied*, 437 U.S. 443, 457 (1978).

73. North American Free Trade Agreement, Canada–Mexico–U.S., Dec. 1992, 32 I.L.M. 289, 605. Free Trade Agreement, Canada–U.S., Jan. 2, 1988, 27 I.L.M. 281.

notable differences between the NAFTA procedures and the WTO procedures. While in the WTO the panelists cannot be citizens of any of the parties, in the NAFTA the disputing parties select two panelists who are citizens of the other party ("reverse selection" of nationals). In the NAFTA, an arbitral panel presents a report to the parties of the dispute and the parties agree on the resolution of the dispute, which "normally" will conform with the determinations and recommendations of the panel. The report of the panel has no binding force. Thus, the NAFTA panel procedures are not arbitration. While panel reports need to be adopted by the DSB in the WTO, they are not subject to adoption by the supervisory political body in the NAFTA. In this respect the NAFTA procedures are more akin to arbitration than the WTO procedures. The name of the panel—"arbitral" panel in the NAFTA—presumably reflects this difference.[74]

The NAFTA incorporates substantive rules of the General Agreement (and equivalent rules of a successor agreement) and makes them part of the NAFTA (e.g., Article 301 incorporates Article 3 of the General Agreement on national treatment; Article 309 incorporates Article 11 of the General Agreement on the prohibition of import and export restrictions; and Article 2101 incorporates Article 20 of the General Agreement on general exceptions). Disputes arising both under the NAFTA and the WTO Agreement may be settled either in the NAFTA dispute settlement procedures or in the WTO dispute settlement procedures at the discretion of the complaining party, except for certain disputes which must be referred solely to the NAFTA procedures (Article 2005).

Under the CFTA, the complaining party selected the CFTA procedures to settle disputes concerning the General Agreement in several cases.[75] In one, the *Salmon and Herring* case, the GATT procedures were tried first, and only subsequently were the CFTA procedures used. The United States filed a complaint first with the GATT that the Canadian prohibition of export of unprocessed salmon and herring was inconsistent with Article 11 of the General Agreement. A panel report accommodating the U.S. contention was adopted by the GATT in 1988.[76] Canada then adopted new regulations which required all salmon and herring caught in Canadian waters to be landed in Canada. The United States again considered the new regulations inconsistent with the General Agreement, and decided on recourse

---

74. For details on the NAFTA dispute settlement procedures, *see, e.g.*, Gary N. Horlick & F. Amanda DeBusk, *Dispute Resolution under NAFTA: Building on the U.S.-Canada FTA, GATT and ICSID*, 27 (No. 1) J. WORLD TRADE 21 (1993).

75. The following disputes were brought to Chapter 18 procedures under the CFTA: West Coast Salmon and Herring from Canada; United States Regulations on Lobster; Treatment of Non-Mortgage Interest under art. 304; The Interpretation of and Canada's Compliance with art. 701.3 with respect to Durum Wheat Sales; Puerto Rico Regulations on the Import, Distribution, and Sale of U.H.T. Milk from Quebec. The *Salmon and Herring* case, the *Lobster* case, and the *U.H.T. Milk* case raised issues on the General Agreement.

76. Unprocessed Salmon and Herring (U.S. v. Can.), BISD, 35th Supp. 98 (panel report adopted on Mar. 22, 1988).

to the CFTA procedures rather than the GATT procedures. A panel was established under the CFTA to examine whether the new regulations were consistent with Article 11 of the General Agreement and whether they would be justified by Article 20 of the General Agreement. The panel concluded in favor of the United States.[77] The dispute was nothing other than a GATT dispute.

Panels established under the NAFTA should apply the NAFTA and the WTO Agreement in accordance with the existing interpretations of the WTO Agreement adopted in the WTO. The CFTA had an explicit provision to this effect (Article 501(2)). This would mean that panel reports adopted in the WTO will have *de facto* precedential value in the NAFTA as well. The CFTA dispute settlement procedures were taken as a model in the Uruguay Round negotiations to improve the GATT dispute settlement procedures, and many of the features of the CFTA procedures were adopted in the WTO by the 1994 Understanding. As a result, differences between the WTO procedures and the NAFTA procedures have diminished. Under the circumstances, it is not very likely that the parties to the NAFTA will select the NAFTA procedures rather than the WTO procedures for the settlement of disputes concerning the WTO Agreement. While a panel report merely represents the wisdom of five individuals in the NAFTA, it receives the endorsement of the supervisory political organ in the WTO. Thus, the political weight of the report is much greater in the WTO.

At the insistence of the EC and Japan, an explicit provision prohibiting unilateral measures has been inserted in the 1994 Understanding. The provision requires the Members of the WTO to refer a dispute concerning the WTO Agreement to the WTO dispute settlement procedures (Article 23). Thus, even though the complaining party is allowed by the NAFTA to choose either NAFTA dispute settlement procedures or the WTO dispute settlement procedures to settle a dispute concerning the WTO agreement, the 1994 Understanding would require referral of the dispute to the WTO dispute settlement procedures. In December 1993, when the text of the 1994 Understanding was substantially agreed upon, the parties to the NAFTA exchanged letters and confirmed that a dispute concerning the WTO Agreement should be referred to the WTO dispute settlement procedures.

b.   The Procedures to Settle Antidumping and Countervailing Disputes (Chapter 19)

The NAFTA procedures to settle antidumping and countervailing disputes (Chapter 19) have two procedural subsets: the statutory amendments review (Article 1903) and the antidumping and countervailing duty determinations review (Article 1904). Both reviews are carried out by a binational panel composed of five members who are citizens of either Canada, Mexico or the United States and are not

---

77. In the Matter of Canada's Landing Requirement for Pacific Coast Salmon and Herring, 2 (No. 2) WORLD TRADE MATERIALS 78 (1990) (panel report of Oct. 16, 1989).

affiliated with any party to the NAFTA. In the statutory amendments review, a party refers an amendment of another party's antidumping or countervailing duty statute to a panel. The panel then issues a "declaratory opinion" as to whether the amendment conforms to the WTO Agreement and the object and purpose of the NAFTA. The "declaratory opinion" has no binding force. The statutory amendments review is thus not an adjudicatory means of dispute settlement. Because the General Agreement and any successor agreement are expressly included among the standards for review, it is manifest that this review has the function of settling disputes concerning the WTO Agreement. This review, however, was never used under the CFTA. How extensively it will be used under the NAFTA is yet to be seen.

The antidumping and countervailing duty determinations review was designed to replace domestic judicial review proceedings. An involved party requests that a panel review an antidumping or countervailing duty determination of an importing state to determine whether such determination was made in accordance with the antidumping or countervailing duty law of the importing state. A private individual, who otherwise would have had the right to appear in domestic judicial review proceedings, has the right to appear before the panel. The panel issues a decision which is binding on the involved parties. The antidumping and countervailing duty determination review is thus an adjudicatory means of dispute settlement. The standards for review are antidumping and countervailing duty laws of the importing state. They are certainly domestic laws of the importing state, but they implement the rules of the WTO Agreement. A CFTA panel declared in 1990 that the domestic law of the importing country "should be construed in a manner consistent with the GATT."[78] Thus, the antidumping and countervailing duty determinations review performs the function of settling disputes concerning the WTO Agreement, as do the domestic proceedings which it has replaced.

The rule of exhaustion of local remedies does not apply in the WTO dispute settlement procedures. The NAFTA antidumping and countervailing duty determinations review was intended to replace domestic judicial review proceedings. It follows that an exporting state may refer a dispute regarding an antidumping or countervailing duty determination to the NAFTA panel procedures and the WTO panel procedures simultaneously. A countervailing duty determination was actually reviewed under both the CFTA procedures and the GATT procedures in the *Pork* case. The U.S. Department of Commerce made an affirmative determination of subsidization, levying countervailing duties on pork from Canada, and the U.S. International Trade Commission made an affirmative determination of threat of material injury. The Canadian government and the Canadian Meat Council requested that panels review these determinations under Chapter 19 of the CFTA.[79] Canada also filed a complaint with the GATT, and a

---

78. Replacement Parts for Self-Propelled Bituminous Paving Equipment, 18–20, 2 (No. 3) WORLD TRADE MATERIALS 100, 117–19 (1990) (panel report of Mar. 7, 1990).

79. For details on this case under the CFTA procedures, *see, e.g.*, Andreas F. Lowenfeld,

GATT panel concluded that the countervailing duty determination had not been made in conformity with Article 6(3) of the General Agreement.[80] The United States opposed the adoption of the GATT report, arguing that the CFTA procedures had not been completed. After losing the case under the CFTA, the United States terminated the countervailing procedures. The United States agreed to an adoption of the GATT report only after the case became moot.

VI. CONCLUSION

A notable feature of the WTO dispute settlement mechanism is the availability of various means of dispute settlement. Even though the panel procedures are the most well-known of all the means, there are other means available for the settlement of disputes in the WTO. The WTO Agreement attaches great importance to consultations. Many disputes are settled by bilateral consultations between the parties of the dispute.

Good offices, mediation, and conciliation are not clearly distinguished in the WTO; in general, they correspond to mediation as defined in international law. These non adjudicatory means of dispute settlement have been used infrequently. In recent years, however, some disputes have been successfully settled through "good offices" of the Director-General. One should not adopt a linear approach to dispute settlement and believe that adjudication is the best means of settling any dispute. Adjudication is certainly effective in settling legal disputes. However, for non-legal disputes, in which a party seeks equitable changes in the law, dynamic means of dispute settlement, such as mediation, are more appropriate.

It is noteworthy that the 1994 Understanding has formally recognized arbitration as a means of dispute settlement within the WTO. How extensively arbitration will be used, however, is yet to be seen. Disputes concerning the WTO Agreement may be taken up also by domestic courts or by the NAFTA dispute settlement mechanism. They, too, are important methods for the settlement of disp utes concerning the WTO Agreement.

The Free Trade Agreement Meets Its First Challenge: Dispute Settlement and the Pork Case, 37 McGill L.J. 597 (1992).

80. Countervailing Duties on Fresh, Chilled and Frozen Pork from Canada, BISD, 38th Supp. 30 (panel report adopted on July 11, 1991).

WTO RULES AND PROCEDURES FOR THE SETTLEMENT OF DISPUTES—THEIR FORMATION: A PRACTITIONER'S VIEW

Naoko Saiki[*]

I. INTRODUCTION

After nearly eight years of strenuous and painstaking negotiations, the Uruguay Round of Multilateral Trade Negotiations has been successfully concluded. Its important achievements include the improvement of the rules and procedures governing the settlement of disputes. They are improved not only in the sense that the dispute settlement rules and procedures under the General Agreement on Tariffs and Trade (GATT) themselves are modified, but also that the dispute settlement rules and procedures under the newly created trade body—the World Trade Organization (WTO)—are, on the basis of the GATT rules and procedures, integrated into a single instrument, so that all disputes arising out of any agreement in the WTO are handled under it in a unified way.

This chapter will examine the formation of the WTO's integrated dispute settlement mechanism and, in particular, focus on issues related to panel proceedings.

---

*   The author was the Japanese negotiator in the Uruguay Round dispute settlement negotiations. She is currently Deputy Director of the First Analysis Division, Ministry of Foreign Affairs of Japan. Views expressed in this chapter are solely those of the author and are not attributable in any manner to either the Ministry of Foreign Affairs or the Government of Japan.

II. GATT DISPUTE SETTLEMENT RULES AND PROCEDURES

a. Panel Procedures

In the GATT, there are quite a few provisions concerning the settlement of disputes,[1] among which Articles XXII and XXIII are central. Since these two articles provide rules and procedures governing dispute settlement only in broad, general language and avoid detail, the GATT dispute settlement system has had to or has been able to evolve over the years and has operated on the basis of established practices.

The first few disputes in the GATT's early days were dealt with directly by plenary meetings of the Contracting Parties. In the early 1950s, some cases started to be referred to working parties (small groups established on an *ad hoc* basis and composed of representatives of the concerned and interested contracting parties). By the mid-1950s the first panel with the purpose of settling a dispute was created. While the responsibility to resolve matters which are brought to the Contracting Parties under Article XXIII, paragraph 2 lies solely with them,[2] the Contracting Parties can delegate their power to working parties or panels to a certain extent; both function to assist the Contracting Parties in discharging their responsibilities under the said provision.

Panels, like working parties, are established on an *ad hoc* basis, though panels are composed of three or sometimes five experts, who are either governmental officials or nongovernmental persons and who act in their individual capacities and not as government representatives or as representatives of any organization. A panel examines a case in the light of the relevant GATT provisions and issues a report. The creation of panels is one of the most significant events in the history of the GATT dispute settlement and, perhaps, is one of the most persuasive reasons as to why the GATT dispute settlement system has functioned well.[3]

---

1.   *See, e.g.*, JOHN H. JACKSON, WORLD TRADE AND THE LAW OF GATT 164 (1969). He writes that "[t]here is no single, sharply defined dispute-settlement procedure in GATT that can be readily distinguished from the remainder of GATT activity."

2.   The Council of the representatives was established in 1960 to undertake consideration of matters arising between sessions of the Contracting Parties. In other words, the Council is empowered to act for the Contracting Parties in all areas, including that of dispute settlement. *cf.* GATT, BISD 9th Supp., 8–9 (1961).

3.   For example, Professor Jackson stated that "[t]he step from Working Party to panel ... represents a step toward greater respect for objective international legal obligations and a step away from the political bargaining among nations." JACKSON, *supra* note 2, at 174. Professor Hudec also stated in his recent book that "[t]he adjudication machinery [a panel] is the jewel of the GATT legal system." ROBERT E. HUDEC, ENFORCING INTERNATIONAL TRADE LAW: THE EVOLUTION OF THE MODERN GATT LEGAL SYSTEM, 9 (1993).

b. General Assessment of the Present GATT Dispute Settlement System— Uniqueness of Panel Procedures

It may not be an exaggeration to say that the GATT dispute settlement system is one of the most successful among the international dispute settlement systems in terms of the number of contracting parties which have used it and of its results. This is particularly so in recent times. For example, at the 1982 Ministerial meeting, it was agreed that "no major change is required in this framework."[4] In addition, at the very beginning of the Uruguay Round negotiation, views were expressed by many delegations that the present dispute settlement system had performed reasonably well.

The system is frequently described as "unique."[5] Firstly, it has a variety of ways and means available, beginning with bilateral consultations, good offices, mediation, conciliation and panel proceedings. It is understood that they are pursued in sequence but with flexibility, which means that it is permissible to suspend a course of action, terminate it, utilize two methods simultaneously, or even go back to the previous stage.

Secondly, panel proceedings are quite unique, as very few international agreements, if any, provide similar devices. The nature of the panel proceedings can be interpreted differently depending on which aspect is emphasized. They, in a sense, are a form of third party adjudication of a legal nature, because panelists serve in their individual capacity and examine the matter in accordance with the GATT provisions. In another sense, however, they still contain political elements because panel reports are subject to adoption by the Contracting Parties. Panel reports themselves do not bind the parties to the dispute, let alone other contracting parties. Legal force is not created unless and until the Contracting Parties adopt them. In other words, adoption of panel reports by the Contracting Parties makes the findings contained therein transform those of the Contracting Parties, thereby binding the parties to the dispute. In the GATT system, panel reports are to be adopted by consensus of the Contracting Parties where parties to the dispute are fully involved in the decisionmaking process. In short, the system has both a juridical and political nature.

---

4.   Ministerial Declaration (Nov. 29, 1982) GATT, BISD, 29th Supp., 14 (1983).

5.   *See, e.g.,* Meinhard Hilf, *Settlement of Disputes in International Economic Organizations: Comparative Analysis and Proposals for Strengthening the GATT Dispute Settlement Procedures in* THE NEW GATT ROUND OF MULTILATERAL TRADE NEGOTIATIONS: LEGAL AND ECONOMIC PROBLEMS, 285, 309 (Ernst-Urich Petersmann and Meinhard Hilf eds., 2nd updated ed, 1991); and JOHN H. JACKSON, RESTRUCTURING THE GATT SYSTEM 59 (1990).

Thirdly, in some instances, it is emphasized that the purpose and nature of the GATT dispute settlement system is to resolve a dispute satisfactorily between the parties to the dispute, and in this respect "[a] solution mutually acceptable to the parties to a dispute is clearly preferred" to that arrived at through a panel proceeding or otherwise.[6] Here greater importance is attached to resolution through negotiation. It is also true that in many instances panelists have acted like judges and the panel proceeding has in most cases contributed to the solution to the matter. (It should be noted that recently the Contracting Parties have simply adopted reports without modifying a single word. This suggests that the panel reports have become increasingly viewed as similar to judicial decisions.)

In short, the GATT dispute settlement mechanism, particularly the panel proceeding, effectively combines aspects of conciliation and adjudication. Resolution of a political nature—through negotiation—and of a juridical nature—by third party adjudication—co-exist in an effective way. The Uruguay Round negotiations have brought radical, revolutionary changes to this system, however, which will be examined below.

III. INTEGRATED DISPUTE SETTLEMENT SYSTEM IN THE WTO

a. Consolidation

As mentioned above, the GATT dispute settlement rules and procedures have been developed over time as necessary and have operated on the basis of practice. That development is not reflected in a single complete text but is scattered in several instruments. In order to understand the concrete details as to how the system really works, one would have to refer to various GATT documents and other relevant sources, some of which may not be easily available. Moreover, the Tokyo Round Codes of 1979 further complicate the issue since they have their own dispute settlement rules and procedures even though they have fundametally imported basic ideas from the GATT dispute settlement system.

Against this background, the importance of codifying the various existing texts relating to dispute settlement in a single consolidated instrument was pointed out very early in the Uruguay Round negotiations. At the same time, negotiators were in general agreement that the work on consolidation should not confuse substantive negotiation on improvement of the existing rules and procedures. They agreed, therefore, that efforts should be concentrated first on formulating agreement on the improved rules and procedures and then be spent on consolidating the results of the negotiation and the other existing texts into a simple instrument. Actually, only after the Trade Negotiation Committee at the ministerial level in Brussels failed to

---

6. Annex to the Understanding Regarding Notification, Consultation, Dispute Settlement and Surveillance (Nov. 28, 1979), para. 4, GATT, BISD 26th Supp., 216 (1980).

conclude the Uruguay Round negotiation in December 1990 as had been scheduled originally was substantial work initiated to prepare a single text by consolidating all previous instruments as well as the results of the Uruguay Round. The so-called Brussels text or Draft Understanding[7] dated December 3, 1990, which was forwarded to the said Trade Negotiation Committee, was not able to reflect earlier proposals for consolidation except that Improvements to the GATT Dispute settlement Rules and Procedures (the so-called Mid-Term Review Procedures) were incorporated.[8]

In the course of the Uruguay Round negotiation, consolidation was understood as non-negotiation: that is, substance once agreed upon should not be changed through the work of consolidation. The basic rule was that when an inconsistency existed between two instruments, the one later in time took precedence. Without apparent and clear conflicts with later provisions, therefore, all previous ones were to stand.

As a result, the consolidated document we have today in the WTO Agreement contains various provisions, the historical background of which are so different that its underlying philosophy might not appear uniform. In some parts emphasis is made on the conciliation aspect, while in other parts a legalistic approach is taken as if the whole GATT (WTO) dispute settlement system were a court. This is attributable partly to the characteristics of the present GATT dispute settlement mechanism: the delicate combination of negotiation and adjudication aspects. The consolidation itself has merely kept these characteristics intact. Another, more important attribution is the agreement on the improved rules and procedures on the settlement of disputes, which introduces many new elements which are quasi-automatic, leans strongly toward adjudication, and has undoubtedly resulted in a change in the nature of the mechanism.

b. Harmonization and Integration of the System

Beyond consolidation, harmonization of dispute settlement rules and procedures under the GATT, Tokyo Round Codes, the coming General Agreement on Trade in Services (GATS) and the Agreement on Trade-Related Intellectual Property Rights (TRIPs) was also discussed in an early phase of the negotiation. Harmonizing and integrating various rules and procedures was seen as desirable to avoid further fragmentation of the system, to diminish unnecessary complication and to remove temptation for a party to seek to exploit different rules and procedures or "forum shop." Negotiators felt a particular need to allow a panel to

---

7. The Brussels text is contained in MTN.TNC/W/35/Rev. 1 (Dec. 3, 1990).

8. The Mid-Term Review Procedures were agreed in substance as part of the "early harvest" by the Trade Negotiation Committee in Montreal in Dec. 1988. The GATT Council approved these procedures [Improvements to the Dispute Settlement Rules and Procedures] in Apr. 1989. GATT, BISD 36th Supp., 61–67 (1990).

examine a case in light of all relevant provisions of *all* relevant agreements, irrespective of the will of the parties to the dispute. At present, a panel is requested only to examine a matter in accordance with the agreement under which it was established, and it cannot refer to other agreements unless both parties to the dispute agree; even with such agreement, the panel may not be able to do so, depending on the interpretation of the role of the GATT Contracting Parties and other relevant Tokyo Round Code Committees.

Furthermore, logic led to the conclusion that disputes are disputes in the end. Therefore, why are different rules and procedures necessary to deal with similar matters related to multilateral trade issues one way or another? There was also recognition that the GATT dispute settlement system had been by and large functioning well and was thus adequate as a basis for rearranging the other rules and procedures.

Substantive work to this end was started after the failure of the Ministerial Meeting at Brussels. In fact, after the Brussels meeting, negotiation on dispute settlement was resumed in three parallel sub-issues: (i) issues which had not been resolved before or in Brussels, such as questions of automaticity, timeframe, non-violation complaints, and commitment to strengthen multilateralism; (ii) consolidation; and (iii) harmonization.

In December 1991 Arthur Dunkel, then GATT Director-General, produced the Draft Final Act (Dunkel text) in the capacity as chairman of the Trade Negotiation Committee at the official level.[9] The Dunkel text contained two draft agreements in the area of dispute settlement: a document as a result of consolidation of the new improvements and all the existing GATT dispute settlement instruments, and a document entitled "Elements of an Integrated Dispute Settlement System."[10]

The latter concerned the across-the-board integration of the dispute settlement systems of all the areas covered by the Uruguay Round. Partly due to time constraints, discussions on this subject had not deepened enough to enable negotiators to agree on specific language. What was agreed upon in the winter of 1991 was first, the generally recognized desirability of integrating the system while respecting the special nature of each agreement and second, based on this general recognition, some key concepts for such an integrated system.[11]

In December 1993 the revised Final Act was issued and finally agreed to by the participants, thereby concluding substantive negotiations of the Uruguay Round.[12] Later on April 15, 1994 at Marrakesh, Morocco, the Ministers of the participating countries in the Uruguay Round signed the Final Act to formally conclude the negotiation. Annex 2 to the Agreement Establishing the World Trade

---

9. The Dunkel text is contained in MTN.TNC/W/FA (Dec. 20, 1991).

10. *Id.*, at S.2 - S.23 and T.1 - T.6.

11. These key concepts are in "Elements of an Integrated Dispute Settlement System," *supra* note 10, at T.1 - T.6.

12. The text is contained in MTN/FA (Dec. 15, 1993).

Organization, the Understanding on Rules and Procedures Governing the Settlement of Disputes (Understanding) is the final result of the work.[13] The Understanding was drafted, following the "Elements of an Integrated Dispute Settlement System," on the basis of the consolidated text of GATT dispute settlement, with certain necessary adaptations.

The adaptation work, although not tremendously difficult, was by no means easy. When the drafting work for the integrated system was conducted from 1992 through 1993, substantive agreement in most of the other negotiating areas had been already reached, including provisions regarding dispute settlement. This made it virtually impossible for dispute settlement negotiators (then participants in the Legal Drafting Group) to radically rewrite those provisions in different texts to make the integrated dispute settlement system more logical, more readable and more consistent. The adaptation made both in the texts of various agreements and in the consolidated/integrated dispute settlement text was, therefore, minimal. Ideally, it would have been better to have initiated the work for the integrated dispute settlement system from scratch for the sake of legal beauty. It is, however, almost certain that that work would not have been able to be concluded within a short period of time.

Central elements of the integrated system provided for in the Understanding are noted below.

First, Article 1.1 of the Understanding stipulates its coverage and scope. "The rules and procedures of this Understanding shall apply to disputes brought pursuant to the consultation and dispute settlement provisions of the agreements listed in Appendix 1 to this Understanding (referred to in this Understanding as the 'covered agreements')" and "to consultations and the settlement of disputes . . . under the provisions of the Agreement Establishing the World Trade Organization . . . and of this Understanding . . . ." Thus, all disputes arising from any agreement covered by the WTO, including the Understanding and the WTO Agreement, are subject to the integrated system.

Second, there is an established principle that such special or additional rules and procedures on dispute settlement contained in the covered agreements as identified in Appendix 2 to the Understanding shall take precedence over the Understanding's general rules and procedures when there is a difference between the two.

Third, a Dispute Settlement Body (DSB) will be created to be primarily responsible for the operation of the Understanding.[14] Article IV:3 of the WTO Agreement provides that the General Council, which is expected to play a role similar to that of the GATT Council, "shall convene as appropriate to discharge the

---

13. Understanding on Rules and Procedures Governing the Settlement of Disputes annexed to the Agreement Establishing the World Trade Organization, Apr. 15, 1994, at 353–377.
14. *Id.*, art. 2.1, at 353.

responsibilities of the DSB."[15]

IV. IMPROVEMENTS IN RULES AND PROCEDURES

a. "Package Deal"

The Uruguay Round negotiation was conducted under the principle of "single undertaking." The Punta del Este Declaration stated that "[t]he launching, the conduct and the implementation of the outcome of the negotiations shall be treated as parts of a single undertaking."[16] To put it differently, during the course of negotiations, emphasis was placed on the interrelationship of negotiating areas; thus, rights and obligations among participants must be balanced in their totality, not solely in one negotiating area.

Without being contradictory, this notion of "a package deal" was also applicable to the negotiation on dispute settlement. Certain key issues were closely linked with each other and left unresolved until the end of the negotiation. Agreement on these issues would not have been possible had they not been handled as a package. Key areas included automaticity of the process, timeframe, non-violation complaints, and the commitment to strengthen the multilateral system. The related question of how to improve the quality of panel reports, including the creation of an Appellate Body, was also considered.

Negotiators agreed that it would be meaningless to improve substantive rules without ensuring their enforceability based on a strengthened dispute settlement mechanism. A question was raised in this regard as to whether the GATT practice of consensus decisionmaking should be maintained in actions of the Contracting Parties relating to dispute settlement. To secure the enforceability of the system, it was suggested that the process be made automatic so that veto power no longer be available for, at the minimum, a Contracting Party to which a recommendation is issued when the Contracting Parties adopt the panel report and authorize suspension of the application to that Contracting Party of concessions or other obligations.

With respect to timeframe, although some of the previous agreements did provide for time-limits at some stages in the dispute settlement process, complaints were made that it had taken too much time to complete the whole process and that this delay had caused a serious difficulty in terms of system efficiency.

---

15. It is interesting to note that well before considering the integration of the system, proposals had been made to have the GATT Council hold a meeting in a "dispute settlement mode," dealing only with matters relating to dispute settlement. At that time, the proposals did not gain much support.

16. Ministerial Declaration on the Uruguay Round (Sept. 20, 1986) pt. I.B.(ii), GATT, BISD 33rd Supp., 20 (1987).

On the other hand, others expressed a need for careful examination of the real problems underlying alleged shortcomings of the system: were they false arguments; i.e., did they result from Contracting Parties' behavior in implementing the rules and procedures, rather than from the inherent deficiencies of the rules and procedures? Proponents of this view noted that the current system worked well and that the GATT dispute settlement rules and procedures had been developed gradually from the experience gained with individual cases. They therefore argued against introducing revolutionary elements, such as automatic adoption of reports and a rigid timeframe for each stage, and in favor of reinforcing the already-existing mechanism by further improving the quality of panel reports so as to diminish the possibility of blocking panel reports. A proposal to institute a review mechanism or an Appellate Body was at first one of those proposals, which, to many participants, was apparently linked to the maintenance of the practice of adopting panel reports by consensus. It, however, changed during the course of negotiations, the details of which will be studied below.

In relation to proposals for automaticity, it was stated that since the dispute settlement system was leaning more toward adjudication, it was necessary to redefine the concept of "non-violation" complaints as stipulated in Article XXIII:1 (b) and (c). Otherwise, it was indicated, the system, in particular panel proceedings, would be overloaded.

Another controversial issue was whether to reaffirm the commitment against resorting to unilateral measures inconsistent with the GATT. The vast majority stressed that this commitment to strengthen multilateralism was one of the *sine qua non* for the package agreement as a result of the Uruguay Round negotiations. The United States, criticized as a frequent user of such unilateral actions, countered that since the present GATT dispute settlement rules and procedures were deficient in terms of allowing blockage and delay, each country had the right to resort to measures without exhausting the GATT dispute settlement system. Furthermore, the United States maintained that since the scope of the present GATT substantive rules was too narrow (i.e., not covering, for instance, services or intellectual property rights), it had no choice but to apply its domestic law unilaterally in order to protect its trade interests vis-a-vis foreign countries which did not possess appropriate law standards on those subjects.[17]

b. Major Changes as a Result of the Negotiation

(1) Provisions on timeframe in various stages of the dispute settlement process have been further elaborated, with time devoted to each stage shortened in some areas.

(2) The degree of automaticity of the process has radically increased. Full consensus is no longer required to adopt panel reports and to authorize the

---

17. *See, e.g.,* HUDEC, *supra* note 3, at 193 and 230.

suspension of concessions or other obligations by the DSB. Instead, the DSB shall adopt reports and authorize such suspension unless it decides by consensus to the contrary ("negative consensus"). This means that support by only one voter—very likely the winning party to the dispute—enables the report to be adopted and the suspension of concessions or obligations to be authorized. This is to say that virtually automatic adoption and authorization will occur. This is a critical departure from the GATT practice whereby all decisions by the Contracting Parties are made by consensus. It is particularly so given the history of the GATT dispute settlement, where the rules and procedures have evolved over time on the basis of experience from concrete cases. It should be remembered further that a number of negotiators emphasized the political nature of the relationship between adoption of reports and implementation of recommendations. According to them, reports adopted by full consensus could result in a greater commitment to implementing the recommendation on the part of the Contracting Party to which it was issued since that Contracting Party itself participated in and contributed to the adoption of the report leaving no justification or excuse not to implement the recommendation.

(3) A standing Appellate Body will be established to hear appeals from panel cases. This is also a dramatic departure from the tradition of the GATT dispute settlement.

The GATT dispute settlement mechanism has operated for a long time through an *ad hoc* panel consisting of three or five experts. The role and function of the panel was first codified in the 1979 Tokyo Round Understanding, which sets out: "[t]he function of panels is to assist the Contracting Parties in discharging their responsibilities under Article XXIII:2 . . . . Panels should consult regularly with the parties and give them adequate opportunity to develop a mutually satisfactory solution."[18] According to the mandate, a panel is expected to act not only as judge but also as conciliator to help the parties find a mutually satisfactory solution. In addition, as mentioned above, panel reports themselves do not have legal force and therefore must be adopted by the Contracting Parties, where the parties to the dispute fully participate in decisionmaking together with all other contracting parties. These features suggest that panel proceedings are not genuine third party adjudication. On the contrary, the Appellate Body, first of all, is not supposed to exercise the power of good offices; second, the Appellate Body is a standing body; and third the adoption of Appellate Body reports as well as panel reports will be made by "negative consensus"—virtually automatic adoption. It can be said, therefore, that the Appellate Body, fortressed by the almost automatic adoption of reports, is a clear indication of a tilt toward judicial settlement.

In public international law, there is precedent for accepting appeals from the parties to the dispute: the Convention on the Settlement of Investment Disputes

---

18. Understanding Regarding Notification, Consultation, Dispute Settlement and Surveillance (Nov. 28, 1979), para. 16, GATT, BISD 26th Supp., 213 (1980).

Between States and Nationals of Other States, for example, sets out an appeal system.[19] The Appellate Body in the WTO, however, cannot be regarded as a usual addition to the precedent because the conditions for appeal to the Appellate Body are different from those, for example, of the said convention: the panel examines legal, not proecdural, errors. More importantly, panel proceedings, which have significantly contributed to the smooth operation and thus credibility of dispute settlement under the GATT, are too precious to be jeopardized by experiment. There is no guarantee that such a change will bring about a more workable and credible system.

In the Uruguay Round, proposals to provide for a review mechanism and for an appeal body appeared to have been made initially in order to maintain the practice of adopting panel reports by full consensus. The proposals did not gain enthusiastic support because they were considered to unduly prolong and burden the dispute settlement system. As negotiations progressed, participants grew supportive of an idea to establish an appellate body as a safeguarding device against a new situation in which panel reports would be adopted quasi-automatically. By "safeguarding device" it was meant: (i) protecting the system and concerned parties against erroneous reports; and (ii) enabling governments, in relation to their domestic constituencies, to justify their decision to give up veto power to block unfavorable panel reports.

Having once served as a panelist, the author is somewhat doubtful as to the wisdom of creating another stage after the panel proceeding. First, although "[a]n appeal shall be limited to issues of law covered in the panel report and legal interpretations developed by the panel,"[20] it is foreseeable that almost all panel reports will be appealed since very few members of the WTO, under domestic pressure, will refrain from attempting to obtain a different and favorable result of the case. Second, few will wish to serve on a panel whose decision may be easily modified or reversed by another body. As the Appellate Body is composed of "persons of recognized authority, with demonstrated expertise in law, international trade and the subject matter of the covered agreements generally,"[21] one would certainly respect those persons and the Appellate Body itself. Being asked to serve as a panelist, however, is a different matter; one may feel uncomfortable and hesitant about being judged as having been wrong by the Appellate Body after having engaged in time-consuming unpaid work. One of the key elements of the present GATT dispute settlement system is the high quality of panel reports. If this quality is not secured, the credibility of the entire system will be endangered.

It is provided in the Decision on the Application and Review of the Understanding on Rules and Procedures Governing the Settlement of Disputes that

---

19. Convention on the Settlement of Investment Disputes Between States and Nationals of Other States, Mar. 18, 1965, art. 51–52, 575 U.N.T.S. 159, 190–192.

20. The Understanding, *supra* note 13, art. 17.6, at 364.

21. *Id.*, art. 17.3, at 364.

a full review of the Understanding shall be completed within four years after the entry into force of the WTO Agreement and that a decision shall be taken whether to continue, modify or terminate the rules and procedures set out in the Understanding.[22] Since all decisions shall be taken by consensus in the WTO following the GATT practice, the decision referred to in the above Decision must also be made by consensus.[23] It is interesting to note in this respect that the decision is not only whether to terminate or modify, but also, to continue the rules and procedures; in order to merely continue the Understanding, a consensus will be required. The reason for this was perhaps the creation of the Appellate Body, which was very new to the system, or, for some negotiators, the drastic change from consensus decisionmaking by the GATT Contracting Parties in some areas contained in the Understanding.

The commitment not to resort unilaterally to GATT inconsistent measures, thereby strengthening the multilateral system, was one of the most difficult subjects agreed upon in both the Uruguay Round and in the negotiation on dispute settlement. This commitment to respect the multilateral system is an essential element of the security and credibility of the system and, in fact, was one of the objectives of the Uruguay Round negotiation.

Article 23 of the Understanding, entitled "Strengthening of the Multilateral System," was finally agreed upon as part of the package deal. The first paragraph of the article reads: "[w]hen Members seek the redress of a violation of obligations or other nullification or impairment of benefits under the covered agreements . . ., they shall have recourse to, and abide by, the rules and procedures of this Understanding."[24] The second paragraph specifically stipulates that (a) no unilateral determination as to the question of GATT consistency will be made except through recourse to the Understanding, (b) the Understanding will be followed to determine the reasonable period of time, and (c) DSB authorization will be obtained before imposing countermeasures in response to the failure of the member concerned to implement the recommendation, and the Understanding will be followed to determine the level of such countermeasures.

The exclusiveness of the WTO dispute settlement rules and procedures has thus been established as a means to resolve disputes arising out of the agreements administered by the WTO; the vast majority of the GATT Contracting Parties were waiting for reaffirmation of this principle. As far as disputes under the WTO are concerned hereafter, parallel access to other ways and means, whether of a unilateral or bilateral nature, is prohibited. One must resort to the built-in dispute

---

22. Decision on the Application and Review of the Understanding on Rules and Procedures Governing the Settlement of Disputes in the Uruguay Round Final Act 419 (Apr. 15 , 1994).

23. Agreement Establishing the World Trade Organization, Apr. 15, 1994, art. IX:I, at 13.

24. The Understanding, *supra* note 13, art. 23.1, at 370.

settlement mechanism in the WTO.

From a strictly legal point of view, this article may not seem to add anything new; what is contained is a restatement or confirmation of the already existing obligations of GATT Contracting Parties (WTO Members). Against the background that some contracting parties did not act under their obligations, however, agreement to this article by all, including those contracting parties, is quite important.

As for non-violation complaints described in Article XXIII, paragraph 1(b) of the GATT, they will be subject to the general rules and procedures of the Understanding except that certain special procedures, taken from relevant parts of the Annex to the Understanding regarding Notification, Consultation, Dispute Settlement and Surveillance of 1979 and re-stipulated as legal requirements, will apply. On complaints described in Article XXIII, paragraph 1(c) of the GATT, rules and procedures of the Understanding relating to the adoption of reports and surveillance of implementation of recommendations and rulings will not apply, but the equivalent rules and procedures in the Mid-Term Review Procedures will govern. The reason for this treatment was clearly that the whole dispute settlement system, and, in particular, panel proceedings, would become more and more juridical, so that this unique type of complaint, not necessarily based on law, should not be dealt with in the same manner as other complaints arising from another member's violation of law.

c. The New Dispute Settlement System in the WTO—Clarifications on Some Aspects of Panel Proceedings

The Understanding changes the basic nature of dispute settlement under the GATT; quasi-automatic adoption of reports by the DSB, reinforced by the establishment of a standing Appellate Body, will inevitably make the whole system more judicial. Incidentally, given the fact that working parties have not been used recently as a vehicle to solve disputes, the reference to "working parties" has been eliminated completely in the Understanding through the consolidation exercise.

The Understanding provides that a panel shall not and cannot create rights and obligations.[25] A panel preserves the rights and obligations of members under the covered agreements and clarifies the matter in the light of their provisions. In this connection, the Uruguay Round negotiation made clear who can make authoritative interpretations of provisions of the covered agreements. Article IX:2 of the WTO Agreement provides that "[t]he Ministerial Conference and the General Council shall have the exclusive authority to adopt interpretations of this Agreement and of the Multilateral Trade Agreements." [26] Ambiguity which existed with respect to

---

25. The Understanding, *supra* note 13, art. 19.2, at 366.
26. Agreement Establishing the World Trade Organization, *supra* note 23, art. XI: 2, at

the effect of adoption of panel reports by the Contracting Parties—whether general interpretation or specific application of the law for the resolution of individual cases—will no longer exist.

As for the precedential value of reports, in theory, a panel does not have to follow past panel reasoning and interpretation of GATT provisions and is free to deviate from them without demonstrating grounds to do so, based on a panel's terms of reference requiring independent judgment. In practice, however, past panel reports are frequently cited by later panels and thus have contributed to the creation of a body of law of the GATT. By this practice, the whole GATT system has become clearer, more consistent and more predictable. The Understanding on this point stipulates that "[t]he dispute settlement . . . serves to . . . clarify the existing provisions of those [covered] agreements in accordance with customary rules of interpretation of public international law."[27] This codifies and advances the current practice. A panel and the Appellate Body will be obliged more or less to follow past cases when interpreting provisions of the covered agreements because past panel reports, adopted and, to a certain degree, unadopted as well, are very likely to constitute part of "subsequent practice" in the meaning of Article 31 of the Vienna Convention on the Law of Treaties.[28]

V.   CONCLUSION

As a result of the Uruguay Round, the GATT dispute settlement rules and procedures have radically changed and been transformed into the Integrated Dispute Settlement System in the WTO. At this juncture, it should be emphasized that the successful operation of the WTO dispute settlement system relies heavily on the political commitment of each member to abide by the rules and procedures. (Needless to say, members are under the legal obligation to observe them.) The most important commitment is to use the WTO system exclusively to resolve disputes under the covered agreements.

It should be remembered that a quick and automatic adoption of panel and Appellate Body reports or an authorization of the suspension of concessions and other obligations is not the purpose of the dispute settlement mechanism of the WTO. The purpose is to secure a positive solution to a dispute: first to help the disputing parties find a mutually satisfactory solution to the matter and second, if this is not possible, to secure the prompt withdrawal of the measure found to be inconsistent with covered agreements by making best use of devices, such as panels. Fulfilling this objective will contribute to establishing the credibility of not only the dispute settlement system but also of the whole WTO system.

13.

27.   The Understanding, *supra* note 13, art. 3.2, at 354.

28.   Vienna Convention on the Law of Treaties, May 23, 1969, art. 31, 1155 U.N.T.S., 331, 340.

Moreover, rules in substantive areas are supplemental to dispute settlement rules since the more precise, detailed and unambiguous the substantive rules are, the more efficient, effective and enforceable dispute settlement rules and procedures can be expected to be; it would be meaningless to have a powerful juridical dispute settlement system in the absence of good substantive rules. The reverse is also true; unless enforcement of the substantive rules is assured by the credible dispute settlement system, the mere existence of good rules in the substantive areas would again be of little meaning.

It is, therefore, fair to wait before concluding that the new dispute settlement system, which is surely one of the most significant achievements of the Uruguay Round, will work well in the future. How the new organization, the WTO, functions with respect to the operation of covered agreements and how members abide by their obligations and commitments must first be observed.

SUPPLEMENTAL PROCEDURAL RULES OF INTERNATIONAL NON-JUDICIAL PROCEEDINGS

Toshio Sawada[*]

I. Introduction

The most widely used means of nonjudicial dispute resolution is arbitration. While frequent resort to arbitration is due partly to the time costs and expense of litigation, this is not the *most essential* reason for a developing tendency to avoid litigation.[1] Arbitration and conciliation, domestic or international, often can offer flexible or more reasonable solutions which litigation cannot, and they are dispute resolution alternatives which coordinate with litigation.

Arbitrators and conciliators do need procedural rules to guide them in carrying out their duties. The extent to which detailed directions are provided differs with types of arbitration and conciliation. In this chapter, the rules providing for a general framework of the proceedings will be called "General Rules" and the more detailed norms on the conduct of the proceedings will be called "Supplemental Rules." General Rules usually cover a limited number of procedural issues, leaving the rest to be dealt with at length in Supplemental Rules.

Such rules as the Understanding on Rules and Procedures Governing the Settlement of Disputes of the new World Trade Organization and the Rules of Conciliation and Arbitration of the International Chamber of Commerce (ICC Rules) are examples of General Rules. The Supplementary Rules Governing the

---

*   Professor of Law (International Transactions), Sophia University, Tokyo; Vice-Chairman, ICC International Court of Arbitration, Paris. The views expressed herein are those of the author alone and not the views of the Court.

1.   Toshio Sawada, *Conciliation - Prospects of Success in International Transactions*, World Intellectual Property Organization (WIPO), WORLDWIDE FORUM ON THE ARBITRATION OF INTELLECTUAL PROPERTY DISPUTES (1994).

Presentation and Reception of Evidence in International Commercial Arbitration (1983) prepared by the International Bar Association (IBA Rules on Evidence) is a typical example of Supplemental Rules.[2] No system of arbitration or conciliation can function only with General Rules. Supplemental Rules are also indispensable. This chapter will discuss when Supplemental Rules must be ready and how detailed they should be.

II.   EXTENT TO WHICH PROCEDURAL DETAILS ARE PROVIDED

When an institution adopts arbitration or conciliation as a means of dispute settlement for the first time, or when preparation of Supplemental Rules that apply to all cases is not feasible or desirable, no ready-made Supplemental Rules are available. A case in point is the dispute settlement mechanism of the World Trade Organization (WTO). According to the Understanding on Rules and Procedures governing the Settlement of Disputes, good offices, conciliation, mediation, panel procedures and arbitration are offered as modes of settling disputes. The Understanding contains detailed rules on panel procedures which have been tested by the GATT for a number of years. While such rules even include provisions on multiple complainants and the Standing Appellate Body, they offer no procedure applicable to conciliation, mediation and arbitration. Under Section 5 of the Understanding, "Good Offices, Conciliation and Mediation are procedures that are undertaken voluntarily if the parties to the disputes so agree" and "the Director-General may, acting in an ex officio capacity, offer good offices, conciliation or mediation with the view to assisting Members to settle a dispute," but there is no instruction as to how these procedures are to be carried out.

Arbitration could take place in connection with a determination of a period of time for compliance with recommendations or rulings of the Dispute Settlement Board[3] and before suspension of concessions, but also more generally "as alternative means of dispute settlement."[5] The last merits attention as providing a dispute resolution mechanism for general application. Such arbitration is "subject to mutual agreement of the parties which shall agree on the procedures."[6] Since arbitration must be "expeditious,"[7] it is obvious that any agreement of the parties on the procedure must ensure expeditious arbitration. The issues must be "clearly

---

2.   International Bar Association, *Supplementary Rules Governing the Presentation and Reception of Evidence*, X Y.B. COMM. ARB. 145 (1985).

3.   Understanding on Rules and Procedures Governing the Settlement of Disputes, *Final Act Embodying the Results of the Uruguay Round of Multilateral Trade Negotiations*, art. 21.3(c) (1994) [hereinafter Understanding].

4.   Understanding, *supra* note 3, art. 22.6.

5.   Understanding, *supra* note 3, art. 25.1.

6.   Understanding, *supra* note 3, art. 25.2.

7.   Understanding, *supra* note 3, art. 25.1.

defined"[8] at the outset, but beyond that, the General Rules are silent as to procedure, and, because of the mutual agreement requirement of Art. 25.2, arbitration will not take place unless the parties will have agreed on the procedural standards.

Arbitration is a new dispute settlement mechanism for the WTO. The draftsmen of the WTO Understanding did not choose to fix detailed procedural rules presumably because it was felt advisable to see them develop gradually over a period of years. The ICC Rules have been in use for decades and include articles touching upon pleadings, written statements and notifications, but the ICC has deliberately refrained from enacting more detailed rules for the sake of flexibility. On the other hand, some lawyers desire sets of written Supplemental Rules, and the creation of the IBA Rules on Evidence is indicative of such a desire.

III. DIFFERENT APPROACHES TO PROCEDURAL DETAILS

Thus, there are several approaches for dealing with details:

1) One approach is to *require* the parties to agree on the procedural details, as in the case of the WTO Understanding.

2) Another approach is to leave such details to the *arbitral tribunal* (and the parties) without providing for particulars in the General Rules or attempting to prepare Supplemental Rules. The ICC takes this approach.

3) Still another approach is to create Supplemental Rules covering at least some aspects of the procedure as attempted by the IBA Rules on Evidence. It is recommended that the parties incorporate them by reference into their agreement in advance in order to supplement any General Rules of their choice. In cases where the parties do not make use of the rules in that way, the arbitrators are expected to use them as a guide.[9]

4) The United Nations Commission on International Trade Law (UNCITRAL) presents guidelines which can be used to formulate Supplemental Rules in conjunction with Approaches 1 and 2 above.[10] In 1976, UNCITRAL prepared arbitration rules for *ad hoc* (non-institutional) arbitrations, which came to be used in the well known Iran-U.S. Claims Tribunal and have been adopted in numerous international business agreements.

---

8. *Id.*

9. *Id.*, at Introduction.

10. *Draft Guidelines for Preparatory Conferences in Arbitral Proceedings*, UNCITRAL, A/CN.9./396/Add. 1 (1994) [hereinafter UNCITRAL *Guidelines*].

It is natural that users of arbitration or conciliation rules become more concerned with detail after they have applied the General Rules in various cases. In 1994, UNCITRAL thus proposed Guidelines for Preparatory Conferences in Arbitral Proceedings, which cover procedural particulars. The Guidelines present a checklist of topics which the arbitral tribunal might wish to include in the "agenda" for a preparatory conference.

IV. TIMING OF ADOPTING SUPPLEMENTAL RULES AND THEIR CONTENTS

No conciliation or arbitration proceedings should begin without fixing procedural rules, and the meeting convoked for such a purpose is called a preparatory conference in the UNCITRAL Guidelines. The term preparatory conference is more appropriate than "pretrial conference" or "prehearing meeting"; words like "trial" that can be associated with litigation should be avoided, and a "hearing" may not take place at all. The UNCITRAL Guidelines do not make recommendations as to the timing of a preparatory conference. The Guidelines state merely: "[i]n some cases, it is considered useful to hold a conference before the claims and defenses have been fully stated. In other cases, it is considered appropriate to convene a preparatory conference shortly after the submission of the statements of claim and defence."[11] The arbitrators and the parties will hold a meeting at the place of arbitration or at some other, appropriate place, and "it may be sufficient if under the coordination of the presiding arbitrator consultations are carried out by telecommunications."[12] The ICC Rules do not use the term "preparatory conference," but when a request for arbitration and its answer have been exchanged, the arbitrator, having perused such pleadings and documents,"[b]efore proceeding with the preparation of the case, . . . shall draw up . . . his Terms of Reference."[13]

The Terms of Reference are usually prepared at a conference attended by the arbitrators and the parties, and this is the meeting which the UNICTRAL Guidelines call a preparatory conference. Under the ICC Rules, the Terms of Reference, in addition to the parties' and the arbitrators' names and addresses, a summary of the claims, definition of the issues and the place of arbitration, must include particulars of the applicable procedural rules and, if such is the case, reference to the power conferred upon the arbitrator to act as amiable compositeur, as well as such other particulars as may be required to make the arbitral award enforceable or may be regarded as helpful.[14]

---

11. UNCITRAL *Guidelines, supra* note 10, at para. 29.

12. UNCITRAL *Guidelines, supra* note 10, at para. 24.

13. INTERNATIONAL CHAMBER OF COMMERCE, RULES OF CONCILIATION AND ARBITRATION, art. 13 (1988) [hereinafter ICC RULES].

14. *Id.*

This indicates that the Terms of Reference could include Supplemental Rules, but their content is left to the arbitrators and the parties. They are free to draw up rules applicable only to their particular case or to adopt existing Supplemental Rules. They may, for instance, agree to incorporate a part of the IBA Rules on Evidence into their Supplemental Rules, since the IBA rules are reasonable and partial to neither common law nor civil law traditions. Adoption of a set of ready-made rules, including the procedural norms of a national law, is, however, dangerous because such rules not only could unduly fetter the arbitrators, but also could conflict with the General Rules. The ICC Court of International Arbitration would not set a case into motion if the parties chose the procedural law of a particular country and stated that the ICC rules would apply on matters on which such procedural law is silent. The ICC Terms of Reference often include Supplemental Rules on the language of the proceedings, exchange of documents, testimonies and other aspects of evidence.

The next section of this chapter will discuss the items suggested in the UNCITRAL Guidelines for possible inclusion in Supplemental Rules. The most important provision of any Supplemental Rules will be a provision that gives the arbitrator (or Chairman, if there are three arbitrators) the power to make procedural rulings from time to time. As long as such a provision is included, Supplemental Rules could be relatively brief and the parties free from the danger of being caught in their own trap.

V. EXAMINATION OF UNCITRAL GUIDELINES

The UNCITRAL Guidelines are quite extensive, dealing with twenty items ranging from the composition of a tribunal to costs, and many of them apply both to *ad hoc* and institutional arbitrations. Some Guidelines refer to the corresponding rules and practices of the ICC Court. The UNCITRAL Guidelines, as to most of the twenty topics, propose one or more Agenda(s) of the preparatory conference and "Remarks" are added to each. The Agendas call to the attention of the parties that they might need a clause on that subject in the Supplemental Rules.

a. Rules Governing Arbitral Procedure

Under this heading, the Agenda says: "[i]f the parties have not agreed on arbitration rules, enquire whether they now wish to do so." In most international arbitration cases, however, it would be rare that the parties have not agreed upon General Rules, and, for the purpose of preparing Supplemental Rules, this usually would not be relevant.

b. Jurisdiction and Composition of the Arbitral Tribunal

The Agenda recommends that the parties enquire whether there is an objection as to the jurisdiction or composition of the tribunal. While alerting the parties to this issue, the Agenda cautions that raising this matter is not always desirable because it may create an incorrect impression that the jurisdiction or the composition of the tribunal is in doubt. This appears to be an overly prudent piece of advice. Although it is generally recognized that the arbitrators have the power to rule on their own jurisdiction, a provision of the Supplemental Rules should confirm the jurisdiction of the tribunal to avoid subsequent controversies which will delay the proceedings.

The Agenda does not explain what is meant by the composition of the tribunal. So far as the number of arbitrators is concerned, if institutional arbitration is chosen, it usually can be determined by the arbitral institution. An institution like the ICC often decides the number of arbitrators on the basis of the financial amount involved in the dispute. Even if the amount is not substantial, the parties are in a better position to decide whether the controversy would merit a tribunal of three arbitrators and whether they are ready for the additional expenditures that a plural-arbitrator tribunal entails. It is highly desirable for the parties to agree on the number of arbitrators at a very early stage.

The same can be said about the qualifications of the arbitrators. Although these matters are often clarified before the preparatory conference, the parties may use that occasion to confirm the arbitrators' qualifications or their independence, if independence is required.

c. Possibility of Settlement

The Agenda suggests that the parties enquire whether they are willing to inform the tribunal about the status of settlement discussions which might have taken place. More important in the case of arbitration is the permissibility of meditation or conciliation. The parties can decide whether they wish the arbitrator to act as a mediator, who acts somewhat passively in the parties' settlement discussions, or as a conciliator, who proposes the terms of settlement.

There is a view that arbitrators should not be allowed to mediate or conciliate for the reason that if mediation or conciliation fails, they would be influenced by what they learned while engaging in mediation or conciliation. Many arbitrators, including the author, however, have not experienced such difficulty. In Japan, where conciliation is very widely practiced, it is quite normal that judges try media-tion or conciliation in court proceedings. If the parties are uncomfortable at having the arbitrators act in such a capacity, they may consider the possibility of concurrent mediation or conciliation by another person.

Whether the parties will attempt conciliation needs not be decided at the beginning, but it could well be an agenda item, and, if a positive decision is made, a provision to that effect may be included in the Supplemental Rules.

d-e. Issue Definition, Decision Order; Undisputed Facts or Issues

Defining the issues should be one of the essential purposes of the preparatory conference. Since the parties often prepare their pleadings in quite different ways, it is desirable for the arbitrators themselves to prepare a summary and present it to the parties or to help the parties articulate the issues. These are matters to be clarified in Terms of Reference, but not for inclusion in Supplemental Rules.

f-k. Evidence: Documentary, Physical and of Witnesses and Experts; Written Submissions and Other Writings

More than a third of the text of the Guidelines is devoted to six topics relating to evidence. This is, however, the area where the tribunal should be able to function with least constraint. Arbitration should be as expeditious as required in the WTO Understanding, a possiblity only when (1) discovery is limited and (2) the arbitrators enjoy maximum discretion.

In America, it is widely recognized that discovery—the pre-trial device permitting each party to obtain facts and information from the other—causes serious delay before a trial in civil litigation, and an advantage of arbitration over litigation is that discovery in aid of arbitration is severely limited. As Wigmore points out, "[a] main object of a voluntary submission to arbitration is the avoidance of formal and technical preparation of a case for the usual procedure of a judicial trial."[15]

It is feared that detailed UNCITRAL agendas on evidence may drive the users to prepare unnecessarily elaborate stipulations. A provision of the ICC rule plainly states: "[t]he arbitrator shall proceed within as short a time as possible to establish [the] facts of the case by all appropriate means."[16]

Commenting on the section on evidence of the International Arbitration Rules of the American Arbitration Association, Hans Smit wrote: "[a]ll of these problems could have been avoided by a simple provision granting the tribunal the authority to order the production of all evidence it deems necessary or appropriate."[17]

The UNCITRAL agenda enumerates, among other things, "a time schedule for submitting documentary evidence," and answering the question "whether the parties agree to submit jointly a single set of documentary evidence." These are procedurally important matters, but articles in Supplemental Rules on such points should be broad enough to enable the arbitrators to issue orders to suit the occasion.

As between documents and oral testimony, oral testimony carries greater weight in common law procedure, while the civil law tradition tends to attach more importance to documents. In the ICC practice, "[a]fter study of the written

---

15. 1 WIGMORE EVIDENCE § 4(e) (3d ed. 1940).

16. ICC Rules, *supra* note 13, art. 14.1.

17. Hans Smit, *The New International Arbitration Rules of the American Arbitration Association*, 2–1 AM. REV. INT'L ARB. 19 (1991).

submissions of the parties and of all documents relied upon, the arbitrator shall hear the parties together in person if one of them so requests; and failing such a request he may of his own motion decide to hear them."[18] Study of documents precedes a hearing, and a hearing is held only if a party or the arbitrator so decides. One should not conclude that this reflects a civil law bias. In international arbitration, it would be natural to place reasonable emphasis on documents as overseas trips for hearings would involve great time and expense.

The UNCITRAL Guidelines refer to written submissions. Initial written submissions of documents are of vital importance in any arbitration, but this usually takes place before a preparatory conference. For instance, in the ICC arbitration, a preparatory conference is held after the parties have exchanged their pleadings.

The Guidelines most appropriately call the parties' attention to the importance of "summaries, tabulations, charts, extracts or samples" in connection with documentary evidence.[19] The arbitrators usually find such materials most helpful in grasping the parties' submissions, and the Supplemental Rules could include a provision that the parties must submit those materials whenever requested by the arbitrators.

l.   Hearings

The Agenda lists "the expected length of hearings," its "time limit" and four other items, and here again the laboriously prepared Agenda seems to be overly concerned with minute detail, as exemplified in the item "notetaking." The Supplemental Rules should lay down some basic rules as to whether: a) only the presiding arbitrator or all arbitrators may question witnesses where there are three arbitrators; and b) both direct and cross examinations may be conducted. It is highly advisable to allow both. The tribunal and the parties should ascertain the ability of the interpreter, if one is to be hired. The tribunal usually retains stenographers, but, if it does not do so, how to prepare a summary record and how to verify its accuracy should also be decided.

m.   Language

The Agenda appropriately reminds the parties to decide on the language or languages of the proceedings, although a choice is often made beforehand in the arbitration agreement. The Supplemental Rules should also specify the language of the award.

---

18. ICC RULES, *supra* note 13, art. 14.1.
19. UNCITRAL *Guidelines, supra* note 10, § F(iv).

n-o. Administrative Support and Secretary

Unless the parties choose arbitration by an institution which provides administrative support, such assistance is indispensable, particularly in large, complex cases. As pointed out in Remarks on the Agenda, the major duties of the secretary are clerical assistance to the arbitrators; handling funds; reservations of meeting rooms; travel and hotel bookings for the arbitrators; and securing and supervising the services of such staff as stenographers and interpreters. As pointed out in the same Remarks, assigning legal research to the secretary is controversial. The service of the arbitrator is personal and the Supplemental Rules should specify the extent to which the secretary may perform research.

p. Place of Arbitration

The Agenda urges the parties to choose the place of arbitration and to emphasize the need for conducting a part of the proceedings outside such location. Careful selection of the place of arbitration, and possible reconsideration of the place even at the stage of the preparatory conference, is important legally because the degree of court intervention varies with the venue. The choice also affects the cost of travel and other expenses.

q. Mandatory Provisions Governing Arbitral Proceedings

The Agenda here first suggests that the tribunal request the parties to express their views on whether there is any mandatory law that adds requirements not expressed in any arbitration rules and then inquire of the parties the necessity of filing an award with an authority. The Arbitrators should go further and themselves inquire into a possible conflict between the Supplemental Rules and any mandatory law. It is thus apt that the Guidelines go on to remind that "it is a duty of the arbitral tribunal to obtain knowledge of and interpret the applicable procedural law." The ICC Rules indeed require the Arbitrators to "make sure that the award is enforceable at law."[20] What the arbitrators are required to do is not only apply the substantive law correctly, but also refrain from adopting procedural rules that could ultimately invite challenge to the award. Supplemental Rules thus may include a clause that the rules are subject to modification if it is discovered later that they conflict with laws.

---

20.   ICC RULES, *supra* note 13, art. 26.

r. Multi-Party Arbitration

The Agenda is brief on this point. It says merely: "[w]hen the arbitration involves more than two parties, consider the organization of the proceedings." This brevity obviously is due not to the draftsman's unawareness of the importance of the problem, but rather to its complexity.

It is desirable in the preparatory conference to ascertain (1) who should be the parties to the arbitration, and (2) the number of arbitrators. There are various types of situations that involve actual or potential multi-party disputes:

1) *A*, *B* and *C* are parties to an agreement to explore mining resources. *A* initiates arbitration against *B*. *C* proceeds against *B*.

2) *A*, *B* and *C* are parties to a consortium agreement with an arbitration clause. *A* files a request for arbitration against *B* and *C*, who maintain that there should be two separate arbitrations (*A* against *B*; *A* against *C*).

3) *A* and *B* concluded a joint research and development agreement containing an arbitration clause, and *B* and *C* entered into a licensing agreement under which Court *X* would have exclusive jurisdiction over *B-C* disputes. *A* files a request for arbitration against *B*, but *C*, non-signatory to the arbitration agreement, starts court proceedings against *A* and *B*. *A* wants a single arbitration.

4) *A* and *B* concluded a joint venture agreement and *B* made "assignment" of a part of its rights and obligations to *C*. *A* files a request for arbitration against *B*. *C*, who has an interest in protecting *B*, wants to be a party.

5) *A* wants to start an arbitration against *B*, who designed a plant for *A*, and also against *C* who, under a separate agreement, built the plant for *A*.

One shortcoming of arbitration based on the parties' agreement is that compulsory joinder or consolidation of cases is not possible, while national courts are often empowered to issue an order compelling the parties to take part in single proceedings. Another problem involving multi-party disputes is the number of arbitrators and the constitution of the tribunal. It is impracticable to expect a tribunal of four or more arbitrators to function efficiently unless such numerous arbitrators can devote their full time to the case. Thus, a tribunal normally consists of one or three arbitrators. In a case of type 2) above, the ICC Court, following its established practice, required *B* and *C* jointly to nominate one arbitrator, but the Court of Cassation of France held that the right of equality of the parties should be respected at all times and the exercise of such right cannot be waived by an agreement made before a dispute has arisen.[21]

Thus, how the parties' agreement is worded is of importance, and, even where it lacks clarity, the defects could be rectified by a new agreement at the preparatory conference through the parties' deliberation on possible joinder and the constitution of the tribunal. When such complex issues are taken up, there can be more than one preparatory conference and third parties might be invited to participate.

Even where such adjustment is not required, a multi-party arbitration requires careful planning. How Supplemental Rules should be drafted depends on the circumstances. It is important to conduct the proceedings in such manner, so to avoid a complaint that a party was not given an opportunity to present its case properly. The rule on the discretionary power of the arbitrator can be made more specific than in the case of a bilateral arbitration with respect, for instance, to the manner of conducting hearings.

s-t. Deposit for Costs and Other Matters

Supplemental Rules could have provisions on the methods of sharing costs, and, as one of "other matters," they may deal with the question as to whether the arbitrator could apply the governing law flexibly.

VI. CONCLUDING REMARKS

The authors of the UNCITRAL Guidelines, which offer "agendas" for preparatory conferences, expect that discussions on these items will lead to "decisions" which "add more details or new requirements" to the General Rules of the arbitrators. Supplemental Rules, which reduce such decisions to writing, are desirable in any arbitration.

The UNCITRAL Guidelines are for international commercial arbitration, but their agendas, as well as discussions about them, are applicable to conciliation and in some measure also to noncommercial arbitration.

Although it should be possible to prepare sample Supplemental Rules to suit different arbitration regimes and varied circumstances, tailor-made rules are required in most cases.

Supplemental Rules and the arbitrators's procedural orders ought not conflict with the applicable General Rules and mandatory procedural laws. Subject to such limitation, rules must vest maximum discretion in the arbitrators. Rules can then be relatively brief and general.

---

21. Siemens AG and BKMI Industrieanlagen GmbH v. Dutco Consortium Construction Company Ltd., Decision of the Cour de Cassation, Jan. 7, 1992, *reprinted in* 3 REVUE DE L'ARBITRAGE 470 (1992).

INTERNATIONAL DISPUTE RESOLUTION: LESSONS FROM MALTA

Michael K. Young

I. INTRODUCTION

The Helsinki Final Act of the Conference on Security and Cooperation in Europe (CSCE) must certainly be counted among the most successful international documents in modern history. The document's articulation of certain basic human rights that each country ought to afford its people was well drawn and, as it turns out, highly useful. The real genius of the Helsinki Final Act, however, was not the substance of the human rights provisions, however artfully drawn. Rather, the triumph of the CSCE Final Act was its imposition of an obligation to hold regular meetings, during which the parties would assess each other's compliance with the various Helsinki commitments.

This combination of commitment and regular review legitimized under international law each country's concern for the behavior of its sister nations. The deeply ingrained political and legal barriers to "meddling" in the so-called internal affairs of other countries had been broken. Claims that such interest violated principles of sovereignty or intruded upon matters of purely domestic moment were no longer complete bars to discussing human rights.

This process, in turn, generated powerful human rights monitoring and lobbying groups that were ultimately highly effective in focusing the attention of member states—and the world in general—on the compliance of each country with the human rights commitments of the Helsinki Final Act. The Helsinki Final Act changed the way countries think about the problem of human rights. The way in which a country treated its own citizens was no longer entirely a matter of mere domestic concern, but instead became a legitimate topic of discussion between two sovereign nations.

The CSCE's enviable record in human rights is as yet unmatched in the other fields with which it has grappled, however. The CSCE has had some successes in

431

the security area, particularly with respect to the so-called "confidence building measures,"[1] but even these have been limited.[2] And in other areas, its successes have been even less apparent. It has produced interesting, but ultimately almost totally ignored documents in the area of economic development. It has also produced a variety of reports on issues important to Europe and North America, such as treatment of minorities, but, so far, these documents have been largely of academic interest, with little or no observable impact.

Perhaps the greatest gap between effort and result is in the area of Peaceful Settlement of Disputes (PSD). PSD has been on the CSCE's agenda since the original Helsinki Consultations (1972–75). Yet, despite the tremendous need for more peace, the CSCE did not even reach agreement on an approach until June of 1991 when the CSCE Council of Foreign Ministers adopted the Valletta Report and agreed to place the so-called Valletta Mechanism under the auspices of the Director of the Vienna Conflict Prevention Center. To date, moreover, despite additions and refinements to the original Valletta agreements, the process has yet to be employed. Notwithstanding the late date at which the CSCE finally reached accord, the CSCE experience might contain interesting lessons for the international community, especially regarding the creation of dispute resolution mechanisms. It might also inspire some hope for reconceptualizing PSD in ways that may change the way countries think about it, in much the same way the Helsinki Final Act encouraged countries to rethink human rights. This CSCE document may therefore be worth closer examination.[3]

II. PACIFIC SETTLEMENT OF DISPUTES IN THE CSCE

a. History of PSD in the CSCE

The history of PSD in the CSCE is long and tortuous. Attempts at a comprehensive PSD document began at the CSCE's conception, when the Swiss raised the issue in the original Helsinki consultations. At those initial consultations, the Swiss championed a proposal developed by Rudolf Bindschedler, which

---

1.   Confidence building measures are activities undertaken to ease tension and insure other countries of a nation's good intentions. In the military area, for example, they include agreements to give notification of various activities relating to troop and armament movements and to avoid certain kinds of movements altogether.

2.   The arms negotiations that have occurred in relationship to the CSCE have been appreciably more successful. These are not strictly part of the CSCE process, however, but rather occur along a parallel track. If viewed as a part of the CSCE process, they can certainly be counted as a success, but they are technically outside the CSCE process proper.

3.   I served as the Head of the U.S. Delegation to the Experts' Meeting on the Pacific Settlement of Disputes in Valletta, Malta, in January 1991. The views expressed in this paper are entirely my own, however, and in no way represent the views of the U.S. government, then or now.

contained both binding and non-binding elements and moved the parties to a dispute through a graduated series of steps, including negotiation, inquiry, mediation, conciliation, and, ultimately, binding arbitration, until the dispute was finally resolved.

The Soviets were adamantly against including PSD in the Final Act. At that time, the Soviets were particularly uncomfortable with any form of binding dispute resolution that might allow an examination of their actions towards the Eastern European nations under their sway. Their implacable opposition, coupled with a general lack of enthusiasm on the part of most other countries for the Swiss proposal, decisively quashed Professor Bindschedler's ambitious agenda. The Swiss were able to engineer only a brief reference to PSD as part of the so-called Basket I of the Final Act.

That brief reference was enough, however, to allow the Swiss to lobby successfully for inter-sessional meetings to examine the subject. The first such meeting devoted entirely to PSD was held in Montreux in 1978. The Swiss again advanced their proposal, while the Soviets countered with a proposal that required consultations and negotiations, but rejected everything else, particularly arbitration or adjudication. A number of Western countries combined to advance a third option that began with relatively "soft" forms of dispute resolution, such as negotiation and mediation, but would have ended with stronger methods, such as binding arbitration, for a limited number of disputes that had a clear legal basis (e.g., "justiciable" disputes). The meeting ended in deadlock, but the parties recommended that PSD be discussed again in the future.

That future arrived in Athens in 1984, where another inter-sessional meeting on PSD was held. The Soviets and their allies again opposed any form of compulsory, binding arbitration or adjudication, while the Swiss again championed binding arbitration. The remaining Western nations agreed that some type of compulsory third-party involvement was necessary, but disagreed on the form it should take. Some supported legally-binding processes, such as arbitration or adjudication for a narrow range of disputes; others wanted only mediation or conciliation.

It was at this meeting that the United States first offered a compromise of sorts that foreshadowed the results finally reached seven years later in Valletta. The U.S. proposal provided for a number of mechanisms, including good offices and mediation, to which the parties were required to have recourse. The results were not binding except in the very final stage (i.e., arbitration), and then only if the parties agreed in advance that the results would be such.[4]

Even the U.S. plan could not break the deadlock, however, and the Athens meeting ended without any consensus. The same tensions that permeated the

---

4. The U.S. also circulated a document that proposed the establishment of various bilateral and joint commissions that would be empowered to make recommendations on disputes within the CSCE context. In the end, however, this document was not formally tabled at the meeting.

Montreux meeting were evident in Athens. This time, however, after weeks of discussion and again no agreement, the patience of the parties had worn even thinner. In their concluding document, the parties simply noted that "no consensus was reached on a method" for PSD. There was not even a call for further meetings, for most of the parties did not feel there was a sufficient basis of agreement to make such a meeting worthwhile.

The Ministers did not give up, however, and in the Vienna Meeting (1986–89), they repeated the Final Act's initial formula regarding PSD and scheduled yet another meeting on PSD, this time to take place in Valletta in January of 1991.

In some ways, the climate for success had improved considerably by the time of the Valletta meeting. Mikhail Gorbachev had taken power in the Soviet Union and had clearly signalled that his country would no longer operate with such a heavy hand in Eastern Europe. Moreover, his country's human rights record improved. Even some of the doubters came to believe that progress on PSD might finally be possible.

At the same time, with the unification of Germany and the elimination of the Soviets' stranglehold on the Eastern Bloc, the possibility of instability, ethnic strife, large-scale migration, and border disputes in that area of the world had grown dramatically. The need for more effective PSD devices became strikingly more apparent. Even some previous skeptics began to consider positively the need for creating effective PSD mechanisms, especially mechanisms that reflected European culture, traditions, heritage and ideology.

Against this backdrop, the irrepressible Swiss, emboldened by the new international environment, dusted off and updated Professor Bindschedler's proposal and made the rounds of the various member states. The member states were finally persuaded that the issue ought to be revisited in light of the changes in the world situation. They called for a meeting of experts to be held in Valletta in 1991 to reexamine the possibility of creating a CSCE-based PSD mechanism. Switzerland's day had finally come.

At the same time, however, the United States and some other countries, while in agreement that some institutionalization of PSD in the CSCE context would be immensely useful, became increasingly unsure of the wisdom of the rigid, constrained Swiss approach, and even more comfortable with the approach first outlined in the previously offered U.S. compromise.

In the first place, many arbitral and adjudicatory bodies already did exist and were, to put it mildly, vastly underutilized. There was little need to create yet another.

Moreover, in the intervening years since the first meeting in Montreux, the U.S. experience with binding, third-party arbitration had not been entirely happy, politically speaking. After the adverse decision in the *Nicaragua* case in the International Court of Justice, the United States had even withdrawn from the compulsory jurisdiction of the Court. Enthusiasm for binding arbitration was not running high in the United States.

The United States also examined carefully the types of disputes likely to arise in Europe, especially Eastern Europe—which were the putative targets of CSCE-based PSD mechanisms—and concluded that these types of disputes were not likely to be resolvable or resolved in a binding, third-party arbitral forum. Rather, something much more mediatory in form and content seemed desirable and the United States, echoing the earlier compromise proposal it first offered at the Athens meeting, made a counterproposal that took a quite different tack from that of the Swiss.

The U.S. proposal first emphasized that dispute resolution was only one aspect of peaceful relations between countries. Countries disagree all the time and should take steps to avoid disputes where possible and, where that is impossible, manage the disputes in a manner so as not to disrupt peace and security.

Second, the United States recognized that countries have many different kinds of disputes and that no single mechanism is appropriate to solve all. Moreover, any dispute resolution process that requires all disputes to be moved from one mechanism to another in a rigid, pre-determined, linear fashion is not likely to contribute much to effective and efficient dispute resolution. A mechanism that ignores the fundamental nature and characteristics of a dispute and simply forces the disputants to move from some less intrusive means (e.g., negotiation, conciliation) to increasingly more intrusive methods (e.g., arbitration, adjudication) is not likely to result in a process that will be any more used than the dozens of virtually idle international arbitral bodies and courts that already exist.

To address these and the other concerns that will be discussed below, the United States proposed that the CSCE dispute resolution mechanism be designed to allow the parties to a dispute to play a large role in both selecting the most appropriate dispute resolution mechanism for their particular dispute and developing the substantive solution to the problem at hand.

Finally, unlike the Swiss proposal that contained very broad exceptions to the application of its mechanisms for disputes relating to national security, territorial claims, and a host of others, the U.S. proposed that virtually all disputes be subject to PSD mechanisms. The United States reasoned that if the mechanism were relatively "soft" then use of the mechanism could not adversely affect national security interests, territorial claims, and the like. Thus, the United States proposed that the exceptions to the application of the dispute resolution mechanism be very narrowly drawn.

After weighty and often tense negotiations, the parties finally agreed upon a joint recommendation to the Council of Ministers,[5] which the Ministers adopted in June 1991 in Berlin. The experts who gathered at Valletta, in their final recommendation to the Ministers, drew upon many specific suggestions of the U.S. proposal, though they substantially modified many and created large categories of disputes that are excepted from the application of the so-called Valletta

---

5.   Report of the CSCE Meeting of Experts on Peaceful Settlement of Disputes, Valletta 1991 (all General Principle number and section number citations hereinafter will refer to this Report unless otherwise indicated).

Mechanism.[6] Nevertheless, the heart of the proposal remains and is sufficiently different from most multilateral dispute resolution mechanisms that it merits further study.

b. The Valletta Report and the Valletta Mechanism

The Valletta Report begins by committing states to the prevention of disputes and, in the event disputes cannot be prevented, to "tak[ing] particular care not to let any dispute among them develop in such a way that it will endanger international peace and security, and justice" (General Principle 5). A variety of suggestions is offered to implement both goals.

The states then agree to use all means available, including "negotiation, enquiry, good offices, mediation, conciliation, arbitration, judicial settlement or other peaceful means of their choice" to resolve disputes that arise (General Principle 6). In particular, the Parties commit to "endeavor to agree upon a settlement procedure suited to the nature and characteristics of the particular dispute" (General Principle 6(b)). No particular order or preference is given to the various devices.

This section is interesting for two main reasons. First, it recognizes that not all disputes can be solved by the same mechanism, but rather that some disputes are more suitable for resolution in one mechanism and other disputes in another. Second, this section involves each party very directly in the selection of the dispute resolution mechanism *for the particular dispute at hand.* In other words, rather than simply relying on a set mechanism to which the parties must have recourse or on a particular order of mechanisms through which a dispute must pass, the parties are enjoined to consult and, if possible, agree on the type of mechanism most suited— legally and politically—to their particular disagreement.

The parties next agree in General Principle 6(d) to accept the involvement of a third party when a dispute cannot be settled by other peaceful means. At this stage, however, the role of this third party is unique, at least as far as international

---

6.   This Mechanism was amended and supplemented in a subsequent meeting in Geneva in 1992. The Valletta Mechanism itself was streamlined and improved. In addition, the experts proposed (and the Ministers subsequently adopted) two additional mechanisms. The first was a more formal arbitral process within the CSCE context for a limited number of disputes. This was proposed by the French and ultimately agreed to by all the parties on the condition that, unlike all other CSCE commitments, not all countries are required to join. Rather, participation is optional. Second, for certain kinds of disputes, the experts developed a more formal conciliation procedure to which countries could commit themselves. Both of these mechanisms, but especially the second, are interesting and worth closer examination. Both, however, are somewhat more conventional and familiar in international law circles than the Valletta Mechanism. Moreover, in many ways, the initial conceptual breakthrough is contained in the Valletta Report. For those reasons, and reasons of space, I will limit my discussion to the Valletta Report.

dispute resolution treaties are concerned. Unlike other dispute resolution treaties, the role of the third party is not to issue a binding (or, at least in the first instance, even a non-binding) decision regarding the dispute at hand.

Instead, the first obligation of the third party (parties, actually[7]) is to "assist the parties in identifying suitable procedures for the settlement of the dispute" (Section VII). The third-party may offer general or specific advice or comments, but all by way of suggestion, unless the parties specifically agree otherwise. The parties, in turn, are required to consider the advice and counsel of the third-party in good faith and in a spirit of cooperation (Section IX). In other words, the parties are required to consult a third party but, at least in the first instance, the design of the third-party intervention is not to resolve the substance of the dispute, but rather to help the parties find a dispute resolution mechanism suitable for resolving their particular dispute. The focus is still on finding a mechanism that will not merely satisfy the sensibilities of international lawyers, but that will genuinely resolve the problem that has given rise to the disagreement among the parties.

In the event this first stage conciliation does not work, then the parties may request a second stage conciliation on the substance of the dispute itself. Again, the third-party may provide general or specific comment or advice on the substance of the dispute, "in order to assist the parties in finding a settlement in accordance with international law and their CSCE commitments" (Section XI). And again, the parties agree to consider the advice in good faith and cooperatively.

The parties commit to bring, at the request of one side or the other, all disputes, except those specifically excluded, to these third-parties.[8] Unfortunately, the final list of specifically excluded disputes is quite broad and includes cases where "another party to the dispute considers that because the dispute raises issues concerning its territorial integrity, or national defence, title to sovereignty over land territory, or competing claims with regard to the jurisdiction over other areas, the Mechanism should not be established or continued" (Section XII).

Either before or during the process, the parties may, by mutual consent, modify the procedure in a number of ways, including authorizing the third-party to conduct fact-finding, engage experts, prepare and submit a formal report, or even make a binding decision (Section XIII).

---

7.   Section V provides that a "CSCE Dispute Settlement Mechanism consists of one or more members, selected by common agreement of the parties to a dispute from a register of qualified candidates maintained by the nominating institution." If the parties cannot agree on members, Section V also provides a complicated process whereby the Senior Official of the nominating institution nominates a certain number of candidates and then the parties may veto a certain number of such candidates, resulting ultimately in a board of at least three people even when the parties have exercised every possible right of rejection.

8.   Of course, parties may bring even excepted disputes to the Dispute Resolution Mechanism by mutual consent.

III. THEORY UNDERLYING VALLETTA REPORT AND VALLETTA MECHANISM

a.   International Dispute Resolution in General

A brief examination of international dispute resolution theory and practice may help us better understand the approach taken in Valletta. It is against this backdrop that the Report and Mechanism were developed and against which its utility must be judged.

The norm in international relations is not the absence, but rather the *presence*, of disputes between countries. Equally importantly, a high degree of disputation does not necessarily indicate a high degree of hostility. To the contrary, it usually underscores a high degree of interaction and friendliness. The United States, for example, has far more "disputes" and "disagreements" with its closest friends and allies than with more politically and geographically distant countries. The United States argues much more with Canada, Japan and the European Union than with all the former Eastern Block countries put together. True, the nature of disagreements between allies, on the one hand, and less friendly countries, on the other, is quite different. But in terms of number, and often intensity, disagreements with friends dwarf disputes with others.

The goal, then, of international law and the role of international legal institutions cannot be the elimination of disputes. Rather, international law and its attendant institutions must be intended—and designed—to facilitate the routine, peaceful settlement of such disputes.

Even more important, the international regime should strive to develop and deeply ingrain patterns of peaceful interaction at every layer of society and government. These habits of interaction cannot merely be imposed or proclaimed. They must be cultivated through the pursuit of shared interests under conditions of respect for agreed standards of conduct.

For many countries, these habits are part and parcel of the daily engagement in the mainstream of Western and Asian democracy. Most international documents envision that a high degree of peaceful interaction among signatory states will become the *norm* rather than the exception.

The principal formal response of the international legal community to these seemingly obvious realities is a curious one, however. Rather than create formal institutions and mechanisms that are used frequently and that become an integral part of the policy and decisionmaking framework, the international law community by and large has created formal dispute resolution institutions that have as their singular characteristic an almost total lack of engagement by the countries they are designed to help.

The International Court of Justice and the large number of arbitral bodies (with the possible—and I stress possible—exception of those in the international trade arena, i.e., the GATT and its successor, the WTO, dispute resolution processes) are most interesting not for what they have accomplished, but for the extraordinary little use to which they have been put. One can count on one hand, usually with fingers left over, the number of cases filed with the ICJ every year. In most cases, one would not run out of fingers on two hands even if one were to add in all the formal arbitrations to which countries agree in a given year.

Moreover, with a few notable exceptions, this focus on formal adjudicatory or arbitral tribunals has been the principal preoccupation of much of the international law community when engaged in thinking, writing and recommending about international dispute resolution mechanisms, as evidenced by the Swiss, and later the French, in the CSCE context. A brief, non-random, non-scientific survey of the major case books on public international law in the United States confirms this preoccupation. Most casebooks devote five to eight times as much space to arbitration and adjudication as they do to other forms of peaceful dispute resolution.

Hence one of the most interesting curiosities in international law: disputes are common place—indeed, the rule, not the exception—and international law rightly focuses much attention on their peaceful resolution; at the same time, however, the formal rules and institutions on which the international community most commonly focuses are employed only infrequently.

One might add another incongruity in the focus on arbitral or adjudicatory type mechanisms. Even a casual examination of international relations makes clear that disputes are much more easily resolved among parties that have some habit and practice of intercommunal dialogue. Countries that interact frequently on many issues at many levels, such as Canada and the United States, tend to resolve their disputes with a minimum of fuss and certainly without any of the acrimony or violence that often attends international dispute resolution. Accordingly, one might think that a primary goal of any PSD institution should be to increase cooperative interaction among the parties.[9]

Of course, one might object to the above analysis on the grounds that some countries historically have had relatively friendly relations or that the disputes that generally arise between them are not highly politically or emotionally charged (e.g., a simple trade dispute, in contrast to a border or territorial dispute). Thus, the objection continues that the parties can more easily resolve their disputes through mutual discussion than can parties with a greater history of acrimony or disputes that go more to the core of national identity. In other words, success has less to do with the nature of the dispute resolution mechanism than with other variables, such as history and the nature of the dispute.

There is certainly much force to this objection and it would be wrong to discount the importance of history and, as discussed later in this paper, even more problematic to dismiss the importance of the nature of the dispute. Nevertheless, it would also be at least as wrong to dismiss the significance of the dispute

---

9. This is particularly true in the CSCE context where many of the countries have no deeply ingrained patterns of interaction or genuine, non-coerced cooperation. The goal always should be to increase the extent to which CSCE countries are required to work together in cooperative ways, in large part to help develop the patterns of voluntary, peaceful, cooperative interaction that form the true basis for peaceful international relations.

resolution culture that develops between two countries.

One is again drawn to the United States and Canada for at least anecdotal instruction. Viewed from a historical perspective, relations between these two countries have been far from amicable. Note that most of the major gun embankments in old Canadian fortresses, such as Quebec City, all face not out to sea, but south. Indeed, as late as 1938, when the Canadian Government reviewed the major battle plan for the defense of Canada in light of the emerging threat of Nazi Germany, staff officers found that the whole battle plan was designed to repeal an invasion from the United States. Moreover, disputes between the United States and Canada have not merely focused on trade, but have included everything from acid rain to serious, on-going border disputes involving significant amounts of territory. Nevertheless, over the years, the two sides have devised a broad array of dispute resolution mechanisms that de-politicize these disputes, that create an environment in which politically and legally acceptable solutions can be jointly devised in a spirit of mutual cooperation, and that establish a culture of cooperative resolution of even the most politically sensitive disputes. Relations among other countries, such as the Western European nations, the members of ASEAN, and the U.S. and Mexico, also teach variants of this same lesson.

Ironically, however, the theoretical focus (and almost seeming preference) for arbitral or adjudicatory solutions points countries in precisely the opposite direction. It polarizes the dispute and reduces dialogue, rather than forcing the parties together to find mutually acceptable solutions.[10] This approach somehow seems wrong under the circumstances.

Despite these apparent incongruities, however, a poll of international lawyers would probably reveal that most believe the international legal community is on the right track. International adjudicatory institutions are necessary, we argue, as courts of last resort to resolve disputes before they devolve into war. It is true that countries do not use these institutions as much as we think they should, but, we assert, that lack of use is merely a result of political necessity—many would say political short-sightedness—within the various member states of the international community. We should continue to create and improve these institutions and then encourage the various countries in the world to use them more.

Thoughtful analysts also suggest that these adjudicatory institutions may not be used because the legal rules they apply have not been developed with sufficient clarity, specificity and predictability. In that case, the task of the international community is to engage forthwith in the process of rule formation. Then, we might suppose that countries will feel more comfortable using the adjudicatory and arbitral tribunals for disputes of national moment.

---

10. Adjudication may be such an unpleasant option, of course, that the parties will work together to find a solution, but that is somewhat like saying that we ought to enshrine war as a dispute resolution mechanism because the parties will then be more encouraged to cooperate.

It is also possible that countries decline to engage these dispute resolution institutions because the countries believe that the rules they apply will reflect values different than those held by the disputing parties. Developing countries or countries that were once colonies might believe, for example, that the international rules applied by the major international institutions have been created largely by the developed countries or the former colonial powers. Accordingly, the major international institutions would promulgate solutions ill-suited to the needs of third world countries.

However true these observations might be, it is nevertheless hard to credit that belief as a prime deterrent to the use of binding, third-party arbitral or adjudicatory type dispute resolution mechanisms. In the first place, individuals from third-world countries are relatively well represented on the decision making panels of many of the major international dispute resolution institutions. Second, even those binding arbitral and adjudicatory dispute resolution bodies established, staffed and run entirely by representatives from less developed countries or former colonies are only very occasionally used by their sponsoring countries. Whatever the ideological or national composition of the body or the disputants, if the body provides binding third party arbitration or adjudication, no country seems very willing to use it.

In part, of course, the problem might be viewed as circular. Without more clear-cut, predictable, and certain international rules, very few countries will be willing to commit disputes of genuine importance to binding adjudication or arbitration. Without more decisions from such tribunals, however, certain and predictable rules cannot develop adequately.

Viewing this as the problem, most analysis therefore approaches resolution of this dilemma from one of the two halves of the circle. Some suggest that we push countries to commit more disputes to arbitration and adjudication in order to develop a sufficient critical mass of clear international rules. Others suggest that we develop the rules first, perhaps through international negotiations that result in treaties, codes and the like; then, countries will feel more comfortable with adjudication and more naturally resort to its employ.

One might wonder, however, whether either of these solutions—exhorting countries to greater use of the ICJ or quicker formation of adequately clear international rules through the treaty-formation process—has even the remotest likelihood of success. Wishful thinking obviously will not—and, at least so far, eloquent urging has not—alter the political will of nations sufficiently to occasion a substantial increase in their use of international adjudicatory institutions. Nor could any sane person who has actually negotiated an international treaty think that this process is capable of creating clear-cut international rules with dispatch sufficient to occasion a real change of behavior with respect to the use of international adjudicatory institutions. In short, the proposed solutions to our problem are generally quite improbable or entirely unworkable.

b.   Rethinking International Dispute Resolution in Light of PSD Practice and Domestic Dispute Resolution Theory

The approach ultimately taken at Valletta does not utilize either of these two "solutions" to the problem. The Experts' Report is instead premised on the notion that the international community might be on quite the wrong track conceptually, wishing for the wrong thing and, in the bargain, getting neither what it wishes for nor what it really needs, namely, a substantial enhancement of pacific dispute resolution processes in the international arena. The Valletta Report embraces the possibility that the problem may not lie in the political will of the participants or the clarity of the rules, but rather in the very way the international community conceptualizes disputes, their resolutions, and the dispute resolution process itself.

The Valletta Report posits that as an initial step to rethinking international dispute resolution, instead of first developing preferred types of institutions and then trying to shoehorn all disputes into those institutions, nations first ought to determine precisely what kinds of disputes occur between countries and exactly which institutions are best suited to their resolution. Second, instead of explaining in ever greater detail what countries should do ideally, the international community should examine more intensely what countries *actually* do to resolve disputes. Then, institutions that appeal to countries and that are truly suited to the disputes these countries have, rather than processes that appeal to some preferred— but currently non-existent and possibly uncreatable—international order, may then naturally result.

Examination of some of the more recent literature on dispute resolution, especially domestic dispute resolution, provides insight to both how *and* why the authors of the Valletta Report departed from much of the conventional wisdom on international PSD. Such literature teaches much about what kinds of approaches to dispute resolution are most effective and most satisfying to the parties, and provides a convenient conceptual framework to understand better what went on at Valletta.

(1) Dispute Avoidance and Dispute Management

First, much of the literature on dispute resolution makes the obvious, but often ignored point that effective dispute resolution practice really starts not with *resolution*, but rather initially with dispute *avoidance*, and then with dispute *management*. A variety of devices can facilitate dispute avoidance, including requirements that parties notify each other of actions they intend to take that will effect the rights or interests of the other; agreements to consult before taking such action; and mutual study groups that anticipate possible problems and facilitate the timely development of mutually acceptable solutions.

Effective dispute management can also be accomplished through many techniques, but might include, for example, commitments not to take any position that would prejudice the outcome of the dispute until it is satisfactorily resolved; agreements that necessary action can be taken without sacrificing legal positions; agreements to keep issues confined to certain fora; and agreements to refrain from certain sorts of action calculated to escalate the intensity of a dispute.

The lesson in this for the international community is obvious. When structuring international arrangements, mechanisms and processes that facilitate the avoidance of disputes and the management of disputes that cannot be avoided are as important as mechanisms that resolve disputes once they arise.

That is the first useful insight learned from the Valletta Accord as well. The parties commit, in many cases for the first time, to attempt to avoid and, if that is impossible, at least to manage disputes so they do not escalate and disturb the peace and security of the CSCE community. Mechanisms to avoid and manage are suggested. Moreover, the CSCE institutions that manage the PSD process are now also charged with developing information and giving advice about various mechanisms that countries might use to accomplish these tasks.

(2) Participation in Selection of Appropriate Processes and Appropriate Solutions

Second, this dispute resolution literature, especially with respect to domestic dispute resolution in the United States, helps illuminate precisely which characteristics of the various possible dispute resolution processes the parties find most satisfying. In other words, what kinds of processes do the parties themselves generally consider best suited to resolve their particular disputes?

This is a particularly important issue in international dispute resolution because domestic and international political considerations simply preclude states from committing a large range of international disputes to determination by independent arbitral or adjudicatory bodies. However much the executive branch of a government would like to submit a dispute to arbitration, legislators and the domestic citizenry often strongly oppose the resolution of a dispute of particular national moment by someone or something over which the domestic government does not have virtually total control. This is especially true, of course, when the domestic political constituencies think that their country has the upper hand in the dispute. But, as a matter of practical observation, it appears only *slightly* less true even when a country cannot possibly hope to secure a satisfactory outcome without the intervention of some external force.

So, what does the literature tell us is most likely to satisfy parties? A variety of elements appears important, but, interestingly, a high correlation exists between the amount of input the parties themselves have in the *choice* of the dispute resolution process and the degree to which the parties are willing to accept the results. A sense of fairness of substantive result and of process are important, but actual satisfaction appears to be as much a function of a sense on the part of the parties that they participated in choosing the mechanism *and* that they actively participated in shaping and molding the substance of the resolution. In other words, parties generally consider it very important to have some say in both the choice of dispute resolution fora and in picking (or at least agreeing to) the result of that process.

From these observations, one might draw our second major lesson in this reconceptualization of international dispute resolution, namely, a primary goal should be the creation of mechanisms that allow the executive branch of any government to claim two things: first, that it chose the process and second, that it has the final say in the ultimate substantive resolution of the dispute. In other words, the resolution of the dispute was derived from a process that the parties had a hand in choosing, and second, that the decision was largely agreed upon, *not* imposed.

The Valletta Accord allows the parties considerable—often dispositive—input into the choice of dispute resolution mechanisms. Moreover, the mandatory fall-back mechanism, the Valletta Mechanism itself, allows the parties to participate—again, usually in a dispositive way—in the development of a substantive solution to the dispute at hand.

(3) Processing Disputes through Mechanisms Appropriate to the Characteristics of the Dispute

A third, highly significant observation culled from the same dispute resolution literature, particularly with respect to dispute resolution in the United States, is that not all disputes are suitable for resolution in the same kinds of fora. Some disputes are simply more easily resolved in some kinds of dispute resolution mechanisms and other disputes in other kinds. This leads to the obvious conclusion that a substantial degree of flexibility in the range of the available dispute resolution mechanisms is essential to their successful employment.

This insight also leads to another less obvious, but no less important conclusion, namely, that dispute resolution mechanisms must be tailored to the essential nature or characteristics of the dispute. Not only must a broad range of mechanisms be available to the disputants, but it is important to include in that list of possibilities both mechanisms and processes that are suitable for resolution of the most important disputes likely to arise between countries.

A brief example may clarify this point. To vastly oversimplify, adjudicatory-type institutions are best suited to deciding "rights"- based disputes. A "right" is, of course, something to which a person has an entitlement and, in most cases, with respect to which someone or something else has a duty or responsibility. This responsibility or duty might be a positive obligation to do something affirmative; alternatively, it might be a duty to refrain from certain sorts of actions. Most critically, however, because the enforcement machinery of the state might be brought to bear to reshape or constrain the behavior of someone or something, the basis of the right and its correlative duty must be relatively clear, predictable and certain. The essence of a rights-based dispute is that at least one of the parties has expectations of vindication of a perceived entitlement. Indeed, courts, at least in the

United States, come under the most severe criticism—and their actions require the most justification—when they create rights and duties that are not generally accepted as heretofore adequately clear and certain, either as a legislative or judicial matter.

In contrast to rights-based disputes, parties may be engaged in an "interest"-based dispute. These disputes involve competing interests with respect to which neither party has an entitlement, but both parties may nevertheless have a strong desire or interest. In contrast to a perceived rights-based dispute, parties in an interest-based dispute might be viewed as without expectations, but with hopes and desires.

This might be most understood easily in the context of resolution of labor disputes. Parties to a labor agreement may have a *rights*-based dispute if one party, the union, for example, believes that the other has violated some expectation mutually agreed upon and enshrined in the contract. The contract may promise an annual cost-of-living adjustment in workers' wages. If the company refuses to increase wages or the proffered adjustment is, in the union's view, too miserly, the union may go to court and claim a "right" has been violated.

For the courts, this is familiar dispute resolution territory. They have a relatively clear, certain, and predictable specification of an entitlement. One might debate precisely how much the cost of living has increased or dispute which of the various cost-of-living indices is the most appropriate and accurate (and the court might even refuse to enforce the "right," if the standard against which the contractual language is to be measured is too vague or imprecise in expression or potential execution), but, generally speaking, the courts can enforce this contractual language. They have clear, legally familiar landmarks to guide them and within which to maneuver. The case may be difficult to resolve, but the processes and techniques are clear. There is a more or less correct answer from a legal perspective, or, at least, from a judicial process perspective.

On the other hand, once the contract has expired the parties may dispute the size of the wage increase to be included in the next contract. Of course, there is no "right" to a certain size increase. Nor does the employer have an "obligation" to increase wages in any certain amount, or, for that matter, to increase wages at all. Not surprisingly, submission of this type of dispute—a dispute over competing interests, not over rights and duties—to a court is appreciably less appropriate. The court has no standard by which it can determine a "legally" correct answer. Neither party has a legally created expectation that the court can determine and enforce. For any of a variety of reasons, the parties may turn the dispute over to an arbitrator to determine, but none of those reasons relates to any sense of entitlement that either party brings to the process (unless, of course, that entitlement comes from practices or rules outside the four corners of the contractual document).

The range of disputes that might be considered "interest" based, rather than "rights" based, on an international level is, of course, infinitely larger than on a domestic level. Far fewer international legal rules exist, and most of the existing international rules are much less precisely defined and have far less clarity and certainty in application than domestic legal rules.

The most obvious conclusion is that at least until the international rules become much greater in number and richer in content, adjudicatory or arbitral-type decision-making processes are not particularly well suited to the resolution of most international disputes. Moreover, even if such disputes are forced into adjudication, the majority of participants is unlikely to acknowledge the legitimacy of the results. At the current stage of development of international law, more disputes cannot be forced into adjudication; nor is it clear from a conceptual perspective that there should be.

The principle that emerges from this discussion is relatively straight-forward. Perhaps international dispute resolution mechanisms would be used more often if they offered a range of mechanisms, including mechanisms particularly suited to the types of disputes that actually arise in international relations, or, at least, the types of disputes that actually arise in light of the current state of development of international legal rules. Adjudicatory and arbitral mechanisms should be created for rights based disputes, but something else (or a variety of something elses) should be available for interest-based disputes.

Again, the Valletta Accord makes a nod to these observations. In the first place, it invites the parties to use any of a large number of dispute resolution mechanisms, chosen according to the characteristics of the dispute, the political and legal situation within the disputing countries, and the tastes of the parties. Second, and perhaps most significantly, it implicitly recognizes that the potentially most disruptive disputes in Europe are likely to be "interest"-based disputes. Accordingly, it contains a fall-back, mandatory mechanism that is tailored precisely to deal with those kinds of disputes. It remains for the CSCE countries to develop the political will and imagination to employ it.

c.   International PSD Practice

Of course, the CSCE is not the only international organization to recognize and implement the above principles. Even a cursory observation of what states really do among themselves suggests that the problem of PSD is not that the states refuse to implement many of the ideas discussed above, but rather that the current theory of international PSD lags behind actual practice. Whatever the case, examples of application of at least some of these theoretical insights can be found well beyond the CSCE context.

(1) Dispute Avoidance and Dispute Management in Practice

Numerous treaty-based attempts at dispute avoidance and dispute management exist. For example, in a variety of bilateral agreements between the United States and Canada, the parties are committed to the process of dispute avoidance through such techniques as prior notification and consultation regarding unilateral action by one state that might affect significant interests or concerns of the other.[11] Some of these treaties also establish bilateral commissions, consultative mechanisms and fact-finding bodies. All are designed to create an environment in which potential areas of disagreement or friction are identified before they become "disputes" and, if at all possible, handled in a way that eliminates the conflict before it arises.

Prior notification of activities that might occasion harm as an approach to dispute avoidance is particularly evident in the environmental area. For example, environmental impact assessments of proposed activities likely to cause significant transboundary impacts are required under the ECE Draft Convention on Environmental Impact Assessment in a Transboundary Context. Notification to potentially affected states of proposed activities is required under that same Draft Convention, and notification of nuclear accidents is required under the IAEA Convention on Early Notification of Nuclear Accidents.

Environmental agreements also lead the field by requiring consultations regarding potentially problematic activities. The ECE Draft Convention, the U.S.-Mexico Border Environment Agreement and a variety of U.S.-Canada border environment agreements all require consultations and discussions.

A range of practical solutions to dispute management has also been devised. For example, *modus vivendi* and other practical solutions allow the parties to advance their interests without compromising their political and legal positions. The most famous example, of course, is the Antarctic Treaty,[12] under which the parties basically have agreed not to act on their sovereignty claims. The U.S.–Canada Arctic Cooperation Agreement is another example. This allows U.S. icebreakers to transit the Northwest Passage in a manner that allows each party to maintain that its legal position on the status of the Passage has not been prejudiced. Joint resource sharing arrangements, such as that between France and Spain over their maritime boundary, are yet other examples of this practical approach to the problem.

To manage disputes effectively, parties may also simply agree to disagree, without taking any action on their disagreement. For example, the United States has agreements with both Canada and Russia not to enforce their claims of territorial sovereignty against each other's flag vessels in disputed waters. In some cases, the

---

11. For excellent discussions of the broad variety of mechanisms established to address disputes between the U.S. and Canada, *see, e.g.*, Bilder, "When Neighbors Quarrel: Canada–U.S. Dispute-Settlement Experience," Disputes Processing Research Program, Working Papers, Series 8 (May 1987)(Institute for Legal Studies, University of Wisconsin-Madison Law School); "Canada–U.S. Relations," in THE REPORT OF THE CANADIAN STANDING SENATE COMMITTEE ON FOREIGN AFFAIRS (3 vols.)(1975); Smith and Biniaz, "Beyond Dispute: An Air Quality Agreement in the Context of a Consultative Relationship," Presentation to the Canada/U.S. Law Institute (Apr. 13, 1991)(Case Western Reserve University School of Law); WILLOUGHBY, THE JOINT ORGANIZATIONS OF CANADA AND THE UNITED STATES (1979).

12. Antarctic Treaty, concluded at Washington, Dec. 1, 1959, entered into force, June 23, 1961. *See* U.N.T.S. 71, 12 UST. 794, T.I.A.S. No. 4780, 19 I.L.M. 860 (1980).

parties agree not to take any action at all. Neither the U.S. nor Canada drills in the disputed Beaufort Sea area; moreover, before the maritime boundary agreement was reached, neither the U.S. nor the former Soviet Union drilled in the disputed Bering Sea area.

(2) Obligation to Negotiate

Many international treaties also impose upon the parties an obligation to attempt initially to settle all disputes by negotiation.[13] Moreover, the United Nations General Assembly may discuss any problem it considers likely to harm the general welfare or friendly relations among nations and recommend measures for the peaceful settlement of that problem. In the vast majority of cases on which the General Assembly has offered suggestions, it has recommended that the parties resolve their dispute by negotiation, though such resolutions often also suggest "other peaceful means," without further specification.[14]

(3) "Alternative" Dispute Resolution

International treaties also occasionally require the parties to take steps beyond negotiation, but short of arbitration or adjudication. For example, treaties occasionally require the parties to negotiate for a certain period of time and, if the dispute is still unresolved, to then seek resolution through conciliation or some other mediatory mechanism.[15] Other forms of international dispute resolution are also commonly employed, including inquiry, good offices, mediation, and conciliation. Occasionally these devices have also been enshrined in certain international agreements.

International agreements have also established an extraordinarily broad array of actual dispute resolution devices. Some of these devices are very unintrusive, such as agreements to negotiate in good faith at the political level or, in a number of cases, at the technical level even before engaging the political level. In other situations, the parties agree to engage the good offices of some independent entity or even to participate in non-binding conciliation or mediation.

In still other situations, the devices chosen may be closer to the strong end of the dispute resolution spectrum, including prior or *ad hoc* agreements to submit the

---

13. *See, e.g.,* 1979 Agreement Governing the Activities of States on the Moon and Other Celestial Bodies (General Assembly Resolution 34/68, annex, art. 15, para. 1); the 1975 Vienna Convention on the Representation of States in their Relations with International Organizations of a Universal Character (art. 84); 1959 Antarctic Treat (art. VIII, Para. 2).

14. Manila Declaration (section II, para. 3(a).

15. *See, e.g.,* 1975 Vienna Convention on the Representation of States in their Relations with International Organizations of a Universal Character (arts. 84, 85); 1978 Vienna Convention on Succession of States in respect of Treaties (arts. 41, 42); 1981 Treaty Establishing the Organization of Eastern Caribbean States (art. 14).

disputes to binding arbitration, to a Chamber of the International Court of Justice (ICJ), or to the full ICJ. Such approaches are particularly prevalent when the treaty provisions are relatively specific and detailed and create an adequate legal standard against which the compliance or non-compliance of the parties can be measured.

(4) Limits on Current Practice

Nevertheless, despite the examples cited above, the major lessons extracted from the alternate dispute resolution literature have not often been applied in international, and particularly multilateral settings. Even those treaties that require something other than arbitration rarely give the parties a genuine, meaningful role in the selection of the mechanisms. The parties are obligated, at the behest of one of the parties, to negotiate and, if that fails, to conciliate, and, if the dispute is still unresolved, to arbitrate or adjudicate.

Second, even treaties that list more than one type of dispute resolution mechanism generally structure the choice of these mechanisms in some linear fashion in which the parties graduate from one mechanism to another until the dispute is resolved. At the behest of one of the parties, the disputants move from less intrusive means (e.g., negotiation, conciliation) to increasingly more intrusive methods (e.g., arbitration, adjudication) in lockstep. Regardless of the nature of the dispute, the parties must move along a rigid, predetermined path. Thus, if these non-adjudicatory type mechanisms do not resolve the dispute, even disputes ill-suited to resolution by adjudication must be submitted to some form of arbitration or adjudication, at the request of only one of the parties.

Moreover, the more generic dispute resolution treaties that exist almost all focus very largely on arbitration or adjudication, containing only the briefest references to any other means. When these treaties include alternatives to arbitration or adjudication, moreover, they generally treat them with appreciably less imagination than the multitude of more subject-matter oriented treaties discussed above. Moreover, these generic dispute resolution treaties also usually adopt a linear, graduated, lock-step approach, with negotiation at the beginning and arbitration or decision by the ICJ at the end. Virtually no generic dispute resolution treaties regard dispute avoidance and dispute management as seriously as they do dispute resolution. Indeed, very few pay any attention at all to it.

IV. CONCLUSION

The Valletta Report and Mechanism is an interesting attempt to deal with some of the more difficult conceptual and practical problems of international dispute resolution. While far from perfect, and obviously the product of a committee—a particularly fractious one at that—when viewed from a more conceptual perspective, this approach deserves to be studied with more care by international lawyers. Then, perhaps countries will be more comfortable trying them out, which may, in turn, lead to a substantial reconceptualizing of the theory of international dispute resolution, and, subsequently, its practice. Such a revolution is admittedly a great deal to hope for, but a revolution regarding human rights was perhaps even more unlikely in 1975. The CSCE stimulated that. Perhaps it can stimulate this as well.

PART V
INTERNATIONAL PEACEMAKING AND PEACEKEEPING ACTIVITIES IN THE POST—COLD WAR WORLD AND ITS RELATIONSHIP TO DOMESTIC IMPLEMENTATION OF INTERNATIONAL OBLIGATIONS

| SUMMARY

Matthew Anderson

INTRODUCTION

The end of the Cold War marked the end to a certain simplicity in international affairs. The polarization of the U.S.S.R. and the United States ironically created stability. Without such a structure, many smaller nationalistic and civil conflicts have erupted. In response to these conflicts, the role of the United Nations Peace Keeping Operations (PKO) have evolved and expanded. This growth, while a reasonable adaptation to changing times, must be evaluated. What follows is a summary of the symposium discussion, based on previously prepared papers, concerning the various political and legal issues that have arisen in this context from the trilateral perspective of Canada, Japan, and the United States. Participants addressed the Security Council's authority under the United Nations Charter to carry out these operations as well as domestic legal and political issues such operations raise.

DISCUSSION

Canada has had a strong tradition of involvement in peacekeeping operations, states Professor Copithorne. Canada is unique in that its participation rarely has been questioned on a legal basis. The absence of a constitutional court or similar institution with the jurisdictional authority to review the government's involvement in United Nations (U.N.) activities indicates the relative freedom that Canada enjoys with respect to its U.N. involvement. Canada's parliament has what amounts to virtually unlimited plenary power. Its involvement with the U.N. does not trigger any review of its constitutionality. In fact, such discussions are "irrelevant." Thus, when Canada was asked to help establish the legal guidelines for further U.N. peace- keeping operations, a senior Canadian official stated that in practice, there is general agreement that PKOs are consistent with the primary purposes of the United Nations. Implying that it had broad freedom to act, the official continued that the U.N., "as the only global organization with Charter

453

authority to promote international security, must be able to exercise that authority effectively."

Without fully endorsing it, Copithorne introduced the chaos theory as offering some support to Canada's approach. Rather than a world of ordered advancement and certain progression, the chaos theory describes history and societal development in terms of change, flux, chance, and the exclusive relevance of the present: progression is not inevitable. With this perspective, the ability to act on an *ad hoc* basis, unrestricted by obsolete laws and irrelevant precedence, becomes paramount.

Professor Franck and Ambassador Owada both expressed doubt concerning the sufficiency of precedence. They pointed to examples where U.N. participation exceeded what they thought was authorized in the language of the Charter. Their espousal of a devaluation of precedence, however, was in an effort to argue that there should be more restraint on the U.N. PKOs. In contrast, Copithorne implied that precedence is insignificant in that past events are unique to those circumstances and are therefore seldom similar enough to be instructive. Thus, the U.N. must be free to deal with entirely new situations as the unique circumstances dictate. Although this is not a blank-check authorization, in Canada the only real challenge to U.N. participation is political.

Historically, Canada has been proud of its active participation in various PKOs. It may be due partially to this support that there has been little need to establish or adhere to any guidelines for U.N. PKOs in which Canada has participated. Currently, however, Copithorne describes the Canadian people as suffering from "donor fatigue." In other words, support for future activity appears less reliable. He attributes the apparent shallow support to at least three factors. First, the uncertainty of the mandates and objectives of the operations makes it difficult for the public to assess the operation's success. Such ambiguous success taxes public enthusiasm. Second, troop-contributing nations desire more involvement in the decisionmaking process. Third, the benefits of such operations are questionable when weighed against increased casualties.

Donor fatigue is not unique to Canada. In the face of increasingly complex conflicts, many countries have become wary of risking troops for uncertain PKOs. The changing nature of the conflicts confronting the U.N. demands a questioning of the role and the type of the response. Professor Franck compared the past U.N. role to that of a strong, magnificently virile bull sent *only to observe* cattle that weren't able to breed. Recent activities manifest a definite trend, if not transformation, from observer to active participant. Ambassador Owada warns that the extent to which that role should change must be investigated. That there is a trend toward a new type of U.N. operation does not in and of itself justify its existence. As we consider such a change, Franck suggests that we consider the rest of the world, particularly those countries with little influence in U.N. politics. Whether such developments are in the best interests of the international community is dependent partially on its ability to gain worldwide political legitimacy.

Japan is representative of the caution with which the U.N. expansion is being perceived. Anxious to be involved at the policy level of international PKOs, Japan has delineated a five-point plan that serves as a guideline for Japan's foreign policy and future involvement in U.N. sponsored operations. This marks an increased willingness to contribute to such activities. And yet, the tension this creates with the passivist nature of its constitution cannot be ignored. While any increased military involvement may be skeptically viewed by Japan's neighbors, this commitment is valuable encouragement to the U.N. quest for legitimate and appropriate expansion of its own role.

Japan's military contribution to international peacekeeping operations is intensely debated by the people of Japan. Although the discussion began in 1958 concerning U.N. activities in Lebanon, it was not until the outbreak of the Gulf War that the debate over the propriety of Japanese participation reached a practical level. In the Japanese Diet, a bill was submitted to provide logistic support to the coalition forces in Kuwait. The Socialist and Communist parties, however, combined to defeat this proposal. Despite this unsuccessful attempt, Yanai recalls that the debate produced some positive results. The most striking was an unprecedented three-party coalition (the Liberal Democratic Party, the Democratic Socialist Party and *Kōmeitō*, which formed to create a substitute bill. Secondly, through the debate on the bill, the Japanese public became much more aware of the need for Japan to become more involved with U.N. PKOs. Until that time, the general public did not understand that Japan's lack of participation in such activities was compromising its world position. Thirdly, this led to an open discussion of the need to explore and define the new role of the Japanese defense forces. Until that time, any discussion of alternative roles for these forces had been taboo. This new bill signaled the beginning of a new era of Japanese involvement in U.N. peace-keeping operations.

The resulting International Peace Cooperation law, discussed more fully in Yanai's chapter, is not, however, a major departure from contemporary Japanese foreign policy. It is rather limited in scope, but does allow for traditional PKOs. The law carefully authorizes new types of peace enforcing operations. All operations in which Japan participates must also comply with the five PKO principles. Regrettably, Yanai adds, some of the provisions were frozen due to political concerns.

Fears of a remilitarization of Japan have severely handicapped the mobilization of the neighboring Self Defense Forces (SDF). The constitutional provisions were frozen because they were to be carried out by these forces, not because the nature of the duties were objectionable. The activities, such as monitoring the exchange of prisoners, marking the lines of ceasefire and ensuring against ceasefire violations can be carried out legally by an individual officer but not by the SDF. Japanese lawmakers were particularly sensitive to any operations performed by SDF. To many people, the SDF represent the Japanese military, and, therefore, any mobilization of those forces is perceived as akin to overt military action. Yanai notes that this has caused many parliament members to be very skeptical of an increased role for these forces.

Japanese resistance to increased participation in PKOs is emotionally as well as constitutionally founded. The validity of increased participation in newer types of U.N. PKOs under Article 9 of the Japanese Constitution is the central issue. Since World War II, Japan has considered itself to be a passivist nation. Article 9 often has been touted as the archetype of passivist law. This is not only a source of pride for the Japanese but a stabilizing force in the peace that East Asia currently enjoys. However, as Japan has increased in international stature, its limited participation in PKOs has become more conspicuous. Demands that it participate more liberally in collective security efforts originate from within as well as from outside the country. This creates a strong tension between the constitution and Japan's growing role in the international community.

Professor Onuma, Mr. Yanai and Ambassador Owada were all in agreement that the Constitution need not be amended now. The current language does not prohibit self-defense, nor does it prevent Japanese participation in PKOs as they interpret it. However, Professor Matsui and many others did not agree. They held that the constitution prohibits any mobilization of Japanese military forces, even if for a U.N. PKO. Perhaps in response to this tension, both Professor Onuma and Mr. Yanai believe that an amendment to the constitution will be necessary in the future. This prediction may be based on another prediction that the evolution of PKOs will eventually extend beyond the scope of the current language. An alternative explanation is that participation in current PKOs is marginally *outside* of constitutional limits and that an amendment would be appropriate now were it not for political externalities that make an amendment impossible.

It is feared that even if an amendment were to fail, neighboring countries would interpret the attempt as signaling a return to imperialist Japan. While East Asia currently enjoys relative calm, suspicions run rampant. Past victims of Japanese aggression are keenly sensitive to any mobilization of Japanese forces. While these fears exist, it will be very difficult for Japan to make any overt steps to upscale its involvement in U.N. PKOs.

Mr. Yanai attributes this largely to Japan's failure to confront and adequately face "war guilt." Nations like Korea and China will continue to be fearful until Japan acknowledges that their past military aggressions were wrong. Without referring to past injustices, Ambassador Owada recognized that there is a general consensus that the constitution should not be changed in order to preserve the peace of that region. Before any changes are made in Japanese foreign policy, a cost/benefit analysis should be made, with specific emphasis on the potential reactions of its neighbors. Ambassador Owada believes that there are no benefits in the near future that would justify amending the constitution.

Japan's newly articulated commitment also presents obstacles for the U.N. itself. If Japan is successful in obtaining a permanent seat on the Security Council, it will gain power to veto any U.N. involvement. Although five countries currently enjoy this power, veto power in the hands of the Japanese could confine U.N. involvement to the observer-bull role. If it is widely held within Japan that increased U.N. activism violates both the U.N. Charter and the Japanese constitution, Japan would be compelled to veto all such operations. In effect, Japan's participation could halt the U.N.'s current evolution towards more activist PKOs. Professor Franck argues that while Security Council members will not allow such a situation to occur, the potential may initiate much needed debate over the Security Council's authority to expand its own role in peacekeeping and peace enforcing operations.

Nevertheless, Japan's chances of actually becoming a permanent member of the Security Council are seriously reduced. Professor Franck stated that if Japan is perceived as having such a restrictive approach toward U.N. involvement, other members who support the expansion of U.N. operations would oppose Japan's bid for permanent membership.

Other than domestic concerns unique to each country, Professor Franck raises a concern that many in the international community share regarding the absence of any kind of a check on the expanding role of the U.N. To the extent that the U.N. PKOs can stay well within the specific objectives of the authorized mission, there will be few abuses of power. However, Professor Franck pointed to the *Lockerbie* case as an example of the U.N. acting beyond its established mission and consequently outside its authority. Along with the *Lockerbie* case, Ambassador Owada views the establishment of a war crimes tribunal in Yugoslavia as another instance of extralegal activity inconsistent with the stated mission.

Ambassador Owada attributed the potential for abuse to the vague nature of the Charter language, which creates a dangerously fertile ground for unlimited growth. The only definite boundaries on Security Council authority to act are operations that infringe on established international law (as in the above-mentioned war crimes tribunal) or infringe on the authority of other U.N. organs. Professor Franck suggested that challenges to the Security Council's authority to act could be heard in an international court that would serve to check the expansion of the Security Council's power. And, in the event that the challenged activity survives judicial review, the operation would receive valuable legitimization. This kind of judicial or quasi-judicial system would be an ideal forum in which past Security Council decisions could be reviewed.

Professor Franck suggested that the arms embargo on the former Yugoslavia should be subject to such a review. While at the time the decision to prohibit arms sales to Yugoslavia was sound, the situation has significantly changed, rendering that decision obsolete. The current situation, he contended, has evolved to the point where the embargo clearly disadvantages the victims (the Bosnians) and aids the Serbian aggressors. In such a forum, Bosnia would be able to argue that the embargo amounts to a denial of their Article 51 right to self-defense. Without an opportunity for review, U.N. actions may become outdated. The inability to update U.N. actions to a change in circumstances exposes those actions to unilateral review and possible dissolution of the accord. The United States' recent threat to withdraw from the embargo is a case in point. Such a withdrawal, regardless of the wisdom of the decision, damages the legitimacy and reputation of UN's solidarity.

While Professor Franck did not agree with the priorities established in Presidential Policy Directive 25 (PPD 25), some kind of similar explicit standard is necessary to control the growth of U.N. PKOs. He suggested a standard that would not approve any actions unless there are: (1) a probability of success; (2) a willingness to make a long term-commitment (of at least five years); and (3) a restoration of order that would foster independence. A standard could help evaluate the appropriateness of U.N. involvement and serve to reassure other, less involved countries that the Security Council is operating within a set of reasonable goals and is reasonably limited in its powers.

Professor Franck reminded the audience that the American Revolution started as a protest against unchecked political powers. He sensed the beginning of a revolt by the third-world countries who are unsatisfied with what they see as unchecked, unlimited political power in the hands of the Security Council. As it is now, the Security Council is sometimes perceived as little more than an instrument of its most powerful members. It is therefore worth considering different ways that the Security Council can become more principled and less secretive.

Professor Onuma agreed with Professor Franck that many of the newly developing PKOs are legal, but was concerned that domestic national interests supersede international priorities. This phenomenon further subjects the U.N. to criticism that it is merely a puppet of its most powerful member states. He specifically referred to United States Senator Robert Dole's proposal that the President obtain Congressional approval before committing troops to the Security Council. While Senator Dole bases part of his argument on language in the U.N. Charter, the proposal heavily emphasizes the domestic issues of the United States over the best interests of the international community. That U.S. interests will be first priority is explicitly stated in PPD 25. While Professor Smith observed that the effective execution of U.N. objectives *is* a U.S. interest, both he and Professor Onuma expressed concern over the blatant reservation of the right to act unilaterally.

Professor Onuma argued that an explicit emphasis on national interests has ramifications that extend beyond skewing the U.N. agenda towards the interests of one country. Other participating countries are adversely affected by this policy as well. Member states may follow suit and reprioritize domestic issues above those of the Security Council. Also, participating states may become disillusioned and discouraged, concerned that the U.N. is constrained by the interests of one very powerful member state. He acknowledged the need to protect domestic concerns and that it is naive to expect a government to ignore its own interests. If, however, all members participated only when it is to their own direct benefit, the U.N. would be reduced to an international coalition of marginal effect.

In PPD 25, the President also reserves the right for the United States to act unilaterally or in concert with regional organizations. Professor Smith feared that, as member states act unilaterally or with other regional organizations, they will be perceived as acting under the aegis of the U.N.: France's recent involvement in Rwanda and Desert Storm are two examples of *ad hoc* arrangements that may detract from the legitimacy of U.N. operations.

Presidential Policy Directive 25 also articulates the President's unwillingness to contribute to a standing U.N. force. Contrary to recommendations from many sources, including the American Bar Association, the executive branch has consistently resisted a standing U.N. force largely because of its unpopularity with the U.S. public. In PPD 25, the U.S. did express interest in some alternative measures: increasing U.N. Department of Peace Keeping Operations staff, and creating a rapidly deployable headquarters staff and perhaps even a trained civilian reserve corps. Professor Copithorne added that Canada has gone one step further, providing a list of what would be available in the event of an emergency. While it does not guarantee troops or equipment for U.N. deployment, it provides specific information as to what will be available if Canada participates: a ready, but not standing force. The U.S. President, on the other hand, perceives that the public is unwilling to commit to any measure that might compromise U.S. sovereignty.

Smith contended that these explicit reservations of U.S. power to act unilaterally are a direct result of what he called the CNN factor. The president reserved the ability to quickly respond to the public's reactions to press coverage. "The ability to risk U.S. troops," he continued, "is almost totally determined by the popular response to the press reporting of those events." The CNN photographs of Somalia dramatically shifted the U.S. public's attitudes toward deployment. While, in this instance, press coverage broadened support for U.N. efforts in Somalia, the CNN factor is unpredictable, affecting different states differently. Professor Smith expressed concern that the UN's ability to effectively deal with a problem may become entirely dependent on the press coverage the problem receives. This would create a sporadic, if not chaotic approach to delicate international conflicts.

Mr. Yanai, however, illustrated the positive effect that the media can have on public support of U.N. operations. The media can be a highly effective means of persuasion. When Japan sent its SDF troops to Cambodia on a PKO, the Japanese public and many members of the Diet were extremely skeptical of the nature of the project. Three hundred media personnel accompanied the initial deployment of 600 troops. During the preceding parliamentary debates, many had expressed fears that although the troops were only armed with small weapons, they were indeed going to battle. The detailed photographs of troops building bridges and repairing roads dispelled those fears. The Japanese popular support of U.N. PKOs has been greatly enhanced by the CNN factor.

Because of the CNN factor and the general success of Japanese involvement in PKOs, Japan will most likely become more responsive to future PKO opportunities. Also, because of the minimal amount of armed conflicts in recent operations, Mr. Yanai believes that those frozen provisions will be reviewed and hopefully re-activated in an upcoming session of parliament.

SUMMARY

Among the panel members, there was a general consensus that most of the recent PKOs were within the authority granted the Security Council. Yet most shared Professor Franck's concern with the lack of institutional checks on these operations. Confronted with new and complex demands on the PKOs, the panel expressed anxiety about the potential for those forces to exceed their authority and compromise the legitimacy of the U.N. operations.

The domestic concerns of the individual countries produce differing restrictions on the member states' ability to participate in these new types of PKOs. According to Professor Copithorne, Canada is relatively unconcerned with the absence of specific Charter authority for these newer activities. Yet, a recent swelling of "donor fatigue" is a source of political discontent that must be addressed. The United States participation has become increasingly dependent on the public's reaction to media coverage of the event in question. Professor Smith observed that this could introduce a substantial chaotic element into the agenda of the United Nations Security Council. Finally, while some in Japan interpret their constitution as forbidding participation in most PKOs, both Professor Onuma and Mr. Yanai believe that Japan can constitutionally participate in current PKOs. In the future, however, they believe the constitution should be amended.

THE TRAVAIL OF A MIDDLE-AGED PEACEKEEPER: CANADA AND THE NEW CHALLENGES OF PEACEKEEPING

Maurice Copithorne

Canada will continue to participate because we are good at it, it makes us feel good, and it contributes to creating the type of world in which we want to live.
Major General Lewis MacKenzie[1]

I. INTRODUCTION

Much has been written about the new activism of the Security Council in the post–Cold War world and the many problems that have accompanied the huge expansion in peacekeeping operations. The growth has reflected conceptual as well as practical change in the number and type of operations the Security Council has mounted to address threats to international peace and security. Many of the traditional precepts of U.N. peacekeeping have been put aside as the Security Council responds, both aggressively and intrusively, to the ethnic and civil strife that has become so prevalent in the aftermath of the Cold War. This chapter will focus on the views of one country: Canada, a long-term faithful supplier of peacekeepers.

It is said—at least in Canada—that Canada has been the peacekeeping country *par excellence*, having contributed to virtually every peacekeeping operation; it is the only country with such a record. Since 1948, some 100,000 Canadians have served abroad in forty-four peacekeeping operations; about one hundred Canadians have died in the process. At the beginning of 1994, approximately 3,500 Canadians were serving abroad in fifteen peacekeeping operations. Canada was one of twelve countries that the United Nations Secretary-General had traditionally turned to;

---

1. *In* THE CHANGING FACE OF PEACEKEEPING 48 (Alex Morrison ed., Canadian Institute of Strategic Studies, 1993) [hereinafter THE CHANGING FACE].

today peacekeepers are being drawn from more than forty countries, with Canada's share dropping from ten percent to three percent of the total.

II. THE EARLY YEARS

Over the years, peacekeeping has become a popular symbol in Canada, cited by politicians as evidence of Canada's humanitarian concerns.[2] For Canada, peacekeeping has been a comfortable activity, widely supported by public opinion and a central feature of bipartisan foreign policy. The activity was regarded as a legacy of the Lester Pearson years as foreign minister, an era in which so-called middle powers were seen to wield significant albeit circumscribed influence on world events. There was no significant public debate in Canada either about committing Canadian troops to the cause of peacekeeping, or over the government's unfettered capacity to do so. It was simply a non-issue, a pleasant reminder that in a changing world, Canada could still play a useful role.

There has always been a strong impulse in Canadian foreign policy in favor of multilateral international arrangements, an impulse born in no small part from living next door to a large and powerful neighbor. As a strong supporter of peacekeeping, Canada was meeting a self-perceived need to express itself as an independent political entity making a contribution to foreign policy issues, and thus contributing to its sense of independence from its large neighbor. The present government has invoked the spirit of Lester Pearson, whose foreign policy it recently described as "independent, original, forward-looking, based on truly Canadian values but requiring at the same time a sustained involvement in international organizations such as the United Nations and NATO."[3] Succeeding governments made various, more specific efforts to promote a separate Canadian identity, particularly in the economic field: these by and large failed. The advent of the Canada–United States Free Trade Agreement marked a major turning point in this respect. Nevertheless, the desire for a way to offset the influence the United States has on Canada, and for a distinctive foreign policy remains.

The Canadian government itself has not always been unreservably enthusiastic about peacekeeping. In the early days of the United Nations, the government was distinctly cool to what it regarded as an imposition on limited military resources.[4]

---

2.   For a thoughtful overview of the history and prospects for Canadian involvement in U.N. peacekeeping, *see* JOSEPH JOCKEL, CANADA AND INTERNATIONAL PEACEKEEPING (Canadian Institute of Strategic Studies, 1994).

3.   Foreign Minister Ouellet, House of Commons Debates (Mar. 15, 1994) at 2258 (drawing upon Geoffrey Pearson's characterization of his father's view of how Canadian foreign policy should be shaped).

4.   *See* Jack Granatstein, *Peacekeeping, Did Canada Make a Difference? And What Difference Did Peacekeeping Make to Canada?*, *in* MAKING A DIFFERENCE? CANADA'S FOREIGN POLICY IN A CHANGING WORLD ORDER (English and Hilmer eds., 1992). *See also* JOCKEL, *supra* note 2, ch.2.

Public opinion became involved, however, after Mr. Pearson received the Nobel peace prize in 1957 for his role in the creation of a U.N. peacekeeping force to end the Suez crisis. The government nevertheless remained lukewarm through the early 1960s, and apparently committed troops to the Congo only in response to public and media pressure. During the following decades, a strong identification developed in the public mind between Canada and peacekeeping, and it came to be said that Canada had in fact invented the concept. By the 1980s, the image of the "Blue Helmets" appeared in the recruiting material of the Canadian Armed Forces, and in various governmental appeals to national pride. Following the award of the Nobel prize in 1988 to the peacekeepers of the world, a large monument to them was erected in Ottawa in a prominent public square.

There have been a few critics of Canada's easy assumption of peacekeeping responsibilities. The noted Canadian diplomat and scholar, John Holmes, warned years ago:

> Ours is not a divine mission to mediate. Our land is strengthened by acknowledged success, but it is weakened if planting the maple leaf becomes the priority. Too often Canada's participation in peacekeeping operations (PKOs) has had some of this planting the flag idea about it, a sense that we must maintain our record as the country that has served on more PKOs than any other—whether or not those operations made sense, had much chance of success, or exposed our servicemen and service-women to unnecessary risks in an unstable area of the world.[5]

Professor Granatstein has suggested that "for too many Canadians peacekeeping has become a substitute for policy and thought."[6]

III. THE POST–COLD WAR WORLD

Over the past few years, as the international community has struggled with the threats to peace and security in the post–Cold War world, significant doubts have arisen within Canada as to its proper role in the new environment. The new Liberal government took office in October 1993; in its pre-election manifesto the party had stated that it would strengthen Canada's leadership role in international peacekeep-ing in part through a reorientation of Canadian defense policy and procurement practices to emphasize the key priority of peacekeeping.[7] Consideration was to be given to creating a special peacekeeping brigade comprising volunteers with both military and nonmilitary expertise. The manifesto also stated that the Liberal party believed Canadians wanted their government to play a more active, independent,

---

5.   Granatstein, *id.* at 223.

6.   Granatstein, *supra*, note 4 at 234.

7.   THE LIBERAL PARTY OF CANADA, CREATING OPPORTUNITY—THE LIBERAL PLAN FOR CANADA 106 (1993).

international role in the changing world, and that they did not want Canadian foreign policy to be determined solely through special personal relationships between world leaders. This was a reference to what was perceived to be an inappropriately cozy relationship between Prime Minister Mulroney and Presidents Reagan and Bush.

One of the first acts of the new government was to place Canada's commitment to peacekeeping in the former Yugoslavia on the parliamentary agenda. In a January 1994 debate, Minister of Foreign Affairs André Ouellet noted that the previous government had committed troops without consulting Parliament.[8] While the new government would strengthen Canada's leadership role in international peacekeeping, it wanted to examine the way this should be done. The Minister used the occasion to set out the guidelines that had been developed over the years to govern Canada's participation in peacekeeping, and which were today still valid:

- there must be a clear, achievable mandate from a competent political authority, such as the Security Council;
- the parties to the conflict must undertake to respect a cease-fire, and must accept the presence of the Canadian troops;
- the peacekeeping operation must undergird a process aimed at achieving a political settlement;
- the number of troops and international composition of the operation must be suited to the mandate. The operation must be adequately funded, and have a satisfactory logistical structure.[9]

The Minister suggested that the previous government's commitment of troops to the former Yugoslavia had not met Canada's own criteria and drew attention to the element of force that was increasingly being introduced into U.N. operations, as well as the risk factor for the troops involved. He also noted the political challenges that the international community took on when it assumed responsibility for situations that were traditionally viewed as the internal affairs of the states involved.

The new government was clearly not only attempting to distance itself from its predecessor's policies, but was also responding to the changed circumstances that were by then all too evident to the Canadian public. Canadian troops were much more obviously in danger in these operations than they ever had been in the past.[10] Moreover, the achievements if not the purposes of these operations were not always self-evident. Public opinion polling suggested that support for peacekeeping, while

---

8.   House of Commons Debates (Jan. 25, 1994) at 263.

9.   *Id.*

10. In Yugoslavia, ten Canadians have died and fifty have been seriously injured. Jeff Sallot, *Reluctant Ottawa Agrees to Keep Troops in Bosnia*, THE GLOBE AND MAIL, Sept. 24, 1994 at A14.

widespread in the past, had been relatively shallow and that it should no longer be taken for granted.[11]

IV. YUGOSLAVIA: THE TURNING POINT?

Nowhere was this more evident than in the debate over the Canadian commitment in the former Yugoslavia. Indeed, no foreign policy issue had been more hotly debated within the government and within Parliament since the 1993 election. Two special House of Commons debates on this subject were held in the Government's first year of office. An apparently inspired press story reported that from mid-1992 to the end of 1993 Canada had spent nearly $1 billion in military deployments to Yugoslavia—about twenty times the $50 million given in humanitarian assistance.[12] Foreign Minister Ouellet stated, in the course of one of the Parliamentary debates:

> [t]he task in Bosnia is an infinitely more difficult and dangerous one than that which our peacekeepers have traditionally faced. In addition to the dangers of simply operating in a war zone, we must face the fact that some of the actors do not always want the humanitarian aid to get through.[13]

Among the arguments of the media critics was the assertion that Canada had become involved in a commitment in Yugoslavia that was disproportionate to that of most of its allies and outstripped Canada's political influence on the international efforts to coax the parties into a settlement.[14] Prime Minister Chrétien was himself reportedly uncomfortable with Canada's involvement in the new peacekeeping, of which Yugoslavia was a prime example. In Parliament, opposition speakers argued that the government had no coherent policy as to when to commit troops to new peacekeeping missions. Prime Minister Chrétien indicated that there were indeed no hard and fast rules, and stated that the government would be guided by "common sense" and the views of members of the Parliament.[15]

The rapid growth in the cost of U.N. peacekeeping for Canada also had become an issue. With some 68,000 U.N. peacekeeping troops in the field, Canada's financial share (3.11percent) had risen from approximately $12 million in 1991 to $130 million in 1994. The actual incremental cost to Canada of its 1994

---

11. *See, e.g.*, THE DECIMA QUARTERLY REPORT, Spring 1993, at 75.

12. Paul Koring, *Price of Peacekeeping Dwarfs Aid*, THE GLOBE AND MAIL, Jan. 4, 1994 at A1.

13. House of Commons Debates (Jan. 25, 1994) at 265.

14. *See, e.g.*, Giles Gherson, *Too Many Canadian Troops Stuck in the Bosnian Quagmire*, THE GLOBE AND MAIL, Apr. 26, 1994 at A22.

15. Jeff Sallot, *Policy on Peacekeeping Urged*, THE GLOBE AND MAIL, June 15, 1994 at A4.

U.N. commitments—that is, the costs on top of the regular defense budget—are about $225 million.[16]

V. THE DEMANDS UPON THE MILITARY

There were also the demands being made upon the Canadian military. The rapidly growing commitment of Canadian troops to peacekeeping operations, particularly infantry, had become a major challenge for military planners. Traditionally less than one percent of Canada's military personnel—mainly specialists—was occupied with peacekeeping. This translated into a bench mark of some 2,000 troops that the military undertook to have available for peacekeeping activities. It was a relatively small and manageable task within a larger military context. Yet at one point in 1992, caught between a shrinking military budget and growing international obligations, more than five percent of Canada's military was being assigned to peacekeeping activities. If one includes the units under training to go abroad as peacekeepers and those recovering from it, there were arguably as many as 12,000 troops committed to this activity. Canada then scaled back its commitments most notably by the withdrawal of its troops from Cyprus—where they had been for twenty-nine years— and by the winding down of commitments in Somalia and Cambodia. By September 1994, however, the commitments had risen again—this time to 3,800.[17] The Canadian army is scheduled to undergo a further reduction to some 20,000 regular troops: a peacekeeping commitment of 3,000–4,000 of this number will be a formidable management challenge.[18]

Two other dimensions of the military aspect of peacekeeping are under scrutiny: equipping the Canadian armed forces and training them for peacekeeping. It has recently been revealed that Canadian troops in Somalia faced serious equipment problems: the Canadians arrived ahead of their communications; their vehicles were immobilized by unannounced shipping measures of draining the oil and removing the batteries; the accuracy of their rifles was seriously impaired by the desert conditions; and their issue maps of some critical areas were "mostly blank."[19]

More generally, some critics of the Canadian military have called for a move away from the "combat culture" that determined equipment priorities and training during the Cold War.[20] For them, the appropriate response to declining military budgets was to redeploy financial resources away from sophisticated combat

---

16. Jeff Sallot, *Ottawa May Cut Forces in Bosnia*, THE GLOBE AND MAIL, Sept. 21, 1994 at A1.

17. Canadian Press, *Canada Is Cutting Forces in Rwanda*, THE GLOBE AND MAIL, Sept. 23, 1994 at A6.

18. *See* JOCKEL, *supra* note 2, at ch. 3.

19. Ron Eades, *Peacekeeping Done Peacemeal in Somalia*, THE VANCOUVER SUN, Oct. 14, 1994 at A10.

20. Ernie Regehr, *The Failure of Peacekeeping, in* THE CHANGING FACE at 22.

technology to low-tech peacekeeping equipment. The military, for their part, were understandably wary. While traditional peacekeeping was acceptable enough as an ancillary peacetime function—particularly as Canada supplied primarily military specialists rather than infantry—current trends in peacekeeping often involved a wide spectrum of civilian activities not associated with traditional military ones. The growing emphasis on peacekeeping held the risk for the military that they could gradually be deprived of the skills and equipment necessary to perform traditional military functions. The contrary view is that faced with further cutbacks in the aftermath of the Cold War, the military would do well to build up its popular support by emphasizing its peacekeeping role, actual and potential.[21]

There is the related issue of appropriate training for peacekeeping. The position of the Canadian military has been that general purpose combat training produces an efficient, reliable, and flexible peacekeeper.[22] Although this point of view no doubt had much validity in the traditional peacekeeping context, it is at least arguable that the increasing range of different tasks being required of peacekeepers is taking the Canadian military well beyond the skills of conventional soldiering. The need for peacekeeping-specific training and education was reinforced by the highly publicized death of a Somali in the custody of Canadian troops that led to a series of courts martial, including that of the Commanding Officer concerned. Post-traumatic stress disorder has been prevalent in the less peaceful peacekeeping operations. According to a study by the military, fifteen percent of Canadian troops that had served in Yugoslavia had symptoms of the disorder.[23]

Canada's peacekeepers clearly have some lessons to learn from Somalia, Bosnia, Haiti and Rwanda. The government has dedicated a decommissioned military training facility in Nova Scotia for a new existence as "The Pearson Peacekeeping Center," to be operated by a civilian agency, the Canadian Institute of Strategic Studies. It is to be a university-level institution to conduct research, education, publishing, and training in peacekeeping. At full strength, it is to have about one hundred staff and one thousand students, for varying lengths of time.[24] It is to be open to the training of peacekeepers from other countries.

---

21. *See* JOCKEL, *supra* note 2, at ch. 4.

22. John Bremner, *Canadian Preparation for Peacekeeping, in* THE CHANGING FACE at 103. *See also* Report of the Senate of Canada, Meeting New Challenges: Canada's Response to a New Generation of Peacekeeping, Ottawa, Feb. 1993 at 11 [hereinafter Meeting New Challenges].

23. Michael Hanlon, *Keeping the Peace Takes High Toll,* THE TORONTO STAR, Dec. 28, 1993 at A28.

24. Canadian Press, *Centre Named in Honour of Former P.M.,* THE GLOBE AND MAIL, Sept. 15, 1994 at N6.

VI. THE CHANGING FOREIGN POLICY CONTEXT

The foreign policy context in which all of this debate is taking place is also changing. There is little doubt that the commitments entered into by the Canadian government in 1991–1992 significantly overextended the Canadian military, and were done without a clear appreciation of the political and military implications. Some media critics have suggested that this reflected the previous Prime Minister's desire for Canada to actively promote the then-voguish new world order. The present Foreign Minister has returned to the earlier view of Canada as a relatively small country which should not overestimate its influence in the world.

While the present government invokes what it describes as the Pearsonian legacy, some critics suggest that this is simply another example of the "rearview mirror" tendency of Canadians, a wish to portray internationalism as an integral part of the Canadian character.[25] For these critics, Canada's middle-power internationalism was a function of the Cold War context within which it developed. The bipolar distribution of power created a demand for a middle power function which Canada developed with great skill. In fact, however, Canada's capacity to shape its own environment is severely limited. Indeed, some critics have suggested that it was the relative stability of the postwar world that afforded Canada the luxury of pursuing a distinctive diplomatic agenda. Peacekeeping, an activity seen to be increasingly managed by the United States, may be losing its value to Canada as a niche activity played in large part by a group of smaller states. While the moral imperative of peacekeeping is, if anything, enhanced in the post–Cold War world, its continuing usefulness in a broader foreign policy context of middle power diplomacy may be considerably diminished.

Two issues that have grown out of the Bosnian conflict have captured the Canadian public's attention and created particular problems for the Liberal government. The first is the cases of harassment and in some instances the detention of Canadian and other peacekeepers by Serb forces. A December 1993 incident in which a squad of Canadian peacekeepers was briefly detained and roughed up by drunken Serb militia became a front page story in Canadian media. In April 1994 another troop of Canadians was captured and held by Serb forces for some days before being released unharmed.[26] These cases only heightened public concern about the safety of Canadian troops and doubts as to whether their commitment was making a contribution to the resolution of the Bosnian dispute.

At about the same time, the use of NATO air strikes in support of U.N. ground operations in Bosnia became a sensitive issue in Canada.[27] There were a thousand

---

25. *See, eg.*, Leigh Sarty, *Sunset Boulevard Revisited? Canadian Internationalism after the Cold War*, XLVIII INTERNATIONAL JOURNAL 749 (September 1993).

26. Paul Koring, *Serbs Hold Canadians Hostage*, THE GLOBE AND MAIL, Apr. 15, 1994 at A1.

27. Jeff Sallot, *Canada Wins Safeguards for Troops*, THE GLOBE AND MAIL, Sept. 21, 1994 at A11.

Canadian troops on the ground, some in extremely exposed positions. Canada, France, Britain, and other countries with troops in Bosnia expressed doubts at various times over U.S. proposals to use air power against Serb positions. In part, the issue was portrayed as one of safety for the U.N. troops. It was also suggested that a larger issue was at stake, that of the nature of Canada's original commitment of troops as part of the U.N.'s effort to protect convoys of food and humanitarian supplies; it was not the result of any commitment as a member of NATO. The argument was also made that the use of air strikes against one party to a conflict could seriously tarnish the U.N.'s profile as a neutral broker. Finally, Canada's best-known peacekeeper as well as other military figures argued that the use of air strikes would be useless without the support of 70,000 to 80,000 ground troops. In the end, Canada, France, and Britain—the largest troops contributors in Bosnia—successfully insisted that United Nations military commanders on the ground have a veto over air strikes if the commanders felt the strikes might endanger ground troops.

It became evident early on that the Chrétien government was uneasy about Canada's commitment in the Balkans and was looking for a way out—particularly from Bosnia. In the summer of 1994, the objective seemed to be to transfer this commitment to Haiti, a conflict that this government had from the beginning a strong interest in.[28] Canada was a member of the "Friends of Haiti," whereas in Yugoslavia it had apparently been excluded from the "contact group" of countries steering settlement efforts. Moreover, there was a domestic political factor at work, comprised of the large Haitian community in Montreal as well as the Québec missionaries serving in Haiti.

In the end, however, and under pressure from Britain and France, the Canadian government agreed to leave its troops in Bosnia for another six months from October 1994.[29] The argument of the British and French was that solidarity among the three troop contributors would make it more difficult for Washington to lift the arms embargo on Bosnia. There was a consensus in Ottawa that lifting the embargo would make Bosnia a much more dangerous place for U.N. troops in general, especially the Canadians who were often stationed in the remoter centers. As in the matter of NATO air strikes, Ottawa found itself resisting Washington on an issue that involved the safety of Canadian troops.

VII. BROADER CONCERNS

Turning to less peculiarly Canadian concerns, there remains the underlying current of concern and criticism among some U.N. member states regarding the adventurous nature of the Security Council's recent peacekeeping operations. These

---

28. Jeff Sallot, *Ottawa May Cut Forces in Bosnia*, THE GLOBE AND MAIL, Sept. 21, 1994 at A1.

29. Jeff Sallot, *Reluctant Ottawa Agrees to Keep Troops in Bosnia*, THE GLOBE AND MAIL, Sept. 24, 1994 at A14.

have been most recently expressed in the report of the 1994 meeting of the Special Committee on Peacekeeping Operations:

> Some delegations underscored that all aspects of peacekeeping operations should strictly adhere to the principles and purposes of the Charter, in particular, the principles of respect for sovereign equality, territorial integrity of states and non-interference in their internal affairs. In their view, peacekeeping operations should be impartial, of a non-intrusive and non-interventionist nature, mandated on the basis of the consent of all the parties concerned and in principle at the request of Member States involved. Use of force should be limited to self-defence, and recourse to Chapter VII should in principle be a measure of last resort.[30]

As for Canada, in this respect, at least, the present government appears to agree with its predecessor: Canada must put aside its traditional view that state sovereignty inhibits forceful action on human rights and in particular humanitarian intervention. In what amounts to a striking turnaround both the Mulroney government in its later stages and the Chrétien government have clearly accepted that intervention in some circumstances is not only a right but probably also a duty. In the words of the present Foreign Minister:

> It is my profound belief that the concept of intervention as a right and a duty represents a turning point in the history of humankind. The world has only recently understood and accepted this concept which, to some, constitutes interfering in a country's domestic politics but to many others is a sign of hope.

> I say this because I have seen the results. In Haiti I spoke to Canadian members of religious orders who work in that country, and these quite remarkable people taught me that intervention could be a duty. Considering Canada's intervention capability, we cannot afford not to use that capability to advance the cause of human rights. We cannot remain indifferent to the fact that throughout the world, millions of human beings—millions—are being denied their most basic rights.

> Indifference is the modern barbarism. Considering Canada's intervention capability, we cannot afford not to use that capability to advance the cause of human rights. We cannot remain indifferent to the fact that millions of human beings—millions—are being denied their most basic rights. Indifference is the modern barbarism. . . .[31]

---

30. *Report of the Special Committee on Peacekeeping Operations*, U.N. Doc. A/48/403 S.26 450 (1994).

31. Foreign Minister Ouellet, House of Commons Debates (Mar. 25, 1994) at 2253.

Under the rubric of "Political Direction and Control," Canada has called for peacekeeping mandates to be viable, achievable, and appropriately resourced. It has argued that flexible implementation of the mandate is essential. It has also pressed for a "Code of Conduct" to be agreed on by all member states. The Security Council has repeatedly emphasized the need for it to maintain sufficient flexibility to respond on a case-by-case basis to each situation as it arises. In May 1994 the President of the Security Council issued a statement on behalf of the Council that cautiously moved the matter forward.[32] The statement declared the Council to be conscious of:

> the need for political goals, mandate, costs and, where possible, the estimated time-frame of the United Nations peacekeeping operations to be clear and precise. . . . The Council will respond to situations on a case by case basis without prejudice to its ability to do so and to respond rapidly and with flexibility as circumstances require, the Council considers that the following factors among others should be taken into account in establishing new peacekeeping operations:
>
> a) whether a situation exists the continuation of which is likely to endanger or constitute a threat to international peace and security;
> b) whether regional or sub-regional organizations and arrangements exist and are able to assist in resolving the situation;
> c) whether a cease-fire exists and whether the parties have committed themselves to these processes intended to reach a political settlement;
> d) whether a clear political goal exists and whether it can be reflected in a mandate;
> e) whether a precise mandate for a United Nations operation can be formulated; and
> f) whether the safety and security of the United Nations personnel can be reasonably ensured including in particular whether reasonable guarantees can be obtained from the principle parties or factions regarding the safety and security of the United Nations personnel.

One may reasonably question how many existing U.N. peacekeeping operations would meet these criteria.

---

32. Statement by the President of the Security Council, U.N. SCOR, 3372nd. mtg., U.N. Doc. S/PRST/1994/22, May 3, 1994.

VIII. SUPPLYING THE PEACEKEEPERS

Another major concern for Canada has been the need for greater coordination in New York, particularly between the Security Council, the United Nations General Assembly, the troop-contributing nations (TCNs) and the Secretary-General. The TCNs, and particularly Canada, have complained about a lack of transparency in the Security Council's deliberations, as well as a failure by the Security Council to consult them as mandates are being developed. There is a pronounced feeling among some TCNs that the Security Council does not take their perspective into account. For its part Canada has insistently pressed for an enhanced role for TCNs, perhaps through a TCN Advisory Committee. Foreign Minister Ouellet commended New Zealand for having launched a process of regular consultation with troop contributors to the Rwanda operation while New Zealand had been president of the Security Council in April 1994.[33]

This leads into the issue of command and control, that is to say, the need to confirm the Secretary-General's overall control and political direction of peacekeeping operations. Somalia and Bosnia, and perhaps Cambodia, have shown the problems that can arise. The Secretary-General has made his view quite clear: "the existence of independent lines of communication between commanders and their national authorities violates the unity and integrity of the mission."[34] In its May 1994 statement, the Security Council had words both soothing and equivocal: "as a leading principle, United Nations peacekeeping operations should be under the operation and control of the United Nations." Canada has repeatedly expressed concern regarding this subject, particularly in the light of the Somalia experience. There has, however, been little progress; in April 1994 the Foreign Minister noted that "the broader challenge of ensuring effective command and control remains."[35]

The shortage of willing and appropriate states volunteering troops has reopened the debate over alternate sources. Across the spectrum of possibilities from a continuation of the present clearly inadequate process to a permanent U.N. army, focus has recently fallen on the Secretary-General's plans for the establishment of "standby arrangements."[36] Under such arrangements, TCNs would undertake to provide an agreed number of troops at an agreed level of readiness and agreed levels of equipment, within fourteen days, subject only to the state consenting to deploy to a particular peacekeeping operation. As of October 1994, some thirty

---

33. Speech by Foreign Minister Ouellet of Apr. 29, 1994 to the *Peacekeeping Brainstorming Session* in Ottawa, Statement Series 94/18 at 4.

34. *Improving the Capacity of the United Nations for Peacekeeping;* REPORT OF THE SECRETARY-GENERAL U.N. GAOR, 48th sess., Agenda Items 87 and 138, U.N. doc. A/48/403, S26450, p.7 (1994).

35. Speech by Foreign Minister Ouellet *supra* note 33, at 4.

36. *See Improving the Capacity of the United Nations for Peacekeeping, supra* note 34, at 5. The Security Council has welcomed these plans. *See* Statement by the President of the Security Council, May 3, 1994, *supra* note 32, at 3.

countries had pledged more than 54,000 troops of a goal of 100,000 infantry and various specialist troops.[37] It has been suggested that this concept be extended to equipment procurement from commercial sources as well as from member states. Canada has welcomed the concept of standby arrangements and has indicated the resources it is prepared to commit on this basis.

In his speech to the General Assembly in September 1994, Foreign Minister Ouellet ventured a step further and proposed a permanent U.N. peacekeeping force.[38] The concept of a permanent force is not a new one, but Ottawa now appeared to be more committed to the idea than other governments, at least until now.[39] The Foreign Minister announced that Canada would be carrying out a major study of the concept with international input and hoped to submit the report to the U.N. in the course of 1995. Canadian officials were quoted as saying that Canada "no doubt would make a significant contribution" to such a permanent force.[40]

The training of peacekeepers has also been a subject that Canada has pursued internationally.. Experience in several recent peacekeeping operations suggests that troops often arrive inadequately trained for the role of peacekeepers and unprepared for the coordination of military operations among troops from different nations, who often have differing military traditions. The Secretary-General is being asked to promulgate common standards and curricula. There have also been suggestions for UN-sponsored courses to train the trainers and for a U.N. staff college.

IX. A MORE SELECTIVE ROLE

As for Canada's role in the new environment, it seems inevitable that it will have to adopt a selective approach to the commitments it undertakes. The government has already said it can no longer commit to every U.N. operation.[41] Such a policy will require criteria such as the existence of Canadian national interests. This would clearly be a major departure for Canada, one that has been

---

37. However, according to a U.N. official the standby arrangements are little more than an inventory of what might or might not be available in particular circumstances. Jeff Sallot, *Strains on Resources and Politics Will Ignite Talk of a United Nations Military Brigade*, THE GLOBE AND MAIL, Oct. 8, 1994, at D1.

38. Speech by Foreign Minister Ouellet to the 49th General Assembly, Sept. 29, 1994, Government of Canada Statement 94/55. *See also* Meeting New Challenges *supra* note 22, at 6, which draws in turn from the Secretary-General's Agenda for Peace.

39. *Canada Proposes U.N. Army*, THE GLOBE AND MAIL, Sept. 30, 1994, at A1.

40. *Id.*

41. Jeff Sallot, *Balkan Force May Be Cut, Ouellet Hints*, THE GLOBE AND MAIL, Sept. 22, 1994 at A4. For a considered survey of Canada's post–Cold War foreign policy on peace and security issues, *see* Keating and Gammer, *The New Look in Canada's Foreign Policy*, XLVIII INT'L J. 220 (Autumn 1993).

suggested in Parliament by the opposition and denounced by the government.[42] Alternatively, Canada might confine its participation to traditional peacekeeping, an activity that Canadian troops clearly perform well. However, Foreign Minister Ouellet has apparently ruled this out in his support for the new interventionism of the Security Council. Canada's refusal of such assignments—which are likely to be the most serious international crises—would likely be widely criticized in Canada as a shirking of international responsibility and could only harm Canada's credibility as a major player in the U.N. A third approach to selectivity could relate to the nature of the chosen role. Canada could opt to supply primarily a variety of specialist services, thus performing a functional specialization.

The government seems to have opted for the latter approach. Foreign Minister Ouellet has said that Canada should focus on roles in U.N. operations involving "what we do best."[43] Further, Canadian contributions should not only be useful in the peacekeeping phase, but also make a contribution to the broader reconstruction of society—the peacebuilding phase. Canada, he said, should be:

> open and responsive when needs arise quickly and when the international community requires an urgent response. . . . There are no hard and fast rules about Canadian participation. There should be no arbitrary limits to Canada's contributions. What we do in each situation must be judged in light of our interests, in light of the requirements and in light of our ability to participate. [44]

X. CONCLUSION

Canada is as much caught up as any nation in the dilemma of concept and process as the world community seeks to adjust to the harsh realities of the post–Cold War world. Threats to international peace and security, disintegrating national states, and gross abuses of human rights all demand the attention of the Security Council. Unprepared and underfunded, the U.N. as an institution has had great trouble in accommodating the demands seeming to be placed upon it. This situation in large part reflects the fact that member states themselves have been going through their own often agonizing reappraisal of their moral and legal responsibilities—to their own citizens as well as the world community. The process is no less intense in Canada as it seeks to adjust to a world in which doubt has suddenly been cast on an activity that has been a source of national pride and has served to legitimize a distinctive foreign policy.

---

42. An Opposition spokesman had proposed that Canada should quit the peacekeeping mission in Rwanda "because it is in a far-off African country that is of little economic significance to Canada."

43. Foreign Minister Ouellet, House of Commons Debates (Sept. 21, 1994) at 5953.

44. *Id.*

THE SECURITY COUNCIL UNLEASHED? POST–COLD WAR U.N. PEACEKEEPING AND PROSPECTS OF U.S. PARTICIPATION

Thomas M. Franck *

I. INTRODUCTION: COLLECTIVE SECURITY OR COLLECTIVE SELF-DEFENSE

The long-moribund Security Council has sprung to life since the end of the Cold War. Some observers consider this a profound transformation of the international system. Others caution that we are only witnessing the sort of transformation that persons undergo when captivated by a temporary infatuation, as contrasted with falling deeply in love. Whichever view is correct, the Council's recent activism has created ample precedents for a new view of peacekeeping and peacemaking. Whether those precedents are followed consistently in the near future may be less remarkable than that they have been set at all.

While the Security Council is a body composed of states, the members function collegially, rather like the prince-electors of the Holy Roman Empire. The Council is not merely a meeting of sovereign states. It has the collective power to make decisions. When it acts, it may preempt powers ordinarily exercised by members of the United Nations system as incidents of their sovereignty.

It is sometimes assumed that, whatever the potential of the Security Council to restrict the autonomy of states, it cannot affect the sovereignty of the five veto-wielding permanent members. Such a conclusion, while initially attractive, would be wrong, as the Council's recent actions have illustrated. For example, the Council enacted a mandatory arms embargo on all the states of the former Yugoslavia.[1] True, any permanent member could have vetoed this sanctions resolution; however,

---

*   Parts of this essay are based on Lecture 9 of the author's General Course in Public International Law given at The Hague Academy in 1993.
1.   S. C. Res. 724 para. 5 (1991) and S. C. Res. 727 para. 6 (1992).

once it had passed, every member of the United Nations, including the permanent members, was prohibited from arming any of the warring parties. To *lift* the embargo on Bosnia, the Council would have had to have acted collectively, through a new resolution. No permanent member, acting alone, could rescind the Council's action. This presents a significant limitation on the sovereign power even of permanent members of the Council to act as they please in what they perceive to be their national interest.

This tidal transformation was barely noticeable during the forty-five-year Cold War because it was hidden beneath a frozen surface of inaction. Now, the thaw has unlocked the potential of the Charter's radical text, nowhere more dramatically than in the matters covered by Chapter VII. Not for 350 years has there been such possibility for genuine systemic transformation, or such trepidation at the prospect of change.

The rules pertaining to the exercise of the Council's powers are both flexible and straightforward. While Article 2(7) ordinarily precludes United Nations intervention in matters "essentially within the domestic jurisdiction" of a state, this limit is suspended when the Council decides to take enforcement measures under Chapter VII. To take such measures, the Council must decide that (1) there is a "threat to the peace, breach of the peace or act of aggression"; and (2) the circumstances warrant recourse to mandatory sanctions or collective military measures under articles 41 or 42 of the Charter.

Once the Council has made these determinations, articles 41, 42, and 43 place at its disposal an array of diplomatic, fiscal, commercial, and military options for enforcing peace and defeating aggression by collective action under United Nations authority and command. The collective security "window" created by the Charter is intended to make the peace and security of *each* state the responsibility of *all* states—with the Security Council as the powerful organ for giving effect to that radical vision.

In practice, however, a "second window" of quasi-collective action has been opened: first by the United Nation's response to North Korea's attack on the South and, more recently, in answer to Iraq's invasion of Kuwait. In both instances, the Security Council determined that there had been a breach of international peace and security,[2] but, instead of marshalling international forces under United Nations command, had called on member states to take designated action against the aggressor.[3]

In the Korean War, the Council invited members to provide "military forces and other assistance" for a "unified command under the United States" and authorized it to use the blue and white United Nations flag.[4] In some respects, this Council improvisation resembled the radical vision of Articles 42 and 43. Fifteen

---

2.   S.C. Res. 82 (June 25, 1950); (Korea); S. C. Res.660 (Aug. 2, 1990) (Iraq).

3.   S.C. Res. 83 (June 27, 1950) (Korea); S. C. Res. 661 (Aug. 6, 1991); S. C. Res. 665 Aug. 25, 1991; S. C. Res. 670 (Sept. 25, 1991); S. C. Res. 678 (Nov. 29, 1991) (Iraq).

4.   S.C. Res. 84 (July 7, 1950).

countries participated.[5] President Truman congratulated the Council for "creating a unified command. . . ."[6] However, while technically a U.N. force, the unified command was essentially an American operation. United Nations Secretary-General Trygve Lie, although supportive of that leadership, was "concerned with the 'solo' role . . . assumed by the United States."[7] Those two evaluations sum up the benefits and the costs of this approach: fast, incisive reaction to aggression *versus* overdependence on a single member state.

In the collective action against Iraq, the Council, after deciding that there had been an "invasion of Kuwait by Iraq"[8] asserted its "responsibility under the Charter . . . for the maintenance of international peace and security," imposing mandatory sanctions on the aggressor,[9] just as Article 41 intended. Later, the Council authorized "Member States cooperating with the Government of Kuwait . . . to use all necessary means" to evict Iraq from the territory it had occupied.[10] This, too, resembles, but is not a literal instance of, the radical vision spelled out in Article 42. Although more than twice as many states fought together under United Nations authorization in Kuwait than in Korea,[11] this operation, too, was led and dominated by the United States.[12] Of greater jurisprudential importance is that the force created to repel Iraqi aggression, like that in Korea, consisted of contingents voluntarily deployed and commanded by states and not of the United Nations forces envisaged by Article 43. This draws the spotlight to another set of benefits and costs of this *ad hoc* approach to collective security. It permits a *form* of collective response in the absence of Article 43 forces under United Nations command; but the relative success of the improvised alternative dampens the impetus to set about the creation of a genuine UN-commanded multinational force as envisaged by the Charter. And the improvised alternative depends heavily on U.S. willingness to lead with its own military forces, command structure, and logistical support. It also depends significantly on improvised funding by transfers from donor states directly

---

5. THOMAS M. FRANCK, NATION AGAINST NATION 37 (1985).

6. HARRY S. TRUMAN, 2 MEMOIRS 347 (1955–56).

7. TRYGVE LIE, IN THE CAUSE OF PEACE 336 (1954).

8. S. C. Res. 661 (Aug. 6, 1991).

9. *Id.* at pmbl. and para. 3.

10. S. C. Res. 678 (Nov. 29, 1990).

11. Approximately thirty countries participated in the Gulf War Coalition. Major military contributors were the United States, Australia, Bangladesh, Belgium, Britain, Canada, Egypt, France, Italy, Morocco, the Netherlands, Pakistan, Spain, Syria, and Turkey, as well as the nations of the Gulf Cooperation Council (Saudi Arabia, Bahrain, Oman, United Arab Emirates, Qatar, and Kuwait). Frank Viviano, *Americans Want More from Allies*, S.F. CHRON., Jan. 29, 1991, at A1.

12. The United States contributed 475,000 troops, 2,000 tanks, 1,300 aircraft and 100 ships to the fighting in the Gulf; 150,000 troops were contributed by the countries of the Gulf Cooperation Council and 112,000 troops by all other countries. (The total for "all other countries" does not include the 100,000 troops Turkey assigned to the Turkish-Iraqi border.) *Id.*

to the coffers of the U.S. treasury.

What, then, was the legal status of these improvised operations authorized by the United Nations in 1950 for Korea and in 1990 for the Gulf? Articles 2(7) and 42–47 of the Charter call for the Council to "take such action by air, sea, or land forces as may be necessary to maintain or restore international security." Its options include "operations by air, sea, or land forces . . ."[13] that members will "make available . . . in accordance with a special agreement," including "facilities. . . ."[14] These the Council is authorized to deploy with the aid of a "Military Staff Committee,"[15] to be composed of the Chiefs of Staff of the Council's five permanent members.[16]

Obviously, the Council's military responses to aggression in Korea and the Gulf, conceptually and logistically, differed significantly from this radical vision of collective security spelled out in the text of Chapter VII, leading some to argue that they were not collective Council measures at all, that they should rather be seen as thinly veneered instances of "individual or collective self-defense" by sovereign states acting under Article 51.[17] In this view, the Council's authorization of the force and its use was convenient but legally unnecessary as Article 51 use of force requires no benediction from the Council.

The issue is far from academic. Article 51 is a relic of the old "just war" system of state sovereignty—a safety net for use when the new collective security system fails. Those who interpret the Korean and Gulf actions as examples of Article 51 in action are probably influenced by a belief that in the future, as in the past, states should rely on their own judgment and military power to defend their interests, and not submit to a new and untested U.N. system of collective security and decisionmaking. The choice between these alternatives is now facing us.

II. THE USE OF FORCE IN SELF-DEFENSE

The right of a state—acting within the customary law's strictures regarding proportionality—to respond in self-defense to an armed attack is acknowledged by Article 51. The right is described by the text as "inherent," which is to say that it is a carry-over from the customary law applicable to sovereign states under the Westphalian system, an incongruous appendage to the new radical vision of Chapter VII—which otherwise deals with collective enforcement by the Security Council. This appendage manifests the drafters' prescient suspicion that Chapter VII might

---

13. U.N. CHARTER art. 42.

14. *Id.* at art. 43.

15. *Id.* at arts. 46 and 47(1).

16. *Id.* at art. 47(2).

17. This is the view of Professor Eugene Rostow, *Until What? Enforcement Action or Collective Self-Defense* 85 AM. J. INT'L L. 506 (1991). A different position is taken by Professor Oscar Schachter, *United Nations Law in the Gulf Conflict* 85 AM. J. INT'L L. 452 (1991).

not work, and for forty-five years, the Cold War amply verified that calculation.

Article 51's "collective self-defence" model does not fit together comfortably with the new "collective security" model. The Charter envisages the use of sovereign force in self-defense only until the Security Council assumes responsibility and authority for repelling the aggressor. Article 51 thus is a temporary expedient and an exception to the new rule of Council-run collective measures.

While, superficially, this seems clear enough, ambiguities latent in the text are significant and potentially troubling. The first is institutional: *who* determines whether an "armed attack," in the sense of Article 51, has occurred? Second, *who* determines whether the "Security Council has taken measures necessary to maintain international peace and security"?

There are three contenders for making these key decisions. The first is the state claiming to have been attacked or a state willing to go to its defense. The second is the appropriate U.N. political organ. The third is the International Court. Let us examine the three alternatives, bearing in mind the need for fairness and legitimacy as well as the practical consequences of implementing each option.

Some writers interpret Article 51 to allow the professed victim of an armed attack and its allies to decide whether, when, and how to fight.[18] This is unexceptionable as far as it goes. The real problem, however, is not in interpreting the *right* of a state to act in self-defense, but in applying that right to the facts. Has there been an "armed attack"? If the state alleging a *right* of self-defense is the sole judge of whether *in fact* an "armed attack" has occurred, then any state capable of uttering a simple lie could slip the bonds of the Charter to engage in unfettered use of force against any party of its choosing. Moreover, this crucial question of fact, "has an armed attack occurred?," becomes even more amenable to manipulation by aggressors bent on self-serving justification if the requisite "armed attack" is interpreted as a metaphor, denoting any conduct arousing alarm.

The first four decades of the Charter system are littered with just such self-serving unilateral exculpations: from North Koreans baldly purporting to be acting in self-defense against an armed attack from the South, to United States forces purporting to be acting in self-defense against hostilities initiated by the Republic of Panama.[19]

There are numerous other examples of the problem created by the vulnerability

---

18. *See* DEREK W. BOWETT, SELF-DEFENCE IN INTERNATIONAL LAW 185 (1958); LELAND M. GOODRICH & EDUARD HAMBRO, CHARTER OF THE UNITED NATIONS COMMENTARY AND DOCUMENTS 344 (1946).

19. U.N. SCOR, at 32, U.N. S/PV.2899, (Dec. 20, 1989) (Ambassador T. Pickering). President Bush stated that he was responding to "General Noriega's reckless threats and attacks upon Americans in Panama. . . ." and his U.N. ambassador claimed the right to occupy Panama "under Article 51." *Id.* at 36. Had not "Noriega declared a state of war against the United States?" he demanded. U.N. SCOR, at 13, U.N. S/PV.2902, Dec. 23, 1989) (Ambassador Pickering). *See* R. Wedgewood, *The Use of Armed Force in International Affairs: Self-Defense and the Panama Invasion,* 29 COL. J. TRANSNAT'L L. 609 (1991).

of Article 51 to self-serving auto-interpretation, and the lack of credible legitimating institutional process to patrol its limits. To say the least, an aura of unfairness hangs over the claim that the United States, in 1963, resorted to a forcible naval blockade of Cuba to avert imminent attack by Soviet nuclear missiles stationed in that country.[20] True, the notion of anticipatory self-defense has some logical validity in the age of nuclear weapons.[21] What is unacceptable is a system in which each state is free to make its own determination of when anticipatory self-defense justifies a waiver of the law prohibiting aggression, freeing it to use force precisely as if the rest of the Charter system had never been established.

This concern might be mitigated if a claim to have been attacked, or threatened with imminent attack, were subject to the prior—or even subsequent—methodical review and scrutiny of a body representative of the international community, or by an impartial tribunal. Such review is not inconceivable. For example, the Security Council was able to conclude, in 1951, that Egyptian interference with Israeli shipping passing through the Suez Canal did not constitute a bona fide exercise of "self-defense."[22] The Security Council was also able to decide that it was North Korea, contrary to its claim, that had launched an unprovoked attack on the South.[23] In making that determination, its members were aided by an on-site team of United Nations observers[24] and by timely reporting of the facts by the Secretary-General.[25] More recently, the General Assembly, after hearing from all parties, overwhelmingly rejected the United States' argument that it had acted in self-defense under Article 51 in invading Grenada.[26]

---

20. Proclamation 3504, *Interdiction of the Delivery of Offensive Weapons to Cuba*, 47 DEP'T ST. BULL. 717 (1963); L.C. Meeker, *Defensive Quarantine and the Law*, 57 AM. J. INT'L L. 515 (1963); Q. Wright, *The Cuban Quarantine, id.* at 546; A. Chayes, *The Legal Case for U.S. Action on Cuba*, 47 DEP'T ST. BULL. 763 (1962).

21. However, the notion of anticipatory self-defense is rejected as illegal under the Charter by many authorities. *See* IAN BROWNLIE, INTERNATIONAL LAW AND THE USE OF FORCE BY STATES 275–78 (1963); MICHAEL AKEHURST, A MODERN INTRODUCTION TO INTERNATIONAL LAW 222–23 (4th ed., 1982); K. Skubiszewski, *Use of Force by States, in* MANUAL OF PUBLIC INTERNATIONAL LAW 739, 767 (M. Sorensen ed., 1968); Louis Henkin, *Force, Intervention and Neutrality in Contemporary International Law, Proceedings of the Annual Meeting*, 57 AM. SOC'Y INT'L L. 147, 150 (1963).

22. U.N. Doc. S/2298/Rev.1 (1951).

23. S.C. Res. 82 (1950).

24. The observers, asleep in Seoul at the time of the mission, were nevertheless useful. They (the United Nations Commission for the Unification and Rehabilitation of Korea, UNCURK) were created by the General Assembly. G.A. Res. 195(III) (1948).

25. U.N. SCOR, 5th Year, 473rd Mtg., U.N. at 18, (June 25, 1950).

26. The self-defense argument turned upon both arts. 51 and 53. The United States argued that its citizens in Grenada were in mortal danger *and* that its intervention had been requested by the Eastern Caribbean association of states. *See* WILLIAM C. GILMORE, THE GRENADA INTERVENTION (1984). The General Assembly, by 108 votes to 9, with 27 abstentions, called the action a "flagrant violation of international law. . . ." U.N. Doc.

Judicial review is also conceivable, and, indeed, there are some precedents. The International Court of Justice has considered whether a claim of self-defense validated intrusive British minesweeping in Albanian waters off Corfu,[27] or United States raids on Nicaraguan harbors.[28] In theory, there is no reason why the ICJ could not review the bona fides of any state's claim to be acting in actual or anticipatory individual or collective self-defense. At the initiative of the Security Council, or the General Assembly, the judges could be asked to render an advisory opinion on the legality of any state's unilateral resort to force. While such a determination of the applicability of Article 51 would normally be *post hoc*, it could have forward-looking legal implications for indemnity claims and would enrich the normative matrix applicable to future situations. Such routine review of the legitimacy of recourse to force justified by Article 51 would reduce the temptation to cheat while also legitimating appropriate usage. It would do much to redeem a public perception of the system's fairness.

The same analysis applies to the residual ambiguity as to who determines when unilateral measures in self-defense have become redundant as a result of "necessary measures" taken by the Security Council. While the U.N. managed to finesse this question in the Gulf crisis, that conflict demonstrates the potential for future trouble if Article 51 is not clarified. In the Gulf War, the Security Council decided on August 6, 1990, both to affirm the right of Kuwait and its allies to use force in collective self-defense[29] and also to invoke mandatory collective sanctions against Iraq under Article 41.[30] These two moves can be complementary. On November 29, however, the Council again affirmed the right of states to act unilaterally under Article 51 even while authorizing members, after a date certain, to use "all necessary means" against Iraq.[31]

In this resolution, the Council decided the parameters of forcible action: who was authorized to use force, when action could commence, and what were the objectives. This no longer resembles Article 51 self-defense: no Council authorization is needed under that provision. Moreover, it is evident that difficulties could arise from a conflict between autonomous self-defense and Council-orchestrated collective measures. Suppose, for example, the autonomous "self-defense" forces had decided—as, arguably, they had a right to do under Article 51—to launch a New Year's Day surprise attack on Iraq instead of awaiting the expiration of the Council-ordained January 15, deadline. Other nations' forces, deployed in response to the Council's November 29 resolution, might then have found themselves unwilling participants in an unauthorized engagement.

A/RES/38/7 (1983).

27. Corfu Channel, 1949 I.C.J. 4.

28. Military and Paramilitary Activities in and against Nicaragua (Nicar. v. U.S.), 1986 I.C.J. 14 (June 27) (merits judgement).

29. S.C. Res. 661 (1990), pmbl.

30. *Id.* at art. 3 and subsequent resolutions.

31. S.C. Res. 678 (1990), pmbl. and para. 2.

To avoid such cacophony, Article 51 provides that the right to self-defense ends when "the Security Council has taken measures necessary to maintain international peace and security." Who decides when that condition has been met? There are those who argue that Article 51 leaves that decision, as well, entirely to the discretion of each state engaged in individual or collective self-defense. As Professor Eugene Rostow has observed, this "is not simply a nice and rather metaphysical legal issue, but an extremely practical one. The question it presents is whether the control and direction of hostilities in the Gulf, their termination, and the substance of the settlement they produce were handled by the Council . . . as a campaign of collective self-defense, or as the United Nations' first 'international enforcement action.'" According to Rostow, the latter interpretation "would enviscerate Article 51, make the exercise of each state's 'inherent' right of self-defense subject to the permission of the Security Council, threaten the veto power of the permanent members," and "could even destroy the United Nations."[32]

III. COLLECTIVE MEASURES AGAINST AGGRESSION: ARTICLE 43

That apocalyptic vision is not necessarily mandated by the terms of the potentially newly activated new collective security system. Many of the states capable of providing forces to repel aggression may actually prefer to do so under the collective mandate of Article 42, rather than in the unilateral mode envisaged by Article 51. It is not merely the law of the Charter that pulls nations to multi-lateralize resistance to aggression by moving away from the Article 51 self-defense mode to Article 42 collective measures whenever, and as soon as, possible. Such a move is dictated primarily by self-interest, even though it entails some potential loss of state autonomy as the system draws up the modalities of the collective engagement.

That may be a price worth paying, and the Gulf conflict could be used as one example. While the United States, as principal military power in the Gulf, might have chosen to act autonomously under cover of Article 51, in practice, a politically sensitive administration in Washington realized, almost from the day Iraq invaded Kuwait, that the United States could not act alone, or solely with Kuwait and Saudi Arabia. In expounding an "unjust enrichment" claim against Kuwait's ruling Sabah family, Iraq earned considerable sympathy in the region and elsewhere. The United States and Kuwait needed to counter with the legitimization of their cause, which only a collectively authorized military action could provide. That is the reason that they had recourse to authorization by the Security Council. Such legitimization comes at a price. When the fifteen states on the Security Council are invited to authorize action against aggression, they, and other states that respond, must have a say in determining the action's parameters. To a state victimized by aggression, "calling in the U.N." thus has benefits and costs. The architecture of Chapter VII builds these cost-benefit factors into the system. States seeking to invoke that

---

32. Rostow, *supra* note 17.

system must bear them in mind.

"Calling in the U.N.," however, is not always a deliberate act of a state seeking help against an aggressor. A more difficult case is posed by the situation in which, fighting having broken out between A and B, the Council orders a cease-fire and a return to the pre-existing boundaries, and imposes an arms embargo on both belligerents. When the fighting persists, it becomes apparent that A is unwilling to give up captured territory. Thereupon, the majority of the Council proposes lifting sanctions against B, but is prevented from doing so by the opposition of a permanent member. What is the legal consequence of this? Are states now free to ignore the U.N. blockade and to assist B under Article 51? A technical parsing of the Charter would seem to preclude recourse to Article 51 unless, as in the 1991 Gulf crisis, B's Article 51 option had been preserved by the Council itself from the very beginning of the Council's involvement.[33]

Options are not always preserved, however. In the Bosnian case, for example, the resolution imposing the Article 41 embargo equally on all parties made no effort to preserve autonomous rights of self-defense.[34] Subsequent consideration of selectively lifting the embargo to benefit Bosnia, which had agreed to a U.N. peace proposal that the Bosnian Serbs had rejected, faced the probability of a veto by a permanent member. Bosnia thereupon asked the International Court of Justice to declare the Security Council's embargo invalid insofar as it constrained its inherent Article 51 rights.[35] Such a request from Bosnia was not entertained by the Court for want of jurisdiction. The results might have been different, however, had the Court's opinion been sought by a request for an advisory opinion, possibly by the General Assembly.

Certainly, Bosnia had not "called in the U.N." That state was not yet even a member of the U.N. at the time the Security Council imposed its mandatory Chapter VII arms embargo. Can the Council decide to end a sovereign state's Article 51 right to defend itself against aggression before providing it with an effective alternative defense against its aggressor under Articles 41 to 47? Can sovereign states be prohibited, by decision of the Council, from exercising what is denoted in Article 51 as their "inherent" right to aid victims of aggression? These are not academic questions. They arise directly out of Bosnia's experience: invaded from all sides, yet prohibited by the Council from receiving military aid.

---

33. S.C. Res. 661, pmbl. (1990). This was incorporated by reference into the Council's subsequent resolutions: S.C. Res. 662 (1990); S.C. Res. 667 (1990); S.C. Res. 670 (1990); S.C. Res. 674 (1990); S.C. Res. 678 (1990); S. C. Res. 686 (1991); S.C. Res. 687 (1991).

34. S.C. Res. 713 para. 6, (1991).

35. The Court chose not to address the question of Bosnia's rights under art. 51 in its decision concerning provisional measures. Application of the Convention on the Prevention and Punishment of the Crime of Genocide, Provisional Measures, 1993, I.C.J. 3.

IV. THE COLLECTIVE USE OF FORCE BY THE UNITED NATIONS

The delegates to the founding San Francisco Conference fully recognized that the collective security enforcement provisions of Chapter VII are "the teeth of the United Nations."[36]

How and in what circumstances are Articles 42–47 to be implemented by the Security Council? Has the Council's practice begun to create discernible normative patterns?

There are, of course, procedural patterns or norms fixed by the Charter itself. As noted, the Council, either implicitly or explicitly, must first determine that there is a "threat to the peace, breach of the peace or act of aggression."[37] Next, under Article 42, it must conclude that measures not involving the use of armed force "have proved to be inadequate." Thereafter, however, the text becomes normatively quite fuzzy. Article 42 empowers the Council to engage "air, sea or land forces as may be necessary," including recourse to "demonstrations, blockade, and other operations. . . ."

The drafters of the Charter envisaged that these forces would be made available to the Council, not on an *ad hoc* basis but in the form of a militia ready to be deployed "on its call."[38] This force was to be created by bilateral agreements between the Council and individual members. Under Article 43, these agreements would specify "types of forces, their degree of readiness, and general location, and the nature of the facilities and assistance to be provided."[39] Negotiating such agreements was a mandatory obligation of U.N. membership.[40] The "plans for combined action" of such forces were to be drawn up by the Council, assisted by the Military Staff Committee.[41]

In practice no such agreements have been negotiated, and the Military Staff Committee hitherto has been celebrated primarily in somewhat derisory anecdotes. In 1945, in the first flush of Charterist optimism, the United States Congress actually did authorize the president to negotiate an Article 43 agreement with the Council for the permanent deployment of a U.S. contingent in a U.N. military force: subject to approval of that agreement by "appropriate act or joint resolution" of Congress.[42] Notably, the law did not require the president, once such an agreement had been approved, to obtain further congressional authorization for actual

---

36. SECRETARY OF STATE, 79TH CONG., 1ST SESS., REPORT ON THE RESULTS OF THE SAN FRANCISCO CONFERENCE (Comm. Print, 1945).

37. U.N. CHARTER, art. 39.

38. *Id.* at art. 43(1).

39. U.N. CHARTER, art. 43(2).

40. *Id.* at art. 43(1) ("undertake") and (3) ("shall be negotiated"). The rapporteur of the drafting committee reported that this article "renders sacred the obligation of all States to participate in the operations." Doc. III, 881/3/46, 12 UNCIO Docs. 766.

41. U.N. CHARTER, at arts. 45, 46.

42. Pub. L. No. 79–264, ch. 583, 59 Stat. 619 (1945); 22 U.S.C. §§ 287–287e (1988).

deployment of the forces by the Security Council.[43]

Once it became clear that no Article 43 agreements were in the U.N.'s foreseeable future, the Secretary-General proposed an alternative: troop standby agreements,[44] which would make available national contingents for U.N. duty while postponing their actual deployment until such time as a specific need would arise and subject to the consent of the donor state. The United States has made clear that it will not make even such a contingent commitment, regarding it as a restraint on its sovereignty. No other permanent member of the Council has offered its forces on a standby basis. If this is the response of permanent members, it gives a better excuse for demurral by those U.N. members that have no permanent seat and thus no veto over Council decisions to deploy such forces.

Article 43 thus assumed an act of faith and a spirit of optimism. Pessimists believe that its moment may have passed.[45] Even if they are right, this need not necessarily signal the demise of the Charter's central vision of real collective security through measures implemented by the Council. It has become evident that when a limb of the Organization envisaged by the Charter, such as the Article 43 standing military force, is amputated by political circumstances, the Organization tends to grow another in its stead. For example, the Charter makes no provision for U.N. forces except through Chapter VII. Nevertheless, at the height of the Cold War, the concept of peacekeeping forces evolved—the so-called "Chapter 6 1/2"[46]—as a way to compensate for the veto-disabling Chapter VII. As Judge Spender said in the *Certain Expenses* case:

> A general rule is that words used in a treaty should be came into existence. But this meaning must be consistent with the purposes sought to be achieved. Where, as in the case of the Charter, the purposes are directed to saving succeeding generations in an indefinite future from the scourge of war, . . . the general rule above stated does not mean that the words in

---

43. *See* M.J. Glennon, *The Constitution and Chapter VII of the United Nations Charter*, 85 AM. J. INT'L L. 74, 78 (1991). *See also* T.M. Franck & F. Patal, *U.N. Police Action in Lieu of War: "The Old Order Changeth,"* 85 AM. J. INT'L L. 63 (1991).

44. N.Y. TIMES, Mar. 28, 1993, at 10 (International).

45. Secretary-General Boutros-Ghali appears to think otherwise. He stated in 1992:
    Under the circumstances that now exist for the first time since the Charter was adopted, the long-standing obstacles to the conclusion of such special agreements [under art. 43] should no longer prevail. The ready availability of armed forces on call could serve, in itself, as a means of deterring breaches of the peace. . . .
An Agenda for Peace: Preventive Diplomacy, Peacemaking and Peacekeeping. Report of the Secretary-General pursuant to the statement adopted by the Summit Meeting of the Security Council on Jan. 31, 1992, A/47/277; S/24111 of June 17, 1992 [hereinafter *An Agenda for Peace*].

46. "Chapter 6 1/2" connotes the grey area between the U.N. Charter's Chapter 7 (mandatory enforcement measures) and Chapter 6 (nonbinding peaceful measures of adjustment).

the Charter can only comprehend such situations and contingencies and manifestations of subject-matter as were within the minds of the framers of the Charter.[47]

V. COLLECTIVE MEASURES UNDER ARTICLE 42

Thus, while the framers may have rested the collective enforcement system on the assumption that states would commit forces to the use of the Council by Article 43 agreements,[48] this intention is not chiseled into the text. If Article 43 cannot be implemented in practice, the Charter's larger purpose is not necessarily thwarted. A cardinal purpose, made explicit in Article 42, is to enable the U.N. to "take such action by air, sea, or land forces as may be necessary to restore international peace and security" deploying "air, sea or land forces of Members. . . ." Article 42 does not mention Article 43, making it possible to conclude that the latter is but *one* possible way to make Members' forces available to restore peace and security. The Charter does not preclude the Council from devising other means to accomplish this paramount institutional purpose.

Thirty-five years ago, Professor Louis Sohn noted that "the Security Council may establish a U.N. Force under Article 42 independent of Article 43,"[49] since the latter does not limit the Council's using "any forces" it "might be able to obtain by other methods."[50] Prophetically, Sohn concluded that, as the "forces contemplated by Articles 43 and 45 of the Charter have not been established, it might be considered essential to establish a limited substitute Force able to perform at least some of the functions assigned by the Charter to the missing forces."[51]

Such a creative interpretative mode is supported by the ICJ's advisory opinion concerning *Reparations for Injuries Suffered in the Service of the United Nations*, which declared that the U.N. "must be deemed to have those powers which, though not expressly provided in the Charter, are conferred upon it by necessary implication as being essential to the performance of its duties."[52] Article 42 sets a task for the U.N. and, if the means envisaged by Article 43 are not at hand, other

---

47. Certain Expenses of the United Nations (art. 17, para. 2, of the Charter), 1962 I.C.J. 151, 182, 186. (Advisory Opinion of July 20) (Separate Opinion of Judge Sir Percy Spender) (citations omitted).

48. *See, e.g.,* "General Principles Governing the Organization of the Armed Forces Made Available to the Security Council by Members of the United Nations," Special Report of the Military Staff Committee to the Security Council, 2 U.N. SCOR Spec. Supp. No. 1 (Annex), Apr. 30, 1947.

49. L. Sohn, *The Authority of the United Nations to Establish and Maintain a Permanent United Nations Force*, 52 AM. J. INT'L L. 229, 230 (1958).

50. *Id.*

51. *Id.* at 230.

52. Reparation for Injuries Suffered in the Service of the United Nations, 1949 I.C.J. 174, 182.

means not precluded by the Charter may surely be devised. The Council may create a force under its command to enforce a decision "to restore peace and security" and, for that purpose, enter into agreements with governments willing to commit troops solely for that specific operation.

Chapter VII forces may also be established by the Council on an *ad hoc* basis without any formal agreements. Or, states may simply decide to contribute forces, as in Korea, in response to a Council "recommendation,"[53] or, as in the Gulf, to a Council-specific "call"[54] and "authorization."[55]

Other pragmatic models have been devised. Dealing with the crisis in the former Yugoslavia, the Council "decided" to establish a "Protection Force" (UNPROFOR) to be deployed, initially, for twelve months. It was entrusted to the command of the Secretary-General,[56] under the overall direction of the Council.[57] The Council "requested" states to provide "appropriate support" for UNPROFOR.[58] It established the force's objective: "to create the conditions of peace and security required for the negotiation of an overall settlement of the Yugoslav crisis,"[59] even while stopping short of authorizing its use to impose a settlement.[60] In April, the Council, having five months earlier ordered a ban on combatants' military flights over Bosnia and Herzegovina, and having authorized UNPROFOR to monitor compliance,[61] asked NATO to enforce it by shooting down violators.[62]

Another example of collective military measures organized *ad hoc* by the Security Council is afforded by the United Nations response to the Somali civil war. In a letter to the President of the Security Council of November 29, 1992, the Secretary-General laid out several options. These options represent the Secretary-General's thinking about the pragmatic possibilities for using force under Chapter VII, in the absence of the U.N. army envisaged by Article 43. One option is that the Council authorize a "countrywide enforcement action undertaken by a group of

---

53. S.C. Res. 84 (1950).

54. S.C. Res 670 para. 8 (1990).

55. S.C. Res. 678 (1990).

56. S.C. Res. 743 para. 3 and 4 1992).

57. *Id.* at para. 7.

58. *Id.* at para. 12.

59. *Id.* at para. 5.

60. While UNPROFOR was not designed as an exercise of collective security enforcement, this merely represents a policy choice, not a limitation on the Council's powers. Whatever the logistical obstacles, there can be no legal question that UNPROFOR, at any time, could be authorized to enforce a Council-designed solution to what has already been designated a threat to, or breach of, international peace and security. S.C. Res. 757 pmbl. (1992) ("Acting under Chapter VII of the Charter. . . ."). *See also* S.C. Res. 770 pmbl. (1992) and S.C. Res. 807 ppmbl. (1993).

61. S.C. Res. 781 (1992).

62. *U.N. Approves Plan to Enforce Bosnia Flight Plan*, N.Y. TIMES, Apr. 1, 1993, at A12; S.C. Res. 816 (1993).

Member States" acting under Council authorization.[63] The Secretary-General was careful to emphasize that the Council "had a legitimate interest in the manner in which such an operation was carried out even though it would not actually command the forces."[64] Specifically, he proposed that it be authorized only "for a specific period of time" and that the Council attach a "liaison staff to the Field Headquarters" of the forces.[65]

The Secretary-General also outlined a second option: an "enforcement operation to be carried out under United Nations command and control, exercised by the Secretary-General under Security Council mandate and supervision."[66] Such an operation, he pointed out, would require immediate commitment of forces and personnel from member states that "would take their orders from the United Nations and not from their national authorities."[67] Even though such a force would not be the standing army envisaged by Article 43, he saw no legal obstacle to creating an *ad hoc* single-operation U.N. force. It "would be consistent with the recent enlargement of the Organization's role in the maintenance of international peace and security," he observed; moreover, such a precedent "would strengthen . . . long-term evolution as an effective system of collective security. . . ."[68]

At the time, in December, 1992, the Council chose the first option, authorizing a U.S.-led operation under Chapter VII and charging it with restoring peace and security in Somalia.[69] As in Resolution 678, which had authorized states to take military action in the Gulf, the Council called "on Member States which are in a position to do so" to join the operation.[70] But, in a nuanced change, it also authorized the Secretary-General, in conjunction with participating states, to arrange the "unified command and control of the forces."[71] The Council also appointed "an *ad hoc* commission" of all members of the Council to "report on the implementation of this resolution"[72] and asked the Secretary-General to appoint a "liaison staff" to be attached to the new Unified Task Force (UNITAF) operation's headquarters.[73] It instructed the Secretary-General to draw up a plan of transition to full United Nations operational control "upon the withdrawal of the [United States–led] unified command. . . ."[74]

---

63. U.N. Doc. S/24868 (1992).

64. *Id.*

65. *Id.*

66. *Id.*

67. *Id.*

68. *Id.*

69. S.C. Res. 794 para. 7–10 (1992).

70. *Id.* at para. 10.

71. *Id.* at para. 12.

72. *Id.* at para. 14.

73. *Id.* at para. 15.

74. *Id.* at para. 19.

UNITAF deployed approximately 37,000 troops in southern and central Somalia, and, by March 1993, its command had reported to the Secretary-General that "all areas are stable or relatively stable," despite incidents of violence and occasional resumptions of fighting.[75] At its peak, however, UNITAF controlled only about forty percent of the country. The Somali north, to which UNITAF did not extend its operations, was relatively quiet but in a state of virtual secession.[76] Nevertheless, UNITAF prepared to turn over its pacification and rescue mission to a successor operation in which the U.S. role would be much reduced. The outlines of another option thus began to take shape. The successor, UNISOM II, had what the Secretary-General described as far-reaching political, legal, and logistical, as well as fiscal, consequences for the U.N. system.[77]

The resolution authorizing the creation of UNISOM II was passed by the Council on March 26, 1993.[78] It called for a large multinational force operating under the authority of the Secretary-General, armed with Chapter VII enforcement powers to prevent a resumption of hostilities. It is also authorized to enforce the Addis Ababa agreement of January 1993, in which the factions agreed to create a secure and humanitarian environment for the reconstruction of Somalia, complete the disarmament of factions, enforce the arms embargo, and extend these measures to the northern part of Somalia.[79] The resolution also demanded "that all Somali parties, including movements and factions, immediately cease and desist from all breaches of international humanitarian law and reaffirm[ed] that those responsible for such acts be held individually accountable."[80] This was the first time a U.N. commander not seconded from the U.S. military would be in charge of an international force that included U.S. detachments. The results of this experiment are mixed, and must be assessed carefully and deliberately in order to glean important factual and logistical lessons therefrom.

These recent instances illustrate ways in which the Council has improvised, potentially filling the gap left by the non-implementation of Article 43. In authorizing the creation of *ad hoc* operational forces, the Council has established control over the forces' objectives, composition, and *modus operandi*, and has authorized them to repulse threats to the peace, breaches of the peace, and acts of aggression. In 1993, the United Nations had more than a dozen military deploy-

---

75. Further Report of the Secretary-General Submitted in Pursuance of Paragraphs 18 and 19 of Resolution 794 (1992). U.N. Doc. S/25354 (1993).

76. *Id.* at 3.

77. *Id.* at 12.

78. S.C. Res. 814 (1993).

79. *Id.*, part B. para. 14 speaks of the "expansion and maintenance of a secure environment throughout Somalia. . . ."

80. *Id.* at para. 13.

ments on four continents involving approximately 90,000 troops.[81]

All this has been possible in the post–Cold War climate. But will the thaw endure? What if the Security Council were again paralyzed by the veto? This was the position during most of the Cold War era, and such circumstances might recur. If so, Section C of the General Assembly's Uniting for Peace Resolution[82] might be resurrected. This provides for "armed forces which could be used collectively" upon the Assembly's "recommendation."[83] Such Assembly-authorized forces would not be able to assert the broad powers conferred on Chapter VII–based militias. They would need to rely on voluntary contributions of states, in keeping with the Assembly's power to recommend, but not order, action. For the same reason, such a force could not be deployed against a non-consenting state, rendering it of limited use in repelling acts of aggression. An Assembly-authorized force could, however, operate when a threat to peace arises from a civil war, provided its presence is requested by the recognized government. This was done in the Congo, where ONUC operated, in part, under the direction of General Assembly resolutions passed in response to requests of the central government.[84] This Assembly-mandated use of force was approved by the I.C.J.'s subsequent advisory opinion which established that the Assembly had "secondary"—that is, supplementary to the Security Council—responsibility under Article 24 of the Charter "for the maintenance of international peace and security."[85] Conceivably, an Assembly-authorized voluntary force might again be deployed in civil war situations at the request of a government. Such a force might even be authorized by the Assembly to carry out humanitarian purposes when the civil authorities of a nation have so disintegrated as to be incapable of giving (or withholding) consent to a U.N. peacekeeping action on its territory.

It is also conceivable that deadlock could return to the Security Council through opposition by nonpermanent members to authorization of a further military measure under Chapter VII. In that hypothetical situation, the permanent members might consult under Charter Article 106 "with a view to such joint action on behalf of the Organization as may be necessary for the purpose of maintaining international peace and security." This provision, however, has never been invoked.

Another possible consequence of renewed Security Council deadlock is that states would revert to the old order preserved by Article 51. It should be noted, however, that Article 51 is far less versatile than Article 39 of Chapter VII. In

---

81. Forces are deployed in Israel, India/Pakistan, Cyprus, Golan Heights, Lebanon, Iraq/Kuwait, Angola, El Salvador, Western Sahara, Yugoslavia, Cambodia, Somalia and Mozambique. Eight of these were deployed since 1991. *See* Carnegie Endowment National Commission, *Changing Our Ways*, AMERICA AND THE WORLD, Table 8, at 65 (1992).

82. G.A. Res. 377A(V) (1950). *See* HANS KELSEN, RECENT TRENDS IN THE LAW OF THE UNITED NATIONS 953–90 (1951); Sohn, *supra* note 48, at 232–34.

83. *Id.*, pmbl.

84. G.A. Res. 1474 (1960). ONUC is the United Nations Operation in the Congo.

85. Certain Expenses of the United Nations, *supra* note 47.

particular, it is not an option for dealing with civil wars, since Article 51 presupposes a cross-border armed attack. Only the Security Council (or, perhaps, the General Assembly) may authorize an intervention such as those undertaken by the United Nations in former Yugoslavia and Somalia. This is as it should be, for unilateral interventions by foreign states in other states' civil wars invite counter-interventions that readily can lead to war.

VI. WILL THE UNITED STATES PARTICIPATE?

Since the United States has a veto in the Security Council, no collective security operations under Article 42 can be envisaged without the consent of the United States (and, of course, of the other permanent members and a voting majority of the Council as a whole). If U.S. consent is legally necessary, it is also necessary as a practical matter. To what extent can the United States be counted upon to approve and participate in future U.N. peace efforts involving the deployment of armed forces?

There has recently been an active debate within the executive and congressional branches of the U.S. government as to the modalities that ought to govern U.S. consent to, and participation in, future Article 42 collective security operations. The subject can be considered under three related but separate issue-headings:

1) Under what circumstances will the United States vote for a collective security operation?
2) When will the United Syates participate in such an operation?
3) Is the president constitutionally empowered to commit U.S. forces to a Chapter VII, Article 42 collective security operation mandated by the Security Council?

Although an executive policy has been outlined to address these issues, the debate has barely begun within the domestic U.S. political fora. Certainly, the enthusiasm of the U.S. public and government for assuming the leading role in policing the world has dimmed notably since the euphoria of the quick and cheap victory over Iraq in the Gulf War. The withdrawal of U.S. forces from Somalia and reluctance to commit ground forces to the former Yugoslavia are reflected in new executive policy positions and congressional initiatives.

a. Under What Circumstances Will the United States Assent?

According to published reports,[86] the policy set by the administration requires that it be satisfied that international security is threatened, that a major disaster requires urgent relief, or that it is imperative to redress a gross violation of human

---

86. N.Y. TIMES, Jan. 29, 1994, at 1, 5.

rights. Only if the White House is satisfied as to at least one of these conditions will its representative in New York vote and agree to help pay for a Security Council authorized collective military operation.

b.   When Will the United States Participate in Such an Operation?

According to the same reports,[87] the preceding conditions would need to be augmented by evidence that the national interests or security of the United States were at stake in order that the United States commit its own forces to such an operation. On the other hand, only the three conditions outlined in part (a) would need to be satisfied in order that the United States commit forces to a "Chapter 6 1/2" peacekeeping operation in which U.N. forces would operate with the consent of, and under an agreement between, the parties.

c.   Is the President Constitutionally Authorized to Commit U.S. Forces?

This issue has been extensively debated in the political forums and in scholarly journals. Senator Robert Dole, the leader of the Republican minority in the Senate, has proposed legislation that would require congressional approval before the U.S. representative to the Security Council may cast a vote in favor of any U.N. operation involving U.S. forces or expending U.N. funds to which the U.S. is required to contribute.

The Republican proposal is radical. But is it legal under the Charter and under the U.S. Constitution? The answer to both of these questions is in the negative. The Dole proposal would violate Article 25 of the Charter by which "Members of the United Nations agree to accept and carry out the decisions of tne Security Council in accordance with the present Charter." A unilateral rewriting of so fundamental a provision of the Charter would likely spell the end of the collective security system, leaving the U.N. a useless relic of the idealism that briefly flickered at the conclusion of World War II and again at the end of the Cold War. In U.S. law, the Dole Resolution clearly constitutes an unconstitutional usurpation of the president's executive power as commander-in-chief[88] and as the voice of the nation speaking to other nations.[89]

Moreover, a decision under Chapter VII of the Charter to deploy force, once made by the Security Council, is a treaty obligation binding on the United States,[90] and is part of the law of the United States by virtue of Article VI, section 1 of the

---

87. *Id.*

88. U.S. Const., art. II, § 2(1).

89. *Id.* art. II, sec. 2(2) and 3.

90. *Cf.* Diggs v. Schultz, 470 F.2d 461 (D.C. Cir. 1972) and U.S. v. Palestine Liberation Organization, 695 F. Supp. 1456 (S.D.N.Y. 1988). *See also* Applicability of the Obligation to Arbitrate Under Section 21 of the United Nations Headquarters Agreement of June 26, 1947, 1988 I.C.J. 12.

Constitution. The president is obliged by Article II, Section 3 to "take care that the laws be faithfully executed. . . ." While Congress could legislate to compel the United States to act in violation of a treaty (for example, by ordering that no U.S. forces ever be deployed in response to a decision of the Security Council under Chapter VII), it could not legislate to require the president to act in violation of the obligations imposed on him by the Constitution. Finally, the decision as to how a U.S. diplomat casts her or his vote in the Security Council is clearly an executive discretionary act in which Congress may not participate under the doctrine of the separation of powers. The president would be right to treat such Congressional encroachment on his plenary powers as unconstitutional usurpations.

A different but related question is raised by the War Powers of the Constitution. Must the president get the consent of Congress before committing U.S. forces to combat? Normally, the answer to this question is clear. When U.S. troops are deployed to defend a state that has been attacked, or otherwise are deployed to enforce peace against an opponent, it is the Congress that is empowered by the Constitution to "declare war."[91] A decision to use U.S. forces under Article 51 of the Charter ("collective self-defense") thus would require a declaration of war or other form of consent by Congress.

What if U.S. forces were committed under Article 42 of the Charter ("collective measures")? In the War Powers Resolution,[92] Congress has stated its view that authority to use U.S. forces in combat "shall not be inferred from any treaty. . . ."[93] That would seem to bar the commitment of U.S. forces even under the treaty obligations imposed by Articles 25 and 42 of the Charter. The constitutionality of that provision is challenged, however, by the executive branch and by many scholars. Moreover, the "war power" of Congress, which this provision of the War Powers Act purports to implement, does not necessarily cover the participation of U.S. forces in actions ordered by the Security Council under Article 42. To understand the limits of congressional power to declare war, it is important to examine the intent of its authors. The decision to commit the war power to Congress was based on fear of concentrating in the sole discretion of the president the power to deploy the nation's citizen's lives and treasure in foreign military adventures. This fear is not applicable where the president's decision to commit U.S. forces is made after the extensive debate and collective decisionmaking that characterizes action by the U.N. Security Council.[94]

The practice has been inconclusive. President Truman committed U.S. troops to the defense of South Korea without a congressional declaration, citing authorization obtained from the Security Council. In commiting U.S. forces to combat in the Gulf, President George Bush both sought and obtained congressional

---

91. *Id.* art. I, § 8(11).

92. 50 U.S.C.A. § 1541–1548.

93. 50 U.S.C.A. 1541–1548, § 8(a)(2).

94. Franck & Patel, *supra* note 43. *But see* Glennon, *supra* note 43.

authorization.[95] This undoubtedly was the right way to proceed. The Security Council's resolution authorizing members of the U.N. to "use all necessary means" to get Iraq out of Kuwait[96] does not constitute a decision requiring the commitment of U.S. troops under Article 25. It does not require the president to "faithfully execute" the Council resolution by dispatching American troops. While the resolution invokes Chapter VII, it does not specifically require any state to use force. More important, the U.S. Government itself took the position that the resolution rests not on collective security measures (Article 42) but merely authorizes the United States to do what it has a right to do without Council authorization: go to the aid of Kuwait in exercise of its "inherent" right of self-defense under Article 51 of the Charter.[97]

The current position of the Executive is that the president will consult congressional leaders before committing U.S. forces to a situation in which combat may be involved, but that the decision to deploy forces is not constitutionally committed to the Congress; nor does Congress have the constitutional power to determine when the United States may participate in forceful collective security measures under Chapter VII.

Yet it is necessary to remind ourselves that the U.S. Constitution works best when its limits are not tested. It would be wise, therefore, to assume that only in extraordinarily urgent circumstances would the U.S. president commit forces to a U.N. combat operation without previously securing the consent of Congress.

Beyond law there is public policy. Given the lack of public enthusiasm in the United States for expending American lives to teach Somalis or Bosnians to live in peace and mutual tolerance, it should not be expected that there will be much U.S. participation in those sorts of endeavors—except when, as in Kuwait, the essential national interest demonstrably coincides with the mandates of international law and the U.N. Charter.

---

95. H.J. Res. 77, 103d Cong., Pub. L. No. 102–1, (1991).
96. S.C. Res. 687 (1990).
97. This position is spelled out by Rostow, *supra* note 17.

UNITED NATIONS' ACTIVITIES FOR PEACE AND THE CONSTITUTION OF JAPAN

Yoshiro Matsui

I. NATIONALIST AND INTERNATIONALIST ARGUMENTS FOR REVISION OF THE CONSTITUTION

The Constitution of Japan, which renounces wars of aggression, prohibits maintenance of any military forces, and denies the right of belligerency of the state (Article 9), has similar roots as the Charter of the United Nations, which prohibits the threat or use of force in international relations in most situations (Article 2, paragraph 4). Both documents have as their background the long standing effort of mankind to eradicate the threat or use of force in international relations and both were the direct products of the World War II. Though they share a common objective, they differ in their methods for its realization. The United Nations Charter stipulates a system of collective security, which contemplates military enforcement measures—albeit as a last resort—against an aggressor. In contrast, the Constitution of Japan renounces all military forces and other war potential. This difference in method seems to originate from the different historical positions surrounding their adoption. The United Nations Charter was a product of the joint war efforts of the United Nations against aggressors during the World War II, and the Constitution of Japan was proof of sincere self-criticism of the Japanese people as an aggressor nation.

One more possible factor contrasting the Constitution of Japan to the United Nations Charter was the atomic bombings of Hiroshima and Nagasaki. Charles Overby, who organized a movement to disseminate the spirit of Article 9 of the Constitution of Japan in the United States, argues that "the U.N. Charter was signed six weeks before the Hiroshima and Nagasaki atomic bombings and almost two years before the Peace Constitution went into effect. The Peace Constitution, therefore, reflects the new awful truth of the nuclear age, something the U.N.

Charter does not."[1] In fact, the tragedy at Hiroshima and Nagasaki seemed to influence strongly the drafters of the Constitution of Japan. Hitoshi Ashida, chairman of the House of Representatives Special Committee on the Draft Revision of the Imperial Constitution, reported to the Plenary that

> [o]ur new Constitution, which completely removes the possibility of armament and renounces all war, may perhaps be a pioneer in the world. No one would deny that, as a result of atomic bombs produced by modern science, a future war occuring between major powers would produce immeasurable calamity to the human race. It goes without saying that we are ready to propose renunciation of war not only because we have fully realized the abominableness of war from the damage of past wars but also because we hold an ideal of sparing the world from civilizational destruction by any such a future war.[2]

The United Nations Charter and the Constitution of Japan also have had a common destiny throughout the almost fifty years of their existence. Their provisions have never been completely realized in practice.

Successive Japanese governments under the Liberal Democratic Party (LDP) have concluded and maintained that the Japan–U.S. Security Treaty and strengthened Self-Defense Forces (SDF) are permissible by interpreting the Constitution of Japan as not renouncing the right of individual self-defense—in contrast to the right of collective self-defense, which is prohibited by the Constitution—and as not prohibiting the maintenance of military power within the limits of self-defense. The LDP lost power in August 1993, and was succeeded by a coalition government of various parties. These LDP policies and the accepted constitutional interpretation have not been changed, however, even though the government now in power is headed by the chairman of the Japanese Socialist Party (JSP). By relying on the doctrine of political question or other interpretative manipulations, the Japanese judiciary has also consistently avoided, with two prominent lower court exceptions,[3] judging the constitutionality of the SDF or the

---

1.   Charles Overby, *A Quest for Peace with Article 9*, JAPAN QUARTERLY 149, Apr.–June 1994.

2.   The Plenary, House of Representatives, July 24, 1946, in TEIKOKU KENPŌ KAISEI SHINGIROKU: SENSŌ HŌKI HEN [MINUTES ON THE REVISION OF THE IMPERIAL CONSTITUTION: RENUNCIATION OF WAR] 210–11 (Secretariat of the House of Councilors, ed., 1952).

3.   In the *Sunakawa* case, the Tokyo District Court decided that to permit the US forces to station in Japan under the Japan-U.S. Security Treaty of 1952 "cannot but come under maintaining land, sea, and air forces, as well as other war potential, prohibited under art. 9, para. 2, the first sentence, of the Constitution of Japan, and therefore, the conclusion is inescapable that the existence of the U.S. forces stationed in Japan is impermissible under the Constitution." Judgment of Mar. 30, 1959, 1 Kakeishū 776, 781–783, *rev'd*, 13

Japan–U.S. Security Treaty.

It is sometimes said that Article 9 has contributed to restricting the size of the increases in Japanese military forces by focusing public opinion and movements for the defense of the Constitution. The Constitution of Japan has no provision on the power to declare war or on command and control of the armed forces; it had been interpreted as prohibiting the overseas dispatch of the SDF. Japanese military expenditure has been relatively low compared with Japan's GNP and Japan has maintained *Hikaku San-Gensoku* (three principles on non-nuclear armament, namely, not to have, not to produce and not to introduce nuclear weapons), as well as *Buki Kinyu Gensoku* (principle not to export weapons).

On the other hand, even according to the *Defense White Paper, 1993*, with expenditures of U.S. $16,464 million, Japan ranks sixth in the world. Moreover, the SDF has 237,000 personnel, 1,200 tanks, 164 warships, and 1,096 airplanes, almost all of it highly sophisticated equipment.[4]

This large military buildup has brought the contradiction between reality and constitutional requirements almost to the breaking point. Moreover, the restrictions on Japanese military efforts, imposed directly or indirectly by the Constitution, have increasingly become obstacles for Japan to be considered a normal state, a state which protects its growing overseas rights and interests by its own military power.

Under these circumstances, the Japanese government's constitutional interpretation, which aims to effect a *de facto* revision of the Constitution, has become increasingly untenable. It is well known that the right wing of the LDP and the Democratic Socialist Party (DSP) have demanded revision of the Constitution to authorize expressly the maintenance of self-defense forces. These arguments for express revision have never gained much support from politicians, lawyers or the public. These two traditional arguments for revision may be called nationalist arguments because their main ground is for the country to defend itself, though strengthening the Japan–U.S. Security Treaty is also included.

The strongest justification for the revision of the Constitution—the threat of the Soviet Union—disappeared with the breakdown of that military superpower in 1991. The argument was resurrected by the seeming *Kamikaze* (divine winds) that blew in the form of new U.N. activism made possible by unanimity among the five permanent members of the Security Council, including the newly cooperative

---

Keishū 3225 (1959). In the Naganuma case, the Sapporo District Court, affirming legal interest of the applicants based on the right to live in peace derived from the Preamble of the Constitution, judged that the SDF is clearly . . . an armed force, and therefore, the land, sea, and air SDFs must be said to amount to 'forces,' the maintenance of which is prohibited under art. 9, para. 2, of the Constitution. Judgment of Sept. 7, 1973, 19–9 Shomu Geppō 1, 121, *rev'd on other grounds*, 22 Shomu Geppō 202, 1 (1976) and 36 Minshū 1679 (1982).

4.   BŌEI HAKUSHO [DEFENSE WHITE PAPER], 146–48, 279, 367–69 (Defense Agency, ed., Printing Bureau of the Ministry of Finance, 1993).

Russia and China. Thus, new arguments emerged for the revision of the Constitution, which may be characterized as "internationalist arguments," since they intend to clear the way for the use of force as a means of *kokusai kōken* (international contribution), mainly through the United Nations. From this standpoint, the usual arguments for the defense of the Constitution have been criticized as *ikkoku heiwashugi* (selfish pacifism). This criticism has exerted discernible influence on the arguments for the defense of the Constitution, and such theories as *sōkenron* (creative development of the Constitution) and *gōkenteki kaikenron* (defensive revision of the Constitution) have emerged. Though claiming to defend "the spirit of the Constitution," these new theories admit, in one form or another, the legitimacy of the SDF under the Constitution and its use abroad in "international contribution."

The JSP, which has hitherto been the most influential defender of the Constitution and the most consistent objector to the constitutionality of the SDF and of the Japan–U.S. Security Treaty, changed its policy upon accession to power in coalition with the LDP in June 1994. The Prime Minister and the Chairman of the JSP, Tomiichi Murayama, announced to the Plenary Session of the House of Representatives on July 20, 1994, that "I understand that the SDF, which is the necessary minimum armed organization for self-defense, is recognized as constitutional." This policy change, incorporated in the new JSP security policy, *A Challenge for Peace*, was ratified by an extraordinary Party Congress held on September 3, 1994.[5] This policy change was bitterly criticized by Japanese constitutional lawyers. In a statement issued on August 12, 1994, they proclaimed that

> the SDF is one of the strongest armed forces in the world, organized and composed in order to use force. Without doubt, this SDF is a war potential which is prohibited to maintain under Article 9, paragraph 2, of the Constitution. A large majority of the constitutional lawyers of Japan, in view of the world trends and upon a strict interpretation, have consistently argued that the SDF is unconstitutional. This academic viewpoint must not be treated lightly by the political power. If those who are in power do not respect and defend the Constitution, the basis of constitutional politics would be lost.[6]

---

5. *Shushō Jietai Gōken o Meigen: Shatō no Kihon-Seisaku Tenkan [Prime Minister Declared SDF Are Constitutional: JSP Changed Its Basic Policy]*, ASAHI SHINBUN, July 21, 1994, at 1; *Shatō ga Shin-Anpo-Seisaku-Sōan [JSP Proposed New Security Policy]*, ASAHI SHINBUN, Aug. 31 , 1994, at 1 & 7; *Shatō-Taikai Shin-Seisaku o Shōnin: Jieitai Gōken ni Tenkan [JSP Congress Approved New Security Policy: Changing to Constitutionality of SDF]*, ASAHI SHINBUN Sept. 4, 1994, at 1.

6. *Imakoso Kenpō Dai 9 Jō o Mamori Hirogeyō: Murayama Sōri no Kenkai ni Kansuru Kenpō-Gakusha no Seimei [Just Now, We Appeal to Defend and Disseminate Article 9 of the Constitution: A Statement of Constitutional Lawyers Concerning a View of Prime*

The constitutional arguments in Japan about the SDF have not yet been concluded.

II. THE UNITED NATIONS COLLECTIVE SECURITY AND THE CONSTITUTION OF JAPAN

Article 9, paragraph 1 of the Constitution stipulates "(a)spiring sincerely to an international peace based on justice and order, the Japanese people forever renounce war as a sovereign right of the nation and the threat or use of force as a means of settling international disputes." As is rightly pointed out by Yasuaki Ōnuma, the use of force "as a means of settling international disputes" means aggressive war according to the normal terminology of international law, and, therefore, this paragraph, as such, does not renounce the use of force in self-defense or participation in military enforcement measures of the United Nations.[7] This interpretation, though not necessarily supported by constitutional lawyers, enjoys substantial support among Japanese international lawyers.

If Article 9 as a whole does not prohibit maintaining armed forces for the purposes of self-defense or military enforcement measures, it would raise problems of compatibility with paragraph 2, which reads: "(i)n order to attain the aim of the preceding paragraph, land, sea, and air forces, as well as other war potential, will never be maintained. The right of belligerency of the state will not be recognized." In order to avoid this difficulty, proponents rely on an understanding that "the aim of the preceding paragraph" denotes the renunciation of aggressive war only. This understanding seems to be incompatible with natural and ordinary meaning of the terms of paragraph 2, however, according to which "the aim" has to be interpreted as "the aim of the preceding paragraph" as a whole, namely, "(a)spiring to an international peace based on justice and order." Thus, this phrase in paragraph 2 is intended not to restrict the scope of renunciation of forces, but to clarify the motive underlying the paragraph.

This interpretation of paragraph 2 is widely shared in Japan by constitutional lawyers and international lawyers. One international lawyer, Yuichi Takano, has argued that the above-mentioned phrase expresses the motive underlying paragraph 2, and does not restrict the renunciation of forces in this paragraph by specifically taking up the restrictive phrase as a means of settling of international disputes of paragraph 1 and bringing it into paragraph 2. Takano further points out that quality or quantity of military forces does not determine their uses, whether they are used for aggression, settlement of disputes, or self-defense. Moreover, as today's international legal order prohibits states from using force except in self-defense, it would be almost meaningless to argue that the Constitution admits only forces for

---

Minister Murayama], SHŪKAN KINYŌBI, Aug. 26, 1994, at 10-11.

7.   Yasuaki Ōnuma, *Heiwa Kenpō to Shūdan Anzenhōsho* [*Japan's Peace Constitution and Collective Security*], 92 KOKUSAIHŌ GAIKŌ ZASSHI 44, 62–63 (1993).

the purpose of self-defense and prohibits other forces.[8]

The drafters of the Constitution intended Article 9 to prohibit military forces even for the purpose of participating in enforcement measures under the U.N. Charter. During the deliberations on the new constitution in the House of Lords at that time, Kijuro Shidehara, then Minister of State and a supposed originator of Article 9, answered that

> [w]e sympathize with most of the objects and purposes of the United Nations, therefore, we will cooperate with it. But, as we have Article 9 of the Constitution, we must formulate a reservation on its application. If we are asked to cooperate with a sanction against some State in contravention of our neutrality, we cannot do it at all.[9]

In fact, the Japanese application for membership in the United Nations, dated June 16, 1952, was accompanied with a declaration by Katsuo Okazaki, Minister for Foreign Affairs, stating that "the Government of Japan hereby accepts the obligations contained in the Charter of the United Nations, and undertakes to honor them, *by all means at its disposal* . . ."[10] Whether it was a formal reservation or not, it clearly indicated the intention of Japan at that time that Japan could not cooperate with the United Nations by means not at its disposal, i.e., with armed force.

This interpretation of Article 9, which has long been shared by successive Governments, is now under attack by the internationalist arguments for the revision of the Constitution. For example, in *A Proposal for International Security*,[11] the author proposes that "under Article 43 of the U.N. Charter, 'All Members of the United Nations . . . undertake to make available to the Security Council . . . armed forces, assistance, and facilities . . . necessary for the purpose of maintaining international peace and security.' On entering into the United Nations, Japan made this undertaking, and participation in a United Nations Force is an unavoidable obligation for Member States," and that

---

8.   Yuichi Yakano, *Kenpō Dai 9 Jō: Kokusaihōteki ni Mita Sensō Hōki Jōkō* [*Article 9 of the Constitution: Article on the Renounciation of War from the Standpoint of International Law*], *in*, 2 NIHONKOKU KENPŌ TAIKAI: MIYAZAWA, TOSHIYOSHI SENSEI KANREKI KINEN [SYSTEM OF THE CONSTITUTION OF JAPAN: IN COMMEMORATION OF 60TH BIRTHDAY OF PROFESSOR TOSHIYOSHI MIYAZAWA], 107, 154–156 (1965).

9.   Special Committee on the Draft Revision of the Imperial Constitution, House of Lords, Sept. 13, 1946, Secretariat of the House of Councilors, ed., *supra* note 2, at 452–53.

10.   1 NIHON GAIKŌ SHŪYO BUNSHO NENPYŌ [BASIC DOCUMENTS AND CHRONOLOGY OF JAPANESE DIPLOMACY] (1941–1960), 523–24 (Kashima Heiwa Kenkyusho, ed., 1983) (emphasis added).

11.   Presented by the Japanese Center for Strategic Studies, the president of which is Mr. Ichiro Ozawa, one of the most influential conservative politicians in Japan.

by correcting the Government's existing interpretation [of the constitution] as soon as possible, and in accordance with the undertaking under the U.N. Charter, Japan has to establish a system to participate, along with the other Members, in a United Nations Force on the call of the Security Council, and to exercise the right of collective self-defense if necessary.[12]

This is indeed a novel interpretation of Article 43 of the Charter. By acrobatically selecting words from Article 43, an impression is created that participation in a United Nations Force is a legal obligation for member states. Omitted, however, is that under Article 43, paragraph 1, participation by the members in military enforcement measures is to be "in accordance with a special agreement or agreements," and that according to paragraph 3 of the same Article, the agreement or agreements shall be concluded between the Security Council and members (or groups of members) and "shall be subject to ratification by the signatory States in accordance with their respective constitutional processes." Participation in military enforcement measures provided for in Article 42 is thus not obligatory for member states.[13]

Those who argue for Japan's participation in the United Nations military enforcement measures and demand revision, or at least a new interpretation of, the Constitution, might nevertheless base their argument on political or moral grounds. They might reason that Japan, as an economic power, must play a more active role in international community efforts to maintain or restore peace and security.

This argument seems to have two defects: first, it lays too much emphasis upon military enforcement measures among the many means at the United Nations disposal to maintain or restore international peace and security; second, it idealizes the United Nations system of collective security too much and somewhat loses sight of the U.N.'s actual functions.

As to the first defect, it must be noted that military enforcement measures are a last resort under the Charter. It is true that the Charter does not require enforcement measures to be applied step by step,[14] but the structure of the Charter advocates the idea that international disputes should be settled by peaceful means provided for in Chapter VI of the Charter (Article 2, paragraph 3); when peaceful

---

12. NIHON SENRYAKU KENKYŪ CENTER, ED., SEKAI NI IKIRU ANZENHŌSHO [SECURITY FOR SURVIVAL IN THE WORLD] 8-9 (Harashobo, 1994) (omissions in original).

13. This is a unanimous view of Commentaries on the U.N. Charter. See, e.g., LELAND M. GOODRICH, EDVARD HAMBRO & ANNE PATRICIA SIMONS, CHARTER OF THE UNITED NATIONS, 316 (3d ed., 1969); BURUNO SIMMA, CHARTA DER VEREINTEN NATIONEN, 593-94 (C.H. Beck, ed. 1991); JEAN-PIERRE COT ET ALAIN PELLET, LA CHARTE DES NATIONS UNIES, 712, 718 (2d ed., Economica, 1991).

14. GOODRICH et al., supra, note 13, at 314; SIMMA, supra note 13 at 587-88; COT ET PELLET, supra note 13, at 708-10.

settlement has failed and the existence of any threat to the peace, breach of the peace, or act of aggression is determined by the Security Council (Article 39), non-military enforcement measures should be resorted to first (Article 41), and, if this is considered or proved to be inadequate, military enforcement measures under Article 42 may be taken. The U.S. delegation observed in its *Report to the President on the Results of the San Francisco Conference* that

> the responsibilities of the Security Council are two-fold: primarily to induce, by every conceivable method, peaceful solutions of international disagreements: and, secondly, *as a last resort*, to apply force, even to the employment of military measures, in order to maintain peace or to suppress any breach of the peace.[15]

As to the second defect, military enforcement measures provided for in the Charter imply a *de jure* as well as a *de facto* double standard. The *de jure* double standard is that the five permanent members of the Security Council have a veto right, and therefore they and the states under their protection can never be the objects of military or nonmilitary enforcement measures. The *de facto* double standard is that these powers have military capabilities, including nuclear weapons, incomparable to those of the other members. Even without the right of veto, therefore, military enforcement measures against them would create another world war involving the use of nuclear weapons, which no one state would or should dare attempt.

The Secretary-General, in his report, *An Agenda for Peace*, noticed these double standards inherent in military enforcement measures. In recommending to the Security Council that negotiations be initiated to conclude special agreements foreseen in Article 43, he admitted that, "[f]orces under Article 43 may perhaps never be sufficiently large or well enough equipped to deal with a threat from a major army equipped with sophisticated weapons. They would be useful, however, in meeting any threat posed by a military force of a lesser order."[16] These double standards were severely criticized by medium and small states at the San Francisco Conference, and have constantly been attacked by non-aligned members since then. Without overcoming these inequalities, the United Nations system of collective security can never function effectively because it will lack the support and confidence of the international community as a whole.

---

15. CHARTER OF THE UNITED NATIONS: REPORT TO THE PRESIDENT ON THE RESULTS OF THE SAN FRANCISCO CONFERENCE BY THE CHAIRMAN OF THE UNITED STATES DELEGATION, THE SECRETARY OF STATE 67 (St. Dept. Pub. 2349, 1945) (emphasis added).

16. *An Agenda for Peace: Preventive Diplomacy, Peacemaking and Peace-keeping— Report of the Secretary-General Pursuant to the Statement Adopted by the Summit Meeting of the Security Council*, U.N. GAOR, 47th Sess., item 10, para. 43, U.N. Doc. A/47/277–S/24111 (1992).

Now is therefore not the time for Japan to talk about participation in military enforcement measures by revising the Constitution or by changing its interpretation. Instead, there seems to exist a wide range of possibilities for cooperation in this field, if the Japanese abide strictly by the terms and spirit of their Constitution. Four steps, among others, will aid in effecting such cooperation.

First, in order to promote the peaceful settlement of international disputes, Japan should endeavor to settle its own disputes with other states by peaceful means, to offer good offices and mediation to help other states in solving disputes between themselves, and to develop further legal norms and mechanisms for peaceful settlement of international disputes. In this respect, Japan's active participation in the Cambodian peace process must be appreciated, though there may be some reservations regarding the actual role it played.[17]

Second, Japan should participate unreservedly in nonmilitary enforcement measures taken under Article 41 of the Charter, which clearly constitutes a legal obligation for Japan. To implement this obligation domestically, Japan's Foreign Exchange and Foreign Trade Control Law subjects specific service technology transactions and the export of goods considered to be obstructive to the maintenance of international peace and security to a license of the Minister of International Trade and Industry (Article 25, paragraph 1 (1) and Article 48, paragraph 1).[18] Japan should also render assistance to states confronted with special economic problems which arise from the carrying out of enforcement measures (Article 50 of the Charter). Japan, it should be borne in mind, was regarded with suspicion because of its dubious attitude toward nonmilitary collective measures against South Africa, although this was decided not by the Security Council but recommended by the General Assembly.

Third, Japan should contribute to democratization of Security Council decisionmaking. Japan should endeavor to render Security Council deliberation more transparent, so that the Council may operate under the watch of world public opinion. Japan's recent quest for a seat as a permanent member of the Security Council would merit support if it held democratization of this body as one of its aims. In a comment submitted pursuant to General Assembly Resolution 47/62, Japan pointed out that the Council is expected to act on behalf of all member states

---

17. Apart from its participation in the U.N. Transitional Authority in Cambodia, discussed elsewhere, Japan served as a co-chairman, together with the UNDP, at the Ministerial Conference for Recovery of Cambodia, held in Tokyo in June 1992. The Conference established an International Commission for Recovery of Cambodia, and Japan was designated as its chair. Japan also made abortive efforts in cooperation with Thailand to persuade the Pol Pot faction to abide by the ceasefire from July to October 1992. *See* 1992 GAIKO SEISHO [DIPLOMATIC BLUEBOOK] 206–211 (Ministry of Foreign Affairs, ed., 1993).

18. Law No.228 of 1949 as amended by Law No.65 of 1979 and Law No.89 of 1987. *See* Shinya Murase, *Trade versus Security: the COCOM Regulations in Japan*, 31 JAPANESE ANN. INT'L L. 1 (1988).

in carrying out its responsibility, and argued that "the legitimacy and credibility of [the Security Council's] action will be enhanced to the extent [the Security Council] accurately reflect[s] the general will of the member states."

Emphasizing that "the Council should provide a forum where a comprehensive approach—an approach that includes not only political and military, but also economic and other factors —to issues concerning world peace and security can be taken," Japan proposed to enlarge the Council to have around twenty members by adding a certain numbers of permanent and nonpermanent seats.[19] This line of argument seems very persuasive. Omitted in the Japanese comment is that in order to democratize the Council, it is more important to reexamine the Council system which gives the permanent members a privileged position.

Above all, Japan should take the initiative toward regional and universal disarmament. If the eradication of nuclear weapons and a significant reduction in conventional arms can be attained, this would lessen, if not eliminate, the double standard inherent in the U.N. system of collective security. A byproduct of such an achievement would be enhancement of confidence among nations and the release of resources that could be used by developing countries for developmental purposes. In the comment cited above, Japan brought up the issue of "peace dividends," arguing that "the [Security] Council should strengthen its commitment to arms control and disarmament with a view to promoting the diversion of the world's human and economic resources away from armaments to other purposes."[20] This seems to be the most important possible contribution to the strengthening of the collective security under the Charter that could be made by Japan, the only state that was a victim of nuclear weapons and has a constitution prohibiting the maintenance of military forces.

In fact, Japan has recently made some efforts towards arms control and disarmament. For example, Japan played a leading role in establishing a Register of Conventional Arms in 1991.[21] On June 30, 1992, the Japanese cabinet adopted the *ODA Taikō (Charter of Official Development Assistance)*, in which the government announced its intention, when providing ODA, to pay full attention to the trends in recipient countries regarding, *inter alia*, military expenditures; development and production of weapons of mass destruction and missiles; and the export and import of arms.[22]

At the same time, these disarmament efforts have centered almost exclusively upon the disarmament of developing countries and have neglected the nuclear

---

19. *Question of Equitable Representation on and Increase in the Membership of the Security Council: Report of the Secretary-General*, at 52–55, U.N. Doc A/48/264 (1993).

20. *Id.* at 54.

21. G.A. Res. 46/36 L , Transparency in Armaments, adopted on Dec. 9, 1991, with 150 in favor, none against, with two abstentions.

22. *See* Junji Nakagawa, *Legal Problems of Japan's ODA Guidelines—Aid and Democracy, Human Rights and Peace*, 36 JAPANESE ANN. INT'L L. 76 (1993).

disarmament of nuclear-weapons holding states. This one-sidedness seems to be a consequence of Japan's adherence to the doctrine of nuclear deterrence, which was declared by the General Assembly to be "the most dangerous collective fallacy that exists."[23] The result will be a consolidation of the prominent military status of nuclear-weapon states, which runs counter to the elimination of the double standard inherent in the U.N. system of collective security.

Thus, it must be admitted that Japan has not done much in support of the U.N. system of collective security, though not because of Article 9 of the Constitution. Notwithstanding Article 9, Japan has not always been able to do something worthy of the article.[24]

III. U.N. PEACEKEEPING OPERATIONS AND THE CONSTITUTION OF JAPAN

Arguments over Japan's participation in U.N. peacekeeping operations have existed since Japan was admitted to the United Nations. The problem again materialized suddenly on the occasion of Gulf War, when the coalition forces strongly pressed for Japan's military and financial cooperation. In response, the Japanese Cabinet presented *Kokuren Heiwa Kyōryoku Hōan* (Bill on Peace Cooperation with the United Nations) to the Diet. This bill was intended to cover not only U.N. peacekeeping operations, but also other activities conducted under United Nations decisions for maintaining international peace and security, i.e., activities akin to those of the coalition forces in the Gulf War. Though this bill failed because of strong resistance on the part of opposition parties and public, the government used the occasion to make the first breakthrough in dispatching the SDF abroad, done in the form of sending SDF's mine sweepers to the Gulf after the ceasefire.

A new *Kokusairengo Heiwa Ijikatsudotō ni taisuru Kyōryoku ni kansuru Hōritsu* (Law concerning Cooperation for United Nations Peacekeeping Operations and Other Operations) was adopted and promulgated on June 19, 1992.[25] The purpose of this law was to permit cooperation with United Nations Peacekeeping Operations and Humanitarian International Relief Operations (Article I). Under this law, International Peace Cooperation Assignments include such activities as monitoring the observance of ceasefires; stationing in, and patrolling of buffer

---

23. *Report of the Secretary-General: Comprehensive Study of Nuclear Weapons*, U.N. GAOR, 35th Sess., provisional agenda, item 48(b), para. 519, U.N. Doc. A/35/392 (1980).

24. YOICHI HIGUCHI, MŌICHIDO KENPŌ WO YOMU [READING THE CONSTITUTION ONCE AGAIN], 197–198 (Iwanamishoten, 1992).

25. Law No. 79 of 1992 (English translation in 36 JAPANESE ANN. INT'L L. 272 (1993)). Contents and background of this law are analyzed in detail by Shunji Yanai, *Law Concerning Cooperation for United Nations Peace-Keeping Operations and Other Operations: Japanese PKO Experience*, 36 JAPANESE ANN. INT'L L. 33 (1993).

zones; supervising or managing elections and plebiscites; advising or guiding police administration; and so on (Article III, paragraph 3). In order to assuage constitutional doubts, operations of a military character are currently "frozen" (Article II of the Additional Provisions). Under this law, the SDF has already participated in the United Nations Transitional Authority in Cambodia (UNTAC); the United Nations Operation in Mozambique (ONUMOZ); and the United Nations Observer Mission in El Salvador (ONUSAL). In addition, the dispatching of the SDF for Humanitarian International Relief Operations around Rwanda has been put into practice.

This *fait accompli* seems to have weakened considerably the opposition of the Japanese people to participation by the SDF in peacekeeping operations. For example, the JSP, once strongly opposed to the adoption of the law, changed its policy and declared its support for the SDF's participation in United Nations peacekeeping operations under the law.

Before concluding this problem, the character of the peacekeeping operations and, above all, its recent changes following the end of the Cold War, must be examined. As is well known, peacekeeping operations have no express basis in the Charter provisions. Rather, peacekeeping operations emerged from the practice of the United Nations. As products of the Cold War, they were invented to cope with the inability of the U.N. system of collective security. And they were intended to block intervention by the two superpowers, thus preventing a regional conflict from escalating into a global conflict. Peacekeeping operations are generally accepted by U.N. members as constitutional under the Charter insofar as they abide by such principles as the consent of the parties concerned, impartiality in the dispute, control by the United Nations, noninterference in internal affairs, and nonuse of force except in case of self-defense.[26]

Among these principles, the principle of consent of the parties concerned seems the most essential. As early as 1958, Dag Hammarskjöld, in summarizing the experiences of the United Nations Emergency Force (UNEF) and the United Nations Observation Group in Lebanon (UNOGIL), observed that

> as the arrangements discussed in this report do not cover the type of force envisaged under Chapter VII of the Charter, it follows *from international law and the Charter* that the United Nations cannot undertake to implement them by stationing units on the territory of a Member State without the consent of the Government concerned. It similarly follows from the Charter that the consent of a Member nation is necessary for the United Nations to use its military personnel or material.[27]

---

26. SHIGERU KŌZAI, KOKUREN NO HEIWA IJI KATSUDŌ [U.N. PEACEKEEPING OPERATIONS], 349–421 (Yuhikaku, 1992).

27. *Report of the Secretary-General: Summary Study of the Experience Derived from the Establishment and Operation of the Force*, para. 155, U.N. Doc. A/3942 (Oct. 9, 1958)

When the International Court of Justice, in its opinion on *Certain Expenses of the United Nations*, recognized tacitly the constitutionality of the UNEF and the United Nations Operation in the Congo (ONUC) under the Charter, it reasoned that the actions in question were within the scope of the function of the United Nations, though neither UNEF nor ONUC was an enforcement action under Chapter VII. These actions were based on the consent of the nations concerned and the relevant resolutions were adopted unanimously or without dissenting vote, and thus acquired general acceptance by U.N. members.[28]

The Court apparently would not have recognized the UNEF and the ONUC as constitutional without the consent of the nations concerned. In fact, resolutions of both the Security Council or General Assembly not based on Chapter VII are recommendations, because neither body can order members to send or accept peacekeeping forces without their consent. Moreover, peacekeeping operations, not being enforcement actions, cannot be conducted without the consent of the parties concerned when the operations intrude into matters essentially within the domestic jurisdiction of states (Article 2, paragraph 7, of the Charter).

Since the time of the UNEF, peacekeeping operations have generally played positive, though restricted, roles in maintaining and restoring peace. As a consequence of profound changes in the international community after the Cold War, peacekeeping operations have expanded qualitatively as well as quantitatively, and the foundations of some of their established principles have been threatened. Four major problems have emerged.

First, peacekeeping operations have been implemented side by side with enforcement measures under Chapter VII. Immediately after the Iraqi invasion of Kuwait, the Security Council decided to take nonmilitary enforcement measures against Iraq.[29] After the formal ceasefire established by Resolution 687, the Council decided to set up the United Nations Iraq-Kuwait Observation Mission (UNIKOM) by Resolution 689 of April 9, 1991. The mandate of UNIKOM was not different from that of normal peacekeeping operations, but it did have some distinctive features. For example, it was not based on Iraq's genuine consent and its members were mainly composed of coalition forces.[30]

(emphasis added).

28. Certain Expenses of the United Nations, 192 I.C.J. 151, 164–72, 175–77 (July 20, 1962).

29. S.C. Res. 661 of August 6, 1990.

30. *See Report of the Secretary-General on the Implementation of Paragraph 5 of Security Council Resolution 687 (1991)*, U.N. SCOR, U.N. Doc. S/22454 (Apr. 5, 1991). Resolution 689 (1991) was adopted by the Security Council acting under Chapter VII of the Charter of the United Nations. Therefore, it may be doubted whether the UNIKOM is a peacekeeping operation in the established meaning.

In the case of the former Yugoslavia, the Security Council established the United Nations Protection Force (UNPROFOR) by Resolution 743 of February 21, 1992, and then adopted nonmilitary enforcement measures against the Federal Republic of Yugoslavia (Serbia and Montenegro) by Resolution 757 of May 30, 1992. Both Resolutions 661 and 757 stated only that the Security Council "act[ed] under Chapter VII of the Charter of the United Nations." They did not specify on what Article(s) of the Charter they were based, though it was apparently Article 41. This phenomenon seems to have made vague the originally clear distinction between enforcement measures envisaged in Chapter VII and peacekeeping operations devoid of an enforcement character.

Second, also contributing to the blurring of the distinction between enforcement measures and peacekeeping operations is that peace-enforcement units, which are conferred wider authority to use force under Chapter VII than are ordinary peacekeeping operations, have been conceived of and put into practice. The Secretary-General Boutros Ghali, in his Report *An Agenda for Peace*, recommended that the Security Council consider utilizing peace-enforcement units, which are more heavily armed than peacekeeping forces, to enforce compliance with ceasefire agreements.[31] The Secretary General's recommendation has been put into practice on various occasions.

Examples of the broadened authority of peace-enforcement units include: (1) the Security Council[32] expanded the size and mandate of the United Nations Operation in Somalia (UNOSOM) to include enforcement action under Chapter VII to secure a ceasefire and to implement the disarmament of the contending parties and factions (UNOSOM II); (2) after an armed clash on June 5, 1993, between the United Somali Congress (USC/SNA) and UNOSOM II operating under this resolution, the Council adopted Resolution 837 on June 6, 1993, which authorized UNOSOM II to use all necessary measures to arrest and detain those responsible for the attack; (3) UNPROPOR is authorized by Security Council Resolution 836 of June 4, 1993, to take measures, including the use of force, necessary to deter attacks against safe areas.

The peace-enforcement units have serious constitutional problems, to be discussed below, and they have not succeeded in improving the specific situations as yet. Indeed, the situations have deteriorated in Somalia and in Bosnia and Herzegovina. The Security Council seems to have admitted its failure by deciding to change the mandate and to decrease the size of the UNOSOM II.[33] A report of the Secretary General, based on which Resolution 897 (1994) was adopted, attributed this change to two factors: failure to secure cooperation of the Somali parties; and unavailability of necessary human and financial resources for

---

31. An Agenda for Peace, *supra* note 16, para. 44.
32. S.C. Res. 814 of Mar. 26, 1993.
33. S.C. Res. 897 of Feb. 4, 1994.

UNOSOM II.[34]

More serious problems seem to have motivated this change. The report of the Commission of Inquiry, established[35] to investigate armed attacks on UNOSOM II, concluded that "peace enforcement by UNOSOM II inside Somalia within the context of a civil war did not enhance the United Nation's peaceful and humanitarian image," and that "in hindsight it seems that the mandate given to UNOSOM II, at least as it was interpreted, was too pretentious in relation to the instruments and to the will to implement it."[36] Thus, it was recommended that "the United Nations should refrain from undertaking further peace enforcement actions within the internal conflicts of states."[37] Therefore, it must be concluded that beyond various technical problems the main cause of failure of UNOSOM II was its mandate of peace enforcement as such.

Third, the principle of consent of the parties concerned has been loosened. When recommending the establishment of UNPROFOR to the Security Council, the Secretary-General admitted uncertainty about the likelihood of receiving necessary cooperation from parties concerned but continued that

> after careful deliberation I have come to the conclusion that the danger that a United Nations peace-keeping operations will fail because of lack of cooperation from the parties is less grievous than the danger that delay in its dispatch will lead to a breakdown of the cease-fire and to a new conflagration in Yugoslavia.[38]

In the case of UNOSOM II, endowed with enforcement powers under Chapter VII, deployment was to be at the discretion of the Secretary-General and "such deployment would not be subject to the agreement of any local faction leaders."[39]

This loosening of the principle of consent seems to pose a serious problem regarding the constitutionality of these peacekeeping operations. The principle of consent is the main constitutional pillar of the peacekeeping operations, which are not enforcement measures and lack explicit basis in the Charter. The Secretary-

---

34. *Further report of the Secretary-General submitted in pursuance of paragraph 4 of resolution 886 (1993)*, U.N. SCOR, U.N.Doc. S/1994/12, paras. 44-61 (Jan. 6, 1994).

35. S.C. Res. 885 (1993).

36. Dated Feb. 24, 1994, and circulated as a Council document on June 1, 1994.

37. *Report of the Commission of Inquiry Established Pursuant to Security Council Resolution 885 (1993) to Investigate Armed Attacks on UNOSOM II Personnel Which Led to Casualties Among Them*, U.N. SCOR, paras. 252, 261, 270, U.N. Doc. S/1994/653 (1994) [hereafter Commission of Inquiry Report].

38. *Further Report of the Secretary-General Pursuant to Security Council Resolution 721 (1991)*, U.N. SCOR, para. 28, U.N. Doc. S/23592 (1992).

39. *Further Report of the Secretary-General Submitted in Pursuance of Paragraphs 18 and 19 of Resolution 794 (1992)*, U.N. SCOR, para. 97, U.N. Doc. S/25354 (1993).

General considered "peace-enforcement units to be warranted as a provisional measure under Article 40 of the Charter," and pointed out that they should not be confused with the forces constituted under Article 43.[40] Though included in Chapter VII, provisional measures under Article 40 are not obligatory, and therefore cannot relieve peace-enforcement units from the principle of consent. On the other hand, the Secretary-General stressed that UNOSOM II was endowed with enforcement powers.[41] Therefore, it must be concluded that UNOSOM II was not a peace-enforcement unit, as it was generally believed to be. Enforcement powers might relieve UNOSOM II from the principle of consent, but then on which articles could it be based except Article 42?

This situation also gives rise to serious problems of command and control. Enforcement action under Chapter VII of the Charter must be strictly under the command and control of the Security Council. It was true that UNOSOM II was established under the authority of the Security Council and placed under the direction of the Secretary-General through his special representative and the force commander. However, UNOSOM II operated side by side with the United States Quick Reaction Force (QRF) and a special task force of United States Rangers, and both were outside the command of UNOSOM II. This situation was bitterly criticized by the Commission of Inquiry, which stated in its Report that

> UNOSOM II . . . was probably also handicapped in prosecuting that war because the US QRF and the latter the ranger operation. . . were not under UNOSOM's control. If these operations were not under UNOSOM II the question arises as to whether they were authorized by the United Nations. If they were not, then the SNA's right to defend itself was even more appropriate . . .[42]

The fourth major peacekeeping operations problem is the drastic expansion of their sphere of activity. According to the Paris Agreement on a Comprehensive Political Settlement of the Cambodia Conflict[43] and a report of the Secretary General,[44] the mandates of the UNTAC encompassed not only military matters, but

---

40. *An Agenda for Peace, supra* note 16, para. 44.

41. U.N. Doc. S/25354, *supra* note 39, para. 58. The Commission of Inquiry stressed that the operations of UNOSOM II were peace enforcement actions. Commission of Inquiry Report, *supra* note 37, para. 250.

42. U.N. Doc. S/1994/653, *supra* note 37, para. 233. SNA denotes the Somali National Alliance, one of the most influential factions in Somalia.

43. *Letter dated 30 October 1991 from the Permanent Representatives of France and Indonesia to the United Nations addressed to the Secretary-General, Final Act of the Paris Conference on Cambodia*, U.N. GAOR 46th Sess., item 24, U.N. Doc. A/46/608–S/23177 (1991).

44. *Report of the Secretary-General on Cambodia*, U.N. SCOR, U.N. Doc. S/23613 and

also such civilian matters, such as organization and conduct of elections; fostering respect for human rights; and control over almost all the administrative agencies of Cambodia, including those relating to foreign affairs and the civil police. Security Council Resolution 814 (1993) and a report of the Secretary-General mandated that the UNOSOM II, in addition to performing the enforcement actions referred to above, provide assistance to the people of Somalia in such fields as repatriation of refugees and displaced persons; political reconciliation and reestablishment of national and regional institutions; reestablishment of police forces; and creation of conditions for the functioning of civil society.

It may be feared that the enlargement of peacekeeping operations mandates will tend to encroach on the right of self-determination of the concerned people without their genuine consent. The report of the Secretary General is not reassuring in this respect when it states that

> UNOSOM II cannot and must not be expected to substitute itself for the Somali people. Nor can or should it use its authority to impose one or another system of governmental organization. *It may and should, however, be in a position to press for the observance of the United Nations standards of human rights and justice.*[45]

The Commission of Inquiry challenged this interpretation of the mandate of UNOSOM II under Resolution 814. According to the Commission's Report, the Security Council distinguished between two powers of UNOSOM II. UNOSOM II was empowered to enforce disarmament of Somali parties by the use of force under Chapter VII, if necessary. On the other hand, with respect to rebuilding Somalia's political structure and organs of governance, UNOSOM II's role was limited to rendering assistance rather than imposing solutions upon the Somali people. The Commission criticized UNOSOM II for overstepping its mandate in this latter respect, and recommended that

> the United Nations should not insist on a particular political formula for the resolution of the Somali conflict, but should within the framework of the fundamental principles and goals of its charter assist all Somali political movements to reach consensus on Political reconciliation and the re-building of the institutions of governance.[46]

In light of these circumstances, Japan's participation in U.N. peacekeeping operations becomes contentious. The Secretary-General, though emphasizing "new departures in peacekeeping," observed that "the established principles and practices

---

Add/1 1 (1992), *approved by* S.C. Res. 745 (1992).

45. S/25354, *supra* note 39, para. 92 (emphasis added).

46. S/1994/653, *supra* note 37, paras. 51–53, 200–209, 263.

of peacekeeping have responded flexibly to new demands of recent years, and the basic conditions for success remain unchanged."[47] It is undeniable, however, that "the established principles" of peacekeeping operations have eroded considerably in recent years, to the point that their constitutionality under the Charter is in serious doubt.   Under these circumstances, it is necessary for Japan to have peacekeeping operations based strictly on established principles, including the principle of consent of the parties concerned.   Observance of the established principles must be the condition *sine qua non* for Japan, as well as for the other members of the United Nations, to participate in peacekeeping operations.[48]

This does not mean, however, that the Security Council has no competence to establish peacekeeping operations outside the express provisions of the Charter or the pre-established principles of peacekeeping operations. In order to cope with human tragedies prevalent in many parts of the world after the Cold War, the Council has set up many new types of peacekeeping operations, and, since each tragedy has its own features, each of these peacekeeping operations is unique. It is also true that the Council has a wide range of discretion in matters of maintenance and restoration of international peace and security. In discharging its duties in this regard, however, the Council, as an organ of the United Nations composed of sovereign member states, "shall act in accordance with the Purposes and Principles of the United Nations"[49] and within the general consensus of the member states. The Council has been criticized for overstepping even this overly wide and overly vague confine.   Thus, in the 1994 session of the Special Committee on Peacekeeping Operations, "some delegations underscored that all aspects of peacekeeping operations should adhere strictly to the principles and purposes of the Charter, in particular the Principles of respect for sovereign equality, territorial integrity of States and non-interference in their internal affairs."[50]

This situation not only seriously affects the legitimacy of new types of peacekeeping operations in general but also, by making uncertain the extent of cooperation to be supplied, fosters particular concern among troop-contributing nations. This concern has caused unmistakable signs of fatigue among these nations[51] and may explain, at least partly, the rather stringent conditions set by troop-contributing nations for participation in peacekeeping operations, as

---

47. *An Agenda for Peace, supra* note 16, para. 50.

48. Art. Ill, para. 1 of the Japanese *Law Concerning Cooperation for United Nations Peace-keeping Operations and Other Operations* stipulates the established principles of the peacekeeping operations as a condition of Japan's participation in them.

49. United Nations Charter, art. 24, para. 2.

50. *Report of the Special Committee on Peace-keeping Operations*, U.N. GAOR 49th Sess., item 81, para. 23, U.N. Doc. A/49/136 (1994).

51. U.N. Doc. S/1994/12, *supra* note 34, at para. 46.

exemplified, for example, by the recently announced United States policy.[52] It seems necessary to formulate principles and guidelines for new types of peacekeeping operations that stipulate conditions for their establishment, the scope of their possible mandates and functions, and their command and control structures. These principles and guidelines may be complemented by such documents as status-of-force agreements, agreements with member states contributing personnel and equipment, and a convention on the safety and security of U.N. and associated personnel, all of which are currently under consideration by various U.N. organs.

It is natural for the Security Council to be negative regarding the formulation of principles and guidelines that would restrict its discretion. A *Statement by the President of the Council*, while enumerating some factors to be taken into account in establishing new peacekeeping operations, stated that "the Council will respond to situations on a case-by-case basis," and that the mentioned factors were "without prejudice to its ability to do so and to respond rapidly and flexibly as circumstances require."[53] In a deliberation of the Special Committee, the idea of principles and guidelines was once criticized because "each operation was different in its scope, objective and organizational structure."[54]

However, the Committee's Report of its 1994 session, "taking into account the principles that have guided peacekeeping operations, stresses the importance of the elaboration of a set of principles and guidelines."[55] Such principles and guidelines would enhance the predictability of peacekeeping operations and assure respect for Charter principles. The legitimacy of peacekeeping operations thus would be strengthened and it would be easier for member states to contribute personnel and equipment. This is certainly a path to be pursued not only by Japan but also by the United Nations as a whole.

Even if these problems concerning the legitimacy of peacekeeping operations under the Charter could be cleared, there would remain constitutional problems in order for Japan to participate in these operations. Many Japanese constitutional lawyers believe that Japan's participation in military activities of peacekeeping operations is unconstitutional. The typical reasons for this are as follows: though the use of force by peacekeeping operations may not be a "war as a sovereign right of the nation" renounced by Article 9, paragraph 1, of the Constitution, an act of the Japanese state, dispatching the SDF for peacekeeping operations cannot be but an exercise of "a sovereign right of the nation," and therefore prohibited by the Constitution. Even on the premise that what the Constitution prohibits is

---

52. *See United States: Administration Policy on Reforming Multilateral Peace Operations*, 33 I.L.M. 795 (1994).

53. *Statement by the President of the Security Council*, at 1-2, U.N. SCOR, U.N. Doc. S/PRST/1994/22 (1994).

54. *Report of the Special Committee on Peace-keeping Operations*, para. 33, U.N. Doc. A/47/253 (1992).

55. U.N. Doc. A/49/136, *supra* note 50, para. 49.

maintenance of "armed forces" which exceed the limit necessary for self-defense, contingents dispatched to peacekeeping operations engaged in armed action are simply "armed forces" as such and therefore prohibited by Article 9, paragraph 2, of the Constitution.[56]

These arguments are not wholly convincing from the standpoint of international law, although it must not be forgotten that proponents of SDF participation in U.N. peacekeeping operations aim to legitimize the existence of the SDF under the Constitution, under the aegis of the United Nations, and eventually to open the way for Japan to dispatch the SDF overseas for Japan's own ends. Arguments over the SDF participation in military or civilian peacekeeping operations cannot be made without examing the constitutionality of SDF. Shigejiro Tabata, one of the most prominent international lawyers in Japan, observed that

> participating in a United Nations Force having the character [of peacekeeping operations] may be said, if independently argued, not to contradict the pacifism of the Constitution. But, also in this case, armed forces participating in such a United Nations Force retain their character as national contingents, and therefore, we cannot argue about it in the abstract before we resolve the question whether Japan can maintain any armed force under Article 9 of the Constitution.[57]

As noted above, the peacekeeping operations recently have drastically expanded their sphere of activities. As pointed out by the Secretary-General, these forays by peacekeeping operations increasingly require that, "civilian political officers, human rights monitors, electoral officials, refugee and humanitarian aid specialists and police play as central a role as military."[58] So far, Japan has sent only a few personnel—political officers, elections observers and the like—to these civilian activities of the peacekeeping operations. Provided that the established principles of, or the principles and guidelines to be formulated for peacekeeping operations are observed, Japan can and should actively participate in these activities under the present Constitution, which proclaims internationalism as one of its basic principles.

---

56. YASUHIRO OKUDAIRA, IKASO NIHONKOKU KENPŌ [MAKING THE MOST OF THE CONSTITUTION OF JAPAN] 109–114 (Iwanamishoten, 1994).

57. Shigejiro Tabata, *Shūdan Anzenhōsho Seido to Dai 9 Jō* [*System of Collective Security and Article 9*], *in* 1 KENPŌ KŌZA [COURSE OF THE CONSTITUTION OF JAPAN] 247, 260 (Shiro Kiyomiya & Isao Sato eds., 1963).

58. *An Agenda for Peace*, *supra* note 16, para. 52.

IV. "AUTHORIZATION" FOR USE OF FORCE BY THE SECURITY COUNCIL AND THE CONSTITUTION OF JAPAN

Another recent form of the use of force under the U.N.'s auspices is the "authorization" by the Security Council for member states to use force. Apart from the experience of the Korean War more than four decades ago, the first such "authorization" was that accorded to the coalition forces during the Gulf Crisis. Council Resolution 665 of August 25, 1990, was interpreted to authorize coalition forces to impose a *de facto* blockade against Iraq in order to ensure implementation of Resolution 661 (1990). The Council, acting under Chapter VII of the Charter, authorized the coalition forces, "unless Iraq on or before January 15, 1991 fully implements . . . the foregoing resolutions, to use all necessary means to uphold and implement resolution 660 (1990) and all subsequent relevant resolutions and to restore international peace and security in the area."[59]

In the case of Somalia, the Council, acting under Chapter VII of the Charter, "authorized the Secretary General and Member States . . . to use all necessary means to establish as soon as possible a secure environment for humanitarian relief operations in Somalia."[60] Under this resolution, the Unified Task Force (UNITAF) led by the United States was active in Somalia from December 1992 to May 1993, when it was succeeded by UNOSOM II.

A third set of these authorizations was that relating to the situation in the former Yugoslavia. The Security Council called upon states "to take nationally or through regional agencies or arrangements all measures necessary to facilitate in coordination with the United Nations the delivery by relevant United Nations humanitarian organizations and others of humanitarian assistance to Sarajevo and wherever needed in other parts of Bosnia and Herzegovina."[61] Council Resolution 816 of March 31, 1993, authorized member states, "acting nationally or through regional organizations or arrangements, to take . . . all necessary measures in the airspace of the Republic of Bosnia and Herzegovina . . . to ensure compliance with the ban of flights" referred to in the same resolution. The Council also decided by Resolution 836 that

Member States, acting nationally or through regional organizations or arrangements, may take, under the authority of the Security Council and subject to close coordination with the Secretary-General and UNPROFOR, all necessary measures, through the use of air power, in and around the safe areas in the Republic of Bosnia and Herzegovina, to support UNPROFOR in the performance of its mandate. . . .

---

59. S.C. Res. 678 (Nov. 29, 1990).
60. S.C. Res. 794 (Dec. 3, 1992).
61. S.C. Res. 770 (Aug. 13, 1992).

These precedents were followed on two subsequent occasions. The Council, by Resolution 929 of June 22, 1994, and acting under Chapter VII of the Charter, authorized the member states cooperating with the Secretary-General to conduct "a temporary operation under national command and control aimed at contributing, in an impartial way, to the security and protection of displaced persons, refugees and civilians at risk in Rwanda." The Council also adopted Resolution 940 of July 31, 1994, which, acting under Chapter VII of the Charter, authorized member states to

> form a multinational force under unified command and control and, in this framework, to use all necessary means to facilitate the departure from Haiti of the military leadership, . . . the prompt return of the legitimately elected President and the restoration of the legitimate authorities of the Government of Haiti, and to establish and maintain a secure and stable environment that will permit implementation of the Governors Island Agreement.

Apart from the problem of constitutionality of these "authorizations" under the Charter, which will be dealt with briefly below, the most serious question regarding these "authorized" actions seems to be the degree to which the United Nations is in control over them. Huge civilian casualties brought about by the Gulf War, which was conducted under Resolution 678 (1990) and did not provide for any control by the Security-Council, prompted then Secretary General Javier Perez de Cuellar's tacit criticism:

> the enforcement action was not carried out exactly in the forms foreseen by Chapter VII; the experience in the Gulf suggests the need for a collective reflection on questions relating to the future use of the powers of the Council under Chapter VII, including the mechanisms required for the Council to satisfy itself that the rule of proportionality is observed and that the rules of humanitarian law complied with . . . enforcement is a collective engagement which requires a discipline all its own.[62]

Thus, subsequent "authorizations" have begun to impose a greater measure of U.N. control. Resolution 794 (1992) provided for the following United Nations control mechanisms over the UNITAF: arrangements of the Secretary-General and the states concerned for unified command and control of the forces involved; appropriate mechanisms for coordination between the United Nations and the members' military forces; and an *ad hoc* commission composed of members of the Council to report on the implementation of the resolution. These provisions of

---

62.   JAVIER PEREZ DE CUELLAR, REPORT OF THE SECRETARY-GENERAL ON THE WORK OF THE ORGANIZATION, 1991 at 8–9 (1991).

Resolution 794 apparently reflect lessons from the Gulf experience.[63]

In the case of the former Yugoslavia, "authorized" actions were to be taken "in coordination with the United Nations" (Resolution 770), or "subject to close coordination with the Secretary-General and UNPROFOR" (Resolutions 819 and 836). Again, "authorized" measures in Rwanda, as well as in Haiti, were to be conducted in close coordination with the peacekeeping operations deployed in these countries—the United Nations Assistance Mission for Rwanda (UNAMIR) in the former case, and an advance team of the United Nations Mission in Haiti (UNMIH) in the latter.

During Council deliberations, a great number of representatives voiced concern about "authorization" of member states to use force without, or with insufficient, control by the Council. Resolution 678 (1990) was criticized by the representative of Yemen as "a classic example of authority without accountability." The Yemeni representative voted against the Resolution 678 because it was not related to any specific article of Chapter VII and, hence, the Council would have no control over authorized forces. Even the Malaysian representative, who voted in favor, noted that the resolution did not clearly reflect the centrality of the United Nations role in the maintenance of peace and security, and that it did not adequately specify the accountability of the authorized countries to the Council. He warned that it would be "a precedent that may not bode well for the future."[64]

As for Resolution 770 (1992), the Indian representative stressed as a question of principle that it would be imperative for an operation involving the use of force to be under the command and control of the United Nations. The representative of Zimbabwe was of the view that any necessary measures had to be undertaken as a collective enforcement measure under the full control of and with full accountability to the United Nations.[65] The Chinese representative also expressed concern about Resolution 794 (1992), noting that it assumed a form which authorized certain countries to take military actions, potentially adversely affecting the collective role of the United Nations.

The Indian representative favored a countrywide enforcement operation in Somalia carried out under United Nations command and control.[66] In the case of Rwanda, the representative of New Zealand also called for an expanded U.N. operation under Chapter VII and criticized the running of two separate parallel operations with different command arrangements. The Nigerian representative concurred, arguing that under the current situation in Rwanda—which constituted

---

63. U.N. SCOR, 3,145th mtg, at 32 (Austria) & 48 (Hungary), U.N. Doc. S/PV.3145 (1992).

64. U.N. SCOR 2,963d mtg. at 33 (Yemen) & 76 (Malaysia), U.N. Doc. S/PV.2963 (1990).

65. U.N. SCOR, 3,106th mtg. at 12–13 (India) & 15 (Zimbabwe), U.N. Doc. S/PV.3106 (1992).

66. U.N. Doc. S/PV.3145, *supra* note 63, at 17 (China) & 50 (India).

a threat to international peace—the United Nations, through the Security Council, should retain the primary responsibility.[67]

Even those who favored the "authorizations" argued that they were "to fill the gap" until the full deployment of UNAMIR, or to be used "as imperfect solutions when no perfect solutions are available."[68] Why, though, were "perfect solutions," i.e., operations under direct U.N. command and control, not available? This was due to member states' refusal to surrender command and control of their forces to the United Nations, which caused a dearth of available forces for United Nations operations. In the case of Somalia, the Secretary-General presented five options to the Security Council, of which the fourth was to authorize member states to undertake a countrywide enforcement operation, and the fifth was a countrywide enforcement operation to be carried out under U.N. command and control (the first three options were rejected as ineffective or impracticable). The Secretary General favored the fifth option "because it would be consistent with the recent expansion of the Organization's role . . . and . . . strengthen its long-term evolution as an effective system of collective security," but, admitting that member states might find U.N. command and control difficult to accept when many lives and much valuable equipment may be at stake, he recommended the fourth option—with which the United States had already expressed its readiness to cooperate—as an alternative.[69] After describing his abortive efforts to get troops and equipment for the expanded UNAMIR on the one hand and the deteriorating humanitarian situation in Rwanda on the other, the Secretary-General recommended that "in these circumstances" the Council consider the French offer to undertake a multinational operation under French command.[70]

The constitutionality of these "authorizations" under the Charter deserves detailed consideration. Many factors must be taken into account in this analysis, including, among others, the purposes of the authorized actions—(military in the case of Gulf War, humanitarian in the cases of Somalia and Rwanda, partly military and partly humanitarian in the case of the former Yugoslavia, and political in the case of Haiti), the circumstances of authorization, and the degree of control by the United Nations. Since the limited scope of this chapter does not permit a detailed analysis of these points, an overview follows.

In light of the lack or insufficiency of control by the United Nations through the Security Council as elucidated above, the possibility that the authorized actions are enforcement measures of the United Nations under Article 42 of the Charter

---

67. U.N. SCOR, 3,392d mtg. at 7 (New Zealand) & 10 (Nigeria), U.N. Doc. S/PV.3392 (1994).

68. *Id.* at 6 (France) & 8 (USA).

69. *Letter dated 29 November 1992 from the Secretary-General addressed to the President of the Security Council*, U.N. SCOR, U.N. Doc. S/24868 (1992).

70. *Letter dated 19 June 1994 from the Secretary-General addressed to the President of the Security Council*, U.N. SCOR, U.N. Doc. S/1994/728 (1994).

must first be excluded.[71] Hence, these actions are not those of the United Nations, but those of the authorized member states. On the other hand, since there are no express Charter provisions permitting the Council to authorize member states to use force, this entirely depends on the Council's "implied competence" or the subsequent practice of the Organization.

It seems impossible for the Council to relieve member states from the principle of non-use of force by virtue of its "implied competence." Non-use of force is expressly stipulated as one of the most important principles of the Charter, and is recognized generally as one of the peremptory norms of general international law (*jus cogens*). Although in the *Nicaragua* case the International Court of Justice did not directly state that the principle of nonuse of force was a rule of *jus cogens*, it did use an obvious quotation from a Report of the International Law Commission to state "that the law of the Charter concerning the prohibition of the use of force in itself constitutes a conspicuous example of a rule of international law having the character of *jus cogens*."[72]

The practice of the Council in this respect seems not to amount to what "has been generally accepted by Members of the United Nations and evinces a general practice of the Organization," to use the words of the International Court of Justice.[73] Votes on relevant resolutions are almost always accompanied by some abstentions, and, in one case, even dissenting votes.[74]

Moreover, each situation under which "authorization" was accorded was thought to be unique, thus requiring an exceptional response. Resolution 794 recognized "the unique character of the present situation in Somalia and . . . its deteriorating, complex and extraordinary nature, requiring an immediate and exceptional response," (2nd preambular paragraph). Resolution 929 recognized that "the current situation in Rwanda constitutes a unique case which demands an urgent response by the international community" (9th preambular paragraph). The second operative paragraph of Resolution 940 also expressed the same recognition for Haiti as was made in the case of Somalia. Representatives who participated in the Council's debates on these resolutions stressed, in one way or another, that the

---

71 . As to this point in the case of the Gulf War, *see* Yoshiro Matsui, *The Gulf War and the United Nations Security Council*, *in* ESSAYS IN HONOR OF WANG TIEYA, (R. St. J. MacDonald, ed., 1993).

72. Military and Paramilitary Activities (Nicar. v. U.S.) 1986 I.C.J. 4, 100 (June 27) (quoting 2 Y.B. INT'L L. COMM. 247 (1966), U.N. Doc. A/CN.4/Ser.A/1966).

73. *See* Legal Consequences for States of the Continued Presence of South Africa in Namibia (South West Africa) Notwithstanding Security Council Resolution 276 (1970), 1971 I.C.J. at 16, 22 (June 21).

74. U.N. Doc. S/PV.2963, *supra* note 64, at 64/65; U.N. Doc. S/PV.3106, *supra* note 65, at 26; U.N. Doc. S/PV.3392, *supra* note 67, at 5. For example, Resolution 678 was adopted by 12 votes in favor, 2 against, and 1 abstention, Resolution 770 by 12 in favor, none against, and 3 abstentions, and Resolution 929 by 10 votes in favor, none against, and 5 abstentions.

unique situation in those countries required exceptional action.

The only possible legal basis for these "authorizations" under the Charter thus seems to be the right of collective self-defense (Article 51). If the Security Council is authorizing collective self-defense, then the legal conditions for the exercise of that right must be met. According to the I.C.J., these conditions are: (1) declaration by the state for whose benefit this right is used that it views itself as the victim of an armed attack; (2) a request by that state; (3) the conditions of necessity and proportionality; (4) and, in case of the law of the U.N. Charter, a report to the Security Council on the measures taken in self-defense.[75]

In any case, the right of collective self-defense could afford a plausible legal ground only for the case of the Gulf War and some aspects of the case of the former Yugoslavia. The other cases, which were basically domestic in nature, had nothing to do with the right of collective self-defense. Not being enforcement measures under Chapter VII of the Charter, and without request or consent of the parties concerned, these cases related to matters which were essentially within the domestic jurisdiction of states concerned, in which the United Nations had no authority to intervene.[76]

What, then, is the Japanese position vis-a-vis such an "authorized" action? It must be emphasized first that such an authorized action is attributed not to the United Nations, but to the authorized states. Participation in it is therefore cooperation not with the United Nations, but with the authorized states. On the one hand, if the constitutionality of an authorized action under the Charter is open to doubt, participation in such an action would undermine the authority and integrity of the United Nations, not only for Japan, but also for other members of the United Nations. On the other hand, if an "authorized" action has any legal basis in the Charter, it must be nothing but the right of collective self-defense, which Japan is prohibited to exercise under Article 9 of the Constitution according to the interpretation by its successive governments. Therefore, there is absolutely no possibility for Japan to participate in any case in an armed action authorized by the Security Council. Rather, Japan along with all the other Members of the United Nations, has a responsibility to act in this organization in order that any use of force abide strictly by the Charter provisions.

---

75. *See* Military and Paramilitary Activities, *supra* note 72, at 103–105. In the present case, the legal right rests on the right of collective self-defense, because the authorized states are not the direct objects of armed attack.

76. Among them, only the case of Haiti may be said to be based on the consent of the legitimate Government. At the 3,413th meeting of the Security Council, during which Resolution 940 was adopted, the permanent representative of Haiti expressed the consent of the legitimately elected president of Haiti to the draft resolution (U.N. Press Release SC/5887, at 1 (July 31, 1994)).

V. SOME CONCLUSIONS

One of the most serious flaws of "internationalist arguments for revision of the Constitution" seems to lie in their reducing cooperation with the United Nations to cooperation with its military activities for maintaining or restoring international peace and security. The recent activities of the United Nations may give the same impression. For example, the oft-cited and oft-argued Secretary-General's Report, *An Agenda for Peace,* focussed mainly on this field of activities. It was natural for this Report to be so restricted because it was prepared in response to the Statement of the President of the Security Council of January 31, 1992, which invited the Secretary-General to prepare a Report on ways to strengthen and make more efficient the capacity of the United Nations for preventive diplomacy, for peacemaking, and for peacekeeping.[77]

In an effort to correct a "distorted view" disseminated by the media that the work of the United Nations centered around the multiple tasks of peacekeeping operations to the near exclusion of other activities, the Secretary-General stressed the comprehensive nature of the activities of the United Nations as follows:

[t]he second generation of peace-keeping is certain to involve not only military but also political, economic, social, humanitarian and environmental dimensions, all in need of a unified and integrated approach. Development is now understood to involve many dimensions: it is no longer merely a matter of economic policy and resources. Political, social, educational, and environmental factors must be part of an integrated approach to development. A new, workable and widely agreed concept of development still eludes us. Until it is achieved, the United Nations will continue to face a sequence of conflicts. There can be no flowering of development without the parallel advance of another key concept: democratization. Peace is a prerequisite of development; democracy is essential if development is to succeed over the long term.[78]

In spite of this assertion by the Secretary-General, there is no denying that the recent activities of the United Nations have been inclined toward military action when faced with actual conflicts, while somewhat neglecting long-term objectives for building a foundation for peace. A General Assembly resolution may have implied some measure of criticism toward *An Agenda for Peace* in this respect, when it emphasized that "international peace and security must be seen in an integrated manner and that the efforts of the Organization to build peace, justice,

---

77.   U.N. Doc. S/PV.3046, 141–47. (1992); *Note by the President of the Security Council*, U.N. SCOR, U.N. Doc. S/23500 (1992).

78. BOUTROS BOUTROS-GHALI, REPORT ON THE WORK OF THE ORGANIZATION, 1993 at 2, 6 (1993).

stability and security must encompass not only military matters, but also, . . . relevant political, economic, social, humanitarian, environmental and developmental aspects" and recognized the need to "complement 'An Agenda for Peace' with 'An Agenda for Development.'"[79]

Throughout its history, the United Nations has emphasized the importance of activities for building a foundation for peace. According to the Preamble of the Charter, these include the pursuit of fundamental human rights, the dignity and worth of the human person, the equal rights of man and woman and of nations large and small; justice and respect for obligations arising from treaties and other sources of international law; and social progress and better standards of living in larger degrees of freedom. Though it has not necessarily attained the expected results, the United Nations has engaged in such diversified activities for these purposes as decolonization, drafting and implementing of various instruments on human rights, progressive development and codification of international law, and economic and social development of the developing countries.

It is in these activities that Japan has the greatest possibilities for cooperation. Japan's Constitution recognizes in its preamble "that all peoples of the world have the right to live in peace, free from fear and want," that it desires "to occupy an honored place in an international society striving for the preservation of peace, and the banishment of tyranny and slavery, oppression and intolerance for all time from the earth," and that it pledges "our national honor to accomplish these high ideals and purposes with all our resources."[80]

---

79. *An Agenda for Peace: Preventive Diplomacy and Related Matters*, preamb. paras. 6 and 7, G.A. Res. 47/120 (1992). The Assembly officially requested by Resolution 47/181 (*An Agenda for Development*) (1992) that the Secretary-General submit a report on an agenda for development. Pursuant to this latter resolution, the Secretary-General submitted on May 6, 1994, to the Assembly *An Agenda for Development: Report of the Secretary-General*, U.N. GAOR 48th Sess., item 91, U.N. Doc. A/48/935.

80. Kenpō [Constitution] preamb.

JAPANESE WAR GUILT, THE "PEACE CONSTITUTION," AND JAPAN'S ROLE IN GLOBAL PEACE AND SECURITY

Yasuaki Ōnuma

I. INTRODUCTION

No nation can play an international role that defies its domestic and historical conditions.[1] Japan is no exception. According to the prevailing view, Japan's role in the maintenance of international peace and security has been extremely limited during the postwar period. Japan has not been a "normal" state with full military sovereignty. Even the constitutional legitimacy of its Self-Defense Forces (SDF) has consistently been challenged by pacifist-oriented Socialists, intellectual leaders, and influential media. The Japanese people have been so naive as to assume that by maintaining Article 9, a pacifist provision of the Constitution,[2] they can enjoy peace. Thus, it is the "Peace Constitution,"[3] it is said, that has prevented Japan from playing an active role in maintaining international peace and security.

The proponents of this view argue that reliance on the "Peace Constitution" is not only naive but also selfish. Naive, because no constitution by itself can guarantee the peace and security of an independent nation. Even if a nation adheres to its pacifist constitution, other nations may attack it. Selfish, because even though

---

1.   Even the United States, the superpower in postwar international society, has been restrained by its domestic structure (*e.g.*, the Senate as the "graveyard of treaties") and its historical predicaments (*e.g.*, recurrence of strong isolationism).

2.   *See infra* section III.a.

3.   In this article, the "Peace Constitution" means the "living Constitution" of postwar Japan, focusing on Article 9 and the Preamble. This "Peace Constitution" has been valid in the political process of postwar Japan, which has been characterized by aversion to war and the antinuclear sentiment of the Japanese people. *See* Yasuaki Ōnuma, *"Heiwa Kempō" to shudan anzen hosho* [Japan's "Peace Constitution" and Collective Security], 92 KOKUSAIHO GAIKO ZISSI 1 at 5 n. 1 (1993).

Japan has enjoyed peace, many other nations have suffered from armed conflicts during the postwar period. Japan, as a rich, powerful, and influential nation, should have contributed more positively to international peace and security.

This view, however, fails to take into account important contributions made by the "Peace Constitution" to regional and global peace during the postwar period. By strictly restraining Japan's military capability and fostering a pacifist psychology in postwar Japan, the Constitution has mitigated the possibility of confrontation between Japan and its neighbors. It has prevented Japan from becoming a merchant of death that produces and exports high-technology military weaponry, although Japan has long maintained such capabilities. It has further contributed to the spread of antimilitary and antinuclear ideas, not only in Japan, but also among those in other nations who find in Article 9 a pacifist ideal.

Had Japan been fully armed and dispatched its armed forces abroad, as other influential powers have done during the postwar period, Japan would have provoked more suspicions, repercussions, and even more militaristic policies among its neighbors. Such an aggressive "international peace and security" policy would have contributed not to a stable peace and security in Asia, but to tensions and conflicts in the region.

Furthermore, critics of the "Peace Constitution" fail to grasp an important factor responsible for the passive postwar peace policy[4] in Japan: the failure of the Japanese people to squarely face the problem of war guilt. Because postwar Japan could not overcome its guilt for its aggressive wars from 1931 through 1945 and colonial rule in Asia, it was difficult for Japan to play a significant role in the field of international peace and security. Japan's adherence to the "Peace Constitution" played a substitute role for an admission of war guilt.

In the early 1990s, however, two events brought about fundamental changes in the above conditions. First, the Gulf War had a tremendous impact on Japan. It raised a serious question among the Japanese people as to whether an enduring policy of passive peace is an appropriate posture for a powerful, influential new Japan in the 1990s and in the twenty-first century. Second, a coalition government supplanted the Liberal Democratic Party's (LDP) government. The new Prime Minister Morihiro Hosokawa admitted in an unreserved manner that Japan's past wars were aggressive wars[5] and made clear apologies. These statements greatly

---

4.   The "passive peace policy" is the inward-looking policy of solely sticking to the language of Article 9 of the Constitution, and failing to proselytize its idea of peace to other nations and to take responsibility for the maintenance of international peace and security.

5.   James Sterngold, *Japan's Leader Vows Action on Political System*, N.Y. TIMES, Aug. 24, 1993, at A8. Hosokawa failed to specify which wars he believed to be aggressive on the part of Japan. It is apparent, however, the wars he referred to are those which Japan waged from 1931 through 1945, except the war launched by the Soviet Union in the final days of World War II, in violation of the Japan-Soviet Neutrality Pact of 1941.

mitigated the suspicions and criticism of Japan's history among Asian nations. They will further facilitate Japan's role in regional as well as global peace and security.[6]

The change is visible not only in Japan but in international society as a whole. Instead of East-West confrontation, control of regional, ethnic, and religious conflicts is a primary factor in global security. Desperate poverty in the South, a situation that has contributed to these conflicts, is another serious challenge. Disagreements between the North and the South (or, East and West in the civilizational sense) over human rights, the environment, and religious and cultural values are likely to threaten global peace and security.

Japan's role in global peace and security must be explored against this domestic, historical, and international background.

II. JAPANESE WAR GUILT

It has been said repeatedly that postwar Japan has failed to confront the problem of war guilt. I myself have consistently criticized this failure, and emphasized that the Japanese people must take responsibility for their past.[7] Failure to take responsibility for aggressive wars (1931–1945) and colonial rule over Korea and Taiwan dulled the moral sensitivities of the Japanese and prompted them to view foreign relations only in economic and political terms. This attitude in turn has prevented Japan from assuming a more positive role in global peace and security.

There have been four major periods when the problem of war guilt was seriously discussed in Japan.[8] The first occurred immediately after World War II.

---

6.   The term "global peace and security" is used in a similar sense to "international peace and security", the term employed in the Charter of the United Nations. However, the term "international security" has often been used to imply a security system mainly based on strategic ideas and military measures. This usage, together with a usage stressing the significance of military measures in the U.N. enforcement system of Chapter 7, has somewhat colored the term "international peace and security" to mean "peace maintained by force."   To achieve a global peace, however, not only military sanctions against delinquent states but also measures seeking disarmament, policies strengthening the legitimacy, peaceful means of settling disputes and the system of peaceful change in the U.N., and other measures for positive peace are extremely significant. The term "global peace and security" is adopted for expressing not only peace by force, but peace created through such nonmilitary activities.

7.   Yasuaki Ōnuma, *Beyond Victors' Justice*, 11 JAPAN ECHO 63–72 (1984); YASUAKI ŌNUMA, TOKYO SAIBAN KARA SENGO SEKININ NO SHISŌ E [FROM THE TOKYO WAR CRIMES TRIAL TO THE PHILOSOPHY OF JAPANESE POSTWAR RESPONSIBILITIES FOR WAR] 11–14 *passim* (3rd ed., 1993). Section II, *infra*, is based on this book.

8.   Since the early 1990s, there have been strong demands for the Japanese government to fulfill its duty to pay postwar compensation to non-Japanese nationals who suffered from Japan's aggressive wars and colonial rule and yet did not receive individual reparations. These claims have naturally involved a wide range of controversies over Japanese war guilt.

Leftists—especially communists—who were persecuted during the war severely criticized the wartime leaders. Concurrently, the former Allied Powers tried wartime Japanese political and military leaders at the Tokyo War Crimes Trial. These leaders were found guilty of crimes against peace as well as ordinary war crimes.

Postwar criticism by the Communists was not widely shared by the ordinary citizens because it was considered too partisan. The Tokyo Trial did have some impact upon the Japanese people as it revealed Japan's aggression and atrocities, and belied the cause of the "Greater Asian War" in which they had believed. However, ordinary Japanese citizens thought that the trial charged only leaders or dignitaries. Most Japanese, who suffered greatly during and after World War II, shared a strong sense of victimization. They regarded the problem of war guilt not as their own, but as their leaders. They were also somewhat skeptical about the trial. A cynical sense of "might makes right" prevailed. The failure of the Allied Powers to apply the law to their own conduct—such as the atomic bombings of Hiroshima and Nagasaki, the Soviet Union's violation of the Japan-Soviet Neutrality Pact, and many postwar events—further undermined the legitimacy of the Trial and strengthened Japanese cynicism.[9]

Disputes over war guilt emerged for the second time in the mid-1950s. The guilt of intellectual leaders, the Showa Emperor and the Communists—all untouched in the previous controversies—was heatedly discussed. Again, however, the focus rested on the guilt of leaders, not on the responsibility of the Japanese people as a whole for invading and damaging other nations. Even the idea of Japanese responsibility for wartime wrongs did not occur to most citizens.

It was not until the early 1970s that the idea of the responsibility of the Japanese as a whole came to be fairly widely discussed. Two events prepared the way for this new, third stage of war guilt controversies. First, the students' revolts and new left movements of the late 1960s raised serious ethical questions: Had not Japan achieved its economic prosperity by exploiting other Asian nations? Had not the Japanese people tacitly suppressed Korean and Chinese minorities whose very existence in Japan was a consequence of its colonial rule over Korea and Taiwan? Had the Japanese mentality toward other Asian peoples ever changed? Had not Japan maintained an attitude of superiority toward other Asian peoples despite having lost the "Greater Asian War?" These questions urged a reappraisal of the very premise and framework of war guilt controversies.

One may thus characterize the early 1990s to the present time as the fifth period of war guilt controversies.

9.   In addition, many trials of ordinary war criminals were biased and conducted with poor interpreter facilities and insufficient knowledge of the Japanese military system. As a result, some of these trials yielded apparently unreasonable judgments, including death penalties imposed on innocents. These facts further strengthened cynicism among the Japanese about war crimes trials conducted by the Allied Powers. *See* Shunsuke Tsurumi, *What the Tokyo Trial Left to the Japanese People, in* THE TOKYO WAR CRIMES TRIAL 134–45 (Chihiro Hosoya et al. eds., 1986).

The normalization of relations with China resulted in a more direct impact on the question of war guilt. Of all the nations victimized by Japan's aggressive wars, China suffered most seriously. Thus, the reestablishment of formal relations with China provided ample opportunity for scholars and journalists to explore the crimes there committed by Japanese military forces. Prominent journalists revealed a huge number of atrocities committed by Japanese armies in China from 1931 through 1945.[10] Various media institutions—newspapers, journals, TV stations, and others—carried reports and confessions of wartime atrocities and inhumane conduct. Guilt, not only on the part of Japanese leaders but on the part of ordinary people as well, began to be perceived.

This new perception was further strengthened in the early 1980s, the fourth period of war guilt controversies. At this time, *de facto* censorship of history textbooks by the Japanese government to conceal distasteful historical facts, such as aggression against China, was severely criticized from both within and abroad. Scholars who since the early 1970s had explored the war guilt issue from the new perspective of Japanese guilt formulated the idea of postwar responsibilities toward the Asian people: the Japanese as a whole had failed to confront war guilt, and were responsible for remorse and compensation.[11]

These controversies over war guilt involved various leading figures, including politicians, historians, novelists, lawyers, and journalists. They failed, however, to motivate the LDP government to confront the problem of war guilt. Prime Ministers of successive LDP governments sought to avoid characterizing wars—from the "Manchurian Incident" (1931) through the "Greater Asian War"—as having been aggressive. What can explain this failure to admit such manifest historical facts?

Many postwar LDP leaders found it difficult to accept that the wars for which their friends and relatives died were aggressive. Conservative leaders, including the LDP leadership, were reluctant to recognize that the Showa Emperor, whom they venerated, bore guilt for aggressive wars and atrocities. In one sense, they accepted the verdict of the Tokyo Trial: those guilty of aggression, represented by Hideki Tōjō, had already been punished. Those who were not judged at trial, including the Emperor and other leaders, should therefore be immune from responsibility. On the other hand, they regarded the Tokyo Trial as a typical example of victors' justice. "Might makes right," they repeated cynically, casting serious doubt on the trial's legitimacy. The failure of the Allied Powers to apply the law of the trial to their own wartime and postwar conduct strengthened this cynicism. Furthermore, some postwar conservative leaders argued that Asian nations attained independence from

---

10. Katsuichi Honda, who published CHŪGOKU NO TABI [A JOURNEY IN CHINA] (1972) and CHŪGOKU NO NIHON GUN [THE JAPANESE ARMY IN CHINA] 1992, is representative of these journalists.

11. The term *sengo sekinin*, literally meaning "postwar responsibilities" and implying the duty to take responsibilities which should have been taken long before, began to be accepted in the 1980s by major media institutions such as the Asahi Shimbun.

European colonial rule at least partially as a result of Japan's wars against European colonial powers.

As for ordinary Japanese, most considered themselves victims rather than wartime aggressors. Having suffered more than three million deaths, strategic bombings of their cities, and conditions of near starvation during and after World War II, they clung to this perception of victimization. The fact that citizens of Hiroshima and Nagasaki were the first victims of nuclear warfare strengthened this sense. Most importantly, since the middle of the nineteenth century, the Japanese had concentrated on catching up with the West and paid little attention to the lives and fates of non-Western peoples in general. This indifference made it easier for the Japanese to ignore the many Asians victimized by Japan's aggression.

The foregoing does not mean that Japan did not learn any lessons from the wars. Postwar Japan's policy of concentrating on economic development and minimizing its military forces apparently reflected a strong condemnation of the prewar policy of seeking military hegemony in Asia. The very fact that postwar Japan maintained an almost visionary pacifist constitution substituted for squarely facing the problem of war guilt.

III. THE "PEACE CONSTITUTION"

a. Origin, Significance, and Reality of the "Peace Constitution"

The "Peace Constitution" was a product of war. The idea of a pacifist Japan was first expressed by Prime Minister Kijūrō Shidehara during a conversation with General Douglas MacArthur, Supreme Commander of the Allied Powers then-occupying Japan. MacArthur was enthusiastic about the idea and ordered his staff to draft a clause stating that "war as a sovereign right of the nation is abolished."[12] The clause, together with other draft articles of the present Japanese Constitution, was shown to the Japanese government, slightly amended, and finally adopted by the Japanese National Diet.

Article 9 of the Constitution reads:

Aspiring sincerely to an international peace based on justice and order, the Japanese people forever renounce war as a sovereign right of nation and the threat or use of force as means of settling international disputes.
In order to accomplish the aim of the preceding paragraph, land, sea, and air forces, as well as other war potential, will never be maintained. The right of belligerency of the state will not be recognized.[13]

---

12. NIHON KOKU KENPŌ SEITEI NO KATEI [THE BIRTH OF JAPAN'S CONSTITUTION], 98–101, 272 (Kenzo Takayanagi et al., eds. 1972).
13. 1 EHS LAW BULLETIN SERIES JAPAN, AA4 (1948).

The "Peace Constitution" has contributed to regional as well as global peace in a number of ways. First, it constituted an important step in the development of the outlawry of war in international law. Together with Article 2(4) of the United Nations Charter, it furthered the notion of the unlawfulness of war expounded by the Kellogg-Briand Pact of 1928. Its restriction is far more thorough than that of similar constitutions, such as the French, German, or Filipino.[14]

The "Peace Constitution" has contributed to the reconstruction of postwar Japan as a pacifist nation. In sharp contrast with other major powers, such as the Soviet Union, the United States, the United Kingdom, France, China, and India, Japan has never resorted to military measures during the postwar period. Whether done in the name of self-defense, to rescue nationals abroad, by invitation of other governments, for national self-determination or other justifications, Japan has never sent its SDF abroad solely in pursuit of its national interest.

The "Peace Constitution" has further prevented Japan from becoming a merchant of death. Although it has had sufficient industrial and technological capabilities to produce weaponry, including nuclear weapons, and to make a profit by exporting them, Japan has refrained from exporting weapons to countries involved in armed conflicts.

Finally, the "Peace Constitution" has functioned as a substitute for open acknowledgment of guilt and responsibility for its aggressive wars. When the present Constitution was enacted in 1947, the former Allied Powers and other Asian nations were still extremely suspicious of Japanese militarism. Japanese political leaders knew that Japan could not prosper, nor even rejoin international society, unless it could convince the world that there would never be a resurgence of Japanese militarism. This was one of the major reasons that Japanese political leaders accepted the almost visionary pacifist provision of Article 9 when they were presented with its draft by the occupation forces.[15] When the draft articles of the new Constitution were discussed in the National Diet, most members of the Diet, including the cabinet, construed Article 9 as prohibiting even the use of force for self-defense.[16]

The majority of Japanese was not conscious of the nexus between the "Peace Constitution" and the suspicion of neighboring nations. Rather they more genuinely believed that Japan should never again resort to arms. The majority accepted and supported the idealistic Article 9 mainly due to the sense of victimization as well as war-weariness and believed that the Imperial Army and Navy had led Japan into

---

14. *See* CHŪICHI HUKASE, SENSŌ HOKI TO HEIWA TEKI SEIZON KEN [THE RENUNCIATION OF WAR AND THE RIGHT TO LIVE IN PEACE] 150–59 (1987).

15. *See* Statement of Prime Minister Shigeru Yoshida (House of Representatives, Plenary Session of the Amendment of the Constitution, June 26, 1946), which alludes to this nexus. TEIKOKU KENPŌ KAISEI SHINGIROKUI [PROCEEDINGS OF THE AMENDMENT OF IMPERIAL CONSTITUTION] pt. 5 at 49 (SANGIIN JIMUKYOKU [SECRETARIAT OF THE HOUSE OF COUNCILORS], eds. 1958).

16. *Id.*

disastrous wars.[17] This sense of victimization prevailed during the postwar period and even today prevents any attempt to revise Article 9. The preservation of Article 9 also sends a tacit message to the world: "We did wrong. We shall never do it again." In this way, fulfillment of the "Peace Constitution"—including restriction of the military budget to around one percent of gross national product, maintenance only of defense weapons, and limitation of other military institutions or activities—has functioned as a tacit admission of war guilt.

On the other hand, the fundamental policy of maintaining the "Peace Constitution" has been marred by a serious flaw. Since its enactment there has been a gap between the apparent meaning of Article 9 and Japan's actual postwar security policy. Article 9 has framed too lofty an ideal to uphold in postwar international society. The U.N. collective security system, upon which a nation should rely in case of attack by other nations, was doomed to malfunction as a result of East-West confrontations. The United States, eager to disarm Japan when Japan enacted its Constitution, soon wanted an armed Japan, with its military bases and supply facilities for U.S. forces, to cooperate with the United States to effectively restrain Soviet military forces.

Since the enactment of the Constitution, the Japanese people have had two major options. One was to adopt a policy of nonarmament and neutrality. The Socialists, critical of "American imperialism," urged this option. This policy meant pursuance of the pacifist ideal of Article 9 to its fullest (and perhaps most naive) interpretation. The other was to ally with the United States, and substantially revise the original intention of Article 9. The conservatives, suspicious of communist regimes, insisted that Japan rely on the United States. Various factors contributed to the victory of the conservatives. These factors included: (1) the need for economic aid from abroad and a market for Japanese goods to recover from a desperate economic situation after the end of World War II; (2) a sense of vulnerability and crisis instigated by the Korean War; (3) the attractiveness of America's economic prosperity and popular culture; and (4) popular dislike of the Soviet Union, aggravated by its violation of the Japan-Soviet Neutrality Pact, detention of many Japanese prisoners of war, and the occupation of the northern islands. In the 1950s, Japan thus concluded a security pact with the United States, and created the SDF.

There have naturally been many conflicts between this policy of alliance with the United States and Article 9 of the Constitution. The U.S. government has consistently demanded that Japan have more effective military forces to restrain their common potential enemy, the Soviet Union. To implement such a policy, however, would mean a further departure from the original spirit of Article 9. The Japanese government has thus slowly and gradually changed its position. After hesitating for some years, it finally adopted the interpretation that maintenance of

---

17. *See* KIJŪRŌ SHIDEHARA, GAIKŌ GOJŪ NEN [FIFTY YEARS OF A DIPLOMAT'S LIFE] 211–13 (1974).

minimal forces for self-defense is not prohibited under Article 9.[18] The Japanese people, on the whole, have accepted this interpretation and the policy to gradually increase Japan's military capabilities under the Japan-U.S. alliance.

As explained below, this attitude may be justifiable from a political perspective, but is difficult to defend from a normative perspective. It contributed, in a sense, to the development of a double standard in Japanese society: on the one hand, Article 9 exists as a supreme ideal; on the other hand, it has been construed as allowing the existence of effective armed forces. This tension surfaced in controversies over the Gulf War and Japan's participation in U.N. peacekeeping operations.

b. The New Situation

When Iraq invaded Kuwait, Japan's reaction was conditioned not only by the foregoing factors but by other considerations as well. First, the invasion was such a manifest aggression that it was difficult to overlook. Many LDP members, pro-American opinion-makers and mass media institutions, such as the Yomiuri newspaper, argued that not only was nonmilitary support to the coalition forces authorized by the U.N. Security Council, but a real need existed to participate in, or at least cooperate with, the coalition forces. The need to cooperate with the Western powers (especially the United States) in maintaining international order and securing oil resources was their primary concern. They thus argued that Japan should make available the SDF for these purposes.

Socialists, some Liberals and "progressive" mass media institutions such as the Asahi and Mainichi newspapers, however, were reluctant to use the SDF for such purposes. Although a majority of Japanese had accepted the existence of the SDF, they were extremely cautious about assigning it a positive role. According to a widely shared interpretation, the "use of force" is prohibited under Article 9 even when Japan acts as a member of the U.N. forces. The Cabinet Legislative Bureau construed that, while dispatching the SDF personnel was not itself prohibited by the Constitution, dispatching the SDF troops to engage in the use of force abroad was not allowed under any circumstances.[19]

Many Socialists and some Liberals in Japan, as well as several neighboring Asian nations, especially Korea and China, were still wary of a possible "resurgence

---

18. Unified view of the Government given by Shūzō Hayashi, Director of the Cabinet Legislative Bureau, at the House of Representatives, Standing Committee for Budget, Dec. 21, 1954, cited in KENPŌ DAI KYU (9) JŌ [ARTICLE NINE OF THE CONSTITUTION] 76–77 (Yuhikaku ed., rev. ed., 1986).

19. Statement of Shūzō Hayashi, Director of the Cabinet Legislative Bureau, at the House of Representatives, Standing Committee for Cabinet, Mar. 28, 1958. 22 KOKKAI SHUGIIN NAIKAKU IINKAI GIJIROKU [HOUSE OF REPRESENTATIVES, STANDING COMMITTEE FOR CABINET, PROCEEDINGS] 5–6. This view has been confirmed repeatedly by subsequent Japanese governments. *See* SHIGERU KOZAI, KOKUREN NO HEIWA IJI KATSUDŌ [THE U.N. PEACE-KEEPING OPERATION] (1991).

of Japanese militarism."[20] They feared that the overseas dispatch of the SDF under the authority of the United Nations would pave the way to expanded SDF activities abroad for Japan's own sake. Furthermore, there were suspicions that the United States was abusing the authority of the U.N. for its own selfish purposes: to secure its vested interests in oil resources and to maintain its hegemony in the region.

Heated debates arose involving a wide range of people—politicians, scholars, lawyers, journalists, other intellectuals, and ordinary citizens. A bill to permit cooperating with the United Nations and participating in other related activities by the coalition forces was proposed by the LDP government but defeated. This result was only natural because some of the proponents of the bill wanted to use this opportunity to fully legitimize the SDF, especially its activities abroad. Such a motivation naturally led to strong resistance by a wide range of citizens, who sensed manipulation by the hard-liners of the LDP.

On the other hand, debates over the bill revealed a somewhat selfish, isolationist aspect to Japan's postwar pacifism. It is true that part of the opposition was rooted in genuine pacifism, or the belief that Japanese soldiers must never again engage in aggression. One cannot deny, however, that this strong opposition was also motivated by a selfish belief that the Japanese not shed their blood for any reason. A national sentiment of "peace at any cost," or, more precisely, "Japanese peace at any cost," revealed itself.[21]

---

20. Arguments that emphasize the (possible) "resurgence of Japanese militarism" fail to grasp a deeply rooted pacifism in postwar Japan. It is difficult to find a country which shows fewer indications of militarism than postwar Japan: postwar Japan has never sent its forces abroad; it has never used its SDF as a means to threaten other nations; its SDF personnel are rigidly restricted as to speech; the budget of the SDF has been kept at around one percent of GNP, compared with three to six percent in the Western European states and the US, and more than ten percent in the former Soviet Union and many developing countries. The SDF has been allowed to have weapons only for defense purposes; no offense weapons, such as bombers or missiles with a range capable of reaching neighboring nations, are allowed.

Four major factors are responsible for this myth of a "resurgence of Japanese militarism." First, Japanese Socialists and Communists argued that those in the camp of "American imperialism" are militarists, whereas those in the communist camp are pacifists—a completely distorted view. Second, the memory of Japanese aggression and the cruel behavior of Japanese soldiers during the war survived and was conveyed to new generations in Asia even after the end of the war. Third, the failure of postwar Japan to admit its war guilt further strengthened this memory, and resentment and suspicions among Asian nations who were victims of prewar Japanese militarism. Fourth, people tend to project their own way of thinking onto others and assume that others will behave according to this projection. Recently, some American experts have predicted that Japan will seek to have nuclear weapons to cope with nuclear threats from North Korea. This is a typical example of such a projection and of the failure to grasp the deeply rooted pacifism and antinuclear sentiment among Japanese.

21. One way to understand postwar pacifism in Japan is to recall the significance and flaws of American pacifism during the interwar period. American pacifism contributed to the birth of the Kellogg-Briand Pact, and played a major role in establishing the global normative consciousness against war. Japanese pacifism has sustained the lofty ideal of Article 9 and

This attitude of isolationist pacifism has gradually yielded to a more internationalist approach to peace and security. As the Gulf War was attracting worldwide attention, another important event was taking place. Japan and other interested parties were working hard to bring about peace in Cambodia, where civil wars had occurred since the 1970s. In October 1991, the Agreement on a Comprehensive Political Settlement of the Cambodia Conflict and other related agreements were concluded. Japan played an important role in persuading the conflicting parties to accept the peace agreements. When the U.N. decided to establish the U.N. Temporary Authority in Cambodia (UNTAC) to carry out these agreements, Japan naturally was expected to participate in this grand peacekeeping operation. The Japanese government proposed a bill to enable the SDF to participate in the UNTAC. After heated debates again in the National Diet, in academic and legal circles, in the media and among ordinary citizens, the Law Concerning Cooperation for U.N. Peace-Keeping Operations (PKO) and other Operations was enacted on June 15, 1992.

The PKO Cooperation Law authorizes the government to engage the SDF and other personnel in (1) U.N. peacekeeping operations, and (2) humanitarian relief operations, based on resolutions or requests by the U.N. or other U.N. organizations such as the U.N. High Commissioner for Refugees. Unlike the aborted bill of October 1990, referred to earlier, the Law does not allow the SDF to join or cooperate with forces organized under the "authorization" of U.N. resolutions such as the coalition forces acting in accordance with Security Council Resolutions 661, 665, and 678 in the Gulf War. Furthermore it remained frozen until a separate law was enacted to set the date for implementation, participation of the SDF in such activities as monitoring the observance of cease-fire arrangements, patrolling in a buffer zone, and participation in other "PKF" activities that might involve the use of force. These restrictions were provided to appease strong domestic critics and assuage the suspicions of Asian neighbors, as well as to comport with the long-standing restrictive interpretation of the Constitution. As a result, the participation of the SDF was limited to such nonmilitary U.N. activities as election monitoring, police administration, provision of medical services, and logistical support for other military forces that participated in the U.N. peacekeeping operation.

Still, passage of the Law was epochal in that it overcame the long-standing isolationist pacifism that had characterized postwar Japan. Three months later, two thousand SDF soldiers, together with civilian personnel, were dispatched to Cambodia for participation in the UNTAC. Although there were some setbacks, including the death of a police officer and a volunteer, Japan's participation in the UNTAC was on the whole a great success. Criticism of the "resurgence of Japanese militarism," a specter haunting Japan and other Asian nations, dissipated. Although

---

played an important role in fostering and disseminating antiwar, antinuclear sentiment. Both were combined, however, with isolationism, and ignored the need of each nation to participate in the international security system. *See* YASUAKI ŌNUMA, SENSŌ SEKININ RON JŌSETSU [PROLEGOMENA TO THE RESPONSIBILITY FOR WAR] 70–97, 105–11, 121–57 (1975).

it was possible that SDF members would be compelled to use weapons, this eventuality did not occur.

Japan must, however, overcome a number of problems in order to fulfill its role in securing global peace. Many legalistic, artificial restraints written into the PKO Cooperation Law, referred to earlier, are conspicuous examples. More fundamentally, Japan has to formulate fundamental principles in order to play a far more positive role in global peace and security. In order to achieve this grand design, it is necessary to analyze norms and actualities on the use of force in contemporary international society and map out an appropriate role for Japan to play.

III. CONTROL OF FORCE IN THE INTERNATIONAL LEGAL ORDER

a.   Norms and Realities Governing the Use of Force

The Allied Powers established the United Nations as a keystone of the postwar international security system. The norms and ideals of the United Nations, however, followed a path similar to that of Article 9 of Japan's Constitution. On the one hand, the norms of Articles 2(4) and 51 of the U.N. Charter, which prohibit the use of force except for self-defense, have been sanctified through repeated citation, confirmation, and reconfirmation by the member states, resolutions of the U.N. and major international conferences, judgments of the International Court of Justice, and the media institutions. On the other hand, many states, including the permanent members of the Security Council, have time and again resorted to armed force.[22] Most of these unilateral uses of force fail to pass muster under a literal interpretation of Article 51. In this way, by the end of the Cold War period, a gap became apparent between the norms and the realities of the use of force by states.[23]

Many experts have said that the malfunctioning of the Security Council was responsible for this gap. Norms banning the individual use of force by states were

---

22.   An array of literature dealing with armed conflicts during the postwar period exists. According to *An Agenda for Peace, Report of the Secretary-General Boutros Boutros-Ghali*, U.N., 47th Sess., U.N. Doc. A/47/277/S/24111 (1992), there have been more than one hundred armed conflicts and twenty million victims.

23.   Various justifications for the use of force beyond what would be allowed under a strict interpretation of Article 51 have been given: (1) a customary right of self-defense remains in addition to the right of self-defense under Article 51; (2) since the ban on the individual use of force presupposes a collective security system, member states are released from their obligations under the Charter if the system does not function well; (3) humanitarian intervention to rescue thousands of innocent people is not prohibited even if it involves the use of armed force by individual states; (4) the unilateral use of force to protect nationals abroad is lawful either in itself or as a matter of self-defense; (5) the use of force in case of necessity is not prohibited either in itself or as a matter of self-defense; (6) the use of force for liberation from colonial rule is legitimate. *See* ŌNUMA, *supra* note 7, at 185–87, 198 n. 47.

backed by sanctions under Chapter 7 of the U.N. Charter, and resort to sanctions required a unanimous decision of the permanent members of the Security Council. The Soviet-U.S. confrontation, however, made this unanimity impossible. Although these explanations for the gap between norms and realities are not incorrect, there are other factors responsible as well.

First, U.N. sanctions require participants to make great sacrifices. For nations that maintain substantial trade relationships with a delinquent state, economic sanctions often result in an abrupt end to essential imports from, or profitable exports to, the delinquent state. Military sanctions are *de facto* wars, which may entail loss of life, huge military costs, and other sacrifices on the part of the sanctioning states. It is difficult for leaders to persuade their own citizens to make such sacrifices for the lofty cause of a collective security that does not necessarily involve their direct interests. Second, a literal interpretation of Article 51 does not address strategic considerations in the age of missiles and nuclear weapons. Third, the use of force to liberate people from colonial rule or end genocide is difficult to condemn, even if it does not satisfy the requirements of Article 51. Fourth, U.N. mechanisms do not provide remedies for victims of unlawful acts that do not constitute armed attacks. Nor are U.N. mechanisms adequate to rectify an unjust status quo. Partly because of these flaws, major powers capable of protecting their rights and interests by their own means have often resorted to the use of force for such purposes. Although these unilateral actions have been criticized, many have nonetheless been carried out with success. Fifth, while the U.N. security system basically assumes that the interstate use of force is a wrong to be suppressed, most postwar armed violence has taken the form of civil war or a combination of civil war and interstate war. The categorical differentiation between Chapter 6 and Chapter 7 is ill-suited to this reality. Finally, the United Nations does not contemplate the use of sanctions against major military powers, such as the permanent members of the Security Council. As such, the United Nations inherently lacks impartiality and tends to invite resentment on the part of small states and nonpermanent members of the Security Council.[24]

It is therefore understandable that many people, although enthusiastic about the United Nations immediately after the decline of the Soviet-Eastern European Bloc, soon became more "realistic," and now talk about "selective interventions" by the United States, or a conflict management system administered by a limited number of powerful, developed countries. These ideas, however, ignore other important

---

24. An overriding need for effective U.N. enforcement actions and to avoid armed conflicts among major powers may justify this apparent impartiality, which a far larger number of less powerful or smaller nations must accept. However, this impartiality is so manifest that it easily invites resentment and frustration unless the composition and the behavior of the permanent members are judged legitimate by other member nations. Over-representation of European powers, double standards for U.N. sanctions and frequent unilateral resort to armed forces by the permanent members have undermined this legitimacy. Recent demands for an increase in or a restructuring of the permanent membership of the Security Council reflect such dissatisfaction among nonpermanent members.

factors that will characterize our globe in the twenty-first century: a gradual but irreversible change in the distribution of power in favor of non-Western nations, continuing frustrations in the developing countries despite this shift in power, and a keen need for intercivilizational or transcivilizational legitimacy in the global security system.

b. Peace and Security in the Twenty-First Century

In the last decade of the twentieth century, the world changed. It is no longer the world of 1945, the year that the United Nations was founded on the basis of Allied victory over the Axis Powers. It is no longer the world of the postwar period, in which any concern or problem was subjugated to the fear of nuclear war between the superpowers. It is a world of constant civil wars, ethnic and religious violence, and more than twenty million refugees. It is a world in which "ethnic cleansing" and manmade starvation plague one part of the globe, while elsewhere people watch these appalling developments on television, perhaps discuss possible solutions, but basically do nothing.

People refer to such ethnic and religious antagonism, suppressed during the Cold War period, as a major cause of this gloomy picture. The destructive forces of religious "fanatics" and "fundamentalists" are said to be the most serious threat to global peace and security. Although I do not categorically deny this view, I believe that we must be aware of the more basic historical trends underlying these destructive forces.[25] One historical trend is the relative "decline" of the West. The other is the globalization of modern Western civilization. These historical trends apparently involve conflicts: conflicts within each respective trend as well as conflicts between them. Despite these conflicts, these two trends will simultaneously persist into the twenty-first century, and this very fact will bring about constant violence on a global scale.

In terms of political rule, economic production, and military strength, the Western powers were at their peak in the early twentieth century. Although the United States entered its heyday in the two decades following the end of World War II as the heir of the European powers, it cannot be denied that the West has seen its dominance and influence decrease in the late twentieth century. Decolonization on a global scale; the emergence of Japan as an economic power; the shift of economic activity from the North Atlantic to East Asia; and high crime, weakening family and communal values, and the huge gap and residential segregation between the educated, rich elites and the uneducated, poor masses (a "Third-Worldization" of the American society) are all symptomatic of this relative decline of the West. [26]

---

25. YASUAKI ŌNUMA, WAKOKU TO KYOKUTŌ NO AIDA [BETWEEN THE COUNTRY OF "WA" AND THE "FAR EAST"] 192–204 (1988).

26. Support for these arguments can be found in ŌNUMA, *supra* note 25; Yasuaki Ōnuma, *Remarks* In *Promoting Training and Awareness—The Tasks of Education in International Law,* 75 PROCEEDINGS OF THE AMERICAN SOCIETY OF INTERNATIONAL LAW 163-70 (1983);

More precisely, this is not a decline of the West. From the beginning of colonization through the twentieth century, Western powers exerted their power and ideology far out of proportion to their population and territory. Even as late as 1800, production in Europe and North America occupied less than thirty percent of the world production, whereas production in China and the Indo-Pakistan area occupied some fifty-five percent. It was only at the end of the nineteenth century that Europeans and North Americans, constituting about twenty percent of the world population, produced eighty-five percent of the world's goods and services.[27] Thus, the relative "decline" of the West is merely a return to normalcy: a more proper situation wherein peoples in various regions and with different cultures occupy their positions in a relatively equitable manner.[28]

At the same time, the "rise of the East" is due to the adoption of key aspects of modern Western civilization by the people of the East. Only by making full use of the tools of modern Western civilization could the people of the East attain independence, modernize their societies, fight against Western colonial powers, achieve economic progress, and enjoy constitutional freedoms and democracy. From one perspective, this may be viewed as a triumph of Western civilization. The "rise of the East" paradoxically reveals that at least some aspects of modern Western civilization have universal validity and utility beyond the boundaries of religion, culture, and civilization.[29] However, one cannot deny that this process of adopting Western tools has been, is, and will be accompanied by the transformation, and even destruction, of important aspects of Eastern civilization. This is one of the major reasons why this process involves conflict, resistance, and violence.

Let us take two examples: Japan and China. It is said that Japan represents a successful case of modernization, i.e., westernization.[30] It is true that the contemporary Japanese enjoy a constitutional democracy, a high standard of education and human rights, a prosperous market economy, the longest life expectancy in the world, high technology, and other similar advantages. Although Japan already had an economic, administrative, and intellectual basis for these achievements before westernization, it cannot be denied that many of these are the fruits of westernization. However, one should not forget that Japan once waged a

---

and Yasuki Ōnuma, *Pitfalls of Internationalization*, Vol. 4 No. 4 IHJ BULLETIN 1–5 (1984).

27. PAUL KENNEDY, THE RISE AND FALL OF THE GREAT POWERS 148–50 (1988).

28. By the same token, it is extraordinary that Japan, with two percent of the world population, produces more than fifteen percent of world GNP. This level cannot be maintained, and should be corrected in the future.

29. Samuel Huntington, in his alarming *Clash of Civilizations?* (FOREIGN AFF., Summer 1993, at 22–49), fails to grasp this paradoxical relationship between East and West. For a persuasive argument against Huntington, *see* Makoto Iokibe, *Shin sekai muchitsujo ron wo koete [Beyond the Theory of Chaotic World Order]* 31 ASUTEION 1–33 (1994).

30. In Eastern societies, modernization was more or less forced by dominant Western powers. As such, modernization in the East has taken the form of westernization and has been perceived, at least in part, as forced from outside.

war in the name of liberating Asia from Western dominance. Moreover, underlying Japan–U.S. economic frictions are various cultural factors deeply rooted in the respective societies.

It is true that culture does change over time. Japan has enormously transformed its culture, and sacrificed its traditional cultural identity to obtain the fruits of modernization. Loss of the traditional architecture and cityscape in Kyoto and other traditional regions, the decline of traditional arts such as Noh, Kyōgen, Bunraku, and many local folk arts, and the deterioration of traditional morals and ethics associated with family structure all demonstrate how much the Japanese people have sacrificed in the process of westernization. Still, the Japanese case involves relatively few sacrifices and psychological conflicts. Within East Asian civilizations, Japan had long been a peripheral nation, accustomed to accepting thoughts and ideas from the center of the civilization (i.e., China), and digesting and refining them according to its fashion. To Japan, acceptance of Western ideas and institutions has simply meant changing the source of importation. Even so, Japan has maintained significant cultural tensions with the West.

China posed, and will pose, an even more serious case of cultural conflicts. China, for most of its history, regarded itself as the center of the world. It was only a little more than a century ago that China had to abandon its long-lived sinocentrism to adopt foreign ideas and westernize its society. Today, the Chinese people are eager to learn from the outside world. However, as China becomes more powerful in economic and military terms, there will certainly arise far greater tensions and conflicts between China and the Western powers, especially the United States.

These tensions and conflicts will be far more serious than those seen today between Japan and the United States. On the one hand, it will be difficult for Western nations, especially the United States, to modify their didactic, missionary, sometimes self-righteous posture—based on their deeply rooted idea of universal values and a sense of superiority—toward China as well as other nations. On the other hand, the Chinese will find it difficult to accept various demands from the West as China becomes more powerful and self-confident. This tension will not be limited to relations between China and the United States. It arises, and will arise, more or less in any case involving emerging Eastern nations and the West.[31]

Still, many nations in Africa and South Asia will remain poor and chaotic in the first half of the twenty-first century. These regions will experience continuous armed conflicts due to economic, religious, ethnic, and other tensions and

---

31. Even Lee Kwan Yu, a Western-educated and Western-oriented statesman, has turned out to be one of the most ardent critics of Western arrogance and self-righteousness. *See* Lee Kwan Yu, *Jinken gaikō wa machigatte iru* [*Human Rights Diplomacy Is Wrong!*] SHOKUN 140–149 (Sept. 1993). I am somewhat critical of him because his claim can be easily abused by authoritarian regimes to rationalize serious violations of human rights. However, I share his view that unless the Western powers, especially the United States, become less arrogant and try to understand different cultures, even the lofty task of enhancing human rights on a global scale will be regarded as cultural imperialism.

antagonisms. In all probability, there will continue to be acts of terrorism coming from such regions. These peoples will remain frustrated as a result of the continuing economic gap between the North and South, and within the South itself; as a result of the double standards the North applies in "sanctions" against delinquent states; and because the United Nations often appears to be a tool for political maneuvering by the North.

Western powers have responded to such threats by sending forces abroad with various justifications: to protect their citizens abroad, for self-defense, at the invitation of legitimate government, for humanitarian reasons, for the sake of democracy, and for other "lofty" principles. Under the "selective intervention" scenario, or a "North-centric" conflict-management scenario, Western powers, especially the United States, will not refrain from such unilateral military intervention, although they will try to obtain authorization from the United Nations in order to legitimize their actions.

Such unilateral actions, however, cannot bring about fundamental solutions. They may prove to be successful as temporary solutions, but will further strengthen resentment by the South. Consolidated U.N. enforcement actions are much more desirable, but there is no assurance that China will agree to actions that lack global legitimacy. In addition, even U.N. actions are not free of the flaws of North-centric conflict-management. Unless the South regards the United Nations as an impartial organ equitably representing the global community, even U.N. enforcement actions will be viewed as interventions by the North in disguise.

Thus, neither an unipolar nor a collective North-centric conflict management system can support a stable universal security system of the kind needed to cope with the conflicts and violence foreseeable in the coming world. Even the consolidated U.N. security system is by itself insufficient. A conflict management system that minimizes the frustration of the poorer, less developed South and incorporates the power and pride of the emerging Eastern nations must be established. Simply put, a global security system with intercivilizational legitimacy is needed. This entails a number of tasks,[32] but in this article I limit myself to two points: overall disarmament both in the North and in the South, and the strengthening of the United Nations.

Disarmament and collective security are fundamentally complementary to and dependent upon one another. For U.N. military sanctions to function in an effective and relatively impartial manner, armament by a possible peace-breaking state, i.e., any member state, must be minimal. Otherwise, other member states will fear losing their own citizens when fighting the delinquent state and will hesitate to participate in U.N. enforcement efforts. The reluctance of Western nations to resort to military sanctions to end the tragedy in Bosnia-Herzegovina typifies this difficulty. Those who simply argue for the strengthening of the U.N. collective security system ignore this vital problem.

---

32. For a more comprehensive argument, *see* Ōnuma, *supra* note 7, at 191–201, 204–29.

On the other hand, for a state to radically disarm itself, an effective collective security system is needed. Otherwise, a state cannot be assured of its vital security and will seek military alliances based on the collective right of self-defense. This will impede the goal of collective security. A major reason that Japan concluded the Japan-U.S. Security Treaty was precisely this. The global collective security system, which Japan's idealistic Constitution assumed, proved to be ineffective immediately after it was enacted.

Naturally, global disarmament is not easily realized. Nor can it be expected that the United States and other major powers will refrain from the unilateral use of force in the immediate future. Still, some basic steps can be taken that will have a tremendous impact on the future of global security. If the U.N. collective security system becomes more effective, the unilateral use of force by major powers who do not resort to such a system can be more legitimately criticized. Such augmented legitimacy will make it difficult for decisionmakers to contemplate the individual use of force, and will thus contribute to its decline, if not its elimination. If substantial disarmament on the part of the present major military powers is accomplished, there will be a more legitimate basis for discouraging states such as China from seeking to increase their military capabilities. Conversely, if our efforts to strengthen the United Nations and to achieve a gradual disarmament are abandoned, the world will continue to face "selective" (i.e., arbitrary) intervention by self-righteous military powers, control by an illegitimate center over the use of force, and outbursts of (largely unpunished) violence. However futile they might appear, efforts must be made to strengthen the United Nations and global disarmament. Japan, with its precious heritage stemming from the "Peace Constitution," can lead this undertaking.

IV. PROMOTING GLOBAL PEACE AND SECURITY

There are at present three major options presented by politicians and opinion leaders regarding Japan's role in promoting global peace and security. First, Japan could adopt the policy of a "conscientious objector nation."[33] Proponents of this policy argue that Japan must not participate in any activity that may involve armed forces—even if such activity is organized as a U.N. enforcement or peacekeeping operation. Instead of engaging in military activities, they argue, Japan must contribute to global peace by engaging in solely nonmilitary activities. Policies aiming at positive peace rather than negative peace must be carried out. Second, Japan could pursue the policy of a "global civilian power."[34] Proponents of this view do not object to Japan's participation in U.N. peacekeeping activities. They are reluctant, however, to participate in U.N. enforcement actions involving armed

---

33. Toshiki Mogami, *Ryōshin teki heieki kyohi koku no akashi no tame ni* [*A Plea for a Conscientious Objector Nation*] *in* 23–34 SEKAI (Nov. 1990).

34. NIHON SENRYAKU SENGEN [CIVILIAN MANIFESTO] 13–18 *passim* (Yōichi Hunabashi ed., 1991).

forces. They also emphasize that Japan must make full use of its huge nonmilitary capabilities to establish a stable peace and an equitable global order. Third, Japan could attempt to become a "normal state."[35] At present, the most influential proponent of this view does not argue that Japan should make use of the SDF as a means of pursuing its national interests. The very image of a "normal state," however, is borrowed from the United States and other Western powers; thus, this view does not exclude the possibility of sending the SDF to protect Japanese nationals and vested interests abroad.

I basically share the second view. At the same time, I believe that previous discussions of Japan's peace and security policy have paid excessive attention to the question of whether it involves the use of force, and have failed to consider another important issue: whether such force is used to pursue Japan's national interests or to realize international public values under the internationally authoritative organization such as the United Nations. If this perspective is appreciated, I see no reason why proponents of the second view should differentiate between U.N. peacekeeping operations on one hand, and the activities of peace enforcement units and U.N. forces under Articles 42 and 43 on the other.

In the field of disarmament and strengthening of the U.N. referred to earlier, Japan's major tasks should be threefold: to propound an aggressive disarmament policy based on its economic power, to make impartial efforts to restructure the U.N., and to gradually "internationalize" the SDF.

As described in Section III, the pursuit of global disarmament is essential to a stable and less violent global order. One way to pursue this global disarmament policy is to combine it with the Official Development Aid (ODA) policy, thereby making full use of Japan's mighty economic power.

Japan has long failed to articulate its world view and the ideals underlying its enormous ODA. As described in section II, postwar Japan has been firmly committed to the value of peace and has pursued an exceptionally pacifist policy among major powers. Since the end of the war, Japan has never sent its military forces abroad in pursuit of its own interests. Unlike other industrialized nations, Japan has not gained enormous profit by exporting arms. These facts should put Japan in a legitimate position to assert that other nations should follow suit. Yet the Japanese government has failed to take advantage of Japan's distinctive status.[36] It relied on the "Peace Constitution," which has been an important basis of the pacifist policy, only as an excuse to resist U.S. pressure to radically increase Japan's

---

35. ICHIRO OZAWA, NIHON KAIZO KEIKAKU [A PLAN FOR RESTRUCTURING JAPAN] 102–105 *passim* (1993).

36. One reason for this failure is another failure of the government to admit Japan's war guilt. Since the Japanese government was humiliated by not having admitted its manifest guilt, it was difficult to make use of its legitimate pacifist position and to urge other nations to follow suit.

military budget and capabilities.[37]   As late as June 1992, the Japanese government adopted the Four Basic Guidelines of its ODA, which in part expresses considerations for peace and disarmament. The Guidelines require Japan to:

- refrain from [allowing Japan's ODA to be] used for military purposes and for facilitating international disputes;
- maintain and strengthen international peace and stability, as well as pay attention to trends in recipients' military expenditures and their policy on development and production of missiles and mass destruction weapons, and importation of weaponry.

These guidelines are better than nothing, but not enough. Japan should make it explicit that it will use a substantial portion of its ODA to encourage recipients' efforts toward gradual disarmament. Although "conditionalities" have become almost synonymous with coercion and arrogance on the part of the North, it still should be possible to use ODA as a positive sanction for the realization of common values such as global peace and human rights.[38] This is especially true in Japan's case, for Japan's ODA policy has been less conducive to the realization of such values than the policies of other donor nations. For example, a certain portion of Japan's ODA should be earmarked for converting a recipient's military industry to civilian industry and for training former military personnel for civilian jobs and other civilian purposes.

Japan's second major task is to support a radical restructuring of the United Nations. The present U.N. system reflects the power structure of 1945 and fails to correspond to present realities and emerging global aspirations. If Japan and Germany continue to be excluded from permanent membership on the Security Council, they will continue to seek an equivalent position in the Group of Seven (G7). This is not desirable, because the G7 possesses neither global legitimacy nor legal and organizational restraints on dominant powers, which the United Nations, though insufficiently, does. Similarly, if the developing countries continue to be underrepresented in the Security Council, their frustration and resentment will be

---

37. Military threats by the former Soviet Union have been a major reason for this negative attitude. Since Japan relied on the military power of the United States to defend itself, the successive LDP governments felt it difficult to vocally assert the universal value of Japan's pacifist policy.

38. A considerable number of Western nations has taken into consideration the human rights situation of ODA recipient nations. However, they have been reluctant to consider factors affecting miliatry budgets and other military-related matters from international public perspective, partly because they have profited themselves by exporting weapons to such recipient nations. (The U.S. strategic consideration in its ODA policy has been based on the perspective of its own interest, not necessarily the perspective of global peace and security.) Japan must take a lead in changing this "merchant of death" policy of the developed countries.

so augmented that even their relatively more rational leaders will find it difficult to rein in extremists and to control outbursts of violence in and from the South.

A restructuring of the United Nations will certainly undermine the excessively privileged status of the United Kingdom and France. It will also impair the present cooperation among the Permanent Five (or at least among the Permanent Four). An inability to act promptly, irritating even today to some of the interventionists in the North, especially in the United States, may become even more conspicuous due to difficulties in reaching consensus among the extended permanent members. To minimize these flaws, developed countries must constantly demand and pressure countries representing the South to behave rationally. In addition, the U.N. decisionmaking mechanism should be changed: for example, the votes of at least two permanent members should be required to block an enforcement action.

Tardiness is often a cost of global consensus. We live in a world where some people must live with U.S. $100 per capita national income and others enjoy U.S. $30,000 or more. It is a world in which, for the majority, nation-building is the most important task, yet for some, democracy, human rights, and the environment, all surpassing the value of the nation, are absolute values. It is a world gradually moving from Eurocentrism to multiculturalism and intercivilizationalism. In such a world, we need global institutions and mechanisms that can equitably represent the shifting power, values, interests, and aspirations of the emerging global community. If we maintain the institutions and mechanisms that reflected the power structure and the dominant values of 1945, and fail to recognize new realities and aspirations, such institutions can neither adjust to nor solve the vital problems of our globe. The European powers, especially the United Kingdom and France, should realize that a decrease in their weightiness within global decisionmaking institutions is a part of the "return to normalcy" process described above. This realization would greatly contribute to a more equitable and less violent future global order.

Together with the restructuring of the United Nations, Japan should fully participate in the peacekeeping and peace-enforcing activities of the United Nations. These activities include traditional peacekeeping operations as well as maintenance of peace enforcement units and the U.N. forces under Article 43 of the Charter (provided the latter two become institutionalized). This would require a radical change in the peace and security policy of postwar Japan. According to the established interpretation by the government, the use of force is prohibited by the Constitution even if it is under the auspices of the United Nations.[39] This interpretation fails, however, to distinguish between the use of force by individual states in pursuing their own interests and the use of force by the U.N. to maintain and restore international peace. It is possible to construe the present Constitution as allowing such international public action. Thus, full participation by Japan in U.N. peacekeeping and peace enforcement activities is possible even under the present Constitution. It may well be said that such activities are in complete consonance with the spirit of the Constitution because its Preamble provides that

---

39. *See supra* note 19.

"We, the Japanese people . . . have determined to preserve our security and existence, trusting in the justice and faith of the peace-loving peoples of the world. We desire to occupy an honored place in international society striving for the preservation of peace. . . ."[40]

On the other hand, one may doubt whether it is desirable to bring such a radical change in the fundamental policy concerning the peace and security of Japan and the international society by means of a change in interpretation of the Constitution. To avoid possible cynicism among ordinary citizens, who may doubt that such fundamental change is possible by merely changing the interpretation of the Constitution, it is probably more desirable that this change be made by means of amending the Constitution. Moreover, Japan's peace policy, including participation in the U.N. peacekeeping and peace enforcement operations, must be pursued into the twenty-first century. By then the present Constitution will be more than fifty years old, and likely in need of other amendments as well to respond to realities and aspirations of the time. These include such issues as the protection of the environment, intergenerational equity, protection of ethnic minorities, and distribution of power between central governments and local municipalities. Thus, there may be other reasons as well to amend the Constitution in the twenty-first century.[41] Possible negative reactions by neighboring Asian nations against the amendment of Article 9 should be mitigated if Japan assumes full responsibilities for its past aggressive wars and colonial rule, restricts the dispatch of the SDF to only contributing to U.N. forces, and strictly maintains the pacifist policy taken thus far.

This will lead us to Japan's third task: to gradually "internationalize" its SDF. To appreciate the importance of this task, one must understand the peculiar features of the Japan-U.S. Security Treaty. The Treaty provides in Article 5 for a U.S. commitment to defend Japan but not for Japan's commitment to defend the United States: hence the argument that Japan is a free rider. On the other hand, Article 6 of the Treaty grants the United States the use of military facilities and areas in Japan, not only for the security of Japan but also for the "international peace and security of the Far East."[42] When and how this requirement is satisfied is to be judged mainly from the perspective of U.S. global strategy. Hence the argument that Japan would become entangled in American wars against the former Soviet Union.

The Treaty was a product of the Cold War, reflecting a power gap that then existed between the United States and Japan. In the early twenty-first century, the

---

40. *See supra* note 13.

41. I do not argue that Japan should amend Article 9 immediately. Such a hasty move is neither desirable nor politically feasible. I do argue, however, that Japanese people should seriously consider Japanese fundamental ideals and philosophies in the twenty-first century global community. This requires, among other things, a serious national debate over the possible amendment of the present Constitution.

42. SHUYŌ JŌYAKU SHŪ [COLLECTION OF MAJOR TREATIES] 115–16 (Gaimushō Jōyaku Kyoku [Ministry of Foreign Affairs, Treaty Bureau] ed. 1986).

Treaty will likely be revised. Otherwise, both parties will be frustrated, though for different reasons: the United States, although appreciating the Treaty's importance as a keystone of multilayered bilateral relations, will be frustrated by an apparent unilateral obligation under Article 5; Japan, though sharing a similar appreciation, will be frustrated by a possible entanglement in armed conflicts as a result of Article 6 (especially in China) and its apparent inequality.

On the other hand, some Asian nations are still fearful of a resurgence of Japanese militarism. Given the deeply rooted pacifist sentiment of the Japanese people, influential pacifist mass media institutions, and strict civilian control in Japan, this fear is groundless. In fact, this fear has steadily been decreasing.[43] Nevertheless, if Japan amends Article 9, the fear will inevitably be heightened. It will be heightened even further if Japan and the United States revise the Japan-U.S. Security Treaty and the former obtains a more independent status. These new circumstances would certainly invite further suspicions from neighboring nations.

To avoid such suspicion, Japan should seek to conclude an agreement with the United Nations to the effect that the United Nations will have a certain influence over Japan's decision to send the SDF abroad. The purpose of this agreement would not only be to avoid suspicion. Article 51 of the U.N. Charter requires member states to report to the Security Council measures taken in the exercise of the right of self-defense and seeks to control the unilateral use of force as much as possible.[44] The past failure to meet this requirement on the part of many member states claiming self-defense is simply wrong and must be rectified. Most importantly, it is essential for the survival of the human species in the twenty-first century that a portion of national sovereignty gradually be delegated to international organizations. If Japan can take the lead in subjecting its SDF to a kind of dual jurisdiction wielded by Japan and the United Nations, it will provide a model for other nations.

Naturally, such an undertaking cannot be easily executed. Japan, as an independent sovereign nation, must carefully observe whether the restructured U.N. is sufficiently reliable to assume this role and whether other conditions are favorable to such a critical decision. However, even if Japan should use force when required to fulfill its role in U.N. activities to maintain global peace and security, it must not spoil its precious heritage: the spirit of peace. In the twenty-first century, Japan should, and most likely will, amend its present Constitution and perform its global

---

43. The success of the peace-keeping operations in Cambodia [UNTAC], in which the SDF was a contingent, greatly contributed to mitigating the suspicion of a "resurgence of Japanese militarism."

44. Article 51 of the U.N. Charter intends to control the right of self-defense by limiting its exercise "until the Security Council has taken the measures necessary to maintain international peace and security" and by providing that "[m]easures taken by Members in the exercise of this right of self-defense shall be immediately reported to the Security Council and shall not . . . affect the authority and responsibility of the Security Council . . . to take . . . such actions as it deems necessary in order to maintain or restore international peace and security."

tasks. At the same time, however, the spirit of peace symbolized by the present Constitution must be strictly preserved. For it is the most precious legacy that the Japanese were given, and have fostered, through the sacrifice of a huge number of victims, both Japanese and non-Japanese, in the war.

THE UNITED NATIONS AND NATO: THE LIMITS OF COOPERATION BETWEEN INTERNATIONAL ORGANIZATIONS

Edwin M. Smith

Because of changes in the global order, international institutions must now face both new opportunities and new problems. These new opportunities and problems have forced both general and limited international organizations to evaluate their founding assumptions and their accepted institutional routines and traditions. In fact, serious crises confront both types of international organizations founded in the aftermath of World War II. The continued survival of those organizations may well depend on the ability to adapt to a changed reality by combining their strengths and capabilities to respond to evolving crises. International institutions may also find that effective responses to international emergencies may depend on the cooperation and support of particular member states. If an international organization must depend either on other international institutions or on powerful member states to accomplish its ostensible objectives, then legal analyses of the organization's constitutional documents may lead to a false expectation that it will have the practical power to respond to international emergencies. On the contrary, constraints generated by those whose assistance is necessary can create an image of an organization that is subservient to alien and partisan interests.

New opportunities for international organizations have been touted because institutions which were paralyzed by cold war confrontation have apparently been freed to take action. In some cases, collective undertakings have been initiated that would have been unthinkable in the context of the superpower standoff. For example, an unaccustomed unanimity among the five permanent members of the United Nations Security Council created the appearance that new common objectives were shared on a broad range of issues, allowing institutional arrangements long dismissed as beyond repair to be deployed in novel ways to meet unanticipated emergencies.

The same changes that appeared to create new opportunities for international organizations have provided catalysts for frightening new dangers. The collapse of a rigid bilateral order increased the importance of new and different actors in the international arena. Long accustomed to being the sole claimants of legitimate recognition in the international arena, states began this century by conceding some status to the international organizations which were their creations. By the middle of the century, the evolution of new norms of international human rights raised the potential for individuals to be claimants of rights as against states. At the same time, groups claiming selfdetermination asserted collectively authorized rights against reluctant and resistant colonial rulers. Ethnic conflicts that had been constrained within autocratic states have erupted in ghastly profusion, raising the danger of widespread crossborder insecurity.

As part of their responses to these new problems and opportunities, multilateral institutions have initiated new means of cooperating in response to the changing order. Two of these organizations, the United Nations and the North Atlantic Treaty Organization (NATO), have faced particular difficulties in making these adjustments.[1] The United Nations, a universal political body with a mandate to respond generally to international threats, has recognized that it needs assistance in bringing the appropriate capabilities to bear on the new types of threats. The U.N. has begun to explore modes of cooperation with more limited functional bodies that have particularly essential capabilities. NATO, a limited alliance made up of like-minded Western democracies, has begun to face the disappearance of the threat that justified its existence for more than forty years, seeking ways to maintain its usefulness by exploring new forms of cooperation with other multilateral institutions. The U.N. and NATO, sharing incentives that appear to be compatible, have begun some new cooperative initiatives. Recent joint operations involving the U.N. and NATO in the former Yugoslavia provide examples of these new patterns. In practical terms, officials of these organizations have developed new practical understandings of the implications of the traditional concept of "regional organizations" under Chapter VIII of the United Nations Charter. While these new understandings may offer new possibilities in fashioning responses to international crises, they also raise some serious new risks to accepted roles and responsibilities among these institutions.

International changes have also forced the leaders of member states of these organizations to reevaluate the risks and rewards of involvement in international organizations. As multilateral institutions engage in new and different activities in changed circumstances, member states have been forced to confront fundamental questions about the foundational assumptions upon which original membership had

---

1.   For an excellent survey of the recent literature on the United Nations, *see* Gene M. Lyons, *A New Collective Security: The United Nations and International Peace*, 17 THE WASHINGTON QUARTERLY 2 (Spring 1994).

been based. In most developed democracies, this reconsideration of traditional multilateral involvements occurs during a period of some skepticism among citizens about the costs and risks involved in any sort of international involvement. This skepticism has led some democratic leaders to respond with reserve when requested to commit troops and resources to multilateral peace operations. Other leaders, recognizing the greater likelihood of domestic acquiescence to action to protect important national interests, have indicated greater willingness to resort to forceful unilateral action in such cases while rejecting the constraints and risks that are inherent in significant involvement in new multilateral initiatives toward peace operations. In the United States, the adoption of Presidential Decision Directive 25 on Peace Operations reflects a sobering rethinking of prior assertions of commitment to multilateral responses to international threats.

New questions raised by political groupings among democratic electorates have forced elected officials to recalculate the value of international involvement. At the same time, these political groupings continue to press their domestically framed interests in ways that frustrate the consistent formation of official foreign policy. In addition, advances in international travel and communications have made it possible for these subnational groupings of citizens to contact like-minded citizens in other states, enabling them to generate crossborder pressures and to exploit personal transnational connections in pursuit of goals that are, in effect, subnational foreign policies. These subnational foreign policies serve to make formal international commitments by state governments more controversial to enter into and more troublesome to implement.

In order to examine more closely the potential for cooperation between international organizations under these circumstances, this chapter will now explore the increasing number of instances of joint action between the United Nations and NATO. Several important questions remain as to the types of organizations that can engage in this cooperation and the types of joint activities that show a reasonable prospect of success. By inquiring into recent initiatives involving NATO and the U.N., it may be possible to reach realistic general conclusions about the probable results of combined efforts in pursuing peace operations. At the same time, it may be possible to develop a better understanding of the limitations imposed on any collective action in peace operations by the frailties of national and international political consensus.

I. DISTINCTIONS: LIOs, GIOs, FUNCTIONAL IOs, AND POLITICAL IOs

Many commentators may promote regional organizations as potential partners for universal organizations. Both types of entities face the same limiting foundational assumptions: the primacy of the interests and concerns of individual member states in both defining threats and implementing responses. Universal organizations and regional groupings face many of the same constraints in responding to threats to international peace and security. More importantly, regional and universal organizations may occasionally possess compatible and complementary abilities for responding to threats to international peace and security. Greater refinement of our understanding of the variations among existing organizations might facilitate analysis of the potential for cooperation among international organizations.

In considering the evolving interaction between the United Nations and other organizations, some preliminary observations may clarify the issues. International organizations may be considered along two dimensions.[2] International organizations may have general membership, holding themselves open to all qualified states who may wish to pursue membership. Alternatively, they may limit their membership by some agreed-upon intrinsic criteria, allowing only certain states to join. At the same time, international organizations may pursue general political goals related to all aspects of the relations among their member states, or they may pursue specific functional objectives related to narrowly specified elements of the relationships among the member states. Both general and limited organizations may be either political or functional. Under this analysis, the U.N. exemplifies a general political organization, while the Organization of American States would constitute a limited political organization. Similarly, the International Labor Organization qualifies as a general functional organization, while the European Free Trade Association fits the category of limited functional organizations.

To the extent that threats to peace and security do not come from states, limited international organizations (LIOs) may be no more capable than general international organizations (GIOs) in providing solutions. On the other hand, if viable conflict resolution strategies can be found, LIOs or GIOs with functional capabilities may have special capabilities in playing functional roles. At present, many of the necessary capabilities are now found in specialized international organizations, some of which may have arisen out of a regional initiative. In fact, since most current international organizations have been established for specialized functional purposes, LIOs may be the principal repositories for many necessary political and technical capabilities.

Several hypotheses should be explored to clarify possible roles for LIOs in responding to crises involving international peace and security. First, unless LIOs have either a political or technical capability, they can rarely offer much to the dispute resolution process that is not otherwise available through GIOs. LIOs may have special political competencies or organizational relationships that allow them to play a significant role. Along these lines, the Organization on Security and Cooperation in Europe may provide the legitimacy that would permit multilateral action that might otherwise appear to be problematic. Other LIOs may bring

---

2. For an illuminating analysis on these lines, *see* CLIVE ARCHER, INTERNATIONAL ORGANIZATIONS 38–70 (2d ed. 1992). With due recognition of the growing artificiality of the categorization, this part of the discussion is limited to relations between states in intergovernmental organizations.

particular military or technical capabilities that are essential for the success of peace operations. In either of these cases, LIO participation may be valuable. Without these special capacities, the contribution of LIOs may remain doubtful.

Second, even without any formal involvement by an LIO, individual member states of LIOs can play useful roles in GIO initiatives whenever appropriate. For example, NATO member states participated in the Persian Gulf coalition without the imprimatur of formal NATO authorization. In the same conflict, member states of the Western European Union also participated without the formal involvement of their organization. The common training and doctrine of these individual member states played an important role in Operation Desert Storm, while the military infrastructure of NATO greatly facilitated the movement of forces to the Gulf region.

Finally, unless LIOs themselves have a functional component involving unique technical or military capabilities, they can contribute little to risky peace operations. While member states may offer troops or facilities, most LIOs lack the ability to make unique practical contributions to these initiatives. The Organization of African Unity proved to be unable to offer these essential elements to UNISOM II[3] in Somalia. In contrast, NATO has provided such technical capabilities to UNPROFOR[4] in the former Yugoslavia.

For the purposes of this discussion, it is helpful to think of the United Nations as a general political organization that is seeking the assistance of other organizations in tailoring its responses to international crises. If NATO is considered on first analysis to be a functional limited organization, it appears to offer special capabilities that have a particular value for the United Nations in the conduct of peace operations. The purpose of this general discussion is to evaluate the viability of interorganizational cooperation based on such assumptions.

II. THE UNITED NATIONS AND NATO

In adjusting to the demands of the changed international context, the United Nations has sought new relationships with other organizations, including the North Atlantic Treaty Organization. Faced with its own limitations in peacekeeping, the U.N. has recognized that "[t]he sheer size and complexity of peacekeeping operations makes it imperative to explore new avenues of cooperation with regional organizations such as NATO."[5] At the same time, certain limited

---

3.   United Nations Operation in Somalia II, authorized under S.C. Res 814 (Mar. 26, 1993).

4.   United Nations Protection Forces, authorized under S.C. Res 743 (Feb. 21, 1992).

5.   Kofi Annan, *U.N. Peacekeeping Operations and Cooperation with NATO*, 41 NATO REVIEW, No. 5 (Nov. 1993), WWW URL gopher://gopher.nato.int:70/00/natodata/ NATOREVIEW/1993–1994/9305–1. Annan is United Nations Under-Secretary -General for Peacekeeping Operations.

552 Trilateral Perspectives on International Legal Issues

multilateral institutions designed for narrow, specific purposes related to perceived security threats have witnessed the disorienting disappearance of historic confrontations that provided the *raisons d'être* for their existence. In particular, the North Atlantic Treaty Organization struggled with the demise of the Soviet Union, removing the massive conventional threat that had provided the impetus for the formation of the transatlantic security alliance. As a consequence, NATO has repeatedly announced its commitment to involvement "in a framework of interlocking institutions" so that international organizations will be able "to make available their specific assets and expertise for the settlement of regional crises or conflicts in a complementary way . . . ."[6] The United Nations has been expressly included as one to the organizations within that framework.[7]

Both the United Nations and NATO have sought means by which they can collaborate in responding to threats to international peace and security. Both organizations have adopted formal declarations which reflect early considerations of the relative roles that each might play in regard to questions of international peace and security. With respect to the former Yugoslavia, the United Nations has repeatedly authorized cooperation with regional organizations in peacekeeping.[8]

---

6. John Kriendler, *NATO's Changing Role: Opportunities and Constraints For Peacekeeping*, 43 NATO REVIEW, No. 5 (July 1993), WWW URL gopher://gopher.nato.int:70/00/natodata/NATOREVIEW/1993–1994/9303–4. Kriendler is Deputy Assistant Secretary-General for Political Affairs and Director, Political Directorate, of NATO.

7. *Id.*, citing Final Communiqué of the Ministerial Meeting of the North Atlantic Council, Brussels, Belgium, Dec. 17, 1992, NATO Press Communiqué M-NAC-2(92)106.

8. In   S.C. Res. 781, para. 5 (Oct. 9, 1992), the Security Council authorized cooperation with regional organizations to enforce a ban on military flights in Bosnia and Herzegovina, and "[calling] upon States to take nationally or through regional agencies or arrangements all measures necessary to provide assistance to United Nations Protection Force, based on technical monitoring and other capabilities . . . ."

In S.C. Res. 787, para. 12   (Nov. 16, 1992), the Security Council authorized cooperation with regional organizations to enforce economic sanctions by inspection of naval vessels:

[a]cting under Chapters VII and VIII of the Charter of the United Nations, [the Security Council] calls upon States, acting nationally or through regional agencies or arrangements, to use such measures commensurate with the specific circumstances as may be necessary under the authority of the Security Council to halt all inward and outward maritime shipping in order to inspect and verify their cargoes and destinations and to ensure strict implementation of the provisions of resolutions 713 (1991) and 757 (1992).

In S.C. Res. 836, para. 10 (June 4, 1993), the Security Council expanded its authorization of the reliance on regional organizations to include the protection of UNPROFOR forces within declared safe havens:

[m]ember States, acting nationally or through regional organizations or arrangements, may take, under the authority of the Security Council and subject to close coordination with the Secretary-General and UNPROFOR, all necessary

NATO has officially expressed its willingness to become involved selectively in United Nations peacekeeping.[9]

However, substantial room for disagreement and misunderstanding still remains. While the parties who drafted the U.N. Charter contemplated a function for regional organizations in the preservation of peace and security, they did not anticipate that regional organizations would develop into sophisticated institutions offering superior capabilities of the sort necessary for U.N. operations. After some initial disagreement, the drafters of the Charter established an arrangement in which the United Nations held primary authority for managing the collective response threats to international peace and security. The proposed Dumbarton Oaks mechanism allowed use of regional organizations for enforcement only when authorized by the Security Council.[10] However, criticisms in San Francisco of the

---

measures, through the use of air power, in and around the safe areas in the Republic of Bosnia and Herzegovina, to support UNPROFOR in the performance of its mandate . . . .

Note that none of these resolutions refers specifically to NATO as a "regional organization or arrangement."

9.   The North Atlantic Council, the governing body of NATO, affirmed its readiness to cooperate with the United Nations:

[w]e confirm today the preparedness of our Alliance to support, on a case-by-case basis and in accordance with our own procedures, peacekeeping operations under the authority of the U.N. Security Council, which has the primary responsibility for international peace and security. We are ready to respond positively to initiatives that the U.N. Secretary-General might take to seek Alliance assistance in the implementation of U.N. Security Council Resolutions. We have asked NATO's Secretary General to maintain in this respect, under the guidance of the Council in Permanent Session, the necessary contacts with the Secretary-General of the U.N. regarding the assistance that the Alliance could provide.

Final Communiqué, *supra* note 7. That commitment was recently reiterated:

[w]e reaffirm the importance we attach to enhanced relations with other institutions. Over the past six months, the Alliance's relationship with the U.N. has developed greatly. The Alliance has demonstrated its readiness and its capacity to support on a case by case basis, peacekeeping and other operations under the authority of the U.N. Security Council. We will work for further improvement in the mutual understanding and the close cooperation between NATO and the U.N.

Press Communiqué M-NAC-1(94)46 (June 9, 1994), Final Communiqué of the Ministerial Meeting of the North Atlantic Council in Istanbul, June 9, 1994.

10.   I LUARD, A HISTORY OF THE UNITED NATIONS 51–54 (19xx). The initial proposal formed the basis for the provision of the Charter that addresses the role of regional organizations. U.N. CHARTER, art. 53, para. 1. The Dumbarton Oaks draft "came under sustained attack at San Francisco, from the Latin Americans in particular. These states had only recently joined in setting up their own regional system . . . under which each member undertook to defend others which were under attack." LUARD at 52.

Dumbarton Oaks proposals led to revisions of the proposed Charter to legitimate immediate interim collective response to threats as "self-defense."[11] Even this hierarchial system of regional arrangements was overtaken by Cold War confrontation, as the United States and its allies formed a system of regional security organizations that operated outside of the authorization of the Security Council.[12] These regional security organizations dominated the scene for some time, but their era seemed to have ended with the demise of the Cold War. However, recognition by the United Nations of its need for assistance in coping with new crises coincided with the realization by NATO that its mission had to be adapted to the post–Cold War era. Unfortunately, while the interests and incentives of these organizations may appear to be similar, disparities in their capabilities and orientations may cause significant dilemmas.

At present, the relative strengths and weaknesses of NATO and the United Nations have generated demonstrable problems in joint responses to crises. Recent events in the former Yugoslavia illustrate some of the difficulties involved in joint action by the United Nations and NATO. After a smooth initiation, frictions have developed which reflect differences in the purposes, structures and cultures of these international institutions. Few problems arose in NATO's initial implementation of air patrols in Operation Deny Flight and naval patrols in Operation Sharp Guard in support of U.N. resolutions related to protection of humanitarian assistance and economic sanctions respectively.[13] However, once pressures arose to employ NATO air power to terminate Serbian action against declared safe havens, differing perceptions of appropriate preconditions for air strikes and inconsistent command and control procedures caused some difficulties.[14] In other contexts, criticism of U.N. management of peacekeeping and peace enforcement operations heightened the skepticism of the organization's capabilities in these areas.[15]

While the United Nations has received criticism for its failure to respond

---

11. U.N. CHARTER, art. 51. That provision preserves "the inherent right of individual *or collective* self defense if an armed attack occurs . . . until the Security Council has taken measures necessary. . . ." (emphasis added). *See* LUARD, *supra* note 10.

12. ROBERT E. RIGGS & JACK C. PLANO, THE UNITED NATIONS: INTERNATIONAL POLITICS AND WORLD ORGANIZATION 111–12 (2nd ed. 1994).

13. In fact, the latter operation was conducted jointly with another regional organization, the Western European Union. For recent reports on the actions of these two operations, *see* Allied Forces South, Fact Sheet on the NATO/WEU Operation "Sharp Guard," June 2, 1994; Allied Forces South, Fact Sheet on the NATO/WEU Operation "Deny Flight," June 2, 1994 (copies on file with the author).

14. Nicholas Doughty, *NATO Poised for Gorazde Strikes as Deadline Nears*, Reuters, Apr. 23, 1994.

15. A recent unpublished U.N. report on problems in the events surrounding military operations in UNISOM II rehearses many of the difficulties. *See, e.g.,* Stanley Meisler, *A Red-Faced United Nations Keeps Lid On Somalia Report*, L.A. TIMES, May 21, 1994, at A2.

decisively to the dangers of the new international situation, many have also criticized NATO for its lack of readiness to respond to the bloody conflict on its doorstep in the former Yugoslavia.[16] Even NATO officials have indicated that the alliance would not act unilaterally unless clear security threats to member states were involved:

> NATO is not prepared to undertake a peacekeeping operation on its own initiative; it is unlikely that such an approach would find consensus among the Allies. It is essential, as we see in the case of the former Yugoslavia, to work closely with the United Nations which has, in accordance with its Charter, the responsibility for the maintenance of international peace and security and can mandate the peacekeeping and, if necessary, peace enforcement action.[17]

While NATO may have overcome legally-based resistance to involvement in "out of area" exigencies, no political consensus exists in favor of aggressive action to restore international peace in the absence of overt aggression. The United Nations, having overcome political paralysis, faces doubts about its practical ability to undertake action extending beyond diplomacy and consensual interpositional deployments. The NATO alliance, having the necessary competence to impose significant coercive force, lacks the collective political will to take initiative.

Because of growing dissatisfaction with failures of multilateral institutions to address emergencies, citizens and governments of states have voiced skepticism about participation in collective responses to these crises. At the same time, responding to combined perceptions of the disappearance of traditional security threats and the upsurge of concern for economic performance, voters in democracies have expressed doubts that their governments should become substantially involved in risky and expensive ventures controlled by foreign bureaucrats. Very few political leaders find that there is political gain to be made from involvement in multilateral peace operations unless vital national interests are clearly involved. Given the central importance of domestic economic concerns in almost all democracies, peace operations have little relevance to the perceptions of "national interest" that drive national politics in those democracies. Their governments, recognizing the political dangers facing leaders held responsible for committing troops to peacekeeping missions involving the risk of casualties and accomplishing vague diplomatic objectives, have been reluctant to commit forces to peace operations.

These concerns have led to various political responses. For some states, the

---

16. *See* Edwin M. Smith, *NATO and the European Community: Troubled Transitions*, USC LAW 2–11 (Fall 1992).

17. Kriendler, *supra* note 6.

level of risk leads to a willingness to commit forces that will only play a narrowly defined technical role involving minimal risk. Other states, after an initial willingness to provide peacekeeping contingents, find that mounting casualties cause such hostile political reactions that the contingents must be reduced or withdrawn. As pressures mount on the leaders of the member states of NATO, the ability of the organization to take concerted action diminishes. This difficulty demonstrates the deeply political nature of the decisions that NATO has been asked to make in support of United Nations action.

This political dimension of alliance decisionmaking shows the limits of the perception implicit in judgments that NATO, a limited functional organization, could serve a technical role under the direction of the general political authority of the United Nations. Although NATO may have technical military capabilities, the alliance is fundamentally political in its character. While much of NATO's organizational structure is devoted to the management of military operations, NATO's evolution has reflected many of the basic issues of the Cold War. In seeking to cooperate with NATO, the U.N. has expected to maintain control over the final political choices involved in peace operations.[18] That expectation is probably rooted in the perceived primacy of the Charter in issues of international peace and security. Unfortunately, the legal structure of the Charter only provides a set of outer parameters for determination of authority to act. The Charter's legal rules cannot dictate practical outcomes for the day-to-day political interplay between the extensive and specialized bureaucracy of NATO and the less operationally sophisticated staff of the Secretariat when practical decisions in peace operations are under consideration. This interaction is made even more complex by the dual roles in NATO and the Security Council played by the United States, France, and the United Kingdom. Far from being a subordinate technical entity, NATO is an equally capable political player with essential technical capabilities. Instead of following the U.N.'s lead in peace operations, NATO may have the ability to set the pace whenever it chooses to do so.

However, since even NATO may not have the political will to take the initiative, pressures abound for unilateral decisions either to take or withhold action. When peace operations cause national forces to suffer casualties, national political leaders face intense pressures to act to demonstrate that they are in control.

---

18. Under-Secretary-General Kofi Annan wrote:

[t]here can be no doubt that the Security Council is the ultimate legal and political authority in deciding on a United Nations operation. The Council uses this authority guardedly and generally insists on retaining control over the operations to maintain international peace and security which it has mandated. In most cases, the Council entrusts the Secretary-General with the responsibility of overseeing the faithful implementation of its resolutions.

Annan, *supra* note 5. Under-Secretary Annan went on to recognize that working out the detail of that interaction could pose significant difficulties because of the political structure of NATO. *Id.*

The most recent U.S. review of policies related to American participation in peace operations demonstrates one outcome of those pressures.

III. THE UNILATERAL PERSPECTIVE: PDD–25

Officials of the U.S. executive branch, attributing significant responsibility for casualties in Somalia to the United Nations bureaucracy, have seriously reviewed the circumstances in which the United States will support multilateral peacekeeping and peace enforcement initiatives. Based on that review, President Clinton has issued a decision directive outlining the conditions under which the United States will participate in those initiatives.[19] Pursuant to the terms of that directive, the United States conditioned its support of a Security Council resolution expanding the peacekeeping and humanitarian assistance mission in Rwanda.[20] Since the United States stands in a particularly strong position because of its relative military, financial and technical capabilities, its reservations about the expansion of United Nations peacekeeping sets a constraint on the possibility of that organization's multilateral response to international crises.[21]

Although the provisions of Presidential Decision Directive 25 (PDD-25) remain classified, the Clinton Administration has distributed an unclassified white paper describing the contents of the document.[22] The paper describes six primary areas of reform addressed in PDD-25. Four of them are most relevant here. They involve:

- [m]aking disciplined and coherent choices about which peace operations to support—both when we vote in the Security Council and when we participate in such operations with U.S. troops;

- [r]educing U.S. costs for U.N. peace operations, both the percentage our nation pays for each operation and the cost of the operations themselves;

- [d]efining clearly our policy regarding the command and control of American military forces in U.N. peace operations;

---

19. Office of the Press Secretary, The White House, *President Clinton Signs New Peacekeeping Policy*, May 5, 1994.

20. S.C. Res. 918, (May 17, 1994).

21. In many respects, this is implicit in the role contemplated in the adoption of the veto in the United Nations Charter.

22. *United States: Administration Policy on Reforming Multilateral Peace Operations*, 33 I.L.M. 795 (1994).

•   [r]eforming and improving the UN's capability to manage peace-
     keeping operations.[23]

Each of these guidelines implies a set of constraints that the United States will
impose on the United Nations in peacekeeping operations.[24] President Clinton has
observed that "[t]he United Nations simply cannot become engaged in every one
of the world's conflicts." As a result, "the United Nations must know when to say
no."[25] The Clinton administration asserts that these limitations are necessary
because the U.N. has not shown the ability to cope with many of the tasks that it
has now undertaken.[26] The United States has offered the guidelines of PDD-25 as
a mechanism to constrain the expansion of peacekeeping until the institutional
capability of the United Nations is improved.[27] The standards of PDD-25 will be
applied to all proposals for peacekeeping or peace enforcement operations that
require U.S. support even when no US forces are involved.

The Secretary-General expressed a commitment to continue to propose
additional peacekeeping missions whenever he deems them appropriate for new
international crises.[28] That commitment may be futile, since the permanent seat
held by the United States on the Security Council provides practical control over
all missions that require authorization under Chapter VII of the Charter. If a
pattern develops of Secretariat initiative frustrated by the constraining hand of the

---

23. *Id.*, at 798–799.

24. President Clinton indicated a number of these constraints in his most recent address
to the General Assembly:

In recent weeks in the Security Council, our nation has begun asking harder
questions about proposals for new peacekeeping missions: Is there a real threat
to international peace? Does the proposed mission have clear objectives? Can
an end point be identified for those who will be asked to participate? How much
will the mission cost? From now on, the United Nations should address these
and other hard questions for every proposed mission before we vote and before
the mission begins.

Speech of President Clinton to the United Nations General Assembly, Sept. 27, 1993.

25. *Id.*

26.   According to Ambassador Albright: "the U.N. has not yet shown a capacity to
respond decisively when the risk of combat is high and the level of local cooperation is
low. The U.N.'s impartiality can be a key to diplomatic credibility, but it is of less help
when military credibility is what is required. And the U.N.'s resources have been stretched
perilously thin." *Tensions in U.S.-U.N. Relations,* Hearing of the International Security,
International Organizations and Human Rights Subcommittee of the House Foreign Affairs
Committee, May 17, 1994 (opening comments of Ambassador Albright).

27.   Interview with Ambassador Madeline Albright, *see* MacNeil/Lehrer News Hour,
May 19, 1994, Thursday, Transcript #4930, available in LEXIS, NEXIS CURNEWS
file.

28. *See* Stanley Meisler, *Rwanda 'Genocide' Angers, Frustrates U.N. Chief,* L. A. TIMES,
May 26, 1994, at A6.

United States, the prospects for collective response may be severely diminished. Continued confrontation between the Secretary-General and the U.S. could create the irony of US prevention of peace operations in which there would be little risk to American forces, even though other states may be willing to contribute forces.

In the case of Rwanda, a glint of that irony has become visible. The principles of PDD-25 led the U.S. to impose particular requirements on the terms of the Security Council's resolution authorizing expansion of the peacekeeping force already deployed in that country. In the resolution, the Secretary-General is requested "to report as soon as possible on the . . . deployment including, *inter alia,* on the cooperation of the parties, progress towards a cease-fire, availability of resources and the proposed duration of the mandate . . . ."[29] In pursuing these specific questions, the United States sought to give content to the authorization, since it "[does not] do any good to pass resolutions that are hollow promises."[30] Security Council Resolution 918 may be the first result of the policy stated in PDD-25.[31]

Unfortunately, some do not appreciate this development. In particular, they contend that the Rwanda crisis provides an inappropriate occasion for this policy. Because the U.S. is a permanent member, any expression of its disapproval of a proposed Security Council resolution is a *de facto* veto, requiring all other members of the Council to comply with U.S. concerns. Although Clinton Administration officials dispute the point, press reports indicate the PDD-25 criteria caused the U.S. Mission to withdraw its acceptance of a draft of Resolution 918, forcing postponement of its passage until the requirement of progress reports as a precondition to the deployment of peacekeeping forces could be included in the language.[32] That exercise of power raised the ire of other members of the Council. During debate on the final resolution, the permanent representative of New Zealand bluntly stated his dissatisfaction with the imposition of the reporting requirements on the Secretary-General.[33] Following the vote, one Western block permanent representative rejected the idea that initiatives of the Security Council should be constrained by any unilaterally determined criteria.[34] When reacting to the Rwanda situation after the passage of Resolution 918, the Secretary-General maintained that the Secretariat must continue to pursue peace operations in the face

---

29. Security Council Resolution 918, para. 7.

30. Interview of Ambassador Albright, *supra* note 24.

31. *See* Stanley Meisler, *Albright Defends Rwanda Troop Delay,* L.A. TIMES, May 18, 1994 at A4.

32. Stanley Meisler, *Crisis in Central Africa; Bitter Taste of 'Realism' Causes Row over U.N. Peacekeeping in Rwanda,* L. A. TIMES, May 23, 1994, p. A8. *But see* Albright Interview, *supra* note 24.

33. Summary of the 3377th Meeting of the Security Council (Night Meeting), May 16, 1994, SC/5843, take 9.

34. Stanley Meisler, *supra* note 28.

of impending international emergencies even when risks were present.[35] However, he later acknowledged that the criteria of PDD-25 could be implemented in a manner consistent with his own ideas of the proper role of the Security Council.[36]

Admittedly, application of the criteria of PDD-25 may serve the interests of the United States while also forcing necessary discipline and responsibility on the Secretariat and the Security Council. Unfortunately, imposition of those guidelines in the Rwanda crisis generated several problems. Because of the apparent frustration of an established Security Council consensus through the unilateral assertion of the PDD-25 criteria, the grudging acceptance of this new U.S. approach has been tinged with some anger. If the United Stataes continues to impose these conditions over the long run, the legitimacy of the Security Council as a neutral participant could be crippled while claims of American dominance in the Security Council would gain new credibility. Under such circumstances, any official who attempts to justify that dominance through reliance on the veto in the legal structure of the Charter or on the geopolitical influence of the United States will miss the point. If multilateral responses are to have any value, they cannot be perceived by most participants and observers as covers for the pursuit of unilaterally determined goals and policies.

IV. POLITICAL CONSTRAINTS ON COOPERATION IN PEACE OPERATIONS: DOMESTIC AND INTERNATIONAL

Those Clinton Administration officials involved in the drafting of PDD-25 faced conflicting concerns. On one hand, the Administration has frequently expressed its desire to rely on multilateral responses to international crises whenever feasible. Although the strength of the emphasis on multilateral strategies

---

35. In a recent speech, Secretary-General Boutros-Ghali stated:
[t]he problem is that simply because the United Nations intervenes in a crisis somewhere in the world, that does not mean that you are bound to be successful. We can be successful, or we can have a set-back. We had a setback in Angola. So we must accept the fact that in certain operations we will not be successful, and the fact that you have not been successful in certain operations must not be an obstacle to carrying out additional operations all over the world if the protagonists to the dispute are asking for our participation or our mediation or intervention. It is like being a hospital—you cannot say "I do not want to take this case." There is a moral responsibility; the raison d'etre of this Organization is to help Member States to solve peacefully their internal disputes and their international disputes if they are ready to accept the rules of the game.
Secretary-General Boutros Boutros-Ghali Press Conference at United Nations Headquarters (May 25, 1994), Press Release SG/SM/5297 at 5.
36. Boutros Boutros-Ghali, Address at School for Advanced International Studies Commencement, May 26, 1994, Press Release SG/SM/5301, at 2 (May 26, 1994) (observing that PDD-25 could be consistent with *An Agenda for Peace*).

has decreased, the Administration continues to affirm the value of collective rather than unilateral responses. The review that resulted in PDD-25 has been portrayed as an effort to increase the effectiveness of multilateral initiatives.[37]

On the other hand, the administration has been sensitive to the political backlash that follows the loss of casualties in a multilateral peace operation. That sensitivity has led to shifts in American policy regarding multilateral peacekeeping, leaving room for some to criticize the Clinton policy as inconsistent and unreliable.[38] Other criticisms have centered on the American urging of policies that increase the risks faced by peacekeeping troops on the ground when the United States is unwilling to deploy ground forces. Whatever the criticisms, the political reality remains. The continuing cross-pressures of public opinion will force American officials as well as those in other democratic governments either to change policy or to risk severe political liabilities. Unless clear national interests are involved, few democratic electorates will support risky foreign commitments.[39] The status of the United States as the sole remaining superpower cannot insulate American officials from those internal pressures.

Just as American officials hesitate to incur the risk of peacekeeping casualties because of public opinion, leaders in other democracies respond in the same way. The Secretary-General has attributed recent refusals of member states of the United Nations to provide troops for deployment to Rwanda under Resolution 918 to "fatigue of the donor countries."[40] Vaclav Havel has attributed the failure of democracies to take risks to preserve international peace and security to the lack of "a willingness to sacrifice for the common interest something of one's own particular interest, including even the quest for larger and larger domestic production and consumption."[41] Just as the changing international order has released new groups of actors to complicate matters in international trouble spots, similar changes have enhanced the transnational role of domestic groups. Those domestic groups assert political pressure to prevent foreign policies that they see as threatening to their particular interests; most of them see multilateral peace operations as involving only economic costs and physical risks to nationals. Democratic governments, responding to their citizens, have few incentives to

---

37. *See* Comments of Albright, *supra* note 26.

38. *See* Transcript of CNN Telecast of a Global Forum with President Clinton on May 3, 1994, White House Press Release dated May 4, 1994 (question from Sarajevo).

39. *See* Lyons, *supra* note 1, at 194. When asked the following question
   [d]o you think that American military forces should be used for peacekeeping purposes, even if our own national interests are not at stake, or should the American military be used only when our own national interests are at stake?
Sixty-two percent of American adults responded that U.S. troops should be deployed only when American national interests are involved. NBC News/Wall Street Journal Poll, Apr. 30-May 3, 1994, available in LEXIS, Nexis Library, RPOLL file.

40. *See* Press Conference of Secretary-General Boutros-Ghali, *supra* note 35, at 2.

41. Vaclav Havel, *A Call for Sacrifice*, FOREIGN AFFAIRS 6 (Mar./Apr. 1994).

become involved in peace operations in far off lands.

If we shift our attention to international institutions, little changes. The same constraints on participation in peace operations continue to apply. Unfortunately, the consensus decisionmaking structure of most international organizations causes the institution to restrain from action unless the most conservative member agrees to that action. Organizations with larger and more diverse memberships will have proportionately greater difficulties in taking the initiative in peace operations. In most instances, those organizations will find it impossible to respond decisively. If an individual state remains determined to act in spite of the lack of consensus within the international organization of which it is a member, that state must forego the full legitimizing aura afforded by that organization by resorting either to unilateral or *ad hoc* multilateral action. Unfortunately, the alternative to *ad hoc* coalitions or unilateral action may be complete inaction.

Where more than one organization is involved, the probability of timely action in initiating peace operations is reduced even further. In that case, consensus must be reached independently in each of the organizations as to the necessary action, and the action contemplated must be agreeable to both. When implementation of the action is initiated, both organizations must share a common standard for judging success or failure. If one organization plays a political role while the other exercises more technical judgments, an allocation of responsibilities may be reached more easily. However, where both organizations play political roles, judgments may conflict. In that case, a limited organization made up of more like-minded members, may establish a stronger consensus among its members than is possible for the general organization.

Even after a joint decision to act is reached, if one of the organizations has particular capabilities essential for implementation, that organization can exercise significant power over the course of the collective response, leaving the other organization less than fully satisfied with the outcome. If that organization combines strong political consensus with technological expertise, its position is even stronger. Upon consideration, the potential for difficulty in arranging collective responses between two international organizations becomes apparent. Again, the resort to *ad hoc* coalitions or to unilateral action may provide the only feasible alternative.

If one member state brings unique political status and technical capabilities, that member state can oblige any organization of which it is a member to pay special attention to its views. If that member state is an essential member of a limited organization upon which a general organization seeks to rely, that state can dictate the directions possible to both organizations. When a state like the United States plays an essential role in both the limited and the general organizations, the policies of that state may play a dominant role by limiting the options of a much larger collective.

Multilateral peace operations based on broadly understood principles such as those contained in the Charter must be the preferred course whenever possible. Limited international organizations can play a role in providing the skills and capabilities necessary to reinforce the capacity of the United Nations in conducting peace operations. NATO has already engaged in military action in support of peace operations of the United Nations. If the relationship between the general organization and the limited organization can be developed, the prospects for both are enhanced.

At the same time, cooperation can increase the vulnerability of all concerned. If consensus is required, difficulties in getting the cooperation of member states and of organizational bureaucracies can frustrate collective actions that may even have the support of a substantial majority of members. If a single dominant state possesses unique capabilities, then that state may exercise its power in ways that threaten the perceived legitimacy of any collective endeavor. These frustrations may promote a preference for *ad hoc* or unilateral action.

One author has concluded that the United Nations has demonstrated its inability to muster either the political will or the technical capability needed to undertake coercive peace operations.[42] Michael Clough has argued that the initial post–Cold War belief in United Nations engagement in military responses to international crises flows from portrayals of "the U.N. Charter as a sacred text that was regularly defiled by superpower antics during the Cold War." He challenges the conclusion that the U.N. can now undertake aggressive action because the Cold War is over as being equally mistaken. Clough asserts that U.N. military initiatives have little likelihood of consistent success because "[t]he effective use of force requires a degree of consensus and resolve that the Security Council can only muster in extreme circumstances." Recent actions in the Gulf War and in Somalia succeeded because of American leadership which pressured the member states to move toward more consensus. Clough notes that, while a number of reforms have been suggested, none of them would solve this problem of initiative. In addition, Clough points out that U.N. military operations entail the risk of protracted involvement in guerilla wars while, at the same time, they destroy any potential for an impartial U.N. role in settlement negotiations. Clough concludes that the U.N. should concentrate on efforts in the areas of international criminal enforcement of human rights, preventive diplomacy, and collective political sanctions in international organizations.

Regardless of the merits of his prescriptions, Clough makes a number of sound observations. Of particular merit is his recognition of both the importance and the rarity of the consensus requisite for U.N. collective action. The United Nations, acting alone, can rarely maintain a supportive consensus on risky action for an extended period, although Security Council procedures may enable operations to continue even when the supporting consensus may have weakened. When the U.N. involves itself with another organization in a joint peace operation, any consensus that has been reached becomes even more fragile: members of either organization

---

42. Michael Clough, *The U.N. Must Abandon its New Military Role*, L.A. TIMES, May 29, 1994, at M1. Clough is a senior fellow of the Council on Foreign Relations.

having reservations can manifest their dissatisfaction at any stage of implementation.   Advocates of greater U.N. cooperation with regional organizations should acknowledge the potential for both costs and benefits.

At the same time, regional organizations can fail in several different ways to play an effective role in peace operations. Most critics have portrayed regional organizations as lacking the financial and military capabilities necessary for managing peace operations. In many cases, proponents of this generalization convey an accurate image. However, NATO, a limited functional organization possessing significant financial and military capability, has failed to offer strong leadership in peace operations because of collective political uncertainties. While this apparent lack of political commitment contrasts most sharply with the UN's passage of strongly worded resolutions advocating action, similarities exist between NATO and the U.N. in their unwillingness to take the initiative in implementation where risky peace operations have been at issue. Even where wealth and power exist, political will remains fundamental.

So long as no collective multilateral bodies can marshall the political will to take the risks involved in conducting peace operations, the initiative will be left to those of international actors willing to take risks. Under those circumstances, many members of the international community may express dissatisfaction. However, until the international community can find effective means of risky collective action based on shared political will, that result will be unavoidable. Those who complain about powerful states pursuing unilateral action can take solace in the political difficulty confronting even the most independent of democratic states where peace operations are concerned. In the final analysis, the most likely action in the face of international crises is no coercive action at all.

V. CONCLUSION

The end of the Cold War opened up the international system in ways that encouraged many to conclude that there were new options for multilateral organizations. In particular, both politicians and pundits pointed to the United Nations as a revitalized international force. At the same time, pressures to respond to new conflicts and humanitarian emergencies caused some observers to conclude that the United Nations should take the opportunity to provide remedies. Once the U.N. began to respond, it recognized that it lacked many of the specific practical capabilities necessary for effective action. Many observers suggested that regional organizations might provide some of the necessary capabilities.

While this advocacy of regional organizations has been criticized because of their lack of capacity, this chapter has taken a different approach. If an analysis based on limited functional rather than geographically based regional organizations is developed, it becomes clear that the opposite result is possible. In fact, limited organizations may have much greater relative influence on multilateral initiatives than membership numbers would suggest. Those who have the capabilities, the skills and the resources can call the tune. Since political will plays the most important role, those international actors capable of combining political will with practical capability,in order to undertake the necessary operations will set the agenda for all concerned. Action that is truly collective will occur only when there is a broadly shared commitment to accept the costs and the risks entailed. Even then, collective action will not succeed until those capabilities necessary for success are shared among many rather than dominated by a few. Until that time, neither general nor limited international organizations can be expected to rise to meet each new crisis that poses a threat to international peace and security. In the near future, any peace operations involving significant military deployment will probably be undertaken by individual states acting unilaterally or as members of *ad hoc* coalitions.

JAPAN'S LEGAL FRAMEWORK FOR PEACEKEEPING OPERATIONS AND INTERNATIONAL HUMANITARIAN RELIEF OPERATIONS

Shunji Yanai[1]

I. LEGISLATIVE BACKGROUND

The Law Concerning Cooperation for United Nations Peace-Keeping Operations and Other Operations[2] (Law) gave Japan a legal framework for its participation in UN peace-keeping operations (PKOs) and international humanitarian relief operations carried out under the auspices of the United Nations and other international organizations. For many years, the Ministry of Foreign Affairs studied various aspects of peacekeeping operations and canvassed the opinions of scholars on the matter, but the studies remained essentially academic until the Gulf Crisis broke out. The government of Japan prepared a Bill on Peace Cooperation with the United Nations and presented it to the House of Representatives (the Lower House) on October 17, 1990. The Bill contained provisions concerning logistic support for the Coalition Forces, certain peacekeeping operations activities and humanitarian assistance, authorizing the government to use the Self-Defense Forces (SDF) for such purposes. The most controversial point was the dispatch abroad of Self-Defense Forces units, even

---

1. Deputy Minister for Foreign Affairs of Japan from August 1993 to July 1995. The views expressed are solely those of the author and do not represent the views of the Government of Japan, the Ministry of Foreign Affairs or the Prime Minister's Office.

For greater detail on this topic, *see* Shuji Yanai, *Law Concerning Cooperation for United Nations Peace-Keeping Operations and Other Operations—The Japanese PKO Experience*, 36 JAPANESE ANNUAL INT'L L. 33-75 (1993).

2. *Kokusairengō Heiwa-ijikatsudō to ni taisuru Kyōryoku ni kansuru Hōritsu*, adopted June 15, 1992, effective Aug. 10, 1992.

though the purpose was limited to noncombat logistical support for the Coalition Forces.

Major opposition parties objected to the bill strongly, from the points of view both of the constitutionality and the policy appropriateness of becoming more directly involved in the Gulf Crisis. In the face of this very strong opposition, the government and the Liberal Democratic Party decided to withdraw the Bill after about three weeks of heated debate in the Special Committee of the House of Representatives. Nevertheless, on November 9, 1990, just before the bill was formally withdrawn, the Liberal Democratic Party, the *Kōmeitō* and the Japan Democratic Socialist Party (*Minshatō*) agreed to cooperate on the preparation of a new bill, the scope of which would be limited to peacekeeping operations and humanitarian relief operations.

It was against this background that the International Peace Cooperation Bill was presented to the Diet on September 19, 1991, with the support of the Liberal Democratic party, the *Kōmeitō* and the Japan Democratic Socialist Party.

II. BASIC ISSUES TO BE SETTLED

Before entering on the drafting of a bill on peacekeeping operations and humanitarian relief operations, the government of Japan had to settle the following basic issues:

a.) Would the Self-Defense Forces or a separate organization to be established specifically for such operations carry out peacekeeping operations and humanitarian relief operations?

b.) Is the use of weapons normally allowed on peacekeeping operations compatible with the provisions of Article 9 of the Japanese Constitution, which prohibits the threat or use of force?

c.) How would civilian control of Self-Defense Forces units participating in peacekeeping operations be ensured? Should the dispatch of such units be subject to Parliamentary approval?

As to the first issue, namely the organizational question, the aforementioned three-party agreement of November 9, 1990, stated that an organization separate from the Self-Defense Forces should be established and entrusted with the task of cooperating in peacekeeping operations and humanitarian relief operations, including disaster relief operations. The idea of setting up a new organization was introduced in consideration of a certain hesitation in Japan about using the Self-Defense Forces as such for these operations abroad. The above three parties and the government, however, abandoned the idea of establishing a separate organization after having taken a fresh look at it in the stage of drafting the International Peace Cooperation Bill. They arrived at this conclusion particularly because the Self-Defense Forces are the most self-sustaining organization suitable for the difficult environment immediately following a ceasefire. In additon, the establishment of a new separate organization would be redundant and entail a considerable duplication of investment. They also considered the fact that public support for the Self-Defense Forces was steadily increasing.

The second issue, which was the most controversial, is related to the question of the compatibility of the use of weapons permitted under the established practice of U.N. peacekeeping operations and the prohibition of the use of force under Article 9 of the Japanese Constitution.[3] This issue arose particularly when the drafters considered the question as to whether or not provisions concerning "peacekeeping forces" should be included in the bill. The term "peacekeeping forces" is neither clearly defined nor often used internationally, but was understood in Japan to mean infantry or other units carrying small arms which are given such missions as monitoring the observance of a ceasefire, being stationed in and patrolling buffer zones, inspecting or identifying the carrying in or out of weapons, disposing of abandoned weapons, and so forth.

Careful study of the U.N. peacekeeping operations up to the time the bill was presented to the Diet in 1991[4] showed that traditional or conventional peacekeeping operations were initiated and carried out on certain premises, in particular: the existence of a ceasefire agreement between the belligerent parties and the consent of the parties and the host country to accept United Nations peacekeeping operations in its territories. These peacekeeping operations maintained strict impartiality. It was also established U.N. practice that if certain peacekeeping operations components such as "peacekeeping forces" are allowed to carry small arms, they are authorized to use such arms only in accordance with strictly defined procedures and only when the lives of peacekeepers are threatened or their mission is obstructed by force by an aggressive party.

On the other hand, Article 9 of the Japanese Constitution is interpreted as prohibiting the dispatching of the Self-Defense Forces abroad on any mission which may entail the use of force. In this context, in particular, three questions regarding the "use of force" arose repeatedly during the drafting process of the bill. First, is the use of weapons allowed under the U.N. PKO practice not to be considered as a use of force prohibited under Article 9 of the Japanese constitution? Secondly, if the ceasefire agreement is broken, or the consent of the host country

---

3.   Article 9 of the Constitution of Japan (Renunciation of War) reads as follows:
      Aspiring sincerely to an international peace based on justice and order, the
      Japanese people forever renounce war as a sovereign right of the nation and the
      threat or use of force as means of settling international disputes.
      In order to accomplish the aim of the preceding paragraph, land, sea and air
      forces, as well as other war potential, will never be maintained. The right of
      belligerency of the State will not be recognized.
Kenpō [Constitution] Ch. II, Art. 9 (Japan).
    4.   Before the International Peace Cooperation Bill was presented by the government of
Japan to the House of Representatives on Sept. 19, 1991, twenty-two U.N. peacekeeping
operations had been established (from UNTSO, established in June 1948, to MINURSO,
established in Sept. 1991).

or the belligerent parties is withdrawn, will the Japanese units participating in U.N. peacekeeping forces not become involved in armed conflict once fighting is resumed between the belligerent parties? Thirdly, can Japan withdraw its units from U.N. peacekeeping forces when any of the essential premises of peacekeeping operations no longer exists even though the United Nations continues its operations?

The Ministry of Foreign Affairs, the Defense Agency, the Cabinet Councilor's Office on External Affairs and the National Legislation Bureau of the Prime Minister's Cabinet, which were the government agencies directly concerned with the drafting of the bill, thoroughly examined and discussed these issues. They arrived at the following conclusions. As to the first question, the National Legislation Bureau, which is responsible for the interpretation of the constitution within the government, concluded that the use of weapons for self-defense by Japanese peacekeepers when their lives are threatened should not be considered as the use of force prohibited under Article 9 of the Japanese Constitution. It did, however, doubt the constitutionality of their use of weapons to prevent possible obstruction of their mission by an aggressive party. In light of the history of the use of weapons by U.N. peacekeepers known to the drafters, in most cases when force was used to obstruct a mission, the lives of U.N. peacekeepers were also endangered. The difference between the two cases therefore did not seem significant in practice.[5]

The second question was studied, because if the ceasefire agreement breaks down or the consent of the host country or the belligerent parties is withdrawn and armed conflict resumes between the parties, U.N. peacekeeping forces may become involved in such a conflict, which may entail more serious types of use of weapons by peacekeeping forces. In such a case, it was feared that the use of weapons by peace-keepers would escalate beyond the degree of self-defense permitted under

---

5. Article XXIV of the International Peace Cooperation Law provides for the use of arms. The main points of the provisions of art. XXIV are:

a.) [International Peace Cooperation] Corps personnel engaged in International Peace Cooperation Assignments in receiving countries to whom small weapons have been lent. under the provisions of para. 1 of art. XXIII above may use such small weapons within the limits considered reasonably necessary in the circumstances, if it is deemed that the unavoidable need exists on reasonable grounds in order to protect their own lives or persons or these of other Corps personnel present with them on the same spot.

b.) [Similar provisions concerning the Maritime Safety officers (coastguard officers) engaged in International Peace Cooperation Assignments].

c.) [Similar provisions concerning the members of the Self-Defense Forces engaged in International Peace Cooperation Assignments].

d.) The use of small weapons or arms under the provisions of the foregoing paragraphs shall not cause harm to persons, except for cases corresponding to the provisions of art. 36 [self-defense] and 37 [necessity] of the Penal Code (Law No. 45 of 1907).

Article 9 of the Constitution. This question is, however, related to the third question concerning the suspension or termination of peacekeeping operations or withdrawal therefrom, since the suspension, termination or withdrawal might resolve the question of getting involved in armed conflict between the belligerent parties. As the existence of a ceasefire agreement and the consent of the host country or the belligerent parties to accept U.N. peacekeeping operations is the very basis of traditional peacekeeping operations, it is to be expected that the United Nations would suspend or terminate the operations concerned, if any such premises ceases to exist. In such an extreme and obvious case, the judgment of the United Nations and that of individual troop-contributing member countries may coincide with each other.

The real issue is therefore whether or not a contributing country can withdraw its contingent when it considers that the ceasefire agreement or the consent of the host country or the belligerent parties no longer exists, even if the United Nations holds a different view and continues its operations. It was considered possible that a contributing country might withdraw its contingent at its own discretion as a last resort, especially when any of the basic premises of peacekeeping operations ceases to exist. This assessment was arrived at because of the several cases in which troop-contributing countries withdrew their troops for one reason or another though the peacekeeping operations as such were not terminated. In addition, there was a provision reflecting the established U.N. practice in the model agreement[6] .prepared by the U.N. Secretariat to be concluded between contributing countries and the United Nations, in effect, requiring such countries to give prior notice before withdrawing their contingents.

In view of the U.N. practice in various peacekeeping operations established after the Congo[7] and as a result of the considerations mentioned above, the government of Japan formulated the following guidelines for Japan's participation in U.N. peacekeeping forces, on the basis of which relevant provisions should be drafted into the bill.

---

6. The U.N. Secretariat prepared a model agreement between the United Nations and member states contributing personnel and equipment to United Nations peacekeeping operations and distributed it as an attachment to the Report of the Secretary-General of May 23, 1991 (A/46/185). Para. 26 of the model agreement provides for notification of withdrawal:

> The Government of (Participating State) shall not withdraw its personnel from [the United Nations PKO] without giving adequate prior notification to the Secretary-General of the United Nations.

As of June 1994, no actual agreement has been concluded after the above-mentioned model agreement.

7. The relevant United Nations resolutions concerning the United Nations Operation in the Congo (ONUC) are Security Council Resolutions 143 (July 14, 1960) and 161 (Feb. 2, 1961).

The "guidelines," which later became better known as the "PKO five principles," read as follows:

1. Agreement on a ceasefire shall have been reached among the parties to the conflict.
2. The parties to the conflict, including the territorial State(s), shall have given their consent to the deployment of peacekeeping forces and Japan's participation in such forces.
3. The peacekeeping forces shall strictly maintain impartiality, not favoring any party to the conflict.
4. Should any of the above guideline requirements cease to be satisfied, the Government of Japan may withdraw its contingent.
5. Use of weapons shall be limited to the minimum necessary to protect personnel's lives, etc.[8]

These five guidelines provided the answers to the aforementioned questions relating to the Japanese constitution and formed the basis for the drafting of the bill. The Ministry of Foreign Affairs of Japan sent a mission to New York to explain the "PKO five principles" to the U.N. Secretariat, which found them to be acceptable as the principles governing Japanese participation in U.N. peacekeeping operations. It should be noted that these five points later became the general principles underlying all Japanese participation in U.N. peacekeeping operations, not just those of the "peacekeeping forces." The spirit of these principles can be found throughout the law, but the principles have been translated into more legal or technical language in the actual legislative provisions.

The third basic issue which had to be settled was how to ensure civilian control of Self-Defense Forces units participating in peacekeeping operations and whether the dispatch of such units be subject to parliamentary approval. On this issue there were two differing schools of thought.

The government held the view that it would suffice to incorporate the aforementioned "PKO five principles" into the bill, since these principles would determine the government's decision as to whether or not the Self-Defense Forces units should be sent on a particular PKO mission. According to this view, such a decision should not be subject to parliamentary approval, as that would prevent the Government from making a timely decision. Consequently, the bill presented by the government did not contain any provisions concerning parliamentary approval, providing only for reporting to the Diet. The Liberal Democratic Party and the Kōmeitō supported this view of the government.

The second school of thought, represented by the Japan Democratic Socialist Party, was shared by some members of the Liberal Democratic Party. They considered the dispatch of SDF units abroad on peacekeeping forces missions, even

---

8.   Guidelines for Japan's Participation in United Nations Peacekeeping Forces.

if armed only with small weapons for self-defense, as requiring the utmost caution. They therefore advocated strong civilian control in the form of required Diet approval. Those who supported this view proposed in both Houses that provisions obliging the government to obtain approval of the Diet for dispatching Self-Defense Forces units on "peacekeeping forces" missions be included.

As a result of negotiations between the proponents of these two schools of thought, it was agreed by compromise in the House of Representatives (the Lower House) that a new paragraph to Article VI of the bill be added. In effect, it said that the government shall obtain approval of the Diet when it intends to continue to operate on a particular "peacekeeping forces" mission beyond two years after the initial participation.

In the House of Councilors (the Upper House), however, it was further agreed among the parties in favor of the bill to include a more straightforward paragraph in the same Article VI. This new paragraph provided, in substance, that the government shall obtain prior approval of the Diet regarding the dispatch of the Self-Defense Forces units on a "peacekeeping forces" mission, provided that if the Diet is not in session or the House of Representatives is dissolved, such approval shall be sought without delay in the first Diet session subsequent to the dispatch of those units.

III. FEATURES OF THE INTERNATIONAL PEACE COOPERATION LAW

a. Background

To the best of the author's knowledge, only a handful of countries, such as some of the Nordic countries and Austria, have laws which specifically govern peacekeeping operations. In the case of Japan, it was considered necessary to clearly spell out the terms and conditions under which the Self-Defense Forces might participate in peacekeeping operations in legislation, since the dispatch of units or personnel abroad for such purposes is a highly sensitive issue both constitutionally and politically.

The International Peace Cooperation Law therefore has 27 articles of detailed provisions under the following five chapters: General Provisions, International Peace Cooperation Headquarters, International Peace Cooperation Assignments, Cooperation in Kind and Miscellaneous Provisions. It also has additional provisions in nine articles and an appendix listing the international humanitarian relief organizations.

b. Main Features of the Law

(1) Purpose

The purpose of the International Peace Cooperation Law is to enable Japan to take part in U.N. peacekeeping operations and international humanitarian relief operations.

(2) Definitions

Under this law, peacekeeping operations and international humanitarian relief operations are defined as follows:

a. "United Nations peacekeeping operations" means operations that are conducted under the control of the United Nations, and upon the basis of resolutions of the General Assembly or the Security Council of the United Nations, to ensure compliance with agreement to prevent the recurrence of armed conflict among the parties to such conflict (hereinafter referred to as "the parties to armed conflict"), to assist in the establishment of a governing machinery by democratic means after the termination of armed conflict or to maintain international peace and security in coping with disputes, provided that such operations be implemented by two or more participating countries at the request of the Secretary-General of the United Nations (hereinafter referred to as "the Secretary-General") and by the United Nations, without partiality to any of the parties to an armed conflict, in case where agreement to cease armed conflict and maintain the cessation has been reached among the parties to an armed conflict and where consent for the undertaking of such operations has been obtained from the host country and the parties to the armed conflict, or from the host country alone where armed conflict has not occurred.

b. "International humanitarian relief operations" means operations, other than those implemented as United Nations peacekeeping operations, conducted in a humanitarian spirit, and upon the basis of resolutions of the General Assembly, the Security Council or the Economic and Social Council of the United Nations or at the request of international organizations listed in the Appendix, to rescue inhabitants and other persons actually suffering or likely to suffer as a result of conflict which is likely to endanger international peace and security (such conflict is hereinafter referred to simply as "conflict;" such inhabitants and persons are hereinafter jointly referred to as "affected people") or to make restoration out of damage caused by conflict, provided that such operations be implemented by the United Nations or other international organizations, or the Member States of the United Nations or other countries (referred to in (4) below as "the United Nations and others"), in case where consent to the undertaking of such operations has been obtained from host countries and, should the host countries be parties to an armed conflict, agreement to cease armed conflict and maintain the cessation has been reached among the parties to the armed conflict.[9]

(3) Assignments or Missions the Government of Japan is Authorized to Carry Out Under the International Peace Cooperation Law

The following are the assignments or missions the government of Japan is authorized to carry out under the International Peace Cooperation Law for peacekeeping operations and international humanitarian relief operations:

(a) monitoring the observance of cessation of armed conflict or the implementation of relocation, withdrawal or demobilization of armed forces as agreed upon among the parties to armed conflict;

(b) stationing and patrol in buffer zones and other areas demarcated to prevent the occurrence of armed conflict;

(c) inspection or identification of the carrying in or out of weapons and/or their parts by vehicles and other means of transportation or travelers on foot;

(d) collection, storage or disposal of abandoned weapons and their parts;

(e) assistance in the designation of ceasefire lines and other assimilated boundaries by the parties to armed conflict;

(f) assistance in the exchange of prisoners-of-war among the parties to armed conflict;

(g) supervision or management of the fair holding of congressional elections, plebiscites and other elections or voting assimilated thereto;

(h) advice or guidance on and supervision of police administrative matters;

(i) advice or guidance for administrative matters not included in (h) above;

(j) medical care, including sanitary measures;

(k) search for or rescue of affected people or assistance in their repatriation;

(l) distribution of food, clothing, medical supplies and other daily necessaries to affected people;

---

9.   Art. III, The Law Concerning Cooperation for United Nations Peacekeeping Operations and Other Operations, June 15, 1992.

(m) installation of facilities or equipment to accommodate affected people;

(n) measures for the repair or maintenance of facilities or equipment damaged in conflict necessary for the daily life of affected people;

(o) measures for the restoration of the natural environment subjected to pollution and other damage by conflict;

(p) transportation, storage or reserve, communication, construction, or the installation, inspection or repair of machines and apparatus not included in (a) to (o) above; and

(q) other tasks assimilated to those mentioned in (a) to (p) above, as prescribed by Cabinet Order.[10]

(4) Scope of Peacekeeping Operations Covered by the Law

As quoted earlier, Article III, paragraph 1 defines the term "United Nations peacekeeping operations" as operations which are conducted under the control of the United Nations, and upon the basis of a resolution of the General Assembly or the Security Council of the United Nations. The law thus covers U.N.-sponsored PKOs but does not contemplate Japan's participation in peacekeeping operations which may be established and carried out by international organizations or individual states outside the United Nations.

As stated above, the law authorized the government of Japan to send contingents or personnel on peacekeeping operations satisfying the above-mentioned "PKO five principles" underlying the law. In other words, the law covers the traditional or conventional type of peacekeeping operations which gradually developed through U.N. practice after the unsuccessful operation in the Congo but it leaves "peace enforcement"-type operations outside its scope.

(5) Scope of Activities in the Area of International Humanitarian Relief Operations

Under the International Peace Cooperation Law, international humanitarian relief operations may be undertaken as operations separate from peacekeeping operations. The tasks mentioned in (j) to (p) of Article III, paragraph 3 have a humanitarian character, but when those tasks are undertaken within the framework of pace-keeping operations, they are not included in "International Humanitarian Relief Operations" according to the definition of the law. (The definition of international humanitarian relief operations is given in Article III, paragraph 2 quoted above).

---

10. Art. III, para. 3, The Law Concerning Cooperation for United Nations Peacekeeping Operations and Other Operations, June 15, 1992.

The law authorizes the government of Japan to carry out the activities from among the "international peace cooperation assignments" enumerated in Article III, paragraph 3, sub-paragraphs (j) to (p), quoted above. It is to be noted that the law provides only for conflict-related humanitarian relief operations, since disaster-related activities are already provided for by the law concerning Dispatch of Japan Disaster Relief Teams of 1987.

(6) Cooperation in Kind

In addition to the provisions concerning the dispatch of troops or personnel for peacekeeping operations or international humanitarian relief operations, the International Peace Cooperation Law also provides for cooperation in kind. Paragraph 1 of Article XXV provides: "The Government [of Japan] may extend cooperation in kind, if the Government deems it appropriate to extend such cooperation in order to cooperate in United Nations peace-keeping operations or international humanitarian relief operations."

The purpose of cooperation in kind, free of charge or at a price lower than the current price, is to assist the United Nations in carrying out peacekeeping operations or the United Nations and others in implementing international humanitarian relief operations by providing them with necessary equipment and materials other than those carried by the troops or personnel dispatched by the government of Japan under the law.

IV. ACTUAL IMPLEMENTATION OF THE INTERNATIONAL PEACE COOPERATION LAW

The United Nations Angola Verification Mission II (UNAVEM II) and the United Nations Transitional Authority in Cambodia (UNTAC) were the first peacekeeping operations in which Japan participated under the law. In September 1992, the government of Japan decided on the Implementation Plans and established the International Peace Cooperation Corps for UNAVEM II and UNTAC, respectively. Subsequently, the government decided in May 1993 to dispatch a Self-Defense Forces unit and headquarters staff officers to the United Nations Operation in Mozambique (ONUMOZ). In March 1994, a Cabinet decision was taken for the sending of election monitors to participate in the United Nations Observer Mission in El Salvador (ONUSAL). These are the four peacekeeping operations to which Japan has to date contributed civilian and/or military personnel under the law. In the cases of UNTAC and ONUMOZ, Self-Defense Forces units were dispatched. In September 1994, the Government of Japan dispatched approximately 400 Self-Defense Forces personnel and about ten civilians to provide the United Nations High Commissioner for Refugees with self-contained services in Zaire such as medical assistance, sanitation, water management and airlifts. This assistance to Rwandan refugees is the first "international humanitarian relief operation" implemented under the International

Peace Cooperation law.

V. REVIEW OF THE LAW

The International Peace Cooperation law has a built-in review clause in its Additional Provisions. Article III of the Additional Provisions provides as follows:

Upon the passage of three years after the entry into force of this Law, the Government shall carry out a review concerning the arrangements for the execution of this Law in the light of the state of the actual implementation of this Law.

Since Japan had no experience in peacekeeping operations when the International Peace Cooperation Bill was drafted, it was felt that the law should be reviewed at an appropriate time after its enactment on the basis of Japan's own experience gained in peacekeeping operations and international humanitarian relief operations to be carried out under the Law. By August 1995, three years will have passed since the Law's entry into force.

Another point to be mentioned in this connection is the provisions concerning the "freezing of peacekeeping forces" assignments. Article II of the Additional Provisions provide that certain International Peace Cooperation Assignments undertaken by Self-Defense Force units shall not be implemented until a date to be set forth in a separate law. These assignments include such missions as monitoring the compliance with a ceasefire, being stationed in and patrolling buffer zones and so forth. Unlike the above-mentioned review clause, this provision regarding the so-called "freezing of peacekeeping forces" does not provide for any specific timing, and the "defreezing" may take place at any time the Diet so decides. Since such a decision has not been taken so far, two years after the enactment of the Law it is likely that the question of "defreezing" will be discussed when other provisions are reviewed in 1995.

VI. CONCLUSION

In his report, *An Agenda for Peace*, Secretary-General Boutros-Ghali analyzed the world situation and made a number of valuable proposals on such important subjects as preventive diplomacy, peace-making, peacekeeping, post-conflict peace-building, cooperation with regional arrangements and organizations, safety of personnel and financing. Among the Secretary-General's proposals, preventive deployment and peace enforcement units are perhaps those which have been talked about most often.

In the area of preventive diplomacy, the Secretary-General proposed preventive deployment at the request of or with the consent of all parties concerned, or of only one party depending upon the circumstances. He pointed out that "United Nations operations in areas of crisis have generally been established after conflict has occurred" and that "the time has come to plan for circumstances warranting preventive deployment, which could take place in a variety of instances and ways." This idea was put into practice under Security Council Resolution 795 in the former Yugoslav Republic of Macedonia, where no armed conflict had yet occurred.

The Secretary-General recommended that "the Council consider the utilization of peace-enforcement units in clearly defined circumstances and with their terms of reference specified in advance." According to his proposal, such units would be more heavily armed than peacekeeping forces. UNOSOM II in Somalia and UNPROFOR in Bosnia and Herzegovina appear to be close in character to the concept of peace-enforcement units.

While the circumstances and backgrounds to the conflicts in Somalia and the former Yugoslavia are entirely different, the developments in Somalia and Bosnia and Herzegovina nevertheless show how difficult it is to keep peace in areas where there is no cease fire agreement among the parties to a conflict.

As is well known, there is no mention of U.N. peacekeeping operations in the United Nations Charter; PKOs were devised and developed through practical application over the years, and, hence, are still evolving. Questions such as how to deal more effectively with actual conflict remain. It is true that today there are situations like the cases above in which traditional PKO functions cannot cope adequately with ongoing crises. These have afforded the opportunity to put some of the Secretary-General's proposals into practice. Nevertheless, the principles and practices of peacekeeping operations carried out by the United Nations for more than forty years are still both appropriate and valid today, and will continue to be so in the future.

As for Japan's participation and cooperation in U.N. peacekeeping operations, Japan still needs to gain a lot more experience, since it has only recently begun to participate. Although there are notable constraints with regard to Japan's arrangements even where the traditional PKO functions are concerned, Japan can continue, and perhaps even increase, its contributions to international efforts in connection with peacekeeping and humanitarian relief. In 1995, the Government of Japan will review the International Peace Cooperation Law after having had accumulated more experience.

CONTRIBUTORS

JONATHAN I. CHARNEY:

Professor of Law at Vanderbilt University in Nashville, Tennessee. Professor Charney is Vice-President of the American Society of International Law, as well as a member of the Board of Editors of the *American Journal of International Law,* the Board of Editors of the journal *Ocean Development and International Law,* the Board of Advisors of the International Boundary Research Unit, the Council on Foreign Relations, and the American Law Institute. He is the author of numerous publications on international law and on the law of the sea.

MAURICE COPITHORNE:

Professor of international law at the University of British Columbia and practices with Ladner Downs in Vancouver, British Columbia. Professor Copithorne was a Canadian career foreign service officer serving at various times as Legal Advisor, Ambassador to Austria, and Assistant Undersecretary of State for Asia and the Pacific. He has recently been appointed as United Nations Special Representative on the Human Rights Situation in Iran.

MASATO DOGAUCHI:

Associate Professor of Private International Law, University of Tokyo, Graduate School of Law and Politics, Tokyo. Professor Dogauchi is a member of the Legislative Council on Private International Law of the Ministry of Justice, and the Editorial Board of the *Kokusaihō Gaiko Zashi (Journal of International Law and Diplomacy).* In addition, he is Secretary to the Japanese Branch of the International Law Association. Professor Dogauchi is author of many articles on conflict of laws, especially on international civil procedure and on international trade law, including a recent article in English in J. Fawcett, ed., *Declining Jurisdiction in Private International Law* (Oxford, 1995). Professor Dogauchi has also been a Visiting Scholar at the School of Law of Columbia University and at the University of Michigan Law School. He earned his B.A. from the University of Tokyo.

581

H. SCOTT FAIRLEY:

Partner in the law firm of Lang Michener in Toronto, practicing in civil litigation with an emphasis on international business and public law issues. Dr. Fairley is also an Adjunct Professor of Law at the University of Windsor and a Member of the Faculty of Graduate Studies at the University of Ottawa. He is the Immediate Past-President of the Canadian Council on International Law, and serves on the executive boards of the Canadian Bar Association National and Ontario sections for constitutional law and international law, for which he served as National Chair, 1991-93. He has written widely in Canada and abroad on constitutional and international law issues. Dr. Fairley received his post-secondary education Queen's University B.A., LL.B.; New York University LL.M. and Harvard University S.J.D.

THOMAS M. FRANCK:

Murry and Ida Becker Professor of Law and Director of the Center for International Studies at New York University. He is the author of 25 books and numerous articles covering international law, international organizations, international relations, national security law, the foreign policy process and ethics, and has thrice received the ASIL Certificate of Merit for publications. Professor Franck is currently Counsel to the Government of Bosnia and Herzegovina in the Case Concerning Application of the Convention on the Prevention and Punishment of the Crime of Genocide before the International Court of Justice.

KEITH HIGHET:

Attorney who has practiced law for 36 years and has served as counsel, advocate and advisor in 14 litigated cases before the International Court of Justice. Of these, 11 have concerned the drawing of boundaries in areas of shared natural resources. He has served as legal counsel to 15 governments, to the United Nations Organization in the 1988 PLO Case, and to OPEC, and as president of an ICSID arbitration tribunal. He was president of the American Society of International Law, and is a member of the Board of Editors of *The American Journal of International Law*. Mr. Highet is currently a Visiting Professor at the School of Law of George Washington University and has taught at a number of other schools. He is a member of the Executive Board of the Law of the Sea Institute and a Trustee for the Procedural Aspects for International Law Institute.

RYUICHI IDA:

Professor of law of International Organizations, Kyoto University, Graduate School of Law, Kyoto. He was the Director of Study, The Hague Academy of International Law, Rapporteur of the Committee of

Regional Economic Development Law and Alternate Member of the Committee of the Legal Aspects of Sustainable Development for the International Law Association. He is also a member of the Steering Committee of the "U.N.U. Global Seminar, Kobe Session," and the Editorial Board of the *Kokusaihō Gaikō Zasshi (Journal of International Law and Diplomacy)*. He is the author of many articles on international law, international law of development and law of international institutions, including *Kokusai_Keizai Hō (International Economic Law)* (1993) (co-author); "Formation des normes internationales en mutation—critique de la notion de Soft Law," in *Melangés Michel Virally*. He earned his B.A. and LL.M. from Kyoto University, his D.E.A. in France, *Enseignant invité Université de Paris 2*.

MAUREEN IRISH:

Professor of Law at the University of Windsor in Windsor, Ontario. Professor Irish is author of *Customs Valuation in Canada* (1985) and several articles on international trade law. She is also a co-editor of *The Legal Framework for Canada-United States Trade* (1987) and *International Trade and Intellectual Property: The Search for a Balanced System* (1994). She earned a B.A. and LL.B. degrees from the University of Toronto and LL.M. and D.C.L. degrees from McGill University.

YUJI IWASAWA:

Associate Professor of International Law, Osaka City University, Faculty of Law, Osaka. Included in his professional career are positions as a Visiting Scholar at the University of Virginia and Cambridge University. He was a member of the Faculty, Asia-America Institute in Transnational Law at Duke University and a Rapporteur for the Committee on International Human Rights Law and Practice of the International Law Association. He is the author of numerous books and articles in Japanese as well as in English on international law, international human rights law, and international economic law, including *Jōyaku no Kokunai Tekiyo Kanōsei (Domestic Applicability of Treaties)* (1985) and *WTO no Funsō Shori (Dispute Settlement of the WTO)* (1995). He earned his B.A. from the Univeristy Tokyo, and his LL.M. from Harvard.

JOHN J. JACKSON:

Hessel E. Yntema Professor of Law at the University of Michigan, Ann Arbor. He served as General Counsel of the United States Office of the Trade Representative. Professor Jackson is a member of a number of professional and learned societies and is or has been a member of editorial boards of a number of Journals, including the *American Journal of International Law,* and he has been consultant to various parts of the U.S. government, including the Senate Finance Committee during the 1979 implementation of the Tokyo Round negotiation results. In addition to his 1969 GATT book, *World Trade and the Law of GATT*, Professor Jackson is author (*inter alia*) of *Legal Problems of International Economic Relations* (3rd ed. with W. Davey & A. Sykes, 1995) and *The World Trading System: Law and Policy of International Economic Relations* (1989).

ATSUKO KANEHARA:

Associate Professor of International Law, Rikkyo University, Faculty of Law, Tokyo, Japan. She is currently a Visiting Scholar at Harvard Law School. Professor Kanehara teaches public international law, law of the sea, and law of state responsibility. Her publications include *Kokkasekininho Ni Okeru "Ippanrieki" Gainen Tekiyo No Genkai (The "Legal Damage" to be Remedied by the Law of State Responsibility-A Critical Review)* (1995), *Tikyu Kankyohogo Ni Okeru Songai Yobo No Hori ("Precautionary Remedies" in the Conventions on Global Environmental Protection)* (1994), and *The Significance of Japanese Proposal of "Pledge and Review" Procedure in Growing International Environmental Law* (1993).

SUSAN L. KARAMANIAN:

Shareholder in the law firm of Locke, Purnell, Rain, Harrell in Dallas, Texas. She represents clients, including agencies of foreign governments and foreign private parties, in federal and Texas courts and before arbitration tribunals. She has authored and delivered various papers on federal and Texas civil procedure. Ms. Karamanian is a member of the Executive Council of the American Society of International Law and has served in other capacities with the Society. She has been a Term Member of the Council of Foreign Relations. She is principal organizer of the Dallas Warburg Chapter of the American Council on Germany, a Research Fellow of the Southwestern Legal Foundation, and has served as a director of numerous nonprofit organizations.

SHIGEO KAWAGISHI:

Professor of International Law, Kobe Gakuin University, Kobe. He is a member of the Japan National Committee for International Law, a division of the Science Council of Japan. He is the author of several articles on international law and international economic law, and a coeditor of *Kokusai Kikō (International Institutions)* (1992). Professor Kawagishi is a recipient of a Fulbright-Hays Faculty Development fellowship and scholarships from the French Government and the Hague Academy of International Law. He has a B.A. from Doshisha University, an LL.M. from Kyoto University, and a *Doctorat d'Université from Université de Paris.*

MAMORU KOGA:

Professor of International Law, Seinan Gakuin University, Faculty of Law, Fukuoka. He has also been a Visiting Scholar at Harvard Law School, a Legal Advisor to the Deep Ocean Minerals Association (Japan's entity for Resolution II of the United Nations Convention on the Law of the Sea) and was sent to the U.N. Conference on the Law of the Sea (1976–82). Professor Koga is a member of the editorial board of the *Kokusaiho Gaiko Zasshi (Journal of International Law and Diplomacy)*. He is co-author with R.L. Friedheim et al., *Japan and the New Ocean Regime* (1984), and author of several articles on the regulation of vessels on the high seas, the sea-bed development regime and the law-making procedures. He has an M.A. from Chuo University.

AKIRA KOTERA:

Professor of International Law, University of Tokyo, Department of International Relations, Tokyo. He is the Supervising Associate Editor of the *Japanese Annual of International Law* and a member of the editorial board of *Kokusaihō Gaikō Zasshi (Journal of International Law and Diplomacy)*. He is the author of numerous publications on public international law, in particular the law of international organizations and the law of international telecommunications, including a recent article in English entitled "Deregulation of International Telecommunications Business in Japan," 34 *Japanese Annual of Intenational Law* (1991).

SHIGERU KOZAI:

Professor of International Law, Faculty of International Studies, Osaka Gakuin University. Dean of the Graduate Schools and Professor Emeritus, Kyoto University. He has been a Visiting Scholar at Columbia University and Harvard Law School. He is the former president of the Japanese Association of International Law and of the Japanese Association of World Law. Professor Kozai is a Member of the Science Council of Japan. He is author *of Kokuren no Heiwa Iji Katsudō (UN Peace-Keeping Operations)* (1991), and co-editor of *Kokusai Kikō Jōyaku Shiryōshū (Treaties and Documents on International Organizations)* (1986).

YOSHIRO MATSUI:

Professor of International Law and former Dean, Nagoya University, School of Law, Nagoya. Professor Matsui was a Visiting Scholar at the London School of Economics. He has also served as Editor-in-Chief, *Kokusaihō Gaikō Zasshi (Journal of International Law and Diplomacy),* and Secretary-General, Law Section of the Association of the Democratic Scientists, Japan. He is a member of the Committee on Legal Aspects of Sustainable Development, International Law Association. Professor

Matsui is author of *Gendai no Kokusai Kankei to Jiketsuken (Contemporary International Relations and the Right to Self-Determination)* (1981); and *Wangan Sensō to Kokusai Rengō (The Gulf War and the United Nations)* (1993). He earned his B.A. and LL.M from Kyoto University.

ARMAND DE MESTRAL:

Professor of Law, McGill University, formerly of the United Nations Secretariat and the Department of Justice, Ottawa. Counsel to Gottlieb and Associates, Montreal. Professor deMestral's research and writing specializes in international trade and the law of international integration. He has authored and co-authored many books and articles in these areas including, with L. Reif, *Canada, Japan and International Law,* Proceedings of the 1990 Annual Conference of the Canadian Council on International Law, C.C.I.L., Ottawa, (1992), and deMestral & T. Gruchalla-Wesierski, *Extraterritorial Application of Export Control Legislation: Canada and the U.S.A.*, (1990). Professor de Mestral was Associate Editor of the *Canadian Yearbook of International Law*. He was honored *Docteur Honoris Cause*, Université Jean Moulin, Lyon-3.

YASUAKI OHNUMA:

Professor of International Law in the Graduate School of Law and Politics of the University of Tokyo. His professional career has included Visiting Scholar positions at Harvard Law School, Yale Law School and Princeton University. He was the Visiting Professor, Montague Burton Chair of International Relations at the University of Edinburgh, as well as a Visiting Lecturer at Yale Law School. He has written many books and articles including *Tan-itsu Minzoku Shakai no Shinwa o Koete (Beyond the Myth of a Monoethnic Society)* (1988); *Tokyo Saiban Kara Sengo Sekinin no Shiso e (From the Tokyo War Crimes Trial to the Philosophy of Japanese Postwar Responsibilities for War)* (1987). His English language publications include *The Tokyo War Crimes Trial: An International Symposium* (co-ed., 1986); and *A Normative Approach to War: Peace, War and Justice in Hugo Grotius* (ed., 1993).

HISASHI OWADA:

Permanent Representative of Japan to the United Nations, Ambassador Owada held the post of Vice-Minister for Foreign Affairs prior to his U.N. appointment. He became a career foreign service officer in 1955, and was appointed Private Secretary to the Minister for Foreign Affairs in Japan. After a number of appointments around the globe, Ambassador Owada returned to Tokyo to be Director-General of the Treaties Bureau, Principal Legal Advisor to the Foreign Ministry and concurrently Director-General for the Law of the Sea in the Ministry of Foreign Affairs. Mr. Owada has also taught at a number of academic institutions, including the University of Tokyo, Columbia University, Harvard University, and New York University where he is the Inge Rennert Distinguished Visiting Professor. He is the author of numerous writings on international political, economic and legal affairs. He earned his degree from Tokyo University and continued his post-graduate studies at Cambridge University in England.

LINDA C. REIF:

Associate Professor of Law, University of Alberta, Canada. Professor Reif teaches public international law, international business transactions, international environmental law, and private international law. Professor Reif has published in the areas of international environmental law, international business law, and professional human rights law. She has a variety of editorial and professional responsibilities, including editing the publications of the International Ombudsman Institute and serving as a member of the Board of Directors of the Canadian Council on International Law and of the Academic Council on the United Nations System. Professor Reif received her LL.B. from the University of Windsor, and her LL.M. from Cambridge University.

NAOKO SAIKI:

Deputy Director of the Department of Staff Recruitment and Placement, Ministry of Foreign Affairs of Japan, Tokyo. Mrs. Saiki has served in various Departments in the Ministry, including Policy Planning and Analysis, Arms Control and Disarmament, and Legal Affairs. Her latest overseas assignment was to the Permanent Mission of Japan in Geneva. She was a negotiator in the Uruguay Round dispute settlement negotiations and a member of the Banana I Panel (1993) of the GATT. She received her B.A. from the University of Tokyo.

MASAO SAKURAI:

Professor of International Relations Law, Keio University, Faculty of Policy Management, Kanagawa. Professor Sakurai is the former Director of Economic Cooperation Department, Institute of Developing Economies (affiliated with the Ministry of International Trade and Industry). He was a Research Fellow at Pontificia Universidade Católica do Rio de Janeiro and a Consultant to ECAFE and ESCAP, United Nations. Professor Sakurai is a member of Transnational Corporation Study-Committee, a Special Member to the Industrial Structure Council and Chairman for the Study Committee on Multilateral Agreement on Investment, all of the MITI. He is the author of *Kokusai-Keizai-Hō no Kihon Mondai (Fundamental Problems of International Economic Law)* (1992); *Kokusai Keizai Hō Kenkyū (Studies on International Economic Law)* (1977); *Kokusai Kaihatsu Kyōryoku Ho (Law of International Development Co-*

operation) (1994).

TOSHIO SAWADA:

Professor of Law of International Transactions, Sophia University, Faculty of Law, Tokyo. He is the Vice Chairman of the ICC International Court of Arbitration, Paris, and also a Judge for the Administrative Tribunal of the Asian Development Bank. He has served as counsel, arbitrator or advisor in cases before the International Court of Justice, municipal courts or arbitral tribunals involving issues of international public, financial or business law. He holds advanced degrees from Columbia University and the University of Michigan. He has delivered lectures in various countries on GATT-WTO, project finance and other financing devices as well as on dispute resolution.

EDWIN M. SMITH:

Leon Benwell Professor of Law and International Relations, University of Southern California Law Center, Los Angeles, California. Professor Smith has served on the Executive Council and the Nominating Committee of the American Society of International Law, and is now chair of the International Organizations Interest Group. He is a member of the Council on Foreign Relations and has been an International Affairs Fellow of the Council (1987) and participated in a variety of Council study groups, including Study Groups on Collective Involvement in Internal Conflicts and Self-Determination. He was also a member of the Council's NATO/European Community Briefing Delegation in May 1992 and has lectured on, and testified before Congress on, cooperation between the United Nations and NATO in peacekeeping matters. His writings include *The United Nations in a New World Order* (co-authored with M.G. Schechter); "Changing Conceptions and Institutional Adaptation," in *The United Nations in the Twenty-First Century* (K. Krause and A. Knight, eds., forthcoming); and "NATO and the European Community: Troubled Transitions," *USC Law* 2-11 (Fall 1992).

PETER D. TROOBOFF:

Partner in the law firm of Covington & Burling, Washington, D.C., with concentration on international trade matters, including United States national security and foreign policy trade controls. Mr. Trooboff was president of the American Society of International Law in 1990–92 and is a member of Board of Editors of the *American Journal of International Law*. He was elected in 1991 as the American member of the Curatorium of The Hague Academy of International Law and also serves on the Secretary of State's Advisory Committee on Private International Law.

DETLEV VAGTS:

Bemis Professor of Law at Harvard Law School. Professor Vagts is editor in chief of the *American Journal of International Law*. He has served as Counselor on International Law in the U.S. Department of State (1976–77) and as associate reporter of the Restatement (Third) of the Foreign Relations Law of the United States (1979–86).

EDITH BROWN WEISS:

Professor of Law at Georgetown University Law Center. She is president of the American Society of International Law, and a member of the Board of Editors for the *American Journal of International Law*. She received the 1994 Elizabeth Haub Prize in International Environmental Law from the Free University of Brussels and the International Council on Environmental Law. She is a member of the Commission on Geosciences, Environment and Resources at the U.S. National Academy of Sciences/National Research Council, and was a member of that organization's Water Science and Technology Board and Environmental Studies Board. Professor Weiss has been a consultant to the United Nations University and the United Nations Environment Programme. She holds an Honorary Doctor of Law from Chicago-Kent College of Law.

SHUNJI YANAI:

Deputy Minister for Foreign Affairs, Ministry of Foreign Affairs of Japan, Tokyo. He has served as Consul-General in San Francisco, Director-General of the Treaties Bureau (Ministry of Foreign Affairs), Executive Secretary of the International Peace Cooperation Headquarters (Prime Minister's Office), and Director-General of the Foreign Policy Bureau (Ministry of Foreign Affairs). Mr. Yanai was involved in the drafting of the Law concerning Cooperation for United Nations Peace-Keeping Operations and Other Operations in 1991. He was the Executive Secretary of the International Peace Cooperation Headquarters when Japan participated in peacekeeping operations in Angola, Cambodia and Mozambique. Mr. Yanai is author of "Law Concerning Cooperation for United Nations Peace-Keeping Operations and Other Operations - The Japanese PKO Experience," 36 *Japanese Annual of International Law* (1993). Mr. Yanai graduated from University of Tokyo, Faculty of Law.

JUN YOKOYAMA:

Professor of Private International Law, Hitotsubashi University, Faculty of Law, Tokyo. Formerly Professor of Dokkyo University Faculty of Law. Professor Yokoyama is a member of the Legislative Council on Private International Law, Ministry of Justice. He is the Japanese delegate to the 18th Session of The Hague Conference of Private International Law. Professor Yokoyama earned his B.A. and LL.M from Hitotsubashi University and also had the opportunity to work as a research student at the University of Glasgow.

HYUCK-SOO YOO:

Associate Professor of International Law, Yokohama National University, Graduate School of International and Business Law, Yokohama, Japan. Professor Yoo is currently a Visiting Scholar at Harvard Law School. He is the author of publications on international law and international economic law, including *GATT 19 to Kokusaitsūshōhō no Kino (GATT Article XIX and the Function of International Trade Law)*. He earned his B.A. from Yonsei University, and his LL.M. and S.J.D. from the University of Tokyo.

MICHAEL K. YOUNG:

Fuyo Professor of Japanese Law and the Director for the Center for Japanese Legal Studies and the Center for Korean Legal Studies, Columbia University, New York City. During the Bush Administration, Professor Young served as Ambassador for Trade and Environmental Affairs, as well as Deputy Under-Secretary for Economic and Agricultural Affairs and Deputy Legal Adviser, at the U.S. Department of State. He is currently a member of the Council of Foreign Relations and chairman of the Business Advisory Council for the Japan Society. He has authored in both English and Japanese numerous articles on comparative law, especially Japanese law, and on international trade law. He was the Chief legal adviser to the U.S. delegation to the Two-Plus-Four German Unification Talks, as well as Head of Delegation to the Conference on Security and Cooperation Negotiations on the Pacific Settlement of Disputes, Valletta, Malta, 1991 and Alternative Head of Delegation to the United Nations Conference on Environment and Development (UNCED, Rio de Janiero, Brazil, 1992)..

INDEX